Kinship and Famil

Blackwell Anthologies in Social and Cultural Anthropology
Series Editor: Parker Shipton, Boston University

Drawing from some of the most significant scholarly work of the nineteenth and twentieth centuries, the *Blackwell Anthologies in Social and Cultural Anthropology* series offers a comprehensive and unique perspective on the ever-changing field of anthropology. It represents both a collection of classic readers and an exciting challenge to the norms that have shaped this discipline over the past century.

Each edited volume is devoted to a traditional subdiscipline of the field such as the anthropology of religion, linguistic anthropology, or medical anthropology; and provides a foundation in the canonical readings of the selected area. Aware that such subdisciplinary definitions are still widely recognized and useful – but increasingly problematic – these volumes are crafted to include a rare and invaluable perspective on social and cultural anthropology at the onset of the twenty-first century. Each text provides a selection of classic readings together with contemporary works that underscore the artificiality of subdisciplinary definitions and point students, researchers, and general readers in the new directions in which anthropology is moving.

Kinship and Family

An Anthropological Reader

Edited by

Robert Parkin and Linda Stone

Blackwell Publishing

Editorial material and organization © 2004 by Blackwell Publishing Ltd

350 Main Street, Malden, MA 02148-5020, USA
108 Cowley Road, Oxford OX4 1JF, UK
550 Swanston Street, Carlton, Victoria 3053, Australia

First published 2004 by Blackwell Publishing Ltd

Library of Congress Cataloging-in-Publication Data

Kinship and family: an anthropological reader / edited by Robert Parkin and Linda Stone.
p. cm. — (Blackwell anthologies in social and cultural anthropology; 4)
Includes bibliographical references and index.
ISBN 0-631-22998-1 (hardback: alk. paper) — ISBN 0-631-22999-X (pbk.: alk. paper)
1. Kinship. 2. Family. I. Parkin, Robert, 1950-II. Stone, Linda, 1947-III. Series.

GN487.K53 2004
306.85—dc21

2003056028

A catalogue record for this title is available from the British Library.

Set in 10/12pt Sabon
by Kolam Information Services Pvt. Ltd, Pondicherry, India

For further information on
Blackwell Publishing, visit our website:
http://www.blackwellpublishing.com

Contents

Preface

The purpose of this collection is to trace, through selected examples, the development of mainstream kinship theory and to provide a kind of intellectual genealogy of the treatment of this important topic in anthropology. As will be argued, despite a reduction in interest in kinship in the 1970s and 1980s, it is a topic that has been consistently central to anthropological practice and theory, and, what is more, it has helped form both. All this activity and thought down the years has demonstrated that there are few aspects of kinship that are universal cross-culturally beyond the basics of biology, and that even these basics are subject to variation in the way they are interpreted, if they are recognized indigenously at all. Ultimately, though, however much cross-cultural variation there might be, no society is without something we can recognize and treat as kinship, and comparative studies are once again being seen as both feasible and desirable. Comparison does not necessarily imply a search for uniformities: it can raise questions about the reasons for variations, and even suggest answers, at least in the local context. Thus although kinship has repeatedly been dismissed as a category of use in analysis, it refuses to go away, as the recent spate of books on the topic demonstrates.

An overview of what these new studies are both building on and seeking to go beyond is therefore timely. In general, the temptation to try and cover all the innumerable topics that have been discussed under the rubric of kinship has been resisted in the present collection. Instead the focus has been on the development of theory that, in broad terms, has approached kinship as a form of social organization or given reasons for querying or rejecting this association. The collection should therefore be regarded as representative rather than comprehensive, given the limitations on selection. However, references are given to other material, much of which will lead the reader off in other, more specialized directions.

Following the General Introduction, which offers the sort of overview mentioned above, the book is divided into two parts. Part I covers descent and alliance theory, covering the history of anthropological kinship up to the 1970s. Part II covers the demise and later revival of kinship in anthropology from the early 1970s to the present. Each part is subdivided into two sections. In Part I the first of these sections covers the dominance of descent or lineage theory in the century or so after the 1860s, an approach which was intimately bound up with the very different schools of evolutionism and functionalism. This approach was even dominant enough to determine, not to say distort, theories of marriage in this period. Some of the critical reaction to it from about 1960 is also covered here. The second section focuses on another part of this reaction, namely the replacement of descent theory by alliance theory as the dominant school from the 1950s to the 1970s. This was linked with the arrival of structuralism, which similarly replaced functionalism in this period.

In Part II the first section deals in broad terms with the shift from social organization to culture, whose influence has spread more recently, since it is seen as a better way of understanding indigenous notions of kinship or "relatedness" than the more analytical schools of the past. The second section focuses on some of the new directions kinship studies are now taking. There are many different approaches. We have not tried to cover all of them or all specific topics, but have preferred to concentrate on those that sum up a key trend or that represent the shift to "culture" in a particularly apt way. We have provided introductions to the readings for general guidance and to highlight what we would regard as the key points (of course, other authors might choose different emphases). These introductions also contain significant references to other work.

Kinship is not the most straightforward topic in anthropology to grasp immediately, and many of the concepts routinely used by professional anthropologists cause difficulties to students and fellow academics outside the field. We have tried to define and explain the main ones used here, and a glossary has been provided, but the reader is directed to one of the introductory books if further enlightenment is required. A selection of the more recent of these is given below:

Ladislav Holy, *Anthropological Perspectives on Kinship*. London and Chicago: Pluto Press, 1996.
Sound, critical, and up to date in the main, but rather weak on affinal alliance and especially kinship terminology.

Robert Parkin, *Kinship: An Introduction to Basic Concepts*. Oxford: Blackwell, 1997.
Defines key terms, provides a potted history of the main aspects of the topic, and discusses a number of ethnographic examples.

Linda Stone, *Kinship and Gender: An Introduction*. 2nd edition. Boulder: Westview Press, 2000.
Good on definitions and with extended discussions of a number of ethnographic examples.

A couple of older books are also useful, though the first is currently out of print:

Alan Barnard and Anthony Good, *Research Practices in the Study of Kinship*. London: Academic Press, 1984.
Written basically for the fieldworker, but discusses a lot of key theories and concepts in a very sound way.

Robin Fox, *Kinship and Marriage*. Harmondsworth: Penguin, reissued 1983 Cambridge: Cambridge University Press, 1967.

Now old, but a highly readable and generally sound text, though rather reliant on biological concepts in the early chapters.

Earlier collections of readings include especially the following (now all out of print, but probably still available in libraries):

Paul Bohannan and John Middleton, eds., *Kinship and Social Organisation*. New York: Natural History Press, 1968.

Brings together many key early texts on kinship terminology, both unilineal and cognatic descent, and Australian marriage systems, though missing out much obvious work on affinal alliance which was already available.

Paul Bohannan and John Middleton, eds., *Marriage and the Family*. New York: Natural History Press, 1968.

Does a similar job as the previous book for marriage and family organization.

Jack Goody, ed., *Kinship: Selected Readings*. Harmondsworth: Penguin, 1971.

Nelson Graburn, ed., *Readings in Kinship and Social Structure*. New York and London: Harper & Row, 1971.

Both are very comprehensive collections of material published until that time.

Robert Parkin and Linda Stone

April 2003

Acknowledgments

The editors and publishers wish to thank the following for permission to use copyright material:

1. Lowie, Robert H., 1950 Unilateral Descent Groups. Social Organisation, pp. 236–66; 421–3; 428–51. London: Routledge & Kegan Paul.

2. Evans-Pritchard, E. E., 1940 The Nuer of the Southern Sudan, *In* African Political Systems. M. Fortes and E. E. Evans-Pritchard, eds. pp. 271–96. London etc.: Oxford University Press.

3. Kuper, Adam, 1982 Lineage Theory: A Brief Retrospect. Annual Review of Anthropology 11: 71–95. Copyright © 1982 by Annual Review of Anthropology, www.annualreviews.org. Reprinted with permission.

4. Barnes, J. A., 1962 African Models in the New Guinea Highlands. Man 62: 5–9. Reprinted with permission of Blackwell Publishing.

5. Rivière, Peter, 1993 The Amerindianization of Descent and Affinity. L'Homme 33/2-4: 507–16; edited. Reprinted by permission of L'Ehss Publishing, France.

6. Goody, Jack, 1969 Inheritance, Property, and Marriage in Africa and Eurasia. Sociology 3: 557–6; edited. Reprinted with permission of Sage Publications Ltd.

7. Rivers, W. H. R., 1968 Kinship and Social Organization, Lecture One. Kinship and Social Organization, London: Athlone Press pp. 39–54, 110–11. Reprinted by permission of The Continuum International Publishing Group.

8. Lévi-Strauss, Claude, 1963 Structural Analysis in Linguistics and Anthropology. Structural Anthropology 1: 31–54. Harmondsworth: Penguin. English translation copyright © 1963 Basic Books, Inc. Reprinted by permission of Basic Books, a member of Perseus Books, L.L.C.

9. Leach, Edmund, 1958 Concerning Trobriand Clans and the Kinship Category 'Tabu'. The Developmental Cycle of Domestic Groups, Jack Goody, ed. pp. 120–45, Cambridge: Cambridge University Press. Reproduced with permission of Cambridge University Press.

10. Dumont, Louis, 1953 The Dravidian Kinship Terminology as an Expression of Marriage (including correspondence with Radcliffe-Brown). Man 53: 34–9, 112, 143. Reproduced with permission of Blackwell Publishing.

11. Good, Anthony, 1981 Prescription, Preference and Practice: Marriage Patterns among the Kondaiyankottai Maravar of South India. Man (n.s.) 16: 108–29. Reproduced with permission of Blackwell Publishing.

12. Needham, Rodney, 1962 Analysis of Purum Affinal Alliance. *In* Structure and Sentiment: A Test Case in Social Anthropology, pp. 74–100, 127–30. Chicago: The University of Chicago Press. Reproduced with permission of The University of Chicago Press.

13. Allen, N. J., 1986 Tetradic Theory: An Approach to Kinship. Journal of the Anthropological Society of Oxford 17: 87–109. Reprinted by permission of the Journal of the Anthropological Society of Oxford.

14. Schneider, David M. 1972 What is Kinship All About? Kinship Studies in the Morgan Centennial Year. Priscilla Reining, ed. pp. 32–63. Washington, D.C.: The Anthropological Society of Washington; edited.

15. Yanagisako, Sylvia Junko and Jane Fishburne Collier 1987 Toward a Unified Analysis of Gender and Kinship. *In* Gender and Kinship: Essays Toward a Unified Analysis. Jane Fishburne Collier and Sylvia Junko Yanagisako, eds., pp. 14–50. Stanford: Stanford University Press. Copyright © 1987 by the Board of Trustees of the Leland Stanford Jr. University. Used with permission of Stanford University Press, www.sup.org; edited.

16. Scheffler, Harold W., 1991 Sexism and Naturalism in the Study of Kinship. *In* Gender at the Crossroads of Knowledge: Feminist Anthropology in the Postmodern Era, Micaela di Leonardo, ed., pp. 361–82. Berkeley: University of California Press. Reproduced with permission of The University of California Press.

17. Carsten, Janet, 1995 The Substance of Kinship and the Heat of the Hearth: Feeding, Personhood and Relatedness among Malays in Pulau Langkawi. American Ethnologist 22: 223–41. Reproduced by permission of the American Anthropological Association. Not for sale or further reproduction.

18. Ragoné, Helena, 1994 Surrogate Motherhood and American Kinship. *In*, Surrogate Motherhood: Conception in the Heart. Helena Ragoné, pp. 109–37. Boulder: Westview Press. Copyright © 1994. Reprinted by permission of Westview Press, a member of Perseus Books L.L.C.

19. Kahn, Susan Martha, 2000 Eggs and Wombs: The Origins of Jewishness. *In* Reproducing Jews: A Cultural Account of Assisted Conception in Israel, Susan Martha Kahn, pp. 112–39. Durham: Duke University Press. All rights reserved. Used by permission of the publisher; edited.

20. Hayden, Corinne P., 1995 Gender, Genetics and Generation: Reformulating Biology in Lesbian Kinship. Cultural Anthropology 10: 41–63. Reproduced by permission of the American Anthropological Association. Not for sale or further reproduction.

21. Stone, Linda, 2002 Has the World Turned? Kinship in the Contemporary American Soap Opera. (Original contribution.)

22. Han, Hua 2002, Kinship, Gender and Mode of Production in Post-Mao China: Variations in Two Northern Villages. (Original contribution.)

23. Fox, Robin, 1975 Primate Kin and Human Kinship. *In* Biosocial Anthropology, Robin Fox, ed. pp. 9–35. New York: John Wiley and Sons; edited.

24. Bloch, Maurice and Dan Sperber, 2002 Kinship and Evolved Psychological Dispositions: The Mother's Brother Controversy Reconsidered. Current Anthropol-

ogy 43(5). Copyright © The Wenner-Gren Foundation for Anthropological Research. All rights reserved.

Every effort has been made to trace copyright holders and to obtain their permission for the use of copyright material. The authors and publishers will gladly receive any information enabling them to rectify any error or omission in subsequent editions.

General Introduction

Robert Parkin with Linda Stone

The present reader brings together a number of items tracing the broad lines of development of thought in a key area of social anthropology – kinship. It has proved impossible within the scope allowed to give coverage to all trends and topics in the subject. The selection is therefore of texts that represent the main intellectual genealogy of this topic: it does not claim to be comprehensive. Accordingly, the focus is on the relationship of kinship to certain forms of social organization, and to the development of anthropological theory. This ought to be explained a little more before we proceed further.

Naturally, social organization means many things – not only kinship, but also social formations that owe little or nothing to kinship, except perhaps metaphorically, such as the state, the community, divisions of labor, friendship, economic relations, slavery, etc. But for much of the existence of anthropology, kinship has been seen as constituting social organization in most of the societies anthropologists have chosen to study. Given that the origins of anthropology lie in part in Victorian intellectuals' self-affirmation of their own sense of superiority and civilization, the study of "primitives" was almost bound to be of intense interest. In addition, the idea of evolution, which had roots in philology as much as in Darwin as far as the infant social sciences were concerned, had both extended the time depth of the sense of the past, and helped stimulate an interest in "origins." The latter motivation had also been stimulated by an interest in archaeology, which had developed as a largely amateur discipline in its own right since the eighteenth century. The general desire to know more about the origins of humanity, and of human social life, in these circumstances – which were ones of increased opportunity as well as altered perspectives – led to an interest in contemporary "primitive" peoples in the Americas and in European overseas empires. The assumption was that these peoples represented survivals from an earlier stage of history, which western Europe and North America, at any rate, had moved away from in making "progress." Such peoples could therefore tell "civilized" Victorians something about their own pasts – indeed, explicit but misleading parallels were frequently made, for example, between the clans of contemporary peoples in the Empire and those of ancient Greece and

Rome. And for the more radical minds of the period, there was every chance that "primitives," however backward and ignorant at the present time, would catch up with the "civilized." At least this perspective recognized the basic unity of the human species, a position that itself had to be fought for in the new science of anthropology.

Such are the basic reasons for the importance of kinship in early attempts to understand the fundamentals of "primitive" social organization. And while anthropology has managed to rid itself of the prejudices associated with these mid-Victorian attitudes, the centrality of kinship in anthropological theory persisted up to about 1970. This was for the very similar reason that it seemed to be at the core of the social organization of the peoples who were still being studied most in anthropology, who were mostly extra-European. By contrast, the study of European societies was for long prone to silent dismissal as a "soft" topic (cf. Cole 1977), and Euro-American kinship contributed virtually nothing to theory in the century or so between Morgan and Schneider.

Kinship has also been important in anthropology in the sense that many of the major developments in the discipline have been related to its study. Kinship, unlike religion, say, is one of the comparatively few topics that anthropology has managed to make its own. In this respect, it has only really faced competition from the sociology and history of the family, and neither of these has managed to become central to its respective discipline. In fact, most of the major figures who have made contributions to anthropology have done so in the area of kinship. This will hopefully become apparent in what follows in the selected texts and our introductions to them, as well as in the brief history of the anthropological treatment of kinship offered in this introduction. First, however, we need some idea of what kinship is and what it is not.

The Idea of Kinship in Anthropology

Kinship obviously involves relationships, which in the Western, quasi-scientific view frequently means relationships that are based on the biological connections created through sex and birth, or conception and parturition. The view that is conventional in the Western part of the developed world, at any rate, is that children are the biological issue of both parents equally, and that groups of children that are the issue of a particular couple are siblings. Yet even here a certain and, in some parts of the Western world, increasing number of relationships of kinship can only be described as social, since there is open recognition that they are essentially substitutes for a relationship that is normally defined biologically, as with adoption, fostering, and step-relations. In addition, the popular view of kinship in the West is far from being entirely scientific, since it makes reference even to bodily substances in a metaphorical way. The frequent use of blood as indicating a certain sort of relationship, for example, is ultimately arbitrary, and therefore culturally determined: other societies may choose flesh or bone. Another aspect of this is the feeling that a child may actually "take after" one parent more than the other – again quite arbitrarily as far as biological relationship is concerned. There is also a conventional acceptance that nurture is as important as nature, that a proper upbringing is required and not just biology. Even in our own liberal world, children are generally seen as needing some form of disciplining, for their own as well as society's good, whether through persuasion or chastisement, whether at home or at school. This "socialization," as it is called academically, is seen as being as much a part of upbringing as the care and protection of infants until they are mature enough to stand on their own feet, which is what a biological approach may tend to stress. Even genealogy, or the calculation of relationships through one-to-one links between relatives, that anthropologists have relied on so extensively as a method of analysis, has been claimed not to fit American ideas about kinship at all exactly, despite widespread assumptions to the contrary (cf. the item by Schneider, below, Chapter 14).

Then there is marriage, in virtually any society an important institution that is often regarded as the foundation for the legitimate birth and upbringing of children. It therefore may be seen as legitimizing the biological activities, especially sex, that underpin these. Yet it is usually seen as a contractual rather than biological relationship in itself, even in societies with cross-cousin marriage, where the affinal (i.e., marriage) relationship itself may be regarded as inherited. The ambiguous position of marriage meant that it was separated from consanguinity (or "kinship" in the narrow sense of, literally, "blood" ties) as an analytical category for a long time in anthropology, before the alliance theorists of the 1950s, 1960s, and 1970s fused the two categories together as "kinship." This, together with the other non-biological factors just mentioned, reinforced the longstanding argument, going back to the start of the modern anthropological treatment of kinship in the 1850s and 1860s, that kinship is essentially social in nature.

For the social anthropologist, therefore, much is both missed and misunderstood in approaching kinship solely as if it were biology. Certainly, a number of anthropologists have repeatedly pointed out that biology must be involved in kinship, since only this explains the physical continuity of the human population as a whole. One example here is the philosopher turned anthropologist Ernest Gellner (1957, 1960), whose argument along these lines was dismissed by Needham (1960), J. A. Barnes (1961), and Beattie (1964), writing from a more purely social anthropological point of view. The whole debate, which is discussed by Harris (1990: 27–39), led to Beattie practically dismissing kinship as an independent field of study, on the basis that kinship only ever appears in the context of something else, which is usually political, economic, or ritual. This point of view was criticized in its turn by Schneider (1964), who was already beginning to develop his view of kinship as culturally specific (see his item below). In addition, he pointed out that one could just as easily learn something about politics, economics, and ritual from kinship as the other way round. But Schneider's own dismissal of kinship as an anthropological category that can be compared (his item below; also 1968, 1984) has led to Gellner's basic point being repeated more recently by, for example, Scheffler (1991) and Stone (2001: 8). In fact not even human biologists in the main, let alone any of these particular anthropologists, would deny either the existence or the significance of the social aspects of kinship. Lévi-Strauss represents what might be called the orthodox position in social anthropology (cf. his item below, Chapter 8), namely that kinship is distinctively social, or in his terms cultural, precisely insofar as it deviates from the biological. For the social anthropologist the biological aspects cannot be denied; but, being uniform, they cannot explain cultural variation and are therefore uninformative in relation to the issues that concern social anthropologists the most.

In any case, the more one moves away from modern, Western societies and out into the rest of the world, the less appropriate the applicability of this model becomes. In the first place, ideas of birth and conception may differ radically from even the quasi-scientific view of popular Western discourse, varying the parts played by the respective parents in the creation of a new life, or denying one or even both parents any part in it at all. As noted above, the substance, or substances, that are thought to link parents and children, or siblings, may differ, and there may be a belief in supernatural intervention of some sort. There may be radical differences in family organization, not to mention ideas of what the family is for: the former Western ideal of the monogamous nuclear family "for life" is far from being uniform to all humanity, and indeed hardly corresponds to uniform practice in the West itself any longer, especially given the ideological challenges to it since the 1960s.

Larger structures, based on notions of kinship, also exist in many parts of the world, especially descent groups, which are often conceived as long chains of parent-to-child ties stretching back for generations. However, even these structures are unlikely to be perfect representations of relationships in reality: intervening generations may be collapsed, ancestors forgotten or mythologized, and collateral lines allowed to lapse from the record. Some may be very shallow, with people scarcely remembering their grandparents. In addition, there may be radical differences in how such relationships are traced, which has important consequences for the constitution of such groups: they may be patrilineal, tracing relationships through male links only; matrilineal, through female links only; or cognatic, tracing links through either gender indifferently (nor does this entirely exhaust the variation anthropologists have encountered). A further source of variation is what, if anything, such groups do: they may regulate marriage, channel inheritance, or simply be a form of classification providing a cognitive map of the universe of kinship. Conversely, it has struck many anthropologists that such groups may actually be founded on co-residence and not kinship, or at least not on descent per se, at all, or that a mixture of these principles may be involved. The first group of articles is chiefly concerned with this topic of descent, what it means, and whether it really exists at all.

Marriage is another fruitful source of variation. Apart from some sense of it regulating sexual intercourse for particular ends, there is little theoretical agreement on its purpose in human societies. Thus it may be thought that it legitimates children or property relations; provides a channel of communication, and of other gifts and services, between whole social groups; provides mutual support and companionship, and so on. At least there is no argument concerning the variety of its forms. Societies may recognize plural or polygamous marriages (either the polygyny of one man having more than one wife, or its reverse, polyandry) as well as monogamous ones; there may be requirements to marry within certain groups (the endogamy of Indian castes, of whole ethnic groups) and/or outside of others (the exogamy of many though certainly not all descent groups); the requirement to marry a certain category of kin, typically defined in the literature as cross-cousin marriage; the permission or prohibition of divorce; different sorts of marriage payment, either bridewealth in exchange for a wife or a dowry being given along with her; in some societies, working for one's bride through bride service, etc. Systems of affinal alliance that are based on cross-cousin marriage – a staple anthropological topic for years, though also a controversial and demanding one – are a main concern of many of the second group of articles.

In short, while anthropology has always had its great synthesizers and comparativists, it is the variations that have struck professionals the most, as well as making the subject exciting and relevant. In kinship, these extremes of variation, together with the failure of biology, or even genealogy, to account for all its aspects, have led to two principal sorts of suggestion. One is that there is no such thing as kinship, theoretically speaking (e.g., Beattie 1964; Needham 1971: 3–5; Schneider 1984, all of whom have their own reasons for coming to this conclusion), and that its use as an analytical category should be abandoned. The other is that we should replace it with "relationship" (a very 1960s view, associated with the alliance theorists, with their greater focus on marriage, though it is foreshadowed in some of Rivers's work 50 years earlier), or more recently with something like "relatedness" (Carsten 2000). The standard answer to such suggestions is that they muddy the divide between relationships based on kinship and those that are not, such as friendship, citizenship, employee–employer relationships, and so on (cf. Holy 1996: 168). This goes back to an original distinction, made in print as early as 1861 by Sir Henry Maine, between kinship as a status that one has, because one is born with it, and contract as something that has to be negotiated, or at least affirmed. This fuzziness may nonetheless seem justified, given that one is born a citizen as well as a child, and that kinship itself may not be seen as a settled status in all societies, but may have to be negotiated and affirmed too, or at least developed over time (cf. the item by Carsten, below, Chapter 17). The traditional Western anthropologists' view of kinship as a fixed structure of relationships – itself rooted, it has been alleged, in the Western quasi-scientific folk model (cf. Schneider, below, Chapter 14) – has therefore been replaced with a view of kinship as process, at least in some cases (cf. Carsten, below, Chapter 17). This and other unsettling issues are represented by the third group of articles in this selection.

A Brief History of Kinship in Anthropology: Roots in Morgan

Henry Lewis Morgan did not exactly invent the anthropological study of kinship: even ignoring precursors from Herodotus to Joseph Lafitau, an eighteenth-century French missionary to the Iroquois, there were still plenty of nineteenth-century scholars who contributed in this area, some of whom we shall meet later. Nonetheless, Morgan's was the first grand theory, and to a large extent the subsequent history of the treatment of kinship in anthropology has been one of unraveling his discoveries, insights, and errors. Given this, and the fact that the first item in each of the three sections into which this collection is divided engages in some sense with Morgan's ideas, it is pertinent to begin by looking at these ideas in some detail. They are enshrined in his two major works, the *Systems of Consanguinity and Affinity of the Human Family* of 1870, and *Ancient Society* of 1877.

Morgan's story has been told repeatedly, and there are good modern accounts of both his career and the controversies he engaged in, on which I draw freely here (see Service 1985, Kuper 1988, Trautmann 1984, 1987). A lawyer born in 1818 in upstate New York, a part of the United States then still in process of modern development, Morgan had become interested in the Iroquois, a local Native American tribe, while still a student, through his membership of a student fraternity that modeled itself on them and therefore collected ethnographic data from them. Later, Morgan was to act for the Iroquois in land rights cases. This must have involved a full recognition that their social organization was matrilineal. But in the course of his involvement with them, Morgan also discovered (or rather rediscovered, given Lafitau's earlier work among the tribe) that their kinship "system" was very different from that of the "civilized" whites. By kinship system, Morgan meant what would today be called the kinship terminology, or inventory of terms for relatives and the patterns they create. This discovery was the foundation of a basic distinction Morgan made between the so-called "classificatory" and "descriptive" systems of relationship.

Although these two descriptors were frequently misunderstood early on (cf. White 1958), and their aptness has just as frequently been challenged, there should be little disagreement today as to what Morgan himself meant by them. A classificatory terminology, typical of "primitive" societies for Morgan, merged lineal kin (that is, kin in ego's direct line of descent) with collateral kin who were linked through the same sorts of tie, and distinguished them from collaterals who were not. In other words, while father's brother is classified as a father (both having the same ties through men), mother's brother had a separate term (being related differently). Similarly, while parallel cousins (linked through same-sex parental ties, namely FBC and MZC) were classed with siblings, cross cousins (linked through opposite-sex parental ties, namely FZC and MBC) had separate terms. And while the children of one's same-sex sibling (brother's children for a man, sister's for a woman) were classed with one's own children, those of opposite-sex siblings were also classed separately.

Morgan's descriptive system, conversely, classified all collaterals together and kept them separate from lineal kin. This corresponds, amongst others, to the English system, in which parents are distinguished from all collaterals, who themselves have common terms, regardless of line of descent (namely uncle, aunt, cousin, nephew, niece), and in which remoter cousins tend to be forgotten or treated ambiguously as kin. To Morgan and his contemporaries this was the "natural" system, since it expressed the known scientific fact that children were the offspring of both their parents. The classificatory system, by contrast, mixed relationships in a way that was not simply confusing, but also to many of Morgan's contemporaries – especially his friend and supporter, the Reverend Joshua McIlvaine – uncivilized and fundamentally immoral. It seems to have been McIlvaine who persuaded Morgan, despite the latter's evident misgivings, that this system was associated with primitive promiscuity – another form of "confusion" and of an absence of discrimination. In effect this is the first version of the idea that, in societies with these and similar systems, the whole tribe conceives itself as being interrelated, regardless of genealogical connection. In fact, of course, any terminological system discriminates – otherwise it would have no reason to exist – it simply does so in different ways. Anthropology has long abandoned any notion that such systems demonstrate confusion as ethnocentric.

Morgan's researches might have ended at this point, a time when he was apparently more concerned with his professional obligations to the Iroquois than with scholarship. However, a brief encounter with an Ojibwa Indian on a business trip further west showed him that this tribe had a similar terminology to the Iroquois, even though they spoke a completely unrelated language. This meant that, in modern terms, the pattern was structural, not historical, much less random, and it might therefore represent a "primitive type" found in other parts of the world too. This discovery stimulated Morgan to extend his researches comparatively, to Asia as well as to the rest of North America. His goal at this stage was simply to prove the Asiatic origin of the Indians by identifying similar terminologies in Asia. He accomplished his researches magnificently, in the sense that he ended up with some two hundred schedules of kin terms from these areas, acquired partly through question-naires sent to local collaborators, and partly through his own researches over four summers in parts of the American Midwest.

Ultimately these researches were to have far more impact on the anthropology of social organization worldwide than on the archaeology of the prehistoric migrations of Native Americans from Asia. One important discovery was that the Tamil and Telugu populations of south India had very similar kinship terminologies to those of the Iroquois and Ojibwa. This later came to be called "Dravidian kinship," from the language family to which these two south Indian languages belonged (see Trautmann 1981 for a modern overall account of south Indian kinship). At least as significant for Morgan's theoretical development was the discovery of a "vari-ation" on the classificatory type, which Morgan called Malayan but modern anthro-pology calls Hawaiian or generational. This type has come to be associated especially with Polynesia, but in fact it is quite a widespread principle, at least in parts of a terminology. In it, all the males of each generation have one term, all the females another (there may be different terms for affines, or relatives by marriage). In other words, there is no distinction of line between patrikin and matrikin, lineal and collateral, only distinctions of generation and, possibly, gender (although gender itself may not be distinguished, especially in generations junior to ego's).

Such variations in kinship systems induced Morgan to produce a global explanation of them in terms of their evolution from a supposed prior form of primitive promiscu-ity, which itself was no longer evident anywhere in the world. Primitive promiscuity was in essence seen as a primordial situation in which the human population was divided into amorphous hordes with no form of marriage or restriction on sexual intercourse. This supposedly created a situation in which children could identify their mothers with near-certainty, their fathers not at all in most cases. The immediate evolutionary outcome of this for Morgan was his Malayan system. Here there is still terminological confusion between senior males and senior females, such that one's parents could not be distinguished from uncles and aunts, but there is now what Morgan called the "consanguine family," based on communal marriage – which therefore makes its appearance here in some form – between groups of brothers and groups of sisters. As Service points out (1985: 40 n. 5), what Morgan was probably identifying here was what the modern literature calls sororate and levirate, that is, the marriage of sisters to one man or brothers to one woman, not necessarily simultaneously.

Another key stage for Morgan – I am collapsing some of his less significant variations in this account – was linked to four-section systems in Australia, like the Kamilaroi version he referred to, or the Kariera "type" of the later literature. Here, there is a double distinction within the kinship system, running both vertically and horizontally, yielding four classes, two in one generation (A and B, let us say), and two in the next (X and Y; then repeating A and B, and so on). The system works on the assumption that persons born into A will marry a spouse from B, and that their children will be in either X or Y, depending on the section membership of the respective parents. Similarly, spouses from X and Y will intermarry, the children of these unions being in A or B. This therefore produces a cyclical, not a lineal progression of generations (cf. the item by Allen, below, Chapter 13). It is also a way of pursuing bilateral cross-cousin marriage (see Good's item, below, Chapter 11;

though his people do not have sections) without referring to genealogy. It was at this stage, according to Morgan, that brother–sister incest avoidance was introduced.

Morgan himself resisted any attribution of cross-cousin marriage to these "primitive" systems, not least perhaps because he himself – a representative of "civilization" – had married his own cross-cousin (Trautmann 1984). For him, these Australian systems indicated instead a development of group marriage such that one group of spouses were siblings but not the other. In fact, all the kin of a single generation in any one section are likely to be classed as siblings, their counterparts in their opposite, same-generation section as cross-cousins, whom they should marry. Later anthropologists, culminating in Radcliffe-Brown (especially 1931), finally determined that, although sections may be involved, and terminological categories always were, actual marriages were individual affairs, not group ones in the way Morgan meant.

Next in Morgan's sequence came the Iroquois, who had clan exogamy, with which Morgan associated the classificatory system as he had first encountered it (and as described initially above). By this time, he was quite properly seeing the cross–parallel distinction associated with classificatory terminologies like the Iroquois as a separate type from the Malayan or Hawaiian. The fact that Iroquois clans were matrilineal was also significant to him, since he believed that such clans were the earliest type of political organization, coming before patriliny. After a few more variants, including the polygyny of a "patriarch," which we may pass over in silence here, Morgan arrived at the modern, "civilized" type of monogamous marriage within the nuclear family, whose perfection came from its being "natural" (nuclear families consisting of just parents and their children). The story of how Morgan stimulated Marx and Engels by suggesting that it was the arrival of property relations that produced this last change is among the most famous in anthropology.

One large question for Morgan and many of his early commentators and interlocutors was the relationship between kinship terminology and social organization. Morgan recognized the cultural aspect to many things in kinship, such as the element of choice in mode of unilineal descent – which involved stressing links through one gender and subordinating or suppressing those through the other – and the different forms of marriage. In other respects, however, he was probably more reliant on genealogical and biological notions than any of his successors, or even contemporaries, who for the most part fully acknowledged the social aspect of kinship. He did not recognize, as later anthropologists have been compelled to, the distinction between genetic parents (genitor, genetrix) and social parents (pater, mater). Also, for him, the kinship terminology existed to denote actual biological and affinal relationships, not categories or classes, as in much later anthropology. In other words, to his mind both kinship terminology and the structure of the family reflected the actual biological relationships that different types of marriage generated. There was thus a jural basis to the variation, which nonetheless had biological outcomes.

In addition, in defining different types of marriage and the family, Morgan frequently extrapolated back from the kinship terminologies, which he claimed were more resistant to change than either marriage or family type. This was based partly on existing philological arguments about the slower rate at which words change in form compared to either their meanings or the situations that give rise to them. Kin terms are words, after all, and Morgan's evolutionism seemed to be based on these pre-

Darwinian ideas rather than the narrowly biological form of the doctrine associated with Darwin himself. In the event, though, this merely provided him with quite a few forms of social organization, quite apart from primitive promiscuity, for which there was no evidence in even the exiguous ethnography of the day, let alone later. This approach was nonetheless revived by Rivers some fifty years later (see the item by him below, Chapter 7). It is not necessarily wrong – for example, in the case of cross-cousin marriage – but even here it needs to be used with care, and was soon found not to be feasible as a blanket explanation of variation in social organization. Morgan also recognized the egocentric nature of kinship terminologies, compared to the ancestor-focused nature of descent groups in particular. This position was temporarily abandoned by those who preferred to see kinship terminology precisely as the expression of descent groups (e.g., Radcliffe-Brown). In this respect, theory since has rightly preferred Morgan's position (cf. the item by Dumont and the attached exchange with Radcliffe-Brown, below, Chapter 10).

It can be seen, therefore, that Morgan initiated discussion of many of the defining topics of kinship, namely descent, marriage, kinship terminology, the relationships between these, and the nature of kinship as a social phenomenon. He did not provide all the answers, nor get all the answers he did provide right, but he laid important foundations for later discussion. In this sense his contribution has been significant, and it undoubtedly represents a great personal achievement.

The Reaction to Morgan, ca. 1860–1925

Morgan was not the only purveyor of the matrilineal hypothesis, or of its linking to "primitive promiscuity." There was a clear convergence here with the ideas of a Swiss lawyer, Johann J. Bachofen (1861), which Morgan only encountered after developing his own ideas independently. Bachofen postulated an original "matriarchate," in which women ruled society, before a mirror-image "patriarchate" developed because of the way marriage and the family evolved. Also adhering to this basic idea was another lawyer, a Scot, John McLennan, for whom the significant indicators were "survivals" – in reality, mostly ritual expressions – of bride capture and female infanticide in the contemporary ethnographic record (1865). The reasoning here was that, among early hunter-gatherers, women were a liability as daughters but an asset as wives. Daughters were killed off, which supposedly led to competition for wives, eased by the practice of polyandry – another situation in which the identity of mothers is allegedly more certain than that of fathers. Only with the arrival of settled agriculture and rights in property did patriarchy come about, basically because men were more involved in this form of economic activity.

Dismissal of McLennan's hypotheses is not difficult with reference to more recent ethnography. In practice, polyandry does not necessarily reduce paternity certainty (cf. Stone 1997: 186–94). Female infanticide is more likely to be practiced in patrilineal groups that have an extreme level of concern for the purity of daughters in circumstances where it may be difficult to marry them all off (e.g., Rajputs in north India). As for marriage by capture, while it may be operative in some cases and certainly occurs in ritual contexts, it is hardly the way most peoples of the world marry. However, McLennan has become equally famous for criticizing Morgan's interpretation of kinship terminology as reflecting aspects of social organization such as marriage practices or mode of descent. For McLennan, kin terms were merely "salutations," that is, modes of address to relatives. Although more attention has been given to terms of reference than to terms of address as such in subsequent anthropology, McLennan started an alternative trend to Morgan's, that is, a trend toward interpreting kin terms in their own right (as systems of classification, especially), rather than in respect of external factors like social organization. This idea was to be taken up again over forty years later by the Boasian, Alfred Kroeber (1909; see further below).

As regards marriage and the priority of one particular mode of descent, the opposite, "patriarchal" tendency, against which McLennan was writing in part, was pursued by yet another lawyer, the highly conservative Sir Henry Maine, who was eventually to acquire administrative experience of India (1861). Basing himself on early Indo-European data, Maine claimed that the earliest form of social organization was the patrilineal family under the absolute authority of the father-husband. Later descent groups developed out of them, partly through direct parent/child ties, but also as accretions – that is, these "descent groups" were often really legal fictions, like units in ancient Greece and Rome, and the Scottish clan. Maine recognized from the outset that much "kinship" was in fact social, involving rules of inheritance through only the male line, adoption, etc. – that is, involving cultural variation that could not be reduced to the biological. The later accretions became more and more political in nature, until we arrive at the state. By this point, kinship, seen as a status one is born with, is definitely taking a back seat to contract, or the negotiation and affirmation of relationships on other bases than kinship, such as territory, citizenship, fealty, economic agreement or subjection (slavery or serfdom).

Maine thus placed the family at the start of social evolution, and saw it building up to much larger polities like the state, though he also thought that the family itself became progressively smaller in parallel with this process, as well as less purely patrilineal and more cognatic. This contrasts with Morgan and other matrilinealists in at least two ways. First, there is no "state of nature": Maine jumps straight in with a distinctly authoritarian form of social organization, human freedom only increasing with the arrival of the state. The matrilinealists, by contrast, started from large, amorphous groups and progressively reduced the size of social groups as more and more discriminations were made, thus placing the nuclear family at the end of the process. For them, too, in being more "moral," the family offered less freedom than earlier forms of social organization, though that freedom was, of course, closer to anarchy. In that Maine starts with a structure that involves cultural discrimination, which is absent from the alternative idea of a horde, he is perhaps being more realistic, though whether his actual choice of the patriarchal family was the right one is anyone's guess. The key question here is at what point human society began to make distinctions between different sorts of relative and began to demarcate different social groups internally. Given the ability of the existing primate species that are closest to humans to recognize at least near relatives, the best guess is that this ability was inherent in human evolution. The idea of amorphous, promiscuous hordes is in reality nothing more than a nineteenth-century version of the state of nature that social theorists from Rousseau to Morgan have held up as a mirror to human society and, even more implausibly, derived it from.

The debate over the historical priority of clan or family did not go away, but persisted well into the twentieth century. In the later nineteenth century another group of writers entered the field, including especially W. Robertson Smith (1885,

1889) and Sir James Frazer (1910) in Britain, and Emile Durkheim (1912) in France, who linked the development of clans with early forms of religion involving blood sacrifice and totemism. Durkheim in particular associated the latter with early forms of religion as represented by present-day native Australians. Totems are essentially emblems, often but not always animal species and therefore drawn from what the modern West would call the natural world, which may be used to identify descent groups from one another. As we now know they may exist for other purposes, and not all societies with descent groups have them. But in many Australian societies, Durkheim alleged, totems were the focus of special attitudes and worship, which, because of the representative nature of totems, amounted to the group worshipping itself – a key point in Durkheim's sociology of religion. Incest, too, was connected with the taboo on spilling the blood of a woman's first intercourse where it was shared within the clan (1898). In another, earlier major work (1893) Durkheim had compared societies divided into clans (mechanical solidarity) from more modern, developed societies organized around a division of labor (organic solidarity). The former had units, the clans, which were essentially similar, so that they could occasionally die out without impairing the society as a whole. In the case of the latter, each trade or craft group or political class had narrower, more specific functions, such that the disappearance of one would impair the whole society by leaving it bereft of a key function.

By the time Durkheim wrote *The Elementary Forms of the Religious Life* in 1912, the associations made between totemism and forms of social organization had already been shown to be ethnographically unsound by Alexander Goldenweiser, a follower of Franz Boas in the United States (1910). Durkheim's interpretation survived little better in the long run. Although Radcliffe-Brown attempted to revive it in modified form (1952: 117–32), as an all-embracing theory it was finally put out of its misery by Lévi-Strauss in a slim volume published in 1962. For the latter, looking for the function of totemism in terms of social control or organization is futile: what is at issue is the notion of classification and the relations between both the categories in a classification, and different classifications as wholes. Totemism and clan organization are related analogously as series within separate domains of discourse: thus the relationship of clan A to clan B is like that of, say, bear to fox in some North American tribes, or cobra to tiger in Orissa, India (these species being exemplary totems). There is also a difference, in that species are endogamous, clans exogamous. If totemism has a function, therefore, it is merely a cognitive one, providing an understanding of social universes (see also Lévi-Strauss 1963) by analogy, not the formation of one mode of classification on the other. Of course, the same objections can be produced to this interpretation, and on much the same ethnographic grounds, as above; in addition in this case, clans are not always exogamous.

The alternative approach to the question of which had priority, descent group or family, was best exemplified in the early twentieth century by Bronislaw Malinowski. For him the nuclear family was the fundamental unit in society, and had priority for this reason (1913, 1930a). This reflected the influence of Edward Westermarck, a Finnish scholar and colleague of Malinowski at the London School of Economics. He had developed a theory of the family as universal in all societies at all periods, thus explicitly contradicting the evolutionists' tendency to confine it to one or other period of human history (1891). Malinowski took this further by replacing any reference to history with a functionalist approach allied to the revolution wrought by Durkheim (although Malinowski was influenced at least as much by Frazer). For Malinowski, society existed to fulfill basic human needs like food, shelter, and explanations of existence. The prime site in which these needs were fulfilled was the nuclear family, in which both parents had a role, regardless of descent mode or the exact nature of belief in birth and conception (Malinowski famously denied that the matrilineal Trobrianders had a belief in paternity). Although wider units such as the clan might be recognized, they were based on extending that recognition outward from the family. Children were especially supposed to do this, as part of socialization and learning. This meant reducing social forms that pre-existed the individual to psychological explanations focused on the individual (another influence on Malinowski was the psychologist Wundt), and most post-Durkheimian anthropologists have rejected such interpretations as mixing domains that ought to be kept separate. Malinowski's psychologism is also reflected in his interest in human motives and their working out in practice, and not just the formal aspects of social organization and classification.

Malinowski also applied this "extensionism" to kinship terminology, which, in opposition to Rivers, he otherwise dismissed as "kinship algebra" (1930b). This position is heavily reliant ultimately on notions of genealogy that are certainly not always ethnographically appropriate, and has subsequently been dismissed by most authorities on kinship, for this very reason. However, it found some allies in the 1950s and after in the United States, especially in formal semantic analyses of kin terms, which are based on very similar propositions (see below). In particular, the main proponents of this school, Harold Scheffler and Floyd Lounsbury, have both defended Malinowski against his more recent critics, including Edmund Leach (see the latter's item below, Chapter 9).

Malinowski therefore did not have much sympathy with the Morgan school, diverging from it in respect of his anti-evolutionary functionalism, his focus on the family in place of descent groups, and his dismissal of the significance of kinship terminology. By the time Malinowski was writing, the Boasians in the United States had already been taking Morgan's work apart for some time. This was principally an attack on the evolutionary uniformities of the 1860s and 1870s, and was based on ethnographic researches mainly in North America, which were now available in much greater abundance than they had been in Morgan's day. Below we shall encounter Robert Lowie refuting Morgan's evolutionary stages in precisely this manner. Later, in the inter-war period, the Boasian rejection of evolutionism also came to involve a repudiation of race as a determinant of social organization or cultural variation. This was something that some evolutionists, though less so Morgan himself, tended to slip into, if not explicitly assume. By the 1930s it was becoming urgent, as a result of the rise of fascism. But evolutionism also tended to postulate fixed stages in a determinist way. The Boasian paradigm replaced this with one of cultural relativism, that is, of the contingency of social and cultural forms, in which known but extremely varied and unpredictable historical circumstances took the place of the neat, settled, inevitable patterns of the evolutionists. The Boasians certainly recognized the significance of the past, therefore, but saw it in terms of variable history, not uniform evolution. Part of the dismissal of Morgan accordingly took the form of repudiating the priority he and others gave to matrilineal over patrilineal descent, but it also involved the suggestion that descent was actually a less significant principle of recruitment to social groups than residence or, more generally, territory. In fact, this is scarcely a more sound proposition as a general principle, though it certainly corresponds to some ethnographic realities (see the items by Good and Barnes, below, Chapters 11 and 4). Descent is frequently dispersed territorially (see the item by Good, below, Chapter 11), and those related by it actually live together relatively infrequently.

Among the more significant Boasian articles for the future study of kinship was Alfred Kroeber's 1909 article on the classificatory form of relationship. As White showed (1958), Kroeber, like many of his colleagues, misunderstood what Morgan meant by this, because he argued that all kinship terminologies denote classes and that therefore all were "classificatory" in one sense or another. However, like McLennan before him Kroeber suggested that a kinship terminology should be studied in its own right, with reference to its general nature as a classification in language and to such internal characteristics as age, generation, laterality, etc. (an approach taken up in the 1950s by Ward Goodenough; see 1956). In particular, ever the skeptical Boasian, Kroeber argued that kinship terminologies have nothing necessarily to do with social organization, though there might be a correlation in particular cases.

This stimulated a Morganesque reply from W. H. R. Rivers in Britain, represented in the item by him below (Chapter 7). Until his death in 1922, Rivers was regarded as the leading contemporary specialist in kinship. This was partly because of his advocacy of the "genealogical method" of collecting kin terms (cf. 1900, 1910), which he pioneered in the western Pacific, and his guarded approach to descent, in which he advocated rigorously separating descent as a mode of recruitment to social groups from either the inheritance of property or succession to office, since these might proceed in different modes even in the same society. He was also among those who saw only unilineal descent, not cognatic descent, as true descent, because of the alleged amorphousness of the latter and the choice of membership in different groups that might be claimed if one's parents were in different groups (1924). In general, the former suggestion has proved happier than the latter (cf. Parkin 1997: 19–22).

But Rivers also deserves to be remembered as an experimenter who, although generally deductive in his reasoning (cf. Kuper 1988: 166, 185 n. 24), was also not afraid to change theoretical tack if the data provided overwhelming proof that this was required. Originally a psychologist with an interest in the physiology of the senses, he sought to apply the principles of natural science to anthropology. His "genealogical method" (cf. Bouquet's critique, 1993, 1996) was initially designed to elicit "true," that is, biological relationships in order to help him understand the inheritance of psychological traits. This led to an interest in anthropology, and in the work of Morgan. However, while retaining Morgan's methods, he revised his interpretation of the past, casting doubt on primitive promiscuity, seeing the Malayan or Hawaiian system as relatively advanced rather than truly primitive as did Morgan, and arguing that cross-cousin marriage depended on paternity recognition and therefore could not be connected with any form of group marriage. At the end of his life, indeed, he abandoned strictly evolutionary explanations for diffusionist ones. These focused on the mutual influence of societies through trade, migration and so on, and at their extreme accounted for the whole of human history and society in terms of the spread of influence from centers of "civilization" like ancient Mesopotamia or Egypt. Briefly popular in Britain at this time, diffusionism, like evolutionism, quickly fell victim to the new anti-historical functionalism. Rivers's reputation suffered undeservedly as a result, though ironically this shift brought him nearer to the Boasians, who retained a greater interest in diffusionist ideas.

The Retreat from History

Rivers's sense of history was thus initially evolutionist in the conventional sense, and only later diffusionist. Both positions became discredited under functionalism, for whose supporters both approaches represented merely "speculative history" of no use in analysis. Both Malinowski and Radcliffe-Brown – originally a student of Rivers – in their different ways replaced all historically based perspectives with versions of functionalism. For Malinowski, as we have seen, the functionalism of society was largely a matter of fulfilling basic human needs, with a focus on the nuclear family more than on descent groups. For A. R. Radcliffe-Brown, who was much more influenced by the rigorously anti-psychological sociology of Durkheim, it was a matter of the mutually sustaining balance of the different institutions in a society, from the family to descent groups, from witchcraft to totemism, and from ritual to expected stereotypes of behavior (joking and avoidance relationships, and the avunculate).

For Radcliffe-Brown and his followers and associates, especially Meyer Fortes and E. E. Evans-Pritchard, the descent group was a major functionalist instrument of this sort. Such groups were seen as discrete groups recruited through descent, with tendencies toward proliferation as they expanded and segmented through time, and with segments periodically breaking off to form new groups. They were usually seen as being defined by their exogamy and by having unilineal rather than cognatic rules of descent. It was well into the post-war period before cognatic descent and descent groups began to be seen as objects worthy of study in their own right (e.g., Goodenough 1955; Firth 1957, 1963; Davenport 1959; Murdock 1960), a period that also saw the publication of Freedman's examination of the bilateral, ego-centered kindred (1960). In the standard view of lineage theory, since descent groups allotted both rights and duties to their members, they had to be discrete and non-overlapping to prevent conflicting claims, attributes that cognatic descent groups, which allowed ego to establish claims in the groups of either parent, did not have.

This basic approach was developed further in one direction by Fortes, who contrasted this "politico-jural" aspect of unilineal social organization with the "domestic" domain of the bilateral family (1945, 1949). This was a development of Malinowski's ideas of the relationship between the two (like Malinowski, Fortes had an early interest in psychology, and was never as Durkheimian as Radcliffe-Brown). Among the Tallensi of what was to become Ghana, for example, the patrilineal descent group was the location of political activities among men, while the family was essentially a bilateral instrument of day-to-day nurture and sustenance. One consequence of this approach was the tendency that developed for a time to separate "kinship," viewed as the totality of an ego's bilateral relationships in all directions, from descent, seen as ego's connections with senior relatives in a direct line. This separation was reflected in publication, both Fortes and Evans-Pritchard dealing with the two topics in separate ethnographies (Fortes 1945, 1949; Evans-Pritchard 1940, 1951). Descent groups were also described as "corporate" because they survived the deaths of individual members, a label that could also be used to suggest that they owned property in common, possibly something intangible like custody of a particular ritual.

For Radcliffe-Brown, the doctrine of the "unity of the descent group" became something of a mantra, balanced by his parallel doctrine of the "unity of the sibling group," which allegedly survived the post-marriage separation of brothers and sisters through exogamy (e.g., 1950, 1952: 49–89). It was consistent with this view of descent-group unity that descent groups, being typified as exogamous, were reliant on each other only for marriage partners. Otherwise functionalists tended to play down the significance of marriage, though this was perhaps less true of Radcliffe-Brown than Fortes or Evans-Pritchard. Fortes, for instance, interpreted relations between ego's own and ego's mother's descent group among the patrilineal Tallensi as involving ego's "complementary filiation" or relationship with the mother. For Dumont and other "alliance theorists" (see below, Chapter 10), on the other hand, this was really an alliance relationship between whole groups, given that ego's father and mother's brother were themselves affines. Even here, therefore, Fortes preferred a descent perspective to the fact that ego's parents had married (and had come from different groups in order to do so). Only Evans-Pritchard escaped this static, substantivized model to some extent and gave it both dynamism and a relational structure (see his item below, Chapter 2). He did so, however, with reference to the operation of the feud, not marriage, and then in ethnographic circumstances that many have questioned subsequently. Kuper (see his item below, Chapter 3) takes us through the repeated construction and deconstruction of the descent model, which, in the quasi-universal form it was so often given, seems finally to have been laid to rest.

The obsession with descent was also indicated by the reduction of at least certain types of kinship terminology to the status of epiphenomena or reflections of social structure. One example were so-called Crow–Omaha terminologies, which were seen to reflect lines of descent because of the vertical equations they make in what are actually lines in the kinship terminology – matrilineal in the Crow case, patrilineal in the Omaha case. In fact, there is much variation in such terminologies, and in any case they do not necessarily coexist with the actual mode of descent their patterns indicate; also, unilineal descent systems occur with quite different sorts of terminology, not only Crow–Omaha ones (cf. Radcliffe-Brown 1952: 49–89). Needham's dismissal of them as a discriminable type (1971: 13–18; cf. also McKinley 1971) is famous, though not quite the last word. Radcliffe-Brown also did a lot of ethnographic survey work on Australian marriage systems (e.g. 1931), of the sort we have already encountered in reviewing Morgan's stages. While the association of terminological pattern and social organization is more obvious in the case of cross-cousin marriage, Radcliffe-Brown still saw the former as a reflection of the latter, which itself was based on a genealogically defined rule of marriage (see his reply to Dumont's item, below, Chapter 10).

At least Radcliffe-Brown recognized that marriage sections and moieties were not essential to such systems. But he and others still found a way of interpreting them in terms of descent, in the form of either patrilineal or matrilineal moieties uniting one section from each generation in the direct line (father to son or mother to daughter), the moieties themselves continuously exchanging spouses. This view of continuous descent generation after generation violated the common indigenous view of alternate generations "recycling" each other through reincarnation or some similar idea (cf. Allen's item, below, Chapter 13). What is more, even with clear moiety organization in one descent mode (say, patrilineal), moieties of the other descent mode (i.e., matrilineal) were imagined as a "submerged" or "hidden" descent line. Such marriage systems were then explained as resulting from the intersection of the two sorts of moiety, or so-called "double descent." In avoiding both ego's patrilineal and matrilineal moieties in marriage, the argument went, ego only had one section or marriage class left to marry into.

This approach is especially associated with Radcliffe-Brown (1931) and Lawrence (1937), but it also reappears in modified form in Lévi-Strauss's distinction between harmonic and disharmonic systems, in both of which the submerged rule of descent becomes a rule of residence (1949; "harmonic" regimes refer to societies that have both descent and residence connected with the same parent, while "disharmonic" regimes mix them). It was another structuralist, Dumont (1966), who argued most convincingly that this particular version of what he called "the apotheosis of descent" was based too much on supposedly implicit factors that were rarely if at all articulated by informants, and that such systems were best seen in terms of affinal alliance, not descent. One final example of this same apotheosis is the very way in which interrelationships between whole peoples were seen in the nineteenth century; namely, as having "descended" from earlier peoples in genealogical terms (cf. Bouquet 1996).

Thus many in the 1950s and after felt that, here too, Lévi-Strauss rode to the rescue in seeking to replace this increasingly redundant and sterile functionalist approach with a more dynamic, structural approach that focused on relations rather than substance. However, his major work in this field, *The Elementary Structures of Kinship* (1949, 1967, 1969), develops a theory that is also effectively evolutionary and functional in part, not just structural. Briefly, the need for early human groups to communicate led to complex networks of exchange, in which the chief item exchanged was women. In other words, the sisters of one group were exchanged with those of another, who became the first groups' wives. As a result, the incest taboo was introduced to reinforce, even maintain, this rule of exogamy. But also, the regular exchange of spouses took the form of cross-cousin marriage, which is found frequently in the contemporary ethnographic record and which, as we have seen, continues a theme that goes back via Rivers to Morgan (to whom Lévi-Strauss dedicated his work). In fact, as the items by Dumont, Good, and Needham in the collection all make clear, such systems cannot simply be understood as involving marriage to cross-cousins in the narrowly genealogical sense, but rather as a category involving a number of other individuals too. We might also remark here that, although they have attracted a great deal of attention from anthropologists, such systems are not pursued by more than a small proportion of the world's population, concentrated mostly in certain areas like aboriginal Australia, Oceania, Indonesia, upland Southeast Asia, south and central India, the Himalayas, the Amazon, and parts of North America (not, therefore, in Europe, nor in Africa or most of Asia by most modern definitions). No more than descent, therefore, are they a characteristic of "third-world" or non-European populations.

Nonetheless, an important and explicit link was made between such systems and the social organization of the societies that had them. Lévi-Strauss is basically interested in the nature of the relationship between descent groups through the exchange of women in marriage, not in their internal composition or distribution of rights and duties to their members, as with the functionalists. These exchanges were often declared to be the only respect in which descent groups needed one another, although in practice they also exchanged other property and ritual services. They were therefore seen as the "cement" holding such societies together. Lévi-Strauss also acknowledged, as had long been recognized, the association between certain sorts of kinship terminology and different variations on cross-cousin marriage, but unlike the evolutionists and functionalists, he declined to reduce either to the other. This was another example of his structuralism, which was also found in his approach to totemism (see above). Basically both were surface expressions of an underlying mode of thought that operated through binary oppositions, in this case mainly between groups, possibly wife-takers and wife-givers, and between sisters and wives.

Lévi-Strauss's theory also had its evolutionary aspects, but it was not rooted in them like the work of Morgan and his contemporaries. Among types of cross-cousin marriage, he saw what he called "generalized exchange" as being less stable than, and collapsing into, "restricted exchange." The former takes the form of non-reciprocal, unilateral marriages in a circle involving successive groups of wife-givers and wife-takers practicing marriage between MBD and FZS: at least three groups are therefore involved (see Needham's item, below, Chapter 12). The latter takes the form of reciprocal, bilateral marriages between just two groups, who repeatedly exchange spouses through marriages between individuals related simultaneously as MBD and FZD, and MBS and FZS (see the items by Dumont and Good, below, Chapters 10 and 11). These are formal, model-level interpretations, and many more groups and exchange cycles might actually be involved in either case.

Lévi-Strauss called both variations "elementary structures," because they could be expressed through a simple marriage rule (called "positive marriage rule" by Dumont). He contrasted them with so-called "complex structures," which lack such marriage rules and which he placed later in world evolutionary terms. In between come the class of "semi-complex structures," generally associated with the "Crow–Omaha systems" of the functionalist. Lévi-Strauss saw these as lacking positive marriage rules in the sense of enjoining whom one should marry, but retaining the practice of framing some of the prohibitions on marriage in terms of prohibiting specific descent groups as a source of ego's spouse. In fact, seen as systems of dispersing the alliances of any one spouse-exchange group among several such groups, Crow–Omaha terminologies are not required at all (as in north India, for example). Despite the efforts of one of Lévi-Strauss's students, Françoise Héritier, to develop the concept of semi-complex structures with reference to the Samo of Upper Volta (1981), it cannot be said that they form a clear class of kinship system any more than Crow–Omaha.

Lévi-Strauss was accompanied or followed by such figures as Edmund Leach, Louis Dumont, and Rodney Needham, all of whom we shall meet below. All of them, especially Needham in terms of sheer volume, drew inspiration from Lévi-Strauss's model, using it to clear up many difficulties and uncertainties in the way kinship systems actually "work." Leach even anticipated Lévi-Strauss in one respect, by writing an ethnographic account of matrilateral cross-cousin marriage among the Kachin of Upper Burma in the late 1940s (1951; cf. Leach 1961: Chs. 2, 3), and he also discussed the type comparatively at around the same time (1951; both are reproduced in Leach 1961). Although Leach was an unreconstructed functionalist in certain respects, he broadly adopted Lévi-Strauss's structuralist approach here, as well as in debating the finer points of the new alliance theory and the older lineage or descent theory with Fortes, his dyed-in-the-wool functionalist colleague at Cambridge (Leach 1957, 1962; Fortes 1959; Forde 1963).

Since the Boasians, then, kinship studies had been concentrated in, but not on, Europe. But after the second world war things started moving in the United States too. There was the work of George Murdock, chiefly remembered today for the creation of a World Ethnographic Atlas coding ethnographic data from all over the world, and exploited among others by Jack Goody (see item by the latter, below, Chapter 6). Kroeber's approach, advocating the study of kinship terminologies in their own right, resurfaced with the componential analysis of Goodenough, as we saw earlier. Often bracketed with him, though their work is different in detail, are the formal semantic analysts Harold Scheffler and Floyd Lounsbury, and sundry supporters, who, as we have also seen already, built on Malinowski's "extensionism" to develop a highly genealogical form of terminological analysis. This approach was also influenced by the then current vogue for deep linguistic structures pioneered by the transformational linguist Noam Chomsky, which has certain parallels with Lévi-Straussian structuralism.

Like transformational linguistics, formal semantic analysis depended on the alleged logical properties of relationships between terms and, more particularly, of the internal semantic composition of individual kin terms in respect of the kin types they stood for. Much derided by followers of traditional approaches, formal semantic analysis has one significant achievement to its credit in Lounsbury's discovery, from a re-examination of Morgan's data, that the kinship terminology of the Seneca Iroquois was not "Iroquois" in type in the sense that Morgan had defined it (cf. Lounsbury 1964). This has also been the fate of other "types" associated with specific ethnic groups, such as "Eskimo" and "Omaha" (White 1958: 383 n. 30; Barnes 1976, 1984), suggesting that the use of ethnonyms in such cases is best avoided. Lounsbury's discovery nonetheless led to Morgan's Iroquois being defined henceforward by its alternative term "Dravidian," a term already in use to represent a "pure" bilateral cross-cousin type. "Iroquois" was henceforward recognized as a type that does not exploit the cross-parallel distinction consistently, but only in relation to near kin (cf. Trautmann 1981: 82–9). In general, though, the belief that kin terms denote whole categories, not genealogical positions extendable outward from an ego, has tended to prevail, despite Lounsbury's attack (1965) on Leach's item in this collection (below, Chapter 9) and several rearguard actions by Scheffler arguing the extensionist case (1977, 1984, 1985a; cf. Good 1985). Scheffler's suggested substitution of "descent category" for "descent group" in cases where identifiable or significant groups are lacking but descent in the sense of intergenerational links is still present as an idea (1966, 1985b) has received somewhat wider acceptance.

The Schneiderian Turn

The most radical shift since Morgan, however, came from another American, the late David Schneider, who was often dismissed early on as a long-winded maverick determined to upset as many apple-carts as possible (cf. his almost wholly destructive article of 1965), but today has replaced Lévi-Strauss as the new kinship guru (see especially 1968, 1984; also his item below, Chapter 14). Schneider's early work was entirely traditional in type, in the sense that it accepted the conventional categories of kinship analysis (e.g., Schneider and Gough 1961; Schneider 1953). Even later, in one respect Schneider was not at all radical but rooted in the cultural relativism of Boas, with a strong dose of Parsonian sociology thrown in. Yet ultimately his basic position went far beyond any lip service to the social nature of kinship. He began by alleging that, without exception, his predecessors and contemporaries were mired in a basically genealogical way of thinking that rested, if only tacitly, on a view of kinship as ultimately biological. He suggested that this was essentially a Western folk model, based loosely on the natural science foundations of modern Western thought, that bore no relationship whatever to many indigenous views in other parts of the world. In his *American Kinship* (1968) he even declared this to be true of views about kinship held by many modern Americans themselves. This extreme relativist position eventually led him to repudiate much of his more conventional early work on the island of Yap in the western Pacific in a further book published in 1984. Although his cultural relativism took a while to become established in the tradition-ally rather technical subject of kinship, it had become extremely influential as one of the standard approaches to kinship by the 1980s. In the United States especially this may have been aided by the more general dominance of Clifford Geertz, another progressive cultural anthropologist influenced by Parsons and, through him, the nineteenth-century German sociologist Max Weber. Yet not everyone has wanted to follow Schneider all the way to his own dismissal of kinship as a useful analytical category. Although there are differences over how much significance to accord the biological foundations of kinship, a wider measure of agreement has returned that its study should, and can, be comparative (e.g., Carsten 2000, Stone 2001, Galvin 2001). Out and out relativism is now to be tamed by a search for commonalities and suitably articulated differences.

Equally important to the continuation of kinship studies have been new theoretical developments in feminist anthropology. Most notably Sylvia Yanagisako and Jane Collier (1987, reproduced here as Chapter 15) adopted a Schneiderian perspective to point out that "gender," like "kinship," has been a cross-culturally inappropriate concept in anthropology because of its definitional roots in culturally specific West-ern conceptions of biology. They suggested that kinship and gender should be studied together, paying attention to indigenous conceptions of both.

Along with greater sensitivity to local ideas of kinship, or relatedness, contempor-ary kinship studies also came to focus on topics such as the new reproductive technologies and kinship reformulations stemming from rising rates of divorce and remarriage, as seen in a few articles reproduced here. Most such studies have been conducted in the United States and Britain, but also included here is Susan Kahn's (2000) study of assisted reproduction in Israel (Chapter 19). Studies of kinship in relation to political economy is another focus of kinship studies, reflecting wider concerns in anthropology with power, social inequality, and history.

Although post-Schneiderian kinship has continued to sever kinship from biology, another current in anthropology seeks to integrate kinship with biology in an evolu-tionary framework. Illustrating this current in the reader are an older article by Robin Fox (1975) addressing the evolution of human kinship from a primate baseline (Chapter 23), and a recent piece by Maurice Bloch and Dan Sperber (2002) that interprets the avunculate from the perspective of evolved human psychological dispositions (Chapter 24).

Thus, despite a drop in popularity in the 1980s and 1990s, led in part by indigestion brought about by the extremes of Lévi-Straussian formalism, which began to seem more and more unreal to an increasing number of younger researchers, kinship is still a vital topic of study. A recent spate of collections has provided it with renewed coverage and theoretical stimulus (e.g., Carsten and Hugh-Jones 1995; Godelier, Trautmann, and Tjon Sie Fat 1998; Birdwell-Pheasant and Lawrence-Zúñiga 1999; Carsten 2000; Schweizer 2000; Stone 2001). Its continued significance for anthropology, as well as for the lives of those whom anthropology studies, seems assured. (For a detailed overview of recent developments, see Peletz 1995. For interpretations of the current post-Schneiderian theoretical position in respect of kinship, see Carsten 2000: 1–14; Stone 2001: 1–10.)

REFERENCES

Bachofen, Johann J., 1861 Das Mutterrecht. Stuttgart: Krais & Hoffman.

Barnes, J. A., 1961 Physical and Social Kinship. Philosophy of Science 28: 296–299.

Barnes, R. H., 1976 Dispersed Alliance and the Prohibition of Marriage: Reconsideration of McKinley's Explanation of Crow–Omaha Terminologies. Man (n.s.) 11: 384–399.

—— 1984 Two Crows Denies It: A History of Controversy in Omaha Sociology. Lincoln and London: University of Nebraska Press.

Beattie, John, 1964 Kinship and Social Anthropology. Man 64: 101–103.

Bloch, Maurice, and Dan Sperber, 2002 Kinship and Evolved Psychological Dispositions: The Mother's Brother's Controversy Reconsidered. Current Anthropology 43 (5): 723–748.

Bouquet, Mary, 1993 Reclaiming English Kinship: Portuguese Refractions of British Kinship Theory. Manchester and New York: Manchester University Press.

—— 1996 Family Trees and Their Affinities: The Visual Imperative of the Genealogical Diagram. Journal of the Royal Anthropological Institute (n.s.) 2: 43–66.

Carsten, Janet, ed., 2000 Cultures of Relatedness: New Approaches to the Study of Kinship. Cambridge: Cambridge University Press.

Cole, John W., 1977 Anthropology Comes Part-Way Home: Community Studies in Europe. Annual Review of Anthropology 6: 349–378.

Davenport, William, 1959 Nonunilineal Descent and Descent Groups. American Anthropologist 61: 557–572.

Dumont, Louis, 1966 Descent or Intermarriage? A Relational View of Australian Section Systems. Southwestern Journal of Anthropology 2: 231–250.

Durkheim, Emile, 1995 [1912] The Elementary Forms of the Religious Life. New York: Free Press.

—— 1963 [1898] Incest: The Nature and Origin of the Taboo. New York: Lyle Stuart.

—— 1984 [1893] The Division of Labour in Society. London: Macmillan.

Evans-Pritchard, E. E., 1940 The Nuer: A Description of the Modes of Livelihood and Political Institutions of a Nilotic People. Oxford: Clarendon Press.

—— 1951 Kinship and Marriage among the Nuer. Oxford: Clarendon Press.

Firth, Raymond, 1957 A Note on Descent Groups in Polynesia. Man 57: 4–8.

Forde, Daryll, 1963 On Some Further Unconsidered Aspects of Descent. Man 63: 12–13.

Fortes, Meyer, 1945 The Dynamics of Clanship among the Tallensi. Oxford: Oxford University Press.

—— 1949 The Web of Kinship among the Tallensi. Oxford: Oxford University Press.

—— 1959 Descent, Filiation and Affinity: A Rejoinder to Dr Leach. Man 59: 193–7, 206–212.

Fox, Robin, 1975 Primate Kin and Human Kinship. *In* Biosocial Anthropology. Robin Fox, ed. pp. 9–35. New York: John Wiley.

Frazer, James G., 1910 Totemism and Exogamy: A Treatise on Certain Early Forms of Superstition and Sorcery, 4 vols. London: Macmillan.

Freedman, Derek, 1960 On the Concept of the Kindred. Journal of the Royal Anthropological Institute 91: 192–220.

Galvin, Kathey-Lee, 2001 Schneider Revisited: Sharing and Ratification in the Construction of Kinship. *In* New Directions in Anthropological Kinship. Linda Stone, ed. Lanham: Rowman & Littlefield.

Gellner, Ernest, 1957 Ideal Language and Social Structure. Philosophy of Science 24: 235–242.

—— 1960 The Concept of Kinship. Philosophy of Science 27: 187–204.

Goldenweiser, Alexander, 1910 Totemism: An Analytical Study. Journal of American Folklore 23: 179–293.

Good, Anthony, 1985 Markedness and Extensions: The Tamil Case. Man (n.s.) 20: 545–547.

Goodenough, Ward, 1955 A Problem in Malayo-Polynesian Social Organisation. American Anthropologist 57: 71–83.

—— 1956 Componential Analysis and the Study of Meaning. Language 32: 195–216.

Harris, C. C., 1990 Kinship. Milton Keynes: Open University Press.

Héritier, Françoise, 1981 L'Exercice de la parenté. Paris: Gallimard.

Holy, Ladislav, 1996 Anthropological Perspectives on Kinship. London and Chicago: Pluto Press.

Kahn, Susan Martha, 2000 Reproducing Jews: A Cultural Account of Assisted Reproduction in Israel. Durham, NC and London: Duke University Press.

Kroeber, Alfred, 1909 Classificatory Systems of Relationship. Journal of the Royal Anthropological Institute 39: 77–84.

Kuper, Adam, 1988 The Invention of Primitive Society: Transformations of an Illusion. London and New York: Routledge.

Lawrence, William Ewart, 1937 Alternating Generations in Australia. *In* Studies in the Science of Society. George Murdock, ed. New Haven: Yale University Press.

Leach, Edmund, 1951 The Structural Implications of Matrilateral Cross-Cousin Marriage. Journal of the Royal Anthropological Institute 81: 23–53.

—— 1957 Aspects of Bridewealth and Marriage Stability among the Kachin and Lakher. Man 57: 50–55.

—— 1961 Rethinking Anthropology. London: Athlone Press.

—— 1962 On Certain Unconsidered Aspects of Double Descent Systems. Man 62: 130–134.

Lévi-Strauss, Claude, 1962 Totemism. London: Merlin Press.

—— 1963 The Bear and the Barber. Journal of the Royal Anthropological Institute 93: 1–11.

—— 1969 [1949, 1967] The Elementary Structures of Kinship. London: Eyre & Spottiswoode.

Lounsbury, Floyd, 1965 Another View of the Trobriand Kinship Categories. *In* Formal Semantic Analysis. E. A. Hammel, ed. Washington: American Anthropologist Special Publication.

—— 1969 [1964] The Structural Analysis of Kinship Semantics. *In* Cognitive Anthropology. Stephen Tyler, ed. New York: Holt, Rinehart & Winston.

McKinley, Robert, 1971 A Critique of the Reflectionist Theory of Kinship Terminology: The Crow/Omaha Case. Man (n.s.) 6: 228–247.

McLennan, John F., 1865 Primitive Marriage, Edinburgh: Adam & Charles Black.

Maine, Sir Henry, 1861 Ancient Law. London: John Murray.

Malinowski, Bronislaw, 1913 The Family among the Australian Aborigines. New York: Schocken.

—— 1930a Parenthood: The Basis of Social Structure. *In* The New Generation. V. F. Calverton and S. D. Schmalhauser, eds. London: Macaulay.

—— 1930b Kinship. Man 30: 19–29.

Morgan, Lewis Henry, 1870 Systems of Consanguinity and Affinity of the Human Family. Washington: Smithsonian Institution Press.

—— 1877 Ancient Society. New York: Holt.

Murdock, George P., 1960 Cognatic Forms of Social Organisation. *In* Social Structure in Southeast Asia. George P. Murdock, ed. New York: Wenner-Gren Foundation.

Needham, Rodney, 1960 Descent Systems and Ideal Language. Philosophy of Science 27: 96–101.

—— 1971 Remarks on the Analysis of Kinship and Marriage. *In* Rethinking Kinship and Marriage. Rodney Needham, ed. London: Tavistock.

Parkin, Robert, 1997 Kinship: An Introduction to Basic Concepts. Oxford: Blackwell.

Radcliffe-Brown, A. R., 1931 The Social Organisation of the Australian Tribes. Sydney: Oceania Monographs 1.

—— 1950 Introduction. *In* African Systems of Kinship and Marriage. A. R. Radcliffe-Brown and Daryll Forde, eds. London: Oxford University Press.

—— 1952 Structure and Function in Primitive Society. London: Cohen & West.

Rivers, W. H R., 1900 A Genealogical Method of Collecting Social and Vital Statistics. Journal of the Royal Anthropological Institute 30: 74–82.

—— 1910 The Genealogical Method of Anthropological Enquiry. Sociological Review 3: 1–12.

—— 1924 Social Organisation. London: Kegan Paul, Trench, Trubner.

Robertson Smith, W., 1885 Kinship and Marriage in Early Arabia. Cambridge: Cambridge University Press.

—— 1889 Lectures on the Religion of the Semites. Edinburgh: A & C Black.

Scheffler, Harold, 1966 Ancestor Worship in Anthropology: or, Observations on Descent and Descent Groups. Current Anthropology 7: 541–551.

—— 1977 Kinship and Alliance in South India and Australia. American Anthropologist 79: 869–882.

—— 1984 Markedness and Extensions: the Tamil Case. Man (n.s.) 19: 557–54.

—— 1985a Markedness and Extensions: the Tamil Case. Man (n.s.) 20: 547.

—— 1985b Filiation and Affiliation. Man (n.s.) 20: 1–21.

—— 1991 Sexism and Naturalism in the Study of Kinship. *In* Gender at the Crossroads of Knowledge: Feminist Anthropology in the Postmodern Era. Micaela di Leonardo, ed. Berkeley: University of California Press.

Schneider, David, 1953 Yap Kinship Terminology and Kin Groups. American Anthropologist 55: 215–26.

—— 1964 The Nature of Kinship. Man 64: 180–1.

—— 1965 Some Muddles in the Models: Or, How the System Really Works. *In* The Relevance of Models for Social Anthropology. Michael Banton, ed. London: Tavistock.

—— 1980 [1968] American Kinship: A Cultural Account. Chicago: University of Chicago Press.

—— 1984 A Critique of the Study of Kinship. Ann Arbor: University of Michigan Press.

Schneider, David, and Kathleen Gough, eds., 1961 Matrilineal Kinship. Berkeley and Los Angeles: University of California Press.

Service, Elman, 1985 A Century of Controversy: Ethnological Issues from 1860 to 1960. London: Academic Press.

Stone, Linda, 1997 Kinship and Gender: An Introduction. Boulder: Westview Press.

—— ed., 2001 New Directions in Anthropological Kinship. Lanham: Rowman & Littlefield.

Trautmann, Thomas, 1981 Dravidian Kinship. Cambridge: Cambridge University Press.

—— 1984 Decoding Dravidian Kinship: Morgan and McIlvaine. Man (n.s.) 19: 421–431.

—— 1987 Lewis Henry Morgan and the Invention of Kinship. Berkeley: University of California Press.

Westermarck, Edward A., 1891 The History of Human Marriage. London: Macmillan.

White, Leslie A., 1958 What is a Classificatory Kinship Term? Southwestern Journal of Anthropology 14: 378–385.

Yanagisako, Sylvia J., and Janet F. Collier, 1987 Toward a Unified Analysis of Gender and Kinship. *In* Gender and Kinship: Essays toward a Unified Analysis. Janet F. Collier and Sylvia J. Yanagisako, eds. Stanford: Stanford University Press.

Part I

Kinship as Social Structure: Descent and Alliance

Section 1   Descent and Marriage

Introduction

Robert Parkin

This section groups together a number of articles that focus on the question of descent and descent groups, some relying on affirmations of these ideas in what became known as lineage or descent theory, others dismissing them in whole or in part.

It is important to realize at the outset what is involved in lineage or descent theory. No one doubts that human populations recognize links between generations. However, the ways they do so are far from fixed. While some groups maintain extensive genealogies, these will usually be at least partly mythical. In other cases genealogical memories may be shallow, only reaching back two or three generations. Secondly, links may be cyclical rather than linear, with relatives returning after death as reincarnations in their descendants (e.g., Parkin 1988; item by Allen in Section 2, Chapter 13) rather than eventually disappearing after death into an amorphous body of ancestors. Thirdly, people related by acknowledged descent need not act or even live together: descent may easily be dispersed residentially. Fourthly, segments need not be recognized or have any significance.

The standard model that anthropology developed, however, was of an extended descent group (lineage or clan) stretching back for many generations, subdividing into segments through growth over time, yet also acting together in some way (as a "corporate group"), whether economically, politically, residentially, or ritually. One of Kuper's concerns (below, Chapter 3) is to show that attempts to adapt this fundamentally inflexible, single-fit model to all ethnographic situations frequently presented serious difficulties, to the point of their failing entirely. Even more extraordinarily, he points out that post-war deconstructions like his own to some extent represent history repeating itself, given that a number of the students of Franz Boas, of whom Lowie (item below, Chapter 1) was among the most prominent, had succeeded in demolishing the leading nineteenth-century theories (of Morgan and Maine, principally) by early in the twentieth century.

The question of the place of descent in the formation of groups is a separate issue from the respective properties of the chief descent modes – patrilineal, matrilineal, and cognatic – that anthropologists have identified. As we have seen, many of the

earliest controversies surrounded the latter, and in particular presented rival evolutionist explanations of which came first, patriliny or matriliny (or, in the jargon of
the time, patriarchy or matriarchy). For Maine, writing in the 1860s and basing
himself on Roman history and law, patriarchal families first developed through
processes of aggregation into patrilineal descent groups. These later gave way to
state formations based not only on territory, but also on status (as serf, subject,
citizen) rather than kinship as a mode of attachment to groups. The contrary theory
developed by Morgan and others at around the same time postulated instead an
initial human period of fluid populations pursuing hunting and gathering economically in circumstances of "primitive promiscuity," that is, the absence of marriage or
of any other regulation of sexual activity. Since in these circumstances mothers
would enjoy a higher recognition factor than fathers, it was natural for matrilineages
to form from acknowledged mother–child links. Only later, with the arrival of
property and/or male-dominated farming, did property relations become significant,
and with them, patriarchal modes of social organization governed by proper marriage regulations leading on to the monogamous nuclear family.

Thus there was an assumption in Morgan's thought that matrilineal groups
were more primitive and less stable than patrilineal ones. Even after evolutionist
speculations became unfashionable, this attitude persisted as far as the alleged
instability of matriliny was concerned, and it has given rise to the treatment of
matrilineally organized societies almost as pathological in some cases. Despite
various "matrilineal puzzles," however, such as a certain and well-attested tendency
for fathers to seek to divert matrilineal property away from their sister's children
towards their own, such societies are no less viable than any other. Nor, of course, is
there a single "type" of matrilineal society, despite attempts to correlate them, for
example, with particular modes of horticulture (e.g., Schneider and Gough 1961).
Domestic arrangements may center on brother–sister rather than husband–wife
pairs in such societies, but equally they may not. Nor do such societies necessarily
increase the power of women. As Goody has pointed out in discussing Africa
(Goody and Buckley 1973; also his item below, Chapter 6), what is significant
here is not mode of descent but the fact that, in virtually all societies, women are
kept away from inheritance to an extent that would not be possible in the mass
civilizations of Europe or Asia. In many societies organized matrilineally, the fact
that women are channels of relatedness between men does not mean that they
benefit either economically or politically.

It took much longer for cognatic (or bilateral) descent groups to be recognized, or at
least theorized. For many anthropologists, following Rivers (1924: 85), they could
not be true descent groups, since they were allegedly more "optative," to use Firth's
term (1957: 5), in allowing a person to belong to more than one such group at a time.
Much post-war anthropology showed, in effect, that this could be true of patrilineal
groups too, which were sometimes even reinterpreted as cognatic (e.g., Holy 1979, on
Evans-Pritchard's account of patrilineages among the Nuer). The issue of cognatic
systems also entered controversies surrounding double descent – to what extent was
this form of descent in two unilineal modes for separate purposes different from
cognatic descent in the ordinary meaning of the term? More recently, too, Schneider
in the 1960s, and Strathern and others in the 1980s and since, have returned to the
question of cognatic descent in addressing the assumption that kinship is necessarily
bilateral because of its foundation in the biology of reproduction (according to which

everyone is the child of two parents). However scientific this view may be, they argue that this is also a Euro-American folk model that has played an important part in maintaining anthropology's continuing Eurocentrism.

Among the most persistent of Morgan's detractors was Robert Lowie. In his contribution here, he provides a long and detailed description, supported by copious ethnographic examples, of the nature of descent systems, both patrilineal or matrilineal. His distinction of "kin" from "clan," the latter being necessarily exogamous, the former not, is no longer followed, due to the abandonment of the use of "kin" in this sense. Unlike Evans-Pritchard, for whom lineages are formed from known genealogical ties, clans not, Lowie treats them as conceptually the same. He also distinguishes "unilateral" (or as we would say today, "unilineal") descent groups from the bilateral family, and associates them with exogamy, unlike larger bilateral groupings, which may be endogamous. He mentions phratries, or non-segmented associations of descent groups, as well as moieties, a situation where there are just two such groupings. The lack of segmentation is really a matter of its non-recognition by the society concerned. So-called dual organization, in which the moieties regularly exchange spouses through a system of bilateral cross-cousin marriage, are a special case of this phenomenon, much discussed in respect of Australia, where both it and the related four-section system were once thought to indicate "group marriage" (see Introduction). Having moieties obviates any necessity to use genealogical reckoning in working out who is and who is not a suitable spouse: moiety membership should be sufficient. However, as Lowie points out (cf. the discussion of Radcliffe-Brown in the Introduction), there is no one-to-one correspondence: moieties exist for other purposes (cognitive or ritual, for example) than the regulation of marriage, and cross-cousin marriage can operate in the absence of either moieties or any other social group.

Much of the second half of Lowie's chapter is taken up with a refutation of Morgan's derivation of patrilineal descent systems from matrilineal ones, which supposedly represent an earlier stage in the evolution of human society. Although Lowie is interested in history, his is a contingent history rooted in the circumstances of actual field situations, not, as for Morgan and other nineteenth-century evolutionists, a series of uniform stages. Lowie rejects Morgan's invoking of the tendency in matrilineal systems for fathers to divert matrilineal property surreptitiously to their sons as a reason for the breakdown of the system and its transition to patriliny. This occurs in existing matrilineal societies, which are not necessarily threatened by it. Lowie doubts whether a simple transition from one form of descent to the other is feasible anyway, given the strength of matrilineal ideologies in even the most challenging circumstances. In any case, the ethnography indicates that neither form of descent can unambiguously be linked to the earliest forms of social organization. Indeed, hunter-gatherers like the Semang of Malaya, mentioned by Lowie, who still pursue the earliest known form of economic activity, are constituted rather of ad hoc, temporary groups focused on a territory, not descent groups of any description. Nor, despite Bachofen's suggestion, is there any evidence in either history or present-day ethnography of matriarchy in the sense of societies ruled exclusively by women. Even in matrilineal societies men are in control of affairs, while women are by no means denied influence in patrilineal ones. The difference between matrilineal and patrilineal thus lies in cultural particularities, not in either evolutionary history or the gender contrast.

As Adam Kuper shows (see below, Chapter 3), Lowie's and others' dismissals of the bases of Morgan's theories had to be repeated in mid-century, after the lineage model was revived, mainly by British anthropologists working in Africa and the Pacific. Among these was Evans-Pritchard, whose work on the Nuer is justly famous. Alongside his major monograph published in 1940 appeared the present essay, a chapter in a book he edited with Meyer Fortes, *African Political Systems*. This book, as well as being significant for kinship, is also frequently cited as the starting point for an identifiable anthropology of politics. Its main aim is to contrast societies like the Zulu, which were organized as kingdoms before the colonial period, with societies like the Nuer, which were not so organized but instead were acephalous ("without a head"). One purpose was to show that the latter type of society was not chaotic, but had other means of resolving disputes, which in the Nuer case was the lineage system itself. Evans-Pritchard's account of Nuer descent and territorial organization is often taken (by Kuper, for example) as being paradigmatic of the lineage type, though Evans-Pritchard himself says that it is unique even within Africa for the extent of its segmentation. Nonetheless, as we shall see below when discussing Kuper's deconstruction of this model, it was not without its problems.

At the time Evans-Pritchard wrote, the Nuer were a collection of over twenty tribes, and he starts by briefly describing the influence of ecology and livelihood upon their social structure and regional variations in it. He continues with a description of the territorial organization, which ranges from local communities (hamlets, villages) to tribes via various levels of tribal section. The tribe is the largest political community within which the peaceful resolution of disputes is considered both possible and desirable. There is no indigenous central administrative or jural authority for all Nuer, although in the pre-British period certain prophets rose to prominence who were sometimes able to unite some of the tribes, at least temporarily. In the failure of peaceful dispute resolution, tribal sections go to war, subsections at one level supporting one another as a section against another whole section at a higher level of distinction, only to fight among themselves in a different conflict. There is thus a process of fission and fusion in which sections emerge or are absorbed with others, according to the location of the feud.

Tribal sections are therefore seen as being segmented, on the model of the lineage system. Evans-Pritchard represents the latter as shadowing the tribal sections without being wholly congruent with them in terms of membership. That is, although Evans-Pritchard claims that the Nuer recognize agnatic lineages and clans that give their names to villages and other localities, in practice residential groups are formed of matrikin and affines too. This means that the descent structure cross-cuts the tribal structure, even though the former only operates through the latter. This aspect of Evans-Pritchard's interpretation has given rise to doubts about the very existence of descent groups among the Nuer (see Kuper, below). Nonetheless, since Nuer lineages and clans are also highly segmented, like tribal sections, Evans-Pritchard says that there is the same sort of dynamics of fission and fusion in response to different levels of conflict, of the relativity of groups rather than their static existence, of "values and situations" (p. 72). This is quite different from the earlier, often tacit assumption that corporate groups always act together.

Adam Kuper, who originally did fieldwork in southern Africa (e.g., 1982), has turned his attention more recently to reinterpreting the history of anthropology, partly by interrogating theories of kinship (e.g., 1973, 1988). The chapter included here, which dates from 1982, is part of a post-war trend deconstructing interpretations of descent in anthropology of the sort produced by Evans-Pritchard. Kuper himself mentions many of the main writers involved in this process, but they include J. A. Barnes (see below, Chapter 4), Ladislav Holy (1976, 1979), and Andrew Anglin (1979). For Kuper especially, the treatment of this topic is intimately bound up with the history of anthropology and its construction – principally in the nineteenth century, though revived in the mid-twentieth – of the very notion of "primitive" society that anthropology took upon itself to study. In brief, lineages and descent itself were seen as the basis of both social organization and political activity in non-state societies like the Nuer and Tallensi.

For Kuper and others like Holy, what were being revived in the post-war period by authorities such as Radcliffe-Brown, Fortes, and Evans-Pritchard were earlier arguments about the place of descent in the constitution of social groups. The Boasians had used ethnographies of Native North Americans to demolish the evolutionist speculations of matrilinealists like Morgan. These speculations were avoided as a matter of principle by Radcliffe-Brown and the others, who were more concerned to demonstrate the functional integration of social life produced by lineage systems. The only exception was that, like Durkheim, whom they mostly followed, they sometimes resorted to unverified claims that social change had taken place to explain away negative or otherwise inconvenient cases. However, the Boasians had also argued that in many cases territory or locality, not descent, was the basis of social organization in such societies. This effectively contradicted Maine's argument that territory was linked to the state formations of "civilization," not "primitive" peoples such as these. Nonetheless his dichotomy was relaunched in 1940 with the publication of *African Political Systems*, the collection of papers edited by Fortes and Evans-Pritchard discussed briefly above.

Both editors stressed the political importance of lineages in the societies they had studied. For Fortes, the lineage principally established an individual's rights and duties, and in relation to whom. For Evans-Pritchard, what was important was the process of fusion and fission associated with the segmentation of clans and lineages, which in his view was not simply a matter of their development over time. As we have seen, he represented the Nuer as a quarrelsome people, with segment fighting segment repeatedly but also fluidly. There was no fixity of grouping: different levels of lineage segmentation would be apparent, depending on the scope of different feuds and the size of the groups involved in them. This interpretation was an advance in the sense that it forced a recognition not only of the flexibility of lineage structures, and of the need to contextualize them accordingly, but also of the fact that they existed in people's heads as much as on the ground. One result was that Evans-Pritchard came to be seen as a structural-functionalist somewhat like Radcliffe-Brown, and even as a proto-structuralist or structuralist *manqué*, for example, by Dumont (1971). The question was, did lineages exist inside the Nuer's own heads, or only in Evans-Pritchard's? Kuper is only one of many to think that the territorial groups that Evans-Pritchard thought shadowed the lineage organization might actually have been the significant groups from the Nuer's point of view. He therefore brings out clearly the implications of Evans-Pritchard's difficulties in making the Nuer even understand what he meant by lineages for the standard anthropological model of lineage organization.

In doing so, Kuper is relying largely on Evans-Pritchard's own honesty in describing the problems he encountered in working with the Nuer (which were not limited to this aspect). What we are presented with is a naïve attempt on Evans-Pritchard's part to fit an already existing model of an acephalous, "primitive society" to an actual field situation where it clearly does not belong. One result of this, perhaps unintended on Kuper's part, is to undermine Evans-Pritchard's reputation as an excellent fieldworker. But Kuper's main conclusion is to dismiss the model as having any relevance to any field situation anywhere. Certainly, as Kuper shows, this experience has been replicated elsewhere before and since, in Papua New Guinea and the Amazon (see the items by Barnes and Rivière, below, Chapters 4 and 5), as well as in Australia (among Aborigines), Polynesia, and other parts of Africa. But this is not to say that notions of what anthropologists call lineages and clans are absent elsewhere, for example, in the *gotras* of Brahmans and Rajputs, and the lineages and clans reported among various tribal groups in India. It is notable that Fortes, whose work Kuper deconstructs in similar terms but more briefly, relying largely on Anglin's earlier critique (1979) in doing so, lived long enough to answer his critics, to whom he conceded little (1979).

But then unlike Evans-Pritchard – who, when he did debate anything, did so mainly with the dead (see 1981) – Fortes was a practiced campaigner in debates with living colleagues. Not content with praising the achievements of Radcliffe-Brown (whom Kuper has also defended, if less slavishly; Fortes 1955; Kuper 1977) and claiming the development of lineage or descent theory as a great advance in anthropology (1953), he engaged in controversy almost "down the corridor" with his colleague at Cambridge, Edmund Leach, over the respective merits of this theory and what became known as "alliance theory" in opposition to it (see below, Section 2). For Fortes, descent groups were certainly significant politically, not in controlling feuding, as among the Nuer, but more in terms of according their members an identity within society and defining their rights and duties in relation to the latter – whence the "politico-jural" dimension Fortes more usually referred to. His distinction between this and the domestic domain of the family, which was bilateral rather than unilineal, referred to in the Introduction above, is well known and has been much discussed from the point of view of later attempts to fuse kinship with gender. Marriage took a back seat in Fortes's model, being partly a matter of exogamy, whereby descent groups distinguished themselves from others of like kind. The real concentration was on what happened *within* descent groups, in particular the ways in which they distributed rights and duties (in land and other property, but also the right to certain rituals, etc.) to their members, rather than *between* them. The latter was the concern of alliance theory, as is shown by the papers in Section 2 (especially those by Dumont, Good, and Needham, Chapters 10, 11, and 12), in which marriage is supremely important. With Fortes, even these links were seen in terms of descent rather than marriage, through his distinctive idea of complementary filiation. This referred to ego's links with the parent who did not carry the descent mode, that is, with the mother among the Tallensi and other patrilineal groups. Since the mother came from another group, ego was also linked to mother's brother and other matrikin through her. This was also a matter of linking individuals rather than groups. For alliance theorists, on the other hand – represented in this controversy by Leach, who had worked among the Kachin, the paradigm case of matrilateral cross-cousin marriage – it was precisely the ties between groups created by marriage that were significant (for references, see Introduction, above).

Leach was also significant in respect of what was perhaps the most persistent aspect of the recurring debates over the descent model, and the one Kuper ultimately focuses on the most, namely the relationship, and dichotomy, between descent and residence or territory. One who prioritized residence was the Boasian Kroeber (1938), building on the work of earlier colleagues whom Kuper treats in some detail. It is noticeable, however, that Kroeber was still reluctant to let the language of descent go entirely, preferring to preserve it as a "secondary pattern" of social organization than dismiss it altogether. He was followed by Murdock, who established rather more firmly the idea that people were related because they lived together rather than lived together because they were related. This certainly corresponds to many indigenous views, such as those of the Yapese discussed in Schneider's revised interpretation (1984) of his own earlier, more traditional work on this west Pacific island (e.g., 1953). Leach (1961) follows a similar general line in his study of *Pul Eliya*, a village in Sri Lanka, in claiming that landed property (a more tangible manifestation of the territorial) was the major concern of the villagers, and the main aim of the social strategies they developed, not descent. However, it has come to be felt subsequently that Leach picked something of a straw man here: as Kuper himself points out, no one ever suggested that the cognatic, polyandrous Sinhalese, with their fluid marriages and family structures, had strong lineage ideologies anyway. In this respect, the arguments of those like Kuper, who have suggested that territory is more suitable than the lineage model that Evans-Pritchard claimed fitted the Nuer case, have proved more telling in the long run.

Among the more cited and influential revisionist studies mentioned by Kuper is J. A. Barnes's re-evaluation of Papua New Guinea data from 1962 (Chapter 4). Rather like Kroeber, Barnes is cautious and still finds it difficult to escape from the language of lineage theory entirely. Nonetheless his basic message is not only the unsuitability of that theory for many ethnographic situations in Papua New Guinea, but also for describing many situations in Africa itself, despite the input of that area into the generation of lineage theory. He also points out that the earliest work on Papua New Guinea, on the coasts, had not been influenced by the model: it was only following its later importation that problems arose in the Highlands of the interior.

One of the things Barnes is concerned to do in this article is to draw a picture of the typical Highlands village community with which to oppose the Africanist descent model. While recognizing that such villages often have a core of agnates or patrikin, he points out that other categories may be present, namely "matrilateral kin, affines, refugees and casual visitors" (p. 98), the last two categories not having anything intrinsically to do with kinship at all, let alone descent. This both reflects and stimulates a whole set of other circumstances. There is considerably more freedom regarding residence than the Africanist model allows for, with the ability of men in particular to associate with more than one local group. Shallow filiation links, including those of complementary filiation, replace lineages as a mode of recruitment to the group. But it is only one mode, given the fluidity of residence that brings in matrikin, affines, etc. In any case, lineages have little ideological existence, and what descent groups there are hardly act together regularly in any respect. But perhaps the chief difference is in the politics. This is what informs status rather than descent; in the anthropological jargon, status is *achieved* through personal effort in political activity, not *ascribed* by one's birth into a lineage. These are typically "big men" societies, effectively controlled by dominant males who may have no rights in a community through descent or even agnatic filiation, but who depend on personal charisma and their knowledge of how to use oratory and manipulate exchange networks to build up their personal followings and positions. They are thus at least partly concerned to attract outsiders to the communities they dominate, on whatever basis. Exchange relationships and political activities therefore focus on individuals, not groups, as in the Africanist model. And whereas in the latter one's importance as a person depends on one's membership of a successful, dominant lineage, in the Highlands of Papua New Guinea the dominance of a local community, including its agnatic core, depends on the activities of its big men. Finally, just as achievement is more important than ascription, so exchange relationships are more important than patrilineal inheritance in acquiring the resources needed to build up one's influence. Most of these resources will be distributed to one's followers, who in toto form a clientele rather than a lineage, regardless of the "agnatic core."

At the time, however tentative, Barnes's statement seemed radical, but it was also an important step forward. Since then, ethnography in this area has largely freed itself from the language as well as the ideas associated with the Africanist model, and Papua New Guinea in its turn set the pace in anthropological theory, especially in the 1970s and after. A good statement of what was achieved in this area in the 1960s, 1970s, and 1980s is Marilyn Strathern's *The Gender of the Gift* (1988). However, not all ethnography from the area reports the situation outlined by Barnes. Although LaFontaine's attempt to retrieve the situation for lineage theory failed (1973), a decade later Feil (1984) was still positing the existence of a continuum in the Highlands between the sort of situation Barnes described and deeper patrilineal structures in larger communities. Nor does even a more radical voice like Strathern's avoid mention of clans and lineages where appropriate, as in the Mount Hagen area where she worked (cf. ibid.). These and many other studies indicate that many writers are guarding against throwing the baby of descent out with the bath water of descent theory.

Although unlike Barnes writing after Kuper, at the other end of the same decade, Peter Rivière does a similar job to Barnes for the Amazon area, another graveyard of traditional notions of both descent and marriage (or affinal alliance). An early concern here was to revise accounts of matriliny in the area, since many of the societies to which this mode of descent was attributed were ultimately discovered to be constituted around cognatic descent systems with uxorilocal residence instead (the latter, being residence with the wife's kin group, had caused the confusion). Indeed, the Amazon has come to be seen as a region of cognatic systems, though Rivière indicates that any temptation to make this a universal feature should be guarded against in its turn. He also states unequivocally that, although genealogical memory is often shallow, it is still frequently important. Nonetheless, this shallowness, combined with the heavy presence of cognatic reckoning, makes the lineage model just as problematic here as in the New Guinea Highlands. Rivière draws our attention to indigenous notions of descent, in the form of the vines of the Canela, the leaves of the Barasana, etc. He also highlights the importance of personhood and naming in producing the attachment of individuals to social groups, and refers to Lea's suggestion that Lévi-Strauss's idea of "house societies" (1982; cf. Carsten and

Hugh-Jones 1995) may be appropriate in some cases. Thus in practice the area has many images and types of social morphology.

But it is perhaps in respect of their particular treatment of affines or relatives by marriage that Amazonian societies pose the greatest interpretative problems and show the greatest distinctiveness. One conundrum has been the exact place of affines in the systems of prescriptive alliance that predominate here (on the latter, see below, Section 2). There are clear structural similarities with other areas in respect of such alliance systems, especially south India (partly because only these two regions of the world appear to have sister's daughter marriage as a variant of bilateral cross-cousin marriage; cf. Rivière 1966, Lave 1966, Good 1980). Nonetheless Rivière cautions us against producing simplistic comparisons between the two areas by seeing Amazonian kinship terminologies as "Dravidian," that is, as south Indian. He also points out that, unlike in Dumont's model of Dravidian kinship (see below, Chapter 10), affines are not placed permanently in a category that is rigorously separated from, and opposed to, consanguines: as in Euro-American society, they *become* consanguines.

Indeed, there is a strong tendency to remove affinity as rapidly as possible. Rivière refers to the much discussed "concentric dualism" of these societies, with their dichotomy between inside and outside, kin and affines, safety and danger, in two successively remote circles arranged around a center. In fact there may be other, remoter circles, covering potential affines as well as actual ones, alien affines as well as allied ones, non-human beings, the unknown, etc. The dangers are often represented as mystical in the literature, though they may appear real enough to the people themselves, few of whom probably have any notion of a "natural" death not produced by mystical or actual attacks. Rivière mentions the "cannibalistic imagery" involved in many indigenous descriptions of these dangers, with the putrefaction of corpses being seen as their consumption by enemies, and so on. In some cases, the category of affine is unambiguously dangerous. At the same time, one type of affine or another (as well as trading partners, ritual friends, etc.) may be expected to act as an intermediary managing the relationship between these different circles, as well as the mystical dangers they represent. One way of overcoming the ambiguity represented by affines is to convert them rapidly into "safe" consanguines. These ideas appear to be associated with the preferential endogamy of cognatic groups in some cases, which in effect amounts to a preference for marriage with consanguines paralleled by an ideological non-recognition of affines (cf. Overing Kaplan 1973 on the Piaroa). For collections on kinship in this region, see Maybury-Lewis 1979; Kensinger 1984; also Rivière 1984 for a comparative study of the Guiana region in the north.

Also gently deconstructive in its way has been the work of Jack Goody, who is usually bracketed with the functionalists. A prolific writer molded initially by Fortes's influence, though known as much for his work on literacy as on kinship, Goody initially did fieldwork in West Africa, some of which he treated comparatively (see, e.g., 1969), before moving on to extend such comparative work to Europe and Asia as well. Behind this comparison is a declared preference for the idea of "middle-range theories" associated initially with the American sociologist Robert Merton, in which controlled comparisons are intended to produce not universal hypotheses, but rather a more modest and restricted but ultimately perhaps more informative account of one particular problem or ethnographic situation. To this end statistics are freely used, as well as more qualitative material, which in the article presented here come chiefly from the Ethnographic Atlas put together under the auspices of George Murdock in the United States. One of Goody's long-standing interests has been in property and the circumstances influencing its transmission between generations. Much of his doctoral thesis, for example, published as *Death, Property and the Ancestors* in 1962, focused on the redistribution of both property and social status among the bereaved among the LoDagaba of Ghana. At around the same time he also worked with Esther Goody on fostering, adoption, incest, and adultery in West Africa, as well as independently on the nature of double descent and what became known as "the developmental cycle of domestic groups" (1969, 1958), all of which had relevance for his grand project.

In the article presented here, the statistical tables, though not the discussion of method, have been omitted for reasons of space and presentation. It is nonetheless valuable as an early statement of a comparative problem which only came to its fullest fruition in Goody's work over twenty years later (see 1990), though there were significant stopovers on the way (especially 1973, 1976, 1983). His basic argument is that, in respect of the inheritance, or what he calls "devolution," of property, there are fundamental differences between Africa and the mass "civilizations" of Asia and Europe. (The remoter "tribal" groups in Asia are actually more similar to the African situation, and they will not be referred to further here.) As far as the present day is concerned, following the communist revolution in China and more gradual changes in Europe and Japan, it is perhaps India that represents the Eurasian situation best, followed by the Middle East. Goody's account therefore has to be, and is, partly historical. In making his argument, he stresses that he is seeking to establish trends and average or typical correlations between social phenomena, not absolute one-to-one correspondences. Being in the first instance statistical, his procedure assumes no structural or functional essentials at the outset, though both structures and functions can be discerned emerging as trends in the arguments he produces from them.

It may be best to present an account of Goody's argument in the reverse order to which he presents it himself, since we can benefit from hindsight in doing so. Ultimately Goody traces the changes he identifies back to a difference in agricultural systems in Africa and Eurasia, the former having mostly extensive agriculture based on hoe cultivation, the latter intensive agriculture based on the more efficient plow cultivation. While Africa retained subsistence agriculture until modern times, in Europe this greater efficiency rapidly led to the differential accumulation of agricultural surpluses, which in their turn created the conditions for social stratification, a division of labor linked partly to urbanization, and an increase in population. The latter, in its turn, caused shortages of land and the valuing of land as an item of wealth in its own right, possession of which was linked to social status.

As a result, there was a concern to retain property within both one's social stratum and one's own immediate family. One way of doing this was to enjoin marriage within the slightly extended family or shallow patrilineage, as with the preference for marriages between patrilateral parallel cousins (FBS to FBD) in the Middle East (see Holy 1989 for a recent general interpretation of this specific type of marriage) up to the present day in some areas. Another way, of greater interest to Goody, is to confine inheritance within the family, rather than dispersing it into a wider kin group, as may happen in Africa. One tactic here is to adopt a son, perhaps an in-marrying son-in-law, in the absence of a direct male heir, rather than allowing property to disappear into the wider kin group. But there is also a marked tendency to allow at least some rights in property to daughters in Eurasia, preferring them to brothers or remoter patrikin in the absence of a son, and granting them pre-mortem inheritance in the form of a dowry given to them at marriage, even where they have brothers. This institution, which is often represented as offering a higher-status groom an incentive to take a lower-status bride in a system of social stratification (India is an excellent example), may actually leave the daughter with some or all control over the disposal of the property thus transferred. Sometimes, as Goody points out, it originates with the groom himself, a situation he calls "indirect dowry."

A further consequence of this social stratification is the frequently encountered concern to preserve the purity and therefore attractiveness of women by controlling their virginity, perhaps also restricting their ability to divorce or remarry as widows (as in India). In high-status strata that can afford it their movements may also be restricted, and work forbidden them. In a more recent statement (1990), Goody suggests that this valuing of women as more than a source of sex, children, and labor (as typically in Africa, he claims) had a number of consequences for the social position of women. One is their seclusion, which persists in parts of India, Pakistan, Iran and, most notoriously in recent history, Afghanistan. However, he suggests that it is also at the root of the greater freedoms that women enjoy in Euro-American societies today, as well as the notions of romantic love that, ideologically at least, underpin marriage and partner relationships there too. This is also connected with a preference for monogamy in some cases (especially in Europe since antiquity), though elsewhere polygyny may be a norm associated with prestige, signaled by its greater affordability in high-status strata (e.g., Moslems; Rajputs in India). In Africa, by contrast, although women as brides are frequently exchanged for cattle circulating as bridewealth, they may be able to acquire greater personal independence of men even after marriage (e.g., Holy 1985 on the Berti), and are not burdened with notions of purity or romance to the same degree, if at all, as women in Europe and Asia.

Thus in Eurasia one frequently encounters bilateral forms of inheritance (Goody's "diverging devolution") or some other "strategy of heirship" that keeps scarce and valued property within the immediate family. This immediately invites us to modify our view of the Indian and Chinese mass societies as being basically patrilineal in respect of inheritance: India still has clear categories of inheritance from mother to daughter, of clothes or ornaments, that are not at all the product of modern legislation or conditions. The situation in Africa is quite different. Here, says Goody, subsistence agriculture, almost by definition, does not produce a surplus; but historically, at least, there has not generally been any shortage of land, which therefore did not become an item of wealth, unlike cattle in some areas. If it existed at all in the past, social stratification was primarily political, a matter of military elites sustaining themselves from trading and raiding activities rather than classes based on control of land and agricultural surpluses, on which military elites were built in turn. Among ordinary people in Africa, property circulates freely between descent groups, especially but not only cattle, which is used not as dowry, but as bridewealth in direct exchange for a woman in marriage. Generally women do not inherit, and brothers or even quite remote male cousins are preferred to daughters as heirs. In societies with matrilineal inheritance too, although women are channels of non-affinal relatedness between men (typically MB to ZS in the latter), they are not normally the recipients or direct beneficiaries of the property thus transmitted. Women are thus more dependent on men than in Europe, though less encumbered with notions of purity enhancing their value to men in exchange relationships between social strata as in western and southern Asia and, formerly, Europe.

Thus Goody has succeeded in producing a broad, not universal but very general comparison of trends in Africa and Eurasia that sheds light on other aspects of life in these two regions, such as the importance of literacy, art, cuisine (as opposed to mere cooking), and flowers in Eurasia but not, or less so, in Africa (e.g., 1977, 1982, 1993). Basically the idea here is that social stratification encourages snobbery, which is expressed in appreciation of the finer things in life (cooking, art, literature), this appreciation in its turn being used to keep the lower orders at a distance. Literacy was also a scarce resource in many of these societies, giving power in its turn. But in what respect is Goody's overall theory deconstructive, as I suggested earlier? In essence, Goody has transcended the older concern with finding substantive differences between societies in terms of different modes of descent, such that they are routinely correlated with some other set or sets of factors. Recognizing, with others, that this is a fruitless exercise, he suggests instead, and indeed demonstrates, that it is differences in types of inheritance and marriage prestation, not mode of descent per se, that are significant in determining both the gender of heirs and the degree of remoteness permitted from those from whom they are inheriting.

REFERENCES

Anglin, Andrew, 1979 Analytical Models and Folk Models: The Tallensi Case. *In* Segmentary Lineage Systems Reconsidered. Ladislav Holy, ed. Belfast: The Queen's University Papers in Social Anthropology.

Carsten, Janet, and Steven Hugh-Jones, eds., 1995 About the House: Lévi-Strauss and Beyond. Cambridge: Cambridge University Press.

Dumont, Louis, 1971 Introduction à deux théories d'anthropologie sociale. Paris and The Hague: Mouton.

Evans-Pritchard, E. E., 1981 A History of Anthropological Thought. London: Faber & Faber.

Feil, Daryl K., 1984 Beyond Patriliny in the New Guinea Highlands. Man (n.s.) 19: 50–76.

Firth, Raymond, 1957 A Note on Descent Groups in Polynesia. Man 57: 4–8.

Fortes, Meyer, 1953 The Structure of Unilineal Descent Groups. American Anthropologist 55: 17–41.

—— 1955 Radcliffe-Brown's Contributions to the Study of Social Organization. British Journal of Sociology 6: 16–30.

—— 1979 Preface. *In* Segmentary Lineage Systems Reconsidered. Ladislav Holy, ed. Belfast: The Queen's University Papers in Social Anthropology.

Fortes, Meyer, and E. E. Evans-Pritchard, eds., 1940 African Political Systems. Oxford: Clarendon Press.

Good, Anthony, 1980 Elder's Sister's Daughter's Marriage in South Asia. Journal of Anthropological Research 36: 474–500.

Goody, Jack, 1958 The Fission of Domestic Groups among the LoDagaba. *In* The Developmental Cycle in Domestic Groups. Jack Goody, ed. Cambridge: Cambridge University Press.

—— 1962 Death, Property and the Ancestors. Stanford: Stanford University Press.

—— 1969 Comparative Studies in Kinship. Stanford: Stanford University Press.

—— 1973 Bridewealth and Dowry in Africa and Eurasia. *In* Bridewealth and Dowry. Jack Goody and Stanley J. Tambiah. Cambridge: Cambridge University Press.

—— 1976 Production and Reproduction: A Comparative Study of the Domestic Domain. Cambridge: Cambridge University Press.

—— 1977 The Domestication of the Savage Mind. Cambridge: Cambridge University Press.

—— 1982 Cooking, Cuisine and Class. Cambridge: Cambridge University Press.

—— 1983 The Development of the Family and Marriage in Europe. Cambridge: Cambridge University Press.

—— 1990 The Oriental, the Ancient and the Primitive: Systems of Marriage and the Family in the Pre-Industrial Societies of Eurasia. Cambridge: Cambridge University Press.

—— 1993 The Culture of Flowers. Cambridge: Cambridge University Press.

Goody, Jack, and Joan Buckley, 1973 Inheritance and Women's Labor in Africa. Africa 43: 108–121.

Holy, Ladislav, 1976 Kin Groups: Structural Analysis and the Study of Behavior. Annual Review of Anthropology 5: 107–131.

—— 1979 Nuer Politics. *In* Segmentary Lineage Systems Reconsidered. Ladislav Holy, ed. Belfast: The Queen's University Papers in Social Anthropology.

—— 1985 Fire, Meat, and Children: The Berti Myth, Male Dominance, and Female Power. *In* Reason and Morality. Joanna Overing, ed. London and New York: Tavistock.

—— 1989 Kinship, Honour and Solidarity: Cousin Marriage in the Middle East. Manchester: Manchester University Press.

Kensinger, Kenneth, ed., 1984 Marriage Practices in Lowland South America. Urbana and Chicago: University of Illinois Press.

Kroeber, Alfred, 1938 Basic and Secondary Patterns of Social Structure. Journal of the Royal Anthropological Institute 68: 299–309.

Kuper, Adam, 1973 Anthropology and Anthropologists: The British School. Harmondsworth: Allen Lane.

—— ed., 1977 The Social Anthropology of Radcliffe-Brown. London: Routledge & Kegan Paul.

—— 1982 Wives for Cattle: Bridewealth and Marriage in Southern Africa. London: Routledge & Kegan Paul.

—— 1988 The Invention of Primitive Society: Transformations of an Illusion. London and New York: Routledge.

LaFontaine, Jean, 1973 Descent in New Guinea: An Africanist View. *In* The Character of Kinship. Jack Goody, ed. Cambridge: Cambridge University Press.

Lave, Jean Carter, 1966 A Formal Analysis of Preferential Marriage with the Sister's Daughter. Man (n.s.) 1/2: 185–200.

Leach, Edmund, 1961 Pul Eliya, a Village in Ceylon: A Study in Land Tenure and Kinship. Cambridge: Cambridge University Press.

Lévi-Strauss, Claude, 1982 The Way of the Masks. Seattle: University of Washington Press.

Maybury-Lewis, David, ed., 1979 Dialectical Societies: The Ge and Bororo of Central Brazil. Cambridge, MA: Harvard University Press.

Overing Kaplan, Joanna, 1973 Endogamy and the Marriage Alliance: A Note on Continuity in Kindred-Based Groups. Man (n.s.) 8: 555–570.

Parkin, Robert, 1988 Reincarnation and Alternate Generation Equivalence in Middle India. Journal of Anthropological Research 44: 1–20.

Rivers, W. H. R., 1924 Social Organization. London: Kegan Paul, Trench, Trubner.

Rivière, Peter, 1966 Oblique Discontinuous Exchange: A New Form of Prescriptive Alliance. American Anthropologist 68: 738–40.

—— 1984 Individual and Society in Guiana: A Comparative Study of Amerindian Society. Cambridge: Cambridge University Press.

Schneider, David, 1953 Yap Kinship Terminology and Kin Groups. American Anthropologist 55: 215–236.

——1984 A Critique of the Study of Kinship. Ann Arbor: University of Michigan Press.

Schneider, David, and Kathleen Gough eds., 1961 Matrilineal Kinship. Berkeley and Los Angeles: University of California Press.

Strathern, Marilyn, 1988 The Gender of the Gift: Problems with Women and Problems with Society in Melanesia. Berkeley: University of California Press.

1

Unilateral Descent Groups

Robert H. Lowie

Lineage and Kin

In contrast to the bilateral family, lineages and kins ignore one side of the family. This does not mean that the peoples organized into unilateral descent groups take no cognizance of the other side, but merely that for specific purposes – say the transmission of names – only the matrilineal or the patrilineal kindred are significant. Conceptually, lineages and kins are alike and usually so figure in the native mind. But objectively there is a difference: the lineage is made up exclusively of provable blood relatives, i.e., all members are demonstrably descended from a common ancestor or ancestress; members of a kin may *believe* in such community of descent, they may conceivably be right in their belief, but it is impossible to prove it. The kin, then, is made up of two or more lineages.

It may happen that a tribe is divided into unilateral divisions some of which are by definition lineages, others clans. In the Hopi village of Mishongnovi, the Lizard, Eagle, and Squash people proved to be each composed wholly of persons related by blood; other groups included two or even three bodies of true kindred. From the native point of view, however, all ranked as equivalent types of unit.

Either lineages or kins are, like those of the Hopi, settled in pairs or larger numbers which jointly form a political entity, or each unilateral descent group owns a distinct tract of land and is politically autonomous. Of the latter type is

the core of an Australian horde or the Miwok *nena*, landowning patrilineal body of kindred who remembered their exact genealogical relationship to one another. As a consequence the territorial lineage cannot be *socially* independent of other groups, since incest taboos force its members to seek wives elsewhere. On the other hand, the Tongan *haa*, though *described* as lineages, are self-sufficient localized kins, for they embrace putative as well as true kindred and permit marriage except between close blood relatives.[1]

The Clan

By convention most contemporary English-speaking scholars define the clan as a unilateral exogamous group; at one time totemism was added to its criteria, but being frequently absent in America, Africa, and Asia, this trait is best dropped as inessential. The definition adopted coincides with common French usage and is not unusual in Germany; in England, Tylor conformed to it in speaking of Chinese and Iroquois clans. On the other hand, the old Scotch clan corresponded more nearly to a tribe, though its core was doubtless composed of patrilineal kindred. In America, Major Powell restricted the term to what we call "matrilineal clans" and called patrilineal ones "gentes" (Latin *gens*, descendants of one ancestor; originally applied only to patricians). Powell's nomenclature did not gain converts beyond the United States, where it no longer predominates.

Because of the former conflict between British and American usage I suggested the Anglo-Saxon "sib" for unilateral groups irrespective of the rule of descent, but since the proposal was not generally adopted I have reverted to prevalent British and French terminology. Morgan originally spoke of Iroquois "tribes" in the sense of clans, later substituting "gens," not with Powell's restricted meaning, but to include any clan in modern parlance.

To turn to another terminological issue, is exogamy really important enough to distinguish one type of kin from another? It is tempting to answer negatively since genetically the two are often related. We know, for example, that under white influence ancient bars to marriage are often relaxed without the disappearance of the unilateral tie. But functionally the difference is considerable. For, if a sufficient number of persons were to marry within the kin, how could one continue to speak of matriliny or patriliny at all? The children of such a union are no longer able to draw that sharp distinction between maternal and paternal relatives which is so conspicuous in many societies. A Crow in such circumstances loses his bearings and perplexes his tribesmen. For he owes specific obligations to his father's relatives and others to his mother's, who are now hopelessly confounded. The sons of his father's clansmen ought to be his censors, whereas his mother's are bound to shield him from criticism; but now the very same persons are his joking-relatives and his clansmen! The dilemma affects others as well as himself.

Thus a clan is truly a distinct form of kin. On the other hand, Kirchhoff goes too far in casting doubt on the very existence of patrilinear or matrilinear agamy, for too many African and Polynesian societies have been authentically described in these terms. To be sure, they cannot be regarded as uncompromisingly unilateral; yet the reported rule of descent is evidently prevalent, whether the facts betoken a nascent or a decadent clan organization or some special obstacle in the way of complete consistency.

At all events, in view of terminological differences in the past, we must carefully scrutinize any reported "clan" system until we are sure that the author's conception of one conforms to ours. It is equally important not to jump to the conclusion that some old source must refer to clans when it merely registers some phenomenon that might conceivably be so interpreted. Past construction of Spanish chronicles concerning American Indians is especially suspect and requires discriminating analysis. The Chibcha of Colombia, we learn, had a ruler or priest succeeded by his sister's eldest son. The fact evidently harmonizes with matriliny, it quite properly should make us alert to any further diagnostic criteria of matrilineal descent, but by itself it is not proof. As a matter of fact, the chronicles also tell us that sons inherited personal property, and nothing is said about the practices of the common herd. What is positively known thus admits of several interpretations. Conceivably the Chibcha were in a transitional stage toward patriliny, as older theorists would at once assume; conceivably the people were bilinear; conceivably the rulers had principles of descent and inheritance different from the commoners. In short, we do not know.

Again, the *ayllu* of early writers on Peru has often been conceived as a typical patrilineal clan. However, the unit at present so called by Aymara and Quechua Indians is definitely nothing of the sort, being an alliance of *unrelated* joint families, each claiming descent from a separate founder and with a strongly endogamous tendency. The old sources do, indeed, indicate a more or less patrilineal body, but one that also favored endogamy. There can thus be no question of clans. In Mexico the *calpulli* of the Aztecs remains an enigma, some specialists interpreting it as a clan, others as a military association. On the other hand, some of the western and southern Mexicans may really have had patrilineal clans; and the recent Lacandon of Yucatan are credited with preponderantly exogamous moieties, i.e., two major clans.[2]

Phratries

In ancient Athens a *phratria* was one of three political subdivisions of the tribe (*phyle*), kinship originally determining membership. Morgan conveniently applied the English form "phratry" to a group of two or more clans united for certain common objects.

Though most of the tribes he knew happened to group all their clans into two major units so that their phratries were moieties, he correctly spoke of the three phratries of the Mohegan. In the light of our present knowledge it is useful to retain the word for a union of kins, but to designate as "exogamous moieties" (French *moitié*, half) the two major kins, whether undivided or subdivided, that make up many tribes. This type of unit will presently receive separate discussion.

Phratries may or may not be exogamous. The thirteen Crow clans were grouped in six nameless major units, four of which certainly did not regulate marriage. On the other hand, in the Hopi village of Oraibi, the nine anonymous phratries, each embracing from two to six named clans that share ceremonial privileges, are the largest exogamous units known to these people.

Kin unions of different type may coexist in the same society. Of the sixteen Kansas clans, eight formed one exogamous moiety, the remainder the complementary moiety; and this dual division found spatial expression, the men of one half-tribe with their families camping on the left side, the men of the other half on the right side of the circle. But in addition "those who sang together" formed phratries, of which there were six.

When kins are localized within a settlement, the domiciliary arrangements may go with distinctive mutual relations between particular kins. Of the eight Sherente clans living each in a particular part of a semicircle, a clan on the north side is paired with its southern counterpart, so that four phratries result. Each member of a couple is charged with decorating and burying the deceased of the allied clan.

However, such obligations are not dependent on localization within a settlement. The four Lobi kins, too, are paired. At a funeral the mourners of one of the two linked kins are guarded by members of the other kin, who prevent suicidal attempts and comfort the bereaved, for which they receive a proper fee. Joking privileges obtain between the two groups, which also exercise the serious function of peacemakers in domestic quarrels and in armed brawls. In the latter emergency, a blacksmith, a xylophone player, or a diviner intervenes and, on pain of suspending his ser-

vices, orders the fighters of the kin allied to his own to desist. These phenomena correspond to some often typical of moieties, but though the Lobi phratries are half-tribes, the mutual obligations in this tribe obtain not between the moieties, but between the halves of each moiety.

An extremely ineffective alliance of clans, based on putative linguistic affinity or a common totem, occurs among the Murngin, but is of interest mainly as a groping toward major social units.

"Phratry" is evidently nothing but a convenient term for a kin linkage. The features covered by it do not by any means correspond to a single sociological phenomenon.[3]

Moieties

Etymologically, moieties are half-tribes. If exogamous, they are simply major clans, but this does not necessarily imply that the lesser clans comprised in a moiety bear a direct genetic relationship to it. Whether this holds in a given case is to be determined by special evidence.

The dual organization may be regarded from several points of view. We must consider the attributes of moieties; the relations of exogamous to agamous moieties; the unity or multiplicity of origin of moieties.

Attributes of moieties

Moieties may be exogamous, agamous, or (more rarely) endogamous. The Toda units, though subdivided into clans, are of the last category and one of the moieties ranks the other, so that they correspond to the castes found in other parts of India. Agamy may mean that a once exogamous dual organization has relaxed the rule preventing marriage within its fold; but it may also mean that for some reason the sense of kinship has never been extended, or not fully extended, to the moiety.

Exogamous moieties require special attention. They are widely distributed, occurring in most of Australia and parts of Melanesia; in India and neighboring parts of Asia; and in several parts of both Americas. Their complete or virtual absence in certain other vast regions is also noteworthy; except for a few dubious exceptions they are wanting in Africa and seem to be found only in the westernmost part of Siberia, among the Ostyak and Vogul.

An exogamous dual organization differs from a multiple clan system in significant respects. For one thing, if the rule of descent and an individual's moiety are known, the moiety affiliation of all his relations can be logically deduced. For, given two matrilineal tribal halves called Wolf and Eagle, a Wolf individual's siblings are also Wolves since, by hypothesis, all children follow their mother; by exogamy his father and the father's siblings are Eagles, and for the same reason the father's sister's husband must be a Wolf. Thus we can go on indefinitely. But if there should be three clans, the relatives' affiliations are only partly determined, for any individual can choose a mate from *either* of the two clans to which he himself does not belong.

Any dichotomy brings about distinctive mutual attitudes that do not appear when there are several or more groups. The political system of the United States with its two major parties is quite different from that of France and Germany with their numerous discordant factions. Similarly, the dual organization of primitive tribes exhibits distinctive features: complementary moieties owe each other specified services, compete in games, use contrasted decorative paint, occupy separate parts of the camp or village, and may be associated in native consciousness with antithetical aspects of nature. A few illustrations will make this clearer.

Among the Tlingit (Alaska) a man never gives property to one of his own half-tribe or employs him for any services. A Raven always gets a Wolf to put up a house for him, to pierce his children's ears, to initiate the youngsters into secret societies, and vice versa. Feasts are given exclusively for the other half. There is great rivalry between the two parties, "and their endeavors to outdo each other sometimes almost resulted in bloodshed."

In the eastern United States, the Choctaw moieties performed funeral obsequies for each other and were associated with war and peace, respectively. The comparable Winnebago divisions are called "those above" and "those on earth," the former comprising clans named after birds, the latter called after land and water animals. The moieties formerly occupied each a definite half of the village and, as in several other Eastern tribes, were pitted against each other in lacrosse.

Many Brazilian aborigines have corresponding features. The Bororo apportion the north side of a village to one half-tribe, the south side to the other; in one district there is an additional dichotomy, an axis perpendicular to the Vermelho River creating an Upstream and a Downstream moiety. The primary moieties have reciprocal duties: after a person's death members of the opposite half must kill a game animal, and the performers of a dance must be washed by their opposites. The Apinayé contrast their halves as "Lower" and "Upper," though they actually name them after two species of chestnut; they associate one with the sun and red paint, the other with the moon and black paint. The related Canella dichotomize the entire population according to two separate schemes, and males by two further principles of dual division. Moieties of one type are exogamous, matrilineal, and linked with the eastern and western half of the village. Membership in the second type of moiety hinges on a person's names. The resulting halves differ in decorative paint, use distinct battle cries, and run races against each other during the rainy season; they are further associated with complementary phenomena of nature – one moiety with the east, the sun, day, the dry season, fire, earth, and red; the other with the west, the moon, night, the wet season, firewood, water, and black. A third scheme sets off males according to their affiliation with one or the other of six groups, three of which are ranged as an eastern moiety, while the rest take up positions in the west. These half-tribes figure prominently at the boys' initiation ceremony and at another festival; in associated races the teams are recruited from the complementary moieties. Finally, the four athletically active age classes are localized in pairs, respectively, on the east and the west side of the village plaza, couples competing with each other in races held during the appropriate season.

To take still another example, Australian moieties, often nameless, in part bear such designations as Eaglehawk and Crow, in part names that cannot be translated. The Murngin system duplicates some of the conceptions found in America. At the end of one ceremony the members of the two groups exchange food; at another the men of one half-tribe are privileged and obliged to construct a sacred emblem, for which their opposites compensate them; for ceremonial decoration, one moiety uses red feathers, the other opossum fur. Most interestingly, the Murngin scheme, like one of the four Canella systems, divides the universe between the two halves.

Reciprocity, complementary functions, conceptual antithesis, and rivalry obviously occur in widely distant regions of the globe. It is worth noting that where these functions go with exogamy, they may be nothing more than extensions of the behavior patterns connected with relatives of the paternal and maternal side. For in such an organization every tribesman must belong to either the paternal or the maternal moiety. On the other hand, the implied extension does not occur everywhere, and may be greatly attenuated, so that moiety solidarity is eclipsed by that within the lesser clan or the family.[4]

Exogamous and agamous moieties

Exogamy readily disappears and readily develops in connection with a dual organization. The Iroquois once regarded fellow members of a moiety as siblings and hence barred marriage among them; recently their restrictions held only within the clan. Nowadays, many Canella defy the traditional rule of moiety exogamy – to the chagrin of the older generation. According to the Angami of Assam, whose moieties will be reconsidered presently, the Pezoma and the Pepfüma were once intermarrying moieties, but for some time the taboo has been observed only within a lesser subdivision.

Agamy naturally develops as a sequel to exogamy in a dual organization. For one thing, a prosperous moiety grows so large that its members lose a sense of kinship or find it greatly weakened. Second, the usual difficulty of finding a mate would make a regulation very irksome that ruled out fully half the men or women of the tribe as sex partners.

But the undoubted loss of the exogamous feature in some instances does not prove that all agamous moieties observed must once have

prohibited marriage. Whether such a hypothesis is at all probable depends on the total context. To take the agamous moieties of the Apinayé, this tribe is of the Ge stock, which includes its closest relatives, the Canella to the east, the Northern Kayapo to the west. With both these groups they share matriliny, localization of the moieties within the settlement, their association with ceremonial and with the same form of sport. As among the Kayapo, the half-tribes are referred to as "upper" and "lower"; as among the Canella, red and black paint are the contrasting decorations used, and each moiety owns a set of personal names. Given the established linguistic affinity of the three tribes, the facts are best interpreted by the assumption of descent with modification. Each of the tribes in course of time developed specific features, the Apinayé dropping the restriction concerning sex relations.

On the other hand, the Pueblo Indians of New Mexico present a rather different condition of affairs. In the eastern villages dichotomy is conspicuous, the halves being connected with summer and winter, turquoise and squash, respectively, but in no case have they anything but ceremonial significance. At Santa Ana, persons of certain clans belong by that fact to the Squash ceremonial chamber, those born into the remaining clans to the Turquoise chamber, but the moiety has not developed any feelings of kinship among the several clans of a half-tribe, remaining a purely ceremonial association. In this area, then, evolution has not occurred from an exogamous to an agamous moiety pattern.

But there is another logical possibility. Instead of losing or never having had the marriage-regulating feature, a dual organization may acquire it secondarily. Continued association may ultimately produce a sense of kinship among fellow members of a ceremonial, sportive, or political moiety, this sentiment being reflected in aversion to marriage within the group. This hypothesis may perhaps be plausibly applied to South America. Olson has stressed the wide occurrence there of half-tribes designated as "lower" and "upper," "east" and "west"; and since his paper additional instances have come to light. Some sort of diffusion is certainly indicated, but how is it to be conceived? The dual organizations now known are in part exogamous, in part – as in Bolivia – they are emphatically not so; yet the agamous Uro-Čipaya divisions, precisely like their Canella counterparts, have their quarters in the east and west, respectively, of a village.

Since the higher Andean civilizations are credited with a dual organization, it is tempting to derive its samples among such simpler peoples as the Ge and Bororo from that source. Lévi-Strauss has suggested that the system arose on an intermediate level of culture, persisting both among the Peruvians and Bolivians as they advanced in material equipment and among the simpler tribes, whom he conceives to have fallen from a formerly somewhat higher estate. This is certainly possible, but the hypothesis requires amplification in order to do justice to the facts. For, oddly enough, it is the simpler peoples who have a highly elaborated dual organization with exogamy and other features not paralleled in the Andes so far as we know. Hence what persisted on this assumption was the bare notion of dichotomy plus spatial segregation of the two halves. This colorless scheme must then have been enriched by the decadent tribes to the extent observed, specifically, by attaching exogamy to a hitherto agamous arrangement.[5]

Moieties and clans

Moieties, exogamous or otherwise, commonly comprise lesser clans. What is the historical relation between the two? There are obvious abstract possibilities: a moiety may have several offshoots that retain a sense of kinship; multiple clans may group themselves into two large phratries; of several clans, some may die out, leaving only two; moieties and lesser clans may arise separately, but subsequently be joined in one consistent scheme. For all we know, every one of these events may have been realized in the course of history.

Morgan favored the first hypothesis. A basic clan, he explained, would grow larger and be segmented into several lesser clans; given two original clans both of which split up, yet retain solidarity, the end result is a typical dual organization. That clans have subdivided is a fact, historical instances being known from the Hopi and the Southern Bantu, though in these

particular cases moieties failed to develop. Segmentation is suggested by the very names of certain units, as when three independent Ojibwa clans are called, respectively, Mud Turtle, Snapping Turtle, Little Turtle. However, unless the primary clans number two, the resulting phratries cannot become moieties.

Sometimes the names of tribal halves suggest the contrary process. Such names as Four-clans and Three-clans among the Hidatsa indicate an alliance rather than segmentation. Hopi clans have repeatedly combined in phratries without achieving a dual organization, but illustrating the process which in some circumstances might yield that result. The same holds for South African tribes. That fusion of a different order, i.e., not involving lesser clans, may also result in a moiety system will be shown presently.

The third possibility is of great importance. In Europe, titles of nobility have constantly lapsed because they could be passed on only to sons. As Boas has pointed out, the unilateral groups of aboriginal societies present a parallel. Given a small number of persons in a clan, the time comes when one generation will comprise only males or only females, which means that in the former case the matrilineal, in the latter the patrilineal, group becomes extinct. If we start with only a few clans, they might thus easily be reduced to two. This actually happened in the Hopi village of Shipaulovi; in 1916 I found only two clans there, the Bears and the Suns, but informants recalled two others that had died out; in one case the male survivors had joined the Bears. Thus, a typical dual organization would have come about except for the fact that the Suns so greatly outnumbered the Bears that many had to seek mates outside the village.

Perhaps the virtual lack of a dual organization throughout Africa is in part due to the absence of the conditions just discussed. Negro tribes often have enormous populations compared to those of other natives, and their clans are likely to be numerous. Uganda had thirty-six clans in Roscoe's day and the number of inhabitants, even in a period of decline, was set at a million. Though some clans were absorbed by others, the chances of thirty-six being reduced to two were thus exceedingly slight. To take a less extreme case, the Lobi proper, with only four matrilineal kins, numbered 69,484 in French territory (1931); on British soil a census of the tribe ten years earlier gave the figure of 32,140, said to embrace ten matrilineal kins. Such figures contrast sharply with the barely 100 inhabitants of Shipaulovi in 1916.

The fourth possibility seems to have been also realized in the southwestern United States. As E. C. Parsons has shown, the western Pueblos are organized into matrilineal clans, whereas the easternmost tribes of the region lack them, but have well-developed agamous ceremonial moieties. Where the two schemes came into contact, some adaptation of one to the other would be expectable and actually took place at Santa Ana.

Since in principle clan and lineage are the same, the data from southern California may be cited as relevant. The patrilineage is the fundamental unit in this area. To this some tribes added the moiety concept, probably modeled on the Pueblo pattern, without necessarily allowing it to alter the essence of their social life. Of the more than forty tribelets constituting the Yokuts stock, only a dozen or so had the dual organization with a tendency, but only a tendency, toward exogamy. The principal functions of the moieties were ceremonial and sportive. So many patrilineages were simply grouped together as one half, counterbalancing so many others.[6]

Unity or diversity of origin

The foregoing considerations support a multiple origin for the dual organizations of the world. Undoubtedly particular features of such systems have been borrowed and widely diffused, but this may happen without a diffusion of the structural basis of the system. The Pawnee (Nebraska) split up into a winter or northern moiety and a summer or southern one; and the dual arrangement pervades all their ceremonial. The association with antithetical seasons can hardly have sprung up independently of that found on the Rio Grande; but the most vital principle of all, filiation, did arise independently, for it is at least partly matrilineal among the Pawnee, patrilineal among the Pueblos. All other traits sit more or less loosely on a moiety scheme; hence it is

not surprising that a tribe, observing some sort of dichotomy in a neighbor, should adopt it along with such elements as contrasting ideas or paint. But until the *structure* of the dual divisions is traced to an outside source we have not explained the presence of the system.

Now, the distribution of moiety systems does permit the inference that systems themselves have spread, though not so frequently as, say, the mere idea of teaming some permanent unit of a tribe against another or setting off rival groups of whatsoever constitution by contrasting names and badges. On the other hand, there is positive evidence that moieties are constantly evolving, disappearing, and reappearing. To the example of Shipaulovi we can add a Brazilian and an Assamese instance.

In 1938 two dialectic subgroups of the Nambikuara (Matto Grosso), which had been diminished by feuds and disease, joined forces, but retained their identity and their respective headmen. The Nambikuara regard cross-cousins as ideal mates. In uniting, the adult men of the two units decided to consider one another "brothers-in-law," which automatically made any adult woman of group A the "sister" of the men in group B, and vice versa. In the following generation, then, the offspring of A would intermarry with the offspring of B in precisely the fashion characteristic of moieties. Cross-cousin marriage and the union of our tribelets without loss of identity created a veritable dual organization, even though not labeled as such. Obviously a moiety scheme caught in its hour of birth cannot yet manifest all the characteristics of the full-blown systems of long standing.

Assam, an area full of established moiety systems, illustrates all the same how fluid such systems are. To revert to the Angami Naga, their traditional moieties, Pezoma and Pepfüma, which are subdivided into clans, were once exogamous, but in recent times a village is sometimes made up wholly of either half-tribe and there is no objection to the marriage of fellow members. The inhabitants of Kohima, for instance, are all Pepfüma, but they freely intermarry unless of the same clan. According to the natives, there were only two clans here at one time, the Cherama and the Pferonoma. *In other words, this village had exogamous moieties.* But whereas Cherama remained undivided, Pferonoma split up into six segments, making altogether seven clans at the time of Professor Hutton's researches. In other words, recently a Kohima might marry into any one of the six clans outside his own.

A pertinent observation was made by Rivers among the Toda. One clan had grown to such proportions there that in order to marry at all its members had to take spouses from all the other clans, leaving very few people of the other clans to intermarry among themselves. Thus, there was a close approach to a typical dual organization, the hypertrophied clan assuming the part of one moiety and all the small clans jointly forming its complement.

A moiety system, then, is not an abstruse intellectual creation, but a form of organization that naturally and, in some cases, inevitably arises from demographic conditions. In a multiple clan system the dying out of all but two clans establishes moieties; so does the extravagant growth of one clan at the expense of others. In the absence of clans, the union of two local units in Nambikuara fashion achieves the same end. Thus, even if we consider only exogamous moieties, a diverse origin seems clear. Dual organizations illustrate convergence.

From Lineage to Kin

The evolution of a kin out of a lineage presents no serious difficulty. It implies nothing but the very common primitive tendency to extend the notion of kinship to others than blood relatives. It is true that this tendency is far less pronounced with some peoples than with others; and in such cases the development may be inhibited. The Yokuts are so chary of admitting putative relationship that common totems do not suggest an ultimate bond of blood, and the offshoot of an established lineage quickly loses all solidarity with the parental group. This fact also explains the modest role played by the dual organization even among those tribelets of the stock that have adopted it. A detail of importance in this connection is the anonymity of the lineage: without the convenient label of a name, relationships beyond the third degree are lost sight of.

Contrast with this the Western Apache parallel. Any fellow clansman is *ipso facto* a sibling, mother, maternal uncle, sister's son. The bond is weaker than with true blood relatives of the corresponding category, but it is real. "It is this which makes the clan function as it does." Here the name is an effective symbol of unity. There can be others: in the French Sudan the same taboos create solidarity, regardless of linguistic and religious differences. A pagan Mossi six hundred miles from home is aided and protected by a Moslem Wolof who learns that the stranger is under identical dietary restrictions.

It is not difficult to understand how a man feels toward a remotely or fictitiously related clansman. Except for special reasons the sentiments must resemble those in an extended or in a very large elementary family. The joint family of Polish peasants subordinates personal feeling to a diffuse sense of loyalty toward all. As soon as strictly personal emotions come to the fore, the fact indicates the decay of the larger solidarity. This latter, precisely because it implies little emotional attachment, demands overt expression: a Hopi woman learning of a clansman's death ostentatiously begins howling aloud to manifest a grief she does not experience, cannot possibly experience in a manner proportionate to her demonstration.

The extension of kinship terms, the inevitable dwindling away of numerically weak unilateral groups which join stronger units, conquest and deliberate absorption of alien groups lead from lineage to clans; similarly they may enlarge clans themselves, sometimes into phratries and even tribes. Some historical instances have already been cited, and others are available. Kazak kins repeatedly all but died out from warfare or natural causes, the survivors amalgamating with stronger kins. Hottentot tribes more than once entered a new district, crushed the occupants, and absorbed the remnants in the conquerors' clans. Similar events occurred frequently in Bantu history.

To repeat, the development of clans out of lineages is easily understood. The real problem lies in explaining the origin of the lineage, that is, of unilateral descent.[7]

The Evolution of Unilateral Descent

The nature of the problem

Morgan regarded the conception of unilateral descent as "essentially abstruse," a view more recently entertained by Olson. What worries these writers is why primitive man should have gathered only part of his blood relatives into a unit, excluding the other half though it is biologically quite as close. For this reason Morgan assumed a single center for the origin of the idea; its artificiality, he argued, made "repeated reproduction in disconnected areas" very unlikely. If the unilateral alignment of kindred had been a deliberate and arbitrary affair, it would indeed be improbable that peoples in, say, India and North America should independently hit on the identical way of assigning certain relatives to a group and excluding others from it. But this intellectualistic approach is psychologically unjustifiable. The point is to lay bare conditions that would *spontaneously* yield the observed alignment of relatives.

Forty years ago Swanton clearly formulated the problem for America north of the Rio Grande. In this continent the simplest peoples have only the bilateral family and some local unit; the tribes somewhat more advanced in an economic way are patrilineal; those still more complex, by and large, tend toward matriliny. Swanton did not postulate a necessary sequence; he demanded, however, that we "show tendencies which might point towards an evolution into a social status like that of the Pueblo or Iroquois."

Following in his wake, but not restricting our survey to North America, we shall try to show tendencies toward (a) patriliny, (b) matriliny; and we shall further try to explain (c) the failure for the development of either. Before so doing, it is necessary to discuss the moot question of diffusion.

What is diffused in diffusion?

Several scholars have been greatly impressed by the fact that matrilineal and patrilineal systems adjoin each other. They infer that the unilateral principle which underlies both is the historically basic reality, which merely happens to develop in this or that direction. They support the position by citing many resemblances which usually characterize adjoining unilateral schemes of either order.

The view rests on an intellectualistic misconception. "Unilateral descent" is an abstraction, useful for the sociologist, but nonexistent for the native. *He* knows only that for certain purposes his matrilineal relatives function differently from his patrilineal relatives. For him the two kinds of system are not varying embodiments of one idea, but utterly diverse, antithetical realities. Assuredly either kind of organization may influence the other, but as in the case of moieties we must ask wherein that influence can at bottom lie. Let us examine a feature of clan systems that has undoubtedly been transmitted from tribe to tribe regardless of principles of filiation.

East of the high Plains of the United States an overwhelming number of clans are totemic. This holds equally for the Iroquoian, Muskoghean, Algonquian, and Siouan families. The very same animal species – Bear, Deer, Turtle, Wolf – serve as labels in all of them; and they figure no less among the matrilineal Seneca than among the patrilineal Omaha. The distribution of totems is largely continuous, so that the paths by which they traveled from tribe to tribe are clear. Their cropping up again and again is not due to some vague general psychological tendency, for in the high Plains a radically different scheme of clan nomenclature confronts us. It, too, has spread widely, at least from Alberta to Oklahoma. This area, like the East, harbors Algonquians and Siouans, but they name tribal subdivisions very differently from the custom of the eastern members of the same families.

The Crow actually resemble their fellow Siouans of Nebraska less in this respect than they do the Gros Ventre of Algonquian stock. Characteristic Crow names are Sorelip lodge, Greasy-inside-the-mouth, Tied-in-a-knot, Kicked-in-their-bellies; and Gros Ventre parallels include Ugly-ones, Those-who-water-their-horses-once-a-day and Those-who-do-not-give-away. The Algonquian Blackfoot have subdivisions interpreted as clans by some writers; by others as loose bands. However that be, the problematical units are dubbed Solid-Topknots, Fat-roasters, Short-necks, Small-robes, Liars, and the like. Farther south, the Arapaho of Wyoming and Oklahoma have subdivisions that are unequivocally only bands; they are called Sagebrush men, Red-willow men, Blood-soup men, Ugly people, Ridiculous men.

In other words, the one area uses animal species as labels of tribal subdivisions; the other prefers sobriquets. Broadly speaking, adjoining tribes have similar or even identical nomenclature; the degree of resemblance varies with geographical nearness, which proves more significant than linguistic affinity. Undoubtedly, then, the systems of nomenclature have spread within their respective ranges by migration of peoples and borrowing.

But this undisputed fact has little bearing on the historical relations of the structural units themselves. The matrilineal clans of the Crow are not genetically related to either the Arapaho bands or the patrilineal Gros Ventre clans even though all three bear similar names. In the same way, the diffusion of the name Turtle from matrilineal Iroquois to, say, patrilineal Algonquians (or vice versa) does not prove a genetic tie between the units themselves. For how is such a relationship to be conceived? Assuming that Algonquians in a pre-clan condition become familar with Iroquois matriliny, what is it they discover? Subdivisions bearing animal names. Noting and fancying the latter, they might readily enough introduce a corresponding nomenclature for their bands or whatever other units they had. But by no mechanism conceivable would an alien who observed a matrilineal alignment of kin be prompted to concoct a patrilineal one for his own people. Countersuggestion cannot operate here, for the supposed transmuter lacks the abstraction *we* call "unilateral rule of descent." He may approve and hence borrow a matrilineal arrangement observed by him; he cannot conceivably say to himself, "This is merely one sample of unilateral descent; I will try out its opposite."

In other words, matriliny and patriliny are to be treated as distinct realities. Whether one of them can evolve into the other, as was once generally assumed, will have to be discussed again later on. At present it is enough to state that their basis must lie in totally different cultural conditions.[8]

The origin of patriliny

Under this head fall two separate questions: How can patrilineal kindred be segregated as a distinct group? And how would this lead to the combination of two or more patrilineal units into the usual form of patrilineal clan system?

As Tylor recognized long ago, coresidence is a potent factor; and Steward has plausibly suggested that where men dominate economically, patrilocalism would be the rule. But patrilocalism is not enough: it might produce merely a joint family with loss of females on marriage; whereas the essence of a patrilineal lineage or clan is that members of both sexes permanently remain in it. To be sure, in a few instances we learn of otherwise typical clan systems in which a wife assumes her husband's clan name, as is reported of the Reddi (Hyderabad). However, this tribe, despite its primitiveness, has been in some ways affected by the higher Hindu civilization; what is more significant, being a matter of direct observation, is that even here membership in the natal clan is preserved, though latent, for it governs the selection of a second husband.

Spier has reconstructed the possible evolution of a patrilineage. The Havasupai occupy one permanent village from April to October. A typical subgroup is a joint family made up of a man with his wife and children, and his adult sons with theirs, each elementary family in a separate but neighboring house. Temporarily there may also be a married daughter with her husband, since a son-in-law stays near his wife's father for a year or so before returning to his own father's camp. Farmlands belong to the subgroup, *daughters as well as sons retaining their rights to a share* without, however, having the males' privilege of transmitting it to their offspring. As Spier contends, this is the essence of patriliny. If those with common property rights came to feel as a distinct unit, they would form a patrilineage, whose existence might later be accentuated by a name or other emblem. Close blood relatives on either side would be barred from intermarriage from the start; as the patrilineal descent group crystallized, those bearing its label would fall under the exogamous rule even if only remotely related, whereas the kinship with corresponding persons on the mother's side would be forgotten. In short, patrilocal residence plus patrilineal inheritance would result in complete patriliny.

In this conjectural scheme the position of the daughters is all important. They, too, inherit farming rights, and they retain contact with their natal group. Were it otherwise, there would merely be a parallel to the Yugoslav or ancient Roman joint family. In ancient Rome a daughter was on principle excluded from the inheritance, as she also ceased to take part in the paternal cult. That is precisely what the Havasupai arrangement prevents, so that the extended family can blossom into a lineage.

This likewise holds in Australia with its patrilocal hordes. Here also the females' tie is not ruptured. A married daughter travels fifty miles to visit her mother, her local patriotism is as strong as her brothers', and on dying she is buried in the territory of her birth.

The Ona case is less certain. The tribal area is split into thirty-nine named and sharply circumscribed hunting territories, exploited by patrilineally linked males. Exogamous sentiment is so strong that, for fear of possibly overlooking a remote relationship, men travel great distances in search of a wife. Are, then, these hordes clear-cut lineages? Perhaps, but we remain in doubt because it is not certain how definitely females remain associated with their native districts. They are evidently not compelled to lose the old affiliation in Roman fashion, for widows are known to have settled again in their old homes after their bereavement. Perhaps the data are best interpreted as a patrilineal system in the very process of taking shape. In another part of South America, the northwest Amazons country, the end goal has been reached. The consistently patrilocal Witoto of that region live in communal houses, sometimes assembling well over a hundred patrilinear kinsfolk. Since all those born into a settlement of this type share a patrilineally inherited name, they remain united by this common token.

When two or more lineages have crystallized in this fashion within the same district, their fusion into a village or tribe of intermarrying lineages is easily understood. As Gifford has shown, that has actually occurred in central and southern California. The Miwok once comprised eighty exogamous landowning patrilineages. Hard pressed by white settlers, they were driven out of their ancestral homes and came to amalgamate in villages, where they retained their individuality, thus assuming the part of several unilateral kins of a typical clan system. Other Californians achieved the same result even before Caucasian contact.[9]

The origin of matriliny

As consistent patrilocal residence and patrilineal property interests foster the alignment of patrilineal relatives, so consistent matrilocal residence and matrilineal property interests tend to produce a matrilineal descent group. Obviously it would be necessary for the husband to remain with his wife's group for good, not merely in the initial stages of wedlock; otherwise the children would not become definitely attached to the maternal side of the family. Although information on relevant South American conditions is inadequate for a decisive conclusion, it is interesting that in the one Guiana tribe with matrilineal clans, the Arawak proper, the groom, after a visit to his mother's, "soon returns to his father-in-law's place where he takes up his permanent abode." These people are not unique in this respect, but there are not a few South American tribes which practice only temporary matrilocalism and have remained clanless.

As it was necessary to explain how females could become attached to the male core of a patrilineage, so it is essential to suggest a way of aligning males with the female core of a matrilineage. Where matrilocal residence implies merely that the husband lives with his in-laws, but remains in his home village, he can easily keep up contacts with his own kinsfolk. A Hopi or Canella man thus pays constant visits to his mother's household. The failure of so many South American tribes to achieve matriliny despite matrilocal residence may be correlated with the frequent necessity of a groom's shifting his headquarters to another village. The strictly matrilineal Bororo and Canella, on the other hand, marry without change of settlement.

However, some matrilineal peoples are patrilocal, though not so many as once appeared to be the case. The Iroquois, for example, were described as patrilocal on nineteenth-century evidence, but Fenton has unearthed a source going back to 1644 which proves the Mohawk matrilocal at the time of white contact. Again, the matrilineal systems of northern British Columbia have been reckoned as patrilocal, whereas at least one of them is now reported in association with matrilocalism. Similarly, Rivers's categorical statement that all Melanesian couples live with the husband's people is refuted by Powdermaker's observations in New Ireland.

Nevertheless, the residual cases of matriliny among patrilocal peoples make it desirable to have recourse to a possible determinant besides residence. Here an Australian fact reported by Roth merits attention. In certain districts of Queensland, women individually own clumps of useful plants, their claims being inherited by their daughters. The phenomenon is exactly paralleled in one Paviotso region of eastern California, where pine-nut plots "were owned by women and inherited matrilineally." Since women so frequently are responsible for procuring wild vegetable food, it is not surprising that wherever a particular species had scarcity value the patch containing it should be claimed by the sex that alone would exploit it. Precisely as feminine dress is inherited by girls, not boys, so the tracts in question would automatically pass on to daughters, sisters, sisters' and daughters' daughters.

It would still be requisite to bring males into the scheme in order to achieve a matrilineage. If we assume that the woman and her offspring are linked with the plot she owns by a name defining the locality, this difficulty would be overcome. A somewhat analogously oblique connection of *females* with a group is known from the Colorado River region. In every Mohave clan all the women bear an identical name of totemic significance, the clans themselves being patrilineal and nameless. Among the related Maricopa, however, the clans bore names which often passed on to women, "but only after marriage" – perhaps, we may conjecture, as a safeguard against their losing solidarity with the natal clan. My suggestion concerning a possible origin of matriliny is that the women in an extended family acquire rights to a particular plot of seeds, trees, and so on; that this locality has a name borne by, or connected with, the owners; and that the connection comes to be shared by sons as well as daughters.

The factors proposed as effectively bringing about matriliny are, then, coresidence and coproprietorship by the core of a matrilineage,

with some mechanism for labeling male as well as female offspring of the women belonging to the nascent lineage.[10]

Impediments

If unilateral descent evolves so easily, why is it not universal? Because the conditions set forth above are lacking or only imperfectly developed. Offhand the patrilocal Yurok seem an ideal breeding ground for patriliny; yet clans never arose, and blood relationship alone counted. Looking at the facts more closely, we find that these people were not strictly patrilocal: a man unable to pay the full price for his bride had to live in her father's settlement and work under his direction, thereby losing status for himself and his children. Very nearly one quarter of all marriages – 85 out of 356 known cases – turn out to have been contrary to the norm. Failing consistency with respect to patrilocalism, the Yurok were naturally unable to develop a strictly patrilineal scheme, while the aberrant cases were far too infrequent to set them on the road toward matriliny.

The Semang present somewhat different phenomena. These food gatherers live in minute settlements, which resemble the Yurok villages in being inhabited largely by blood kindred, but differ in being impermanent. The patrilineages have a definite territory to roam in, and within it adult males owned clumps of trees. How far the women continue belonging to their natal horde is not clear. Apart from an initial two years' period of service for his father-in-law, a husband takes his wife to his paternal horde. The population of a camp is often composite: one settlement of only fifty-four inmates living in seventeen windscreens turned out to include members of four distinct kindred groups, each spatially segregated within the camp. In another settlement fifteen windbreaks belonged to natives of the dialectic group called Jehai, while apart from them lay the dwellings of an old man and his sons, who spoke the Sabubn language. These had married Jehai wives and settled with their in-laws, but periodically went off on their own.

Since there is uncertainty about the permanent affiliation of the females, we cannot be sure whether the dominant group in a camp is a lineage or only a joint family. If the former, the first settlement mentioned would parallel the amalgamation of Miwok lineages into a village community. But the Semang alliances seem to lack permanence. A small body of visitors turns up, is allowed to linger without being really welcomed, then flits away again.

Finally, economic conditions may militate against the assemblage of unilateral kindred beyond the elementary family. The Chukchi, the Eskimo, the Yaghan live so precariously that only a handful of persons can keep together for any length of time. Unless that condition is overbalanced, as in Australia, by connecting a larger company with a tract of land, there will be no sizable social unit.[11]

Independent centers

No one asserts that all the recorded kin systems have originated independently of one another. To take the five tribes of the Iroquois Confederacy, all had matrilineal clans; the distribution of clan names was as follows:

Seneca:	Wolf, Bear, Turtle, Beaver, Deer, Snipe, Heron, Hawk
Cayuga:	Wolf, Bear, Turtle, Beaver, Deer, Snipe, Eel, Hawk
Onondaga:	Wolf, Bear, Turtle, Beaver, Deer, Snipe, Eel, Ball
Oneida:	Wolf, Bear, Turtle
Mohawk:	Wolf, Bear, Turtle

Add that the first three tribes certainly grouped their clans in moieties and that the last two in all probability likewise did so, and the evidence for a genetic connection becomes absolute. We are dealing with linguistically related tribes intimately associated with one another and sharing the same general mode of life. Either the basic social structure, then, existed in the tribe parental to all five and was carried away by the several offshoots to be modified by subsequent events, or one of the tribes after differentiating evolved the scheme, which later spread to the others, wholly or in part. Whether (as Morgan believed) the Mohawk and the Oneida lost the clans found among their fellows, or whether (as Fenton has it) the Seneca borrowed the Deer, Beaver, and Heron clans from the Huron, is a detail. Marriage with an alien woman from another matrilineal

people provides an easy mechanism for introducing a new clan; and the geographical position of the tribes favored borrowing. In short, any variant of the original pattern illustrates descent with modification.

The question is not whether evolution from a common pattern has taken place, but how far such a hypothesis can be reasonably extended. For instance, we have previously found that systems may travel freely not only among members of the same stock, but among utterly unrelated tribes. At the same time it became clear that diffusion of special features does not necessarily imply diffusion of the essential structural pattern. However, even that may be proved by specific evidence. The Menomini and the Winnebago are both residents of Wisconsin, but the former are of the Algonquian, the latter of Siouan stock. Both have a clan system characterized by (a) patrilineal descent; (b) totemic clan names, of which over half a dozen agree; (c) moieties linked with the upper and lower worlds, respectively; (d) the ownership of name-sets by clans. Where this pattern, much of which also occurs among the Eastern tribes, ultimately took shape need not concern us now; it evidently was not invented independently by our two tribes, whose observed systems are obviously only variants of a single scheme. That only diffusion across linguistic barriers can account for the resemblances further appears when we compare the Winnebago with their fellow Siouans, the Crow, who have a clan organization without a single feature on the Winnebago and Menomini roster.

But precisely how far must unilateral organizations agree to support the theory of a single origin? On this point scholars differ. Morgan, we saw, believed that unilateral descent originated only once in the history of mankind, spreading from a single center, but the archaic form would be uniformly matrilineal. He fully realized the chasm between matriliny and patriliny and explained how at a much later period the rule of descent might change. Kroeber seems to imply a corresponding evolution in the New World when he outlines the course of social developments among American Indians. Swanton had indicated the rudeness of patrilineal compared with matrilineal tribes north of Mexico, and the still greater simplicity of those loosely organized. Building on this foundation, Kroeber assumes clanlessness as the archaic American condition. At some period Middle America, advancing in other phases of life, also evolved patriliny, he contends, and disseminated it in all directions, though without affecting such marginal peoples as the Eskimo and the Yaghan. Subsequently Middle America turned matrilineal and diffused the new principle, but less widely; and finally the central area dropped unilateral kinship altogether, achieving political integration.

This theory does not purport to explain why Middle Americans switched from patriliny to matriliny, a rather serious gap considering the traditional view that the reverse sequence is natural. Moreover, it assumes a minimum of spontaneous creativeness on the part of the simpler peoples: everything beyond the barest elements of culture is derived from a center of higher civilization. This approach has, indeed, much to recommend it if the trait in question involves a difficult technical accomplishment, such as metallurgy, or an extremely elaborate intellectual achievement, such as a calendar system. In the case of unilateral descent, neither of these assumptions holds: the conditions of residence and inheritance spontaneously screen out individuals who make up a unilateral descent group. This happens as easily in Tierra del Fuego as in Mexico, in Arnhem Land as in China. A multiple origin is therefore indicated both for patriliny and matriliny in the New World and a fortiori in the history of all mankind.

How frequently unilateral descent happened is of course hard to say, but diffusion must rest on the sort of evidence that demonstrates the unity of the Winnebago and the Menomini systems. To make the argument concrete, the matrilineal Crow and the Iroquois organizations are to be considered independent of each other until proof to the contrary appears. Of course, it is *metaphysically* conceivable that in some dim past a matrilineal scheme arose somewhere; and that its surviving offshoots diverged to such an extent as no longer to share anything but the bare rule of descent. All sorts of conjectures can be put forth to suggest the paths of transformation. But such fictions do not yield scientific proof.[12]

General Considerations
Relative chronology of kins

Though half a century ago scholars generally accepted the proposition that all patrilineal peoples had gone through an earlier, matrilineal stage, they did not put matriliny at the very beginning of human society. Morgan explicitly conceived matriliny as a reformatory development that swept away ruder arrangements. And Tylor, in the article on statistical method, declares: "It seems probable that this maternal system arose out of an earlier and less organized and regulated condition of human life." Modern investigators certainly concur in the view that unilateral descent groups arose out of a condition in which descent was not fixed, however different their picture of those early times may be from Morgan's. For reasons already explained, they place the elementary family before the kin, not at the very end of social evolution. Nowadays it seems an historical accident that Morgan laid down the wellnigh universal distribution of the clan at a certain level of culture: he was influenced by what he had observed among the Iroquois, whom he had studied first and most thoroughly; had he begun with the Ute or Paiute or the Andaman Islanders, he would not have scented clans everywhere.

As a matter of fact, it is not easy to correlate clans – rigidly unilateral exogamous kins – with any particular stage of development. They do not occur in Western industrialized nations, but they are still powerful in at least part of so civilized a country as China. On the other hand, the so-called clans of Japanese history do not conform to our definition. The Japanese word *be* that is so translated is, indeed, applied to hereditary groups, but also to corporations of weavers, fishermen, farmers, and the like; and, what is decisive, the oldest historical writings of the country, the Kojiki and the Nihongi, indicate the absence of exogamy. Again, the patrilineal Arab "clans" are proved not to be such by the constant marriage with a father's brother's daughter.

Near the opposite end of the scale, virtually all the Australians have clans, but these do not occur among many of the hunting peoples – the Andaman Islanders, the Eskimo, the Yaghan, the Chukchi. Some stockbreeders, such as the

Masai, have the system; others, like the Lapps, are without it; in still other cases, such as the Kazak, the question of the exogamous unit remains unclear. It is a striking phenomenon that tribes in adjoining areas and sharing the same general type of culture often differ radically in this respect. The Kwakiutl of Vancouver Island are roughly on a plane with the Tsimshian, but are without clans; the Arapaho and the Crow are both typical buffalo hunters, but present the same contrast; the Canella moieties are exogamous, those of the Apinayé agamous.

Undoubtedly an intensive study of such cases may reveal the reason for the difference, but a generalizing statement in broad terms seems impossible. At one time the correlation of clans with agriculture seemed promising, but it can no longer be maintained even for the New World, where it was once applied. In tropical South America, innumerable farming populations of various degrees of complexity are without clans; in northern British Columbia several fishing tribes have them; the eastern Pueblos are not exogamous nor were the Pawnee.

We are on safer ground if we drop exogamy in an attempted correlation. Kins of some sort are not the only means of consolidating groups exceeding the joint family, but they are one very effective means toward that end. Accordingly, we may reasonably expect them above a certain level in the absence of economic deterrents and of equivalent devices for integration. Thus, the clanless Arabs and Japanese certainly did have kins, and the same holds for the Polynesians. As the ideal of nationalism, whether in a dynastic or a popular form, grows in strength, the narrower loyalty must yield to the wider, either becoming subordinated or being wiped out. In southern Albania the people lost their clans in the first half of the nineteenth century as a result of the Turkish overlordship, but the system has lingered on in the isolated northern part of the country.

The utility of the kin thus falls mainly into the field of politics and will be reconsidered in connection with the rise of statehood. The clan, of course, shares this function. Its marriage-regulating attribute it shares with the elementary family: mere clan exogamy would not prevent a father from marrying his daughter among the Crow, or a mother from sex relations with her son among the Murngin.

To sum up, unilateral descent groups do not appear at the very beginning of social evolution; and they tend to be overshadowed or even eliminated when political organization is highly developed.[13]

Chronology of matriliny and patriliny

The earlier theorists considered it self-evident that matriliny must precede patriliny, because fatherhood would be uncertain in the dim past. Whether this premise is valid or not, the inference no longer holds. We now know that physiological fatherhood is a matter of supreme indifference to various primitive groups. Other supposed lines of evidence have also proved deceptive.

The occurrence of double descent in a fair minority of cases puts a new complexion on the problem. It would in each instance require a detailed analysis of the entire cultural setting before we could hazard even a probable guess which of the coexisting systems was prior. Emeneau, the discoverer of the matrilineal Toda clans, has done just that. He finds that in South India patriliny predominates until we reach the Malabar coast with some fully evolved matrilineal clan organizations, but more generally there is a tendency, fluctuating in intensity, to bar unions with matrilineal relatives. Contrary to Rivers's assumption, there is no linguistic affinity between the Toda and the people of Malabar, and only generic or superficial resemblances exist between the two cultures. The Toda have apparently seized upon the moderate repugnance to marrying matrilineal kindred that is common in the whole area and have intensified it, the process culminating in a second exogamous scheme. Here, then, matrilineal clans followed patrilineal ones. It is a local development that need not have been duplicated anywhere else, though it explains how double descent *may* arise.

Apart from the complication introduced by the fact of bilinear peoples, the chronological relations of matriliny and patriliny remain a problem. We must distinguish among (a) the imposition of one of these systems by a dominant power; (b) change by borrowing; and (c) the internal evolution of one into the other. Our government tends to introduce our patrilineal rules of inheritance in place of aboriginal matriliny, rules which might undermine the ancient system, though it is remarkable how long the Iroquois, Navaho, and Hopi have preserved ancient custom. Perhaps Islam might somewhat more effectively alter an earlier matrilineal scheme.

Diffusion has admittedly played a large part in the distribution of unilateral organizations. But we may reasonably doubt whether a people actually organized according to one rule of descent would borrow the opposite rule. Given the differential way of regarding relatives from the two sides, such borrowing would involve a total reorientation. A Crow, borrowing Gros Ventre patriliny, would have to drop his aversion from marrying a tenth or putative cousin through the mother and transfer his repugnance to the patrilineal counterparts; his defenders at all odds and his censors would change places unless, as is quite likely, there would be an utter loss of bearings in all social relations. It is rash to declare that anything is impossible, but the process seems highly improbable.

It is true that Boas reported an often-quoted shift from patriliny to matriliny on the northwest coast. What appears from his later description of the facts, however, is something rather different. The Kwakiutl were primarily without unilateral descent, though favoring the father's side, as many loosely organized tribes do. On coming into contact with matrilineal groups to the north, the northern Kwakiutl adopted this mode of reckoning. Matriliny, then, superseded not patriliny, but a loose bilateral system which, to be sure, might under favorable conditions have evolved true patriliny or, like the Yurok one, might not.

The objection that holds against borrowing of an antithetical rule of descent likewise holds against an internal evolution of either system into the other. Morgan suggested that as property accumulated men would not want to have it inherited by their nephews, but by their sons, and saw in this a motive "sufficiently general and commanding" to bring about the change to patriliny. The motive certainly is a real one: in West Africa and Melanesia, in British Columbia and northern South America, men demonstrably have tried to get around an existing matrilineal code for the material benefit of their sons. To be sure, new forms of wealth

have not been able to sweep away the inveterate matriliny of the Hopi, Navaho, or Iroquois, nor do we know how far the reported paternal efforts quoted just now would actually go toward altering the established system. On the other hand, no comparable motive has yet appeared that would favor an internal shift from patriliny to matriliny. We can, then, fairly state that, *if* a change in the rule of descent occurs, it is more likely to be in the patrilineal direction; but that a change is inherently improbable.

It is otherwise when no crystallized system of unilateral descent is involved, but only certain conditions that are favorable to the evolution of one. The statistics for the Yurok show a prevalence of patrilocalism, but a fair proportion of matrilocal marriages. If general impoverishment should make it necessary for most men to serve for their wives instead of paying the bride price, matrilocalism would, of course, become the norm and *might* set in motion a development toward matriliny.

The conclusion, then, is that a full-fledged matrilineal or patrilineal system does not evolve into its opposite. Contrary to early theories and to some diffusionist doctrines, the two have a distinct history.[14]

The matriarchate

Bachofen, who first treated matriliny in theoretical fashion, conceived it as part of a larger social system – a matriarchate (Latin *mater*, mother; Greek *archos*, ruler) or gynaecocracy (Greek, *gunē*, woman; *gunaikos*, of a woman; *kratein*, to rule). This implied rule of the family by the mother, not the father; control of government by women not men; and the supremacy of a female deity, the moon, not of the male sun. We are here concerned merely with the question whether matrilineal descent is actually correlated with the domestic and political superiority of women.

In the first place, no strictly matriarchal peoples are known ever to have existed. Sporadically, natives tell tales about the former ascendancy of women. The Fuegian form of the story explains petticoat rule as due to the men's ignorance of the masquerade costumes by means of which the women impersonated spirits and cowed their husbands. When men by chance learnt the truth of the matter, a revolution followed that put men at the helm. This is the sort of myth often told by aborigines to account for present usage as the exact opposite of what was customary in the remote past. The historical value of such traditions is nil.

Recent accounts of matriarchal conditions boil down to the fact that some societies recognize certain prerogatives of women that are unusual or contrary to Western law. In this category belongs the Hopi notion that houses must belong to women regardless of how much labor men may have put into their erection or repair. However, we never hear of women as chiefs, and the all-important ceremonials are directed by men. The Khasi women similarly hold all real estate, as well as the family jewels, and at least locally the highest priestly office is held by a woman. Nevertheless, the husband may kill an adulteress, and within the house it is the wife's eldest brother who ranks as the head, not the house-owning wife herself. Again, Iroquois women impeach and nominate chiefs, but no woman is ever chosen for the office.

These are perhaps the most extreme cases recorded; their analysis explodes the notion of any true matriarchate. The sporadic occurrence of feminine rulers, is, of course, wholly beside the point: Queen Elizabeth, Queen Victoria, the Empress Catherine, and Maria Theresa reigned successfully, but without in the slightest degree affecting the status of their female subjects.

But for true perspective it is essential to compare the position of women in the distinctly patrilineal societies. As males are not the downtrodden drudges of termagant wives in matrilineal tribes, so females are by no means the mere toys and slaves of their husbands among patrilineal peoples. Here, too, apparently extreme instances actually refute popular prejudices and lay bare the contrast between theory and reality. Niebuhr, the eighteenth-century traveler previously quoted on Arab polygyny, could discern no great difference in the treatment of women by Moslems and by Europeans: "The women of that country seem to be as free and happy as those of Europe can possibly be." The theoretical right to take four wives was exercised only by "rich voluptuar-

ies" and "their conduct is blamed by all sober men." Legally entitled to divorce a wife at will, "the Arabians never exercise the right of repudiating a wife, unless urged by the strongest reasons." Women enjoyed great liberty "and often a great deal of power in their families." The wife retained control of her dowry, and a poor man might be wholly dependent on his spouse. Niebuhr dismisses as absurd the travelers' tale that all Mohammedan women are slaves. A century and a half later the Seligmans had much the same experience in the Sudan: the Kababish Arab women were anything but obsequious, felt in no way aggrieved, and rather pitied Mrs. Seligman for wearing no jewelry and being obliged to travel without a litter. They had complete disposal of their money and possessions and were often treated with marked respect.

Parallel observations apply to China. Ideologically, woman may be rated an inferior creature, but folk literature teems with tales of henpecked husbands, the Chinese mother is supreme in her household, and at various periods of history some women seem to have exerted a tremendous influence even on public life. It appears, then, that the question of correlation is not at all a simple one. Certainly it is false to accept either rule of descent as a token of unqualified dominance by the ostensibly favored sex.

The question is peculiarly difficult for several reasons. For one thing, there is the observer's personal equation. A naïve American traveler may be outraged by all sorts of things noted abroad. He winces at the arrangement of matches by French parents and is revolted by the sight of a female hod carrier in Austria. It never occurs to him that foreigners have many things to offer by way of countercriticism, and that the average European woman, like her Chinese sister, may be quite contented with her lot. Second, if the recorder has purged himself of his society's preconceptions, what objective criterion is there for deciding that woman's position in a particular community is better or worse than elsewhere? Third, granting that the criterion is known, how easy is it for a stranger to get a fair sampling of the life led by either sex? How much do we know of the intimate relations of our best friends?

To return to the question of patriliny versus matriliny as affecting the position of the sexes, the most promising line of inquiry would be to compare related peoples that differ in the rule of filiation. Further, where possible, we should eliminate the personal equation by considering the same observer's comments on different tribes.

Thus, Nimuendajú, intimately acquainted with a number of South American tribes, was greatly struck with the dominant part played by women among the Palikur, a patrilineal people of Brazilian Guiana. At adolescence the girls begin to put on airs, look down at young men, and henceforth pilfer catches of fish from incoming boats as a matter of privilege. Husbands are conspicuously uxorious, hunting and fishing according to their wives' demands, and a man will miss a chance for lucrative employment if his woman wants him to gather shrimps for her. Even in public affairs women are obviously not without authority, for about 1735 a missionary reports that a sorcerer who had aroused the women's suspicion was killed by them, not by their husbands. Nothing in the division of labor accounts for pronounced feminism: both sexes plant, weed, and harvest; and since fish are as a rule shot with bow and arrow, the task of getting them is a masculine one. Residence is not fixed, but the husband's status is naturally even worse when he lives at his mother-in-law's.

More enlightening than the Palikur case are the phenomena Nimuendajú recorded among the Canella and the Sherente. The Canella, as previously noted, are consistently matrilocal, with women owning dwellings and plantations. This puts the husband at a disadvantage; but since with wedlock he merely shifts dwellings, not settlements, he can in case of conflict return to his mother's and sisters' home, where he plays a significant role. All in all, "neither sex considers the other inferior; the sexes have distinct functions, not higher and lower ones." Only men are councilors and chiefs, but "except in warfare nothing is undertaken without feminine participation." In contrast to this situation, the Sherente husband is in sole control of the home and farm, residence being of course patrilocal, and his wishes prevail. Daughters are trained to be submissive. Yet Nimuendajú saw no instance of a husband's systematically bullying his wife, and one man deceived by his wife, instead of beating her, hanged himself.

These observations among a matrilineal and a patrilineal people of the same stock, offered by the same investigator, are surely suggestive. But we must recall our earlier caution concerning causal connection. Matriliny is not *the* cause of the favorable position of Canella women, when that of their Palikur sisters is even more favorable in a patrilineal community. Matriliny is one descriptive trait that we have isolated from a complex, some other element of which—say mode of residence—may be more important. For a clearer insight into the significance of rules of descent we should require a large series of comparisons like those just indicated for South America. How do the matrilineal Northern Kwakiutl compare with the loosely organized Kwakiutl proper? Is the status of women noticeably better among the matrilineal Crow or Hidatsa than among patrilineal Siouans, such as the Omaha? among their patrilineal neighbors, the Gros Ventre? among loosely organized fellow-Plainsmen, such as the Western Cree or the Arapaho? Corresponding comparisons are necessary in Melanesia, Africa, and other regions. Pending such investigations, any conclusion is necessarily tentative. The indications are that the rule of descent is not highly and only indirectly correlated with the status of the sexes—probably only in so far as the rule is itself connected with the mode of residence. With complete assurance, however, we can assert that matriliny does not automatically involve a matriarchate nor patriliny a patriarchate.[15]

NOTES

1   Gifford 1929, 29–40; id. 1926.
2   Rivers 1924, 19 ff. Tylor 1865, 278, 282. Morgan 1871, 139; id. 1877, pt. II chap. 2. Lowie 1920, III. Powell, LV. Richards 1934. Kirchhoff 1931, 117. Kroeber in Steward ed. 1946, 2:903. J. H. Rowe, ibid., 2:252–256, 262 f. B. Mishkin, ibid., 2:441. H. Tschopik, ibid., 2:539, 544. Beals, Tozzer, 26, 62 f., 99 f. Roys, 31–48. Soustelles, 325–344. Spinden, 186. Vaillant, 108.

3   Morgan, 1877, pt. II, chaps. 2 and 6. Titiev, 58. Dorsey 1897, 230 ff. Nimuendajú 1942, 17, 23. Labouret, 218 ff. Warner, 33 ff.

4   Steinitz. Swanton 1908, 430, 434 f.; id. 1946, 663. Colbacchini, 1–30. Lévi-Strauss 1936. Nimuendajú 1939, 21 f.; id. 1946, 79 et seq. Radcliffe-Brown 1931, 6 et seq. Warner, 29–33.

5   Barbeau. Hutton, 45, 109, 150 et seq., 193. Lowie 1943, 633 f. White, 142 ff. Lévi-Strauss 1944. Parsons 1924. Olson 1933. Métraux 1932, 192–196.

6   Morgan, 1877, pt. II, chaps. 2 and 6. Soga, 23 ff. Lowie 1929, 324 ff., 336. Strong 1929, et seq.; id. 1927. Gifford 1926. Gayton 1945. Boas 1940, 316–323. Roscoe 1911, 6, 138 ff. Labouret, 51. Rattray 1932, 425–451.

7   Murie in Wissler ed. 1912–1916, 549 et seq., 642. Lévi-Strauss 1943 (a); id. 1943 (b). Bose, 29. Hutton, 45, 109, 150 et seq., 193. Rivers 1906, 507. Gayton 1945. Goodwin, 119 f. Thomas and Znaniecki, 1:87 et seq. Delafosse, 3:105 f. Hudson, 13, 98–105. Hoernlé, 12. Soga, 18 f., 25.

8   Morgan 1877, pt. II, chap. 15. Olson 1933. Swanton 1906, 166–173; id. 1905; id. 1946, 654–661. Kroeber 1908, 147 f. Wissler 1911, 21. Kroeber 1902–1907, 7.

9   Steward 1936. Fürer-Haimendorf 1945, 161. Spier 1922. Westrup, 103 et seq. Fenton, 204 ff. Gifford 1926. Kaberry, 132, 176. Gusinde 1931, 302, 319, 419, 425. Kirchhoff 1931, 170–176.

10 Kirchhoff 1931, 149. Roth 1924, 669. Murdock 1934. Steward 1938, 52. Kroeber 1925, 741. Spier 1933, 187. Lowie 1919. Rivers 1914, 2:126. Powdermaker, 32. Fenton, 204. Bachofen.

11 Waterman and Kroeber. Schebesta, 59–69, 78 f., 92 f., 104–109, 225.

12 Morgan 1877, pt. II, chap. 2. Fenton, 204 f., 217 f., 227. Skinner 1921, 47 et seq., 372 f. Radin 1923, 190 et seq. Olson 1933. Schmidt and Koppers, 78 et seq. Kroeber 1923, 355–358.

13 Chamberlain, LI, 58 f., 173, 304, 312. Aston, 1:22, 43, 104, 324, 350, 375; 2:31.

14 Murdock 1940. Emeneau, 173–175. Boas 1940, 356–378. Morgan 1877, pt. II, chap. 14.

15 Bachofen. Gurdon, 66 et seq., 76 et seq., 82, 93. Goldenweiser 1912, 464–475. Niebuhr, 2:212 et seq. Seligman 1918, 150 f. Lin Yutang, 143–146. Nimuendajú 1926, 33 f., 78–82; id. 1946, 113, 125 f.; id. 1942, 32 f.

REFERENCES

Aston, W. G. (translator) 1896 Nihongi. London.

Bachofen, J. J. 1861 Das Mutterrecht. Stuttgart.

Barbeau, C. M. 1917 Iroquois Clans and Phratries (American Anthropologist 19:392–405).

Beals, Ralph L. 1932 Unilateral Organizations in Mexico (American Anthropologist 34: 467–475).

Boas, Franz 1940 Race, Language and Culture. New York.

Bose, J. K. 1934 Dual Organization in Assam (Journal of the Department of Letters, 25:Pt.1:29). Calcutta.

Chamberlain, Basil Hall (translator) 1906 Kojiki. Tokyo.

Colbacchini, D. A. 1925 I Bororos orientali. Turin.

Delafosse, Maurice 1912 Haut-Sénégal-Niger. Paris.

Dorsey, J. O. 1897 Siouan Sociology (Bureau of American Ethnology, Report 15:205–244).

Emeneau, M. B. 1941 Language and Social Forms: A Study of Toda Kinship (in Spier, Leslie, et al., editors, Language, Culture and Personality, 58–179). Menasha, Wis.

Fenton, Wm. N. 1940 Problems Arising from the Historical Northeastern Position of the Iroquois (Smithsonian Miscellaneous Collections 100:159–251). Washington.

Fürer-Haimendorf, Christoph and Elizabeth von 1945 The Reddis of the Bison Hills. London.

Gayton, A. H. 1945 Yokuts and Western Mono Social Organization (American Anthropologist 47:409–426).

Gifford, Edward W. 1926 Miwok Lineages and the Political Unit in Aboriginal California (American Anthropologist 28:389–401).

—— 1929 Tongan Society (Bulletin of the Bernice P. Bishop Museum 61). Honolulu.

Goldenweiser, A. A. 1912 On Iroquois Work (Summary Report of Geological Survey of Canada). Ottawa.

Goodwin, Grenville 1942 The Social Organization of the Western Apache. Chicago.

Gurdon, P. R. T. 1907 The Khasis. London.

Gusinde, Martin 1931 Die Selk'nam. Mödling bei Wien.

Hoernlé, A. Winifred 1925 The Social Organization of the Nama Hottentots of Southwest Africa (American Anthropologist 27:1–24).

Hudson, Alfred E. 1938 Kazak Social Structure (New Haven: Yale University Publications 20).

Hutton, J. H. 1921 The Angami Nagas. London.

Kaberry, Phyllis M. 1939 Aboriginal Woman, Sacred and Profane. Philadelphia.

Kirchhoff, Paul 1931 Die Verwandtschaftsorganisation der Urwaldstämme Südamerikas (Zeitschrift für Ethnologie 63:85–193).

Kroeber, A. L. 1902–1907 The Arapaho (Bulletin of the American Museum of Natural History 18).

—— 1908 Ethnology of the Gros-Ventre (American Museum of Natural History, Anthropological Papers 1:141–281).

—— 1923 Anthropology. New York.

—— 1925 Handbook of the Indians of California (Bulletin of Bureau of American Ethnology 78). Washington.

—— 1946 The Chibcha (in Steward, J. H., ed., Handbook of South American Indians 2:887–909). Washington.

Labouret, Henri 1931 Les tribus du rameau Lobi. Paris.

Lévi-Strauss, Claude 1936 Contribution à l'étude de l'organisation sociale des Indiens Bororo (Journal Société des Américanistes 28:269–304). Paris.

—— 1943 (a) Guerre et commerce chez les Indiens de l'Amérique du Sud (Renaissance 1:122–139).

—— 1943 (b) The Social Use of Kinship Terms among Brazilian Indians. (American Anthropologist 45:398–409).

—— 1944 On Dual Organization in South America (America Indígena 4:37–47).

Lin Yutang 1935 My Country and My People. New York.

Lowie, Robert H. 1919 The Matrilineal Complex (Berkeley: University of California Publications in Anthropology 16:29–45).

—— 1920 Primitive Society. New York.

—— 1929 Notes on Hopi Clans (American Museum of Natural History, Anthropological Papers 30:303–360).

—— 1943 A Note on the Social Life of the Northern Kayapó (American Anthropologist 45:633–635).

Métraux, Alfred 1932 L'organisation sociale et les survivances religieuses des Indiens Uro-Čipaya (International Congress of Americanists 25:191–213).

Morgan, Lewis H. 1871 Systems of Consanguinity and Affinity. Washington.

—— 1877 Ancient Society. New York.

Murdock, George Peter 1934 Our Primitive Contemporaries. New York.

—— 1940 Double Descent (American Anthropologist 42:555–561).

Niebuhr, M. 1792 Travels through Arabia and Other Countries in the East. Edinburgh.

Nimuendajú, Curt 1926 Die Palikur-Indianer und ihre Nachbarn. Göteborg.

—— 1939 The Apinayé (Catholic University of America 8).

—— 1942 The Šerente. Los Angeles.

—— 1946 The Eastern Timbira (Berkeley: University of California Publications in Anthropology 41).

Olson, Ronald L 1933 Clan and Moiety in Native America (Berkeley: University of California Publications in Anthropology 33:351–422).

Parsons, Elsie Clews 1924 Tewa Kin, Clan and Moiety (American Anthropologist 26:333–339).

Powdermaker, Hortense 1933 Life in Lesu: the Study of a Melanesian Society in New Ireland. New York.

Powell, J. W. 1884 On Kinship and the Clan (Bureau of American Ethnology, Report 3:xlvi–lv).

Radcliffe-Brown, A. R. 1931 The Social Organization of Australian Tribes. Melbourne.

Radin, Paul 1923 The Winnebago Tribe (Bureau of American Ethnology, Report 37).

Rattray, R. S. 1932 The Tribes of the Ashanti Hinterland. Oxford.

Richards, Audrey I. 1934 Mother-right among the Central Bantu (Essays presented to C. G. Seligman 267–279). London.

Rivers, W. H. R. 1906 The Todas. London.

—— 1914 The History of Melanesian Society. Cambridge, England.

—— 1924 Social Organization. New York.

Roscoe, John 1911 The Baganda. London.

Roth, Walter E. 1924 An Introductory Study of the Arts, Crafts and Customs of the Guiana Indians (Bureau of American Ethnology, Report 38).

Roys, Ralph L. 1940 Personal Names of the Maya of Yucatan (Carnegie Institute of Washington, Publication 523:31–48).

Schebesta, Paul 1927 Bei den Urwaldzwergen von Malaya. Leipzig.

Schmidt, William and Koppers, William 1924 Völker und Kulturen. Regensburg.

Seligman, C. G. and B. Z. 1918 The Kababish, a Sudan Arab Tribe (Harvard African Studies 2:105–185).

Skinner, Alanson B. 1921 Material Culture of the Menomini (Indian Notes and Monographs). New York.

Soga, John Henderson 1931 The Ama-Xosa: Life and Customs. Lovedale.

Soustelles, Jacques 1935 Le Totémisme des Lacandons (Maya Research 2:324–344).

Spier, Leslie 1922 A suggested Origin for Gentile Organization (American Anthropologist 24:487–489).

—— 1933 Yuman Tribes of the Gila River. Chicago.

Spinden, H. J. 1917 Ancient Civilizations of Mexico: New York.

Steinitz, W. 1938 Totemismus bei den Ostjaken in Sibirien (Ethnos 125–140).

Steward, Julian H. 1936 The Economic and Social Basis of Primitive Bands, in Essays presented to Alfred L. Kroeber, 331–347. Berkeley.

—— 1938 Basin-Plateau Aboriginal Sociopolitical Groups (Bulletin of Bureau of American Ethnology 120).

—— 1946 (editor) Handbook of South American Indians (Bulletin of Bureau of American Ethnology 143), 2 vols.

Strong, William Duncan 1927 An Analysis of Southwestern Society (American Anthropologist 29:1–61).

—— 1929 Aboriginal Society in Southern California (University of California Publications in Anthropology 26).

Swanton, John R. 1905 The Social Organization of American Tribes (American Anthropologist 7:663–673).

—— 1906 A Reconstruction of the Theory of Social Organization (Boas Anniversary Volume 166–178). New York.

—— 1908 Social Conditions, Beliefs and Linguistic Relationship of the Tlingit Indians (Bureau of American Ethnology, Report 26:391–485).

—— 1946 The Indians of the Southeastern United States (Bulletin of Bureau of American Ethnology 137).

Thomas, W. I. and Znaniecki, Florian 1927 The Polish Peasant in Europe and America. New York.

Titiev, Mischa 1944 Old Oraibi; a Study of the Hopi Indians of Third Mesa (Peabody Museum Papers 22:16–201).

Tozzer, A. M. 1941 Landa's Relación de las Cosas de Yucatan (Peabody Museum Papers 18).

Tylor, E. B. 1865 Researches into the Early History of Mankind. London.

Vaillant, George C. 1941 Aztecs of Mexico. Garden City, New York.

Warner, W. Lloyd 1937 A Black Civilization. New York.

Waterman, T. T. and Kroeber, A. L. 1934 Yurok Marriage (University of California Publications in Anthropology 35:1–14).

Westrup, C. W. 1934 Introduction to Early Roman Law; Comparative Sociological Studies. Copenhagen.

White, Leslie A. 1942 The Pueblo of Santa Ana (Memoirs of the American Anthropological Association).

Wissler, Clark 1911 The Social Life of the Blackfoot Indians (American Museum of Natural History, Anthropological Papers 7:1–64).

—— 1912–1916 (editor) Societies of the Plains Indians (American Museum of Natural History, Anthropological Papers 11).

2

The Nuer of the Southern Sudan

E. E. Evans-Pritchard

I write shortly of the Nuer because I have already recorded a considerable part of my observations on their political constitution and the whole is about to be published as a book.[1] They have, nevertheless, been included in this volume for the reasons that their constitution is representative of East Africa and that it provides us with an extreme political type.

I. Distribution

To discover the principles of their anarchic state we must first review briefly the oecology of the people: their means of livelihood, their distribution, and the relation of these to their surroundings. The Nuer practise cattle-husbandry and agriculture. They also fish, hunt, and collect wild fruits and roots. But, unlike the other sources of their food supply, cattle have more than nutritive interest, being indeed of greater value in their eyes than anything else. So, although they have a mixed economy, Nuer are predominantly pastoral in sentiment.

Nuerland is more suited for stock-breeding than for agriculture: it is flat, clayey, savannah country, parched and bare during the drought and flooded and covered with high grasses during the rains. Heavy rain falls and the rivers overflow their banks from June to December. There is little rain and the rivers are low from December to June. The year thus comprises two seasons of about equal duration. This seasonal dichotomy, combined with pastoral interests, profoundly affects political relations.

During the rains Nuer live in villages perched on the backs of knolls and ridges or dotted over stretches of slightly elevated ground, and engage in the cultivation of millet and maize. The country which intervenes between village and village, being more or less flooded for six months, is then unsuitable for habitation, agriculture, or grazing. Anything from five to twenty miles may separate neighbouring villages, while greater distances may divide sections of a tribe and tribe from tribe.

At the end of the rains, the people burn the grasses to provide new pasture and leave their villages to reside in small camps. When the drought becomes severe, the inmates of these intermediate camps concentrate on permanent water supplies. Although these moves are made primarily for the sake of the cattle, they also enable the Nuer to fish, which is generally impossible from village sites, and, to a lesser degree, to hunt and collect wild fruits and roots. When the rains set in again, they return to their villages, where the cattle have protection and the higher ground permits agriculture.

The distribution of the Nuer is determined by the physical conditions and mode of life we have outlined. During the rains, villages are separated, though by no means isolated, from their neighbours by flooded stretches of grassland, and local communities are therefore very distinct units. During the drought, people of different villages of the same district eventually concentrate on permanent water-supplies and share common camps. On the other hand, some families of a village may go to one camp and some to another, though the majority form a local community throughout the year.

Nuer seldom have a surplus of food and at the beginning of the rains it is often insufficient for their needs. Indeed, it may be said that they are generally on the verge of want and that every few years they face more or less severe famine. In these conditions, it is understandable that there is much sharing of food in the same village, especially among members of adjacent homesteads and hamlets. Though at any time some members may have more cattle and grain than others, and these are their private possessions, people eat in one another's homesteads at feasts and at daily meals, and food is in other ways shared, to such an extent that one may speak of a common stock. Food is most abundant from the end of September to the middle of December in a normal year, and it is during these months that most ceremonies, dances, &c., take place.

The Nuer have a very simple technology. Their country lacks iron and stone and the number and variety of trees are small, and they are generally unsuited for constructive purposes other than building. This paucity of raw materials, together with a meagre food supply, contracts social ties, drawing the people of village or camp closer, in a moral sense, for they are in consequence highly interdependent and their pastoral, hunting, fishing, and, to a lesser degree, their agricultural activities are of necessity joint undertakings. This is especially evident in the dry season, when the cattle of many families are tethered in a common kraal and driven as a single herd to the grazing grounds.

Thus, while in a narrow sense the economic unit is the household, the larger local communities are, directly or indirectly, cooperative groups combining to maintain existence, and corporations owning natural resources and sharing in their exploitation. In the smaller local groups the co-operative functions are more direct and evident than in the larger ones, but the collective function of obtaining for themselves the necessities of life from the same resources is in some degree common to all

local communities from the household to the tribe.

These local communities are the monogamous family attached to a single hut, the household occupying a single homestead, the hamlet, the village, the camp, the district, tribal sections of varying size, the tribe, the people, and the international community the limits of which are a Nuer's social horizon. We regard the family, the household, and the hamlet as domestic, rather than political, groups, and do not discuss them further in detail.

The distribution of these local communities is very largely determined by physical conditions, especially by the presence of ground which remains above flood-level in the rains, and of permanent water which survives the drought. In any village, the size of population and the arrangement of homesteads is determined by the nature of the site. When perched on an isolated knoll, homesteads are crowded together; when strung out along a ridge, they are more widely separated; and when spread over a broad stretch of higher ground, several hundred yards may intervene between one hamlet and the next. In any large village, the homesteads are grouped in clusters, or hamlets, the inmates of which are generally close kinsmen and their spouses. It is not possible to give more than a rough indication of the size of a village population, but it may be said to vary from 50 to several hundred souls.

As explained, villages are separated by several miles of savannah. An aggregate of villages lying within a radius which allows easy intercommunication we call a 'district'. This is not a political group, for it can only be defined in relation to each village, since the same villages may be included in more than one district; and we do not regard a local community as a political group unless the people who comprise it speak of themselves as a community by contrast with other communities of the same kind and are so regarded by outsiders. Nevertheless, a district tends to coincide with a tertiary tribal section and its network of social ties are what gives the section much of its cohesion. People of the same district often share common camps in the drought and they attend one another's weddings and other ceremonies. They intermarry and hence establish between themselves many affinal and cognatic relationships which, as will be seen later, crystallize round an agnatic nucleus.

Villages, the political units of Nuerland, are grouped into tribal sections. There are some very small tribes to the west of the Nile which comprise only a few adjacent villages. In the larger tribes to the west of the Nile and in all the tribes to the east of it, we find that the tribal area is divided into a number of territorial sections separated by stretches of unoccupied country, which intervene also between the nearest habitations of contiguous tribes.

As all Nuer leave their villages to camp near water, they have a second distribution in the dry season. When they camp along a river, these camps sometimes succeed one another every few miles, but when they camp around inland pools, twenty to thirty miles often separate one camp from the next. The territorial principle of Nuer political structure is deeply modified by seasonal migration. People who form separate village communities in the rains may unite in a common camp in the drought. Likewise, people of the same village may join different camps. Also, it is often necessary, in the larger tribes, for members of a village to traverse wide tracts of country, occupied by other village communities, to reach water, and their camp may lie close to yet other villages. To avoid the complete loss of their herds by rinderpest or some other misfortune, Nuer often distribute the beasts in several camps.

In western Nuerland, where the tribes are generally smaller than to the east of the Nile, there is usually plenty of water and pasturage, and it is possible, therefore, for village communities of the rains to maintain a relative isolation in the drought. But where, as in the Lou tribe, for example, scarcity of water and pasturage compels more extensive movement and greater concentration, people who are very widely distributed may have more social contact with one another than is the case in western Nuerland. The isolation and autonomy of local communities are broken up by economic necessity and the size of the political group is thereby enlarged. This fact has to be considered in relation to the further fact that to the east of the Nile wider stretches of elevated ground allow larger local concentrations in the rains than is usual to the west of that river. Moreover, seasonal concentration offers an explan-

ation, though by no means a full one, of the location of tribal boundaries, since they are determined not only by the distribution of villages, but also by the direction in which the people turn in their move to dry season pastures. Thus the tribes of the Zeraf Valley fall back on the Zeraf River and therefore do not share camps with the Lou tribe, and that part of the Lou tribe which moves east and northeast make their camps on the Nyanding River and on the upper reaches of the Pibor and do not share their waters and pasture with the Jikany tribes, who move to the upper reaches of the Sobat and the lower reaches of the Pibor. Furthermore, that some of the larger Nuer tribes are able to preserve a degree of tribal unity without governmental organs may in part be attributed to seasonal migration, since, as explained above, the different local sections are forced by the severity of the latitude into mutual contact and develop some measure of forbearance and recognition of common interests.

Likewise, a tribal section is a distinct segment, not only because its villages occupy a well-demarcated portion of its territory, but also in that it has its unique dry-season pastures. The people of one section move off in one direction and the people from an adjoining section move off in a different direction. Dry-season concentrations are never tribal, but always sectional, and at no time and in no area is the population dense.

The total Nuer population is round about 300,000. I do not know the total square mileage of the country, but to the east of the Nile, where there are, on a rough estimate, some 180,000 Nuer, they are said to occupy 26,000 square miles, with the low density of about seven to the square mile. The density is probably no higher to the west of the Nile. Nowhere is there a high degree of local concentration.

Although dry-season movement produces more social interrelations between members of different tribal sections than the rainy season distribution might lead us to expect, these contacts are mainly individual or, when they concern groups, only smaller local communities, and not the larger tribal sections, are brought into association. This is probably one of the reasons for the lack of structural complexity and of great variation of types of social

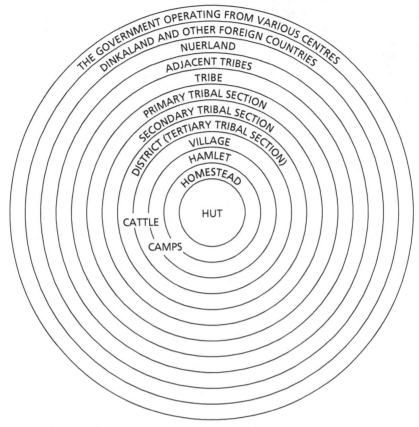

Figure 2.1

relations among the Nuer. Outside small kinship groups and village and camp communities, there are no co-operative economic combinations and there are no organized ritual associations. Except for occasional military ventures, active corporate life is restricted to small tribal segments.

II.   Tribal System

What is a Nuer tribe? The most obvious characteristic is its territorial unity and exclusiveness, and this was even more marked before European conquest than to-day. The population of a tribe varies from a few hundreds among some small tribes to the west of the Nile – if these are rightly regarded as tribes, for very little research was conducted in that area – to many thousands. Most tribes have a population of over 5,000 and the largest

number between 30,000 and 45,000 souls. Each tribe is economically self-sufficient, having its own pastures, water-supplies, and fishing reservations, which its members alone have the right to exploit. It has a name which is the symbol of its distinction. The tribesmen have a sense of patriotism: they are proud to be members of their tribe and they consider it superior to other tribes. Each tribe has within it a dominant clan which furnishes a kinship framework on which the political aggregate is built up. Each also regulates independently its age-set organization.

None of the above-mentioned attributes clearly make a formal distinction between a tribe and its divisions. The simplest definition states that a tribe is the largest community which considers that disputes between its members should be settled by arbitration and that it ought to combine against other communities of the same kind and against foreigners. In these two respects there is no larger political group than the tribe and all smaller political groups are sections of it.

Within a tribe there is law: there is machinery for settling disputes and a moral obligation to conclude them sooner or later. If a man kills a fellow tribesman, it is possible to prevent, or curtail, a feud by payment of cattle. Between tribe and tribe there is no means of bringing together the parties to a dispute and compensation is neither offered nor demanded. Thus, if a man of one tribe kills a man of another tribe, retribution can only take the form of intertribal warfare. It must not be supposed that feuds within a tribe are easy to conclude. There is considerable control over retaliation within a village, but the larger the local community the more difficult settlement becomes. When two large divisions of a tribe are concerned in a feud, the chances of immediate arbitration and settlement are remote. The force of law varies with the distance in tribal structure that separates the persons concerned. Nevertheless, so long as a sense of community endures and the legal norm is formally acknowledged within a tribe, whatever may be the inconsistencies and contradictions that appear in the actual relations between tribesmen, they still consider themselves to be a united group. Then either the contradiction of feuds is felt and they are settled, the unity of the tribe being maintained thereby, or they remain so long unsettled that people give up all hope and intention of ever concluding them and finally cease to feel that they ought to be concluded, so that the tribe tends to split and two new tribes come into being.

Nor must it be supposed that the political limits of the tribe are the limits of social intercourse. People move freely all over Nuerland and are unmolested if they have not incurred blood-guilt. They marry and, to a small extent, trade across tribal boundaries, and pay visits to kinsmen living outside their own tribe. Many social relations, which are not specifically political, link members of different tribes. One has only to mention that the same clans are found in different tribes and that everywhere the age-sets are co-ordinated. Any Nuer may leave his tribe and settle in a new tribe, of which he thereby becomes a member. In time of peace, even Dinka foreigners may visit Nuerland unharmed. Moreover, we must recognize that the whole Nuer people form a single community, territorially unbroken, with common culture and feeling of exclusiveness. Their common language and values permit ready intercommunication. Indeed, we might speak of the Nuer as a nation, though only in a cultural sense, for there is no common political organization or central administration.

Besides being the largest group in which legal obligation is acknowledged, a tribe is also the largest group which habitually combines for offence and defence. The younger men of the tribe went, till recently, on joint raiding expeditions against the Dinka and waged war against other Nuer tribes. Raids on the Dinka were very frequent; war between tribes less so. In theory, if two sections of different tribes were engaged in hostilities, each could rely on the support of the other sections of the same tribe, but in practice they did not always join in. Contiguous tribes sometimes combined against foreigners, especially against the Dinka, though there was no moral obligation to do so, the alliance was of short duration, and the allies conducted their operations independently, even when in collaboration.

At the present time, Nuer are to the west and south bordered by Dinka, who appear to have very much the same kind of political system as their own, i.e. they comprise a congeries of tribes without centralized government. From the earliest times the Nuer have been fighting the Dinka and have been generally on the offensive. We know that during the first half of the last century waves of Nuer broke from their homeland to the west of the Nile on to the Dinka lands to the east of that river and that they conquered and absorbed the inhabitants in most of what is now eastern Nuerland (the Nuer distinguish between *Nath cieng*, the 'homeland', or western Nuer, and *Nath doar*, the 'migrated', or eastern Nuer). Fighting between the two peoples has continued till the present time but there does not appear, if maps made by early travellers are to be trusted, to have been much change of territory during the last fifty years. This eastwards migration is a fact that has to be taken into account, with those related earlier, if we wish to know why the eastern tribes are larger, territorially and numerically, than the western tribes, for it

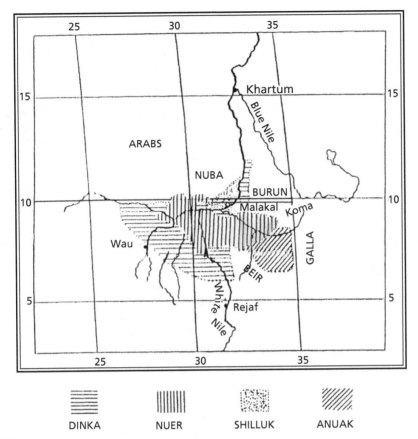

Figure 2.2

may be assumed that the struggle of conquest and settlement, and absorption of Dinka on an unprecedented scale, had some effect on the migrating hordes.

To the north, the Nuer are in varying degrees of contact with Arabs, the peoples of the Nuba Hills, the powerful Shilluk kingdom, and certain small communities in Darfung (Burun and Koma); while to the east and south-east they are bordered by the Galla of Ethiopia, the Anuak, and the Beir. Wherever the Nuer have direct relations with these peoples, they are hostile in character.

Arab slave-raiders from the Northern Sudan intruded here and there into the more accessible portions of Nuerland in the second half of the nineteenth century, but nowhere did they gain the upper hand or, indeed, make a marked impression on the Nuer, who opposed them as strongly as they resisted later the Egyptian

Government, which undertook no serious operations against them. The Nuer likewise treated British rule with open disrespect till, as a result of lengthy military operations between 1928 and 1930, their opposition was broken and they were brought under effective administration. With the exception of this last episode in their history, the Nuer may be said to have reached in their foreign relations a state of equilibrium and of mutual hostility which was expressed from time to time in fighting.

A tribe is divided into territorial segments which regard themselves as separate communities. We refer to the divisions of a tribe as primary, secondary, and tertiary tribal sections. Primary sections are segments of a tribe, secondary sections are segments of a primary section, and tertiary sections are segments of a secondary section. A tertiary section is divided into villages and villages into domestic groups.

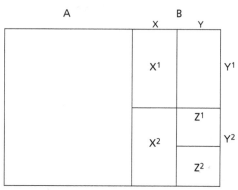

Figure 2.3

A member of Z^2 tertiary division of tribe B sees himself as a member of Z^2 community in relation to Z^1, but he regards himself as a member of Y^2 and not of Z^2 in relation to Y^1. Likewise, he regards himself as a member of Y, and not of Y^2, in relation to X. He regards himself as a member of tribe B, and not of its primary section Y, in relation to tribe A. Thus, on a structural plane, there is always contradiction in the definition of a political group, for a man is a member of it in virtue of his non-membership of other groups of the same type which he stands outside of, and he is likewise not a member of the same community in virtue of his membership of a segment of it which stands in opposition to its other segments. Hence a man counts as a member of a political group in one situation and not as a member of it in a different situation, e.g. he is a member of a tribe in relation to other tribes and he is not a member of it in so far as his segment of the tribe is opposed to other segments. In studying the Nuer political constitution, it is therefore essential that we view it together with those of their enemies as a single political system, for the outstanding structural characteristic of Nuer political groups is their relativity. A tribal segment is a political group in relation to other segments of the same kind, and they jointly form a tribe only in relation to other Nuer tribes and to adjacent foreign tribes which form part of their political system, and without these relations very little meaning can be attached to the concepts of 'tribe' and 'tribal segment'. That the distinction and individuality of a political group is in relation to groups of the same kind is a generalization that em-

braces all Nuer local communities, from the largest to the smallest.

The relation between tribes and between segments of a tribe which gives them political unity and distinction is one of opposition. Between tribes, or federations of tribes, and foreign peoples this opposition is expressed, on the Nuer side at any rate, by contempt and persistent raiding, often carried out in a reckless and brutal manner. Between Nuer tribes, opposition is expressed by actual warfare or by acceptance that a dispute cannot, and ought not, to be settled in any other way. In intertribal warfare, however, women and children are neither speared nor enslaved. Between segments of the same tribe, opposition is expressed by the institution of the feud. A fight between persons of the same village or camp is as far as possible restricted to duelling with clubs. The hostility and mode of expression in these different relations vary in degree and in the form they take.

Feuds frequently break out between sections of the same tribe and they are often of long duration. They are more difficult to settle the larger the sections involved. Within a village feuds are easily settled and within a tertiary tribal section they are concluded sooner or later, but when still larger groups are involved they may never be settled, especially if many persons on either side have been killed in a big fight.

A tribal section has most of the attributes of a tribe: name, sense of patriotism, a dominant lineage, territorial distinction, economic resources, and so forth. Each is a tribe in miniature, and they differ from tribes only in size, in degree of integration, and in that they unite for war and acknowledge a common principle of justice.

The strength of the sentiment associated with local groups is roughly relative to their size. Feeling of unity in a tribe is weaker than feeling of unity within its sections. The smaller the local group, the more the contacts its members have with one another and the more these contacts are co-operative and necessary for the maintenance of the life of the group. In a big group, like the tribe, contacts are infrequent, short, and of limited type. Also the smaller the group the closer and the more varied the relationships between its members, residential relations being only one strand in a network of agnatic, cognatic, and affinal relationships. Relationships by blood and marriage become fewer and more distant the wider the group.

It is evident that when we speak of a Nuer tribe we are using a relative term, for it is not always easy to say, on the criteria we have used, whether we are dealing with a tribe with two primary segments or with two tribes. The tribal system as defined by sociological analysis can, therefore, only be said to approximate to any simple diagrammatic presentation. A tribe is an exemplification of a segmentary tendency which is characteristic of the political structure as a whole. The reason why we speak of Nuer political groups, and of the tribe in particular, as relative groups and state that they are not easily described in terms of political morphology, is that political relations are dynamic. They are always changing in one direction or another. The most evident movement is towards fission. The tendency of tribes and tribal sections towards fission and internal opposition between their parts is balanced by a tendency in the direction of fusion, of the combination or amalgamation of groups. This tendency towards fusion is inherent in the segmentary character of Nuer political structure, for, although any group tends to split into opposed parts, these parts tend to fuse in relation to other groups. Hence fission and fusion are two aspects of the same segmentary principle and the Nuer tribe and its divisions are to be understood as a relation between these two contradictory, yet complementary, tendencies. Physical environment, way of livelihood, mode of distribution, poor communications, simple economy, &c., to some extent explain the incidence of political cleavage, but the tendency towards segmentation seems to be inherent in political structure itself.

III. Lineage System

Tribal unity cannot be accounted for by any of the facts we have so far mentioned, taken alone or in the aggregate, but only by reference to the lineage system. The Nuer clan is not an undifferentiated group of persons who recognize their common kinship, as are many African clans, but is highly segmented. The segments are genealogical structures, and we therefore refer to them as lineages and to the clan as an exogamous system of lineages which trace their descent to a common ancestor. The defining characteristic of a lineage is that the relationship of any member of it to other members can be exactly stated in genealogical terms. His relationship to members of other lineages of the same clan is, therefore, also known, since lineages are genealogically related. Thus, in figure 2.4, A is a clan which is segmented into maximal lineages B and C and these again bifurcate into major lineages D, E, F, and G. In the same manner, minor lineages H, I, J, and K are segments of major lineages E and F; and L, M, N, and O are minimal lineages which are segments of minor lineages H and J. The whole clan is a genealogical structure, i.e. the letters represent persons to whom the clan and its segments trace their descent, and from whom they often take their names. There must be at least twenty such clans in Nuerland, without taking into account many small lineages of Dinka origin.

The Nuer lineage is a group of agnates, and comprises all living persons descended, through males only, from the founder of that particular line. Logically, it also includes dead persons descended from the founder, but these dead persons are only significant in that their genealogical position explains the relationship between the living. The wider agnatic kinship is recognized the further back descent has to be traced, so that the depth of a lineage is always in proportion to its width.

The Nuer clan, being thus highly segmented, has many of the characteristics which we have found in tribal structure. Its lineages are distinct groups only in relation to each other. Thus, in the diagram, M is a group only by opposition to L, H is a group only by

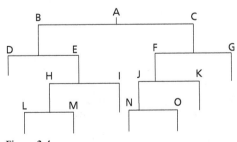

Figure 2.4

opposition to I, D is a group only by opposition to E, and so on. There is always fusion of collateral lineages of the same branch in relation to a collateral branch, e.g. in the diagram, L and M are no longer separate minimal lineages, but are a single minor lineage, H, in opposition to I, and D and E are no longer separate major lineages, but are a single maximal lineage, B, in opposition to C. Hence two lineages which are equal and opposite are composite in relation to a third, so that a man is a member of a lineage in relation to a certain group and not a member of it in relation to a different group. Lineages are thus essentially relative groups, like tribal sections, and, like them, also are dynamic groups. Therefore they can only be described satisfactorily in terms of values and situations.

Nuer lineages are not corporate localized communities though their members often have an association with a locality and speak of the locality as though it were an exclusive agnatic group. Every Nuer village is associated with a lineage, and though the members of it often comprise a small proportion of the community, it is identified with them in such a way that we may speak of it as an aggregate of persons clustered around an agnatic nucleus. The aggregate is linguistically identified with the nucleus by the designation of the village community by the name of the lineage. It is only in reference to rules of exogamy and certain ritual activities that one needs to regard lineages as completely autonomous groups. In social life generally, they function within local communities, of all sizes from the village to the tribe, and as part of them. We cannot here discuss the ways by which residential groups become a network of kinship ties – marriage, adoption, and various fictions – but the result tends to be that a local group is a cognatic cluster round an agnatic core, the rules of exogamy being the operating principle in this tendency.

Nuer clans are everywhere much dispersed, so that in any village or camp one finds representatives of diverse clans. Small lineages have moved freely over Nuerland and have settled here and there and have aggregated themselves to agnatically unrelated elements in local communities. Migration and the absorption of Dinka have been circumstances favouring the

dispersal and mixture of clans. Being a conquering, pastoral people and not having an ancestral cult, the Nuer have never been bound to any particular spot by necessity or sentiment.

Nevertheless, there is a straight relation between political structure and the clan system, for a clan, or a maximal lineage, is associated with each tribe, in which it occupies a dominant position among other agnatic groups. Moreover, each of its segments tends to be associated with a segment of the tribe in such a way that there is a correspondence, and often a linguistic identification, between the parts of a clan and the parts of a tribe. Thus if we compare figures 2.3 and 2.4 and suppose clan A to be the dominant clan in tribe B, then maximal lineages B and C correspond to primary sections X and Y; major lineages D and E correspond to secondary section X^1 and X^2; major lineages F and G correspond to secondary sections Y^1 and Y^2; and minor lineages J and K correspond to tertiary sections Z^1 and Z^2.

We speak of a clan which is dominant in a tribe as the aristocratic clan, although, except on the periphery of Nuer expansion eastwards, its predominance gives prestige rather than privilege. Its members are in a minority – often a very small minority – in the tribe. Not all members of the aristocratic clan live in the tribe where it is dominant, but many are also found in other tribes. Not all clans are associated with a tribe in this manner. A man is only an aristocrat in the one tribe in which his clan is dominant. If he lives in another tribe, he is not an aristocrat there.

There is consequently in every tribe some social differentiation. There are aristocrats, Nuer of other clans, and Dinka, but these strata are not classes and the second and third are properly to be regarded as categories rather than as groups. The Dinka who have been absorbed into Nuer society have been for the most part incorporated into their kinship system by adoption and marriage, and conquest has not led to the development of classes or castes. This is, perhaps, to be attributed, in part at any rate, to the fact that the Dinka, like the Nuer, are chiefly pastoralists and that in other respects their ways of life are very similar.

Without presenting all the evidence and without making every qualification, we attempt an explanation of why Nuer clans, especially the dominant clans, are segmented into lineages to a far greater degree than is usual among African peoples. In our view, they are segmented because the political structure to which they correspond is segmented in the way we have described. Social obligations among the Nuer are expressed chiefly in a kinship idiom and the interrelations of local communities within a tribe are defined in terms of agnatic relationship. Therefore, as the tribe segments the clan segments with it and the point of separation between the tribal sections becomes the point of divergence in the clan structure of the lineages associated with each section. For, as we have seen, clans and their lineages are not distinct corporate groups, but are embodied in local communities, through which they function structurally. Such being the case, it is not surprising that they take the form of the State which gives them corporate substance.

Those clans which are associated with tribes have generally greater lineage extension and depth than those which are not so associated, and the larger the tribe the more significance this association has for the Nuer. It is in the largest tribes, territorially and numerically, and those which have expanded most and assimilated most foreigners, like the Lou and Eastern Gaajak and Gaajok tribes, that we find the greatest attention paid to the distinct and dominant position of the aristocratic clans. Indeed, not only do political relations affect the clan structural form, splitting it into segments along the lines of political fission, but also the clan system may be said to have a corresponding action on the political structure. In a confusion of lineages of different clan origin and in an amorphous network of cognatic links, the political structure is given consistent form, in the language of kinship, by one clan – a single system of lineages – being made to correspond to the tribe and to its structure of opposed segments. Just as a man is a member of a tribal segment opposed to other segments of the same order and yet also a member of the tribe which embraces all these segments, so also he is a member of a lineage opposed to other lineages of the same order and yet also a member of the clan which embraces all these lineages, and there is a strict correspondence between these two sets of affiliations, since the lineage is embodied in the segment and the clan in the tribe. Moreover, the distance in clan structure between two lineages of a dominant clan tends to correspond to the distance in tribal structure between the two sections with which they are associated. Thus the system of lineages of the dominant clan enables the Nuer to think of their tribe in the highly consistent form of clan structure. In each segment the network of kinship ties are given unity and coherence by their common relationship to the lineage of the dominant clan that resides there, and as these separate lineages are composite in relation to other clans so the whole tribe is built around an exclusive agnatic framework. Though the sections may tend to draw apart and to split, a common agnatic value, shared by the dominant lineages contained in them, endures.

IV. Age-set System

Another tribal institution is the age-set system, which is socially more significant among the Nuer than among other Nilotic peoples of the Sudan. Nuer boys pass into the grade of manhood through a severe ordeal and a series of rites connected with it. These initiations take place whenever there are a sufficient number of boys of from about fourteen to sixteen years of age in a village or district. All the youths who have been initiated in a successive number of years belong to one age-set, and there is a four-year interval between the last batch of initiates of one set and the first batch of the next set, and during this interval no boys may be initiated. The initiation period is open for about six years, so that, with the four years of the closed period, there are about ten years between the commencement of any age-set and the commencement of the set that precedes or succeeds it. The age-sets are not organized in a cycle.

Nuer age-sets are a tribal institution in the sense that, in the larger tribes at any rate, all the sections of a tribe have the same open and closed periods and call the sets by the same names. They are also the most characteristic of all Nuer national institutions, for initiation scars are the sign of their communion and the badge of their supremacy. Moreover, though each big tribe has its own age-set organization, adjacent tribes co-ordinate their sets in periods and nomenclature, so that the Western Nuer, the Eastern Nuer, and the Central Nuer tend to fall into three divisions in this respect. But even when a man travels from one end of Nuerland to the other, he can always, and easily, perceive the set which is equivalent to his own in each area. The age-set system, therefore, like the clan system, whilst having a tribal connotation, is not bound by lines of political cleavage.

There is usually in each tribe a man whose privilege it is to open and close initiation periods and to give each set its name. This man belongs to one of those lineages which have a special ritual relationship to cattle and are known as 'Men of the Cattle'. He opens and closes initiation periods in his own district, and other districts of his tribe follow suit. Once a period has been opened, each village and district initiates its boys when it pleases. The age-sets have no corporate activities and cannot be said to have specific political functions. There are no grades of 'warriors' and 'elders' concerned with the administration of the country, and the sets are not regiments, for a man fights with the members of his local community, irrespective of age. In the rites of initiation there is no educative or moral training. There is no leadership in the sets.

There are probably never more than six sets in existence at any time, since six sets cover about seventy-five years. As each set dies its name is remembered only for a generation or two. Each set becomes more senior as the years go on, so that a man rises from a junior to a middle, and from a middle to a senior position in his community as a member of a group. The stratification of the age-set system is thus a further exemplification of the principle of segmentation which we have seen to be a characteristic of the political and kinship systems. There is further stratification within each set, but this is not of great importance, for the set sees itself, and is seen by others, as an undivided group in relation to other sets, and its divisions become merged as the set becomes more senior. A set once complete does not change its membership, but the sets are constantly changing their positions in relation to the whole system. There is also a certain relativity about these stratified sets similar to that we noted about tribal sections and clans, for, while they keep their distinction, there is often a situational fusion of two sets in relation to a third. This is

especially apparent at feasts. Whether a set is regarded as junior or equal depends not only on its position in the age-set structure, but also on the status of a third set concerned in any situation, a tendency due to the connexion between age-sets and generations.

The most evident action of age-sets in determining behaviour is the way duties and privileges are effected by a transition from boyhood to manhood. Also, in virtue of the position of his set in the structure, every male Nuer is in a status of seniority, equality, or juniority towards every other Nuer man. Some men are his 'sons', some his 'brothers', and some his 'fathers'. Without entering here into further detail, we may say that the attitude of a man towards other men of his community is largely determined by their respective positions in the age-set system. Hence age relations, like kinship relations, are structural determinants of behaviour. The age-set system may, moreover, be regarded as a political institution, since it is, to a large extent, segmented tribally and since it divides a tribe – as far as its male members are concerned – into groups, based on age, which stand in a definite relation to each other. We do not consider, however, that it has any direct accord with the tribal structure, based on territorial segmentation, which we have recorded. The politico-territorial system and the age-set system are both consistent in themselves and to some extent overlap, but they are not interdependent.

V.   Feuds and other Disputes

The political system operates largely, we think, through the institution of the feud which is regulated by a mechanism known as the 'leopard-skin chief', a title we retain, although the appellation of 'chief' is misleading. This person is one of those specialists who are concerned, in a ritual capacity, with various departments of Nuer social life and of nature. Leopard-skin chiefs belong to certain lineages only, though not all members of these lineages utilize their hereditary ritual powers. In most of Nuerland, the lineages are not branches of dominant clans.

When a man has killed another, he must at once go to a chief, who cuts his arm so that the blood may flow. Until this mark of Cain has been made, the slayer may neither eat nor drink. If he fears vengeance, as is normally the case, he remains at the chief's home, for it is sanctuary. Within the next few months the chief elicits from the slayer's kin that they are prepared to pay compensation to avoid a feud and he persuades the dead man's kin that they ought to accept compensation. During this period neither party may eat or drink from the same vessels as the other and they may not, therefore, eat in the home of the same third person. The chief then collects the cattle – till recently some forty to fifty beasts – and takes them to the dead man's home, where he performs various sacrifices of cleansing and atonement. Such is the procedure of settling a feud, and before the present administration it had often to be used, for the Nuer are a turbulent people who esteem courage the highest virtue and skill in fighting the most necessary accomplishment.

In so brief a description, one may give the impression that the chief judges the case and compels acceptance of his decision. Nothing could be further from the facts. The chief is not asked to deliver a judgement: it would not occur to Nuer that one was required. He appears to force the kin of the dead man to accept compensation by his insistence, even to the point of threatening to curse them, but it is an established convention that he shall do so, in order that the bereaved relatives may retain their prestige. What seems really to have counted were the acknowledgement of community ties between the parties concerned, and hence of the moral obligation to settle the affair by the acceptance of a traditional payment, and the wish, on both sides, to avoid, for the time being at any rate, further hostilities.

A feud directly affected only close agnatic kinsmen on both sides. One did not avenge oneself on cognates or on distant agnates. Nevertheless, we believe that the feud had a wider social connotation and that therein lies its political significance. We must first recognize that feuds are more easily settled the smaller the group involved. When a man kills a near kinsman or a close neighbour, the matter is quickly closed by compensation, often on a reduced scale, being soon offered and accepted, for when a homicide occurs within a village general opinion demands an early settlement, since it is obvious to every one that were vengeance allowed corporate life would be impossible. At the other end of the scale, when a homicide occurs between primary or secondary sections of a tribe, there is little chance of an early settlement and, owing to distance, vengeance is not easily achieved, so that unsettled feuds accumulate. Such homicides are generally the result of intertribal fights in which several persons are killed. This not only increases the difficulty of settlement, but continues between the sections the mutual hostility that occasioned the fight, for, not only the close agnatic kinsmen of the dead, but entire local communities are involved. Feud, as a choice between direct vengeance and acceptance of compensation, without the necessity of immediate settlement, but requiring eventual conclusion, is especially a condition that flourishes between villages of the same district. The kinsmen of the dead man are near enough to strike at the kinsmen of the slayer and far enough from them to permit a temporary state of hostility between the local communities to which the parties belong. For whole communities are of necessity involved, though they are not subject to the rigid taboos that a homicide imposes on close agnatic kinsmen of slayer and slain, nor are they threatened with vengeance. Nevertheless, their members are, as a rule, closely related by cognatic or affinal ties to the principals and must assist them if there is an open fight. At the same time, these communities have frequent social contacts, so that eventually the mechanism of the leopard-skin chief has to be employed to prevent their complete dislocation. The feud thus takes on a political complexion and expresses the hostility between political segments.

The balanced opposition of political segments is, we believe, largely maintained by the institution of the feud which permits a state of latent hostility between local communities, but allows also their fusion in a larger group. We say that the hostility is latent because even when a feud is being prosecuted there is no uninterrupted endeavour to exact vengeance, but the kinsmen of the dead may take any opportunity that presents itself to accomplish their purpose; and, also, because even when compensation has been accepted the sore rankles and the feud may, in spite of settlement, break out again, for Nuer recognize that in sentiment a feud goes on for ever. The leopard-skin chief does not rule and judge, but acts as mediator through whom communities desirous of ending open hostility can conclude an active state of feud. The feud, including the role played in it by the chief, is thus a mechanism by which the political structure maintains itself in the form known to us.

The leopard-skin chief may also act as mediator in disputes concerning ownership of cattle, and he and the elders on both sides may express their opinion on the merits of a case. But the chief does not summon the defendants, for he has neither court nor jurisdiction and, moreover, has no means of compelling compliance. All he can do is to go with the plaintiff and some elders of his community to the home of the defendant and to ask him and his kinsmen to discuss the matter. Only if both sides are willing to submit to arbitration can it be settled. Also, although the chief, after consultation with the elders, can give a verdict, this verdict is reached by general agreement and in a large measure, therefore, arises from an acknowledgement by the defendant's or plaintiff's party that the other party has justice on its side. It is, however, very seldom that a chief is asked to act as mediator, and there is no one else who has authority to intervene in disputes, which are settled by other than legal methods.

In the strict sense of the word, the Nuer have no law. There is no one with legislative or juridical functions. There are conventional payments considered due to a man who has suffered certain injuries – adultery with his wife, fornication with his daughter, theft, broken limbs, &c. – but these do not make a legal system, for there is no constituted and impartial authority who decides on the rights and wrongs of a dispute and there is no external power to enforce such a decision were it given. If a man has right on his side, and, in virtue of that, obtains the support of his kinsmen and they are prepared to use force, he has a good chance of obtaining what is due to him, if the parties live near to one another. The usual way of obtaining one's due is to go to the debtor's kraal and take his cattle. To resist is to run the risk of homicide and feud. It seems that whether, and how, a dispute is settled depends very largely on the relative positions of the persons concerned in the kinship and age-set systems and the distance between their communities in tribal structure. In theory, one

can obtain redress from any member of one's tribe, but, in fact, there is little chance of doing so unless he is a member of one's local community and a kinsman. The force of 'law' varies with the position of the parties in political structure, and thus Nuer 'law' is essentially relative, like the structure itself.

During the year I spent with the Nuer, I never heard a case being conducted, either before an individual or before a council of elders, and I received the impression that it is very rare for a man to obtain redress except by force or threats of force. And if the Nuer has no law, likewise he lacks government. The leopardskin chief is not a political authority and the 'Man of the Cattle' and other ritual agents (totemic specialists, rain-makers, fetich-owners, magicians, diviners, &c.) have no political status or functions, though they may become prominent and feared in their locality. The most influential men in a village are generally the heads of joint families, especially when they are rich in cattle, of strong character, and members of the aristocratic clan. But they have no clearly defined status or function. Every Nuer, the product of a hard and equalitarian upbringing, deeply democratic, and easily roused to violence, considers himself as good as his neighbour; and families and joint families, whilst co-ordinating their activities with those of their fellow villagers, regulate their affairs as they please. Even in raids, there is very little organization, and leadership is restricted to the sphere of fighting and is neither institutionalized nor permanent. It is politically significant only when raids are controlled and organized by prophets. No Nuer specialists can be said to be political agents and to represent, or symbolize, the unity and exclusiveness of local groups, and, apart from the prophets, none can be said to have more than local prominence. All leaders, in this vague sense of influential persons in a locality, are adults and, except for an occasional prophetess, all are men.

Owing to the fact that Nuer prophets had been the foci of opposition to the Government, they were in disgrace, and the more influential of them under restraint or in hiding, during my visit to Nuerland, so that I was not able to make detailed observations on their behaviour. Nuer are unanimous in stating that they did not arise much before the end of the last century and there is some evidence to suggest that their emergence was connected with the spread of Mahdism. However that may be, there can be no doubt that powerful prophets arose about the time of Arab intrusion into Nuerland and that at the time of British conquest they were more respected and had wider influence than any other persons. No extensive raids were undertaken without their sanction and often they led them, received part of the spoil, and to some extent supervised the division of the rest of it. Though there seems to be good evidence that the earlier prophets were no more than ritual agents, some of the later ones appear to have begun to settle disputes, at any rate in their own districts. However, their chief political importance rather lay elsewhere. For the first time a single person symbolized, even if in a mainly spiritual form, the unity of a tribe, for the prophets were essentially tribal figures, though – and this fact is also of great political significance – their influence often extended over tribal boundaries and brought about a larger degree of unity among adjacent tribes than there appears to have been hitherto. When we add that there was a tendency for the spirits which possessed prophets to pass, at their deaths, into their sons, we are justified in concluding that development was taking place towards a higher degree of federation between tribes and towards the emergence of political leadership, and in explaining these changes by reference to Arab and European intrusion. Opposition between Nuer and their neighbours had always been sectional. They were now confronted by a more formidable and a common enemy. When the Government overthrew the prophets, this development was checked.

VI. Summary

We have briefly described and analysed what we regard as Nuer political structure: the relations between territorial segments within a territorial system and the relations between that and other social systems within an entire social structure. We have examined intertribal relations, and the relations between tribal segments. It is these relations, together with the tribal and intertribal contacts with foreign peoples, that we define as the Nuer political system. In social life the political is combined with other systems, particularly the clan system and the age-set system, and we have considered what relation they bear to the political structure. We have also mentioned those ritual specialisms which have political significance. The political system has been related to environmental conditions and modes of livelihood.

The Nuer constitution is highly individualistic and libertarian. It is an acephalous state, lacking legislative, judicial, and executive organs. Nevertheless, it is far from chaotic. It has a persistent and coherent form which might be called 'ordered anarchy'. The absence of centralized government and of bureaucracy in the nation, in the tribe, and in tribal segments – for even in the village authority is not vested in any one – is less remarkable than the absence of any persons who represent the unity and exclusiveness of these groups.

It is not possible from a study of Nuer society alone, if it be possible at all, to explain the presence and absence of political institutions in terms of their functional relationship to other institutions. At best we can say that certain social characteristics seem to be consistent. Environmental conditions, mode of livelihood, territorial distribution, and form of political segmentation appear to be consistent. So do the presence of clans with genealogical structure and a developed age-set system seem to go together with absence of political authority and of class stratification. Comparative studies alone will show whether generalizations of such a kind are true and, moreover, whether they are useful. We cannot here discuss these questions and will only say, in conclusion, that the consistency we perceive in Nuer political structure is one of process rather than of morphology. The process consists of complementary tendencies towards fission and fusion which, operating alike in all political groups by a series of inclusions and exclusions that are controlled by the changing social situation, enable us to speak of a system and to say that this system is characteristically defined by the relativity and opposition of its segments.

NOTE

1   This record is printed in a series of papers in *Sudan Notes and Records* from 1933 to 1938. The research was done on four expeditions

and was financed mainly by the Government of the Anglo-Egyptian Sudan and partly through a Leverhulme Fellowship. Rather than merely describe again what I have already described elsewhere, I have presented my material in a more abstract form than would be permissible were a descriptive account not accessible.

3

Lineage Theory: A Critical Retrospect

Adam Kuper

Blood and Soil

The establishment of "lineage theory" or "descent theory" is conventionally traced to the publication in 1940 of *African Political Systems, The Nuer,* and *The Political System of the Anuak* (15, 16, 28). Lineage theory dominated the study of social structure in British anthropology immediately after the end of World War II and retained a central position until the mid-1960s when, like British social anthropology more generally and the British Empire itself, it seemed to lose its impetus and to run into the sands. Yet it did not completely vanish. Elements of the lineage model of political organization still embellish phantom protostates in the work of African historians or "the lineage mode of production" in the work of French Marxist anthropologists, or they appear simply as part of the trappings, taken for granted, in dozens of ethnographic monographs. This stubborn half-life of lineage theory warrants consideration.

I have an historical interest in lineage theory also, for although represented at the time as a breakthrough, it was rather a transformation of earlier theories in anthropology. Understanding the way in which the transformation occurred helps us to see how and why anthropology developed as it did.

The organization of my review is roughly chronological, and I shall sketch the genealogy of lineage theory, a genealogy which predict-

ably has been tampered with (by others) to fit later political realities. Evans-Pritchard, for example, pointed out that there is a long history of interest in the central themes of descent theory, that is, in "the reciprocal relations between descent groups and local and political groups, between lineages and clans and local and political communities." He cited particularly the classical studies of Maine, Fustel de Coulanges, Robertson Smith and Pederson – "but I think that one of the first systematic field studies of a lineage system was my own study of the Nuer of the Anglo-Egyptian Sudan, which began in 1929. A more prolonged and detailed study was Professor Fortes' investigation of the Tallensi of the Gold Coast, begun in 1934" (19, p. 10).

Meyer Fortes himself offered a different version. In *Kinship and the Social Order* (26) he constructed a tradition dating back not only to Maine but to Morgan, and developed by Rivers and Radcliffe-Brown before Evans-Pritchard and Fortes himself made their field studies. Fortes also offered a microgenealogy which linked Evans-Pritchard's Nuer study directly to Radcliffe-Brown and to the Boasians:

Evans-Pritchard states in his review of my *Dynamics of Clanship* . . . that the suggestion of how to handle the data of Nuer descent groups came from a conversation with Radcliffe-Brown in 1931 . . . I was present on this occasion. Evans-Pritchard was describing his Nuer observations, whereupon Radcliffe-Brown said, as he stood in front of the fireplace: "My dear Evans-Pritchard, it's perfectly simple, that's a segmentary lineage system, and you'll find a very good account of it by a man called Gifford" (see 34). Thereupon Radcliffe-Brown gave us a lecture on Gifford's analysis of the Tonga system (27, p. viii).

There is some truth in all these versions, but I shall argue that the history of the models is to be grasped not at the level of individual borrowing or development but rather at a deeper level, at which revisions and criticisms and even empirical applications appear as transformations of a single structure.

The development of lineage theory can be divided conveniently into two periods for purposes of exposition, the classical and modern, each marked by three phases. The classical period was inaugurated by the publication of the original models of Maine and Morgan. Almost at once these models were modified by contemporaries, most notably perhaps McLennan. There followed a third phase, in which hypotheses drawn from these models were subjected to empirical testing on the basis of new ethnographic reports, a phase associated particularly with Boas's students in the United States. Then, when the classical models had finally been stripped of all their original pretensions and appeared to be no more than harmless survivals of an earlier period of speculation, they were unexpectedly revived in a new guise in the studies of the British Africanists. This then initiated a new cycle of elaboration and of ethnographic application and criticism.

Throughout these two periods the central issues remained remarkably constant. First there was the question of the relationship between "blood" and "soil," kinship (or descent) and territory. Second there was the relationship between the "family" on the one hand and the "clan" or "gens" or "sib" on the other. These two topics were related to each other, and they were rooted in older questions about "nature" and "culture," "savagery" and "civilization." The underlying issue was the constitution of the primitive polity and the implications for a civilized political order.

Maine, Morgan, and McLennan

Sir Henry Sumner Maine published his *Ancient Law* in 1861. Looking back, many years later, he recalled: "When I began . . . the background was obscured and the route beyond a certain point obstructed by *a priori* theories based on the hypothesis of a law and state of Nature." In contrast, his own view of early society was grounded in the evidence of Greek and Roman authors, particularly the early records of Roman jurisprudence. These led him to formulate the "Patriarchal theory," "the theory of the origin of society in separate families, held together by the authority and protection of the eldest valid male ascendant" (70, pp. 192–93) (Even Homer's Cyclops had been organized in families: "every one exercises jurisdiction over his wives and his children, and they pay no regard to one another"!)

The next step in social evolution was the aggregation of families. When the Patriarch died his sons and their families stayed together, forming the basis of a broader polity. In this way extended ties of kinship became the basis of societies. Only very much later did territorial attachment come to rival blood ties as the basis for social organization.

> The history of political ideas begins, in fact, with the assumption that kinship in blood is the sole possible ground of community in political functions; nor is there any of those subversions of feeling, which we term emphatically revolutions, so startling and so complete as the change which is accomplished when some other principle – such as that, for instance, of *local contiguity* – establishes itself for the first time as the basis of common political action (69, p. 106).

The extended patriarchal family group was a unilineal development out of the family. "It is this patriarchal aggregate – the modern family thus cut down on one side and extended on the other – which meets us on the threshold of primitive jurisprudence" (69, p. 110). It provided the basis for jural order and continuity, since the extended family was a corporation, and this implied persistence in time. "Corporations *never die*, and accordingly primitive law considers the entities with which it deals, i.e.

the patriarchal or family groups, as perpetual and inextinguishable" (69, p. 122).

Maine's fundamental opposition between societies based on kinship and societies based on territory became common currency in the following generation. Opposition arose on different issues. McLennan, Morgan, and others argued that the original state of human society was characterized by promiscuity rather than family life, and that subsequent, more ordered systems of procreation initially highlighted the mother/child bond and so generated matriliny rather than patriliny. Patriliny would represent a later, more sophisticated development, presupposing marriage and the recognition of legal paternity.

Morgan's central thesis, however, echoed Maine.

> . . . all forms of government are reducible to two general plans . . . The first, in the order of time, is founded upon persons, and upon relations purely personal, and may be distinguished as a society (societas). The gens is the unit of this organization. . . . The second is founded upon territory and upon property, and may be distinguished as a state (civitas) (73, pp. 6–7).

"Gentile society" dominated the early history of mankind, and "wherever found is the same in structural organization and in principles of action" (73, p. 634). Moreover, it was a democratic and egalitarian system. "Liberty, equality, and fraternity, though never formulated, were cardinal principles of the gens" (73, p. 85).

The Critical Development

The initial developments of the model were of two main kinds. First, rival theorists rearranged the elements in fresh patterns, to suggest alternative lines of putative historical development.

Secondly, and more interestingly, the model was applied to classical sources and to ethnographic reports from exotic societies. These drew attention to specific local institutions, which were sometimes incorporated into the general models or given greater prominence. McLennan and Morgan stressed the necessity for exogamy in the clan or gens. In Morgan's

formulation the gens established itself in part as a biological mechanism. "As intermarriage in the gens was prohibited, it withdrew its members from the evils of consanguine marriages, and thus tended to increase the vigor of the stock" (73, p. 69; cf. p. 75). "Totemism," discovered in Australia, was soon thought to be a common attribute of kin groups, perhaps even explaining kin group exogamy. Both these ideas owed much to the advocacy of McLennan and the industry of Frazer. On the basis of classical sources, Fustel de Coulanges (32) argued that it was ancestor worship that had led to the enlargement of the patriarchal family into the ancient gens. (Fortes was later to make much of these relationships, though in a functional rather than an historical framework.) Robertson Smith applied McLennan's thesis to ancient Semitic societies and emphasized the importance of the "blood feud." "The key to all divisions and aggregations of Arab groups lies in the action and reaction of two principles: that the only effective bond is a bond of blood, and that the purpose of society is to unite men for offence and defence. These two principles meet in the law of the blood-feud. . . . " (80, p. 56). (Evans-Pritchard was to develop this line of thought.)

Durkheim, in *The Division of Labor in Society* (first published in 1893), tried to work out on first principles how a clan-based society might operate in practice. He argued that the segments of such societies would recognize their mutual similarity and be inspired by a sense of what he termed "mechanical solidarity." Clan-based societies were, however, only a special case of what he called *segmental organization*, societies based on repetitive parts which joined together simply through a sense of mutual resemblance. Clans gave way to territorial segments without disturbing the mode of solidarity. Only later, with the development of the division of labor, did groups emerge which were defined by function. These united with other specialized groups to form a complex organization inspired by a sense of "organic solidarity" (11).

A far more radical development occurred in the early twentieth century, and most significantly in the United States where Boas's students initiated a review of Morgan's model with reference to new American Indian materials. They began, for the first time, systematically to test the relations posited between the elements in the model.

The first important contribution was John Swanton's superb paper, "The Social Organization of American Tribes," first published in the *American Anthropologist* in 1905 (96), not quite three decades after the appearance of *Ancient Society*. Swanton questioned the postulated historical priority of matrilineal clans. Various North American tribes were not matrilineal. Moreover, tribes organized rather on a family basis were by no means more advanced than the matrilineal tribes, as Morgan's theory required. If there was a distinction which could be drawn, it was rather on ecological and regional grounds (96).

Swanton's thesis won rapid acceptance among North Americanists, and in 1910 Goldenweiser took up a suggestion of Swanton's and reviewed the problem of "totemism." In one of the great empirical critiques of the Boas school, Goldenweiser (37) demolished the notion of a unified totemism associated with exogamous clans. When, however, he reexamined the clan model in 1914, his conclusions were more cautious. On the one hand the "univocal" Morgan model was clearly no longer tenable. Moreover, "The significance of territorial units in primitive life has certainly been underestimated" (38). Yet Goldenweiser was remarkably reluctant to challenge the underlying assumptions of the classical model, and for a very telling reason. "A group based on relationship, and one based on local cohabitation, may be designated as natural groups" (38, p. 433). Even many years later, he resisted the logic of his own critique:

The impression might thus be conveyed that the sib represents a wholly fictitious category corresponding to no one reality, that it is but a term, more useful in the scientist's study, with its abstractionist inclinations, than realistic in connotation or univocal in meaning.

Fortunately, it is not necessary to accept so extreme a conclusion. Whatever the differences, clans and gentes, wherever found, have certain traits in common. Among these we can recognize the traits indicated in the definitions of clan and gens: the fiction of blood-relationship, the hereditary character, the unilateral aspect, as well as a sib name (39, p. 306).

This was a sterile conclusion, little more than a tautology, but Rivers, in his discussion of the matter in Chapter 2 of *Social Organization*, had been reduced to similarly empty formulae.

In 1915 the ethnographer Frank Speck pointed out that Algonkian hunter-gatherers were organized on a family basis, and, more significant still, that these families were definitely associated with particular territories. "The whole territory claimed by each tribe was subdivided into tracts owned from time immemorial by the same families and handed down from generation to generation" (92, p. 290).

Lowie provided an authoritative summary of the position of the American empiricists after the critique of Morgan had been completed (see 65–68). First, the historical relationship between the family and the unilineal groups was clarified. "A survey of the data clearly shows that the family is omnipresent at every stage of culture; that at a higher level it is frequently coupled with a sib organization; and that at a still higher level the sib disappears" (67, p. 147). Secondly, there is "no fixed succession of maternal and paternal descent" and "if the highest civilizations emphasize the paternal side of the family, so do many of the lowest" (67, p. 185). Finally, "both the bilateral (family) and the unilateral (clan, sib, moiety) unit are rooted in a local as well as a consanguine factor" (68, p. 66).

Rivers and Radcliffe-Brown

The British anthropologists were engaged more directly with Maine and McLennan than with Morgan, and their empirical evidence was drawn largely from Oceania. Nevertheless, their discoveries closely paralleled those of their transatlantic colleagues, and Rivers, for example, freely cited their conclusions. The debate on the historical priority of "father-right" or "mother-right" was abandoned, the rival theses proving equally untenable (e.g. 79, p. 98). The early existence of the family group was also accepted, as a consequence especially of the work of Westermarck and Malinowski. Clans were generally associated with a particular territory, and "at present we must be content to accept the territorial tie as one form of bond between the members of clan," although Rivers considered it "probable that in all territorial clans the real bond is belief in common descent rather than habitation of a common territory" (79, pp. 22–23).

The "classificatory kinship terminology" identified by Morgan and associated by him with forms of group marriage was now generally linked to the presence of exogamous clans. This was Lowie's view, though he hedged it cautiously at times (66; cf. 12). Rivers, who had earlier experimented with elaborate marriage-rule explanations of kinship terminologies, now advised his readers: "If you are dissatisfied with the word 'classificatory' as a term for the system of relationship which is found in America, Africa, India, Australia and Oceania, you would be perfectly safe in calling it the 'clan' system, and in inferring the ancient presence of a social structure based on the exogamous clan even if this structure were no longer present" (79, p. 82).

So far the American and British writers were broadly at one. If the British writers can be said to have developed a special theme, it was with reference to the corporate role of descent groups. This was a topic which had been raised by Maine in his discussion of corporateness in Roman law. Rivers returned to it, and so especially did Radcliffe-Brown.

Rivers' discussion of "descent" in *Social Organization* was meant to clear up confusion, but has instead caused endless misunderstanding – in part, no doubt, because the book was not completed by Rivers himself but edited posthumously from lecture notes by the diffusionist, W. Perry.

Rivers drew attention to the general failure to distinguish between the use of the term "descent" for "the way in which membership of the group is determined, and for the modes of transmission of property, rank or office." This was unacceptable since "these processes do not always correspond with one another." The term descent should refer to "membership of a group, and to this only." The difficulty arose from his qualification, so often cited afterwards but never explained by Rivers, that "the use of the term is only of value when the group is unilateral. Therefore, the groups to which it applies most definitely are the clan and the moiety. . . . The use of the term has

little sense, and consequently little value, in the case of the bilateral grouping . . . " (79, pp. 85–86). On the very same page, however, Rivers used the term descent also to denote membership of a "class," taking as his example the German and the Polynesian nobilities, groups which were certainly not unilineal in character.

Radcliffe-Brown's essay on "Patrilineal and Matrilineal Succession" provided Rivers' distinction with a rationale (77). He argued that social organization demanded continuity, stability, and definiteness, and that to meet these needs every society required the organization of corporations which transcended individual persons. Such corporations might be organized on the basis either of territorial ties or of kinship ties. Kinship-based corporations would usually be unilineal descent groups, since only unilineal groups would unambiguously define group membership on a descent criterion.

Radcliffe-Brown illustrated his argument with material drawn from Australia, and his short monograph, *The Social Organization of the Australian Tribes* (76), prefigured the "lineage theory" studies which appeared a decade later. In that monograph he described the two bases of Australian Aboriginal social structure as the "family" and the "horde." The horde was a local group which controlled rights in a territory. Its members were recruited by patrilineal descent, and in consequence each horde was associated with a "clan." The clan was usually exogamous and was attached to the local totems found in the territory of the horde. The local clan/horde was the political and war-making unit, "tribes" being no more than linguistic categories. The other kinship groups (moieties, sections, and sub-sections) were also based on unilineal descent, patrilineal or matrilineal.

Kroeber, in one of the most radical critiques of the period, challenged Radcliffe-Brown's insistence on the central importance of descent in Australia. Foreshadowing in his turn many of the critiques which were to be aimed at lineage theory, Kroeber wrote: "Instead of considering the clan, moiety, totem, or formal unilateral group as primary in social structure and function, the present view conceives them as secondary and often unstable embroideries on the primary patterns of group residence and subsistence associations" (53, p. 308). These institutions were "secondary or superstructural even as regards their functional value in many particular societies. They are in a sense epiphenomena to other, underlying phenomena, such as place of residence" (53, p. 307).

The Transformation

I have argued that the central issues raised by Maine and Morgan concerned first the evolutionary relationship between territorial and kinship groups and second the relationship between the family and the clan. The generation of empirical criticism initiated by Swanton and Lowie successfully established an informed consensus on these questions. The institutions and principles of group organization were not related in firm historical sequence. Where clans were important they were always found together with elementary family units. The additional properties which had been associated with clans or sibs (totemism, the blood feud, ancestor worship, and even exogamy) were now known to occur in the absence of clans or sibs. Nor were they necessarily found associated with clans or sibs where such groups were identified.

The clan model did not die, nevertheless, nor did it simply fade away. In America, Murdock tried to clarify matters by distinguishing a totemic and exogamous descent group, which following Lowie he called a "sib," and a localized descent group which he called a "clan" (73a). However, a more successful revival was launched contemporaneously in Britain. In one of the most remarkable transformations in the history of anthropological theory, the moribund "clan model" was resuscitated and relaunched in a new, functionalist guise as the "lineage model" of segmentary political organization. At one level the revival seems to depend on little more than sleight of hand. Clans were pushed into the background, and they were replaced by lineages. Gifford had simply substituted the term "lineage" for "clan," for reasons he never explained (e.g. 33, p. 393), but in the new version the lineage was actively contrasted to the clan. The clan was now a vague entity defined by "putative" descent, and it was not necessarily localized, totemic,

or exogamous. Its importance lay in the fact that "it consists of several lineages, which may be segmented" (72, p. 4). These lineages were corporate, localized, exogamous, unilineal descent groups. In short, they were endowed with all the attributes formerly associated with the clan, sib, or gens.

But more than a sleight of hand was involved. The functionalist version of the old model did more than just change some of the labels. The functionalists were not concerned with sequences of institutional change but rather with the relationship between contemporary institutions. Moreover, they were ethnographers, studying particular systems. The old model was now replaced by specific African examples of "segmentary lineage systems."

The ethnographic paradigms

In their introduction to *African Political Systems*, Fortes and Evans-Pritchard (28) contrasted "states" and "stateless societies" in terms which would have been immediately familiar to Maine and Morgan. The distinction was not, it is true, any longer a simple matter of the presence or absence of territorial or descent units. Rather it depended on a difference in the nature of such units. In states "the administrative unit is a territorial unit; political rights and obligations are territorially delimited . . . In the other group of societies there are no territorial units defined by an administrative system, but the territorial units are local communities the extent of which corresponds to the range of a particular set of lineage ties and the bonds of direct co-operation" (28, p. 10). Political relations in such societies were regulated by the "segmentary lineage system."

But if the segmentary lineages were indeed the old clans in fancy dress, how could they rejuvenate the languishing classic model? To appreciate how this happened it is necessary to consider in some detail the central monographs, particularly *The Nuer* (15) and *The Dynamics of Clanship among the Tallensi* (21), for the new model triumphed by way of what Fortes later called "paradigmatic" cases, concrete ideal types. These lent the model a feeling of reality and considerable persuasive power. The development marked the full exploitation of the Malinowskian premise that a fieldworker, because he could understand the interconnections of a particular culture from within, was in a position not merely to offer descriptive materials for purposes of comparative research (in the Boasian manner) but even to develop a "theory" of a particular society, a theory which might then serve as an exemplary model that could be applied to other societies (cf. 54).

Functionalist field studies aimed at the synchronic analysis of societies. This implied that the associations between territorial groups and descent groups, or between lineages and families, should be treated as sociological questions, not as historical issues. Clans and families coexisted; kinship and territorial bonds were intertwined. How did they interact? These questions led to genuinely novel developments of the old model.

The Nuer: Territory and descent

The outlines of the Nuer paradigm are too familiar to require extensive recapitulation here. Group relations ("social structure") were distinguished from individual networks of relationships. "By structure we mean relations between groups of persons within a system of groups" (15, p. 262). These groups were based either on territory or on descent.

The largest territorial and political community was the tribe, the unit within which homicide should be compensated for by bloodwealth rather than vengeance. The tribal territory was divided into segments, and at each successive level of segmentation the local groups were smaller and more cohesive. These segments had no absolute existence, but emerged

in specific situations, called into being in opposition to like units. If a man in one village killed a man in another, the two entire villages would be forced into confrontation. If a man in either of these villages killed a man in another district, then all the villages in his district would unite against all the villages in the other district. These were the processes of "fission and fusion" which Evans-Pritchard identified as the dynamic of the segmentary political system. These processes were evident above all in the blood feud, whose "function," Evans-Pritchard wrote, was "to maintain the structural equilibrium between opposed tribal segments which are, nevertheless, politically fused in relation to large units" (15, p. 159).

Paralleling the territorial order was a series of descent groups. Each tribe was associated with a dominant clan, and its segments, maximal, major, minor, and minimal lineages, were each associated with a specific level of local organization. The lineage system provided a language, an idiom, in terms of which the territorial political relations were articulated. "The assimilation of community ties to lineage structure, the expression of territorial affiliation in a lineage idiom, and the expression of lineage affiliation in terms of territorial attachments, is what makes the lineage system so significant for a study of political organization" (15, p. 205). Because of this correspondence (thought it is not "exact") the two systems could be represented in a single diagram (15, p. 248; reproduced as figure 3.1).

For the moment it is enough to present just the bare outline of this model, to indicate how elegantly it resolved the classical antithesis between descent groups and territorial groups in political organization. The model has been

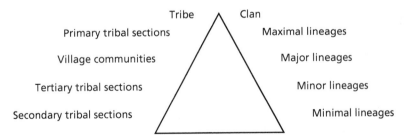

Figure 3.1

discussed by many authors (e.g. 8, pp. 72–75; 10; 35; 42; 47; 52, pp. 290–98; 78). The most common kind of criticism is that it is too formal and idealist to do justice to what happens on the ground. Audrey Richards, whose review of *The Nuer* was perhaps the first published version of this critique, argued, for example, that her own African field experience had taught her that:

nothing is more remarkable than the lack of permanence of particular lineages or "segments"; the infinite variety there is in their composition, their liability to change owing to historic factors, the strength of individual personalities and similar determinants. Such societies, in my experience, are not divided into distinct and logical systems of segments, but rather owe their being to the existence of a number of different principles of grouping . . . (78, p. 51).

Gluckman, introducing an essay of Evans-Pritchard's in 1945 (36), responded that the detailed case materials published in *Sudan Notes and Records* (14), and other data which would appear later, contained the empirical justification for Evans-Pritchard's model. However, this line of defense could not be sustained for long, particularly after the publication of *Kinship and Marriage among the Nuer* (18). That book contained sufficient data on local organization to make it perfectly clear that the model was a poor guide to local community structure.

Evans-Pritchard himself took a very different line – in fact, several very different lines. In his earlier essays in *Sudan Notes and Records* (14), he had suggested that the disjunction between the descent system and the system of territorial political groups arose because the Nuer were in a state of transition from a pure lineage system to a territorially based polity. Generations of war and expansion "broke up clans and lineages to an extent which must have greatly impaired the unifying influence of kinship." Clans were consequently diffused, dispersed "into small lineages which . . . were in frequent feud with their relatives and neighbours. This means that community of living tended to supplant community of blood as the essential principle of social cohesion though in a society based upon ties of kinship the change took

place by assimilating symbiotic [i.e. territorial] ties to kinship ties." He even argued that the clan system now constituted "the main obstacle to political development" (14, pt. 3, pp. 86–87). In short, he offered a traditional evolutionist argument.

The Nuer marked the replacement of this historical model with a synchronic perspective. In the earlier essays the Nuer had been represented as a society in a process of change through conquest and accretion of new peoples. The old clan system was giving way to a more developed territorially based polity. [This is exactly contrary to Sahlins' later idea that the segmentary lineage system was a tool for "predatory expansion" (81).]

In the functionalist model the principles of descent and territory were not historically opposed but functionally united. The empirical discrepancies could, therefore, no longer be attributed to the inevitably untidy process of transition, and Evans-Pritchard no longer argued that the lineage model corresponded to a former type of organization. Nor did he suggest, like Gluckman, that the model referred to actual groups out there, camped along the Nile. The segmentary lineage system was rather "a system of values linking tribal segments and providing the idiom in which their relations can be expressed and directed" (15, p. 212).

The obvious contrast between Evans-Pritchard's model and what he sometimes termed "the actualities" was no longer a source of embarrassment. Evans-Pritchard, indeed, increasingly came to glory in the lack of fit between the model and the empirical reports. This was the source of those famous paradoxes which made Evans-Pritchard a sort of G. K. Chesterton of African anthropology. I cite two examples. Both treat the apparently perplexing importance of kinship ties traced through the mother.

It would seem it may be partly just because the agnatic principle is unchallenged in Nuer society that the tracing of descent through women is so prominent and matrilocality so prevalent. However much the actual configurations of kinship clusters may vary and change, the lineage structure is invariable and stable (18, p. 28).

As Glickman commented, "This statement implies that if the principles were challenged,

descent through women would be less prominent and matrilocality less prevalent" (35,
p. 309n).

> Nuer make *any kind of cognatic relationship
> to several degrees* a bar to marriage and, at
> least so it seems to me, it is a bar to marriage
> because of the fundamental *agnatic* principle
> running through Nuer society (18, p. 47) (my
> emphasis).

(Does this imply that a society based on "a
fundamental *cognatic* principle" would not
ban marriages with cognates?)

The argument is formulated in essentialist
terms. "The underlying agnatic principle is
. . . in glaring contrast to social actualities.
But the actualities are always changing and
passing while the principle endures" (17,
p. 65). The Nuer model was not a description
of "social actualities," nor even of all Nuer
values. Rather it was intended to capture the
deep, unchanging essence of Nuer society, the
core of Nuer values.

Some critics have pointed out that the
model clearly does not capture some basic
Nuer values. Indeed, some Nuer values appear
to contradict it. Holy and Kelly, however, suggest that the values encapsulated in the model
are central to the Nuer, but exist in a state of
conflict with other values which emanate from
other domains of social life (47, 52). My own
position is more radical. I see no reason to
salvage any part of the Nuer model.

In an early essay in *Sudan Notes and
Records*, Evans-Pritchard remarked on the difficulties of his fieldwork conditions and on the
rapid changes the Nuer were experiencing. In
consequence, he confessed:

> I was more successful, for these reasons, in
> grasping their kinship system and the daily
> contacts of cattle camp life than the organiza-
> tion of the less tangible clan and tribal groups
> . . . in the case of the second I had to rely
> largely upon what little information could
> be dragged out of the occasional informants
> by question and answer methods of enquiry.
> I am therefore compelled to generalise upon
> what may sometimes be insufficient data
> and to regard some of my conclusions as
> working hypotheses though I feel that I
> have drawn the outlines correctly (14, Pt. 3,
> p. 76).

There were, however, more fundamental
problems involved in ferreting out the "clan"
model of the Nuer, problems beyond the vagaries of time and chance.

What exactly is meant by lineage and clan?
One thing is fairly certain, namely, that the
Nuer do not think in group abstractions called
clans. In fact, as far as I am aware, he has no
word meaning clan and you cannot ask a man
an equivalent of "What is your clan?" (14, Pt.
1, p. 28).

Some years later, in *The Nuer*, he was a little
more confident:

> . . . it is only when one already knows the
> clans and their lineages and their various ritual
> symbols, as the Nuer does, that one can easily
> place a man's clan through his lineage or by his
> spear-name and honorific salutation, for Nuer
> speak fluently in terms of lineage. A lineage is
> *thok mac*, the hearth, or *thok dwiel*, the en-
> trance to the hut, or one may talk of *kar*, a
> branch (15, p. 195).

Apparently the Nuer, like the British anthropologists, had achieved a new certainty by
abandoning a "clan" model for a "lineage"
model. What, then, was their idea of "lineages," of which they "speak fluently?"

> A Nuer rarely talks about his lineage as dis-
> tinct from his community, and in contrast to
> other lineages which form part of it, outside a
> ceremonial context. I have watched a Nuer
> who knew precisely what I wanted, trying on
> my behalf to discover from a stranger the
> name of his lineage. He often found great ini-
> tial difficulty in making the man understand
> the information required of him, for Nuer
> think generally in terms of local divisions and
> of the relationships between them, and an at-
> tempt to discover lineage affiliations apart
> from their community relations, and outside
> a ceremonial context, generally led to misun-
> derstanding in the opening stages of an inquiry
> (15, p. 203).

When Evans-Pritchard elicited a Nuer diagram of "clan" or "lineage" relations, it was
not at all like the tree and branch imagery he
favored (e.g. 15, pp. 196–98). On the contrary,
the Nuer drew a focus, with lines radiating out
from it. As Holy has pointed out (46, pp. 5–6),
this was obviously a map of a particular set of

territorial relations. Evans-Pritchard commented:

> This representation and Nuer comments on it show several significant facts about the way in which Nuer see the system. They see it primarily as actual relations between groups of kinsmen within local communities rather than as a tree of descent, for the persons after whom the lineages are called do not all proceed from a single individual (15, pp. 202–3).

There is not space for an exhaustive analysis, but it is evident that the Nuer do not clearly distinguish "lineages" from "local groups" (cf. 46, 47). It is extremely doubtful that there is a Nuer folk model which corresponds even loosely to the model of the segmentary lineage system. It is hardly credible that the model captures values which are so powerful and enduring that they *explain* the apparent lack of pattern in Nuer social action. It is more reasonable to conclude that the Nuer model provides reliable guidance neither to Nuer social behavior nor to Nuer values. Even the Nuer are not like *The Nuer*. To what then does the model relate? It relates in the first place to the work of earlier anthropologists, and in particular to the conceptualizations of Morgan, Maine, Durkheim, Robertson Smith, and Radcliffe-Brown. Secondly, it transmutes something of Evans-Pritchard's experience of the Bedouin, as mediated by his reading of Robertson Smith (13, pp. 37, 100).

The Tallensi: Clanship and kinship

The other main source of lineage theory was Fortes's study of the Tallensi. This was less influential than the Nuer study in the field of political anthropology, but it had a profound impact on kinship studies, a field to which Fortes subsequently devoted special attention.

Tallensi "clans" were localized associations containing "lineages" and linking up with like units in a series of cross-cutting associations. The overlapping "fields of clanship" contrasted sharply with the neat, hierarchical, nesting pattern of Nuer segments. Boundaries were uncertain, and segments of "clans" often had different, though partly overlapping, "fields of clanship."

"Clan ties" were constituted, in Fortes's description, by a variety of activities and symbols. They might be based on simple spatial proximity, without any genealogical basis, or on occasional ritual collaboration (e.g. 21, pp. 96–97), or even on intermarriage (although clanship was supposed to imply exogamy); yet Fortes was occasionally obliged further to distinguish a special category of "extra-clan ties of clanship" (21, p. 82). The clans and lineages were not corporate economic units apart from the "nuclear lineage" [or, in simple terms, a man and his sons (21, p. 178)]. Politically, too, "clanship" was less relevant than the system of political offices and the divisions between the Namoos and the Talis.

In a recent critique, Anglin concluded that "the Tallensi do not use agnatic descent as the basic principle of local organization" (2, p. 65), but he suggested that there is a relevant difference between the autochthonous Talis and immigrant Namoos. "Namoo cultural identity is based predominantly on ancestry and Talis identity primarily on locality" (2, p. 50). This is because the Namoos, arguing from descent, can make the most of their prestigious Mamprusi origins, while the Talis, arguing from residence, can claim the ritual authority due to the original owners of the land.

Fortes's Tallensi "paradigm" was less formalized and more nuanced than Evans-Pritchard's starker Nuer model, but in the end Fortes made similar assumptions, which the rich documentation did not support. He argued that "descent" principles were primary in group structure and that this primacy was reflected in Tallensi conceptions. Like Evans-Pritchard, Fortes then had to account for the importance of matrilateral kinship (22). He developed a theoretical explanation which rested on a distinction between "clan" relations, which operate between groups, and in which descent is supposed to be dominant, and "kinship" relations, which join individuals.

Malinowski and Radcliffe-Brown had both attempted to define a psychological relationship between the family and the clan. "Sentiments" generated in the family were projected onto more distant relationships. Evans-Pritchard, and especially Fortes, now proposed a more formal sociological relationship. Individual ties of kinship, generated by familial ties of filiation and siblingship, constituted a specific "domain" of social action, distinct from the public, sociocentric, "politico-jural domain." The discrimination of action into "domestic" and "politico-jural" domains was a matter of context. Interests and values interpenetrated and might even pull a person in different directions. The developmental cycle of the domestic group, for example, was the product of "domestic," moral, sentiments of attachment as well as "politico-jural" considerations, including rules of inheritance, rules of residence at marriage, and the power of the ruling lineage in a particular community. Among the Ashanti, for example, there was a tension between these influences (23). This distinction was so real to Fortes and Evans-Pritchard that they divided their reports into two volumes, each devoted to one of the two "domains" of social life.

Fortes later elaborated the model, developing a complex distinction between "descent" and not only "filiation" but "complementary filiation." If "descent" was the fundamental principle in the constitution of groups based on kinship, "filiation," the relationship of parents and children, and its corollary "siblingship," provided the basis for domestic relationships of kinship. Descent systems gave a special jural role to one of the two lines of filiation, while the other, the line of "complementary filiation," then had to bear the weight of moral sentiment (24).

Typologies and Variants

One line of development from the Nuer and Tallensi monographs was in the form of theoretical elaboration of the model and the definition of typologies. The most important paper in this series was without question Fortes's "The Structure of Unilineal Descent Groups," published in the *American Anthropologist* in 1953 (24). Here he presented the segmentary lineage model as the great theoretical contribution of contemporary British anthropology. "We are now in a position to formulate a number of connected generalizations about the structure of the unilineal descent group and its place in the total social system which could not have been stated twenty years ago" (24, p. 24).

Fortes stressed particularly the corporate and hence putatively perpetual nature of these lineages in Africa, and their political role, especially where political centralization was slight.

With respect to the relationship between territory and descent, Fortes took an extreme position, and one which by no means followed inevitably from his Tallensi analysis. "I think it would be agreed that lineage and locality are independently variable and how they interact depends on other factors in the social structure. As I interpret the evidence, local ties are of secondary significance, *pace* Kroeber, for local ties do not appear to give rise to structural bonds in and of themselves" (24, p. 36).

The family/clan opposition was restated in terms of the new concept of "complementary filiation."

> It appears that there is a tendency for interests, rights and loyalties to be divided on broadly complementary lines, into those that have the sanction of law or other public institutions for the enforcement of good conduct, and those that rely on religion, morality, conscience and sentiment for due observance. Where corporate descent groups exist the former seem to be generally tied to the descent groups, the latter to the complementary line of filiation (24, p. 34).

Other classificatory studies followed (e.g. 6, 31, 40, 72, 90). The issues addressed were the range and type of descent groups, the criteria of corporateness, and the importance which should be attached to unilineality, an issue which especially irked Oceania specialists, who felt that they were being denied use of the model by Africanists. No consequences of any interest were attached to the distinction between "unilineal" and "nonunilineal" or "cognatic" descent groups, and the debate, surely the most arid and scholastic in modern anthropology, serves only to highlight the prestige and influence of the African segmentary lineage model (see 26, 40, 44, 61, 85, 86). Leach attacked typologizing, questioning even the categories of "matrilineal" and "patrilineal" societies, perhaps the most fruitful anthropologists had been able to identify. He yielded to nobody, however, in his faith in Rivers' definition of descent groups, anathematizing those anthropologists who "have been inclined to abandon Rivers' distinctions altogether . . . Having thus created a terminological chaos they have tried to unscramble the eggs again by resort to a tortuous taxonomy" (61, p. 131). Others (e.g. 64) advocated the specification of sets of variables rather than the multiplication of types and subtypes, a position perhaps not too far removed from that of Rivers.

The alliance alternative

During the 1960s it seemed to many that the main challenge to the "descent model" came from a model of primitive social structure developed by Lévi-Strauss, and commonly referred to at the time as "alliance theory" (cf 10, 87). This model also posited the existence of a segmentary organization of unilineal descent groups, but located the articulation of the system in the marriage exchanges between these (putatively exogamous) groups. As Lévi-Strauss argued in a critique of Radcliffe-Brown, the model also offered an alternative interpretation of the relationship between "family" and "clan." Radcliffe-Brown had believed that a universal "family" generated sentiments which were extended along lines of solidary siblingship to larger groupings. In Lévi-Strauss's view the nuclear family was not essential. Sibling groups were linked through the exchange of sisters in marriage (63).

Leach, representing the the alliance school in a dispute with Fortes (25), argued that "complementary filiation" was a blind. Fortes, "while recognising that ties of affinity have comparable importance to ties of descent, disguises the former under the expression 'complementary filiation'" (60, p. 122). In his analysis of the Kachin, Leach argued that both segmentary lineage systems and primitive states could be identified in the region, and indeed that there was a cyclical movement between the two systems. The key mechanism in this dialectic was a system of preferential unilateral marriage alliances, which linked "local descent groups" (58, 59).

The transactional alternative

Another competitive model was neo-Malinowskian in tone. The "clan" was a legal fiction. The rationale of social action was to be grasped at the level of individual manipulation of resources for personal advantage (cf 45). This view was developed in direct opposition to the segmentary lineage model, and may be exemplified again by Leach, this time in

his study of a village in Sri Lanka, *Pul Eliya* (62).

In Evans-Pritchard's studies of the Nuer and also in Fortes's studies of the Tallensi unilineal descent turns out to be largely an ideal concept to which the empirical facts are only adapted by means of fictions. Both societies are treated as extreme examples of patrilineal organisation. The evident importance attached to matrilateral and affinal kinship connections is not so much explained as explained away (62, p. 8).

But, Leach argued, kinship and descent principles do not actually guide men's actions. They are mere idioms, ways of talking about property interests. The community is not defined by kinship or descent; it is "simply a collection of individuals who derive their livelihood from a piece of territory laid out in a particular way" (62, p. 300). The traditional opposition between descent and territory was thus reintroduced. Territory is reality in this version, descent fiction. "Pul Eliya is a society in which locality and not descent forms the basis of corporate grouping; it is a very simple and perhaps almost obvious finding, yet it seems to me to have very important implications for anthropological theory and method" (62, p. 301). "It might even be the case that 'the structure of unilineal descent groups' is a *total* fiction; illuminating no doubt, like other theological ideas, but still a fiction" (62, p. 302).

Leach failed to distinguish "kinship" relations between individuals, which were demonstrably the source of independent interests and pressures in Pul Eliya, from "descent groups," which perhaps few would have expected to find in a Singhalese village in any case. Nor did he attempt to relate this critique to his earlier advocacy of "alliance" models. Nevertheless, *Pul Eliya* stands as a convenient source for another strand in the modern critique of descent theory, albeit, like alliance theory, a critique from within the same historical tradition, a critique which at a profound level adopted the terms of the model it attempted to displace.

Ethnographic Developments: Actors' Models and Systems "on the Ground"

In Africa the application of the model followed a conservative path for some time, though there were some ingenious modifications such as Southall's definition of an intermediate "type," the segmentary state, represented by the Alur (91; cf 43, 72). In some areas the model was more or less neglected. The most notable instance was North American Indian studies. Here the influence of Radcliffe-Brown on the Chicago school was not translated into a concern with aboriginal political structures, perhaps because the Boasian critique could not be ignored. Elsewhere the Africanist model was sometimes applied with a minimum of adaptation, for example by Freedman for China (29, 30; cf 1), or in some studies of Islamic pastoralists (reviewed in 13, Chap. 5). More usually the model was adapted, or rather, particular local systems were presented as variants with more or less significant theoretical consequences. The Middle Eastern segmentary lineage systems, for example, were ideally endogamous, and both Barth and Peters (5, 74) argued that in consequence "lineages" were less directly implicated in power relations, for lineage relations could be modified by political marriages. Elsewhere Kirchoff's model of the internally ranked descent group, the "conical clan," was revived to describe the coexistence of descent models and stratified social systems and, theoretically, to link the "segmentary lineage system" and the "state" (see 31, pp. 4–6). Without question, however, the most interesting ethnographic developments concerned Polynesia and the newly contacted societies of Highland New Guinea.

In New Guinea a younger generation of anthropologists, trained or influenced directly by the British descent theorists, was confronted with societies in which principles of patrilineal descent were given considerable emphasis and where political centralization was minimal. One of the first and most influential monographs, by Meggitt, applied the Africanist model to the Mae Enga (71; cf 4). Yet at an early stage precise and significant objections were formulated to the "African" model, stimulating a debate which provided the context for later field studies and ethnographic analyses.

Barnes set out the issues in a brief but extremely influential paper published in 1962.

The peoples of the New Guinea Highlands first became accessible for study at a time when anthropological discussion was dominated by the analyses of political and kinship systems that had recently been made in Africa. Ethnographers working in New Guinea were able to present interim accounts of the poly-segmentary stateless systems of the Highlands with less effort and greater speed by making use of the advances in understanding already achieved by their colleagues who had studied similar social systems in Africa. Yet it has become clear that Highland societies fit awkwardly into African moulds (3, p. 5).

In part the problem was one of the levels of abstraction. As Langness put it, "the comparisons made are often between jural rules (ideologies) of the lineal-segmentary societies of Africa, and presumed (but not actual) statistical norms of New Guinea" (57, p. 163). But there appeared to be other, more fundamental, difficulties as well.

While a large proportion of men in the local communities were typically related agnatically, local groups often included large numbers of nonagnates, who might be powerful members of the community. Status distinctions within the group did not depend on descent, and descent principles were not greatly elaborated. Further, there appeared to be considerable fluidity in group composition: Highland societies were "loosely structured," as Pouwer had argued (75). Barnes contrasted the multiplicity of individual affiliations to the apparently solidary Tallensi group structures. A corollary was the absence of "predictability or regularity in changes in the segmentary pattern" (3, p. 9). In sum, as Brown complained:

... we may be hard put to decide, for example, whether descent groups are mainly agnatic with numerous accretions, or cognatic with a patrilineal bias. We find that people are more mobile than any rules of descent and residence should warrant, that genealogies are too short to be helpful, that we don't know what "corporate" means when applied to some groups, that local and descent groups are fragmented and change their alignments. (7, p. 57).

The critique was sustained by subsequent research. Reviewing the literature a few years later, de Lepervanche documented and confirmed the reservations which had been expressed (9; cf 83). Strathern suggested that, nonetheless, some traditional questions remained to be dealt with. "Even if we regard descent dogmas as merely 'an expression' of common residence, it is surely interesting that this particular expression rather than others is regularly chosen" (93, p. 38). In his ethnographic studies he pursued the ideological meanings of claims that neighbors are "brothers," and revealed a complex interpenetration of ideas, "a partial fusion of descent and locality ideology" (94, p. 26; 95). The concept of food, giving substance, linking people to the soil, "may be an important mediator between the concepts of identity through locality and identity through descent . . . " (94, p. 33). At the level of political analysis, however, "group" models of all kinds yielded to transactional "big man" models.

The classic Australian models have been subjected to a similar series of critiques (cf 100), and a parallel development can be traced in Polynesian studies (reviewed in 20). A number of American Polynesia specialists began to stress the importance of making a distinction between culture and social action, a distinction authoritatively advocated by Parsons but absent in the model-building activities of both descent and alliance theorists.

In Oceania, local communities were apparently similar to the African local groupings, though based on what the authors sometimes called "cognatic descent." Where, then, lay the difference? Keesing noted:

> The gulf between the way Kwaio (and I as their ethnographer) conceptualize their system and the way Fortes and Goody conceptualize the African systems seems far wider than the gulf between what the Kwaio and Africans *do*. And if the gulf is generated more by the models than by the facts, we had better look very carefully at the models (50, p. 765).

Different ideologies, in other words, might be associated with the same sort of local grouping. "In major territorial descent groups, there is no particular relation between the descent ideology and group composition," Sahlins argued. "A descent doctrine does not express group composition but imposes itself upon the com-

position" (82, p. 104). This line of thought was developed at length by Scheffler, in a penetrating review of descent theory (85). Schneider (88, 89) took a similar position and tried to foster the cultural study of "descent constructs" (cf 41, 51, 52). The culmination of this critique is Schneider's superb new monograph, which contrasts an earlier "lineage theory" model of Yap society with a cultural model in which "lineage," "descent," and "residence" are abandoned as analytical categories (89).

One Africanist has attempted to defend the model against the New Guinea critique (56), but she is obviously struggling against the current. African studies may rather be infiltrated by New Guinea models. Kaberry hinted that "an analysis of some Nuer communities reveals that they have a number of the characteristics attributed by Barnes to many Highland societies" (48, p. 114), and New Guinea models have already been applied to African societies with interesting results by Karp (49) and by Van Leynseele (97). There are two recent general critiques of the segmentary lineage model by Africanists, dealing respectively with Southern Africa (55, Chap. 4), and with Central Africa (98).

Conclusion

The Boasian critique of Morgan's model of gentile society was intellectually unanswerable, and yet the model survived, to be rejuvenated in the form of lineage theory. A generation later, after theoretical debate, ethnographic comparison, and the reanalysis of "paradigmatic" cases, lineage theory appears equally threadbare. Yet it too survives, and not only as a passive element in studies which are really more concerned with something else.

At the height of its vogue the model provided a readily comprehensible framework, facilitating the organization of ethnographic materials. It also had the merit of drawing attention to clearly important issues, such as the organization of local communities, kinship relations, and the regulation of marriage, residence, inheritance, and succession. It was like a verbose but assiduous guide: the patter was often a bore, but at least one was shown many items of interest. Even today the model continues to stimulate the publication of good descriptive articles, which find a theoretical peg in the criticism of some aspect of the model in a particular ethnographic context (e.g. 1, 84.) Some ideas appropriated and developed by descent theorists have been widely used, such as the notion of "segmentary opposition." Yet I would not attempt even a guarded defense of the model. It is theoretically unproductive, and that is the real test.

Verdon has tried to tighten up the model and his experiment is instructive (99). Like LaFontaine (56), he fears that if the critics win out then the whole comparative thrust of anthropology may be lost. Consequently he is determined "to find definitions universal enough to promote the comparative analysis of descent groups across continents." This involves a return to first principles and Verdon's principles are of unprecedented austerity. It is not enough to distinguish folk models and decision models. We must "agree to divorce groups from their behavioral and normative expression and contemplate them as sets from which can be derived a series of properties" (99, p. 147). Descent groups are then further distinguished with equal care. But the price of purifying the criteria is that the model seems no longer to apply to any ethnographic cases: in the end even the Nuer, Tiv, and Talis cannot be said to have "true segmentary lineages." Other examples may be found – the Namoos perhaps, or the Ewe, amongst whom Verdon has worked – but clearly the exercise leaves us with a comparative tool which has few applications.

My view is that the lineage model, its predecessors and its analogs, have no value for anthropological analysis. Two reasons above all support this conclusion. First, the model does not represent folk models which actors anywhere have of their own societies. Secondly, there do not appear to be any societies in which vital political or economic activities are organized by a repetitive series of descent groups.

Yet I do not expect the model to be finally abandoned. It evidently suits modern notions of how primitive societies were organized, perhaps because of what it implies about the relationships between nature and culture, race and citizenship, the community and the individual. The model also fits snugly into a broader class of sociological models, in which closed societies are analyzed into mutually exclusive groups or classes defined by a single principle.

The way in which the model has been repeatedly transformed is of broad interest, since I do not believe that lineage theory is the only branch of anthropology characterized by such transformations. Not only the contemporaries of Maine and Morgan but all the model builders since, including lineage theorists and alliance theorists, have done little more than reorder the elements of the model in novel combinations, like children playing with building blocks. Individual cases have then been presented as "paradigmatic" examples of particular versions of the model, or as local, perhaps transient exceptions. Only in the rare attempts at systematic regional structural comparison were the fundamental assumptions of the model occasionally shaken.

Given this assessment, there is obviously no point in casting about for a substitute. Admittedly, the models can be made increasingly complex by contrasting models of values and models of action, or by seeking still deeper principles of structure which might underlie both, or by positing "conditions" which would explain away obvious weaknesses. Yet a century of often very nimble manipulation of the basic model has yielded no profit. The efforts of generations of theorists have served only to buy time for the model in the face of its long-evident bankruptcy.

LITERATURE CITED

1. Ahern, E. 1976. Segmentation in Chinese lineages: a view through written genealogies. *Am. Ethnol.* 3(1):1–16.
2. Anglin, A. 1979. Analytical models and folk models. See Ref. 45, pp. 49–67.
3. Barnes, J. A. 1962. African models in the New Guinea Highlands. *Man* 52:5–9.
4. Barnes, J. A. 1967. Agnation among the Enga. *Oceania* 37(1):33–43.
5. Barth, F. 1973. Descent and marriage reconsidered. See Ref. 41, pp. 3–19.
6. Befu, H., Plotnicov, L. 1962. Types of corporate unilineal descent groups. *Am. Anthropol.* 64(2):313–27.

7. Brown, P. 1962. Non-agnates among the patrilineal Chimbu. *J. Polynesian Soc.* 71:57–69.

8. Buchler, I. R., Selby, H. A. 1968. *Kinship and Social Organization: An Introduction to Theory and Method.* New York: Macmillan.

9. de Lepervanche, M. 1967–68. Descent, residence and leadership in the New Guinea Highlands. *Oceania* 38(2): 134–58; (3):163–89.

10. Dumont, L. 1971. *Introduction à Deux Théories d'Anthropologie Sociale: Groupes de Filiation et Alliance de Mariage.* The Hague: Mouton.

11. Durkheim, E. 1946. (First publ. in French, 1893). *The Division of Labor in Society.* New York: Free Press.

12. Durkheim, E. 1897. Review of J. Kohler, *Zur Urgeschichte der Ehe* (In French). *Année Sociol.* 1:306–19.

13. Eickelman, D. F. 1981. *The Middle East: An Anthropological Approach.* Englewood Cliffs, NJ: Prentice-Hall.

14. Evans-Pritchard, E. E. 1933–35. The Nuer: tribe and clan. *Sudan Notes and Records,* Pt. 1, 16(1):1–53; Pt.2, 17(1):51–57; Pt. 3, 18(1):37–87.

15. Evans-Pritchard, E. E. 1940. *The Nuer: A Description of the Modes of Livelihood and Political Institutions of a Nilotic People.* Oxford: Clarendon.

16. Evans-Pritchard, E. E. 1940. *The Political System of the Anuak of the Anglo-Egyptian Sudan.* London Sch. Econ. Monogr. Soc. Anthropol. No. 4. London: Lund.

17. Evans-Pritchard, E. E. 1945. *Some Aspects of Marriage and Family among the Nuer.* Lusaka: Rhodes-Livingstone Inst. Paper No. 11.

18. Evans-Pritchard, E. E. 1951. *Kinship and Marriage among the Nuer.* Oxford: Clarendon.

19. Evans-Pritchard, E. E. 1958. Preface to Ref. 72, pp. ix–xi.

20. Feinberg, R. 1981. What is Polynesian kinship all about? *Ethnology* 20(2): 115–31.

21. Fortes, M. 1945. *The Dynamics of Clanship among the Tallensi.* London: Oxford Univ. Press.

22. Fortes, M. 1949. *The Web of Kinship among the Tallensi.* London: Oxford Univ. Press.

23. Fortes, M. 1949. Time and social structure: an Ashanti case study. *Social Structure,* ed. M. Fortes, pp. 54–84. Oxford: Clarendon.

24. Fortes, M. 1953. The structure of unilineal descent groups. *Am. Anthropol.* 55(1):17–41.

25. Fortes, M. 1959. Descent, filiation and affinity: a rejoinder to Dr. Leach. *Man* 59:193–97, 206–12.

26. Fortes, M. 1969. *Kinship and the Social Order: The Legacy of Lewis Henry Morgan.* Chicago: Aldine.

27. Fortes, M. 1979. Preface to Ref. 45, pp. vii–xii.

28. Fortes, M., Evans-Pritchard, E. E., eds. 1940. *African Political Systems.* London: Oxford Univ. Press.

29. Freedman, M. 1958. *Lineage Organization in Southeastern China.* London Sch. Econ. Monogr. Soc. Anthropol. No. 18. London: Athlone.

30. Freedman, M. 1966. *Chinese Lineage and Society: Fukien and Kwangtung.* London Sch. Econ. Monogr. Soc. Anthropol. No. 33. London: Athlone.

31. Fried, M. H. 1957. The classification of corporate unilineal descent groups. *J. R. Anthropol. Inst.* 87(1):1–29.

32. Fustel de Coulanges, N.-D. 1864. *La Cité Antique: Etude sur le Culte, le Droit, les Institutions de la Grèce et de Rome.* Paris: Durand.

33. Gifford, E. W. 1926. Miwok lineages and the political unit in aboriginal California. *Am. Anthropol.* 28:389–401.

34. Gifford, E. W. 1929. *Tongan Society.* Honolulu: Bishop Mus. Bull. No. 61.

35. Glickman, M. 1971. Kinship and credit among the Nuer. *Africa* 41(4): 306–19.

36. Gluckman, M. 1945. Preface to Ref. 17

37. Goldenweiser, A. A. 1910. Totemism, an analytical study. *J. Am. Folklore* 23(88): 179–293.

38. Goldenweiser, A. A. 1914. The social organization of the Indians of North America. *J. Am. Folklore* 27(106): 411–36.

39. Goldenweiser, A. A. 1937. *Anthropology*. New York: Crofts.
40. Goody, J. A. R. 1961. The classification of double descent systems. *Curr. Anthropol.* 2(1):3–25.
41. Goody, J. A. R., ed. 1973. *The Character of Kinship*. London: Cambridge Univ. Press.
42. Gough, K. 1971. Nuer kinship: a reexamination. In *The Translation of Culture*, ed. T. O. Beidelman. London: Tavistock.
43. Gray, R. F., Gulliver, P. H., eds. 1964. *The Family Estate in Africa: Studies in the Role of Property in Family Structure and Lineage Continuity*. London: Routledge & Kegan Paul.
44. Holy, L. 1976. Kin groups: structural analysis and the study of behavior. *Ann. Rev. Anthropol.* 5:107–31.
45. Holy, L., ed. 1979. *Segmentary Lineage Systems Reconsidered. The Queen's University Papers in Social Anthropology*, Vol. 4. Dep. Soc. Anthropol., Queen's Univ. Belfast.
46. Holy, L. 1979. The segmentary lineage structure and its existential status. See Ref. 45, pp. 1–22.
47. Holy, L. 1979. Nuer politics. See Ref. 45, pp. 23–48.
48. Kaberry, P. M. 1967. The plasticity of New Guinea kinship. In *Social Organization*, ed. M. Freedman, pp. 105–23. London: Cass.
49. Karp, I. 1978. New Guinea models in the African savannah. *Africa* 48(1):1–16.
50. Keesing, R. M. 1970. Shrines, ancestors and cognatic descent: the Kwaio and Tallensi. *Am. Anthropol.* 72(4):755–75.
51. Keesing, R. M. 1971. Descent, residence and cultural codes. In *Anthropology in Oceania*, ed. L. R. Hiatt, C. Jayawardena, pp. 121–38. Sydney: Angus & Robertson.
52. Kelly, R. C. 1974. *Etoro Social Structure: A Study in Structural Contradiction*. Ann Arbor: Univ. Mich. Press.
53. Kroeber, A. L. 1938. Basic and secondary patterns of social structure. *J. R. Anthropol. Inst.* 68:299–309.
54. Kuper, A. 1980. The man in the study and the man in the field. *Eur. J. Sociol.* 21:14–39.
55. Kuper, A. 1982. *Wives for Cattle*. London: Routledge & Kegan Paul.
56. LaFontaine, J. 1973. Descent in New Guinea: an Africanist view. See Ref. 41, pp. 35–51.
57. Langness, L. L. 1964. Some problems in the conceptualization of Highlands social structures. *Am. Anthropol.* 66(3), Pt. 2:162–82.
58. Leach, E. R. 1951. The structural implications of matrilateral cross-cousin marriage. *J. R. Anthropol. Inst.* 81:23–55.
59. Leach, E. R. 1954. *Political Systems of Highland Burma*. London: Bell.
60. Leach, E. R. 1961. *Rethinking Anthropology*. London Sch. Econ. Monogr. Soc. Anthropol. No. 22. London: Athlone.
61. Leach, E. R. 1962. On certain unconsidered aspects of double descent systems. *Man* 62:130–34.
62. Leach, E. R. 1968. *Pul Eliya: A Village in Ceylon: A Study of Land Tenure and Kinship*. Cambridge: Cambridge Univ. Press.
63. Lévi-Strauss, C. 1945. L'analyse structurale en linguistique et en anthropologie. *Word* 1:33–53.
64. Lewis, I. M. 1965. Problems in the comparative study of unilineal descent. *The Relevance of Models for Social Anthropology*, ed. M. Bantom, pp. 86–112. ASA Monogr. I. London: Tavistock.
65. Lowie, R. H. 1914. Social organization. *Am. J. Sociol.* 20:68–97.
66. Lowie, R. H. 1915. Exogamy and the classificatory systems of relationship. *Am. Anthropol.* 17:223–39.
67. Lowie, R. 1920. *Primitive Society*. New York: Boni & Liveright.
68. Lowie, R. 1927. *The Origin of the State*. New York: Harcourt, Brace.
69. Maine, H. S. 1861. *Ancient Law*. London: Murray.
70. Maine, H. S. 1888. *Lectures on the Early History of Institutions*. New York: Holt.
71. Meggitt, M. J. 1965. *The Lineage System of the Mae-Enga of New Guinea*. London: Oliver & Boyd.
72. Middleton, J., Tait, D., eds. 1958. *Tribes without Rulers: Studies in African Segmentary Systems*. London: Routledge & Kegan Paul.

73. Morgan, L. H. 1877. *Ancient Society: Researches in the Lines of Human Progress from Savagery through Barbarism to Civilization*. New York: Holt.

73a. Murdock, G. P. 1949. *Social Structure*. New York: Macmillan.

74. Peters, E. 1960. The proliferation of segments in the lineage of the Bedouin of Cyrenaica. *J. R. Anthropol. Inst.* 90: 29–53.

75. Pouwer, J. 1960. "Loosely structured societies" in Netherlands New Guinea. *Bijdr. Taal-, Land-Volkenk.* 116:109–18.

76. Radcliffe-Brown, A. R. 1931. *The Social Organization of Australian Tribes*. Sydney: Oceania Monogr. No. 1.

77. Radcliffe-Brown, A. R. 1935. Patrilineal and matrilineal succession. *Iowa Law Rev.* 20(2):286–303.

78. Richards, A. I. 1941. A problem of anthropological approach. *Bantu Stud.* 15(1):45–52.

79. Rivers, W. H. R. 1924. *Social Organization*. London: Kegan Paul, Trench & Trubner.

80. Robertson Smith, W. 1885. *Kinship and Marriage in Early Arabia*. Cambridge: Cambridge Univ. Press.

81. Sahlins, M. D. 1961. The segmentary lineage: an organization of predatory expansion. *Am Anthropol.* 63(2):322–45.

82. Sahlins, M. D. 1965. On the ideology and composition of descent groups. *Man* 65:104–7.

83. Salisbury, R. F. 1964. New Guinea Highland models and descent theory. *Man* 64:168–71.

84. Salzman, P. C. 1978. Does complementary opposition exist? *Am. Anthropol.* 80: 53–70.

85. Scheffler, H. W. 1966. Ancestor worship in anthropology: or, observations on descent and descent groups. *Curr. Anthropol.* 7(5):541–51.

86. Scheffler, H. W. 1973. Kinship, descent and alliance. In *Handbook of Social and Cultural Anthropology*, ed. J. J. Honigman, pp. 747–93. Chicago: Rand McNally.

87. Schneider, D. M. 1965. Some muddles in the models: or, How the system really works. In *The Relevance of Models for Social Anthropology*, ed. M. Bantom, pp. 25–85. ASA Monogr. No. 1. London: Tavistock.

88. Schneider, D. M. 1967. Kinship and culture: descent and filiation as cultural constructs. *Southwest. J. Anthropol.* 23: 65–73.

89. Schneider, D. M. 1982. *Critique of the Study of Kinship*. Ann Arbor: Univ. Mich. Press.

90. Smith, M. G. 1956. On segmentary lineage systems. *J. R. Anthropol. Inst.* 86(2): 39–80.

91. Southall, A. W. 1953. *Alur Society: A Study in Processes and Types of Domination*. Cambridge: Heffer.

92. Speck, F. G. 1915. The family band as the basis of Algonkian social organization. *Am. Anthropol.* 17:289–305.

93. Strathern, A. 1968. Descent and alliance in the New Guinea Highlands: Some problems in comparison. *Proc. R. Anthropol. Inst. 1968*, pp. 37–52.

94. Strathern, A. 1973. Kinship, descent and locality: some New Guinea examples. See Ref. 41, pp. 21–33.

95. Strathern, A. 1979. "We are all of one father here": models of descent in the New Guinea Highlands. See Ref. 45, pp. 145–55.

96. Swanton, J. R. 1905. The social organization of American tribes. *Am. Anthropol.* 7:663–73.

97. Van Leynseele, P. 1979. *Les Libinza de la Ngiri*. PhD thesis. Univ. Leiden, The Netherlands.

98. Vansina, J. 1980. Lignage, idéologie et histoire en Afrique équatoriale. *Enquêtes Doc. Hist. Afr.* 4:133–55.

99. Verdon, M. 1980. Descent: an operational view. *Man* 15:129–50.

100. Verdon, M., Jorion, P. 1981. The hordes of discord: Australian Aboriginal social organisation reconsidered. *Man* 16:90–107.

4

African Models in the New Guinea Highlands

J. A. Barnes

Introduction

The peoples of the New Guinea Highlands[1] first became accessible for study at a time when anthropological discussion was dominated by the analyses of political and kinship systems that had recently been made in Africa. Ethnographers working in New Guinea were able to present interim accounts of the polysegmentary stateless systems of the Highlands with less effort and greater speed by making use of the advances in understanding already achieved by their colleagues who had studied similar social systems in Africa. Yet it has become clear that Highland societies fit awkwardly into African moulds. When first tackling the New Guinea societies it was a decided advantage to be able to refer to the analytical work available on Nuer, Tallensi, Tiv and other peoples, but it may be disadvantageous if this African orientation now prevents us from seeing the distinctively non-African characteristics of the Highlands.

The central highland valleys of New Guinea have become accessible to travellers only during the last 15 years and early ethnographical research was necessarily undertaken on the coast and in the coastal mountains. These inquiries were made before the work of Evans-Pritchard and Fortes on the Nuer and Tallensi had made its full impact on social anthropology and were carried out among peoples living mainly in politically independent villages whose social organization appeared not to offer any striking parallels with Africa. After 1945 the New Guinea Highlands were opened to a new generation of ethnographers strongly influenced by structural thinking who found here larger societies, apparently patrilineal and lacking hereditary leadership, whose structures invited comparison with Africa. When in several respects these societies were discovered not to operate as an Africanist might have expected, these deviations from the African model were often regarded as anomalies requiring special explanation. Yet in the last year or so a closer examination of the ethnographical facts, the presentation of data from a wider range of Highland societies and, more recently, the discussions about non-unilineal systems in Malayo-Polynesia have considerably weakened what we might call the African mirage in New Guinea.

The Tiv, Nuer, Tallensi and others differ considerably from one another but in making intercontinental comparisons the substantial differences between them have often been overlooked. The possible existence of lineage systems in New Guinea has even been discussed without stating precisely which African lineage systems have been used as type specimens. Comparisons have often been drawn with the more abstract accounts of African societies. as for example Evans-Pritchard's essay in *African Political Systems*, rather than with the detailed descriptions of actual African situations given, for instance, in his paper *Marriage and the Family among the Nuer*. It has been easy to make the mistake of comparing the *de facto* situation in a Highland community, as shown by an ethnographical census, with a non-existent and idealized set of conditions among the Nuer, wrongly inferred from Evans-Pritchard's discussion of the principles of Nuer social structure. The New Guinea hamlet is found to be full of matrilateral kin, affines, refugees and casual visitors, quite unlike the hypothecated entirely virilocal and agnatic Nuer village (though similar to real Nuer villages). This procedure gives an exaggerated picture of the differences between the Highlands and Africa, and although most ethnographers have avoided this error in print, it persists in many oral discussions.

Yet, despite this caveat, major differences in social structure remain between, say, Nuer, Tiv, Tallensi, Dinka and Bedouin on the one hand and, on the other, Chimbu, Enga, Fore, Huli, Kuma, Kyaka, Mbowamb, Mendi and Siane. This is not the place to compare all these systems but rather to suggest topics that should form part of any detailed comprehensive comparison.

Descent

In the Highlands usually a majority, though rarely all, of the adult males in any local community are agnatically related to one another. Most married men live patrivirilocally. Many a large social group is divided into segments each associated with a son of its founder. It is argued that these groups are patrilineal descent groups. Yet several other characteristics of Highland societies make this categorization less certain. These may be summarized as follows:

(*a*) In many instances non-agnates are numerous in the local community and some of them are powerful.

(*b*) It is often hard to detect any difference in status between agnates and non-agnates. If a distinction is drawn it may be made in such a way that the patrilineal descendants of non-agnates after one or two generations are assimilated to the local agnatic group.

(*c*) An adolescent boy, and even an adult man, has some choice in deciding whether he

will adhere to the local group in which his father is an agnate or to some other group to which he can trace non-agnatic connexion. He may be able to maintain multiple allegiance or to shift his affiliation.

(*d*) A married woman neither remains fully affiliated to her natal group nor is completely transferred to her husband's group but rather sustains an interest in both. Yet the division of rights in and responsibilities towards her is not exclusive.

(*e*) Many individuals who assert a mutual agnatic relationship are unable to trace out their connexions step by step and are uninterested in trying to do so.

(*f*) The names of remoter patrilineal ancestors are forgotten; or alternatively the genealogical structure of the group is stated to be a single (or sometimes a double) descending line of males with no remembered siblings leading to a large band of brothers about three generations above living adults; or else there is a gap of unspecified magnitude between the putative remote ancestors who give their names to contemporary segments and the father's fathers or father's father's fathers of the living.

(*g*) Even if the agnates form a recognizable core to the local community there may be no context in which all potential members of this core, including non-residents, act as a unity distinguished from their non-agnatic neighbours.

(*h*) An agnatic ancestor cult either does not exist or else does not provide contexts in which non-resident agnates, or agnates from co-ordinate segments, are brought together.

Hence it seems prudent to think twice before cataloguing the New Guinea Highlands as characterized by patrilineal descent. Clearly, genealogical connexion of some sort is one criterion for membership of many social groups. But it may not be the only criterion; birth, or residence, or a parent's former residence, or utilization of garden land, or participation in exchange and feasting activities, or in house-building or raiding, may be other relevant criteria for group membership. If, as Fortes advocates, we continue to restrict the category 'descent group' to groups in which descent is the only criterion for membership, then in many Highland societies it is hard to discover descent groups. Furthermore the genealogical connexion required for membership may not necessarily be agnatic. Other connexions can be invoked, and this appeal to other cognatic, and sometimes to affinal, ties does not have to be justified by some elaboration of, or dispensation from, an agnatic dogma. In the Highlands the patrilineal ancestors do not act as guardians of the agnatic principle.

These remarks apply unequally to different Highland societies. In some, long lines of agnatic ancestors are remembered while in others genealogical knowledge is poor and not agnatically biased; in some the local incidence of agnates is high, in others it is low; in some there is strong pressure on a man to affiliate himself exclusively with his agnates while in others he can divide his allegiance between two or more kin groups; and there are other dimensions of variation. The Mae Enga, for instance, fit well into an agnatic model whereas the Chimbu and some other peoples can be treated as agnatic societies only with increasing difficulty as we come to know more about them.

Thus although some Highland societies are appropriately classified as agnatic, the area as a whole appears to be characterized by cumulative patrifiliation rather than by agnatic descent. Here I am making a distinction between filiation as a mechanism of recruitment to social groups and to ascribed relationships and descent as a sanctioned and morally evaluated principle of belief. The Tallensi, for example, have both these characteristics. But in most, though not in all, Highland societies the dogma of descent is absent or is held only weakly; the principle of recruitment to a man's father's group operates, but only concurrently with other principles, and is sanctioned not by an appeal to the notion of descent as such but by reference to the obligations of kinsfolk, differentiated according to relationship and encompassed within a span of only two or three generations. In each generation a substantial majority of men affiliate themselves with their father's group and in this way it acquires some agnatic continuity over the generations. It may be similar in demographic appearance and *de facto* kinship ties to a patrilineal group in which accessory segments are continually being assimilated to the authentic core, but its structure and ideology are quite different.

A genealogy in a pre-literate society is in general a charter, in Malinowski's sense, for a given configuration of contemporary social relations. Where there is a dogma of descent, and in particular a dogma of agnatic solidarity, the genealogy must reflect the contemporary situation, or some desired modification of it, in terms of the dogma. But if the dogma is absent, appeal to a genealogy to validate present action is of no avail. Hence it is not surprising that several Highland societies, though again not all of them, neglect their genealogies, either by not revising them or by simply forgetting them. Where revision does take place, it may be simplification rather than the manipulation characteristic of Tiv and Nuer.

Bounded and Unbounded Affiliation

In a poly-segmentary society like Tallensi the main affiliations that govern an individual's status and activities are determined by birth. He has a specified and unique position in the lineage system and cannot escape from it, though within the minimal lineage he can exercise some initiative, as well as in the affinal ties which he chooses to establish, and in the relationships which he enters into outside the lineage system. In Firth's terminology there is little or no optation in the descent system itself. New Guinea societies, on the other hand, seem to be characterized by a considerable degree of optation. The absence or weakness of a dogma of agnatic descent is one aspect of this and the possibility of affiliation with some local group other than one's father's follows from it. In some societies, Mae Enga for example, sooner or later a man must declare his allegiance one way or the other but in other societies he can, and indeed, if he is ambitious, he will, keep open until late in life the possibility of shifting from one group to another. In the southern Highlands, and possibly elsewhere, a man can successfully continue as a member of two or more groups at the same time.

In a unilineal descent system multiple membership or affiliation of this kind is obviously impossible; one of the arguments used against the alleged feasibility of non-unilineal descent systems is precisely this potential or actual plurality of membership. There are three separate issues involved: the distinction between membership of a group and residence on its territory; the feasibility of multiple affiliation in a system of competing groups; and the notion that a man must have a single home with which he is principally identified. Co-residence implies the possibility, but not the necessity, of continual day-to-day face-to-face interaction and in a non-literate society, however clearly their rights are recognized, absent members cannot play as full a part in the activities of the group as do those who are present. But just as co-residence does not necessarily imply co-activity, so some form of co-activity is possible without continuous co-residence. This is particularly relevant to those Highland societies where there is no nuclear family residence and where a man sleeps with his fellows while his wives sleep with their young children and pigs in their own houses. Under these conditions, where a man spends the night is only one indication among many of where his principal allegiances and interests lie. His gardens may be scattered, not only in the sense of being located on various ridges and in various valleys but also by being on land under the control of several local groups. In effect, even in those societies where a man's main allegiance is always to one and only one local group, he may have substantial interests in a number of others. There is no great difference between unilocal residence in these circumstances and the manifest poly-local residence reported from some of the southern Highland societies.

Multiple affiliation may give individuals greater security and room to manœuvre but may be detrimental to group solidarity. A group can either be jealous of its resources and discourage immigrants or it can seek to build up its strength by recruiting new members. The choice it makes will depend at least in part on the availability of garden land and other natural assets under its control and on its strength as a fighting unit *vis-à-vis* its likely or actual enemies. Either it can restrict membership by insisting on agnatic purity or in some other way or it can build up its numbers by recruiting non-agnates and by bringing back agnates who have strayed. Highland societies vary in the choice made; probably enough has been published to make a preliminary comparative survey worth while. No simple answer is likely, for it should be remembered that restrictive policies act both ways. A man whose agnatic group is short of land may support a policy restricting use of the land to agnates, but if he is short of land himself he may be relying on exercising his claims as a non-agnate in the territories of neighbouring groups.

In the Highlands an individual often has allegiances, of the same kind if varying in degree, to several groups which may be either at enmity or amity with one another. This multiple allegiance is quite distinct from the allegiances of different kinds to different groups which occur in even the most determinate unilineal societies. This multiplicity in New Guinea is largely a result of individual initiative and is not due to the automatic operation of rules. A 'rubbish man' is typically a man who is a member of one local group but who has no ties that lead him outside it, whereas a 'big man' is likely to have a great variety of individual and group ties, along with a clear primary identification with one specific group.

Moreover it is proliferation of ties at the individual rather than at the group level that seems to distinguish New Guinea from Africa. As we would expect, both kinds of bond occur in both areas. In most parts of the Highlands there are fairly stable alliances between large groups such as clans and phratries, and sometimes enduring relationships of hostility as well, and these are often expressed in an affinal or fraternal idiom. It is also true that in all the polysegmentary African societies that we are considering, explicit recognition is given to the rights and obligations which a man has with respect to the groups to which he or his agnates are linked matrilaterally. Yet the relative importance of what we might call high-level and low-level non-agnatic (and also pseudo-agnatic) ties seems to differ in the two areas. Complementary filiation plays a greater part in the lives of New Guinea Highlanders and traditional inter-group ties seem less important. It may be argued that this is due to the imposition of colonial peace, for when warfare was endemic inter-group affiliation was presumably more significant than it is now. But the accounts of pre-contact fighting, of the military alliances arranged and the refuges sought after defeat, do not bear this out. In any case pre-colonial fighting is at least as close to the present in New Guinea as it is in the relevant regions of Africa.

The emphasis on low-level rather than high-level affiliation is clearly associated with the greater range of choice in the New Guinea systems, and in particular with the widespread cultural emphasis on ceremonial exchange. Although exchanges and prestations may be spoken of as arranged by the clan or sub-clan and may even be timed on a regional basis, the great majority of these ceremonial transactions are undisguisedly transactions between individuals. In establishing a position of dominance in these transactions a man is seriously handicapped if he lacks the support of his agnates, but he cannot hope to succeed without utilizing in addition a wide range of other connexions, some matrilateral, others affinal and yet others lacking a genealogical basis. If he is successful it is his local group, usually but not invariably consisting of his close agnates, which more than others enjoy his reflected glory. Among Tiv and Tallensi, and less certainly among Nuer, it seems that a man acquires dominance primarily because he belongs to the dominant local group, whereas in the New Guinea Highlands it might be said that a local group becomes dominant because of the big men who belong to it. The contrast is greatest between the Highlands and those African societies where leadership within lineage segments is determined more by rules of seniority than by individual effort.

Two aspects of this contrast require special mention. Fortes, in his discussion of what he calls the 'field principle,' draws attention to the fact that Tallensi matrimonial alliances are established not at random but in accordance with social interests. The pattern of marriages is determined partly by the choices made by individuals within the range of potential spouses permitted by the rules, and partly by the configuration of rules themselves. Prohibition of marriage within one's own clan, or mother's sub-clan, or preference for marriage with a specified kind of cousin, indicate the variety of interest involved. Two alternative trends can be seen. Either marriages are restricted to a certain group, so that enduring connubial alliances, either symmetrical or one-way, are maintained and renewed down the generations, or else every marriage between

two groups is an impediment to further marriages between them. In other words, matrimonial alliances are either concentrated or deliberately dispersed. The latter alternative is more common in the Highlands and accords well with the emphasis on a multiplicity of freshly established inter-personal connexions rather than on group and intergroup solidarity.

The other aspect that should be mentioned is the availability of natural resources. Some of the differences between New Guinea and Africa may be due simply to the differences between pigs and cattle, but obviously this is only part of the story. In the African societies which we are considering a man is largely dependent on his agnatic kin for economic support, but this is less true of the New Guinea Highlands. Inheritance and the provision and distribution of bridewealth play a major part in African societies in determining the structure of small lineage segments and in establishing their corporate qualities. In New Guinea a man depends less on what he can hope to inherit from his father and pays less attention to the ill defined reversionary rights which he may perhaps have in the property of his agnatic cousins. In both areas a man looks first to his agnatic group for garden land, but it seems that in New Guinea he can turn with greater confidence to other groups as well. Before the coming of commercial crops there were in the Highlands, apart from groves of nut pandanus, comparatively few long-lived tree crops or sites of particularly high fertility such as in Africa often form a substantial part of the collective capital of a lineage segment. In New Guinea a man's capital resources consist largely in the obligations which he has imposed on his exchange partners and on his death these resources may be dissipated or disappear entirely. Hence to a greater extent than in Africa every man in the New Guinea Highlands starts from scratch and has to build up his own social position. Once again, we must not carry the contrast too far. Clearly even in New Guinea it is generally an advantage to be the son of a big man, just as in Africa the eldest son of an eldest son does not attain leadership without some personal ability; but the contrast remains.

In general terms this contrast might be phrased as between bounded affiliation in

Africa and unbounded affiliation in the High-lands; or between African group solidarity and New Guinea network cohesion.

Social Division as Condition or Process

Concentration on the network of alliances between individuals and between small groups may perhaps explain why comparatively little attention has been paid in New Guinea studies to the processes whereby groups such as clan and sub-clan segment and divide.

In the analysis of segmentary societies there are always two points of view. On the one hand poly-segmentation is seen as an enduring condition whereby there are in existence, and perhaps have been for a long time, a fixed hierarchy of segments, each segment of higher order containing several segments of lower order. Evans-Pritchard and Fortes's earlier work discusses how in different contexts segments variously oppose and support one another without changing their status in the segmentary hierarchy. The terms 'fission' and 'fusion' were applied to these shifts of opposition and alliance in different contexts. On the other hand we may turn our attention to the ways in which new segments are formed and how existing segments are upgraded, downgraded and eliminated. Many recent writers have followed Forde in using 'fission,' 'fusion' and other terms to refer to these processes of status alteration of segments rather than to the contextual shifts with which Evans-Pritchard and Fortes were initially concerned.

In New Guinea the contemporary pattern of polysegmentation has been documented for many societies. There has been some discussion of how the fortunes of war have led in the past to changes in this pattern, and a little has been said about contextual shifts of opposition and alliance. There has been less analysis of how, for example, increasing population over the years may result in a segment of one order converting itself, gradually or suddenly, to one of higher order. Meggitt's study of the dynamics of segmentation among the Mae Enga, dealing with this process at length, has not yet been published.

This omission arises partly because it is hard to get any reliable time depth from the field material; Highlanders are poor oral historians.

But it is due also, I suggest, to a basic difference between New Guinea and Africa in the way in which over-large groups split up. In Nuer, Tiv and Tallensi we have a clear picture of how, given adequate fertility, two brothers from their childhood gradually grow apart until, after several generations, their agnatic descendants come to form two distinct co-ordinate segments within a major segment. Even if some analytical queries remain the process over at least the first three generations is well understood. This kind of segmentation we may well call chronic, for in a sense the division of the lineage into two branches is already present when the brothers are still lying in the cradle. The details of the process may be unpredictable but the line of cleavage is already determined. Segmentation or fission in New Guinea appears not to take this inexorable form; one cannot predict two generations in advance how a group will split. Instead it seems that within the group of agnates and others there is a multiplicity of cleavages or potential cleavages. In a crisis these are polarized, two men emerge as obvious rivals and each with his followers forms either a new unit or a distinct segment of the existing unit. Segmentation, as it were, is not chronic but catastrophic. The regularities, if any, in catastrophic segmentation are obviously harder to determine than in chronic segmentation. In Africa the dogma of descent acts as a continuously operating principle, providing each individual with an ordered set of affiliations, so that in any crisis he knows his rightful place, even if he is not always there. In New Guinea affiliations are not automatically arranged in order in this way; what might be called the principle of social mitosis, whereby potential recruits to rival co-ordinate segments sort themselves before an impending crisis, is absent; the break, when it comes, appears to come arbitrarily. In addition, changes in the poly-segmentary pattern in New Guinea seem to come about more often than in Africa as the result of defeat in war. The causes of war may be predictable but who is killed and who lives, which group wins and which loses, is in New Guinea as much as anywhere else a matter of luck. Here again we have to deal with an apparently arbitrary process.

This lack of predictability or regularity in changes in the segmentary pattern is, of course, another aspect of the basic contrast between group solidarity and individual enterprise. The sanctions that maintain the segmentary *status quo*, whether derived from economic or physical pressures, or from cult or dogma, are weaker in the Highlands than in Africa and the incentives for change are stronger.

A characteristic of Highland cultures, and perhaps of Melanesia as a whole, is the high value placed on violence. The primitive states of Africa, and even the African stateless societies which we have been considering, are readily likened to the kingdoms and princedoms of mediæval Europe, valuing peace but ready to go to war to defend their interests or to achieve likely economic rewards. Prowess in battle is highly rewarded but warfare is usually not undertaken lightly and most of the people most of the time want peace. In New Guinea a greater emphasis appears to be placed on killing for its own sake rather than as a continuation of group policy aimed at material ends. In these circumstances we might expect to find a less developed system of alliances and countervailing forces, and less developed arrangements for maintaining peace, than we would have in a polity directed to peace and prosperity. Secondly, we would expect that leaders, whatever their other qualities, were moved to violence at least as much as their fellows and possibly more. The Highlands of New Guinea cannot have been the scene of a war of all against all, for the pre-contact population was large and often densely settled; indigenous social institutions preventing excess violence and destruction must necessarily have been effective, for otherwise the population would not have survived. Likewise other qualities than prowess in violence were required for leadership, in particular the ability to engage and co-ordinate the efforts of others in ceremonial exchanges. Yet despite these qualifications I think that it may still be hypothecized that the disorder and irregularity of social life in the Highlands, as compared with, say, Tiv, is due in part to the high value placed on killing.

Conclusion

I have sketched some of the difficulties that follow from assuming that the societies of the New Guinea Highlands can be regarded as variants on a pattern established by the Nuer, Tallensi, Tiv and similar African societies, and I have tried to indicate ways out of these difficulties. There are major ecological differences between the two groups of societies and any full commentary would have to take account of these, in particular the lack of storable food in New Guinea. Despite the great difference in structure, culture and environment, one route to a better understanding of the Highlands lies, I think, through a closer examination of the detailed information available on the stateless societies of Africa. Perhaps this examination may lead incidentally to a clearer formulation of the salient characteristics of these African systems.

It so happens that stateless societies were studied and described in Africa before ethnographical research really got under way in the Highlands. It would be interesting to work out how, say, the Nuer might have been described if the only analytical models available had been those developed to describe, say, Chimbu and Mbowamb. At the same time, if the differences between the patrilineal poly-segmentary stateless societies of Africa and the societies of the New Guinea Highlands are as great as I have suggested, it might be worth while looking for other societies in Africa that could provide closer parallels.

NOTE

1   This paper was presented to Section VII, 10th Pacific Science Congress, in Honolulu on 31 August, 1961. It was written at sea, away from books, and I cannot cite sources. I hope to publish later a fuller discussion substantiating and certainly qualifying the many generalizations in this paper.

5

The Amerindianization of Descent and Affinity

Peter Rivière

In 1975, Jean Jackson, reviewing Lowland South American ethnography, wrote that, despite the significant increase in the quantity and quality of such work, South America remained, anthropologically speaking, the "least known continent". This state of affairs is probably still true despite the fact that the number of publications that have appeared over the past fifteen years far exceeds that from the period Jackson was writing about. Furthermore, in my estimation the recent work done on Lowland South America, with the possible exception of that from Papua New Guinea (there are some fascinating parallels between the two areas that have been little explored so far), is amongst the richest and most innovative that has appeared during that time. Unfortunately there is no space in this review to explore fully the reasons for this relative obscurity, although hints about my thinking on them occur in the text. [. . .]

The topics with which this review is mainly concerned, descent and affinity, fall within the general area of what is called social organization. This may sound dull and prosaic, but I believe that the ideas that have been developed over the past fifteen years have taken us a long way from the standard anthropological definitions of these terms. Indeed it has become clear that within Lowland America it is extremely dangerous to draw a distinction between the social and the cultural, and because of this there is a general lesson for anthropology to learn. [. . .]

Jackson (1975: 319–320) had commented on the fact that there had been a serious revision about the classification of many Lowland South American societies as unilineal, especially those reputedly matrilineal. This applied particularly to the Gê and the Guiana peoples, reclassified as cognatic, among whom uxorilocal residence had given earlier ethnographers the spurious impression of the presence of matrilineal descent groups. However, this was only a first step in what was to become a radical re-appraisal of the concept of descent itself. It is difficult to identify any single individual responsible for this although there is a number of possible contenders. The public and collective revision was made at the symposium on "Social time and social space" at the International Congress of Americanists held in Paris in 1976 (Overing Kaplan, ed., 1977). Here a number of speakers questioned the value of "descent" as the term had become generally to be understood in anthropology. Perhaps one of the most succinct was Irving Goldman who, deploring the lack of an adequate theory of descent, insisted that such a theory must be rooted in an "understanding of the native theory of descent, that is, of the generative process" (Goldman 1977: 182).

Although that conference is widely considered to mark a watershed in Lowland South American anthropology and was the public expression of a general intellectual ambience, one can point to other contemporary works that contributed to the same movement. For example, Roberto Da Matta (1976) pointed to the social as opposed to the biological component of descent among the Apinayé. He later (1979) went further and proposed that continuity among the Northern Gê is achieved by "substitution" rather than "descent" because it occurs between the living and requires little depth of genealogical knowledge. At about the same time, Robert Murphy (1979) queried whether it was wise to import from other areas classical notions of lineage and lineality that did not seem to fit the South American case. It was the publication of "A Construção da pessoa nas sociedades indígenas brasileiras" [The construction of the person in indigenous Brazilian societies] (Seeger *et al.* 1979) that proved decisively influential. These authors rejected what they labelled as the African model with its emphasis on the definition of groups and the transmission of goods and offices, and went on to make some positive proposals. They argued that, in Lowland South America, societies are structured in terms of the symbolic idioms (names, essences, etc.) that relate to the construction of the person and the fabrication of the body. This set of ideas has been very influential, although one suspects that its full impact has been lost because not only that work but much of the resulting literature has been published only in Portuguese. An exception to this is Seeger's 1981 monograph on the Suya. Of similar merit are Manuela Carneiro da Cunha's *Os Mortos e os outros* [The dead and the others] (1978) and Eduardo Viveiros de Castro's *Araweté* (1986, 1992) in which the importance of death and of cannibalism as a basis for a theory of the person is explored at length.

However, the problem of descent and lineality has failed to go completely away – especially as far as the Gê are concerned. Nimuendajú had reported matrilineal groups among the Northern Gê, and although attempts have been made to explain how he made such a mistake, some ethnographers have been reluctant totally to reject his claim. Thus William Crocker (1979), for example, hypothesised that the Canela, even if they no longer had matrilineages, had had them in the past. Christopher Crocker, although he went to some lengths to show that the Bororo are not matrilineal, still found himself writing that "the Bor-

oro can be considered as functionally but not ideologically matrilineal" (J.-C. Crocker 1985: 32). The whole question has been recently and exhaustively re-examined by Vanessa Lea (1986) who insists that the Kayapó legitimise a 'House's' ownership of names and prerogatives *(nekrets)* in terms of uterine descent that may be traced back as many as seven generations. Indeed she argues that to deny that the Kayapó have any notion of descent because their notion does not resemble that classically defined is to throw out the baby with the bathwater (*ibid.*: 399).

Lea's point is well made for there seems to be a problem of language, and in our efforts to rid ourselves of the unwanted connotations that cling to descent, we have left ourselves speechless. It is true that the imagery associated with our word "descent", the idea of descending generations that continually move down and away from some ancestor, is in most cases alien to native Lowland South Americans who use different forms of representation. A good example of this are the Canela who represent the idea of descent in terms of the sweet potato vine with each new potato figuring a more distant female descendant. "Descent" is the horizontal spread of the vines (i.e., matrilines) away from the central plant (W. H. Crocker 1990: 266–267). A more radically different idea is found among the Barasana who represent the succession of generations as leaves piling up on the forest floor and employ ritual means to keep in contact with their origins (S. Hugh-Jones 1977: 209). At the same time, Christine Hugh-Jones (1979) has shown how Barasana ideas of descent involve two components: a one-generational cycle associated with male bone and semen and female flesh and blood, and a two-generational cycle involving the inheritance of patrilineal names. Among the Gê, as well as the shared substance of kinship, there are social units reproduced by means that are overtly non-genealogical: the transmission of name-sets. In the case of the Kayapó, it is the consistent transfer of names and prerogatives across several generations of mothers' brothers to sisters' sons that gives this society the matrilineal colouration of which Lea writes. Christopher Crocker (1985: 32) is clear that as far as the Bororo are concerned, they do not regard members of the same clan as blood relatives; rather membership is based on other shared qualities, refractions of the group's totemic essence. Even so this does not mean that blood relationships are unimportant for they are, in both the uterine and agnatic lines. Thus while the Bororo organize themselves through two relationship systems, these are integrated in a variety of ways. For example, the mode of transmitting names, ownership of which bestows membership in corporate groups, is based on genealogical relationship. On the other hand, in Guiana the absence of social formations means that kinship is more exclusively the idiom of social relationships and shared substance the idiom of kinship. Thus, it would seem that, after all, everywhere in Lowland South America, genealogy, real or classificatory and however shallow, influences the transmission of properties, whatever they may be.

An excessive concern with definitions is not very productive and we should look for other ways in which to describe what is there. Lea (1986) has made a useful proposal. In grappling with the intricacies of Kayapó social organization she came to appreciate that it is the "House", as the owner of names and prerogatives, that is the significant unit in societal continuity. It would appear that it was only after she had reached this conclusion that she became acquainted with Lévi-Strauss's concept of "sociétés à maison". This notion of House has allowed her to look again at the difficult problem of the nature of the social units (domestic clusters) that are located in the residences that encircle the Gê village. The problem has been that these units are not "corporate groups", at least in the usual anthropological sense of the term which almost invariably implies unilineal descent. However, Lea has used the notion of House as "moral person" to good effect in explaining the nature of these institutions as the units that transmit names and prerogatives. Furthermore, following Lévi-Strauss, she suggests that Kayapó Houses are able to accommodate the conflicting principles of social organization that exist in the society. By putting the emphasis on the House, she also finds herself in a position to reconsider the roles of centre and periphery, usually taken as a key feature of Gê and Bororo social organization and often associated with a series of other distinctions such as men and women, and public and private, with the implication that the second terms are inferior. In her view, this characterization is wrong because it is the Kayapó Houses on the periphery that own, control and transmit the names and valuables that are vital for the reproduction of the units (moieties, etc.) that operate in the centre of the village.

It might be said that to introduce the notion of House is merely to muddy the waters further by the addition of another ill-defined concept. I disagree with this on condition that the notion is not used too rigidly and that it has expository value. I find its application to the Northern Gê and the Bororo illuminating. How far it will work elsewhere in Lowland South America remains to be seen. The meaning of the *maloca* in the Northwest Amazon has been extensively explored by Christine Hugh-Jones (1979) and it is clear that here the House is an essential element in Tukanoan society. But these people with their shallow, patrilineal exogamous descent groups seem less in need of the House to counteract opposing principles. In Guiana where, as stated above, social relationships are mainly expressed in the idiom of kinship categories, the notion of House serves to hide the difference between kinship and coresidence, so that coresident non-kin become more kinlike than non-resident kin, thus mediating the opposition of inside and outside. But in neither case is the notion of House likely to elucidate as much as it does for the Gê, where the House takes on the role of the "moral person" with corporate continuity.

Alongside the question of descent there is that of affinity and to some extent the problem here is even greater than it is with descent. Whereas with the latter term, we know that we are referring to the general area of the relationship between generations and the "generative process", we cannot be so certain that what has come to be called "affinity", because of a shadowy similarity with affinity elsewhere, necessarily concerns those related through marriage. The situation has been worsened by the tendency to refer to spouses as affines which they are not in normal English usage nor in many South American cases where they become kin as they increasingly participate in a common substance.

A starting point for considering this problem seems to be the concentric dualism that is pervasive in the symbolic ordering of Lowland South American societies. In this scheme the inside is associated with familiarity, kin and safety, the outside with the other, affines and danger. Joanna Overing Kaplan, in a review article (1981), drew attention to the fact that while different societies manipulate this distinction in different ways, both parts of the cosmos are everywhere equally important because the universe only exists and reproduces itself through the mixing of things that are different from one another. The evidence that affinity is part of this otherness is very strong. Thus, among the Panare the distinction between marriageable and unmarriageable may be expressed in the terms *piyaka* and *tunkonan*, the literal translations of which being respectively "another of the same kind" and "another of a different kind" (Henley 1982: 100–101). However, it is Albert's 1985 study of the Yanomami that has most effectively described the concentrically constructed classification of groups, running from coresidents through friends and allies, enemies, potential enemies to those who are not known. He has further shown that these groups are distinguished not only by particular configurations of exchanges and conflicts but also, in quantifiable terms, by the types of mystical attack that emanate from them. The analysis is then taken a step further and it is shown how enemies, possible enemies and the unknown are tied into a system of reciprocal predation, mystical or actual, which is expressed through the notion of symbolic exo-cannibalism. The putrefaction and decay of the flesh on the exposed corpse are seen as the consumption of the flesh by the predator. Thus the first stage of the funerary ceremony, the exposure of the corpse, is linked in with the wider set of concentric relations. The relationship between a given community and its allies is ritually expressed through the endo-cannibalistic consumption of the ashes of the bones. The crucial role in this is played by classificatory affines of the deceased: in the first part of the funerary ritual by a coresident classificatory affine, and in the second part by a non-resident classificatory affine drawn from the category of friends and allies. People in these positions act as hinges that articulate between the different spheres of the Yanomami's socio-political world, and, in the course of the funeral ceremony, serve to mask such fundamental distinctions as kin/affines, coresidents/allies.

This is just one of a series of works that has drawn attention to the cannibalistic imagery to be found in many Amerindian cosmologies. Although the association of enemy, cannibal and affine is widespread, its exact configuration varies. Thus Overing (1986) has described the abstract role of the cannibal outsider among the Piaroa and shows that it is the means whereby violence is excluded from intra-settlement relationships. This contrasts with the Pakaa Nova whose funerary rituals involve the actual consumption of flesh and bones by real affines (addressed as kin), who are reluctant cannibals compared with strangers (addressed as affines) who are avid cannibals (Vilaça 1990). Viveiros de Castro (1986) describes the role of the cannibal gods in the ontology of the Araweté and more recently (1993) has attempted to generalize a concept that arose from that work. This is what he has called in Portuguese "*terceiro incluído*" and in English, after Peirce, "thirdness". This notion refers to the widely reported presence in Lowland South America of roles mainly external to kinship: formal friends, trading partners, and captives but including the Tukanoan mother's sister's child. They provide the dynamism within the concentric world by mediating between the same and other, the inside and outside, friend and enemy, living and dead. Above all, perhaps, it is the potential or classificatory affine that fulfils this role of thirdness, and why it is that affinity, which suggests something to do with relations through marriage, has also to do with the fact or fantasy of cannibalism.

Clearly more thought will have to be given to this idea of thirdness, but its identification offers some new avenues to explore. For some years it has been apparent that Amazonian affinity presents problems and various terms (such as "affinability") have been coined in order to try and cope with the difficulties. In practice, most of these seem to have been introduced in order to protect the integrity of the dualistic structure of the so-called Dravidian terminologies. The recognition of a "third term" or the "ternary nature" of many terminologies offers a possible escape from the Indologist model (in my own view, nothing has been or is to be gained by referring to Amazonian terminologies as Dravidian) in the same way as the Africanist models of descent have been found wanting. Furthermore, and this is perhaps the important thing, the existence of the third term as a mode of articulation in a concentric dualistic structure is perfectly consistent with the generative process that we call "descent".

This returns us to the beginning of this discussion on affinity, and the fact that creativity comes from the mixing of two unlike things which are potentially dangerous to one another. There is here what Viveiros de Castro (1993) has dubbed the "symbolic economy of predation". The relation of this "symbolic economy" to the other Amerindian economies is best stated in his own words (my translation):

> The relations of predation hierarchically encompass the relations of production. This means that an economy of symbolic exchanges, linked to the creation and destruction of human components [. . .] circumscribes and determines the political economy of marriage and of the allocation of productive resources, a dimension which becomes a specific incidence of the global order of cannibalistic sociality. The simplistic conception of marriage exchange as involving the distribution, circulation and control of individuals (classically women) must give way to a shrewder consideration of the symbolic attributes and properties which circulate, not only in marriage but also in the general order of an assumed predation (Viveiros de Castro, 1993).

In other words the widest social world of the Amerindian is not predicated on the narrow-range exchanges of spouses and things but on symbolic exchanges which even incorporate unknown people. Clearly there is here an idea of some considerable power and there is much evidence to support it although I would query whether this exchange has to use the symbolism of predation. There is one recent work which seems to suggest that an opposite concept might also be an appropriate predicate for such a schema. This is Fernando Santos Granero's study (1991) of the Amuesha

among whom it is the relations of love that hierarchically encompass all other relationships and give legitimation to them. This is not to say that cannibalistic ideas are absent, but the Amuesha associate them with the relatively narrow-range influence of the shamans rather than the wide-ranging moral influence of their priests.

Love or violence, the proposed scheme of far-ranging symbolic exchanges incorporating unknown people, has obvious importance for the study of social organization. The focus of much work has reflected what is often the natives' own view of their social world, consisting of the community and a handful of neighbouring communities, although ethnographers have realized that this ideal isolation and autonomy are, in practice, unachievable. What has been missing is the wider view whereby societal reproduction does not depend on the production and exchange of visible and material items but on invisible but no less real events. The assumed cannibalistic consumption by an outsider of the putrefying Yanomami corpse is no less important than a visible birth for the continuity of society.

I have dealt, but only superficially, with the Amerindianization of two key terms in social organization. More space would allow for the consideration of a similar process with other concepts: hierarchy, gender, property, postmarital residence, for example. One crucial lesson that has emerged from all this work is that social organization is inseparable from culture; even to express it in these terms may be misleading since it suggests that they may be potentially separable. In Lowland South America, at least, all the evidence points in the opposite direction.

Finally, and although it is not in my remit to propose or predict where future studies should lie, the way now seems clear for a genuine comparative approach to Lowland South American sociocultural phenomena. This does not mean that we have all the analytical tools at hand, but rather it is only through comparative studies that appropriate tools can be identified and honed. It says little for Western thought that it has taken 500 years to begin to discover what we have destroyed.

BIBLIOGRAPHY

Albert, Bruce 1985 *Temps du sang, temps des cendres. Représentation de la maladie, système rituel et espace politique chez les Yanomami du sud-est (Amazonie brésilienne)*. Thèse, Université de Paris X.

Balée, W. 1989 "The Culture of Amazonian Forests", in D. A. Posey & W. Balée, eds., 1989: 1–21.

Carneiro da Cunha, Manuela 1978 *Os Mortos e os outros. Uma análise do sistema funerário e da noção de pessoa entre os Índios Krahó*. São Paulo, Editora Hucitec.

Crocker, Jon Christopher 1985 *Vital Souls: Bororo Cosmology, Natural Symbolism, and Shamanism*. Tucson, University of Arizona Press.

Crocker, William H. 1979 "Canela kinship and the question of matrilineality", in M. L. Margolis & W. E. Carter, eds., *Brazil Anthropological Perspectives*. New York, Columbia University Press: 225–249.

—— 1990 *The Canela (Eastern Timbira). I: An Ethnographic Introduction*. Washington, D.C., Smithsonian Institution Press ("Smithsonian Contributions to Anthropology" 33).

Da Matta, Roberto 1976 *Um Mundo dividido: a estrutura social dos Índios Apinayé*. Petrópolis, Editora Vozes.

—— 1979 "The Apinayé Relationship System: Terminology and Ideology", in D. Maybury-Lewis, ed., *Dialectical Societies: The Gê and Bororo of Central Brazil*, I. Cambridge, Mass., Harvard University Press: 83–127.

Goldman, Irving 1977 "Time, space, and descent: the Cubeo example", in J. Overing Kaplan, ed., 1977: 175–183.

Henley, Paul 1982 *The Panare. Tradition and Change on the Amazonian Frontier*. New Haven & London, Yale University Press.

Hugh-Jones, Christine 1979 [1988] *From the Milk River: Spatial and Temporal Processes in Northwest Amazonia*. Cambridge, Cambridge University Press.

Hugh-Jones, Stephen 1977 "Like the Leaves on the Forest Floor . . . : Space and Time in Barasana Ritual", in J. Overing Kaplan, ed., 1977: 105–215.

Jackson, Jean 1975 "Recent ethnography of indigenous Northern Lowland South America", *Annual Review of Anthropology* 4: 307–340.

Lea, Vanessa 1986 *Nomes e nekrets kayapó. Uma concepção de riqueza*. Thèse de Doctorat. Rio de Janeiro, Museo Nacional.

Murphy, Robert F. 1979 "Lineage and Lineality in Lowland South America", in M. L. Margolis & W. E. Carter, eds., *Brazil. Anthropological Perspectives*. New York, Columbia University Press: 217–224.

Overing, Joanna 1986 "Images of Cannibalism, Death and Domination in a 'Non-Violent' Society", in D. Riches, ed., *The Anthropology of Violence*. Oxford, Basil Blackwell: 86–102.

Overing Kaplan, Joanna 1977 "Social Time and Social Space in Lowland South America", in J. Overing Kaplan, ed., 1977.

—— 1981 Review Article: "Amazonian Anthropology", *Journal of Latin American Studies* 13: 51–65.

Overing Kaplan, Joanna, ed. 1977 *Actes du XLIIe Congrès international des Américanistes*, 2. Paris, Société des Américanistes.

Santos Granero, Fernando 1991 *The Power of Love. The Moral Use of Knowledge amongst the Amuesha of Central Peru*. London & Atlantic Highlands, NJ, The Athlone Press ("London School of Economics Monographs on Social Anthropology" 62).

Seeger, Anthony 1981 *Nature and Society in Central Brazil: The Suyá Indians of Mato Grosso*. Cambridge, Mass., Harvard University Press ("Harvard Studies in Cultural Anthropology" 4).

Seeger, Anthony Roberto Da Matta & Eduardo B. Viveiros de Castro 1979 "A Construção da pessoa nas sociedades indígenas brasileiras", *Boletim do Museu Nacional, Antropologia* 32: 2–19. Rio de Janeiro.

Vilaça, Aparecida 1990 *O Canibalismo funerário Pakaa Nova: uma etnografia*. Rio de Janeiro, Programa de Pósgraduação em Antropologia Social do Museu Nacional ("Comunicação" 19).

Viveiros de Castro, Eduardo 1986 *Araweté: os deuses canibais*. Rio de Janeiro, Jorge Zahar Ed.

—— 1992 *From the Enemy's Point of View. Humanity and Divinity in an Amazonian Society*. Chicago, Chicago University Press.

—— 1993 "Alguns aspectos da afinade no dravidianato amazônico", in E. Viveiros de Castro & M. Carneiro da Cunha, eds., *Amazônia: etnologia e história indígena*. São Paulo, Núcleo de História Indígena/Universidade de São Paulo (USP).

6

Inheritance, Property, and Marriage in Africa and Eurasia

Jack Goody

Many of the detailed observations of pre-colonial African society come from West Africa, and especially from the Gold Coast. For this region was not only the closest part of Black Africa but also of the greatest economic interest, especially when the Portuguese lost their monopolistic hold on the coast and the way was open for the Protestant business men of the western seaboard, Holland, England, Scandinavia, and north Germany to develop the interlocking trade in gold, slaves, and firearms which stood them in such stead in the early years of capital accumulation that preceded the development of industry in Europe.

During this period, at the end of the seventeenth century, the Dutch factor, William Bosman, was struck by certain features of social organization of the Gold Coast which he saw as fundamentally different from those he had grown up with in Western Europe. Bosman was on the coast for some 14 years and published his observations in 1704 under the title of *A New and Accurate Description of the Coast of Guinea, divided into the Gold, the Slave, and the Ivory Coasts*. In the twelfth letter of his book, the author writes 'Of the Negroes manner of Marrying'. 'Marriage here is not over-loaded with Ceremonies, nor have they any Notion of a Praevious Courtship to bring on a Match: here are no tedious Disputes on account of Marriage Settlements.... The Bride brings no other Fortune than her Body, nor does the Man want much; 'tis sufficient if

he has enough to defray the Expence of the Wedding-Day' (1967: 197–98). He further observes the corollary of the absence of dowry, that 'Married people here have no community of Goods; but each hath his or her particular Propriety.... On the Death of either the Man or the Wife, the respective Relations come and immediately sweep away all, not leaving the Widow or Widower the least part thereof...' (202).[1]

Thus Bosman sees that not only is conjugal community of property rare, but that a deceased's estate is not called upon to support the surviving spouse. This fact is linked to the absence of a marriage settlement, to the absence of a woman's portion of the patrimony which she brings with her into marriage as a dowry.[2] If a woman brings nothing at marriage, she gets nothing when the union is dissolved. Bosman also notes a related fact, though he does not perceive its interrelatedness. He observes that except at Accra, inheritance is matrilineal. Even in the matrilineal societies property is sex-linked... 'the eldest Son of his Mother is Heir to his Mothers Brother or her Son, as the eldest Daughter is Heiress of her Mothers Sister or her Daughter' (203). This is to say, property descends 'homogeneously' e.g. *between* males, even when it goes *through* females.[3]

In earlier publications, I have emphasized the importance of inheritance as a variable (1958, 1959, 1962) and suggested that in the domestic domain one of the major differences between

African and Eurasian societies lies in the fact that in Eurasia diverging inheritance (i.e. 'bilateral' inheritance, where property goes to children of both sexes) is common, especially in the major civilizations, whereas in Africa it is virtually unknown. The absence of diverging inheritance is linked to the absence of dowry in Africa (cf. Goode 1963: 67), since dowry is essentially a process whereby parental property is distributed to a daughter at her marriage (i.e. *inter vivos*) rather than at the holder's death (*mortis causa*). I therefore include dowry as part of the process of 'diverging devolution'. The property a woman receives through dowry or 'bilateral' inheritance establishes some variety of a conjugal fund, the nature of which may vary widely. This fund ensures her support (or endowment) in widowhood and eventually goes to provide for her sons and daughters.

I have elsewhere tried to analyse the concomitants of diverging devolution in the Eurasian setting and have discussed some of the implications of this difference for comparative sociological studies. In a paper on 'Adoption in Cross-Cultural Perspective' (1968), I have outlined some of the interlinking variables (unavoidably these are mostly 'qualitative variables' in the statistical sense) that I regard as concomitants of diverging devolution. I should add that I see the system of the transmission of property (i.e. devolution) as being the independent variable in some of these instances and as the intervening or dependent variable in others; for in the main it seems to occur where agriculture is intensive and the means of production are in relatively short supply. In this present paper I try to test certain hypotheses concerning diverging devolution by another means, namely, the recent Ethnographic Atlas. The 1967 version of this sample consists of 80 columns of data on 863 societies from all parts of the globe. This instrument enables us to check some of the statements that sociologists generate about societies, usually on the basis of the one or two in which they have worked and the handful they currently have in memory store. Clearly the number of aspects that one can test is limited. For example, it could be suggested that the extent of ceremonial performed at rites of passage in the individual's life cycle is positively correlated with the amount of work (in terms of the handing over

of rights and duties, etc.) that has to be done. Where marriage establishes a conjugal fund (as in dowry systems) the wedding ceremonial will be more elaborate than where it does not; where funerals redistribute the dead man's property, they will be more elaborate than where a holder divests himself of his property during his lifetime (Goody 1962: v). But this information is not coded in the present Ethnographic Atlas and to read through a representative sample of the relevant material would be very time-consuming. In other cases the information exists, though not always in quite the form one optimally needs. When this is so, I have carried out tests of the relevant aspects of the hypothesis.[4] In so doing, I am not seeking to explain all of one 'variable' by another; in the example I gave of the relationship between life-cycle ceremonies and devolution, it is obvious that other factors are at work. The predictions are for a positive association, a significant trend, not a one to one relationship. In many branches of the social sciences a hypothesis is rejected if the probability value is less than .05, while an association of 0.33 on a phi test is understood to be high (the scale runs between −1 and +1); to this convention I will adhere in this paper.[5]

There are two kinds of problem involved in trying to make such a test, namely, those to do with the instrument and those to do with the analytic concepts. From the analytic standpoint, it is the transmission of major items of property that is clearly going to be of greater significance, especially the transmission of basic productive resources (usually land); but in the code the distinction between land and movables is made for inheritance but not for dowry. Secondly, there is a potential difficulty in deciding when property diverges. For example, a daughter may inherit her father's property in her own right or as an epiclerate, that is, a residual heir in the absence of brothers. Nevertheless the overall distinction is clear. In the main Eurasian societies, a close female inherits before a more distant male, even where both are members of the same patrilineal descent group. In Africa south of the Sahara, a woman only inherits male property when there are no males left in the wider kingroup, and even then it is a very rare occurrence.

The specific problems to do with the instrument are twofold. Firstly the composers note that the inheritance data have not been easy to code; indeed they describe the code as inadequate (Murdock 1967: 167). The second point has to do with marriage transactions. Since I define devolution as transmission between holder and heir (see Goody 1962: 312), whether or not it takes place at death, I include dowry in these operations. Indeed I include not only the 'direct dowry' (the property passed from 'parents' to a daughter on her marriage). I also include the 'indirect dowry', that is, property passed by the groom to the bride at marriage. Such prestations are often spoken of as bridewealth or brideprice, but I would limit these terms to prestations that pass between the kin of the groom and the kin of the bride, and that can therefore be used to provide wives for the girl's brothers; in short, they form part of a system of circulating or on-going exchange. I suspect that most accounts fail to make a distinction between these types of prestation, despite the different social implications that they have. Hence what I would regard as (indirect) dowry may sometimes have been reported as brideprice.

As with most kinds of sociological analysis the measuring rods and the measurements themselves are bound to be less than perfect. But however crude, even such rough comparisons provide some degree of confirmation or contradiction of hypotheses about human social organization. On the one hand this procedure gets us out of the unsystematic comparisons upon which so much comparative sociology is based and on the other hand liberates us from certain of the limitations of the structural-functional method. It is no part of my intention to substitute one approach for another; different methods answer different problems. Indeed it is a sign of the relative immaturity of the social sciences that so many of their practitioners presume that there is a single approach to the sociological verities, an attitude which makes them more akin to philosophers than to other behavioural scientists.

Bearing in mind the limitations of this and other methods, I first looked at the distribution of diverging devolution (or the 'woman's property complex')[6] in different continents, that is, the distribution of those systems where diverging inheritance or dowry are found. This information was found in the following form in the Ethnographic Atlas:

(i) all societies where daughters have a share in either land (column 74: c, d) or movable property (76: c, d);

(ii) all societies with dowry as the main or alternative method of marriage transaction (12: d; 13: d).

The negative cases consist of all those that remained once the diverging devolution data had been extracted, less those societies with no individual property rights or no rule of transmission (74: o; 76: o) and those societies where there was no information on the relevant columns (74, 76, 12).

The first run was a purely distributional one, in order to confirm or refute the suggested differences between Africa and Eurasia. The following points emerge from it:

(i) In Africa, diverging devolution is rare, i.e. it occurs in 5 per cent of the cases. Bosman's observation thus has general significance.

(ii) In America, there is a large proportion of societies with no individual property rights or transmission rule. The reason is that in many of the hunting and gathering societies individuals had little property, except personal equipment, and this was often destroyed at death.[7] On-going productive property was minimal.

(iii) In America, the relatively large number of societies with diverging inheritance is in part a question of the importation of European norms through imperial conquest. The Mayan-speaking people of Yucatan have the same practice (Redfield 1934: 61 ff.), but I do not know whether this is an aspect of early Mayan inheritance or a European import (the people of Chan Kom have long been Christian). Eurasian religious and secular codes (including Islam) promote diverging devolution independently of other factors.

(iv) In Eurasia and the Pacific, the number of societies with diverging devolution is approximately 40 per cent of the total. However, this figure includes the major civilizations in the area, whose populations are more numerous and whose influence greater. It is suggested that the societies with homogeneous devolution are mostly those outside the major traditions, i.e. 'tribal' societies of various kinds, especially those without intensive agriculture.

In sum, the distributional table shows that systems of devolution in Africa differ from those associated with the major Eurasian civilizations, being of the homogeneous rather than the diverging kind.

What about the correlates of these differences in devolution? It seems probable that where women are receivers of male property considerable attention will be paid to their marriage arrangements. An heiress is often not allowed to marry just anyone; her spouse is more likely to be chosen for her. Other women too are likely to marry (and to want to marry) within rather than without; for unless a woman marries 'well' her standard of living might drop, and this would be a matter of concern to herself as well as her kinsfolk. It seemed plausible to test this assumption by means of the data on pre-marital virginity (col. 78); a stress on virginity at marriage could be held to indicate, *inter alia*, the degree of control exercised on women by society, kin, and self. It also limits the possibility of conflicting claims on the estate in which a woman has rights.

A further hypothesis is generated by this suggestion that where women are recipients of male property, there will be a greater tendency to control their marriages. When women are heirs, or even residual heirs, they may be encouraged to marry within a certain range of kin; this was the case with the daughters of Zelophehad in ancient Israel as well as in the epiclerate of classical Athens. The Atlas does not permit us to assess the incidence of these kinds of marriages but it does enable us to get an idea of the association of one form of in-marriage, that is, endogamy (in kin, caste, or local group), with diverging devolution. . . . Defined 'culturally', in terms of Hindu ideology, caste is clearly limited to the Indian subcontinent. Defined 'sociologically', as a closed, in-marrying, stratum, caste is still largely confined to the Eurasian continent, or other areas where Eurasian whites have established themselves (e.g. North America, Southern Africa, the Saharan fringes). Racial factors, which because of their visibility provide one of the most universal cards of identity used by man, also enter into the ban on intermarriage. But here

again property is heavily involved, for there appears little reluctance for men to engage in sexual unions, as distinct from marriage, with women of the lower orders. It is the sexuality of their own sisters they are concerned to protect, and the notions regarding the purity of women that attach to caste systems and the concern with their honour that marks the Mediterranean world cannot be divorced from the position of women as carriers of property. [. . .]

Another kind of in-marriage is the union with cousins. Certain of these are property-conserving as far as women are concerned, especially the father's brother's daughter marriage; in societies with agnatic descent groups, this woman falls within a man's own group. [. . .]

Control over property can be exercised by the number as well as the kind of marriage and I predicted a connection between diverging devolution and monogamy. Where both males and females require parental property for the maintenance of their status, and where resources are limited, then large polygynous families are likely to have an impoverishing effect. Only the very rich can afford the luxury of many children without dropping in the economic hierarchy. In dowry systems wives may be thought of as augmenting a man's wealth and hence polygyny could be advantageous to him; but every marriage would establish its own conjugal fund and differentiate each spouse according to the marital property she brings. There are obvious difficulties for a man in setting up a plurality of such funds (though less so when the women are sisters). The test shows a positive association between diverging devolution and monogamy. [. . .]

Like monogamy, polyandry also limits the number of wives and heirs with whom the property has to be divided and this form of marriage again displays a positive association with diverging devolution. Indeed in Tibet the provision of one legitimate heir-producing wife for a group of brothers is explicitly thought of as a way of keeping the balance between people and land (Carrasco 1959: 36). The Atlas includes only four cases of polyandry, three of which are found in conjunction with diverging inheritance.

The residence of a married couple is a further factor likely to be influenced by property considerations; a rich wife can make a poorer husband move to her natal home; and the well-to-do father-in-law may have the same power over (and attraction for) his daughter's husband. Not every woman will display these magnetic powers, which depend essentially upon the differential distribution of wealth; it is only the rich or epicleratic daughter who finds herself in such a position. So that we should not expect a straightforward uxorilocal pattern of postmarital residence but rather an ambilocal one, where a married couple may choose to reside with either the kin of the bride or of the groom depending upon their relative position. There is another possibility: if an independent conjugal fund is established at marriage, bride and groom may also establish an independent (i.e. neolocal) residence.[8]

The results of this test [indicate] that, while bilocal and neolocal marriage are definitely correlated with diverging devolution, the correlation is negative where the alternative forms of marriage represent less than one-third of the total. The latter finding is contrary to my hypothesis. However the determinants of residence are not of course limited to property. Indeed in this instance it seemed possible that the absence of unilineal descent groups (i.e. 'Bilateral descent') would prove to have a close association with the patterns of residence. [. . .]

I return to this question later when I compare 'bilaterality' and 'diverging devolution' as variables. Here I want to point out that it is only in respect of residence that kinship is a better predictor than the transmission of property. Part of the answer emerges from a study of the figures for the residence patterns of societies that have 'no individual property rights or no regular rules of transmission'. The interesting point is the very large proportion of these societies that include marriages of the 'bilocal' or 'virilocal with alternatives' type – no doubt because there is no immovable property to tie anyone anywhere. There are more societies with 'uxorilocal with virilocal alternative' in this category (13) than in the societies with property (9).

Property considerations, in the shape of diverging devolution, also seemed logically connected with kin terms. Only in exceptional cases (where there are no descendants, male, female or adopted) do brothers (or more usually brother's sons) inherit under such systems. So that the three characteristics of this type of transmission are (i) it is inter-generational, (ii) it is direct and (iii) close females are preferred to distant males. Indeed devolution occurs within the nuclear family, while the establishment of separate conjugal funds differentiates sibling from sibling, parents from children. Though cousins may be possible 'intestate' heirs, they rarely inherit. The emphasis is on direct transmission, even if one has to adopt.

It seemed possible that this 'isolation' of the nuclear family, as manifested in conjugal funds and direct inheritance, would be reflected in a kinship terminology that differentiated siblings from cousins (Murdock 1967: 158). There are several ways in which brothers (for I confine the discussion to males) may be set apart from other kin. Firstly, under an 'Eskimo' (e.g. English) system they are distinguished from all cousins. Secondly, cousins may be distinguished not only from siblings but among themselves; this is the case with descriptive terminology ('descriptive or derivative'). [The data show a] positive correlation between terminologies that isolate siblings and diverging devolution.

While I have used inheritance, or rather devolution, as the independent variable, it is independent only in a certain context. For these hypotheses raise a further series of questions concerning the incidence of diverging devolution itself. Why should the African and Eurasian patterns be so different? I suggest that the scarcer productive resources become and the more intensively they are used, then the greater the tendency towards the retention of these resources within the basic productive and reproductive unit, which in the large majority of cases is the nuclear family. There are several reasons for this hypothesis. Intensive agriculture, whether by plough or irrigation, permits a surplus of production over consumption that is sufficient to maintain an elaborate division of labour and a stratification based upon different 'styles of life'. An important means of maintaining one's style of life, and that of one's progeny, is by marriage with persons of the same or higher qualifications.[9] We should therefore expect a greater emphasis upon the direct vertical transmission of property in societies with intensive rather than extensive exploitation of agricultural resources.

This system of direct vertical transmission (i.e. from parents to children) tends to make provision for women as well as men. The position of women in the world has to be maintained by means of property, either in dowry or inheritance – otherwise the honour of the family suffers a set-back in the eyes of others. This also means that they are likely to become residual heirs in the restricted sibling groups that monogamy permits, the property going to female descendants before collateral males, even when these are members of the same agnatic clan.

The other aspect of intensive agriculture bearing upon the conditions for the emergence of diverging devolution is the expansion of population it allows, another factor making for scarcity of land. Where intensive agriculture is dependent upon the plough, the increase in production is partly a result of the greater area a man can cultivate; once again, land becomes more valuable, especially the kind of land that can sustain permanent cultivation by means of the simpler type of plough.

Intensive exploitation of resources can be variously measured. [The data show] the firm association that exists between the presence of the plough and diverging devolution. The information on the absence of plough agriculture is not altogether satisfactory since the absence of an entry in column 39 might mean either no information or no plough; however the presence of the plough is such an obvious feature of human societies that the chance of error should be small.

The Atlas also gives a separate code for intensive agriculture (col. 28, *I*, *J*) and it is possible to retest the hypothesis on this column, though the association is somewhat less strong.

Intensive agriculture is virtually a condition of the extensive differentiation by styles of life that in turn encourages the concentration of property by inheritance and marriage. The concentration of property is maintained by diverging devolution, which takes the form of direct vertical transmission; hence the importance of 'sonship', real and fictional (which includes daughters), in these areas of social action.[10] We would therefore expect to find diverging devolution associated with complex stratified societies of all types, whether charac-terized by caste or class. This hypothesis is linked with the suggestion that diverging devolution encourages in-marriage, which I tested earlier. Endogamy is clearly one way of limiting the consequences of the transmission of property through women. Other systems of complex stratification may restrict marriage *de facto* if not *de jure*.

The same hypothesis can be tested in column 33 which provides 'a measure of political complexity'. I have included here only the larger states. In surveying the major Eurasian civilizations, I found all (in differing degrees) to be characterized by diverging devolution: women were usually residual heiresses to their brothers, in addition to which they received a dowry if they married away. These forms of marriage prestation and inheritance are recorded in the Greek, Roman, and Hebrew and Chinese texts and in Babylonian, Hindu, and Buddhist law-books. For such societies were all literate; indeed testamentary inheritance, as Maine pointed out, was sometimes used to divert property from a man's agnates, who were his residual heirs. But more often and more universally the institution of adoption (often of agnates) and the 'appointed daughter' were used to ensure the direct vertical transmission of property. In general, these literate societies fall into the category of 'large states' (or are closely linked to them) and the association with diverging devolution is shown to be firm.

Alternative Predictions

To test my hypothesis, I predicted that the presence of different types of descent groups would be less closely associated with the variables examined than would the transmission of property. The runs done for diverging devolution were repeated for the nearest equivalent in kinship terms, i.e. bilateral 'descent' or kinship, that is to say those societies which possessed neither patrilineal nor matrilineal descent groups. In every case except for residence diverging devolution has a stronger association with the variables than does 'bilateral kinship'. The general point that I would make here is that while anthropologists have given most attention to kinship factors, there are a number of important areas of social life where the mode of distributing property appears to be more significant. This is not a matter of trying to substitute one monolithic form of explanation for another. Nor yet of equating (as some writers have tended to do) kinship and property. The two variables are closely interlocked in pre-industrial societies where the basic means of production are almost universally transmitted between close kin. My interest is in attempting to specify the way in which they are associated, particularly with a view to ascertaining the influence of differences in systems of transmission upon kinship relations. Causal direction is not of course something one can establish by correlational analysis alone; though causal inferences can be made by means of statistical techniques it needs to be supplemented by a study of changing situations.[11]

I suggested therefore that 'bilateral descent' (or rather 'bilateral kinship') would be a worse predictor. On the other hand, the vesting of landed property in women, as distinct from movables alone, was thought likely to produce more significant results, anyhow as far as residence is concerned. While in every case except residence bilateral kinship (i.e. the absence of unilineal descent groups) is less closely associated with the variables than diverging devolution (as I had suggested), the inheritance of land comes second to diverging devolution and is a worse rather than a better predictor. As I have earlier noted this excludes societies with a landed dowry (and in inheritance of land by women) which may well be a better predictor; but I make no attempt to explain this result.

Conclusions

Tylor long ago pointed out the adaptive functions of exogamy for human societies (1889). Mankind, he remarked, was faced with the alternative of marrying out or being killed out. In-marriage on the other hand is a policy of isolation. One reason (and there are of course others) for such a policy is to preserve property where this is transmitted through both males and females, to encourage marriages with families 'of one's own kind' and thus to maintain property and prestige. The positive control of marriage arrangements (exogamy is a negative control) is stricter where property is transmitted to women. It is a commentary on their lot that where they are more

propertied they are initially less free as far as marital arrangements go, though the unions into which they enter are more likely to be monogamous (or even polyandrous).

In this paper I have tried to test by means of the Ethnographic Atlas a set of hypotheses to do with the concomitants of diverging devolution, derived from a more intensive study of the literature on a number of societies in Eurasia and Africa. Though the information is imperfect and the instrument limited, my basic suggestions are all confirmed (except for caste). Bilateral kinship was a worse predictor except for certain types of residence; on the other hand, the inheritance of land was also worse, which the theory did not anticipate. These results are reinforced by the fact that the hypotheses are interlocked and were formulated in advance.

I have shown that Eurasian and African societies differ in their systems of transmitting property; these differences are correlated with differences in the types of marriage prestation, the extent of control over women, both before marriage and in terms of marriage partners (and probably, too, after marriage though this I could not test). Differences in the nature of a man's estate are indicated in the greater prevalence of terms that isolate the sibling group, an indication of the differences in the type of descent corporation found associated with the systems for the devolution of property and with modes of agriculture. Both the means of production and the relationships of production have certain marked differences.

It is a failure to recognize these differences in the type of descent corporation (even when both can be described as 'patrilineal descent groups') that seems to have caused much of the controversy over the application of descent or alliance models to the study of such societies, and it is significant that so-called 'descent theorists' have generally worked in societies with homogeneous devolution and the 'alliance theorists' in societies with diverging devolution. It should be apparent that where marriage involves a re-arrangement of property rights of the dowry kind, then conjugal, affinal, sibling, and filial relationships are likely to display qualitative differences from systems of the African kind. It also follows that the organization of descent groups will differ under these two conditions. The ball-play between rival 'theorists' has obscured the basic differences in the material they are dealing with.

I shall pursue this point in another place; meanwhile I conclude by pointing to the association of diverging transmission with intensive (and plough) agriculture, with large states and with complex systems of stratification. In such societies social differentiation, based on productive property, exists even at the village level; to maintain the position of the family, a man endows (and controls) his daughters as well as sons, and these ends are promoted by the tendency towards monogamous marriage.[12] Indeed it is significant that the strongest associations of diverging devolution are with monogamy and plough agriculture.

NOTES

Note: The data presented in this paper have subsequently been analysed by a type of multivariate analysis, in fact a combination of pathway and linkage techniques. The results are embodied in a further paper, *Causal inferences concerning diverging devolution*, by Jack Goody, Barrie Irving, and Nicky Tahany, which it is hoped to publish shortly.

1   Bosman was accustomed to the conjugal community of Roman Dutch Law. But the absence of a dowry was apparent even to Englishmen reared under the qualified unity of conjugal property which was a feature of their Common Law. This broad distinction between Africa and Europe still persists. 'Marriage in Ashanti between free persons . . . does not lead to community of property between the spouses, still less to the sinking of the wife's legal persona in her husband's' (Allott 1966: 191).

2   The absence of a dowry is enshrined in local usage of English and French. For the Europeans, having no word for prestations that passed from the family of the groom to that of the bride, used the word they had, 'dot' or 'dowry', for a very different set of transactions. These terms are still sometimes used for 'bridewealth' and other prestations.

3   Barton used the term 'homoparental' but this presents difficulties for matrilineal inheritance.

4   I have used all the data from the Atlas and have not sampled them in the way suggested

by Murdock, 1967: 114. The reasons for this are purely practical and I shall conduct further tests when time allows.

5   The phi coefficient is also known as the Kendall partial rank coefficient (Siegel 1956: 225–26).

6   In speaking of the 'woman's property complex' I refer to her access to property held by males. Under systems of homogeneous inheritance, women have property but it is either inherited from women or self-acquired.

7   Property was also destroyed during the lifetime of the holder in the well-known case of the potlatch.

8   Logically, neolocal residence is less firmly attached to diverging devolution than are bilocal or the less evenly distributed systems of alternative residence. But the boundaries of 'neolocal' residence are difficult to discriminate (how separate is 'separate'?).

9   In my account of the LoWiili of Northern Ghana (1956), I suggested that the increased differentiation of wealth militated against the movement of property outside the co-residential group. The specific feature of this group that inhibits a dispersal of the property is its character as a unit of production. Where self-acquired property (income) begins to play a greater part than inherited wealth (capital), then there will be increasing reluctance to allow property to go outside, as is bound to be the case where the residential pattern is incongruent (or partially so, as in a fully fledged system of double descent) with the mode of inheritance.

10   This point is developed elsewhere (Goody 1968a).

11   I have tried to approach this problem in my comparative work on the LoWiili and the LoDagaba, as well as in a separate essay (Goody 1968b).

12   This paper represents the preliminary results of the comparative research I have undertaken with the help of a grant from the Social Science Research Council. I have hoped for some years to carry out such a survey but it would have been impossible but for the help, by means of this grant, of my assistant in research, Mrs. L. March. I should also like to thank Dr. L. Slater for the programming, and Dr. E. N. Goody, for comments and advice. Little systematic comparison has been carried out in Europe since the work of Hobhouse, Wheeler, and

Ginsberg (1915); like all recent writers on the subject I am much indebted to G. P. Murdock for making his collection of data available in the shape of the Ethnographic Atlas.

BIBLIOGRAPHY

Allott, Anthony N. 1966. The Ashanti law of property. *Zeitschrift für vergleichende Rechtswissenschaft*. 68: 129–215.

Bosman, William. 1967. *A new and accurate description of the coast of Guinea*. London: Frank Cass (First English ed. 1705).

Carrasco, Pedro. 1959. *Land and policy in Tibet*. (Am. Eth. Soc.). Seattle: Univ. of Washington Press.

Driver, Harold Edso. 1961. Introduction to statistics for comparative research, *Readings in cross-cultural methodology* (ed. Frank W. Moore). New Haven: H.R.A.F.

Goode, William J. 1963. *World revolution and family pattern*. New York: Free Press.

Goody, Jack. 1956. *The social organisation of the LoWiili*. London: H.M.S.O. (Second ed. 1967).

Goody, Jack. 1958. The fission of domestic groups among the LoDagaba, *The developmental cycle in domestic groups* (Cambridge Papers in Social Anthropology, No. I). Cambridge: University Press.

Goody, Jack. 1959. The mother's brother and the sister's son in West Africa. *J. R. Anthrop. Inst.* 89: 61–88.

Goody, Jack. 1962. *Death, property and the ancestors*. Stanford: University Press.

Goody, Jack. 1968a. Adoption in cross-cultural perspective. *Comparative Studies in Society and History*.

Goody, Jack. 1968b. Inheritance, social change and the boundary problem, *Lévi-Strauss Festschrift* (ed. J. Pouillon and P. Maranda). The Hague: Mouton.

Goody, Jack. 1969. Marriage policy and incorporation in northern Ghana, *From tribe to nation in Africa* (ed. R. Cohen and J. Middleton). San Francisco: Chandler.

Hobhouse, L. T., Wheeler, G. C. and Ginsberg, M. 1915. *The Material Culture and Social Institutions of the Simpler Peoples*. London.

Murdock, George P. 1960. Cognatic forms of social organization, *Social structure in southeast Asia* (Viking Fund Pubs. in Anthrop. No. 29). Chicago: Quadrangle Books.

Murdock, George P. 1967. Ethnographic atlas: a summary. *Ethnography* 6: 109–236.

Redfield, Robert. 1934. *Chan Kom: a Maya village*. Washington D.C.: Carnegie Institute of Washington.

Siegel, Sidney. 1956. *Nonparametric statistics for the behavioral sciences*. New York: McGraw-Hill.

Tylor, Edward B. 1889. On a method of investigating the development of institutions: applied to laws of marriage and descent. *J. Anthrop. Inst.* 18: 245–269.

Section 2   Terminology and Affinal Alliance

Introduction

Robert Parkin

Another model much loved and discussed by anthropologists is that of affinal alliance, seen in particular as relationships being pursued between groups through cross-cousin marriage, and the associated kinship terminologies. As we have seen (Introduction), the latter can be seen as inventories of terms for relatives in any language, which form distinct patterns, some of which "express" cross-cousin marriage (see the items below). This version of "alliance theory" was essentially a post-World War II phenomenon, thus coming later than descent theory, and it was always linked with structuralism rather than functionalism, which had come to its fullest development in the inter-war period. However, as we have seen, an interest in such systems was nothing new in itself but could be traced back to the reports of the eighteenth-century missionary Lafitau. To recap briefly on the Introduction, Morgan began the discussion of terminologies and their links with social organization in the 1860s, though he was reluctant to associate particular patterns with types of cross-cousin marriage in the way that Rivers was to do later. The work of both men entailed evolutionism, in Morgan's case as a way of linking different terminological patterns in evolutionary sequences, while for Rivers the presence of an appropriate terminology in a society indicated the existence of the associated form of cross-cousin marriage in the past, if not at present. These views were rejected by the functionalists, who in Europe derided both "speculative history" (Radcliffe-Brown) and the "kinship algebra" involved in studying the terminologies (Malinowski). This happened less in America, where people like Fred Eggan managed to combine the two approaches (e.g., 1937). It was only with the massive work of Claude Lévi-Strauss on *The Elementary Structures of Kinship* (1949, 1967, 1969) that an interest in such systems really revived, and then in the form of a structuralism that for the most part was agnostic about history.

One of the oldest controversies in this area has concerned the nature of kinship terminologies. As we saw in the Introduction, for Morgan they denoted actual biological relationships and were associated with different marriage patterns and structures of kin groups and families. For McLennan, they were merely "saluta-tions," that is, modes of address. For Rivers, they denoted the presence or absence of cross-cousin marriage. For Kroeber, they were primarily linguistic phenomena producing classifications, and had no unambiguous social-structural implications. For Radcliffe-Brown, they were expressions of lineage and sibling-group solidarity. For Lévi-Strauss, they were surface manifestations of underlying mental structures, of which various forms of cross-cousin marriage were another expression. For Needham, they were a form of classification. All through this series, however, there is a pattern, or rather two patterns running in parallel. For Morgan, Rivers, and Radcliffe-Brown, terminologies reflected different aspects of social structure. For McLennan, Kroeber, and Needham, they were primarily ways of classifying relatives, any social-structural aspects being contingent, not necessary. This was followed by various sorts of componential analysis (Goodenough 1956) and semantic analysis (e.g., Hammel 1965; Scheffler 1978; Scheffler and Lounsbury 1971), mainly in America, who often used algebraic means of representing terminological systems.

In general, though, anthropologists have always avoided Morgan's strict linking of terminological patterns with actual biological relationships. Despite Schneider's later criticisms of his colleagues (see Part III, below), it was quickly realized that kinship is basically a social phenomenon for the social or cultural anthropologist, and this has been emphasized more and more since Morgan's time. More recalcitrant has been the notion of genealogy, which is hard to avoid totally in the abstract analysis of either kinship systems seen as social structure or terminologies, but does not correspond invariably, if at all, to indigenous representations. This was realized already in the structuralist period, as we shall see below. However, as part of the shift away from structuralism and formal analysis, and toward process and agency, analysis using genealogy has largely been replaced by descriptions of indigenous ideas of kinship and relatedness in their own terms (see also Part III, below).

Such, in a nutshell, is the history of alliance theory, including the theory of kinship terminologies, in anthropology. Rivers's contribution here is an early statement of it in some respects. In other respects, however, it is embedded in the debates of his time, before and around World War I, during which Rivers shifted rapidly from being a psychologist interested in administering psychiatric tests to non-European populations to being an expert in the anthropology of kinship, and successively an evolutionist and a diffusionist theoretically. His insights are still influential. He had been challenged, however, by Kroeber, who in 1909 had rejected (wrongly; cf. White 1948) Morgan's distinction between descriptive and classificatory kinship terminologies on the basis that all terminologies denote classes to some extent. More particularly in the present context, he had also rejected the idea that terminologies were determined by, or at least embedded in, social structure, preferring to see them as linguistic and even psychological in content. Use of the latter term was to cause him much misunderstanding later, and he eventually repudiated it (1952).

Rivers was thus a supporter of Morgan in the main, though he did disagree with him on some points, as we saw in the Introduction. He rose to Kroeber's implicit challenge in a series of three lectures, of which the first is reproduced here. He states right at the outset that he will demonstrate the links between kinship terminology and social organization. He also believes that the former can say something about the history of non-literate, non-European societies, indicating in some cases that they once had cross-cousin marriage, even if they do no longer. As regards the distinction between descriptive and classificatory terminologies, Rivers makes something of a virtue of Kroeber's objection, while keeping the basic distinction between these forms. Western terminologies (Rivers does not use the term "descriptive") may indeed have classes, but they also have terms for a number of individual genealogical positions (F, M, H, W, EF, EM), which a fully classificatory terminology does not.

As far as the social correlates of terminology are concerned, Rivers starts with the system of attitudes or behavior, focusing especially on the position of the mother's brother in many societies in a manner that anticipates the later, more developed hypothesis of Radcliffe-Brown. Briefly, Rivers's hypothesis is the simple (and simplistic) one that the kin term one uses for another individual is linked to, even determines, the socially expected behavior toward that individual. There are many problems with this thesis, not least the fact that – since we are indeed dealing in the main with classes and not genealogical positions – many if not most societies will recognize degrees of relationship within a category. "Real" mother's brothers may indeed be distinguished from other senior matrilateral males even where the latter are covered by the term, and behavior will often be modified accordingly (e.g., Kronenfeld 1973, on the Fanti of Ghana). In many cases, one need not act ritually to a distant MB in the same way, or with the same intensity or formality, as to a close or distant one. For Rivers, however, this was more than just a precept: it underlay the very methods used (the famous "genealogical method") in collecting terminologies in the first place. This method has been modified or abandoned since, with anthropologists in the field now generally using the terminology to establish the genealogies as much as the other way round. This was another respect in which Rivers was closer to Morgan than his successors, despite Schneider's tendency to place them all in the same box (see further below).

For the most part, however, Rivers sees the correlations between terminology and social organization in terms of marriage, or affinal alliance. Recognizing the priority here of the work of the German scholar J. Kohler, he sets out to describe a hypothetical system of cross-cousin marriage (actually MBD–FZS marriage), using his by now extensive knowledge of the ethnography of Oceania to back it up with examples. In many cases he gives the kin terms by which MB is equated with WF, as is logical if male ego is marrying MBD. Unlike later authorities, he tends to assume that the equivalence is genealogical, not categorical. In fact, ego may have a number of genealogical mother's brothers' daughters to choose from, and greater experience was to show that even these were not necessarily actually defined genealogically to begin with. He also firmly believed that the type of terminology was based on the marriage system. Again there is a difference from later authorities. Lévi-Strauss saw both terminology and marriage system as surface manifestations of underlying modes of thought. Needham and his followers came to see the terminology as actually guiding the marriage choices, as well as redefining the kin involved in "wrong" marriages so the system could continue in its proper form (see the items by Dumont, Good, and Needham, below, Chapters 10, 11, and 12).

Rivers persisted with this general theme in the other two lectures, not reproduced here (1968), in which he discussed what we would now term Crow–Omaha and Hawaiian systems with respect to patterns of marriage to particular genealogically defined kin. These arguments have proved much less satisfactory and were quickly abandoned by others. For Radcliffe-Brown (1952: 70–88), Crow–Omaha systems, which typically trace matrilineal and patrilineal descent in certain lines, expressed lineal unity, while for Lévi-Strauss (1966) they were "semi-complex structures" which had the prohibitions but not the prescriptions of elementary structures or cross-cousin marriage (cf. above, Introduction). For Needham, however (1971b: 13–18; cf. McKinley 1971), it makes no sense to see them as a separate, definable class of terminologies at all. Much the same might be said of Hawaiian terminologies, which typically have just one term per generation for male consanguines and one for female consanguines, though for Morgan they had denoted the emergence of group marriage out of primitive promiscuity because of their conflation ("confusion") of fathers and father's brother, sisters and female cousins, patrikin and matrikin, and so on.

Although Rivers's reputation as a pioneer in the anthropology of kinship has survived modern attacks upon him, in the short term his evolutionist and later diffusionist speculations – less apparent here – were rejected by both Malinowski and Radcliffe-Brown as "conjectural history" that, being unknowable, it was pointless to try and re-create. In the area of cross-cousin marriage he was eclipsed by Lévi-Strauss's monumental work, *The Elementary Structures of Kinship*, published in French in 1949, revised in a second edition in 1967, and translated by Needham and colleagues in 1969. This was among the most discussed and most influential works in anthropology, let alone kinship studies, in the 1950s, 1960s, and 1970s. More recently, its reliance on the idea of unconscious structures determining human behavior has come up against the usual objection to the Durkheimian sociology from which it stems, to the effect that it denies human agency and is therefore essentially illiberal. The former, at least, appears to be the decided view of Lévi-Strauss, in that he sees his structures as being unrealized (though not unrealizable) by social actors in acting normally. Nonetheless, in the 1970s these structures began to seem to have taken on a life of their own for many, far removed from real-life situations.

The item included here (Chapter 8) presents an embryonic version of Lévi-Strauss's main theory, as well as a justification for the structuralist method in opposition to the functionalism represented mainly here by Radcliffe-Brown. Lévi-Strauss's main concern is to develop this justification with reference to a Radcliffe-Brownian obsession, namely socially expected systems of attitudes toward different kin types. However, he begins by praising another subject, linguistics, for its scientific achievements as what is essentially a social science, as well as the sensitivity of its practitioners to social facts, not to mention their achievements in that field. It is clear that he sees here a model for anthropology, especially now that linguistics has left its past obsession with history behind and developed structuralist perspectives in the work of such figures as Ferdinand de Saussure and N. S. Trubetskoy. Like Radcliffe-Brown, in fact, Lévi-Strauss is advocating the production of sociological laws, but using structure, not function, as their basis, since the search for a function for every social fact frequently distorts reality and is thus futile.

Language is significant as a model for the new structuralism because, like kinship (and myth, for that matter, in Lévi-Strauss's view), it has a system. In the case of linguistics, this system is based on the phonemes or semantically significant sounds of the language; in the case of kinship, it is enshrined in the terminologies. In both cases, the same patterns recur in different surface situations (different languages or different societies, respectively). However, linguistics is not an exact remedy, since kin terms are whole words, whereas phonemes are parts of words; in addition, unlike phonemes kin terms have both linguistic and social significance. Even more fundamentally for Lévi-Strauss, while language was, until the arrival of structural linguistics, a phenomenon with a known function but an unclear system, kinship terminology has been known to be systematic since Morgan, though its function is still unclear.

In this respect, Lévi-Strauss claims, socially expected behavior toward different kin types, or what he calls the "system of attitudes" – much discussed by both Radcliffe-Brown and Rivers as a reason for terminological patterns – resembles language. Radcliffe-Brown in particular had noticed the different cases in which the father or the mother's brother was the authority figure, and he linked the two situations with patrilineal and matrilineal descent, respectively. Like earlier authorities, Lévi-Strauss focuses on the role of the MB, but argues first, that the correlations claimed by Radcliffe-Brown are far from perfect ethnographically, and secondly that it is not always clear who, father or MB, is actually the authority figure. Certainly there is a correlation, but it is structural, not functional, in nature. Basically, Lévi-Strauss argues, there is always a contrast: if the father is an authority figure, the relationship with MB will be an easy and familiar one, probably with privileged joking (the "avunculate") and vice versa. But moreover, the relationship between husband and wife will be similar to that between father and son, while that between MB and ZS will resemble that between brother and sister. Thus, formally speaking, significant relations occur not only between kin, but between the actual relationships that certain kin types have with others. These "relations between relations" emerge frequently in all Lévi-Strauss's work.

Thus four kin types (or perhaps more accurately, genealogical positions) are needed in this interpretation, not only father and mother's brother, but son/ZS and wife/sister too. For Lévi-Strauss, this is the most fundamental kinship structure – what he calls a "unit of kinship" (p. 153). The first thing to note is that MB no longer appears as a "problem" to be resolved: he is an intrinsic part of the structure to begin with. This structure also obeys Radcliffe-Brown's principle that kinship entails consanguinity, descent, and affinity, since all three are present (respectively, the relationships between brother and sister; father and son, and MB and ZS; and father and MB, or ZH and WB). It is also an expression of the incest taboo, since it shows one man giving his sister in marriage to another to whom he is not related by either descent or consanguinity but who thereby becomes his affine.

For Lévi-Strauss, this structure is thus also the core of an elementary structure based on cross-cousin marriage, in which context it becomes the more famous "atom of kinship." As he explains in *Elementary Structures*, the incest taboo is an expression of the requirement for human groups to communicate with one another by exchanging women in marriage. To do this they must forego their own women, and the incest taboo enforces this requirement (cf. White 1948 for an overview of existing theories of incest). This basic structure thus includes affinal alliance or marriage, which is cultural, not biological. Lévi-Strauss compares this idea with Radcliffe-Brown's choice of the nuclear family of parents and children as the irreducible social structure. However commonsensical this might seem, for Lévi-Strauss it is completely false, not least in being biological, not cultural: human kinship is distinct and significant only to the extent that it uses culture to move away from this basic idea of biology. To do that, it needs marriage, or affinal alliance between groups. And this entails a focus on relations, not substance, the former being at the heart of structuralism, while a focus on the latter perpetuates functionalism. The incest taboo itself is thus significant in that it links the biological or natural with the cultural or social, actually effecting the transition from the former to the latter. As for the avunculate, Lévi-Strauss claims, on no very compelling grounds – not least because of the impossibility of quantifying it – that it is more highly developed in elementary structures than the complex ones (i.e., those lacking cross-cousin marriage) that developed later. As for the various types of elementary structure, or cross-cousin marriage, that Lévi-Strauss identifies, these are described in more detail below, in the items by Dumont, Good, and Needham.

To some extent, the arguments of Edmund Leach in the paper presented here straddle these debates between the two schools of functionalism and structuralism (Chapter 9). Shortly after World War II, Leach had produced the first full account of matrilateral cross-cousin marriage (1945), based on his fieldwork among the Kachin of Upper Burma and other literature, and anticipating Lévi-Strauss by a short period. Until that time, some of the best accounts of this system of affinal alliance, which has terminological characteristics of its own, were to be found in Dutch-language reports from Indonesia, while Lévi-Strauss's great work existed in French only until the late 1960s; both situations inhibited understanding of this system to some extent. Leach, who also wrote comparatively on this topic (1951), was thus the acknowledged expert on it in Britain for some years, and it was one basis of the structuralist side of his thought. (By contrast, systems of bilateral cross-cousin marriage had been well known for decades, and existed in the ethnographic record centuries ago.) However, Leach also retained a species of functionalism derived ultimately from Malinowski's pragmatism. This is more evident in the present, much cited item, though it also has a very structuralist concern with the nature of classification and categories. The article is actually a critical rereading of Malinowski's famous work on the Trobriand Islanders, located off the coast of New Guinea, earlier in the twentieth century.

Leach starts by criticizing Malinowski's pragmatism for its neglect of "the degree to which behavior can serve as a system of symbolic communication" (p. 158). The example he wishes to discuss is the use of kin terms, some of which to Malinowski were simply homonyms being used pragmatically, but which to Leach are category words uniting a number of meanings based on kinship, some of which are clearly metaphorical. In discussing reasons for the use of individual terms, Leach's functionalism comes to the fore. For example, he depends heavily on aspects of the life cycle of especially male egos, who reside with different kin, depending on their present status (children, adults, unmarried, etc.) and on what the whole book containing this item is all about – the developmental cycle of families and other domestic units through time. He does not make much of the "Crow" nature of the terminology, not being interested in Radcliffe-Brown's association of this form with lineal unity, nor, indeed, very interested in the pattern of the terminology overall. The nature of Trobriand descent groups is anyway a problem for Leach. Malinowski had regarded both clans and sub-clans as significant units in the social structure. Leach, on the other hand, sees the significance of the former as being merely cognitive, as symbolizing the four sub-clan hamlets with which male egos will have most to do at various periods of their lives. As for the latter, Leach questions whether they are as significant as the hamlets they represent symbolically. In other words, is it descent, or locality, that Trobriand Islanders think in terms of when they consider their relationships with people in other groups? Leach clearly thinks that, fundamentally, it is the latter.

As far as kin terms are concerned, Leach is also opposing Malinowski's doctrine of extensions, whereby certain meanings of a kin term (father, say) are more basic, and learned earlier by children, than others (FB, MZH, father's patrilateral male parallel cousins, etc.). For Leach, the anthropologist must seek to arrive at some understanding of the whole category that fits all its uses and not privilege one possible or "core" meaning over all others. To this end, he avoids translating kin terms genealogically and uses instead descriptions in words, for example *tama* as "domiciled male of my father's sub-clan hamlet" (p. 160) rather than simply "father" or "mother's husband", as for Malinowski. He also recognizes that seeing a term as a category does not rule out making internal distinctions within it: the ability of the Trobriand Islanders to distinguish real fathers from other relatives included in the category *tama* is not in question. As far as the key term *tabu* is concerned, Leach argues that this does not represent three unconnected homonyms, as Malinowski suggests, but that it is one term uniting all the recipients of ego's father's ritual (*urigubu*) payments of yams and other items. Another term, *kadu*, denotes those who give *urigubu* payments to ego's father (who is in a different sub-clan to ego in this matrilineally organized society). *Tabu* also has a female reference, being opposed to *latu* and *luta* as marriageable to unmarriageable women. Finally, Leach also rejects the argument that the Trobriand Islanders' terminology reflects the practice of marriage between FZD and MBS, which Malinowski had attributed to the Trobriand Islanders as a little-followed ideal. Leach gives reasons for thinking that this is a tactic pursued by status-conscious chiefs to get round the particular dilemmas that the transfer of *urigubu* payments presents them with. Leach therefore finds a functionalist argument to replace the psychological explanation based on a father's affection for his son, which is all Malinowski could come up with. As Leach remarks, it is not only important chiefs who have sons.

In his article on affinal alliance in south India (Chapter 10), Dumont makes many of the same points as Leach as regards the nature of the terminology. However, his is a structural argument that at the same time seeks to associate the terminology firmly with the system of affinal alliance, and even to see the former as an expression of the latter. Unlike Lévi-Strauss, Dumont, who had come late to an academic career, was not a structuralist on grounds of logical principle, but because he felt it best explained the facts of Indian kinship and social structure generally (that is, caste). He was also more prepared to take practice into account than Lévi-Strauss, whose structuralism is much more purely ideological, though Dumont gave a definite priority in the formation of basic social values (e.g., in *Homo Hierarchicus*, 1980) to ideology.

The structuralist nature of Dumont's account can be seen initially in the fact that, unlike Leach, he does not discuss a single kin term but focuses purely on the structure of the whole terminology, that is, the pattern that underlies it and the relationships between terminological positions. This pattern is claimed to be appropriate for virtually all languages and groups in south India, excepting only some Brahman groups and the Nayar, who marry atypically for the area. Dumont rejects previous attempts to describe this terminology by Rivers and Radcliffe-Brown for their reliance on aspects of social structure such as dual organization and the unity of the sibling group. Although dual organization accompanies this form of terminology elsewhere in the world – Australia or sometimes the Amazon, for instance – its absence from the south Indian variants of this system shows that it is not essential to it. Dumont is very clear that kinship terminologies are ego-centered and do not reflect the organization of social groups. In effect, though, Dumont replaces these older suggestions with one of his own, namely the relationship between groups set up by marriages between sets of affines who can also be defined as cross-cousins to one another. Later work was to establish – in the Amazon, for example, or parts of Indonesia – that groups as such are not required for these systems of marriage to function (e.g., R. H. Barnes 1974, on Kédang, Indonesia; Yalman 1962, on the Sinhalese). The idea that they are is a legacy of Lévi-Strauss's influence on Dumont. It can readily be seen too, in fact, that Dumont's account is very much old wine in new bottles, since he is refining and updating interpretations of cross-cousin marriage and allied terminological systems dating back through Rivers to Morgan.

Like Leach, Dumont is opposed to Malinowskian extensionist arguments, citing an earlier article of Hocart's (1937). He was to be subjected to debate on these issues himself later by the neo-Malinowskian Scheffler (1977, 1984). In opposition to this tendency, Dumont has consistently maintained, like Leach, that kin terms express multi-member categories of kin, not one primary genealogical position such as MB. Although discriminations within them can be made using affixes or adjectives, both these and synonyms should be disregarded in establishing either the basic meaning of the terms or the basic structure of the terminology. This view has always scandalized Scheffler, for whom polysemy proceeds by extension from a basic meaning, not the contraction of a global one: that is, Scheffler prefers to build up the meanings associated with a category from their elements, as opposed to the "structuralist disease" of starting from a basic meaning for the whole category and breaking it down into its elements. One consequence of Dumont's position is the way he diagrams the structure, as a matrix of boxes rather than a genealogical network. Although pioneered by Hocart (1937), Dumont popularized this form of representation as more suitable for showing that terminologies are classifications in their own right, and different from genealogical reckoning (cf. Parkin 1996a for a recent interpretation of the significance of this distinction).

Dumont also moves away explicitly from descent theory, interpreting the key relationship between ego's father and mother's brother as a relationship of affinal alliance that involves them directly, and is not mediated through ego's descent from them both. This is at the heart of Dumont's debate with Radcliffe-Brown, also reproduced here. It underlies Dumont's reluctance to extend the cross–parallel distinction to the whole structure, since he prefers to talk in terms of consanguines and affines instead. In essence, cross-cousin categories are not only the key to the system, they are analytically a little ambiguous, being both consanguines and affines simultaneously. This too was debated between Dumont and Radcliffe-Brown, though both recognized the established fact that systems of cross-cousin marriage do not require separate terms for affines. Ultimately, indigenous views are crucial here: as we saw in the case of Rivière's contribution, the notion that cross cousins are intrinsically affinal, which Dumont's account rendered somewhat doctrinal in the work of later authorities, is not suitable for the Amazon, where affines are converted into consanguines as quickly as possible. Dumont, however, provides a picture of a permanent, indeed inherited relationship between sets of cross-cousins seen as affines (who are also necessarily same-sex for him). Affinity precedes marriage in his view, an outcome of the cultural expectation that one should marry a relative for whom one already has a kin term.

Comparative analytical work on systems of prescriptive alliance or – less satisfactorily, for reasons that will become clear later – cross-cousin marriage ultimately indicated two basic forms. In the one form, represented here by Good's analysis of a particular south Indian sub-caste (Chapter 11), the basis assumption is the repeated and direct or symmetric exchange of spouses related to one another as bilateral cross-cousins, that is, related to ego through both patrilateral and matrilateral ties simultaneously (as MBC and FZC). This is Lévi-Strauss's "restricted exchange" and enjoins, or at least allows, the direct exchange of spouses. Included here are two much-discussed variants. One is FZD marriage, which is no longer generally recognized as a separate type because of the lack of any specific terminological pattern expressing it (cf. Needham 1958, 1960a). The other is ZD marriage, which is sometimes recognized as separate (cf. Rivière 1966, Lave 1966, Good 1980), but also appears alongside the bilateral form in south India and the Amazon. The other main form, represented here by Needham's famous and much debated example of the Purum of north-east India (Chapter 12), is asymmetric or, in Lévi-Strauss's terms, "generalized exchange." This is based formally on marriage to cross-cousins linked to ego respectively through matrilateral (male ego) or patrilateral (female ego) links only, that is, marriages between MBD and FZS (not also FZD and MBS). This automatically necessitates a ban on direct exchange and the categorical separation of wife-givers from wife-takers (who are identical in the other system). As a result, these systems tend to be cyclical in form, and are so at the level of the formal model. Any reversal in the direction of spouse exchange does not make the system a symmetric one but simply reorients it.

Needham probably analyzed more kinship systems in the course of his career than even Lévi-Strauss, and he helped clarify many issues in respect of the character of prescriptive systems in particular, as well as the nature of terminologies and their relationship to social structure. One of the persistent objections to the very idea of prescriptive systems was the lack of fit in many ethnographic cases between terminology and alliance system, which Needham had repeatedly demonstrated himself (especially 1966–7). Not only this, there were many such cases in which genealogical first cross-cousins were rarely if ever married. These factors were supposed to undermine the validity of the type altogether. In fact, as all these authorities pointed out, the answer is that the prescribed category represents not a genealogically defined individual but a whole class of potential spouses with, in many cases, no known genealogical links to ego. If the system were restricted to first cousins alone, it would soon become unworkable for demographic reasons: not all individuals have a first cross-cousin whom they can marry.

In an article of 1973, Needham suggested that one way of clarifying these issues, and moving away from the controversies they had generated, was to separate out the data into different levels. One was the level of rules, in this case marriage rules, which was primarily jural and, as Good was to point out (see below), corresponded most closely to the indigenous interpretation. A second was the level of practice or behavior, which was basically statistical and could obviously be seen to deviate from the level of rules in many cases. The third level was perhaps less easy to grasp, but was that of classification, in this case the kinship terminologies that also played a key part in the functioning of such systems. One of the characteristics of this level is that, being an aspect of language, terminologies are taken for granted and are less open to challenge than either rules (which can openly be broken) or behavior (which may indicate broken rules and is therefore subject to moral evaluation; cf. Good, below). Needham suggested that prescription, or the formal representation of cross-cousin marriage, although literally suggesting rules (through the allied notion of "pre-scribed marriage"), was really located at this level. The reason for this was also formal, since prescriptive terminologies articulated best the very categories that were linked through the operation of the marriage rules. One could therefore still talk of prescription while recognizing practical peculiarities. In a sense, the terminologies expressed the structure in its pure form, in a way the other levels did not: behavior clearly violated the rules, which were themselves but an ideal expression of what actually happened. For Good, although rules were much favored in earlier function-alist accounts, they are the least satisfactory level of all. In principle, however, no one level should be given priority in an analysis, for they all reflect a common set of events and circumstances in different ways.

In his article, Good applies Needham's model to his own material on a particular sub-caste in south India, though the level of rules is partly also one of preferences, which have less weighty sanctions against their violation. This Maravar sub-caste have both matrilineal and patrilineal exogamous groups, though only the first, the *kilai*, are a significant item of social knowledge, even though they are residentially dispersed.

People are not really aware of even their own membership in the latter, though in choosing a spouse one must avoid someone with the same hereditary deities, which pass from father to son. Both the latter belong to the same *kottu*, a vaguer patrilineal descent group. Marriage according to the terminology is with the bilateral cross-cousin. The rules and preferences accord with this, but vary it by expressing a preference for marriage between FZDy and MBDe, that is, for a male a younger patrilateral cross-cousin, and for a female an older matrilateral cross-cousin. Thus informants declare a preference that is unilateral, not bilateral, and that also has a relative age component. These kin types even have a claim on one another in marriage, expressed in the term *urimai*. There is no eZD marriage, since this would involve endogamy of the matrilineal *kilai*, against the rule of exogamy. Other data belonging to the level of rules or preferences indicate that there is no tendency here, despite Dumont's model, toward enduring alliances between villages, lineages or families. Nonetheless this is what the terminology expresses, and a spouse should not be completely unrelated. Good also reports varying reasons for and against the direct exchange of spouses, which, as we have seen, is expressed in the terminology but ambiguous where the level of rules and preferences is concerned.

What if an ego has no *urimai* partner? Even asking this question assumes that it is the actual or genealogical cross-cousin that is involved in either case. In fact, as Good, following both Dumont and Needham, shows, what is at issue is a multi-individual category of prescribed spouse, not a genealogically related individual. Other members of the category include the so-called "classificatory cross-cousins," who may be second, third cross-cousins, etc., or simply suitable spouses from previous affinal groups, or even entirely unrelated individuals, with none of whom a genea-logical connection may be traceable within current indigenous knowledge. Even if an ego were to marry a parallel cousin or a relative from a different terminological level, that person would be redefined as a cross-cousin. This shows that the ter-minology ultimately places its own construction on what has actually happened, including "wrong" marriages. This is different from the level of rules, which, once broken, remain broken. Another consequence of this is the diagrams that Good uses: like Dumont, he prefers the matrix to the genealogy to represent the terminologies, precisely because the latter are not genealogical.

Finally, we should examine the level of practice, represented here by Good's statistics of how people actually marry. Of the 58 marriages existing in the community at the time, 18.9 percent were with an actual cross-cousin, a figure rising to 25 percent if all the marriages he recorded, including those of the recently deceased, are taken into account; as Good points out, comparatively speaking this is a high percentage. Contrary to the rules but in conformity with the model suggested by the terminology, there was no unilateral bias between the two types of cross-cousin. Such a bias only emerged when the remaining marriages were taken into account, another 59 percent of which were with a woman from ego's father's *kilai* (which would include FZD but not MBD in this matrilineal situation). What these figures indicate is that, in practice, people tend to marry in accordance with the unilateral preference once they move away from the genealogical cross-cousin as a marriage partner; but there is still no absolute observance of the rules and preferences. Generally, exogamy of the descent lines was observed, or concealed if broken; there was much less concern over breaches of marriage rules, and much less difficulty in uncovering terminologically "wrong" marriages, in which the crucial relatives had simply been redefined, as described above, and which were regarded as inconvenient rather than morally or supernaturally offensive. As for the relative age preference, this was observed in all but one case.

Good's main theoretical point is not just that congruence between these three levels cannot be expected, but that it is impossible in principle anyway. Fundamentally, the terminology provides the classification with reference to which the rules and preferences are formulated. However, the latter is essentially associated with ideals, which are always at least tacitly distinguished from the practice of an imperfect world. Since this level of rules is one of ideals, therefore, one cannot expect the level of behavior to reflect it exactly, and it does not here. Ultimately, though, the lack of fit will not be so great that the three levels contradict one another absolutely. If they were to do so, it might indicate an unstable situation leading to change in social values or social organization.

As already indicated, Needham's contribution below focuses on an example of the asymmetric type of cross-cousin marriage among the Purum, a population of the Indo-Burma borderlands numbering only 303 in 1945. The account, by Das, was therefore already old when Needham exploited it in the context of his long-term study into the nature of prescriptive systems, in which his discussions were mostly based on the previous work of others, not his own fieldwork. We should not object to this, assuming that we are interested in the interpretation of social situations rather than history per se. This particular example has been chosen because it clearly demonstrates Needham's approach to such systems, rather more clearly than in the 1958 article on the same topic, as well as because it generated considerable controversy in this period (cf. Needham's own testy review of these debates, 1971a: lxvi–lxxxi).

This particular item is an exception to most of the others presented here (except the item by Lowie) in that it is drawn from a monograph; it is therefore not a self-contained article. The basic purpose of this monograph, *Structure and sentiment* (1962), was to defend Lévi-Strauss against what Needham regards as a false interpretation of his work by two Americans, the behaviorist-minded sociologist George Homans and the cultural anthropologist David Schneider, whom we shall meet again (Homans and Schneider 1955). The basis of their theory is that systems of matrilateral cross-cousin marriage owe their existence to the spread of male ego's sentiments from ego's mother, via her brother, to the latter's daughter, whom ego will therefore want to marry. This is supposed to be a feature especially of societies which also have patrilineal descent, where, following Radcliffe-Brown (1952: 15–31), fathers are the usual authority figures. Needham rejects this argument, principally because, quite apart from its lack of unambiguous ethnographic support, it confuses the constraints of social organization and social values with the apparently free play of ego's affections. Societies that accord the father an authoritarian role are by no means confined to those with matrilateral cross-cousin marriage. Why have they not also developed such systems? In addition, Needham shows that one is dealing with whole categories of kin defined without necessary reference to such close genealogical connections. Even in societies such as the Purum, few egos marry the genealogical MBD that Homans and Schneider's argument depends on them doing.

The Purum themselves not only have matrilateral cross-cousin marriage, but also five clans, four of which are divided into lineages. It is these descent groups that are the effective exchange units, not families, much less individuals, as Homans and Schneider assume. Wives are taken from recognized wife-giving descent groups and given to wife-taking ones: the two should not be the same for any one group. However, provided this rule is followed, any one descent group may engage in alliances with more than one other in either direction. In fact, as Needham shows, even for a small population of 300 or so, the actual network of alliances is extremely dense and complicated. Again, we are shown that prescribed spouses are defined in relation to categories, not genealogical positions, as Homans and Schneider presuppose. This is demonstrated by the fact that nearly half of all wives came from a clan other than male ego's mother's and, of the other half, a good many appear to have been with a woman other than the genealogical MBD. And again, the terminology simply redefines the relatives involved in any "wrong" marriages as if the rules had been obeyed. As for the pattern of the terminology itself, it conforms to the model of affinal alliance more or less exactly. Needham's way of showing this is typically to list the terms and their designations first, then the formal equations and distinctions they indicate. The Purum terminology is also skewed so that wife-givers (*pu*) are associated with senior generations, wife-takers (*tu*) with junior generations – a not invariable but common device graphically demonstrating the status inequality that normally obtains in these systems, with wife-givers almost always being superior.

But Needham is not content with just demonstrating the way the affinal alliance system works: he is also interested in showing that it is just one part of a "total structural analysis" for which his ultimate inspiration is the holism of Marcel Mauss and the work of Robert Hertz on religious polarity (1973). This structure is based on the figure of binary opposition or "dual symbolic classification" (cf. Needham, ed. 1973), of which the relationship between wife-givers and wife-takers in respect of any marriage is a fundamental example. The second half of the article is therefore taken up with a description of the symbolic aspects of Purum society, including the house, divination, marriage prestations, deities, etc. Needham's work in these respects has been subjected to considerable controversy (see Parkin 1996b: 78–86 for a brief overview), but his ultimate aim is to draw up a table of oppositions which form a structure, and in which the affinal alliance system is implicated. In brief, the opposition between wife-givers and wife-takers is also found in the opposition between different parts of the house, one of which is less accessible to outsiders than the other; "male" and "female" marriage prestations, depending on who is giving to whom; wife-givers as deities and wife-takers as mortals owing one ritual services, etc. For Needham, this kind of holistic structure is most likely to be found in prescriptive systems and becomes much less striking, though it still exists, where these are absent. Other examples of situations similar to the Purum are Needham's studies of the Kom (1959) and Aimol (1960b), also of the Indo-Burmese border area, and the Lamet (1960c), in Laos.

The final item in this section, by Allen (Chapter 13), represents a return to a consideration of history in the context of kinship, not because it initiated it as such, but because it is a particularly highly developed interpretation of this approach. It is therefore rooted in the tradition of Morgan, though Allen has also been influenced by the work of Gertrude Dole, a neglected figure (e.g., 1957). This tradition did not in fact die out but continued "underground" in the functionalist period, especially in the United States. Later Needham and his circle also contributed to this approach at times, one in which there was a particular focus on the evolution of types of terminology as much as on social morphology (see the brief history of this approach in Parkin 1997: 162–9).

Allen's interpretation is set in what he calls "world historical terms." Fundamentally, it takes the form of a back-projection of the four-section system found in Australia and elsewhere described in the Introduction (above), the aim being to arrive at a hypothetical but reasoned model of what the earliest kinship system in human history might have looked like. In its details, this reconstruction has never been recorded ethnographically, unlike the four-section systems from which it derives. What it nonetheless envisages is an initial situation in which social organization, in the form of the marriage system, was exactly congruent with the kinship terminology. Allen argues that the latter, like the former, really requires no more than four terms – hence the designation "tetradic" for this model. Indeed, it did not need terms as such at all, for the sections could have been marked in some symbolic way. This at least makes it possible to envisage such classifications as existing prior to the invention of language.

After discussing the model's characteristics and implications, Allen concentrates on its development, which essentially means movement away from it, in history. This process is seen in terms of variant possibilities rather than Morganesque uniform stages. The exact congruence between terminology and social organization quickly disappears, giving rise to a lesser but still significant degree of convergence between them (cf. the items by Good and Needham, above). The ultimate stage is represented by terminological patterns like those of modern European languages, which have no particular connection with other aspects of kinship – which themselves have a generally reduced importance anyway in modern state societies. Allen's model thus combines informed speculation and a certain reliance on logic with a high degree of plausibility and ethnographic justification, providing a solid foundation for interpretations of kinship set in terms of historical change (cf. Allen 1982, 1989; also 1976 for an ethnographic study of terminological change in the Himalayas).

REFERENCES

Allen, N. J., 1976 Sherpa Kinship Terminology in Diachronic Perspective. Man (n.s.) 11: 569–587.

—— 1982 A Dance of Relatives. Journal of the Anthropological Society of Oxford 13: 139–146.

—— 1989 Tetradic Theory: An Approach to Kinship. Lingua 77: 173–185.

Barnes, R. H., 1974 Kédang: A Study of the Collective Thought of an Eastern Indonesian People. Oxford: Clarendon Press.

Dole, Gertrude, 1957 The Development of Patterns of Kinship Nomenclature. Ann Arbor: University Microfilms.

Dumont, Louis, 1980 Homo Hierarchicus: The Caste System and its Implications. Chicago: University of Chicago Press.

Eggan, Fred, 1937 Historical Changes in the Choctaw Kinship System. American Anthropologist 39: 34–52.

Good, Anthony, 1980 Elder Sister's Daughter Marriage in South Asia. Journal of Anthropological Research 36: 474–500.

Goodenough, Ward, 1956 Componential Analysis and the Study of Meaning. Language 32: 195–216.

Hammel, Eugene A., ed., 1965 Formal Semantic Analysis. Washington: American Anthropologist Special Publication.

Hertz, Robert, 1973 The Pre-eminence of the Right Hand: A Study in Religious Polarity. In Right & Left: Studies on Dual Symbolic Classification. Rodney Needham, ed. Chicago: University of Chicago Press.

Hocart, Arthur Maurice, 1937 Kinship Systems. Anthropos 32: 345–351.

Homans, George C., and David M. Schneider, 1955 Marriage, Authority and Final Causes: A Study of Unilateral Cross-Cousin Marriage. Glencoe: Free Press.

Kroeber, Alfred, 1909 Classificatory Systems of Relationship. Journal of the Royal Anthropological Institute 39: 77–84.

—— 1952 The Nature of Culture. Chicago: University of Chicago Press.

Kronenfeld, David B., 1973 Fanti Kinship: The Structure of Terminology and Behavior. American Anthropologist 75: 1577–1595.

Lave, Jean Carter, 1966 A Formal Analysis of Preferential Marriage with the Sister's Daughter. Man (n.s.) 1: 185–200.

Leach, Edmund, 1945 Jinghpaw Kinship Terminology: An Experiment in Ethnographic Algebra. Journal of the Royal Anthropological Institute 75: 59–72.

—— 1951 The Structural Implications of Matrilateral Cross-Cousin Marriage. Journal of the Royal Anthropological Institute 81: 23–53.

Lévi-Strauss, Claude, 1966 The Future of Kinship Studies. Proceedings of the Royal Anthropological Institute 1965: 13–22.

—— 1969 [1949, 1967] The Elementary Structures of Kinship. London: Eyre & Spottiswoode.

McKinley, Robert, 1971 A Critique of the Reflectionist Theory of Kinship Terminology: The Crow/Omaha Case. Man (n.s.) 6: 228–247.

Mauss, Marcel, 1954 [1922–3] The Gift: Forms and Functions of Exchange in Archaic Societies. London: Cohen & West.

Needham, Rodney, 1958 The Formal Analysis of Prescriptive Patrilateral Cross-Cousin Marriage. Southwestern Journal of Anthropology 14: 199–219.

—— 1959 An Analytical Note on the Kom of Manipur. Ethnos 24: 121–135.

—— 1960a Patrilateral Prescriptive Alliance and the Ungarinyin. Southwestern Journal of Anthropology 16: 274–291.

—— 1960b A Structural Analysis of Aimol Society. Bijdragen tot de Taal-, Land- en Volkenkunde 116: 81–108.

—— 1960c Alliance and Classification among the Lamet. Sociologus 10: 97–119.

—— 1962 Structure and Sentiment: A Test Case in Social Anthropology. Chicago: University of Chicago Press.

—— 1966–7 Terminology and Alliance. Sociologus 16: 141–57; 17, 39–53.

—— 1971a Introduction. *In* Rethinking Kinship and Marriage. Rodney Needham, ed. London: Tavistock.

—— 1971b Remarks on the Analysis of Kinship and Marriage. *In* Rethinking Kinship and Marriage. Rodney Needham, ed. London: Tavistock.

—— 1973 Prescription. Oceania 42: 166–181.

—— ed., 1973 Right & Left: Essays on Dual Symbolic Classification. Chicago: University of Chicago Press.

Parkin, Robert, 1996a Genealogy and Category: An Operational View. L'Homme 139: 85–106.

—— 1996b The Dark Side of Humanity: The Work of Robert Hertz and Its Legacy. Amsterdam: Harwood Academic.

—— 1997 Kinship: An Introduction to Basic Concepts. Oxford: Blackwell.

Radcliffe-Brown, A. R., 1952 Structure and Function in Primitive Society. London: Cohen & West.

Rivers, W. H. R., 1968 [1914] Kinship and Social Organization. London: Athlone Press.

Rivière, Peter, 1966 Oblique Discontinuous Exchange: A New Form of Prescriptive Alliance. American Anthropologist 68: 738–740.

Scheffler, Harold, 1977 Kinship and Alliance in South India and Australia. American Anthropologist 79: 869–882.

—— 1978 Australian Kin Classification. Cambridge: Cambridge University Press.

—— 1984 Markedness and Extensions: The Tamil Case. Man (n.s.) 19: 557–574.

—— and Floyd Lounsbury, 1971 A Study in Kinship Semantics: The Siriono Kinship System. Englewood Cliffs: Prentice Hall.

White, Leslie A., 1948 The Definition and Prohibition of Incest. American Anthropologist 50: 416–435.

—— 1958 What Is a Classificatory Kin Term? Southwestern Journal of Anthropology 14: 378–85.

Yalman, Nur, 1962 The Structure of the Sinhalese Kindred: A Re-examination of the Dravidian Terminology. American Anthropologist 64: 548–575.

7

Kinship and Social Organization

W. H. R. Rivers

The aim of these lectures is to demonstrate the close connection which exists between methods of denoting relationship or kinship and forms of social organization, including those based on different varieties of the institution of marriage. In other words, my aim will be to show that the terminology of relationship has been rigorously determined by social conditions and that, if this position has been established and accepted, systems of relationship furnish us with a most valuable instrument in studying the history of social institutions.

In the controversy of the present and of recent times, it is the special mode of denoting relationship known as the classificatory system which has formed the chief subject of discussion. It is in connection with this system that there have arisen the various vexed questions which have so excited the interest – I might almost say the passions – of sociologists during the last quarter of a century.

I am afraid it would be dangerous to assume your familiarity with this system, and I must therefore begin with a brief description of its main characters. The essential feature of the classificatory system, that to which it owes its name, is the application of its terms, not to single individual persons, but to classes of relatives which may often be very large. Objections have been made to the use of the term 'classificatory' on the ground that our own terms of relationship also apply to classes of persons; the term 'brother', for instance, to all the male children of the same father and mother, the term 'uncle' to all the brothers of the father and the mother as well as to the husband of an aunt, while the term 'cousin' may denote a still larger class. It is, of course, true that many of our own terms of relationship apply to classes of persons, but in the systems to which the word 'classificatory' is usually applied, the classificatory principle applies far more widely, and in some cases even, more logically and consistently. In the most complete form of the classificatory system there is not one single term of relationship the use of which tells us that reference is being made to one person and to one person only, whereas in our own system there are six such terms, viz., husband, wife, father, mother, father-in-law and mother-in-law. In those systems in which the classificatory principle is carried to its extreme degree every term is applied to a class of persons. The term 'father', for instance, is applied to all those whom the father would call brother, and to all the husbands of those whom the mother calls sister, both brother and sister being used in a far wider sense than among ourselves. In some forms of the classificatory system the term 'father' is also used for all those whom the mother would call brother, and for all the husbands of those whom the father would call sister, and in other systems the application of the term may be still more extensive. Similarly, the term used for the wife may be applied to all those whom the wife would call sister and to the wives of all those whom the speaker calls brother, brother and sister again being used in a far wider sense than in our own language.

The classificatory system has many other features which mark it off more or less sharply from our own mode of denoting relationship, but I do not think it would be profitable to attempt a full description at this stage of our inquiry. As I have said, the object of these lectures is to show how the various features of the classificatory system have arisen out of, and can therefore be explained historically by, social facts. If you are not already acquainted with these features, you will learn to know them the more easily if at the same time you learn how they have come into existence.

I will begin with a brief history of the subject. So long as it was supposed that all the peoples of the world denoted relationship in the same way, namely, that which is customary among ourselves, there was no problem. There was no reason why the subject should have awakened any interest, and so far as I have been able to find, it is only since the discovery of the classificatory system of relationship that the problem now before us was ever raised. I imagine that, if students ever thought about the matter at all, it must have seemed obvious that the way in which they and the other known peoples of the world used terms of relationship was conditioned and determined by the social relations which the terms denoted.

The state of affairs became very different as soon as it was known that many peoples of the world use terms of relationship in a manner, and according to rules, so widely different from our own that they seem to belong to an altogether different order, a difference well illustrated by the confusion which is apt to arise when we use English words in the translation of classificatory terms or classificatory terms as the equivalents of our own. The difficulty or impossibility of conforming to complete truth and reality, when we attempt this task, is the best witness to the fundamental difference between the two modes of denoting relationship.

I do not know of any discovery in the whole range of science which can be more certainly put to the credit of one man than that of the classificatory system of relationship by Lewis Morgan. By this I mean, not merely that he was the first to point out clearly the existence of this

mode of denoting relationship, but that it was he who collected the vast mass of material by which the essential characters of the system were demonstrated, and it was he who was the first to recognize the great theoretical importance of his new discovery. It is the denial of this importance by his contemporaries and successors which furnishes the best proof of the credit which is due to him for the discovery. The very extent of the material he collected [1871] has probably done much to obstruct the recognition of the importance of his work. It is a somewhat discouraging thought that, if Morgan had been less industrious and had amassed a smaller collection of material which could have been embodied in a more available form, the value of his work would probably have been far more widely recognized than it is today. The volume of his material is, however, only a subsidiary factor in the process which has led to the neglect or rejection of the importance of Morgan's discovery. The chief cause of the neglect is one for which Morgan must himself largely bear the blame. He was not content to demonstrate, as he might to some extent have done from his own material, the close connection between the terminology of the classificatory system of relationship and forms of social organization. There can be little doubt that he recognized this connection, but he was not content to demonstrate the dependence of the terminology of relationship upon social forms the existence of which was already known, or which were capable of demonstration with the material at his disposal. He passed over all these early stages of the argument, and proceeded directly to refer the origin of the terminology to forms of social organization which were not known to exist anywhere on the earth and of which there was no direct evidence in the past. When, further, the social condition which Morgan was led to formulate was one of general promiscuity developing into group-marriage, conditions bitterly repugnant to the sentiments of most civilized persons, it is not surprising that he aroused a mass of heated opposition which led, not merely to widespread rejection of his views, but also to the neglect of lessons to be learnt from his new discovery which must have received general recognition long before this, if they had not been obscured by other issues.

The first to take up the cudgels in opposition to Morgan was our own pioneer in the study of the early forms of human society, John Ferguson McLennan [1876: 331]. He criticized the views of Morgan severely and often justly, and then pointing out, as was then believed to be the case, that no duties or rights were connected with the relationships of the classificatory system, he concluded that the terms formed merely a code of courtesies and ceremonial addresses for social intercourse. Those who have followed him have usually been content to repeat the conclusion that the classificatory system is nothing more than a body of mutual salutations and terms of address. They have failed to see that it still remains necessary to explain how the terms of the classificatory system came to be used in mutual salutation. They have failed to recognize that they were either rejecting the principle of determinism in sociology, or were only putting back to a conveniently remote distance the consideration of the problem how and why the classificatory terms came to be used in the way now customary among so many peoples of the earth.

This aspect of the problem, which has been neglected or put on one side by the followers of McLennan, was not so treated by McLennan himself. As we should expect from the general character of his work, McLennan clearly recognized that the classificatory system must have been determined by social conditions, and he tried to show how it might have arisen as the result of the change from the Nair to the Tibetan form of polyandry [1876:373]. He even went so far as to formulate varieties of this process by means of which there might have been produced the chief varieties of the classificatory system, the existence of which had been demonstrated by Morgan. It is quite clear that McLennan had no doubts about the necessity of tracing back the social institution of the classificatory system of relationship to social causes, a necessity which has been ignored or even explicitly denied by those who have followed him in rejecting the views of Morgan. It is one of the many unfortunate consequences of McLennan's belief in the importance of polyandry in the history of human society that it has helped to prevent his followers from seeing the social importance of the classificatory system. They have failed to see

that the classificatory system may be the result neither of promiscuity nor of polyandry, and yet has been determined, both in its general character and in its details, by forms of social organization.

Since the time of Morgan and McLennan few have attempted to deal with the question in any comprehensive manner. The problem has inevitably been involved in the controversy which has raged between the advocates of the original promiscuity or the primitive monogamy of mankind, but most of the former have been ready to accept Morgan's views blindly, while the latter have been content to try to explain away the importance of conclusions derived from the classificatory system without attempting any real study of the evidence. On the side of Morgan there has been one exception in the person of Professor J. Kohler [1897], who has recognized the lines on which the problem must be studied, while on the other side there has been, so far as I am aware, only one writer who has recognized that the evidence from the nature of the classificatory system of relationship cannot be ignored or belittled, but must be faced and some explanation alternative to that of Morgan provided.

This attempt was made four years ago by Professor Kroeber [1909], of the University of California. The line he takes is absolutely to reject the view common to both Morgan and McLennan that the nature of the classificatory system has been determined by social conditions. He explicitly rejects the view that the mode of using terms of relationship depends on social causes, and puts forward as the alternative that they are conditioned by causes purely linguistic and psychological.

It is not quite easy to understand what is meant by the linguistic causation of terms of relationship. In the summary at the end of his paper Kroeber concludes that 'they (terms of relationship) are determined primarily by language'. Terms of relationship, however, are elements of language, so that Kroeber's proposition is that elements of language are determined primarily by language. In so far as this proposition has any meaning, it must be that, in the process of seeking the origin of linguistic phenomena, it is our business to ignore any but linguistic facts. It would follow that the student of the subject should seek the antecedents of linguistic phenomena in other linguistic phenomena, and put on one side as not germane to his task all reference to the objects and relations which the words denote and connote.

Professor Kroeber's alternative proposition is that terms of relationship reflect psychology, not sociology, or, in other words, that the way in which terms of relationship are used depends on a chain of causation in which psychological processes are the direct antecedents of this use. I will try to make his meaning clear by means of an instance which he himself gives. He says that at the present time there is a tendency among ourselves to speak of the brother-in-law as a brother; in other words, we tend to class the brother-in-law and the brother together in the nomenclature of our own system of relationship. He supposes that we do this because there is a psychological similarity between the two relationships which leads us to class them together in our customary nomenclature. I shall return both to this and other of his examples later.

We have now seen that the opponents of Morgan have taken up two main positions which it is possible to attack: one, that the classificatory system is nothing more than a body of terms of address; the other, that it and other modes of denoting relationship are determined by psychological and not by sociological causes. I propose to consider these two positions in turn.

Morgan himself was evidently deeply impressed by the function of the classificatory system of relationship as a body of salutations. His own experience was derived from the North American Indians, and he notes the exclusive use of terms of relationship in address, a usage so habitual that an omission to recognize a relative in this manner would amount almost to an affront. Morgan also points out, as one motive for the custom, the presence of a reluctance to utter personal names. McLennan had to rely entirely on the evidence collected by Morgan, and there can be no doubt that he was greatly influenced by the stress Morgan himself laid on the function of the classificatory terms as mutual salutations. That in rude societies certain relatives have social functions definitely assigned to them by custom was known in Morgan's time, and I think it might even then have been discovered that the relation-

ships which carried these functions were of the classificatory kind. It is, however, only by more recent work, beginning with that of Howitt, of Spencer and Gillen, and of Roth in Australia, and of the Cambridge Expedition to Torres Straits, that the great importance of the functions of relatives through the classificatory system has been forced upon the attention of sociologists. The social and ceremonial proceedings of the Australian aborigines abound in features in which special functions are performed by such relatives as the elder brother or the brother of the mother, while in Torres Straits I was able to record large groups of duties, privileges and restrictions associated with different classificatory relationships.

Further work has shown that widely, though not universally, the nomenclature of the classificatory system carries with it a number of clearly defined social practices. One who applies a given term of relationship to another person has to behave towards that person in certain definite ways. He has to perform certain duties towards him, and enjoys certain privileges, and is subject to certain restrictions in his conduct in relation to him. These duties, privileges and restrictions vary greatly in number among different peoples, but wherever they exist, I know of no exception to their importance and to the regard in which they are held by all members of the community. You doubtless know of many examples of such functions associated with relationship, and I need give only one example.

In the Banks Islands the term used between two brothers-in-law is *wulus*, *walus*, or *walui*, and a man who applies one of these terms to another may not utter his name, nor may the two behave familiarly towards one another in any way. In one island, Merlav, these relatives have all their possessions in common, and it is the duty of one to help the other in any difficulty, to warn him in danger, and, if need be, to die with him. If one dies, the other has to help to support his widow and has to abstain from certain foods. Further, there are a number of curious regulations in which the sanctity of the head plays a great part. A man must take nothing from above the head of his brother-in-law, nor may he even eat a bird which has flown over his head. A person has only to say of an object 'That is the head of your brother-in-law', and the person addressed will have to desist from the use of the object. If the object is edible, it may not be eaten; if it is one which is being manufactured, such as a mat, the person addressed will have to cease from his work if the object be thus called the head of his brother-in-law. He will only be allowed to finish it on making compensation, not to the person who has prevented the work by reference to the head, but to the brother-in-law whose head had been mentioned. Ludicrous as some of these customs may seem to us, they are very far from being so to those who practise them. They show clearly the very important part taken in the lives of those who use the classificatory system by the social functions associated with relationship. As I have said, these functions are not universally associated with the classificatory system, but they are very general in many parts of the world and only need more careful investigation to be found even more general and more important than appears at present.

Let us now look at our own system of relationship from this point of view. Two striking features present themselves. First, the great paucity of definite social functions associated with relationship, and secondly, the almost complete limitation of such functions to those relationships which apply only to individual persons and not to classes of persons. Of such relationships as cousin, uncle, aunt, father-in-law, or mother-in-law there may be said to be no definite social functions. A schoolboy believes it is the duty of his uncle to tip him, but this is about as near as one can get to any social obligation on the part of this relative.

The same will be found to hold good to a large extent if we turn to those social regulations which have been embodied in our laws. It is only in the case of the transmission of hereditary rank and of the property of a person dying intestate that more distant relatives are brought into any legal relationship with one another, and then only if there is an absence of nearer relatives. It is only when forced to do so by exceptional circumstances that the law recognizes any of the persons to whom the more classificatory of our terms of relationship apply. If we pay regard to the social functions associated with relationship, it is our own system, rather than the classificatory, which is open to the reproach that its relationships carry into them no rights and duties.

In the course of the recent work of the Percy Sladen Trust Expedition in Melanesia and Polynesia I have been able to collect a body of facts which bring out, even more clearly than has hitherto been recognized, the dependence of classificatory terms on social rights [Rivers 1919]. The classificatory systems of Oceania vary greatly in character. In some places relationships are definitely distinguished in nomenclature which are classed with other relationships elsewhere. Thus, while most Melanesian and some Polynesian systems have a definite term for the mother's brother and for the class of relatives whom the mother calls brother, in other systems this relative is classed with, and is denoted by, the same term as the father. The point to which I now call your attention is that there is a very close correlation between the presence of a special term for this relative and the presence of special functions attached to the relationship.

In Polynesia, both the Hawaiians and the inhabitants of Niue class the mother's brother with the father, and in neither place was I able to discover that there were any special duties, privileges or restrictions ascribed to the mother's brother. In the Polynesian islands of Tonga and Tikopia, on the other hand, where there are special terms for the mother's brother, this relative has also special functions. The only place in Melanesia where I failed to find a special term for the mother's brother was in the western Solomon Islands, and that was also the only part of Melanesia where I failed to find any trace of special social functions ascribed to this relative. I do not know of such functions in Santa Cruz, but my information about the system of that island is derived from others, and further research will almost certainly show that they are present.

In my own experience, then, among two different peoples, I have been able to establish a definite correlation between the presence of a term of relationship and special functions associated with the relationship. Information kindly given to me by Father Egidi, however, seems to show that the correlation among the Melanesians is not complete. In Mekeo, the mother's brother has the duty of putting on the first perineal garment of his nephew, but he has no special term and is classed with the father. Among the Kuni, on the other hand, there is a definite term for the mother's brother distinguishing him from the father, but yet he has not, so far as Father Egidi knows, any special functions.

Both in Melanesia and Polynesia a similar correlation comes out in connection with other relationships, the most prominent exception being the absence of a special term for the father's sister in the Banks Islands, although this relative has very definite and important functions. In these islands the father's sister is classed with the mother as *vev* or *veve*, but even here, where the generalization seems to break down, it does not do so completely, for the father's sister is distinguished from the mother as *veve vus rawe*, the mother who kills a pig, as opposed to the simple *veve* used for the mother and her sisters.

There is thus definite evidence, not only for the association of classificatory terms of relationship with special social functions, but from one part of the world we now have evidence which shows that the presence or absence of special terms is largely dependent on whether there are or are not such functions. We may take it as established that the terms of the classificatory system are not, as McLennan supposed, merely terms of address and modes of mutual salutation. McLennan came to this conclusion because he believed that the classificatory terms were associated with no such functions as those of which we now have abundant evidence. He asks, 'What duties or rights are affected by the relationships comprised in the classificatory system?' and answers himself according to the knowledge at his disposal, 'Absolutely none' [1876: 366]. This passage makes it clear that, if McLennan had known what we know today, he would never have taken up the line of attack upon Morgan's position in which he has had, and still has, so many followers.

I can now turn to the second line of attack, that which boldly discards the origin of the terminology of relationship in social conditions, and seeks for its explanation in psychology. The line of argument I propose to follow is first to show that many details of classificatory systems have been directly determined by social factors. If that task can be accomplished, we shall have firm ground from which to take off in the attempt to refer the general characters of the classificatory and other systems of relationship to forms of social organization. Any complete theory of a social institution has not only to account for its general characters, but also for its details, and I propose to begin with the details.

I must first return to the history of the subject, and stay for a moment to ask why the line of argument I propose to follow was not adopted by Morgan and has been so largely disregarded by others.

Whenever a new phenomenon is discovered in any part of the world, there is a natural tendency to seek for its parallels elsewhere. Morgan lived at a time when the unity of human culture was a topic which greatly excited ethnologists, and it is evident that one of his chief interests in the new discovery arose from the possibility it seemed to open of showing the uniformity of human culture. He hoped to demonstrate the uniformity of the classificatory system throughout the world, and he was content to observe certain broad varieties of the system and refer them to supposed stages in the history of human society. He paid but little attention to such varieties of the classificatory system as are illustrated in his own record of North American systems, and seems to have overlooked entirely certain features of the Indian and Oceanic systems he recorded, which might have enabled him to demonstrate the close relation between the terminology of relationship and social institutions. Morgan's neglect to attend to these differences must be ascribed in some measure to the ignorance of rude forms of social organization which existed when he wrote, but the failure of others to recognize the dependence of the details of classificatory systems upon social institutions is rather to be ascribed to the absence of interest in the subject induced by their adherence to McLennan's primary error. Those who believe that the classificatory system is merely an unimportant code of mutual salutations are not likely to attend to relatively minute differences in the customs they despise. The credit of having been the first fully to recognize the social importance of these differences belongs to J. Kohler. In his book *Zur Urgeschichte der Ehe*, which I have already mentioned, he studied minutely the details of many different systems, and showed that they could be explained by certain forms of marriage practised by those who use the terms. I propose now to deal with classificatory terminology from this point of view. My procedure will be first to show that the details which distinguish different forms of the classificatory system from one another have been directly determined by the social institutions of those who use the systems, and only when this has been established, shall I attempt to bring the more general characters of the classificatory and other systems into relation with social institutions.

I am able to carry out this task more fully than has hitherto been possible because I have collected in Melanesia a number of systems of relationship which differ far more widely from one another than those recorded in Morgan's book or others which have been collected since. Some of the features which characterize these Melanesian systems will be wholly new to ethnologists, not having yet been recorded elsewhere, but I propose to begin with a long familiar mode of terminology which accompanies that widely distributed custom known as the cross-cousin marriage. In the more frequent form of this marriage a man marries the daughter either of his mother's brother or of his father's sister; more rarely his choice is limited to one of these relatives.

Such a marriage will have certain definite consequences. Let us take a case in which a man marries the daughter of his mother's brother, as is represented in Figure 7.1.

One consequence of the marriage between C and d will be that A, who before the marriage of C was only his mother's brother, now becomes also his wife's father, while b, who before the marriage was the mother's brother's wife of C, now becomes his wife's mother.

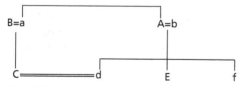

Figure 7.1
Key: Capital letters are used to represent men and the smaller letters women.

Reciprocally, C, who before his marriage had been the sister's son of A and the husband's sister's son of b, now becomes their son-in-law. Further, E and f, the other children of A and b, who before the marriage had been only the cousins of C, now become his wife's brother and sister.

Similarly, a, who before the marriage of d was her father's sister, now becomes also her husband's mother, and B, her father's sister's husband, comes to stand in the relation of husband's father; if C should have any brothers and sisters, these cousins now become her brothers- and sisters-in-law.

The combinations of relationship which follow from the marriage of a man with the daughter of his mother's brother thus differ for a man and a woman, but if, as is usual, a man may marry the daughter either of his mother's brother or of his father's sister, these combinations of relationship will hold good for both men and women.

Another and more remote consequence of the cross-cousin marriage, if this becomes an established institution, is that the relationships of mother's brother and father's sister's husband will come to be combined in one and the same person, and that there will be a similar combination of the relationships of father's sister and mother's brother's wife. If the cross-cousin marriage be the habitual custom, B and b in Diagram 1 will be brother and sister; in consequence A will be at once the mother's brother and the father's sister's husband of C, while b will be both his father's sister and his mother's brother's wife. Since, however, the mother's brother is also the father-in-law, and the father's sister the mother-in-law, three different relationships will be combined in each case. Through the cross-cousin marriage the relationships of mother's brother, father's sister's husband and father-in-law will be combined in one and the same person, and the relationships of father's sister, mother's brother's wife and mother-in-law will be similarly combined.

In many places where we know the cross-cousin marriage to be an established institution, we find just those common designations which I have just described. Thus, in the Mbau dialect of Fiji the word *vungo* is applied to the mother's brother, the husband of the father's sister and the father-in-law. The word *nganei* is used for the father's sister, the mother's brother's wife and the mother-in-law. The term *tavale* is used by a man for the son of the mother's brother or of the father's sister as well as for the wife's brother and the sister's husband. *Ndavola* is used not only for the child of the mother's brother or father's sister when differing in sex from the speaker, but this word is also used by a man for his wife's sister and his brother's wife, and by a woman for her husband's brother and her sister's husband. Every one of these details of the Mbau system is the direct and inevitable consequence of the cross-cousin marriage, if it becomes an established and habitual practice.

This Fijian system does not stand alone in Melanesia. In the southern islands of the New Hebrides, in Tanna, Eromanga, Aneityum and Aniwa, the cross-cousin marriage is practised and their systems of relationship have features similar to those of Fiji. Thus, in Aneityum the word *matak* applies to the mother's brother, the father's sister's husband and the father-in-law, while the word *engak* used for the cross-cousin is not only used for the wife's sister and the brother's wife, but also for the wife herself.

Again, in the island of Guadalcanal in the Solomons the system of relationship is just such as would result from the cross-cousin marriage. One term, *nia*, is used for the mother's brother and the wife's father, and probably also for the father's sister's husband and the husband's father, though my stay in the island was not long enough to enable me to collect sufficient genealogical material to demonstrate these points completely. Similarly, *tarunga* includes in its connotation the father's sister, the mother's brother's wife and the wife's mother, and probably also the husband's mother, while the word *iva* is used for both cross-cousins and brothers- and sisters-in-law. Corresponding to this terminology there seemed to be no doubt that it was the custom for a man to marry the daughter of his mother's brother or his father's sister though I was not able to demonstrate this form of marriage genealogically.

These three regions, Fiji, the southern New Hebrides and Guadalcanal, are the only parts of Melanesia included in my survey where I found the practice of the cross-cousin marriage, and in all three regions the systems of relationship are just such as would follow from this form of marriage.

Let us now turn to inquire how far it is possible to explain these features of Melanesian systems of relationship by psychological similarity. If it were not for the cross-cousin marriage, what can there be to give the mother's brother a greater psychological similarity to the father-in-law than the father's brother, or the father's sister a greater similarity to the mother-in-law than the mother's sister? Why should it be two special kinds of cousin who are classed with two special kinds of brother- and sister-in-law or with the husband or wife? Once granted the presence of the cross-cousin marriage, and there are psychological similarities certainly, though even here the matter is not quite straightforward from the point of view of the believer in their importance, for we have to do not merely with the similarity of two relatives, but with their identity, with the combination of two or more relationships in one and the same person. Even if we put this on one side, however, it remains to ask how it is possible to say that terms of relationship do not reflect sociology, if such psychological similarities are themselves the result of the cross-cousin marriage? What point is there in bringing in hypothetical psychological similarities which are only at the best intermediate links in the chain of causation connecting the terminology of relationship with antecedent social conditions?

If you concede the causal relation between the characteristic features of a Fijian or Aneityum or Guadalcanal system and the cross-cousin marriage, there can be no question that it is the cross-cousin marriage which is the antecedent and the features of the system of relationship the consequences. I do not suppose that, even in this subject, there will be found anyone to claim that the Fijians took to marrying their cross-cousins because such a marriage was suggested to them by the nature of their system of relationship. We have to do in this case, not merely with one or two features which might be the consequence of the cross-cousin marriage, but with a large and complicated meshwork of resemblances and differences in the nomenclature of relationship, each and every element of which follows directly from such a marriage, while no one of the systems I have considered possesses a single feature which is not compatible with social conditions arising out of this marriage. Apart from quantitative verification, I doubt whether it would be possible in the whole range of science to find a case where we can be more confident that one phenomenon has been conditioned by another. I feel almost guilty of wasting your time by going into it so fully, and should hardly have ventured to do so if this case of social causation had not been explicitly denied by one with so high a reputation as Professor Kroeber. I hope, however, that the argument will be useful as an example of the method I shall apply to other cases in which the evidence is less conclusive.

The features of terminology which follow from the cross-cousin marriage were known to Morgan, being present in three of the systems he recorded from Southern India and in the Fijian system collected for him by Mr Fison. The earliest reference [Grant 1870: 276] to the cross-cousin marriage which I have been able to discover is among the Gond of Central India. This marriage was recorded in 1870, which, though earlier than the appearance of Morgan's book, was after it had been accepted for publication, so that I think we can be confident that Morgan was unacquainted with the form of marriage which would have explained the peculiar features of the Indian and Fijian systems. It is evident, however, that Morgan was so absorbed in his demonstration of the similarity of these systems to those of America that he paid but little, if any, attention to their peculiarities. He thus lost a great opportunity; if he had attended to these peculiarities and had seen their meaning, he might have predicted a form of marriage which would soon afterwards have been independently discovered. Such an example of successful prediction would have forced the social significance of the terminology of relationship upon the attention of students in such a way that we should have been spared much of the controversy which has so long obstructed progress in this branch of sociology. It must at the very least have acted as a stimulus to the collection of systems of relationship. It would hardly have been possible that now, more than forty years after the appearance of Morgan's book, we are still in complete ignorance of the terminology of relationship of many peoples about whom volumes have been written. It would seem impossible, for instance, that our knowledge of Indian systems of relationship could have been what it is today. India would have been the country in which the success of Morgan's prediction would first have shown itself, and such an event must have prevented the almost total neglect which the subject of relationship has suffered at the hands of students of Indian sociology.

REFERENCES

Grant, C., 1870. *Gazetteer of Central Provinces*, 2nd ed., Nagpur.

Kohler, J., 1897. Zur Urgeschichte der Ehe. *Zeitschrift für vergleichende Rechtswissenschaft*, **12**, pp. 187–353.

Kroeber, A. L., 1909. Classificatory Systems of Relationship. *Journal of the Royal Anthropological Institute*, **39**, pp. 77–84.

McLennan, J. F., 1876. *Studies in Ancient History*, London.

Morgan, L. H., 1871. *Systems of Consanguinity and Affinity of the Human Family*. Smithsonian Contributions to Knowledge, **17**, Washington.

Rivers, W. H. R., 1914. *The History of Melanesian Society*, 2 vols. Cambridge.

8

Structural Analysis in Linguistics and in Anthropology

Claude Lévi-Strauss

Linguistics occupies a special place among the social sciences, to whose ranks it unquestionably belongs. It is not merely a social science like the others, but, rather, the one in which by far the greatest progress has been made. It is probably the only one which can truly claim to be a science and which has achieved both the formulation of an empirical method and an understanding of the nature of the data submitted to its analysis. This privileged position carries with it several obligations. The linguist will often find scientists from related but different disciplines drawing inspiration from his example and trying to follow his lead. *Noblesse oblige*. A linguistic journal like *Word* cannot confine itself to the illustration of strictly linguistic theories and points of view. It must also welcome psychologists, sociologists, and anthropologists eager to learn from modern linguistics the road which leads to the empirical knowledge of social phenomena. As Marcel Mauss wrote already forty years ago: "Sociology would certainly have progressed much further if it had everywhere followed the lead of the linguists...."[1] The close methodological analogy which exists between the two disciplines imposes a special obligation of collaboration upon them.

Ever since the work of Schrader[2] it has been unnecessary to demonstrate the assistance which linguistics can render to the anthropologist in the study of kinship. It was a linguist and a philologist (Schrader and Rose)[3] who showed the improbability of the hypothesis of matrilineal survivals in the family in antiquity, to which so many anthropologists still clung at that time. The linguist provides the anthropologist with etymologies which permit him to establish between certain kinship terms relationships that were not immediately apparent. The anthropologist, on the other hand, can bring to the attention of the linguist customs, prescriptions, and prohibitions that help him to understand the persistence of certain features of language or the instability of terms or groups of terms. At a meeting of the Linguistic Circle of New York, Julien Bonfante once illustrated this point of view by reviewing the etymology of the word for uncle in several Romance languages. The Greek θεῖος corresponds in Italian, Spanish, and Portuguese to *zio* and *tio*; and he added that in certain regions of Italy the uncle is called *barba*. The "beard," the "divine" uncle – what a wealth of suggestions for the anthropologist! The investigations of the late A. M. Hocart into the religious character of the avuncular relationship and the "theft of the sacrifice" by the maternal kinsmen immediately come to mind.[4] Whatever interpretation is given to the data collected by Hocart (and his own interpretation is not entirely satisfactory), there is no doubt that the linguist contributes to the solution of the problem by revealing the tenacious survival in contemporary vocabulary of relationships which have long since disappeared. At the same time, the anthropologist explains to the linguist the bases of etymology and confirms its validity. Paul K. Benedict, in examining, as a linguist, the kinship systems of Southeast Asia, was able to make an important contribution to the anthropology of the family in that area.[5]

But linguists and anthropologists follow their own paths independently. They halt, no doubt, from time to time to communicate to one another certain of their findings; these findings, however, derive from different operations, and no effort is made to enable one group to benefit from the technical and methodological advances of the other. This attitude might have been justified in the era when linguistic research leaned most heavily on historical analysis. In relation to the anthropological research conducted during the same period, the difference was one of degree rather than of kind. The linguists employed a more rigorous method, and their findings were established on more solid grounds; the sociologists could follow their example in "renouncing consideration of the spatial distribution of contemporary types as a basis for their classifications."[6] But, after all, anthropology and sociology were looking to linguistics only for insights; nothing foretold a revelation.[7]

The advent of structural linguistics completely changed this situation. Not only did it renew linguistic perspectives; a transformation of this magnitude is not limited to a single discipline. Structural linguistics will certainly play the same renovating role with respect to the social sciences that nuclear physics, for example, has played for the physical sciences. In what does this revolution consist, as we try to assess its broadest implications? N. Troubetzkoy, the illustrious founder of structural linguistics, himself furnished the answer to this question. In one programmatic statement,[8] he reduced the structural method to four basic operations. First, structural linguistics shifts from the study of *conscious* linguistic phenomena to study of their *unconscious* infrastructure; second, it does not treat *terms* as independent entities, taking instead as its basis of analysis the *relations* between terms; third, it introduces the concept of *system* – "Modern phonemics does not merely proclaim that phonemes are always part of a system; it *shows* concrete phonemic systems and elucidates their structure"[9] –; finally, structural linguistics aims at discovering *general laws*, either by induction "or . . . by logical deduction, which would give them an absolute character."[10]

Thus, for the first time, a social science is able to formulate necessary relationships. This is the meaning of Troubetzkoy's last point, while the preceding rules show how linguistics must proceed in order to attain this end. It is not for us to show that Troubetzkoy's claims are justified. The vast majority of modern linguists seem sufficiently agreed on this point. But when an event of this importance takes place in one of the sciences of man, it is not only permissible for, but required of, representatives of related disciplines immediately to examine its consequences and its possible application to phenomena of another order.

New perspectives then open up. We are no longer dealing with an occasional collaboration where the linguist and the anthropologist, each working by himself, occasionally communicate those findings which each thinks may interest the other. In the study of kinship problems (and, no doubt, the study of other problems as well), the anthropologist finds himself in a situation which formally resembles that of the structural linguist. Like phonemes, kinship terms are elements of meaning; like phonemes, they acquire meaning only if they are integrated into systems. "Kinship systems," like "phonemic systems," are built by the mind on the level of unconscious thought. Finally, the recurrence of kinship patterns, marriage rules, similar prescribed attitudes between certain types of relatives, and so forth, in scattered regions of the globe and in fundamentally different societies, leads us to believe that, in the case of kinship as well as linguistics, the observable phenomena result from the action of laws which are general but implicit. The problem can therefore be formulated as follows: Although they belong to *another order of reality*, kinship phenomena are *of the same type* as linguistic phenomena. Can the anthropologist, using a method analogous *in form* (if not in content) to the method used in structural linguistics, achieve the same kind of progress in his own science as that which has taken place in linguistics?

We shall be even more strongly inclined to follow this path after an additional observation has been made. The study of kinship problems is today broached in the same terms and seems to be in the throes of the same difficulties as was linguistics on the eve of the structuralist revolution. There is a striking analogy between certain attempts by Rivers and the old linguistics, which sought its explanatory principles first of all in history. In both cases, it is solely (or almost solely) diachronic analysis which must account for synchronic phenomena. Troubetzkoy, comparing structural linguistics and the old linguistics, defines structural linguistics as a "systematic structuralism and universalism," which he contrasts with the individualism and "atomism" of former schools. And when he considers diachronic analysis, his perspective is a profoundly modified one: "The evolution of a phonemic system at any given moment is directed by the *tendency toward a goal*. . . . This evolution thus has a direction, an internal logic, which historical phonemics is called upon to elucidate."[11] The "individualistic" and "atomistic" interpretation, founded exclusively on historical contingency, which is criticized by Troubetzkoy and Jakobson, is actually the same as that which is generally applied to kinship problems.[12] Each detail of terminology and each special marriage rule is associated with a specific custom as either its consequence or its survival. We thus meet with a chaos of discontinuity. No one asks how kinship systems, regarded as synchronic wholes, could be the arbitrary product of a convergence of several heterogeneous institutions (most of which are hypothetical), yet nevertheless function with some sort of regularity and effectiveness.[13]

However, a preliminary difficulty impedes the transposition of the phonemic method to the anthropological study of primitive peoples. The superficial analogy between phonemic systems and kinship systems is so strong that it immediately sets us on the wrong track. It is incorrect to equate kinship terms and linguistic phonemes from the viewpoint of their formal treatment. We know that to obtain a structural law the linguist analyzes phonemes into "distinctive features," which he can then group into one or several "pairs of oppositions."[14] Following an analogous method, the anthropologist might be tempted to break down analytically the kinship terms of any given system into their components. In our own kinship system, for instance, the term *father* has posi-

tive connotations with respect to sex, relative age, and generation; but it has a zero value on the dimension of collaterality, and it cannot express an affinal relationship. Thus, for each system, one might ask what relationships are expressed and, for each term of the system, what connotation – positive or negative – it carries regarding each of the following relationships: generation, collaterality, sex, relative age, affinity, etc. It is at this "microsociological" level that one might hope to discover the most general structural laws, just as the linguist discovers his at the infraphonemic level or the physicist at the infra-molecular or atomic level. One might interpret the interesting attempt of Davis and Warner in these terms.[15]

But a threefold objection immediately arises. A truly scientific analysis must be real, simplifying, and explanatory. Thus the distinctive features which are the product of phonemic analysis have an objective existence from three points of view: psychological, physiological, and even physical; they are fewer in number than the phonemes which result from their combination; and, finally, they allow us to understand and reconstruct the system. Nothing of the kind would emerge from the preceding hypothesis. The treatment of kinship terms which we have just sketched is analytical in appearance only; for, actually, the result is more abstract than the principle; instead of moving toward the concrete, one moves away from it, and the definitive system – if system there is – is only conceptual. Secondly, Davis and Warner's experiment proves that the system achieved through this procedure is infinitely more complex and more difficult to interpret than the empirical data.[16] Finally, the hypothesis has no explanatory value; that is, it does not lead to an understanding of the nature of the system and still less to a reconstruction of its origins.

What is the reason for this failure? A too literal adherence to linguistic method actually betrays its very essence. Kinship terms not only have a sociological existence; they are also elements of speech. In our haste to apply the methods of linguistic analysis, we must not forget that, as a part of vocabulary, kinship terms must be treated with linguistic methods in direct and not analogous fashion. Linguistics teaches us precisely that structural analysis cannot be applied to words directly, but only to words previously broken down into phonemes. *There are no necessary relationships at the vocabulary level.*[17] This applies to all vocabulary elements, including kinship terms. Since this applies to linguistics, it ought to apply *ipso facto* to the sociology of language. An attempt like the one whose possibility we are now discussing would thus consist in extending the method of structural linguistics while ignoring its basic requirements. Kroeber prophetically foresaw this difficulty in an article written many years ago.[18] And if, at that time, he concluded that a structural analysis of kinship terminology was impossible, we must remember that linguistics itself was then restricted to phonetic, psychological, and historical analysis. While it is true that the social sciences must share the limitations of linguistics, they can also benefit from its progress.

Nor should we overlook the profound differences between the phonemic chart of a language and the chart of kinship terms of a society. In the first instance there can be no question as to function; we all know that language serves as a means of communication. On the other hand, what the linguist did not know and what structural linguistics alone has allowed him to discover is the way in which language achieves this end. The function was obvious; the system remained unknown. In this respect, the anthropologist finds himself in the opposite situation. We know, since the work of Lewis H. Morgan, that kinship terms constitute systems; on the other hand, we still do not know their function. The misinterpretation of this initial situation reduces most structural analyses of kinship systems to pure tautologies. They demonstrate the obvious and neglect the unknown.

This does not mean that we must abandon hope of introducing order and discovering meaning in kinship nomenclature. But we should at least recognize the special problems raised by the sociology of vocabulary and the ambiguous character of the relations between its methods and those of linguistics. For this reason it would be preferable to limit the discussion to a case where the analogy can be clearly established. Fortunately, we have just such a case available.

What is generally called a "kinship system" comprises two quite different orders of reality.

First, there are terms through which various kinds of family relationships are expressed. But kinship is not expressed solely through nomenclature. The individuals or classes of individuals who employ these terms feel (or do not feel, as the case may be) bound by prescribed behavior in their relations with one another, such as respect or familiarity, rights or obligations, and affection or hostility. Thus, along with what we propose to call the *system of terminology* (which, strictly speaking, constitutes the vocabulary system), there is another system, both psychological and social in nature, which we shall call the *system of attitudes*. Although it is true (as we have shown above) that the study of systems of terminology places us in a situation analogous, but opposite, to the situation in which we are dealing with phonemic systems, this difficulty is "inversed," as it were, when we examine systems of attitudes. We can guess at the role played by systems of attitudes, that is, to insure group cohesion and equilibrium, but we do not understand the nature of the interconnections between the various attitudes, nor do we perceive their necessity.[19] In other words, as in the case of language, we know their function, but the system is unknown.

Thus we find a profound difference between the *system of terminology* and the *system of attitudes*, and we have to disagree with A. R. Radcliffe-Brown if he really believed, as has been said of him, that attitudes are nothing but the expression or transposition of terms on the affective level.[20] The last few years have provided numerous examples of groups whose chart of kinship terms does not accurately reflect family attitudes, and vice versa.[21] It would be incorrect to assume that the kinship system constitutes the principal means of regulating interpersonal relationships in all societies. Even in societies where the kinship system does function as such, it does not fulfill that role everywhere to the same extent. Furthermore, it is always necessary to distinguish between two types of attitudes: first, the diffuse, uncrystallized, and non-institutionalized attitudes, which we may consider as the reflection or transposition of the terminology on the psychological level; and second, along with, or in addition to, the preceding ones, those attitudes which are stylized, prescribed, and sanctioned by taboos or privileges and expressed through a fixed ritual. These attitudes, far from automatically reflecting the nomenclature, often appear as secondary elaborations, which serve to resolve the contradictions and overcome the deficiencies inherent in the terminological system. This synthetic character is strikingly apparent among the Wik Munkan of Australia. In this group, joking privileges sanction a contradiction between the kinship relations which link two unmarried men and the theoretical relationship which must be assumed to exist between them in order to account for their later marriages to two women who do not stand themselves in the corresponding relationship.[22] There is a contradiction between two possible systems of nomenclature, and the emphasis placed on attitudes represents an attempt to integrate or transcend this contradiction. We can easily agree with Radcliffe-Brown and assert the existence of "real relations of interdependence between the terminology and the rest of the system."[23] Some of his critics made the mistake of inferring, from the absence of a rigorous parallelism between attitudes and nomenclature, that the two systems were mutually independent. But this relationship of interdependence does not imply a one-to-one correlation. The system of attitudes constitutes, rather, a dynamic integration of the system of terminology.

Granted the hypothesis (to which we wholeheartedly subscribe) of a functional relationship between the two systems, we are nevertheless entitled, for methodological reasons, to treat independently the problems pertaining to each system. This is what we propose to do here for a problem which is rightly considered the point of departure for any theory of attitudes – that of the maternal uncle. We shall attempt to show how a formal transposition of the method of structural linguistics allows us to shed new light upon this problem. Because the relationship between nephew and maternal uncle appears to have been the focus of significant elaboration in a great many primitive societies, anthropologists have devoted special attention to it. It is not enough to note the frequency of this theme; we must also account for it.

Let us briefly review the principal stages in the development of this problem. During the entire nineteenth century and until the writings of Sydney Hartland,[24] the importance of the mother's brother was interpreted as a survival of matrilineal descent. This interpretation was based purely on speculation, and, indeed, it was highly improbable in the light of European examples. Furthermore, Rivers' attempt[25] to explain the importance of the mother's brother in southern India as a residue of cross-cousin marriage led to particularly deplorable results. Rivers himself was forced to recognize that this interpretation could not account for all aspects of the problem. He resigned himself to the hypothesis that *several* heterogeneous customs which have since disappeared (cross-cousin marriage being only one of them) were needed to explain the existence of a *single* institution.[26] Thus, atomism and mechanism triumphed. It was Lowie's crucial article on the matrilineal complex[27] which opened what we should like to call the "modern phase" of the problem of the avunculate. Lowie showed that the correlation drawn or postulated between the prominent position of the maternal uncle and matrilineal descent cannot withstand rigorous analysis. In fact, the avunculate is found associated with patrilineal, as well as matrilineal, descent. The role of the maternal uncle cannot be explained as either a consequence or a survival of matrilineal kinship; it is only a specific application "of a very general tendency to associate definite social relations with definite forms of kinship regardless of maternal or paternal side." In accordance with this principle, introduced for the first time by Lowie in 1919, there exists a general tendency to *qualify attitudes*, which constitutes the only empirical foundation for a theory of kinship systems. But, at the same time, Lowie left certain questions unanswered. What exactly do we call an avunculate? Do we not merge different customs and attitudes under this single term? And, if it is true that there is a tendency to qualify all attitudes, why are only certain attitudes associated with the avuncular relationship, rather than just any possible attitudes, depending upon the group considered?

A few further remarks here may underline the striking analogy between the development of this problem and certain stages in the evolution of linguistic theory. The variety of possible attitudes in the area of interpersonal relationships is almost unlimited; the same holds true for the variety of sounds which can be articulated by the vocal apparatus – and which are actually produced during the first months of human life. Each language, however, retains only a very small number among all the possible sounds, and in this respect linguistics raises two questions: Why are certain sounds selected? What relationships exist between one or several of the sounds chosen and all the others?[28] Our sketch of the historical development of the avuncular problem is at precisely the same stage. Like language, the social group has a great wealth of psycho-physiological material at its disposal. Like language too, it retains only certain elements, at least some of which remain the same throughout the most varied cultures and are combined into structures which are always diversified. Thus we may wonder about the reason for this choice and the laws of combination.

For insight into the specific problem of the avunculate we should turn to Radcliffe-Brown. His well-known article on the maternal uncle in South Africa[29] was the first attempt to grasp and analyze the modalities of what we might call the "general principle of attitude qualification." We shall briefly review the fundamental ideas of that now-classic study.

According to Radcliffe-Brown, the term *avunculate* covers two antithetical systems of attitudes. In one case, the maternal uncle represents family authority; he is feared and obeyed, and possesses certain rights over his nephew. In the other case, the nephew holds privileges of familiarity in relation to his uncle and can treat him more or less as his victim. Second, there is a correlation between the boy's attitude toward his maternal uncle and his attitude toward his father. We find the two systems of attitudes in both cases, but they are inversely correlated. In groups where familiarity characterizes the relationship between father and son, the relationship between maternal uncle and nephew is one of respect; and where the father stands as the austere representative of family authority, it is the uncle who is treated with familiarity. Thus the two sets of attitudes constitute (as the structural linguist would say) two pairs of oppositions. Radcliffe-Brown concluded his article by proposing the following

interpretation: In the final analysis, it is descent that determines the choice of oppositions. In patrilineal societies, where the father and the father's descent group represent traditional authority, the maternal uncle is considered a "male mother." He is generally treated in the same fashion, and sometimes even called by the same name, as the mother. In matrilineal societies, the opposite occurs. Here, authority is vested in the maternal uncle, while relationships of tenderness and familiarity revolve about the father and his descent group.

It would indeed be difficult to exaggerate the importance of Radcliffe-Brown's contribution, which was the first attempt at synthesis on an empirical basis following Lowie's authoritative and merciless criticism of evolutionist metaphysics. To say that this effort did not entirely succeed does not in any way diminish the homage due to this great British anthropologist; but we should certainly recognize that Radcliffe-Brown's article leaves unanswered some fundamental questions. First, the avunculate does not occur in all matrilineal or all patrilineal systems, and we find it present in some systems which are neither matrilineal nor patrilineal.[30] Further, the avuncular relationship is not limited to two terms, but presupposes four, namely, brother, sister, brother-in-law, and nephew. An interpretation such as Radcliffe-Brown's arbitrarily isolates particular elements of a global structure which must be treated as a whole. A few simple examples will illustrate this twofold difficulty.

The social organization of the Trobriand Islanders of Melanesia is characterized by matrilineal descent, free and familiar relations between father and son, and a marked antagonism between maternal uncle and nephew.[31] On the other hand, the patrilineal Cherkess of the Caucasus place the hostility between father and son, while the maternal uncle assists his nephew and gives him a horse when he marries.[32] Up to this point we are still within the limits of Radcliffe-Brown's scheme. But let us consider the other family relationships involved. Malinowski showed that in the Trobriands husband and wife live in an atmosphere of tender intimacy and that their relationship is characterized by reciprocity. The relations between brother and sister, on the other hand, are dominated by an extremely rigid taboo. Let us now compare the situation in the Caucasus. There, it is the brother–sister relationship which is tender – to such an extent that among the Pschav an only daughter "adopts" a "brother" who will play the customary brother's role as her chaste bed companion.[33] But the relationship between spouses is entirely different. A Cherkess will not appear in public with his wife and visits her only in secret. According to Malinowski, there is no greater insult in the Trobriands than to tell a man that he resembles his sister. In the Caucasus there is an analogous prohibition: It is forbidden to ask a man about his wife's health.

When we consider societies of the Cherkess and Trobriand types it is not enough to study the correlation of attitudes between *father/son* and *uncle/sister's son*. This correlation is only one aspect of a global system containing four types of relationships which are organically linked, namely: *brother/sister, husband/wife, father/son,* and *mother's brother/sister's son.* The two groups in our example illustrate a law which can be formulated as follows: In both groups, the relation between maternal uncle and nephew is to the relation between brother and sister as the relation between father and son is to that between husband and wife. Thus if we know one pair of relations, it is always possible to infer the other.

Let us now examine some other cases. On Tonga, in Polynesia, descent is patrilineal, as among the Cherkess. Relations between husband and wife appear to be public and harmonious. Domestic quarrels are rare, and although the wife is often of superior rank, the husband "... is nevertheless of higher authority in all domestic matters, and no woman entertains the least idea of rebelling against that authority."[34] At the same time there is great freedom between nephew and maternal uncle. The nephew is *fahu*, or above the law, in relation to his uncle, toward whom extreme familiarity is permitted. This freedom strongly contrasts with the father–son relationship. The father is *tapu*; the son cannot touch his father's head or hair; he cannot touch him while he eats, sleep in his bed or on his pillow, share his food or drink, or play with his possessions. However, the strongest *tapu* of all is the one

between brother and sister, who must never be together under the same roof.

Although they are also patrilineal and patrilocal, the natives of Lake Kutubu in New Guinea offer an example of the opposite type of structure. F. E. Williams writes: "I have never seen such a close and apparently affectionate association between father and son...."[35] Relations between husband and wife are characterized by the very low status ascribed to women and "the marked separation of masculine and feminine interests...."[36] The women, according to Williams, "are expected to work hard for their masters ... they occasionally protest, and protest may be met with a beating."[37] The wife can always call upon her brother for protection against her husband, and it is with him that she seeks refuge. As for the relationship between nephew and maternal uncle, it is "... best summed up in the word 'respect' ... tinged with apprehensiveness,"[38] for the maternal uncle has the power to curse his nephew and inflict serious illness upon him (just as among the Kipsigi of Africa).

Although patrilineal, the society described by Williams is structurally of the same type as that of the Siuai of Bougainville, who have matrilineal descent. Between brother and sister there is "... friendly interaction and mutual generosity...."[39] As regards the father–son relationship, Oliver writes, "... I could discover little evidence that the word 'father' evokes images of hostility or stern authority or awed respect."[40] But the relationship between the nephew and his mother's brother "appears to range between stern discipline and genial mutual dependence. ..." However, "... most of the informants agreed that all boys stand in some awe of their mother's brothers, and are more likely to obey them than their own fathers...."[41] Between husband and wife harmonious understanding is rare: "... there are few young wives who remain altogether faithful ... most young husbands are continually suspicious and often give vent to jealous anger ... marriages involve a number of adjustments, some of them apparently difficult...."[42]

The same picture, but sharper still, characterizes the Dobuans, who are matrilineal and neighbors of the equally matrilineal Trobrianders, while their structure is very different. Dobuan marriages are unstable, adultery is widespread, and husband and wife constantly fear death induced by their spouse's witchcraft. Actually, Fortune's remark, "It is a most serious insult to refer to a woman's witchcraft so that her husband will hear of it"[43] appears to be a variant of the Trobriand and Caucasian taboos cited above.

In Dobu, the mother's brother is held to be the harshest of all the relatives. "The mother's brother may beat children long after their parents have ceased to do so," and they are forbidden to utter his name. There is a tender relationship with the "navel," the mother's sister's husband, who is the father's double, rather than with the father himself. Nevertheless, the father is considered "less harsh" than the mother's brother and will always seek, contrary to the laws of inheritance, to favor his son at the expense of his uterine nephew. And,

finally, "the strongest of all social bonds" is the one between brother and sister.[44]

What can we conclude from these examples? The correlation between types of descent and forms of avunculate does not exhaust the problem. Different forms of avunculate can coexist with the same type of descent, whether patrilineal or matrilineal. But we constantly find the same fundamental relationship between the four pairs of oppositions required to construct the system. This will emerge more clearly from the diagrams which illustrate our examples. The sign + indicates free and familiar relations, and the sign − stands for relations characterized by hostility, antagonism, or reserve (Figure 8.1). This is an oversimplification, but we can tentatively make use of it. We shall describe some of the indispensable refinements farther on.

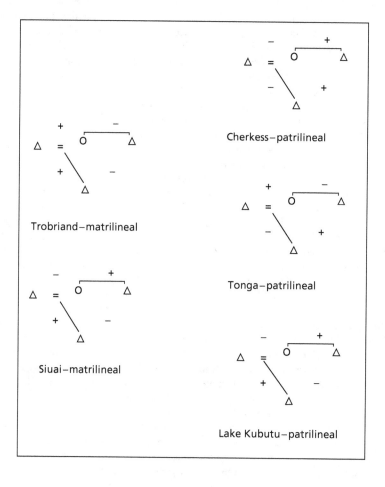

Figure 8.1

The synchronic law of correlation thus suggested may be validated diachronically. If we summarize, after Howard, the evolution of family relationships during the Middle Ages, we find approximately this pattern: The brother's authority over his sister wanes, and that of the prospective husband increases. Simultaneously, the bond between father and son is weakened and that between maternal uncle and nephew is reinforced.[45]

This evolution seems to be confirmed by the documents gathered by Léon Gautier, for in the "conservative" texts (Raoul de Cambrai, Geste des Loherains, etc.),[46] the positive relationship is established chiefly between father and son and is only gradually displaced toward the maternal uncle and nephew.[47]

Thus we see[48] that in order to understand the avunculate we must treat it as one relationship within a system, while the system itself must be considered as a whole in order to grasp its structure. This structure rests upon four terms (brother, sister, father, and son), which are linked by two pairs of correlative oppositions in such a way that in each of the two generations there is always a positive relationship and a negative one. Now, what is the nature of this structure, and what is its function? The answer is as follows: This structure is the most elementary form of kinship that can exist. It is, properly speaking, *the unit of kinship*.

One may give a logical argument to support this statement. In order for a kinship structure to exist, three types of family relations must always be present: a relation of consanguinity, a relation of affinity, and a relation of descent – in other words, a relation between siblings, a relation between spouses, and a relation between parent and child. It is evident that the structure given here satisfies this threefold requirement, in accordance with the scientific principle of parsimony. But these considerations are abstract, and we can present a more direct proof for our thesis.

The primitive and irreducible character of the basic unit of kinship, as we have defined it, is actually a direct result of the universal presence of an incest taboo. This is really saying that in human society a man must obtain a woman from another man who gives him a daughter or a sister. Thus we do not need

to explain how the maternal uncle emerged in the kinship structure: He does not emerge – he is present initially. Indeed, the presence of the maternal uncle is a necessary precondition for the structure to exist. The error of traditional anthropology, like that of traditional linguistics, was to consider the terms, and not the relations between the terms.

Before proceeding further, let us briefly answer some objections which might be raised. First, if the relationship between "brothers-in-law" is the necessary axis around which the kinship structure is built, why need we bring in the child of the marriage when considering the elementary structure? Of course the child here may be either born or yet unborn. But, granting this, we must understand that the child is indispensable in validating the dynamic and teleological character of the initial step, which establishes kinship on the basis of and through marriage. Kinship is not a static phenomenon; it exists only in self-perpetuation. Here we are not thinking of the desire to perpetuate the race, but rather of the fact that in most kinship systems the initial disequilibrium produced in one generation between the group that gives the woman and the group that receives her can be stabilized only by counter-prestations in following generations. Thus, even the most elementary kinship structure exists both synchronically and diachronically.

Second, could we not conceive of a symmetrical structure, equally simple, where the sexes would be reversed? Such a structure would involve a sister, her brother, brother's wife, and brother's daughter. This is certainly a theoretical possibility. But it is immediately eliminated on empirical grounds. In human society, it is the men who exchange the women, and not vice versa. It remains for further research to determine whether certain cultures have not tended to create a kind of fictitious image of this symmetrical structure. Such cases would surely be uncommon.

We come now to a more serious objection. Possibly we have only inverted the problem. Traditional anthropologists painstakingly endeavored to explain the origin of the avunculate, and we have brushed aside that research by treating the mother's brother not as an extrinsic element, but as an immediate *given* of the simplest family structure. How is it then that we do not find the avunculate at all times and in all places? For although the avunculate has a wide distribution, it is by no means universal. It would be futile to explain the instances where it is present and then fail to explain its absence in other instances.

Let us point out, first, that the kinship system does not have the same importance in all cultures. For some cultures it provides the active principle regulating all or most of the social relationships. In other groups, as in our own society, this function is either absent altogether or greatly reduced. In still others, as in the societies of the Plains Indians, it is only partially fulfilled. The kinship system is a language; but it is not a universal language, and a society may prefer other modes of expression and action. From the viewpoint of the anthropologist this means that in dealing with a specific culture we must always ask a preliminary question: Is the system systematic? Such a question, which seems absurd at first, is absurd only in relation to language; for language is the semantic system par excellence; it cannot but signify, and exists only through signification. On the contrary, this question must be rigorously examined as we move from the study of language to the consideration of other systems which also claim to have semantic functions, but whose fulfillment remains partial, fragmentary, or subjective, like, for example, social organization, art, and so forth.

Furthermore, we have interpreted the avunculate as a characteristic trait of elementary structure. This elementary structure, which is the product of defined relations involving four terms, is, in our view, the true *atom of kinship*.[49] Nothing can be conceived or given beyond the fundamental requirements of its structure, and, in addition, it is the sole building block of more complex systems. For there are more complex systems; or, more accurately speaking, all kinship systems are constructed on the basis of this elementary structure, expanded or developed through the integration of new elements. Thus we must entertain two hypotheses: first, one in which the kinship system under consideration operates through the simple juxtaposition of elementary structures, and where the avuncular relationship therefore remains constantly apparent; second, a hypothesis in which the building blocks of the

system are already of a more complex order. In the latter case, the avuncular relationship, while present, may be submerged within a differentiated context. For instance, we can conceive of a system whose point of departure lies in the elementary structure but which adds, at the right of the maternal uncle, his wife, and, at the left of the father, first the father's sister and then her husband. We could easily demonstrate that a development of this order leads to a parallel splitting in the following generation. The child must then be distinguished according to sex – a boy or a girl, linked by a relation which is symmetrical and inverse to the terms occupying the other peripheral positions in the structure (for example, the dominant position of the father's sister in Polynesia, the South African *nhlampsa*, and inheritance by the mother's brother's wife). In this type of structure the avuncular relationship continues to prevail, but it is no longer the predominant one. In structures of still greater complexity, the avunculate may be obliterated or may merge with other relationships. But precisely because it is part of the elementary structure, the avuncular relationship re-emerges unmistakably and tends to become reinforced each time the system under consideration reaches a crisis – either because it is undergoing rapid transformation (as on the Northwest Coast), or because it is a focus of contact and conflict between radically different cultures (as in Fiji and southern India), or, finally, because it is in the throes of a mortal crisis (as was Europe in the Middle Ages).

We must also add that the positive and negative symbols which we have employed in the above diagrams represent an oversimplification, useful only as a part of the demonstration. Actually, the system of basic attitudes comprises at least four terms: an attitude of affection, tenderness, and spontaneity; an attitude which results from the reciprocal exchange of prestations and counter-prestations; and, in addition to these bilateral relationships, two unilateral relationships, one which corresponds to the attitude of the creditor, the other to that of the debtor. In other words there are: mutuality ($=$), reciprocity ($\pm$), rights ($+$), and obligations ($-$). These four fundamental attitudes are represented in their reciprocal relationships in Figure 8.2.

Figure 8.2

In many systems the relationship between two individuals is often expressed not by a single attitude, but by several attitudes which together form, as it were, a "bundle" of attitudes (as in the Trobriands, where we find both mutuality *and* reciprocity between husband and wife). This is an additional reason behind the difficulty in uncovering the basic structure.

We have tried to show the extent to which the preceding analysis is indebted to outstanding contemporary exponents of the sociology of primitive peoples. We must stress, however, that in its most fundamental principle this analysis departs from their teachings. Let us cite as an example Radcliffe-Brown:

> The unit of structure from which a kinship system is built up is the group which I call an "elementary family," consisting of a man and his wife and their child or children.... The existence of the elementary family creates three special kinds of social relationship, that between parent and child, that between children of the same parents (siblings), and that between husband and wife as parents of the same child or children.... The three relationships that exist within the elementary family constitute what I call the first order. Relationships of the second order are those which depend on the connection of two elementary families through a common member, and are such as father's father, mother's brother, wife's sister, and so on. In the third order are such as father's brother's son and mother's brother's wife. Thus we can trace, if we have genealogical information, relationships of the fourth, fifth or n^{th} order.[50]

The idea expressed in the above passage, that the biological family constitutes the point of departure from which all societies elaborate their kinship systems, has not been voiced solely by Radcliffe-Brown. There is scarcely an idea which would today elicit greater consensus. Nor is there one more dangerous, in our opinion. Of course, the biological family is ubiquitous in human society. But what confers upon kinship its socio-cultural character is not what it retains from nature, but, rather, the essential way in which it diverges from nature. A kinship system does not consist in the objective ties of descent or consanguinity between individuals. It exists only in human consciousness; it is an arbitrary system of representations, not the spontaneous development of a real situation. This certainly does not mean that the real situation is automatically contradicted, or that it is to be simply ignored. Radcliffe-Brown has shown, in studies that are now classic, that even systems which are apparently extremely rigid and artificial, such as the Australian systems of marriage-classes, take biological parenthood carefully into account. But while this observation is irrefutable, still the fact (in our view decisive) remains that, in human society, kinship is allowed to establish and perpetuate itself only through specific forms of marriage. In other words, the relationships which Radcliffe-Brown calls "relationships of the first order" are a function of, and depend upon, those which he considers secondary and derived. The essence of human kinship is to require the establishment of relations among what Radcliffe-Brown calls "elementary families." Thus, it is not the families (isolated terms) which are truly "elementary," but, rather, the relations between those terms. No other interpretation can account for the universality of the incest taboo; and the avuncular relationship, in its most general form, is nothing but a corollary, now covert, now explicit, of this taboo.

Because they are symbolic systems, kinship systems offer the anthropologist a rich field, where his efforts can almost (and we emphasize the "almost") converge with those of the most highly developed of the social sciences, namely, linguistics. But to achieve this convergence, from which it is hoped a better understanding of man will result, we must never lose sight of the fact that, in both anthropological and linguistic research, we are dealing strictly with symbolism. And although it may be legitimate or even inevitable to fall back upon a naturalistic interpretation in order to understand the emergence of symbolic thinking, once the latter is given, the nature of the explanation must change as radically as the newly appeared phenomenon differs from those which have preceded and prepared it. Hence, any concession to naturalism might jeopardize the immense progress already made in linguistics, which is also beginning to characterize the study of family structure, and might drive the sociology of the family toward a sterile empiricism, devoid of inspiration.

NOTES

1 Marcel Mauss, "Rapports réels et pratiques de la psychologie et de la sociologie," *Journal de Psychologie Normale et Pathologique* (1924); reprinted in *Sociologie et Anthropologie* (Paris: 1951), p. 299.

2 O. Schrader, *Prehistoric Antiquities of the Aryan Peoples*, trans. F. B. Jevons (London: 1890), Chapter XII, Part 4.

3 *Ibid.* See also H. J. Rose, "On the Alleged Evidence for Mother-Right in Early Greece," *Folklore*, XXII (1911), and the more recent studies by George Thomson, which support the hypothesis of matrilineal survivals.

4 A. M. Hocart, "Chieftainship and the Sister's Son in the Pacific," *American Anthropologist*, n.s., XVII (1915); "The Uterine Nephew," *Man*, XXIII, No. 4 (1923); "The Cousin in Vedic Ritual," *Indian Antiquary*, LIV (1925); etc.

5 Paul K. Benedict, "Tibetan and Chinese Kinship Terms," *Harvard Journal of Asiatic Studies*, VI (1942); "Studies in Thai Kinship Terminology," *Journal of the American Oriental Society*, LXIII (1943).

6 L. Brunschvicg, *Le Progrès de la conscience dans la philosophie occidentale* (Paris: 1927), II, p. 562.

7 Between 1900 and 1920 Ferdinand de Saussure and Antoine Meillet, the founders of modern linguistics, placed themselves determinedly under the wing of the anthropologists. Not until the 1920's did Marcel Mauss begin – to borrow a phrase from economics – to reverse this tendency.

8 N. Troubetzkoy, "La Phonologie actuelle," in *Psychologie du langage* (Paris: 1933).

9 *Ibid.*, p. 243.

10 *Loc. cit.*

11 *Ibid.*, p. 245; Roman Jakobson, "Principien der historischen Phonologie," *Travaux du Cercle linguistique de Prague*, IV (1931); and also Jakobson, "Remarques sur l'évolution phonologique du russe," *ibid.*, II (1929).

12 W. H. R. Rivers, *The History of Melanesian Society* (London: 1914), *passim; Social Organization*, ed. W. J. Perry (London: 1924), Chapter IV.

13 In the same vein, see Sol Tax, "Some Problems of Social Organization," in Fred Eggan (ed.), *Social Anthropology of North American Tribes* (Chicago: 1937).

14 Roman Jakobson, "Observations sur le classement phonologique des consonnes," *Proceedings of the Third International Congress of Phonetic Sciences* (Ghent: 1938).

15 K. Davis and W. L. Warner, "Structural Analysis of Kinship," *American Anthropologist*, n.s., XXXVII (1935).

16 Thus at the end of the analysis carried out by these authors, the term *husband* is replaced by the formula:
$$C^{2a}/2d/^0 \ SU^{1a \ 8}/Ego \ (Ibid.)$$
There are now available two works which employ a much more refined logical apparatus and offer greater interest in terms both of method and of results. See F. G. Lounsbury, "A Semantic Analysis of the Pawnee Kinship Usage," *Language*, XXXII, No. 1 (1956), and W. H. Goodenough, "The Componential Analysis of Kinship," *ibid.*

17 As will be seen in Chapter V, I have now refined this formulation.

18 A. L. Kroeber, "Classificatory Systems of Relationship," *Journal of the Royal Anthropological Institute*, XXXIX (1909).

19 We must except the remarkable work of W. L. Warner, "Morphology and Functions of the Australian Murngin Type of Kinship," *American Anthropologist*, n.s., XXXII-XXXIII (1930–1931), in which his analysis of the system of attitudes, although fundamentally debatable, nevertheless initiates a new phase in the study of problems of kinship.

20 A. R. Radcliffe-Brown, "Kinship Terminology in California," *American Anthropologist*, n.s., XXXVII (1935); "The Study of Kinship Systems," *Journal of the Royal Anthropological Institute*, LXXI (1941).

21 M. E. Opler, "Apache Data Concerning the Relationship of Kinship Terminology to

Social Classification," *American Anthropologist*, n.s., XXXIX (1937); A. M. Halpern, "Yuma Kinship Terms," *American Anthropologist*, n.s., XLIV (1942).

22 D. F. Thomson, "The Joking Relationship and Organized Obscenity in North Queensland," *American Anthropologist*, n.s., XXXVII (1935).

23 Radcliffe-Brown, "The Study of Kinship Systems," *op. cit.*, p. 8. This later formulation seems to us more satisfactory than his 1935 statement that attitudes present "a fairly high degree of correlation with the terminological classification" (*American Anthropologist*, n.s., XXXVII [1935], p. 53).

24 Sydney Hartland, "Matrilineal Kinship and the Question of its Priority," *Memoirs of the American Anthropological Association*, No. 4 (1917).

25 W. H. R. Rivers, "The Marriage of Cousins in India," *Journal of the Royal Asiatic Society* (July, 1907).

26 *Ibid.*, p. 624.

27 R. H. Lowie, "The Matrilineal Complex," *University of California Publications in American Archaeology and Ethnology*, XVI, No. 2 (1919).

28 Roman Jakobson, *Kindersprache, Aphasie and allgemeine Lautgesetze* (Uppsala: 1941).

29 A. R. Radcliffe-Brown, "The Mother's Brother in South Africa," *South African Journal of Science*, XXI (1924).

30 As among the Mundugomor of New Guinea, where the relationship between maternal uncle and nephew is always familiar, although descent is alternately patrilineal or matrilineal. See Margaret Mead, *Sex and Temperament in Three Primitive Societies* (New York: 1935), pp. 176–185.

31 B. Malinowski, *The Sexual Life of Savages in Northwestern Melanesia* (London: 1929), 2 vols.

32 Dubois de Monpereux (1839), cited in M. Kovalevski, "La Famille matriarcale au Caucase," *L'Anthropologie*, IV (1893).

33 *Ibid.*

34 E. W. Gifford, "Tonga Society," *Bernice P. Bishop Museum Bulletin*, No. 61 (Honolulu: 1929), pp. 16–22.

35 F. E. Williams, "Group Sentiment and Primitive Justice," *American Anthropologist*, n.s., XLIII, No. 4, Part 1 (1941), p. 523.

36 F. E. Williams, "Natives of Lake Kutubu, Papua," *Oceania*, XI (1940–1941), p. 266.

37 *Ibid.*, p. 268.

38 *Ibid.*, p. 280. See also *Oceania*, XII (1941–1942).

39 Douglas L. Oliver, *A Solomon Island Society: Kinship and Leadership among the Siuai of Bougainville* (Cambridge, Mass.: 1955), p. 255.

40 *Ibid.*, p. 251.

41 *Ibid.*, p. 257.

42 *Ibid.*, pp. 168–9.

43 R. F. Fortune, *The Sorcerers of Dobu* (New York: 1932), p. 45.

44 *Ibid.*, pp. 8, 10, 62–4.

45 G. E. Howard, *A History of Matrimonial Institutions*, 3 vols. (Chicago: 1904).

[46 *Translator's note*: The "Chansons de Geste," which survive in manuscript versions of the twelfth to the fifteenth century, are considered to be remodelings of much earlier originals, dating back to the age of Charlemagne. These poems of heroic and often legendary exploits also constitute a source of information on the family life of that period.]

47 Léon Gautier, *La Chevalerie* (Paris: 1890). See also: F. B. Gummere, "The Sister's Son," in *An English Miscellany Presented to Dr. Furnivall* (London: 1901); W. O. Farnsworth, *Uncle and Nephew in the Old French Chanson de Geste* (New York: 1913).

48 The preceding paragraphs were written in 1957 and substituted for the original text, in response to the judicious remark by my colleague Luc de Heusch of the Université Libre of Brussels that one of my examples was incorrect. I take this opportunity to thank him.

49 It is no doubt superfluous to emphasize that the atomism which we have criticized in Rivers refers to classical philosophy and has nothing to do with the structural conception of the atom developed in modern physics.

50 A. R. Radcliffe-Brown, "The Study of Kinship Systems," *op. cit.*, p. 2.

9

Concerning Trobriand Clans and the Kinship Category 'Tabu'

Edmund Leach

For social anthropologists Malinowski's ethnographic accounts of Trobriand Island culture are a kind of Domesday Book. Palpably incomplete, palpably imperfect, they yet transcend in some indefinable way everything of like kind. This paper is an attempt to demonstrate from Malinowski's own material that certain of his inferential conclusions were incorrect. It is with no feelings of disrespect that I offer this revision. On the contrary I consider it a tribute to Malinowski's remarkable skill as an ethnographer that he can be shown to have recorded important features of the Trobriand social system of which he himself was unaware. The conclusion which I reach at the end of my paper is a functional one which would have appealed strongly to Malinowski's imagination.

The paper has originated in this way. In an essay contributed to a forthcoming critical symposium on Malinowski's writings (Firth 1957) I have argued that Malinowski's emphasis on the pragmatic consequences of behaviour led him to underestimate the degree to which behaviour can serve as a system of symbolic communication. I have cited his view that classificatory kinship terminologies are to be explained as systems of homonyms as an example of the sociological distortion that results from this kind of pragmatism. The present paper elaborates this argument in detail.

Like the other contributions to this volume my paper bears a certain genetic relationship to

Fortes's essay 'Time and Social Structure' (Fortes 1949(*a*)). The common theme is that the nature of a social system can only be fully understood when we recognize adequately that any particular individual occupies successively a series of different positions in the total structure.

In brief, the problems which I seek to answer are these. First, why do the Trobrianders have four clans?

The common sense explanation is that it is an historical accident. That no doubt is the explanation which Malinowski himself would have offered. That seems to me too simple.

As a matter of fact Malinowski fails to explain why the Trobrianders should have a clan system at all. The clans appear to play no social role as such. The effective social groupings in Trobriand society are the units which Malinowski calls sub-clans. It is these sub-clans which are the landowning units, and which operate efficiently as exogamous corporations. Yet, according to Malinowski, each of these numerous sub-clans is allocated to one or other of four totemic clans, and the number four is, it seems, important:

> Humanity is divided into four clans. Totemic nature is conceived to be as deeply ingrained in the substance of the individual as sex, colour, and stature. It can never be changed, and it transcends individual life, for it can be carried over into the next world, and brought back into this one when the spirit returns by reincar-

nation. This fourfold totemic division is thought to be universal, embracing every section of mankind...(Malinowski 1932: 416).

To use Malinowski's terminology, this is quite clearly a 'mythical charter' for something or other. But for what? Malinowski does not explain; I shall seek to do so.

My second problem concerns the tantalizing Trobriand word *tabu* which Malinowski discusses at some length on several occasions (Malinowski 1932: 423, 450–1; 1935, II: 28, 113).

Malinowski distinguishes several meanings of this word which he regards as homonyms – i.e. as different words of similar sound. Apparently he considered that there were at least three such distinct words:

1. *tabu* = taboo, sacred, forbidden. This, according to Malinowski, is an alien word introduced into the Trobriands by Christian missionaries.

2. *tabu* = grandparents, ancestors, totems.

3. *tabu* = father's sister and, by a process of extension, 'lawful woman' – i.e. a woman with whom sexual intercourse is permitted.

On Malinowski's own showing *tabu* in the Trobriands also has various further meanings, e.g. grandchild, and 'husband of any lawful woman'. It is not clear to me whether Malinowski regarded these as yet further homonyms or as extended meanings of the first three.

Now homonyms occur in most languages and, since Malinowski was a most notable linguist, we should perhaps accept his views on the matter. But this I prefer not to do. I submit the hypothesis that Malinowski was here mistaken and that there is only one Trobriand word *tabu*, all the meanings of which are closely and logically connected.

Finally I shall show how my 'solutions' to these two 'problems' tie in very nicely with a third curiosity of Trobriand ethnography, the celebrated origin myth, whereby various original ancestors are made to emerge from holes in the ground conveniently situated at known sites on ancestral property. In pursuing these inquiries we shall be led to re-examine and partly reinterpret Malinowski's views concerning the nature of Trobriand rules of incest and exogamy.

Let us start by considering the various meanings of *tabu*, regarded as a kinship category. In Malinowski's published writings there is no complete list of Trobriand kinship terminology. The nearest approximation to such a list is to be found in *The Sexual Life of Savages*, ch. XIII, section 6. However, in preparing this paper I have had the advantage of being able to consult Mr H. A. Powell, who carried out anthropological fieldwork in the Trobriand Islands in 1950–1. Mr Powell has not only filled in the gaps in Malinowski's kinship term diagram, he has also explained how in certain particulars Malinowski's diagram is in error. The points at which I rely on Mr Powell's information in lieu of Malinowski's own are noted in the text below.

I must stress that I have used Mr Powell simply as an informant on matters of fact. My use of his material does not in any way imply that he agrees with my theoretical interpretations; indeed I know very well that he does not. For all that, his comments on a preliminary draft of this paper have been extremely helpful.

Considered simply as a system in itself, without regard to cultural context, Trobriand kinship terminology falls into the well-known Crow type which has long been recognized as correlated in a general way with matrilineal descent (Tax 1937: 12 ff.). There are, however, a number of atypical features – e.g. Ego's mother's brother's wife falls into the same term category as Ego's mother. As a consequence, the system as a whole cannot be made comprehensible by a simple lineage analysis of the kind favoured by Radcliffe-Brown and his pupils (e.g. Gilbert 1937: 292). Instead of arguing *a priori* let us then start with Malinowski's own analysis.

As I have already indicated, Malinowski's treatment of the term *tabu*, regarded as a kinship term, starts by distinguishing *tabu* meaning grandmother and *tabu* meaning father's sister as two different words. Of the latter he says:

The primary meaning of this word [*tabu*] is 'father's sister'. It also embraces 'father's sister's daughter' or 'paternal cross cousin' or by extension 'all the women of the father's clan'; and, in its widest sense 'all the women not of the same clan [as Ego]'. In this, its most extensive application, the word stands for 'lawful woman'..... For such a woman the term *lubaygu*, 'my sweetheart', may be correctly used; but this term is absolutely incompatible with the kinship designation, *lu(gu)ta*, 'my sister'. This linguistic use embodies, therefore, the rule of exogamy, and to a large extent expresses the ideas underlying this (Malinowski 1932: 423).

On Malinowski's own showing, this statement is neither comprehensive nor altogether accurate. It ignores the fact that the category *tabu*, regarded as a kinship term, is used by members of both sexes and that, in either case, it includes numerous males as well as females. It is true that most 'lawful' (i.e. 'marriageable') women are classed as *tabu* by a male Ego, but this does not equate, as Malinowski seems to suggest, with 'all women not of the same clan as Ego'. On the contrary, both the wives and the daughters of the men of both Ego's own sub-clan and that of his father are ordinarily categorized by terms other than *tabu*, and this is true also of a large number of other women who, in later life, are connected affinally to Ego through his wife.

Throughout his analysis Malinowski assumes that 'prohibitions on sexual intercourse' and 'rules of exogamy' are interchangeable, coincident, descriptions of the same set of regulations; moreover, in the context cited, he states explicitly that by 'exogamy' he means 'clan incest'. In Malinowski's presentation the exogamous group is defined by the principle of matrilineal descent alone and is influenced by no other factor. His argument is that, in its widest extension, the category *tabu* serves to mark off this exogamous grouping – the women who are *tabu* are the 'lawful women' who are outside the barrier of clan incest. Using exogamy in this sense Malinowski's explanation simply fails to fit the facts which he describes.

But what better explanation can be offered?

It is a cardinal and fundamental assumption in Malinowski's analysis that words employed in kinship terminology have attached to them certain *primary* meanings and sentiments, which derive from a sociological relationship existing between the speaker and a particular individual near-kinsman. The use of kinship terms in a classificatory sense comes about through the gradual extension of these primary

sentiments to a wider and wider range of individuals. Thus, to take a particular instance, the term *tama*, which a Trobriander ultimately applies to nearly all the males of his father's clan, has, in Malinowski's view, the *primary* meaning 'father' or 'mother's husband' and all extended uses of the term are derived from the initial relationship existing between a Trobriand father and his son (Malinowski 1932: 5).

In my own analysis I shall make no such assumption. I do not repudiate the possibility of the 'extension' of meanings from narrow primary to wider secondary contexts, but I do not admit that words used as kinship terms must, *ipso facto*, derive their primary meaning exclusively from a kinship context, nor that the primary application is always to a particular individual rather than to a class of individuals.

For example, I agree with Malinowski that the term *tama* has a primary meaning which later undergoes extension, but, where Malinowski supposes that the primary meaning stems from the context of the nuclear family, so that *tama* = 'mother's husband', I myself would suggest that the primary meaning here stems from the identification of a particular group of males with a particular locality. My own 'primary' translation would be *tama* = 'domiciled male of my father's sub-clan hamlet'. Let me elaborate this distinction.

I fully accept Malinowski's contention that, of all the males whom the child addresses as *tama*, the speaker's own father is the one with whom Ego has the most personal contacts, but that does not make 'father' the primary meaning of *tama*, nor does it imply that every *tama* is looked upon as being, in some sense, 'a kind of father'. The fact that I have a pet dog called Peter does not make Peter the primary meaning of the word *dog*, nor does it imply that I cannot distinguish between my dog and another.

My view is that most words employed in kinship terminologies are category terms rather than individualizing proper names. Malinowski insisted that *tama* refers primarily to a particular individual, the father, and to other individuals only by extension; he supposed that any other view would imply that Trobrianders cannot distinguish between one *tama* and another (Malinowski 1932: 447). My own assumption, on the contrary, is that *tama* refers primarily to a category; this does not imply any suggestion that Trobrianders have any difficulty about distinguishing the roles of different individual *tama*.

Malinowski does not describe for us in detail the actual kinship composition of any particular Trobriand local community, but he explains fairly clearly what the ideal 'theoretical' composition of such a community ought to be according to the Trobrianders' own ideas. Land in the Trobriands is owned by the matrilineal sub-clans (Malinowski 1932: 26, 417; 1935, I: ch. XII). The married males of the sub-clan, numbering it would seem about a dozen individuals, live, each in his own domestic household, in a village, or section of a village, situated on or near the sub-clan land. I shall call this collectivity a sub-clan hamlet.

Here let me emphasize two things. First, the assertion that all the adult males of a sub-clan live in their own sub-clan hamlet is almost certainly an idealization of reality. I imagine that in almost all actual cases there are some married men who are *not* living in the hamlet of their own sub-clan. But this discrepancy between fact and ideal does not, I think, affect my argument. Secondly, my phrase 'sub-clan hamlet' is not meant to be identical with the term 'village' as used by Malinowski.

In Malinowski's writings 'village' ordinarily means the cluster of buildings around a particular central place (*baku*). Although such a 'village' may sometimes be occupied by householders of a single sub-clan, this is not ordinarily the case.

The more usual pattern is that a village comprises several sections each of which is associated with a different sub-clan. The households forming one section of the village belong to married males of one particular sub-clan, and these men collectively exercise certain rights of ownership over parts of the garden land adjacent to the village. The houses in a village section plus the garden lands associated with this village section form a unity which I call a sub-clan hamlet. This analysis is valid even though the houses and gardens of different sections of the same village are immediately adjacent to one another.

In these terms, the 'component village of Yalumugwa' (Malinowski 1935, I: 385) embraces two sub-clan hamlets; Omarakana (1935, I:

430) comprises three sub-clan hamlets, though in this case the male householders of one of the three sub-clans reside in another village. My phrase 'sub-clan hamlet' equates therefore with Malinowski's 'village section' and appears to correspond to a native Trobriand category (1935, 1: 430). The variety of land ownership rights that pertain to a sub-clan hamlet, considered as a corporation, is described in *Coral Gardens* (Malinowski 1935, I: 343–4).

In the course of a lifetime both men and women are ordinarily resident members of two distinct sub-clan hamlets. A girl remains under the control of her parents until she marries, and then joins her husband in a new household established in the husband's sub-clan hamlet; at no stage is she a resident member of her own sub-clan hamlet. The pattern of residence for a boy is more complicated. He ceases to sleep in his parents' house at adolescence and joins a bachelor house (*bukumatulu*) (Malinowski 1932: 53–64). Bachelor houses are not necessarily identified as belonging to any particular sub-clan; boys of different sub-clans may sleep in one house. If a boy's father and his mother's brother live in different villages, he might, it seems, find bachelor accommodation in either community (Malinowski 1935, I: 36, 205, 357). But a boy only sleeps in the bachelor house, he does not eat there.

From an early age a boy plays his part in garden work, but while he starts by working for his father he gradually transfers his productive effort to his mother's brother's lands (1935, I: 60, 191). So long as he contributes directly to his parents' household, he receives food from his mother; when he contributes to his mother's brother's household, he receives food from his mother's brother's wife. The economic consequences of this shift are small, for when the boy works on his mother's brother's land, the produce serves to increase the annual harvest gift (*urigubu*) which the mother's brother's household contributes to the father's household. Thus, in either case, the boy may be said to be working for his parents.

Finally, on marriage, a young man establishes a new independent household in his own sub-clan hamlet. From his garden plots he continues to make *urigubu* payments to his parents and his married sisters.

I must emphasize that although a boy ceases to sleep in his parents' house at adolescence he does not fully renounce his residence rights there until after he is married. Marriage itself is publicly established by the act of cohabitation in the household of the boy's father – *not* that of his mother's brother (Malinowski 1932: 75, 93).

We may describe all this by saying that, in the precise terminology of English law, a Trobriand male is, from the start, *domiciled* in his own sub-clan hamlet but his *residence* varies. During childhood he is resident in his father's sub-clan hamlet; after marriage he is resident in his own sub-clan hamlet; during the interval between adolescence and marriage he has a dual status with residence rights in both communities.

These facts provide the core of my analysis. My thesis is that, as a child, the male Ego identifies himself primarily with his father's household while, as an adult, he identifies himself primarily with the members of his own sub-clan hamlet considered as a corporation. I argue that this time shift in the composition and membership of the group whom Ego (male) regards as 'people like us' is fundamental for our understanding of the nature of Trobriand kinship categories.

The position of a girl is different; though technically domiciled in her own sub-clan hamlet, she is never actually resident there. The analysis which follows is pursued solely from the viewpoint of a male Ego. A separate though comparable analysis would be necessary to explain the system of kinship categories used by a girl.

It follows from what I have said, and from Malinowski's own description of the sex and age categories in Trobriand society (Malinowski 1932: 51), that any particular sub-clan hamlet, at any particular time, comprises the following categories of individuals:

A   Old men – *tomwaya* or *toboma*.[1]

B   Old women – *numwaya* – wives of *A*, widows, etc.

C   Active married men – *tovavaygile*.

D   Active married women – *navavaygile* – wives of *C*.

E   Bachelors – *to'ulatile* – 'sister's sons' to *A* and *C* and resident here only part of the time.

F   Young girls – *inagwadi* – and adolescent girls – *nakapugula* – still under the charge of their parents, daughters of *A*, *B*, *C*, *D*.

G   Young boys – *gwadi* – still living with their parents – sons of *A*, *B*, *C*, *D*.

In this classification *A*, *C* and *E* together comprise the locally resident owners of the sub-clan hamlet. In addition, some other male members of the sub-clan, young boys, live scattered about among other hamlets with their parents. *B*, *D*, *F* and *G* in the above classification are all members of 'alien' sub-clans; that is to say, although their *residence* is in this hamlet, their *domicile* is elsewhere.

Let us now ignore altogether Malinowski's tendentious arguments about the way in which kinship sentiments are first established within the context of the elementary family and then extended outwards. Instead let us simply consider from first principles how a Trobriander might reasonably be expected to classify his kinsmen and acquaintance.

It seems evident from Malinowski's account that the two really fundamental economic facts in Trobriand social organization are (*a*) an individual's rights to the use or produce of the land of his or her own sub-clan, and (*b*) the institution of *urigubu* which results from this principle of land tenure. Rights in the land are possessed by men and women alike, but only the men of the sub-clan have direct access to their land. The men therefore cultivate the land; one major share (*taytumwala*) of the produce is kept by the cultivator for the use of his own household and for seed purposes; another, usually larger, share (*urigubu*) is transferred in harvest gifts to the cultivator's mother and married sisters (Malinowski 1935, 1: 194). Let us assume that these economic facts are the ones which provide the primary criteria for distinguishing categories of kin.

It is plain that the individual Trobriand male experiences the effects of the *urigubu* institution in two distinct phases; first, as a child in his father's household, and secondly, as a married adult in his own household.

In the first phase the implications of *urigubu*-giving are lopsided. The child is a member of a household which regularly receives gifts from members of a sub-clan hamlet which he is taught from the start to regard as his own. These people, his 'mother's brothers' (*kada*), are clearly, in a formal sense, 'friends'. The friendship may indeed be subject to strain, but it is palpably advantageous to 'our household'.

In contrast, a substantial share of the produce of his own father's garden is given away to strangers – the father's mother and the father's sister – from whom Ego receives no benefits. On the contrary, in the long run, the sons of these strangers will appear on the scene and usurp the property which at present seems to be the main source of Ego's livelihood. These people too no doubt are, officially speaking, to be regarded as 'friends', but from Ego's point of view they are very disadvantageous ones. Indeed in many respects these strangers, the recipients of the father's *urigubu* gifts, might seem to be the prototype 'enemy'.

I shall here digress to remind the reader briefly of certain features of Radcliffe-Brown's theoretical discussions of taboo and joking relationships (Radcliffe-Brown 1952: chs. IV, V, VII).

For Radcliffe-Brown *taboo* is a technical term with a narrower range of meaning than the common Polynesian word *tabu*. He discusses taboo in terms of what he calls 'ritual avoidances' which serve to define the 'ritual status' differences existing between two persons in a single social system. The following are some of the characteristics of taboo which emerge from Radcliffe-Brown's analysis: Tabooed persons are respected as sacred, they are the object of ritual avoidance and the recipients of tribute. The tabooed thing or person is 'abnormal', it is separated from that which is normal, but its quality is ambivalent; it is a source of power, but the power may have good or evil consequences, it is sacred and polluting at the same time.

The ritual behaviours which Radcliffe-Brown discusses under the general title of 'joking relationships' are an exemplification of this theme. These behaviours express 'friendship' either by manifesting taboo – e.g. ritual avoidance coupled with gift-giving – or else by the systematic breach of taboo, which amounts to much the same thing – for, in Radcliffe-Brown's argument, anyone who breaks a taboo automatically becomes taboo himself. That taboo should be used in this way to express 'friendship' is the subject of one of Radcliffe-Brown's most penetrating pieces of analysis.

He points out that marriage often serves to unite two potentially hostile groups, and that it

then becomes necessary for members of these 'opposed' parties to assert, by formal behaviour, that they are 'friends'. The 'friendship' involved is of a peculiar and precariously balanced kind: it is 'a relation neither of solidarity nor of hostility but of "friendship" in which the separateness of the groups is emphasized, but open conflict between the two groups or members on the two sides is avoided'. By way of example he refers to his own description of the Andamanese *aka-yat* relationship (Radcliffe-Brown 1933: 81) in which two individuals who scrupulously avoid one another constantly send each other presents. There seems an obvious parallel here with the Trobriand householder who avoids his married sister yet regularly sends her gifts.

Radcliffe-Brown further points out that the kind of ritual friendship which may characterize the behaviour of persons linked by ties of affinity is also frequently characteristic of the behaviour that is expected between members of alternating generations – e.g. between a grandparent and a grandchild – the fact that in some societies a man is expected to marry his 'classificatory granddaughter' exemplifies this similarity (Radcliffe-Brown 1952:79–80, 100).

Radcliffe-Brown's discussion is here not altogether convincing. Since he treats the relationship between grandparents and grandchildren as an example of joking relationship, one might infer that the friendship involved is one in which 'there is an appearance of antagonism, controlled by conventional rules' (1952: 112), yet elsewhere he has maintained that 'in many classificatory systems the terms for grandfather and grandmother are used...as implying a general attitude of friendliness, relatively free from restraint towards all persons to whom they are applied' (1952: 79).

This contradiction disappears if we say that 'friendliness' and 'hostility' are not, properly speaking, exclusive categories; as with the case of 'sacredness' and 'pollution', each is an aspect of 'the same thing'. Radcliffe-Brown's argument would have been more convincing if he had simply opposed 'relations of solidarity', which stem from economic co-operation and common economic interest, and 'relations of separateness', which link persons who are outside this co-operative corporation. His essential theme is that all relations of this latter kind have an ambivalent friendship/hostility content; they are always formally expressed by behaviours indicating 'friendship' but, in especially critical situations, an added element of taboo is present, superimposed on the friendliness. From this digression let us now return to the Trobriand Islands.

That the relationship which links groups of Trobriand affines in bonds of 'friendship' is of a precarious kind is plain enough. Malinowski himself describes the relationship between a man and his father's sister's son as one of 'predestined enmity' (Malinowski 1932: 13). This latent hostility becomes explicitly formalized in the mortuary rituals which follow the death of either the father's sister or her husband or that of either of the father's parents. On these occasions not only are the affinally linked subclans ritually opposed to one another in the clearest possible manner, but the affines of the deceased are very liable to be accused of murder by sorcery. 'It is characteristic of their idea of the bonds of marriage and fatherhood – which they regard as artificial and untrustworthy under any strain – that the principle suspicion of sorcery attaches always to the wife and children' (1932: 137).

The male Ego's own role in this situation is by no means clear cut. As a member of his mother's sub-clan, he is an affine of his father, and thus a kind of logical ally of his father's other affines, who come near to being his father's enemies. My thesis is, however, that the young child, resident in his father's house, is taught to accept a set of kinship categories which are appropriate to the structural situation of that household. In that situation the recipients of Ego's father's *urigubu* form a highly ambivalent category of kinsmen.

Enemies who must be treated as 'friends'; dangerous people who must be appeased by gift giving; this precisely is the context which, in Radcliffe-Brown's terminology, reflects a situation of taboo.

In Radcliffe-Brown's terms, the relationship which Malinowski describes as existing between the givers and receivers of *urigubu* is one of taboo. Consistent with this we find that a man's child is taught to class as *tabu* all the recipients of his father's *urigubu*. The category *tabu* includes:

(*a*) Ego's father's mother.

(*b*) Her husband and the other males of his sub-clan.

(*c*) Ego's father's sister.

(*d*) Her husband and the other males of her sub-clan.

(*e*) The daughters of (*a*) and (*d*).

Accordingly, instead of postulating, as Malinowski does, that the Trobrianders have several different words pronounced *tabu* I assume that they have only one such word and that its meaning approximates to Radcliffe-Brown's concept of taboo.

Malinowski tells us little of the prescribed behaviour that accompanies this verbal category, though it appears that, as Ego begins to grow up, he finds himself in an emphatic joking relationship with his father's sister (Malinowski 1932: 450). On my thesis, it is not to be expected that a male Ego will be required to behave in exactly the same way towards all his *tabu*. In Radcliffe-Brown's terminology 'joking relationship' or 'ritual friendship' includes not only violent and obscene horseplay between cross-cousins but also playful friendliness between grandparents and grandchildren. If then the Trobriand relationship *tabu* is likewise one of 'ritual friendship', there is room for variation.

What seems to happen is that while Ego (male) is still a child in his father's household his 'friendship' with the immediate recipients of his father's *urigubu* is critical enough to involve a relationship of the 'obscene joking' type. But as he grows older and begins to separate off from his father's household, the social distance between himself and these paternal *tabu* steadily increases. Such *tabu* are still 'formal friends' but the stereotype of behaviour now becomes one of playful friendliness rather than obscene horseplay. On this basis the father's sister's daughter is said to be an appropriate object for sexual liaison and ultimate marriage (1932: 295). I shall have more to say concerning this alleged 'preferred marriage' presently.

The young male Ego's *tabu* category is not confined to the recipients of his father's *urigubu*. It extends also to a number of relatives distinguished by their age seniority and their social remoteness from Ego. Thus *tabu* includes Ego's mother's parents. In contexts which are not rigidly formal it also includes classificatory father's mother's mother's brothers and their wives, and classificatory mother's mother's brothers and their wives.[2] Note that it is social distance rather than genealogical distance that matters here. While Ego is resident with his father, it is only the males of the father's sub-clan who are *three* generations senior to Ego who may rate as *tabu*; that is to say individuals who are already, socially speaking, 'almost dead'. In contrast, the males of Ego's own sub-clan who are only *two* generations senior to himself may rate as *tabu*; but of course by the time Ego himself becomes a householder in his own sub-clan hamlet these too will be very old men withdrawn from social life. In relation to Ego all these elderly *tabu* are merging into the other-world of the sacred and ancestral dead.

We can represent the whole system, as so far described, by a diagram (Figure 9.1). Ego at the centre is surrounded by a body of 'near kins-

men', his father's group (*tama*) and his own sub-clan group (*kada*). Beyond this 'circle of active kin relations' in all directions lie the *tabu*, the marginal kin who merge into the outer unknown of dangerous strangers and dangerous ancestral spirits.

The same argument is presented in Figure 9.2, which demonstrates even more clearly that the kinship categories express differences of locality and of age status rather than genealogical relationship.

In this figure the terms listed against leading letters *A–G* correspond to the age categories listed above. Ego (male), resident in his father's hamlet, is thought of as occupying a position at the bottom of col. 3. He classes all the members of his father's father's and father's sister's husband's hamlets as *tabu* except for a few young boys who are members of his own father's sub-clan.[3] He categorizes the members of his father's hamlet as in col. 3 and of his

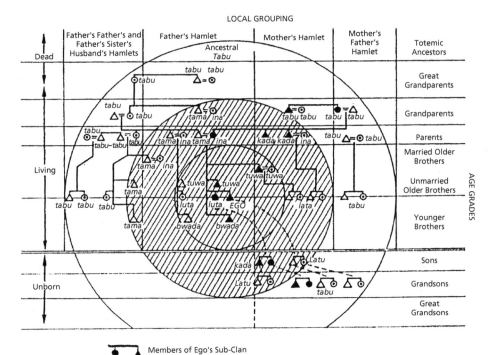

Figure 9.1

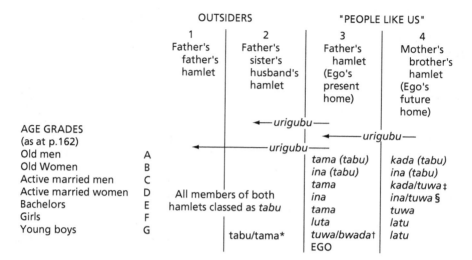

	OUTSIDERS		"PEOPLE LIKE US"	
	1 Father's father's hamlet	2 Father's sister's husband's hamlet	3 Father's hamlet (Ego's present home)	4 Mother's brother's hamlet (Ego's future home)

AGE GRADES (as at p.162)

Old men	A		tama (tabu)	kada (tabu)
Old Women	B		ina (tabu)	ina (tabu)
Active married men	C		tama	kada/tuwa‡
Active married women	D	All members of both	ina	ina/tuwa §
Bachelors	E	hamlets classed as tabu	tama	tuwa
Girls	F		luta	latu
Young boys	G		tama	latu
		tabu/tama*	tuwa/bwada†	latu
			EGO	

◄—urigubu— (between col 2 and col 3)
◄——urigubu— (between col 3 and col 4)
◄—urigubu— (between col 1/2 and col 3)

tama*   —boys of Ego's father's sub-clan.
bwada† —boys younger than Ego.
tuwa‡   —young married men of Ego's generation.
tuwa§   —wives of men classed as tuwa (Source Powell).

Figure 9.2

mother's hamlet as in col. 4 regardless of their sub-clan affiliation.

Although all the information contained in these diagrams is derived directly from the genealogically arranged table of kinship terms given by Malinowski himself (Malinowski 1932: 435), they suggest that the words involved have quite different 'primary meanings' from those given by Malinowski.

Tabu now appears as a general term, undifferentiated as to age or sex, comprising the whole broad category of potentially hostile 'outsiders'. The only individuals in the *urigubu*-receiving hamlets who are not categorized as *tabu* are the male *tama* who are domiciled in (and later residents of) Ego's father's hamlet.

Tama, as I have already suggested, is seen to refer to 'a domiciled male of my father's sub-clan hamlet' (see above and cf. Fortes 1953: 20).

Kada, tuwa, bwada are not here primarily 'mother's brother', 'elder brother', 'younger brother' but rather 'the domiciled males of my own sub-clan hamlet' categorized by age and generation. The use of *tuwa* and *bwada* for the wives of men previously classified by these terms is clearly an extension of the initial meaning.

Ina, which in Malinowski's analysis has the fundamental meaning 'mother', here becomes 'the wife of any senior male of either of my two home hamlets'.

Luta is not simply 'sister' but 'alien girls resident in my father's hamlet'. The phonemically very similar word *latu* represents a corresponding category, namely 'alien children resident in my own sub-clan hamlet'.

These last two terms need further discussion for they affect our understanding of incest and exogamy rules. For Malinowski the primary meaning of *luta* is 'own sister'; it is the fundamental incest category, 'the core of the *suvasova* taboo' (Malinowski 1932: 448). By 'extension' *luta* also comes to cover, first, a number of 'sub-clan sisters' who are regarded as real kinsmen (*veyola*) and to whom the *suvasova* taboo rigidly applies, and secondly, a much wider range of 'clan sisters' who are regarded as pseudo-kinsmen (*kakaveyola*) and to whom the *suvasova* taboo applies only in modified degree.

According to Malinowski, *marriage* with *luta* of all types is strictly prohibited but *sexual intercourse* with *luta* in the *kakaveyola* category, though 'prohibited by legal doctrine', 'is frequently practised, and is, so to speak, at a premium' (1932: 449). Unfortunately Malinowski entirely ignores the fact that most of the *luta* who are Ego's immediate next-door neighbours are not members of Ego's own sub-clan at all. This is true for example of the daughters of Ego's father born of wives other than Ego's own mother; and it is true also of most of the daughters of other males of Ego's father's sub-clan, all of whom are ordinarily resident close to Ego's own father. This is a very serious omission.

Malinowski makes a point of opposing the two categories *tabu* = 'lawful woman' and *luta* = 'prohibited woman' (1932: 423) but he couples this with a suggestion that *luta* are all 'clan sisters' and that it is the clan to which rules of exogamy and incest alike apply. But here he was surely either mistaken or misleading? The 'distant' *luta* with whom Ego is likely to be in most immediate contact, the girls with whom sex relations, though forbidden, are 'so to speak at a premium', are not his clan sisters scattered all over the island but the girls next door!

From Malinowski's elaborately detailed accounts of the amorous adventures of Trobriand childhood it appears that the sexual experiments of infancy and early adolescence are with local playmates. They are affairs which lack all seriousness. Now the most obvious playmates for a boy are the girls of his two home hamlets, the daughters of his *tama* and the daughters of his *kada*. It is surely striking that Ego rates the first as *luta* – 'classificatory sisters' and the second as *latu* – 'classificatory daughters'.

All members of the first of these categories fall, theoretically, under the incest prohibition (*suvasova*). Relations with the second category are not incestuous (*suvasova*) but they are nevertheless improper. According to Malinowski, marriage with such a girl 'is viewed with disfavour and happens only rarely'. The verbal similarity between the two terms perhaps reflects this similarity of valuations. Malinowski's statements, taken as a whole, imply that while a boy can safely have love affairs with any of his *latu* and most of his neighbouring *luta*, he can decently marry neither.

In contrast, serious love affairs of the kind likely to lead to marriage tend to be with girls of other hamlets, most of whom fall into the *tabu* category (Malinowski 1932: 295). Affairs of this latter type are described in section 6 of ch. IX of *The Sexual Life of Savages*. In some cases they evidently entail a substantial element of risk for the lovers and were formerly the occasion of para-military raiding parties, especially if the girls concerned lived outside the local village cluster.

In all, we are left with two equations:

(*a*) The girls of Ego's two home hamlets – classed like 'sisters' and 'daughters' – mostly fair game for a love affair, but not suitable for marriage – *luta* and *latu*.

(*b*) The girls outside Ego's two home hamlets – classed like 'potential enemies' – suitable for marriage – *tabu*.

This is a conclusion which would have satisfied Tylor (White 1948: 416; Tylor 1888: 267). It suggests quite a different picture from that given by Malinowski. In his interpretation, all pre-marital sex relations are to be regarded as trial preliminaries leading to marriage. For Malinowski the typical youthful love affair is with a *tabu*, the 'lawful woman'. Yet I feel he must be wrong. The structure that I have now presented has so many striking parallels in other societies (e.g. Fortes 1949 (*b*): 249; Evans-Pritchard 1951: 44–8), and it makes sense in so many different ways.

Malinowski's analysis rests on the assumption that the fundamental element in the total system is 'clan exogamy'; but Trobriand clans are shadowy amorphous things with no very obvious function. Why and how should such shadowy entities maintain their exogamy? In contrast, the membership of sub-clan hamlets is clear and corporate and economically highly significant. I find it very illuminating to realize that if a Trobriander keeps to the rules which Malinowski describes it is not merely Ego's clan that becomes exogamous; it is the total population of Ego's two home hamlets that is set apart as 'people like us' (see Figure 9.2).

Let me emphasize again that these 'hamlets' are not spatially separate entities immediately discernible on the ground. A single village may contain households of a number of different sub-clans and the members of these sub-clans inter-marry. But the hamlets are defined as entities by the rules of exogamy and the category distinctions of kinship terminology. I have already quoted Malinowski as saying 'this linguistic usage (with respect to *luta*) embodies therefore the rule of exogamy and to a large extent expresses the ideas underlying this'. I would now agree with this but it is the exogamy of local grouping that I am talking about whereas Malinowski thought only of the exogamy of clans.

As to how far the *luta* category – as I have now distinguished it – forms, in fact, an exogamous category, I have no information. That it is ideally considered to be such seems clearly apparent in Malinowski.

The distinction I have now made between casual premarital love affairs with *luta* and *latu*, and serious liaisons with *tabu*, is fully consistent with the kind of meaning I have already attributed to the word *tabu*. It eliminates a striking inconsistency in Malinowski's presentation which makes it appear that marriage, a contractual arrangement of the most serious economic consequences, is the legal outcome of love affairs of the utmost casualness.

In terms of my diagram *latu* are 'the children of the married males of Ego's own sub-clan'. A category of this type is to be expected in any 'Crow-type' system of kinship terminology. Malinowski translates it simply as 'child' (Malinowski 1932: 434–6).

As the Trobriand male child grows up he begins to separate himself off from his parents and for a while has a kind of dual residential status in both his home hamlets – that of his father and that of his mother's brother. During this phase there is little change in the way that Ego's kinsmen are categorized, but the significance of the different categories becomes modified. For example, in terms of Radcliffe-Brown's analysis which I outlined above, the relationship between Ego and his father which was formerly one of 'solidarity' now begins to assume the qualities of 'separateness' and ritual 'friendship', while, on the other hand, the relationship of Ego with the senior males of his own sub-clan, which has previously been one of 'friendship' and 'separateness' now changes to one of 'solidarity'.

It is symptomatic of this change of attitude that Ego who has previously referred to the householders of his own sub-clan hamlet collectively as *kada* (uncles) now begins to refer to the same collectively as *tuwa* (brothers) (Mr Powell's information).

At the same time Ego's father's affines (Ego's paternal *tabu*) move outside the field of Ego's *urigubu* system altogether, they now become remote relatives barely distinguishable from total strangers (*tomakava*). Meanwhile many of the elders of his own sub-clan hamlet will have died. These men, whom Ego referred to as *tabu* while he was living with his father, remain *tabu* even though they now exist only in the world of ancestral spirits.

When finally the Trobriand male Ego marries and settles down the *urigubu* institution assumes for him a new significance. Ego is now resident in his own sub-clan hamlet along with his mother's brother. He is receiving gifts from his wife's brother's hamlet and he is also linked in ties of friendly alliance with his wife's father's hamlet – which was his wife's original home. In turn he is giving gifts to his sister's husband and to his father in the latter's capacity as mother's husband.

At this phase in the boy's development the *urigubu* can no longer be considered as an isolated institution; it is closely enmeshed with the political relationships which bind a man to his chief; it is linked through the institutionalized payments called *youlo* and *takola* with the prestige-gaining activities of the *kula* exchange; it is part of 'a veritable tangle of obligations and duties' which are finally worked out only after the death of the *urigubu* recipients (Malinowski, 1935, I: 56, 190, 372, 406; 1932, 136; 1922: 64). It is Malinowski's thesis that the *urigubu* gifts which a man makes to the husbands of his mother and his sisters are adequately reciprocated by the various benefits, political and otherwise, which he receives in return. Malinowski does not make it very clear just why a Trobriander should have this evaluation, but we must accept the fact that it is so.

It is a symptom of this equality between givers and receivers of *urigubu* that at every phase Ego is, terminologically, in a reciprocal relationship with all the members of his *urigubu* system, other than his own father. As a child Ego classes the recipients of his father's *urigubu* as *tabu* and the givers of his father's *urigubu* as *kada*, both terms are used reciprocally. Now as an adult he uses the term *lubou* both for his sister's husband to whom he himself gives *urigubu* and for his wife's brother from whom he receives *urigubu*. The other males of the sister's husband's sub-clan who are also indirect beneficiaries of Ego's *urigubu* payments fall into the *yawa* category, which is again a reciprocal term.

Marriage establishes a *lubou* relationship between two men, namely the wife's brother and her husband. This relationship is expressed by the payment of *urigubu*. The same marriage puts the hamlets with which the two *lubou* are associated in a vaguer affinal relationship signified by the reciprocal use of the kinship category *yawa*.

The marriage of a male Ego and the marriage of his sister thus puts Ego in affinal relationship with the members of four hamlets – those of his wife's mother's brother, his wife's father, his sister's husband, and more vaguely his sister's husband's father. Nearly all these relatives are *yawa*.[4] The only exceptions are *lubou's* brothers who are also *lubou*; *lubou's* children who are *tabu*, unless they are members of Ego's own clan when they are *kada*; and Ego's wife's unmarried sisters, who are classed as if they were male siblings (*tuwa/bwada*). Marriage with these last is not incestuous (*suvasova*) but is strongly disapproved (Malinowski 1932: 449), presumably because such polygyny would place a double load of *urigubu* liability

on the one set of wives' brothers. Marriage with *kada* females is, of course, incestuous. Marriage with either *tabu* or *yawa* females is legitimate, though marriage with *tabu* is considered preferable.

Roughly speaking therefore the effect of marriage and its associated *urigubu* system is to create for Ego a new 'ring' of relatives which, in social distance, lie somewhere between the near kinsmen of the home groups and the distant marginal kinsmen classed as *tabu*. My Figure 9.3 shows this argument schematically.

As in Figure 9.1 Ego's total kinship system may still be thought of as a series of concentric circles centred about himself. But Ego is now located in the *kada/tuwa/bwada* group, while the *tama* are of declining significance. Indeed, by the time that both Ego's parents are dead the *tama* sub-clan will cease to be regarded as relatives at all.

Beyond the circle of these 'near kin', among whom Ego has residential status, are the affines (*lubou*, *yawa*), established as such by Ego's own marriage and the marriage of his sisters, and beyond them again are the marginal, socially remote, *tabu* relatives who lie outside Ego's personal system of *urigubu* transactions.

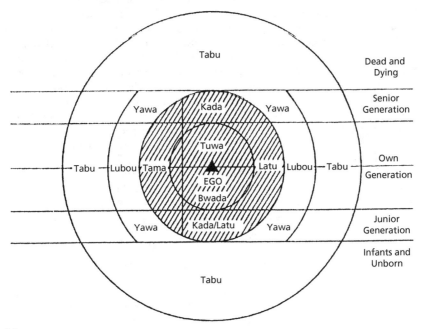

Figure 9.3

All the affines (*yawa* and *lubou*) are potentially hostile 'aliens' whose relationship is modified into a kind of treaty friendship by the fact of marriage and *urigubu* gift giving. It needs to be remembered that there is an avoidance relationship between a man and his sister, and though Malinowski is not very specific on the matter, it seems evident that the *lubou* relationship must be one of marked strain. So far as Ego is concerned, the relationship is based solely on the marriage bond and, if the marriage is terminated by death or divorce, the relationship is terminated also. Thereafter if the members of these affinal groups are categorized at all, they are rated simply as *tabu* or as 'total strangers' (*tomakava*) (Malinowski 1932: 4, 451; 1935, I: 192).

At this stage in the male Ego's development the members of his father's hamlet are also drifting away into a relationship of weak affinity, though here the relationship link is less fragile than in the case of *lubou*. Even after their mother's death, sons will continue to make *urigubu* payments to their father. On the latter's death the sons have important duties to perform in the mortuary ritual (Malinowski 1935, I: 192, 206). So long as either parent survives, a son cannot completely break off 'treaty relations' with his father's hamlet.

I must now make a somewhat lengthy digression to discuss Trobriand rules of preferred marriage. This is necessary not only because it has a bearing on the meaning of the term *tabu* but because it has been the subject of a good deal of unjustified theoretical speculation – as, for example, in Homans and Schneider (1955).

According to Malinowski, Trobrianders maintain a theoretical preference for marriage with the true father's sister's daughter. It is largely on the basis of this alleged preference that Malinowski bases his argument that *tabu* has the extended meaning 'lawful woman', for, in his view, this term refers primarily to the father's sister and her daughter who are, he says, 'the prototype' of the lawful woman (1932: 450).

The argument is unsatisfactory. Actual occurrences of patrilateral cross-cousin marriage seem to be rare and to be largely confined to the families of chiefs. Malinowski's only explanation of the rule is that it is a device whereby, in a matrilineal structure, a man, particularly a

chief, may ultimately transmit his hereditary rights to his own son's son. He has not, however, demonstrated that Trobrianders themselves think of father's sister's daughter marriage as a tortuous legal subterfuge of this kind.

Nevertheless Malinowski cites his Trobriand informants as saying: 'the true *tabu* is the proper wife for us' and he is most emphatic that this means marriage with the *actual* father's sister's daughter (1932: 81, 86, 451). What are we to make of this?

It is of course possible that Malinowski misunderstood his informants, and that they were merely maintaining that most actual marriages are between individuals who are in a *tabu* relationship of one kind or another. This of course is true enough. The rules of exogamy exclude women who are classed as *ina, luta, latu, tuwa, bwada, kada* and this only leaves *yawa* and *tabu* available. But let us consider what would be implied if Malinowski were correct in thinking that marriage with the first cousin *tabu* is preferred.

On the face of it, a marriage convention of this kind appears to be in direct conflict with the principles of *urigubu* gift giving. If normal residence behaviour is adhered to, patrilateral cross-cousin marriage will serve to cancel out the economic bond between Ego and his father's community. While Ego will be contributing *urigubu* to his father (*tama*), his father's sister's son (*tama*) will be contributing *urigubu* to Ego. Such direct reciprocity would make nonsense of the theme that *urigubu* payments represent, among other things, tribute from a political inferior to a political superior.

Moreover it is plain that direct reciprocity of this kind makes no sense to a Trobriander. When marriage with the true father's sister's daughter *does* occur, the residence pattern is abnormal. The husband, instead of taking his wife to live with him in his own sub-clan hamlet, acquires the right to settle in his wife's sub-clan hamlet and to farm his wife's land. In other words, he goes on living in his own father's village, and farms his father's land in company with his father's sister's sons (Malinowski 1932: 83, 86; 1935, I: 206, 354, 385). According to Malinowski this comes about through the personal affection of a father for his son.

It is quite evident that such behaviour is altogether exceptional. The only example that Malinowski cites is that of a chief's son. Further, he states that if an ordinary commoner were to encroach in this way upon his *tama's* territorial privileges he would 'both degrade himself and suffer disabilities' (1932: 83 n.), which perhaps means that he would receive no *urigubu* from his wife's brothers.

Malinowski (1932: 85) does give a genealogy which is said to display three patrilateral cross-cousin marriages within one short pedigree, but in point of fact only one of these is between first cousins. Moreover, although Malinowski omits to mention the fact, the same genealogy also displays two (classificatory) *matrilateral* cross-cousin marriages; the chart therefore gives little support to the view that marriage with the true father's sister's daughter is preferred.

The genealogy in question is indeed revealing, but for reasons other than those suggested by Malinowski. Since the Tabalu chiefs receive their 'tribute' in the form of *urigubu* payments from their wives' brothers, it is a matter of some political significance as to who receives the *urigubu* payments of the chief himself. About this Malinowski tells us very little, but the cross-cousin marriages in his chart all have the effect of making members of the Kwoynama sub-clan recipients of the chief's *urigubu*. Elsewhere we are told that 'this sub-clan is the very one from which a Tabalu chief ought to choose his principal wife' (1932: 113–14). In doing so, he evidently marries a classificatory mother's brother's daughter (*latu*) – a relationship which is nearly incestuous (1932: 87). The implication seems to be that, as an exception to the normal system, a practice of *bilateral* cross-cousin marriage operates between the Kwoynama and Tabalu aristocratic sub-clans which permits these two groups to exchange *urigubu* gifts without prejudice to the political status of either.[5]

The principle involved can be stated thus. Whoever marries the sister of the chief's heir is potentially in a structurally superior position, for the chief's heir must give him tribute. By marrying this girl to his own son and then insisting that the son stays where he is, the chief is not 'favouring his son', he is protecting the rights of his heir! The son pays *urigubu* to his father the chief.

The reverse case is mentioned in a rather vague way by Malinowski (1935, I: 362 f.). If a woman of high rank marries a man of lower rank, she may arrange for her son to marry the sister of her husband's heir. Again the son in question 'stays put' in his father's hamlet, instead of moving to his own. But in this case, unlike the first, he is able to transmit his irregularly acquired land rights to his own heirs – his sister's sons. This, according to Malinowski, is the mechanism whereby aristocratic sub-clans have been able to assert territorial claims in villages where they have no mythological roots.

On this analysis the preferred marriage with a father's sister's daughter, in so far as it exists, has nothing to do with the affection of fathers for their sons. It is simply a straightforward mechanism in the working of the political structure.

It is thus evident that, despite Malinowski, marriage with the 'true' *tabu* is exceptional. For anyone except the highest chiefs it is 'proper' (i.e. desirable) only in the sense that, if achieved, it permits the husband's sub-clan to encroach on the land rights of the wife. It is a status-climbing device. On the other hand the fact that Trobriand chiefs contract marriage alliances which would be more or less taboo for everyone else is strictly in accord with theoretical expectations (Radcliffe-Brown 1952: 138).

The system of terminology discussed above covers all the usage of a male Ego, for, as Ego grows older and acquires married children and grandchildren, the new relationships that are thereby set up are merely the reciprocals of those which Ego himself experienced as a youth. By the time that Ego and his sisters have married the various categories of relationship have received their final form.

Presented in this way the logic of the system is seen to be entirely simple and consistent. In contrast, when the terms are projected on to a genealogical diagram, as is done by Malinowski, the underlying logic is utterly incomprehensible. Anyone who doubts this opinion should compare the analysis given here with that given by Malinowski in *The Sexual Life of Savages*.

But while the term system is complete the diagrams cover the population of only eight particular sub-clan hamlets, namely:

(a) father's hamlet – male owners: *tama*,

(b) own hamlet – male owners: *kada, tuwa, bwada*,

(c) father's sister's husband's hamlet – male owners: *tabu*,

(d) father's father's hamlet – male owners: *tabu*,

(e) wife's brother's hamlet – male owners: *yawa, lubou*,

(f) wife's father's hamlet – male owners: *yawa*,

(g) sister's husband's hamlet – male owners: *yawa, lubou*,

(h) sister's husband's father's hamlet – male owners: *yawa*.

I suggest that this is in fact the initial range of effective kinship; it is the range of active *urigubu* transactions as they affect the individual Ego.

Just how far the various categories are 'extended' beyond this immediate operational context is not clear in Malinowski's writings. Evidently, in principle, all the terms applied to Ego's own sub-clan hamlet are applicable also to all other sub-clan hamlets of Ego's clan. Similarly the terms applied to the father's hamlet should apply also to all other hamlets of the father's clan and also to the hamlet of the mother's sister's husband and so on. But I suspect that much of this wider range of kinship is notional only. Where the category is in doubt the relationship is *tabu*.

Thus construed, the term *tabu*, as used by a male adult, becomes a category of purely marginal relationship. In Radcliffe-Brown's phrase (1952: 69) – 'it is used to mark off a marginal region between non-relatives and those close relatives towards whom specific duties and over whom specific rights are recognised'. It is a negative category (Malinowski 1935, II: 113). *Tabu* comprises all those numerous members of Ego's total society who are *not* in one way or another directly involved in the *urigubu* transactions of which Ego is either giver or receiver.

In terms of genealogy some *tabu* appear to be quite 'closely related' – e.g. the father's sister, the father's parents, the mother's parents. But in terms of structure these people are scarcely relatives at all. The households of which they are members are, socially speaking, remote from Ego; he has virtually no economic contact with them. Only the father's sister, with whom there is a formal joking relationship, is close enough to be regarded as in some respects a member of 'our group'.

Remote kinship is not only vague but ambiguous. According to Mr Powell: 'Kinship terms are used only in contexts where emphasis is on the formal aspects of kinship relations; in ordinary conversation personal names are used more frequently between, and of, persons of all ages and both sexes.' The occasions on which one would require to specify the precise kinship category of a distant clan relative must be rare. The uncertainty as to whether a distant clansman should be regarded as a clan relative (*kada, tuwa, bwada*), some sort of affine (*tama, yawa, lubou*), or scarcely a relative at all (*tabu*), is thus of no great consequence.

But this raises another issue which I mentioned at the beginning of this paper. Why do Trobrianders have a clan system at all? If, as seems to be the case, the operationally functional social groups are the sub-clans, what purpose do the clans serve, and why are there four of them?

In quite a different ethnographic context, that of the North Burma Kachins, I have pointed out that the assertion commonly made by Kachins that 'we have five clans' does not correspond to the empirical facts (Leach 1945). Nevertheless this assertion is a highly important schematic device. The Kachins need five distinct patrilineal categories if they are to explain to themselves the workings of their own society, and the fiction that there are only five clans altogether serves just this purpose. I suggest that in a comparable manner the Trobrianders need four categories to display the workings of their society, and that the four matriclans fulfil this purpose.

What happens in the Kachin case is that a Kachin will say *either* that the social world consists of five clans – Marip, Lahtaw, Lahpai, N'hkum, Maran *or* he will say that it consists of five major categories of kin: (i) *kahpu-kanau* (clan brothers), (ii) *mayu* (matrilateral affines), (iii) *dama* (patrilateral affines), (iv) *lawu* (classificatory grandchildren, 'those below'), (v) *lahta* (classificatory grandparents, 'those above').

Allowing for the fact that the Trobriands are matrilineal while the Kachins are patrilineal the corresponding categories in the Trobriand case would be (i) *kada, tuwa, bwada*, (ii) *tama*, (iii) *yawa/lubou*, (iv and v) *tabu*. Let me elaborate this.

On the analysis I have given in this paper it would appear that the individual Trobriand male is presented with a society which appears to consist of four distinct types of sub-clan hamlet. These are

A. People like us $\begin{cases} (a) \ \textit{tama} \ \text{hamlets} \\ (b) \ \textit{kada, tuwa, bwada} \\ \quad \text{hamlets} \end{cases}$

B. The others $\begin{cases} (c) \ \text{affines} : \textit{yawa, lubou} \\ \quad \text{hamlets} \\ (d) \ \text{marginal relatives and} \\ \quad \text{non-relatives} : \textit{tabu} \\ \quad \text{hamlets} \end{cases}$

From the individual Ego's point of view, this has the appearance of a moiety system. Ego should not seek a wife in (*a*) or (*b*); he should seek a wife in (*c*) or (*d*), especially perhaps in (*d*), since a marriage here will increase 'our' total range of kinship alliances. *Tabu* becomes the stereotype of a suitable wife simply because it is desirable in principle to reduce the number of *tabu* groups and convert them into *yawa*. Also, as I have indicated, a man who marries a *close tabu* may achieve a step up in the rank hierarchy.

Now these four categories of the total society are *not* unilineal descent groups. They are categories of hamlets distinguished according to the kind of people who are resident therein. Nevertheless I suggest that there is a functional connection between this fourfold categorization of Ego's kinship world and the fact that Trobrianders claim to have four clans.

The Trobriand myths of origin which form the basis of Trobriand rules of land tenure (Malinowski 1935, I: 342 f.) specify that the original sub-clan ancestors emerged from various holes in the ground appropriately situated in the midst of sub-clan territory. It is these myths which establish that the members of the sub-clan are the owners (*toli*) of the sub-clan hamlet and its associated lands. The Trobriand sub-clan is a dispersed unit which seldom actually assembles all in one place; the

sub-clan hamlet and its lands is on the other hand a permanent visible entity known to all. It is really an inversion of the facts to say that the continuing units in Trobriand social structure are the sub-clans and that the hamlets belong to the sub-clans. It is much closer to reality to say that the continuing units are the hamlets and that the sub-clan members belong to the hamlets by virtue of the emergence myths. How many kinds of sub-clan hamlet ought there to be in terms of Trobriand mythology?

The sub-clan emergence myths are mostly bald and perfunctory assertions of dogmatic fact, but they are supplemented by a much more elaborate story of the same type. 'Only one myth of first emergence is expanded into a long and dramatized story, and that is the myth of the first emergence of the four ancestors of the four main clans' (Malinowski 1935, I: 343). In this myth the four totemic animals of the four clans emerge one after another from a single hole (Malinowski 1932: 419 f.). Malinowski maintains that the function of this myth is to assert the superior rank status of the Tabalu sub-clan of the Malasi clan, but his argument is weak. To me it seems plain that this 'clan' emergence myth can only be understood if considered along with the 'sub-clan' emergence myths. In that context what the myth 'says' is that while people in general are indissolubly associated with particular domains – sub-clan members with their sub-clan hamlets – there are four distinct kinds of such people.

My thesis is then that the four Trobriand clans are not really to be thought of as four unique and separate lines of descent – Trobrianders indeed seem to have little interest in pedigree. The four clans are an 'expression', a kind of model, of the fact that the Trobriand individual finds himself in a world which contains, so far as he is concerned, four kinds of localized hamlets with their associated sub-clans. From the young male Ego's point of view there are four categories of land-owners – *tama, kada, yawa, tabu* – and they have four categories of daughters – *luta, latu, yawa, tabu*. This explains why the importance of the four clans seems to be constantly emphasized by the Trobrianders themselves, even though the clans scarcely exist as corporate groups and may at times be difficult to identify at all.

Conclusion

In this paper I have sought to demonstrate the advantage of approaching the analysis of a kinship terminology without any preconceived assumption that the 'primary meaning' of this or that particular word must necessarily be defined by genealogy. My general standpoint is that kinship terms are category words by means of which the individual is taught to recognize the significant groupings in the social structure into which he is born. Until we as anthropologists fully understand the nature of that social structure we can hardly hope to understand what the various category words 'mean'. Indeed the meaning of particular terms varies according to the age status of the individual within the total system.

From Malinowski's writings we can safely infer that, in Trobriand social structure, descent group affiliation and residential grouping have an almost equal importance. We can further infer that the *urigubu* payment is the primary and fundamental expression of the various relationships which result from this structure. Assuming this to be the case, I have examined the kinship term categories against the structural background. The result is what seems to me a perfect 'fit'. Where the genealogical analysis of Malinowski leads to a maze of 'anomalies' and to Malinowski's desperate expedient of the doctrine of homonyms, the present analysis displays no exceptions and can in fact be memorized in a few minutes. This consistency convinces me that the pattern I have given comes very near to the Trobrianders' own conception. Further confirmation is provided by the fit between the fourfold categories in the kinship system and the four clans. The supposed preference for patrilateral cross-cousin marriage has been demonstrated as an expression of the rules of exogamy which emerge from other elements in the structure. This much indeed Malinowski himself proclaimed, but where Malinowski argued that exogamy centred in the sub-clan and clan, I have suggested that it is based in the male Ego's dual residential status in the hamlets of his father and his mother's brother.

My further initial purpose was to demonstrate that there is an inherent consistency between all the various meanings of *tabu* which were listed at the beginning of this paper. This I claim to have done. In the context of kinship, *tabu* in all its senses is seen to refer to 'remote and potentially hostile relatives with whom Ego has no direct economic bonds but towards whom an attitude of "friendship" is expected'. It is a category of marginal relationship; it is filled with the 'dangers of the unknown' upon which Malinowski was prone to lay such stress. The category includes remote deceased ancestors and totemic spirits, and this links up the notion of 'sacred-forbidden' with that of 'distant-dangerous'.

Open hostility is not involved, *tabu* are related to one another only by intermediate links, there is no common economic interest which they are likely to fight about. But, for all that, *tabu* are dangerous people, people of power with whom you must be on good terms. It is significant that the only situations in which Malinowski mentions the *tabu* relationship as being ritually important are occasions when the *tabu* influence one another by magic (Malinowski 1932: 185 ff., 295 ff.). The magic in these cases happens to be beneficial, but a Trobriander would never forget that any magician may very easily become a sorcerer.

I hope then that I have disposed of the idea that the various meanings of *tabu* are accidental homonyms as unrelated as *pair* and *pear*.

Yet the puzzle remains. Why should Malinowski have been so keen to insist that the various meanings of the word are wholly unrelated? Why, when he himself laid such stress on the taboo between a man and his sister, should he repudiate the logic by which a boy regards his father's sister as *tabu*?

The answer seems to be that it was because he took over uncritically from his predecessors the bland assumption that the key to the understanding of any system of kinship terminology must always be sought in rules of preferred marriage.

This belief had been dogma for Rivers, and Malinowski regarded Rivers' anthropology as the very quintessence of everything that is wrong-headed and misdirected. Yet Malinowski's pronouncements regarding the term *tabu* seem to derive from the fact that Trobrianders told him that they ought to marry their *tabu*. How could it possibly be that the term which thus described the 'lawful woman' should also mean 'forbidden, dangerous, sacred'? The only possible explanation for Malinowski was that we are here dealing with two or more entirely different words. What he failed to notice was that when a man does marry a *tabu* relative either close or remote, she and her immediate kinsmen forthwith cease to be *tabu*, and come into the much more closely bonded categories of *lubou* and *yawa*. In other words, marriage is a device whereby the dangers of *tabu* are for the time being exorcized.

NOTES

1   Malinowski (1932: 52) translates *toboma* as 'tabooed man' from the general root *boma* ('sacred', 'taboo'). This fits well with the explanation of *tabu* given below.

2   Source Powell. In strict formality father's mother's mother's brothers are *tama*, mother's mother's brothers are *kada*. The informal use of *tabu* here seems to fit with the use of *toboma* for certain respected old men; cf. p. 126.

3   It is possible that some members of either of these two hamlets might be members of Ego's own sub-clan. In that case he would use *kada*, *ina*, *tuwa*, *bwada*, *luta* as appropriate in place of *tabu*.

4   Mr Powell has here corrected Malinowski. The term *ivata* which appears in Malinowski's lists is not used by males and I shall not discuss it. In Malinowski, *yawa* has the restricted meaning of parent-in-law.

5   The Kwoynama sub-clan itself possibly has a similar arrangement with their political inferiors of the Malasi clan in the village of Yalumugwa. Malinowski (1935, I: 389) shows the Kwoynama village headman Yovisi marrying off his sister Aykare'i to his own wife's brother who is a member of the inferior Malasi sub-clan in the same village as Yovisi himself.

Cf. also Seligman (1910: 718) where it is noted that *for chiefs only* the father, the children and the sisters' husbands fall into one ritual category; this would be a logical consequence of bilateral cross-cousin marriage.

REFERENCES CITED

Evans-Pritchard, E. E. 1951, *Kinship and Marriage among the Nuer*, Oxford.

Firth, R. (Editor) 1957, *Man and Culture*, London.

Fortes, M. 1949 (*a*), 'Time and Social Structure: An Ashanti Case Study' in Fortes, M. (ed.) *Social Structure*, Oxford.

——1949 (*b*), *The Web of Kinship among the Tallensi*, London.

——1953, 'The Structure of Unilineal Descent Groups', *American Anthropologist*, 55.

Gilbert, W. H. 1937, 'Eastern Cherokee Social Organization' in Eggan, F. (ed.) *Social Anthropology of North American Tribes*, Chicago.

Homans, G. C. and Schneider, D. M. 1955, *Marriage, Authority and Final Causes*, Glencoe, Illinois.

Leach, E. R. 1945, 'Jinghpaw Kinship Terminology', *J.R.A.I.*LXXV.

Malinowski, B. 1922, *Argonauts of the Western Pacific*, London.

——1932, *The Sexual Life of Savages* (3rd ed.), London.

——1935, *Coral Gardens and their Magic*, 2 vols. London.

Radcliffe-Brown, A. R. 1933, *The Andaman Islanders* (2nd ed.), London.

——1952, *Structure and Function in Primitive Society*, London.

Seligman, C. G. 1910, *The Melanesians of British New Guinea*, Cambridge.

Tax, Sol. 1937, 'Some Problems of Social Organization' in Eggan, F. (ed.) *Social Anthropology of North American Tribes*, Chicago.

Tylor, E. B. 1888, 'On a Method of Investigating the Development of Institutions: Applied to Laws of Marriage and Descent', *J.R.A.I.*LVIII.

White, L. A. 1948, 'The Definition and Prohibition of Incest', *American Anthropologist*, 50.

10

The Dravidian Kinship Terminology as an Expression of Marriage

Louis Dumont

This paper[1] springs from two sources. Field acquaintance with Dravidian kinship terminology made me feel very strongly its systematic, logical character; I could not help thinking that it centred in marriage, and that it should be possible to express those two features in a simple formula. But, in trying to do so, a considerable resistance from current anthropological ideas was experienced. Therefore a few general and critical remarks suggest themselves.

Preliminary

Its main features are well known: classification according to generations, distinction of sex, distinction of two kinds of relatives inside certain generations, distinction of age.

Since Morgan, who based his second or '*punaluan*' family on the Dravidian and the Seneca-Iroquois systems, this type of terminology, known as Seneca or Dakota-Iroquois type, and one of the most widely spread, has challenged anthropologists. Rivers, studying the Dravidian system, saw that its main feature was the distinction of parallel and cross cousins, and rightly connected some of its features with cross-cousin marriage, but, to account for it as a whole, he turned towards a hypothetical previous stage of dual organization. Less satisfactory descriptions, when

found in modern literature, witness to the difficulty scholars encounter in becoming familiar with this important and relatively simple terminology. As late as 1947 we find maintained the denomination of 'bifurcate merging' type introduced previously with the explanation: '...bifurcate, because paternal and maternal kin are distinguished, merging as far as there is a partial merging with the parents,' a definition obviously inaccurate and misleading, as the distinction is not between paternal and maternal sides, which are, on the contrary, treated exactly according to the same principle, as already made clear by Rivers. Even when the 'principle of the solidarity of the sibling group' is emphasized, we return to the same confusion, since the paternal aunt is assimilated with the father, the maternal uncle with the mother.[2]

All this would require an explanation, and some of what I believe to be the factors producing these misconceptions will be found below. But perhaps it may be said in general that the terminology was not considered for a moment in itself but in terms of other aspects of kinship, in fact related to but different from it; at the same time it was still felt as irrational and one hastened to explain without accurately describing. This is so true that when Kirchhoff, on the contrary, only wants to describe it, he comes close to the explanation. He states, in his type

D, that there is 'a common word for father and father's brother, but another word for mother's brother' (etc., in two columns).[3] Let us proceed from this point to some further observations. Here, in the father's generation, there are two kinds, and two kinds only, of male relatives. They are two *classes*, and we should not, because the father and the mother's brother respectively fall into these two classes, by stressing them in fact substitute the idea of a dyadic relationship for that of a class, as we do if we suppose, for example, 'mother's brother' to be the basic meaning, and the others to be extensions.[4] Moreover, the 'mother's brother' is also the 'father-in-law,' and the common assumption that the affinal meaning is here secondary, the cognatic meaning being primary, is based upon nothing but the common notion that one's kinship position necessarily precedes one's marriage, an idea quite out of place here, as only the analysis of the system can reveal the real meaning of the category. All these arbitrary assumptions arise from our own way of thinking, *unconsciously* superimposed upon the native way of thinking. We must, therefore, refuse to indulge them and keep before us the question: what is the principle of the opposition between those two classes of relatives exemplified by what we call father and mother's brother? Provided that we consider this opposition as standing in its own right and do not assume that the principle of the opposition lies in the relation with the Ego, and provided that we view it against the background of the whole system (see note 7 below), we can find some approach to the answer. Briefly, in this case the relationship between father and mother's brother is:

F   M's Br

and it is very likely that the principle of the opposition lies in that relationship. Possibly our preconceived ideas resist such a view, but should they not give way if the facts impose it? This relationship we shall call an alliance relationship, as the relationship arising between two male (or two female) persons and their siblings of the same sex, when a 'sister' (a 'brother') of one is married to the other:

or, more generally:

and

It expresses the fact that if marriage creates a relation between two persons of different sexes, it connects also their groups. As an equivalent formula I shall speak also of two men (or women) having an alliance relationship as male (or female) affines.

There is another way of expressing the same fact, which, although not altogether wrong, is I think less accurate, and the criticism of which will throw some more light on the anthropologist's unconscious resistance to the classificatory idea. It is possible to extend the distinction between parallel and cross cousins and to speak of parallel and cross relatives, the principle of the distinction being that 'there is, or there is not, a change of sex when passing from the direct line to the collateral line.' I followed this doctrine in a monographic study of kinship in a Tamil-speaking community.[5] But the whole passage, although tending to a synthetic view, is, I am afraid, obscure. Moreover, the formula is not satisfactory for two reasons: (*i*) in spite of the fact that the natives do, when tracing relationships, pass from one line to another, these are not among their basic categories and are not in the least expressed in their theory: (*ii*) the system has much to do with marriage, and this should appear more clearly, if possible, in its formula. In fact, it is the anthropologist alone who is responsible for the introduction of this unsatisfactory concept of a 'change of sex'; he does so because he wants to trace through a relative of the opposite sex a relationship which the native conceives – when he thinks classificatorily – in a different manner. For instance we introduce the mother as a link between Ego and his mother's brother, where in fact the latter is just opposed to the father. Two errors converge here: (*i*) the 'extension' tendency confuses a class with the actual mother's brother, (*ii*) the introduction of the latter's compounded, western, descriptive name brings in the mother, who is only relevant at this level as the link by which the relation between father and mother's brother comes into existence. If, however, we agree to consider the terms for the two sexes separately (as is normal in a system where the terms for females are distinct, and not mere feminine forms of the terms for males), and in a classificatory perspective, the difficulty vanishes.

After this lengthy but necessary discussion, we can now define the problem.

Limits and Nature of the Analysis

Since Morgan, it has been recognized that the terminological systems used by most of the communities speaking one of the four written Dravidian languages (round about 70 million people) are very much alike. What does this amount to, when each language uses different terms, when again in each language the actual list of terms differs slightly from one group to another, and when, moreover, only a few such lists are recorded from among the vast number of those which exist? Is it possible to abstract anything like a common terminological system? It is, thanks to the systematic character of a remarkably constant structure. And it will not be denied that the attempt will be logical rather than statistical. Not all groups conform to the perfect schema outlined below – for instance, some Tamil Brahmins alter the system considerably by the introduction of a number of individualizing terms, or Nayar at the present day do not distinguish between cousins (according to Mlle Biardeau) – but on the whole most lists can be said to centre in a common scheme, from which they differ slightly and individually. Both the Tamil lists and the published Kanarese examples illustrate it almost perfectly.[6]

The limits of the analysis will be drawn close to the vital nucleus of the system: I shall consider only the common classificatory features within a range of five generations.

One important point is that the nature of the task compels us to consider the distinctiveness of the terms denoting the classes, quite irrespective of their concrete linguistic form. This is fortunate, because it allows the analysis to develop at the basic level of the structure of the system, whereas such analyses usually become mixed up with linguistic considerations as well as with considerations of attitudes or institutions which belong to a different level of analysis and which are excluded here by the very

diversity of the background. The need to stress the cross-cousin marriage will appear the more striking as our analysis develops.

A brief explanation is needed of the expression used above: 'the distinctiveness of the terms denoting the classes.' The distinctiveness of the terms is the main matter, as they are used to distinguish (*i.e.* to oppose) classes. But conversely, linguistic differences which are not used to oppose classes are irrelevant here, and it is for this reason that I add the words 'denoting the classes.' For instance, different words applied to exactly the same relatives are irrelevant, or again secondary differences within a class (obtained by affixation, etc.) are irrelevant in so far as they do not alter its unity (because for instance the class word or root is kept in all). Again, linguistic resemblances may exist between terms of different classes, in so far as the classes are not in direct opposition. All such facts are of interest, and may even be found to be common to all our terminologies; but they do not form part of the basic structure. (Considerations of space preclude these points being developed and exemplified here as they should be.) Our situation is similar to that of the phoneticist: just as he retains among phonetic particularities only those which differentiate meanings, we here retain from linguistic particularities only those which differentiate relatives, and even (for the time being) the fundamental classes of relatives only.

The system as just defined classifies all relatives of five generations from grandfather to grandson into 16 classes by using 16 distinctive (sets of) terms. The generations are as a rule absolutely distinguished; there is no assimilation of relatives belonging to different generations. Additionally, Ego's generation is split into two by distinguishing relatives older and younger than Ego: this distinction of age will be treated as analogous to the distinction of generations. (The distinction of age in other generations, *e.g.* the father's, is marked, not by distinct terms, but by prefixed adjectives; hence it is not relevant here, as stated in our previous point). Some of the terms have a masculine and a feminine form, some have only one form, either masculine or feminine, and this is the rule wherever the central, critical distinction which follows is fully maintained. In each generation (or age) group, the relatives of the same sex are distinguished into two classes. In the chart (Figure 10.1), every class is designated by a letter, from *A* to *P*, and they are distributed symmetrically to stress the opposition.

Although, for the reader's convenience, I give the ordinary equivalents, we shall not rely upon them in the least, but on the contrary try to deduce the meaning of each class from its situation in the whole.

Some qualifications are necessary, as regards the value of the chart. Class *D* has a tendency to split among the Tamil groups that I studied, but the cleavage is never the same, and the two terms on which it is based are largely interchangeable, so that already in Tamil it is not possible to take it as a general feature. In the region *HILM* I had to choose between two variants, the other variant not applying distinction of age to this group. Both will be found equally consistent. For *N* and *O* this is the Tamil situation, while elsewhere the central distinction and the distinction of sex are more in evidence.

We now proceed to discover, or rather confirm, the nature of the principle of the central opposition, and thus define the fundamental meaning of each class (as distinct from its linguistic meaning; see above), and to try to understand the way in which the different distinctions are combined, and the range of their application.

Generation	△	○	○	△
grandfather		A (+ fem.A')		
father	B	C	D	E
Ego >Ego	F	G	H	I
Ego <Ego	J	K	L	M
son	N(+fem.N')		O[=k+N]*(+fem.O')	
grandson		P(+fem.P')		

* For instance in Tamil, where k probably means 'marriage'. The linguistic connexion between N and O is stressed here as an exception.

A are the 'grandfathers,' B the 'fathers,' C the 'mothers,' D the 'father's sisters' and 'mothers-in-law,' E the 'mother's brothers' and 'fathers-in-law,' F the 'brothers' older than Ego, J the younger, I and M, 'male cross cousins,' older and younger; G, K, 'sisters,' and H, L, 'female cross cousins' respectively older and younger; N the 'sons' (fem. for the 'daughters'); O the 'sons-in-laws' (fem. for the 'daughters-in-law').

Figure 10.1

Father's Generation

We have seen already that the alliance relationship defines the mother's brother by reference to the father. But the father himself is defined by reference to the Ego. Let us consider now the nature of the latter relation and both together. In doing so we should not forget that, although we have taken the particular, genealogical father as example, we are dealing in fact with the 'fathers' as a class. In the relation, or as I prefer to say, in the opposition, between Ego and Ego's father, there are two elements, one of which is common to them both, while the other differentiates them; the element which is common to both terms of the opposition I call the 'basis' of the opposition, the differentiating element I call the 'principle' of the opposition. The principle is clear: it is the distinction between two successive generations. But what is the basis, what is it that is common to Ego and Ego's father? Obviously, the answer lies in the context: what they have in common is opposed to what makes their relation (more precisely the father's relation) with the mother's brother, *i.e.* to the alliance (Figure 10.2).

Father and Ego are related by a link which excludes alliance, and which I propose to call 'kin link.' One qualification regarding sex must be added: whereas the 'fathers' and the 'mother's brothers' are respectively male sibling groups, the sex of Ego is irrelevant (the terms for father, etc., being the same irrespective of the sex of Ego). The two generations opposed to one another in the kin group are

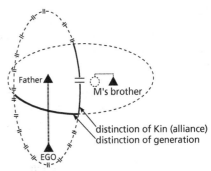

Figure 10.2

one generation of male siblings, and the generation of their children, both male and female. In other words, the distinction of sex, if it is the preliminary condition of the distinction of kin, is unrelated to the distinction of generation; this should be remembered.

If we now consider together the two oppositions between Ego, his father and his mother's brother, we see that Ego and the father are similar in kin and different in generation, while father and mother's brother are similar in generation and different in kin (*i.e.* are allied). Each of the two elements (generation and kin) serves under its negative (differentiating) form as principle of one opposition, and under its positive (uniting) form as the basis of the other.

The two concrete oppositions not only have one term in common (the father), but their concatenation is built upon two abstract oppositions operating crosswise: (*i*) community and difference in generation; (*ii*) community and difference in kin, *i.e.* kin and alliance. The latter, in which the category of alliance is brought to light by opposition to the kin category, is of paramount importance. Compared with Morgan's Malayan system, where the two categories are not distinguished, it emphasizes the importance of alliance, *i.e.* of marriage as a relation between groups. Moreover both ideas are given together, and spring from one another: no kin without alliance, no alliance without kin.

A few more remarks may be added. (*i*) We understand why there are no special terms (at the present level) for affines; the basic meaning of the terms for the 'cross' category is affinal – my mother's brother is essentially my father's affine. (*ii*) We have in fact taken the two oppositions as a way leading *from* Ego to the father and from the father to the mother's brother; are we then perhaps not entitled to speak of a structure *sensu stricto*? But here lies the characteristic of a kinship terminology as compared with other kinship groupings, that it is a constellation revolving around the Ego. The only difference from customary views on the subject lies in the way we have taken, not the way through the mother, as suggested by our own vocabulary, but, I believe, the native way, as imposed by the terminology. (*iii*) What is here called kin has, of course, nothing to do with actual groups, being only an abstraction arising from the oppos-

itions; this again centres in Ego, and is only a part of what the terminology suggests as such, because we had to abstract it on the male side; turning to female relatives, we shall find its feminine counterpart. The whole could be called 'terminological kin' to avoid confusion, and opposed to 'terminological affines'. This is only a framework which is used and shaped by each group according to its particular institutions.

In the same generation, we can deal exactly as above with the opposition between the 'mother' and the 'father's sister,' and connect it with the opposition between Ego and Ego's mother. We shall leave out the intermediary link, this time the father, as a mere agent bringing about (and hence contained in) the alliance relationship between the two women. The kin group arising here will be formed of a generation of female siblings, the mothers (opposed to their female affines), and of the generation of their children of both sexes. This kin category is not different from the preceding one; it is the same, opposed to alliance as above, though we take another view of it in accordance with the distinction of sexes in the system. In order to insist upon the classificatory character, we give here (Figure 10.3) a generalized schema; a similar one could, of course, be drawn for males.

Having ended the part of the demonstration which is most likely to arouse controversy, and before extending it to the other generations, we may pause here and get a first glimpse of the

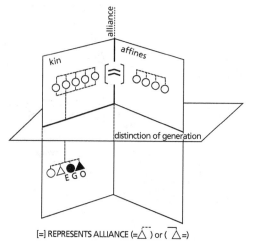

[=] REPRESENTS ALLIANCE (=△) or (△ =)

Figure 10.3

whole. There will be no difficulty, as one can imagine, in showing that Ego's 'cross cousins' are essentially Ego's affines, just as the 'mother's brother' proved to be essentially the father's affine. This means that the alliance which we considered horizontally in one generation acquires a new, a vertical dimension, and runs through generations.

Alliance As an Enduring Institution: Cross-Cousin Marriage

It is not another alliance, but one and the same relationship transmitted from one generation to the next, inherited; what we have considered up to now as an alliance relationship was only a horizontal section of it. And could it be opposed to kin if it did not transcend generations? It is this alliance as an enduring institution that is embedded in the terminology, that provides it with its fundamental and characteristic opposition.

But to say that an alliance relationship is inherited is the same as to say that a certain marriage regulation is observed. Theoretically, to maintain the relation, one marriage in each generation is enough, but the more marriages of that type occur, the firmer the alliance relationship will be. The most immediate and complete, the total formula for that is 'cross-cousin marriage' of any description. In fact, what we are accustomed to call cross-cousin marriage is nothing but the perfect formula for perpetuating the alliance relationship from one generation to the next and so making the alliance an enduring institution – a very particular and queer name for a fact of a very general and logical character. Indeed, it is only the anthropologist's customary and peculiar vocabulary, expressing alliance in terms of kin, which conceals this simple truth instead of revealing it.

Other Generations

How can we in our turn reproduce in other generations what we said in the father's generation? If the alliance relationship may be supposed to be similar, the generation relationship will be different.

In the grandfather's generation, cross-cousin marriage (or an equivalent) leads one to suppose an affinal link between Ego's two grandfathers, and this is the very reason why they cannot be distinguished, and why there is normally only one term for both of them, for both are kin in one way, and affines in another: mother as well as father is kin to the Ego, and so are their fathers, who have at the same time an alliance relationship, so that we may consider one of them A as kin, and the other B as affine, or, equally, B as kin and A as affine: the two categories merge in that generation and the distinction of kin does not apply to it. The same may be said about grandsons: alliance works as a principle of opposition for (two or) three generations only, whereas all relatives merge in the fifth and the first.[7]

There is no theoretical difficulty in Ego's son's generation, but rather a practical one: in Tamil at least, the alliance opposition weakens (the basis is emphasized by the use of the same word, with the addition of a prefix on one side, rather as with 'son' and 'son-in-law'), and at the same time the sex opposition disappears ('daughter' is the feminine of 'son'). This is consistent, but I can offer no structural explanation, although there is probably a common background.

In Ego's generation (males), something interesting happens if we try to apply the same procedure as in the father's generation: on one side the alliance opposition is present, the male affines being sister's husband and wife's brother as well as sons of the father's (male) affines and of the mother's (female) affines. On the other side, the generation opposition vanishes, as Ego and his brothers might be considered indifferently, but a new principle is invoked in order to replace as it were the waning principle, *i.e.* relative age is distinguished, and the generation is split into two halves under Ego's older brother and Ego's younger brother. The two distinctions (generation and age), one of which relieves the other, have a common background of age connotation and are closely connected.[8]

Now we can proceed with the elder brother as with the father: he is opposed to Ego, as older, and he is opposed to the 'cross cousin, older than Ego' as a sibling to an affine. The same for the younger brother, opposed to a 'younger cross cousin' (Figure 10.4*a*), but we here cross the generation axis of the structure, and the age order between Ego and his kin is inverted.

As previously stated, our chart gives for the affines here only one of the two variants actually found. The other variant presents no distinction of age among the affines and has only one term for males equivalent to *HL*. For this we can account very simply: in that variant, Ego's generation is taken as a whole, the male affine is opposed directly to Ego, and the age distinction, although introduced among brothers, does not replace structurally the generation distinction, and therefore is not extended to the affines (Figure 10.4*b*).

Moreover, it is in this part that the actual terminologies differ most from our chart. Several factors are at work, one of which is of a classificatory nature. It is a tendency to stress the relative sex of the person compared to the Ego, as is quite natural where prospective mates are found. This tendency combines in various ways with the elder–younger distinction, and the matter is still more complicated by other factors, so that it requires a special treatment.

In the preceding paragraph we have already anticipated the classification of female relatives, which should be extended from the mother's to the other generations. This is not necessary, as the structure is symmetrical (with the exception just mentioned).

Conclusion

I have shown, I hope, that the Dravidian kinship terminology, and with it other terminologies of the same type, can be considered in its broad features as springing from the combination in precise configurations of four

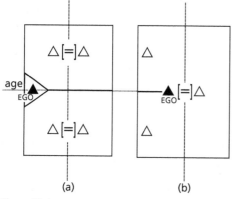

(a)   (b)

Figure 10.4

principles of opposition: distinction of generation (qualified as an ordered scale), distinction of sex, distinction of kin identical with alliance relationship, and distinction of age.

The third distinction (which alone is in no way biological) is the most important; the system embodies a sociological theory of marriage taken in the form of an institution following the generations, and supposes – as well as favours – the rule of marrying a cross cousin as a means of maintaining it. Hence also the fact, well preserved in Indian groups, that the two categories of kin and affines comprehend all relatives without any third category. This may be understood without resorting to dual organization; the opposition between kin and affines constitutes a whole – the affine of my affine is my brother – marriage is in a sense the whole of society, which it unites, and at the same time separates in two from the point of view of one Ego.[9]

No wonder, then, if India makes it the paramount ceremony, and perhaps it is also an explanation for the stability and vitality of the Dravidian terminology which has puzzled many anthropologists since Morgan.

A. R. Radcliffe-Brown's Response to Dumont's Article and Dumont's Reply

Dravidian Kinship Terminology.

I cannot claim that I understand the article on Dravidian kinship terminology by Mr. Dumont though I have read it carefully several times. I should like to be enlightened as to its meaning, and I suspect that there are others in the same position as myself.

As I understand it the fundamental point is the distinction between relations of kinship and what are called 'alliance relationships' which are described as 'the relationship arising between two male (or two female) persons and their siblings of the same sex when a "sister" (a "brother") of one is married to the other.' 'As an equivalent formula,' Mr. Dumont writes, 'I shall speak also of two men (or women) having an alliance relationship as male (or female) affines.' It appears that the relation between a father and son (or mother and son) is one of kinship and so is the relation between siblings.

But the relation of a man to his maternal uncle is described as an alliance or affinal relation, since he is the brother-in-law of the father. The 'mother's brother,' we are told, 'proves to be essentially the father's affine.' It appears similarly that the real relation of a father's sister to Ego is that she is in an 'alliance relationship' with Ego's mother, being her husband's sister. The mother's brother and the father's sister and their children the cross cousins are therefore not kin, but relatives by alliance or affines. 'There will be no difficulty in showing that Ego's "cross cousins" are essentially Ego's affines, just as the "mother's brother" proved to be essentially the father's affine.'

We are not told whether the father's brother and the mother's sister are to be regarded as kinsfolk. Presumably not, since the mother's sister is the wife's sister of the father and therefore an alliance relative. It is customary in English to speak of uncles and aunts as kinsfolk. But when the maternal uncle is referred to as 'mother's brother' this is described by Mr. Dumont as 'the anthropologist's customary and peculiar vocabulary expressing alliance in terms of kinship,' and so concealing the 'simple truth' that the real relationship is that the maternal uncle is the brother-in-law of the father.

When Mr. Dumont asks us to abandon our 'customary and peculiar vocabulary' and speak of the maternal uncle not as a brother of the mother but as a brother-in-law of the father he ought to give us some adequate reason for making the change and explain what will be the advantages. This he has not done. He is asking us to repudiate the idea of cognatic kinship by which persons are cognates if they are descended, through males or through females, from a common ancestor or ancestress. A mother's brother's son is just as much a cognate as a father's brother's son but is classified by Mr. Dumont as an 'affine.' Why?

Mr. Dumont speaks of the Dravidian kinship terminology as belonging to the 'Dacota–Iroquois' type. In my teaching on kinship for more than a quarter of a century I have indicated to students that we ought to recognize what I called the 'Australian–Dravidian' type of terminology existing in Australian tribes, in the Dravidian peoples and in some Melanesian societies. The characteristic feature of the type

is that there are no terms for relatives by marriage, or in the few instances in which such terms are found they are not classificatory but specific for the individual relationship. In the Kariera tribe of Western Australia a man is only permitted to marry a woman who is his *nuba*, the daughter of a man who is his *kaga* and a woman who is his *toa*. After the marriage his wife is still his *nuba* and her father and mother are still his *kaga* and *toa*. Just as he practised rigid avoidance of his *toa* (of any *toa*) before he married, he continues to avoid her after his marriage. The terms '*nuba*,' '*kaga*' and '*toa*,' which are applied to large numbers of persons, are not terms for relatives by marriage.

Mr. Dumont says that in speaking of uncles and aunts as brothers or sisters of the father and mother we *unconsciously* superimpose our own way of thinking upon the native way of thinking. The evident implication is that the Dravidian peoples think of the maternal uncle not as a brother of the mother but as the brother-in-law of the father. It is impossible to believe that this is true of the Nayars where one of the maternal uncles is the head of the *taravad*, exercising authority, and the father is, or formerly was, no more than the *sambandham* lover, or one of the lovers, of the mother. I can assure Mr. Dumont that amongst the Australian natives the maternal uncle is thought of as the brother of Ego's mother and not as the brother-in-law of the father. It is certainly true that my own maternal uncle is the brother-in-law of my father, and that some other man whom I call 'mother's brother' may be the husband of my father's sister. But in neither instance is he thought of as being 'essentially' a relative by marriage. In fact the Australian aborigines have no terms to indicate relatives by marriage, 'alliance' relatives or affines. Yet there is clearly a great similarity between Australian and Dravidian systems of kinship terminology.

A. R. RADCLIFFE-BROWN

Dravidian Kinship Terminology.

Professor Radcliffe-Brown has honoured me by criticizing at some length my article on 'Dravidian Kinship Terminology.' What can I say in its defence? In the first place

I dealt solely with a type of *terminology* common among *South Indian* castes. On this I feel that none of my distinguished critic's arguments has a direct bearing, as I considered neither kinship *behaviour*, nor *Australian* aborigines. When the assumption is renewed that Dravidian and Australian terminologies belong to the same type, I would ask that some attention be given to the difference I mentioned (note 7). The only Indian group which Professor Radcliffe-Brown refers to is the Nayar. They were not included by me (sources, note 6), and their terminology differs widely from the type studied (see K. Gough in *J. R. Anthrop. Inst.*, Vol. LXXXII, Part I (1952), pp. 82f.).

I attempted to show that the simplest way of accounting for the basic distinction between two kinds of relatives in the systems which I considered is to say that it is based on affinity, *e.g.* the father and the mother's brother are distinguished as being affines to one another. The extra-terminological (and therefore strictly speaking irrelevant) Nayar data adduced by Professor Radcliffe-Brown would not seem to go against this, but rather to accord with it: there, the mother's brother is a close relative, while the father on the contrary is 'no more than the *sambandham* lover...of the mother.' (Incidentally, *sam-bandham*, 'con-junction,' means in Sanskrit and in common South Indian usage 'marriage,' 'affinity.') True, the ordinary positions – which alone I mentioned – of father and mother's brother are here reversed, but the principle of the distinction stands, and this is the main matter.

Professor Radcliffe-Brown extends to kinship in general categories which I defined only on the terminological level: the system of kinship terms distinguishes two categories; the principle of the distinction lies in alliance (or affinal) relationship defined as 'the relationship arising between two male (or two female) persons...when a sister (a brother) of one is married to the other.' As against this relationship is defined a relationship excluding alliance, which is called arbitrarily 'kin' relationship. Then the *kinship* terms fall into two categories: 'terminological kin' and 'terminological affines' (p. 37, *in fine*). It is relatively easy to confuse the issue by disregarding

the definition of 'kin' and identifying 'kin' with kinship in general. Professor Radcliffe-Brown ironically asks in which category the mother's sister fits. The answer should be obvious, but, to clear up any doubts, she is present in fig. 3 of my text. He suggests that she might be considered as the father's affine. But this is clearly impossible, as they do not belong to the same sex, whereas affinity is considered only between persons of the same sex in the above definition, which was quoted by Professor Radcliffe-Brown himself a few lines earlier. Also, while I wrote of the 'anthropologist's customary and peculiar vocabulary' only in relation to cross-cousin marriage (p. 38), this is given by Professor Radcliffe-Brown as applying to the maternal uncle.

Is that all? Let us try to see where the disagreement actually lies. Two points seem important. First, Professor Radcliffe-Brown insists on knowing 'how the maternal uncle is thought of' by the people. This, I submit, is not a matter of terminology, but of behaviour. Two different approaches are contrasted here: in the first one, Professor Radcliffe-Brown takes the maternal uncle as the prototype of a whole class of relatives, and enquires into the concrete linguistic form of the term (*e.g.* 'male mother,' etc.), the way the people think of that particular relative, etc. In the other approach, we take the terminological system as a whole and try to determine from its structure what the content of each of its categories is. The latter method obviously implies that the system as a whole is logically consistent, and one might object to that assumption, if one were inclined to consider the kinship vocabulary as being merely a rough reflection of patterns of behaviour. But is this possible in a case where the assumption of consistency is verified? Here, there is some advantage in treating the two sexes separately. In English, it might perhaps be said that the aunt is a female uncle, etc. But it does not lead us very far unless we recognize that the difference between the father and the uncle, the mother and the aunt, the brother (or sister) and the cousin, the son (or daughter) and the nephew (or niece) is one and the same, and is the difference between the direct line and the collateral lines. Here is the main distinction, the axis of the system. Once we have acknowledged this, is not the question how an Englishman 'thinks of' his paternal aunt a different matter altogether? But, if the English system is logical, then is not the Dravidian type (my fig. 1) as logical as the English? If so, then what is the structural principle on which it is based? I may have been mistaken in its identification, but the task of seeking it is inescapable.

A second reason of disagreement lies in contrary assumptions about the importance of affinity. From the fact that in a given system 'there are no terms for relatives by marriage,' Professor Radcliffe-Brown seems to conclude that any affinal content is absent from the terms of that system. Limited as my experience is compared with his, I should conjecture on the contrary that in such a case many terms have an affinal content, which may be important even though unsuspected or understressed by the anthropologist. This is true already of the Kariera examples adduced: 'a man is only permitted to marry a woman who is his *nuba*..., after the marriage his wife is still his *nuba*...,' and then comes the startling conclusion: 'The terms *nuba* (etc.), which are applied to large numbers of persons, are not terms for relatives by marriage.' True, they are not *distinctive* terms but, precisely for that reason, is not the whole category of *nuba* tinged with affinity? Or should we say that the connexions of *nuba* with marriage referred to above are not part of the meaning of the term, on the level on which Professor Radcliffe-Brown considers it?

In general, Professor Radcliffe-Brown objects to widening the concept of affinity. He is satisfied with the current meaning of the word, *i.e.* with a common-sense category of our own society which has not undergone any transformation or adaptation before being applied to different societies, in particular to societies with positive marriage regulations. I submit that this is untenable. If there are prescribed or preferred mates, what does it mean, if not that affinity in a way precedes the actual marriage, that an individual has potential affines before he acquires actual in-laws by marriage, that affinity in a wider sense is inherited just as our 'blood' relationships are?

I can assure Professor Radcliffe-Brown that I have only tried to do justice to my field data by adapting my ideas to them. I do not for a moment equate terminology with the whole of kinship. Of the latter in some South Indian groups I would in fact claim that it is not possible to get a satisfactory picture without widening our notion of affinity. Whether or not, by doing so, I succeed in giving a relatively simple and well connected account, as he instructed us to do, Professor Radcliffe-Brown will judge from an article to be published.

LOUIS DUMONT

NOTES

1 I wish to express my thanks to Professor Evans-Pritchard for his discussion of this paper, and to D. Pocock, for his help in its preparation. The structural approach, although different, is largely influenced by Cl. Lévi-Strauss, 'L'Analyse structurale en linguistique et en anthropologie,' *Word*, New York, Vol. I, No. 2, August, 1945. For a structural approach to attitudes, see E. E. Evans-Pritchard, 'The Study of Kinship,' MAN, 1929, 148, and 1932, 7.

2 Lewis H. Morgan, *Ancient Society*, London, 1877, pp. 424–52; W. H. R. Rivers, *Kinship and Social Organization*, London, 1914, pp. 47–9, 73; see also 'The Marriage of Cross Cousins in India,' *J. R. As. Soc.*, 1907, pp. 611–40.
    'Bifurcate-merging': R. H. Lowie, 'A Note on Relationship Terminologies,' *Amer. Anthrop.*, 1928, pp. 265f.; *cf.* G. P. Murdock, 'Bifurcate-Merging, a Test of Five Theories,' *Amer. Anthrop.*, 1947, pp. 56–68.
    'Solidarity of the Sibling Group': A. R. Radcliffe-Brown, in *African Systems of Kinship and Marriage*, Introduction, p. 25.

3 P. Kirchhoff, 'Verwandtschaftsbezeichnungen u. Verwandtenheirat,' *Zeits. für Ethnol.*, Vol. LXIV (1932), pp. 41–72; *cf.* Lowie, Social Organization (1948), London, 1950, p. 63.

4 For a strong protest against this kind of 'extension' see A. M. Hocart, 'Kinship Systems,' *Anthropos*, Vol. XXXII (1937), pp. 545–51 (reprinted in *The Life-giving Myth*, London (Methuen), 1952, p. 173).

5 Formula from Cl. Lévi-Strauss, *Les Structures Élémentaires de la Parenté*, Paris (P.U.F.), 1949, p. 165. I hope that my emphasis on marriage will be found in keeping with the

general inspiration of that work. L. Dumont, 'Kinship and Alliance among the Pramalai Kallar,' *Eastern Anthrop*. Lucknow, Vol. IV, No. 1., Sept.–Nov. (1950–1), pp. 1–26 (but with many misprints); see pp. 5–12 as a first attempt in the present direction.

6   Most complete are Morgan's lists (*Systems*, pp. 518f.) for Tamil, Telugu and Kanarese. References to recent monographs in Dumont, *loc. cit*. (not restricted to written languages, but see for Kanarese Srinivas, *Marriage* ..., for Malayalam Aiyappan, *Nayadis* ... and *Iravas* ...). Lists of 'common' terms, unspecified and unlocalized, are found in grammars, etc. I have taken here into account lists from several groups in Tamil, to be published.

7   This feature is fundamental, and our analysis rests largely upon it. The whole structure is different when grandson and grandfather are identified, as in Kariera (with two terms for each).

8   The close connexion between age and generation in the structure may constitute the basis of an important exception to the generation principle, rather of a diachronic nature, as stressed by Mrs. I. Karve in a study to be published (oral communication).

9   This does not happen always, but only when certain conditions are present.

11

Prescription, Preference and Practice: Marriage Patterns among the Kondaiyankottai Maravar of South India

Anthony Good

The *koṇḍaiyaṅkōṭṭai maṟavar*[1] of Tamil Nadu, south India, form a large and historically-celebrated sub-caste known to anthropologists mainly for their system of exogamous, matrilineal *kiḷai*. In this article, their marriage system is examined in all its aspects, giving due weight to every level of data. This approach makes it possible to bypass to some extent the controversies which bedevil the study of kinship and which arise in large part because one level or other is accorded analytical primacy.

A three-level model of social reality proposed for heuristic purposes by Needham (1972) is adopted here. This model was developed in the course of studies into prescriptive systems of kinship and marriage (cf. Needham 1967), but is in principle generally applicable. Briefly, it discriminates the following analytically separable levels of data, the glosses for which are my own.

(1) The *statistical-behavioural*, which comprises the aggregate consequences of the behaviour of individual members of the society or group in question. In the particular case of kinship, this level is exemplified by demographic, marital, residential and other observed patterns.

(2) The *jural*, comprising the normative, legal, moral, religious and analytical statements of the society's members. Needham likens such phenomena to what Leach (1964: 285) has called the 'as-if' descriptions contained in indigenous social theory. The common characteristic of jural data is that they refer to ideals held by the studied people themselves and made explicit by them, though not always verbally or in the form which the ethnographer would himself choose. For example, statements of marriage preference belong to this level.

(3) The *categorical*, made up of modes of classification and systems of nomenclature. Kin terminology is perhaps the archetypical example of data at this level. Moreover Needham (1972) has shown that the phenomenon known to anthropologists as prescription is categorical in character and not, as Lévi-Strauss (1969) would have it, jural.[2] Categorical data may perhaps be said to differ from jural phenomena by being implicit. That is, they are taken for granted by the members of society and do not seem to them to require the kinds of explanation, justification and idealisation commonly associated with jural statements.

There are, then, three different levels at which marriageability can be studied. The analyst may choose to examine the prescriptions (if any), preferences or practices of that group. In the past, one of these has indeed tended to be emphasised to the comparative exclusion of the others. It is because kinship can be looked at in these very different and at first sight incompatible ways that we have witnessed such controversy among kinship theorists ever since the original appearance in 1949 of Lévi-Strauss's *Elementary structures of kinship* (see also Barnes 1980: 302).

Some, such as Needham himself (1962; 1967), have emphasised the categorical level. Others, such as Schneider (1965; 1968), have concentrated upon jural or, in the current phrase, ethnosociological data. Finally, there are those – perhaps more appealing to the kind of practical 'common sense' which views terminology, and indeed the whole of ideology whether categorical or jural,[3] as epiphenomenal to the 'hard facts' – who content themselves with recording and reporting kinship behaviour (cf. the village monographs included in the 1961 Census of India).

Yet there is nothing to cause one to believe *a priori* that the content of any one of these levels is necessarily fully determined by or completely *congruent* with the content of any other, as Needham (1967; 1972) has clearly demonstrated. Indeed, there is clear evidence of incongruence in the case of marriageability in south India. On the other hand, it could plausibly be argued that the various levels of data must be *consistent* with one another, at least to the extent that direct *contradiction* is avoided. The central theme of the present article is the examination of the nature and extent of congruence and consistency in the marriage behaviour of one particular south Indian sub-caste. The levels defined here are seen as constituting different aspects of the same social facts, rather than as a taxonomy of ideal types of such facts (cf. Khare 1977: 107). This perspective enables us to clarify the fact that such incongruences and inconsistencies as do occur are indeed present in the data and not merely consequences of the analytic model.

As for the collection of different kinds of data, the various techniques available for recording kin terms, while easy to carry out, prove on comparison to yield data of fundamentally different kinds. Asking abstract questions ('What term do you use for your MBW?', for instance) provides information about the kinds of 'terminological identity' usually regarded as relevant to a determination of the terminological structure *per se*. However, the standard 'genealogical method' (R.A.I. 1951: 52–5) confuses this type of identity with purely contingent 'genealogical identities'. The results obtained by the two methods are not necessarily directly comparable therefore, particularly when 'oblique' marriages with such personages as the eZDy are involved.[4] One reason for choosing the K.K. Maravar as the subject of this article is that such difficulties do not arise, as will become clear.

There is no problem over compiling statistical–behavioural information on such matters as the empirical frequencies of certain types of genealogically close inter marriage, age differences between spouses, the extent of the geographical area from within which these spouses are selected, and so on. At the level of jural rules and preferences things are not as clear-cut though, for it is never known in advance what particular cultural forms such rules may take (Needham 1972: 172–3). There can therefore be no generalisable techniques for collecting such information.

Far from jural data being the most amenable, because they 'mediate in a cognitive sense between actual networks of relationships and unconscious structures of thought' (David 1977: 220),[5] they are in fact the least reliable and most problematic of the three types: least reliable, because of methodological problems in their collecting; most problematic, because it is hard to estimate their explanatory status. Yet jural information was the stock-in-trade of early anthropologists (and in different form, more concerned with exegetical than regulatory indigenous statements, is enjoying a present resurgence in the guise of 'cognitive' or 'ethnosociological' anthropology).

It was on the basis of such jural data, and with a consequent over-emphasis on formalisation, rigidity and (often purely imaginary) cultural elaboration, that the descriptive and typological classification of the world's kinship systems was first carried out. It is to this period of anthropological endeavour in the nineteenth and early twentieth centuries that we owe the term 'Dravidian' as the title of one particular ideal-typical configuration of kinship and marriage (Morgan 1871). The paradox inherent in such typologies is that it is now necessary to question whether many Dravidian-speaking peoples do in fact possess 'Dravidian kinship systems' after all (Good 1981). A second reason for selecting the caste-group dealt with here is that for them the question can be answered in the affirmative.

This article is concerned with prescription, preference and practice in the marriage system of the Kondaiyankottai Maravar of south India. After a brief introduction to the local context, it deals successively with the categorical, jural and behavioural aspects of their marriage behaviour. Finally the interrelationships among these three levels are discussed.

The Ethnographic Context

Fieldwork was carried out in 1976–7, in two villages of the Kovilpatti Taluk, Tirunelveli District, Tamil Nadu. The populations of *terku vaṇḍāṉam* (henceforth TV) and *kaliṅkapaṭṭi* (KP), enumerated in more detail elsewhere (Good 1978a; 1981), are 816 (161 households) and 300 (62 households). Both contain a number of sub-castes (14 in TV, 10 in KP). The Kondaiyankottai (K.K.) Maravar is the largest group in TV (284; 54 households) and the second largest in KP (49; 12 households).

The economies of both villages are almost entirely agricultural, and so the main determinant of wealth is land; on this score the K.K. Maravar as a group are about average. There are a few wealthy households, however, including those of the Panchayat President – an elected official of the modern state – and the KP *talaiyāri*, a traditional policeman who now assists the Revenue Department and draws a government salary. It is still broadly true that the latter office is inherited patrilineally, though this is no longer automatic, and it is usual in this area for the Talaiyari to be a Maravar. This is consistent with the caste's other traditional roles: like the Pramalai Kallar (Dumont 1957b), they installed themselves in villages as paid watchmen (*kāvalkār*), in order to guard against the depredations of their caste-fellows, the watchmen from elsewhere (Pate 1917: 330–9; Rajayyan 1974: 30–2; Reiniche 1978: 139).

Terminological Prescription among the K.K. Maravar

The structure of the K.K. Maravar kinship terminology corresponds almost exactly to the 'Dravidian' ideal type. Such systems are conventionally said to involve 'cross-cousin' marriage in that, among other possibilities and prohibitions, the MBD and FZD are permitted spouses for a male ego whereas the FBD and MZD (the 'parallel cousins') are forbidden. This description is inadequate, at least in the present case. First, a man cannot marry *any* 'cross-cousin', but only one who is in a terminological sense his junior. Secondly, the permitted – or more accurately, prescribed – spouse is not a first, second or even n-th cross-cousin in any genealogical sense, but rather any person standing in that terminological category, relative to ego, to which these cross-cousins belong.

The kin terms used by the K.K. Maravar were obtained in the two ways already mentioned. Most local caste-groups practise elder sister's daughter marriage, as we shall see, and for them the two methods yield different results because of the empirical mixture of intra- and inter-level marriages. For the K. K. Maravar, however, all marriages occur between persons in the same terminological level as one another, with the result that the two methods yield identical answers.

Table 11.1 displays the resulting terminology. The various kin terms, and the levels to which they belong, are listed together with some of the close genealogical referents to which they are applied. In connexion with the latter, it must be re-emphasised that one or other of terms 1–28 applies, in principle, to every member of the sub-caste, whether the exact genealogical connexion to ego is known or not. It should most definitely *not* be concluded that the listed denotata are in any sense the 'real' or 'most essential' meanings of the corresponding kin terms.

Another point merits immediate clarification. When advocating the three-level model outlined earlier, I have often been confronted with the objection that the categorical level has no independent existence: table 1 may be adduced as evidence of the fact that categories (here the kin terms) cannot be either collected

Table 11.1 *The kinship terminology of the Kondaiyankottai Maravar.*

Kinship term	Genealogical referents	Level
1. *tāttā*	FF, MF, FFB, MFB, FMB, MMB	+2
2. *pāṭṭi, ācci*	FM, MM, FFZ, MFZ, FMZ, MMZ	+2
3. *ayyā, appā*	F	+1
4. *periyappā*	FeB, MZH (older than F)	+1
5. *sittappā*	FyB, MZH (younger than F)	+1
6. *attā, ammāḷ*	M	+1
7. *periyammāḷ*	MeZ, FeBW	+1
8. *siṉṉammāḷ, sitti*	MyZ, FyBW	+1
9. *mamaṉ*	MB, FZH, WF, HF	+1
10. *attai*	FZ, MBW, WM, HM	+1
11. *māmiyār*	HM	+1
12. *aṉṉaṉ*	eB, FBSe, MZSe	+0
13. *akkāḷ*	eZ, FBDe, MZDe	+0
14. *tampi*	yB, FBSy, MZSy	−0
15. *taṅkacci, taṅkai*	yZ, FBDy, MZDy	−0
16. *attāṉ*	MBSe, FZSe, WeBe, HeB, eZH	+0
17. *madiṉi*	MBDe, FZDe, WeZe, HeZ, eBW	+0
18. *maittuṉār, macciṉaṉ, māppiḷḷai*	MBSy$_{ms}$, FZSy$_{ms}$, WeBy, WyB, yZH$_{ms}$	−0
19. *koḷundaṉ*	MBSy$_{ws}$, FZSy$_{ws}$, HyB, yZHy$_{ws}$	−0
20. *ḵoḷundiyāḷ*	MBDy$_{ms}$, FZDy$_{ms}$, WeZy, WyZ, yBW$_{ms}$	−0
21. *sammanti, nāttiṉār*	MBDy$_{ws}$, FZDy$_{ws}$, HyZ, yBW$_{ws}$	−0
22. *sammantakkāraṉ*	DHF, DHM, SWF, SWM	± 0
23. *makaṉ*	S, BS$_{ms}$, ZS$_{ws}$, HBS, WZS	−1
24. *makaḷ*	D, BD$_{ms}$, ZD$_{ws}$, HBD, WZD	−1
25. *marumakaṉ*	BS$_{ws}$, ZS$_{ms}$, WBS, HZS, DH	−1
26. *marumakaḷ*	BD$_{ws}$, ZD$_{ms}$, WBS, HZD, SW	−1
27. *pēraṉ*	SS, DS, BSS, ZSS, BDS, ZDS	−2
28. *pētti*	SD, DD, BSD, ZSD, BDD, ZDD	−2

or considered separately from behavioural data (their genealogical denotata). This objection may be rebutted, at least partially. The genealogical denotata are included in the table because anthropological analyses of kin terminologies have always been conducted in these terms and because they provide a nonspeaker of the language with a means of access into what is really a self-contained categorical system with its own internal structure, independent of any *particular* genealogical or any other kind of behavioural usage.

For example, kin terms stand in fixed structural relationships to one another, relationships which exist independently of their various genealogical denotata. The simplest such relationship is that of reciprocity. The so-called 'principle of reciprocal sets' has been claimed as a more-or-less universal feature of kin terminologies (Goodenough 1967; Scheffler and Lounsbury 1971: 77). While empirical evidence does not support this suggestion, the principle does seem to be of fairly wide applicability, with the proviso that it is often precisely those points in a kin terminology at which it does not apply which are of greatest analytic interest and importance (Good 1978*b*).

According to the principle, kin terms may be arranged in sets, such that one set contains all possible reciprocals of one, and only one, other specified set, and vice versa. In the simplest case, for example, the English set 'husband' is the reciprocal of the set 'wife'. In the more complex set 'father' and 'mother', the reciprocal set is 'son' and 'daughter'. These and other more complex types of formal arrangement exist – and the point is clear in 'classificatory' terminologies such as that in table 11.1 – whatever the genealogical context in which the components of the sets are used.

There are, then, various relationships of reciprocity among the kin terms in that table, and while it is true that these relationships are detected in the first instance through behaviour, they exist independently of the particular behavioural context in which they are observed. With kin terms denoted by their assigned numbers, the reciprocal sets found in table 11.1 are as follows:

$$1, 2 \longleftrightarrow 27, 28$$
$$3, 4, 5, 6, 7, 8 \longleftrightarrow 23, 24$$
$$9, 10 \longleftrightarrow 25, 26$$
$$12, 13 \longleftrightarrow 14, 15$$
$$16 \longleftrightarrow 18, 20$$
$$17 \longleftrightarrow 19, 21$$
$$22 \longleftrightarrow 22$$

If it is known what term ego uses to any given alter, it is also known, if the sex of ego is specified, what term will be used in return. In this case, with the partial exception of term 11, an honorific modification of term 9 used only in certain contexts, there is full adherence to the 'principle of reciprocal sets'. This reflects the perfect symmetry characteristic of the ideal 'Dravidian' model, and does not apply to any other caste-groups in TV or KP because of their practice of eZDy marriage.

These are not the only formal relationships which exist, however. Tamils themselves work out terminological usages, when these are not already known, using a set of simple mnemonics which express relations of a second-order kind. If ego knows what term to use for alter A, and also knows what term A uses for alter B, he can easily work out what term he himself should use for B. These are 'extension rules', but not of the type envisaged by componential analysts (Scheffler 1977) since they do not base themselves upon primary genealogical referents. For example, on being questioned about a given person, a woman[6] might say: 'taṅkacci makaḷ,makaḷ'. This means, less cryptically, 'my taṅkacci calls this person "makaḷ", so I too should call her makaḷ'. To translate this as 'my yZ calls her D, therefore I call her yZD$_{ws}$', would be to miss the point. If it really were the yZD to whom the question referred, ego would know the answer already and would not need such a tautologous aide-mémoire in order to work it out. The crux is that the mnemonic is

true of *all* behavioural contexts, because the relationship it expresses is a formal one inherent in the logic of the system of categories.

It is clear that there are formal, structural relationships in the kin terminology which do not derive from particular, behavioural uses to which that terminology may be put. That being so, it is necessary to portray this structure in a way which does not – and does not even appear to – tie it to any behavioural situation. For this reason, the structure should not be represented by means of a pseudo-genealogical diagram. This issue is taken up in the final section below.

An alternative and much more satisfactory mode of portrayal was selected by Dumont for his classic exposition of the formal structure of Dravidian terminology (1953). I re-examine his arguments at length elsewhere (Good 1981) and merely display them here in a briefer and rather different way.

A 'classificatory' kin terminology may be thought of as a structured set of zones or regions which together make up the entire semantic space around an ego, corresponding to the category 'sub-caste'. Every member of ego's subcaste is classifiable into one or other of these zones, at least in principle. Moreover, every zone is labelled with its own distinctive kinship term. The problem is to determine the principles upon which this division of semantic space is based. This is precisely what Dumont set out to do, and it transpired that there were four such principles. By applying these one after another to the overall semantic territory, it is possible to generate the structure depicted by Dumont. The various stages involved are illustrated in fig. 11.1.

The first structural principle, dividing the members of the sub-caste into (in theory equal) halves relative to ego, is the distinction between parallel and cross relatives. This divides the semantic space into the two parts shown in diagram 1(a). Dumont, it should be noted, rejects the terms 'parallel' and 'cross' on the grounds that they refer to an analytic distinction made by the anthropologist which is not conceptualised in this way by the people themselves. He prefers to label these two semantic zones 'consanguines' and 'affines' respectively. In my view, it is precisely the neutral character of the terms 'parallel' and 'cross' which makes their use desirable. Terms

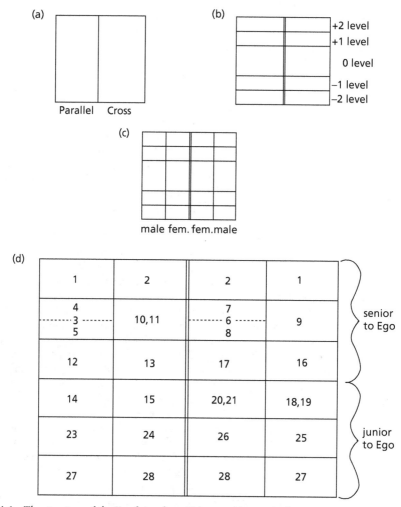

Figure 11.1 *The structure of the Kondaiyankottai Maravar kin terminology.*

such as 'consanguine', if taken literally, can only be applied in the light of information on indigenous theories of 'blood' and the nature of affinity, information which Dumont did not then possess.

The second distinction is that of classification by 'generation', to retain Dumont's phrase. As fig. 11.1(b) shows, the terminology typically distinguishes five generations: ego's own, the two preceding and the two following. The use of the term 'generation' seems unfortunate, especially in view of the complications introduced, for most other local groups, by eZDy marriage. Instead, in this categorical context, it seems preferable to speak of 'ter-

minological levels': the discussion will henceforth be phrased in these terms.

Thirdly, there is classification according to the sex of the referent (i.e. the alter). The effect of this distinguishing principle, which operates at every terminological level, is shown in fig. 11.1(c).

Finally, distinction on the basis of relative age has the effect of dividing ego's own level into two halves, one senior and the other junior relative to him or her. One slight complication arises here, because this principle also applies to parallel relatives in the terminological level immediately above that of ego, where age relative to ego's parents is taken into account.

The overall situation is depicted in fig. 11.1(d). The kin terms listed in table 11.1 are fitted into this diagram and it can be seen that the correspondence is almost exact. The figure also closely resembles that drawn by Dumont himself (1953), and the only significant discrepancy concerns the ± 2 levels, for which there are in each case four boxes but only two different kin terms. Dumont believed that, always and everywhere, there were only two terms in the +2 level. Subsequent ethnography (for example, Beck 1972: 228, 287) has cast doubt on this assumption. In TV the usual situation is that shown in table 11.1, where FF = MF and FM = MM, but there are four possible terms available and some older informants use them (cf. Good 1981). They seem to refer mainly to genealogical grandparents though, and are only rarely used in a classificatory sense. Nevertheless, that particular discrepancy between fig. 11.1(d) and table 11.1 is thus partially resolved. There is, however, no similar evidence for the −2 level.

The most significant point, for present purposes, to emerge from table 11.1 and fig. 11.1 is that the terminologically-prescribed category is *koḻundiyāḷ* (term 20) for a man and *attāṉ* (term 16) for a woman. That is, *a man has to marry a junior cross-relative of his own terminological level and a woman a senior cross-relative of her own level.*

The K.K. Maravar have another classificatory device to be taken into account, namely their celebrated system of exogamous, matrilineal *kiḻai* ('branches') and *kottu* ('bunches'). Fawcett (1903, quoted at length in Thurston & Rangachari 1909: V, 33) cites an 'authoritative' Tamil book, the *Maravar padal*, to the effect that there are eighteen 'septs' (Kilais) grouped three by three into six 'sub-tribes' (Kottus).

In TV and KP, all informants were able to name the Kilai to which they belonged: most could also state their F's Kilai. Few people knew even their own Kottu, however, although almost everyone was aware that such units existed. Awareness of an overall system such as that described by Fawcett was very limited: people tended to concur with his version when confronted with it, but only one man volunteered it spontaneously. He went even further, and introduced a further level of association which he had read about in a book, the *Kilai-*

vagaikottu, kept in the palace of the ex-Zamindar of nearby Kadampur, who was himself a K.K. Maravar. According to this man, the six Kottu are paired, forming three *pavaḷam* ('coral'). No other informants seemed to be aware of this. He named his own Pavalam as Seyavan (an epithet of the god Murugan), but did not know the names of the others. Kadhirvel (1977: 9) states that Maravar women wear coral necklaces called Pavalam after marriage, as well as a *tāli*, but this practice is not current in TV.

Rules and Preferences

Almost every local caste-group permits marriage not only with the 'cross-cousin' but with the eZDy and her more distant equivalents too. The occurrence of the latter form of marriage introduces an inevitable contradiction between preference and practice on the one hand, which involve inter-level marriage, and the prescriptive ideal-typical 'Dravidian' terminology on the other, which is predicated upon the absolute distinction of terminological levels, as shown above. It seems (Good 1981) that most local caste-groups avoid this contradiction by employing a system of categories *not* structured according to the Dravidian ideal type. For them, relative age becomes the sole criterion for classifying cross-relatives of given sex within the ± 1 and ± 0 levels. Moreover, purely contingent genealogical quirks lead to 'genealogical identities' which are not part of the structure itself.

Fortunately, these problems do not arise for the K.K. Maravar. In their case, eZDy marriage is automatically ruled out by the presence of the Kilai. These Kilai may be termed matrilineal descent groups, the term 'descent' being used here in the restricted sense proposed by Dumont (1957a). It refers only to transmission of membership in the exogamous group and not to succession and/or inheritance. In the present case, the K.K. Maravar practice is that both inheritance of land and succession to office obey the rules of *paramparai*, transfer from F to S or the nearest possible agnatic equivalent. Residence after marriage is ideally (and usually) patri-virilocal, so the Kilai are necessarily widely dispersed. They are, then, 'groups' only in the one context of exogamy.

Aiyappan (1934) and Lévi-Strauss (1969: 432–3) have noted that a system such as the K.K. Maravar possess is incompatible with ZD marriage because the MB and ZD belong to the same exogamous group. The K.K. Maravar themselves are quite explicit about this; indeed, it is the only reason they ever offer to explain their ban on such unions. Marriage with a 'classificatory' (i.e. terminological) 'sister's daughter' is not thereby necessarily ruled out, but no instances were observed.

According to Fawcett (1903), the Kottu is also exogamous. He cites a proverb which seems to indicate that even inter-Kottu marriage is subject to restrictions, and that the Kottus may be grouped into three exogamous pairs. This recalls the Pavalam mentioned in the previous section. My informants all agreed[7] that one should indeed marry into a different Kottu. The point was generally an academic one, given that they did not usually know to which Kottu they themselves belonged.

As is normal among south Indian castes, the K.K. Maravar have family deities (*kulateyvam*), which they inherit from their fathers. Such deities are specified by both name and place. For example, several K.K. Maravar families, including those of the Talaiyaris of TV and KP, have as their Kulateyvam the deity *terku vaṇḍānam kāḷasāmi*, that is, the god Kalasami whose temple lies in TV.[8] Altogether, seventeen different localised deities are named as Kulateyvams by the various K.K. Maravar men and women living in TV. Strictly speaking, a wife becomes a worshipper of her H's family deity after marriage, so it is really the H's and WF's deities which are in question here. Their shrines are located in widely-scattered parts of Tirunelveli and Ramanathapuram Districts, so their distribution corresponds more or less to that of the sub-caste itself. The statuses of these deities within the south Indian pantheon are those of 'hero' or 'guardian' (male deities) and 'smallpox goddess' (female). This is consistent with the general status and traditional occupation of the Maravar. The deity TV Kalasami, for example, is commander-in-chief of the god *aiyanār*, who watches over the village territory (Dumont 1970). Likewise, the Maravar Talaiyaris assist the traditional local law-enforcement officer, the *muṇsīp*. In TV, two K.K. Maravar named particular, localised

manifestations of Aiyanar as their Kulateyvams. Aiyanar's status is somewhat higher – see Beck (1970: 794) for a classification of types of family deity – but he is the leader of the 'heroes', so the choice is not inconsistent.

Couples who share the same family deity cannot marry. This is interpreted to mean that both the name and locality of the deity must be the same before marriage is ruled out. Given the patrilineal inheritance of these deities, the empirical situation is therefore that the K.K. Maravar have both matrilineal *and* patrilineal exogamous descent groups, and the cultural stress placed on the former should not blind us to this fact.

Rules of exogamy prohibit marriages between persons of certain groups or categories. Other types of jural regulation express preferences for particular – perhaps genealogically defined – marriage partners within the prescribed or preferred group or category. For example, almost every south Indian sub-caste picks out a single genealogical relative as the ideal, preferred partner. The two potential spouses thus inter-related are said to have an *urimai* ('claim') over each other, and the man refers to his female counterpart as his *urimaippeṉ*, *peṉ* meaning 'girl' and, in this context, 'bride'. In some parts of south India and Sri Lanka, a person must pay a fine or make a gift, the acceptance of which signifies consent, to his or her urimai partner should he or she marry someone else (Beck 1972: 243; Yalman 1963: 27). This is true of other groups of Maravar in Tirunelveli (Dumont 1957a: 18; 1963: 303), but there is no such expectation in TV. Despite this, there is a clearly stated preference among K. K. Maravar for the FZDy as urimai partner. They are in fact one of the few local groups who are all agreed as to the direction of their urimai preference. A similar patrilateral preference is stated by other Maravar sub-castes (Dumont 1963).

So much for formal rules determining the choice of spouse, whether positively or negatively, on the bases of genealogy or exogamy. We now consider briefly more practical rules governing the actual selection of marriage partners. Everyone agrees that there are no especially significant or enduring alliances with particular villages, nor with specific lineages or families of K.K. Maravar elsewhere. They state a vague preference for village exogamy. Nonetheless, they emphasise that the ideal spouse is someone to whom one is already closely related (*sondam*). In such a case, character and wealth are known quantities, marriage prestations are reduced and horoscopes are not required. Not surprisingly, then, isogamy is the norm. People say that 'class' (*vakuppu*)[9] and 'status' (*takuti*) should normally be the same, but that an educated groom of lower status is acceptable. It is not clear precisely what is understood by 'class' and 'status' locally, while the positive value put on education can only be hypothetical as far as the experience of almost every villager is concerned. It seems likely that these statements reflect an awareness of urban preferences which has been diffused through the press, radio and especially the cinema. Urban migration, which might present an opportunity to put such views into practice, is very rare among K.K. Maravar (cf. Dumont 1957*b*: 12 for similar comments on the Pramalai Kallar).

Attitudes to sister-exchange (*sakōtari parimarram*, 'sister transaction') vary within the caste-group. Strangely enough, the same factor is adduced by each school of thought in support of its own position. On one hand, people say that such close inter-relationships are good because serious disputes are thereby rendered less likely, while on the other it is argued that a dispute affecting one marriage would be likely to cause the breakdown of the other as well. In any case, the fact that such marriages are allowed, whether approved of or not, is further evidence of isogamy.

Polyandry does not occur. On the other hand, a man may[10] take a second wife if his first union is childless. There are, however, several instances in KP and TV of polygyny among K.K. Maravar in which the first wife had borne children prior to the second union. One is discussed in the next section: like most but not all cases, it involves sororal polygyny. The first wife's consent is required in every case. If the new wife is indeed the yZ of the first, the wedding may be greatly attenuated.

Divorce is permitted, and is known as *tīrttal* ('causing to be finished'). It may result from a personal or financial dispute between the spouses themselves or their respective families. Another common cause is the husband's pref-

erence for another woman – or the wife's for another man – in spite of which they had formally acquiesced in their parents' choice. I never observed divorce proceedings firsthand, but it is clear from what people said that the most important aspect is the return of the marriage prestations. Nor is this simply a question of a transaction between the divorcing couple alone. Instead, all prestations previously made by relatives on both sides must, as far as possible, be returned individually and exactly.

Divorced K.K. Maravar of either sex are permitted to remarry, as are widows and widowers, though usually a much less elaborate wedding rite will be involved on a second occasion. The rules *vis-à-vis* widowers are the same for all castes, but the K.K. Maravar are the only local caste-group to admit to allowing widows to marry again as a matter of principle – though by no means the only group to condone this in practice. They are also among the very few to permit divorce in principle.

Marriage Practice

Every Maravar adult in TV and KP was interviewed, and each person's genealogy obtained, together with information about their place of birth, date of birth, and the family deity, Kilai and Kottu affiliations of themselves and their parents. All locally resident K.K. Maravar could be linked together on a single genealogical diagram. Although only some five generations deep, this genealogy obviously has a tremendously wide horizontal spread. It contains information about all fifty-eight K.K. Maravar marriages for which at least one spouse is still alive and resident locally, as well as many others involving people elsewhere, or for which both spouses have died. Of these defunct or non-local unions, a further eighty-eight were included in the overall sample because enough was known about both the couple and their parents to be certain whether or not the spouses were first cousins.

Of the fifty-eight local unions, five (8.6 per cent.) were MBDy marriages and six (10.3 per cent.) were FZDy marriages. The corresponding figures for the entire sample of 144 were eighteen (12.5 per cent.) of each type. There is, then, no evidence of any behavioural bias towards the genealogical relative specified by the urimai rules. It is worth remarking that the overall figure of 25 per cent. for first cross-cousin marriages is remarkably high, both relatively in comparison with data from other places in the region (see the table in Beck 1972), and absolutely when demographic factors are taken into account. Since the groom must, given the nature of the terminological prescription, be senior to his bride, and since there is also a strong feeling against too large an age discrepancy between them, at least in the case of a man's first marriage, it is clear that by no means everyone has a suitable first cross-cousin available to marry even should they wish to do so. It is impossible to give exact figures in the absence of precise data on dates of marriage, but it seems safe to conclude that in most cases where a cross-cousin of appropriate age had been available, that person had indeed been married.

The Maravar are far from unique locally in having such a densely intertwined genealogy. The overall figures for TV and KP, taking every caste-group into account, reveal sixty-six (7.6 per cent.) marriages with a MBDy, sixty-five (7.5 per cent.) with an FZDy and seventy-five (9.0 per cent.) with an eZDy, out of a total sample of 859. Marriages with one or other of the three genealogically closest possible spouses therefore comprise 24.1 per cent. of the total. The K.K. Maravar are about average in this regard.

In all, seven Kilai names were represented in the two villages. No informant could give any Kilai names apart from these seven, so it seems reasonable to assume that only these were found among their relatives elsewhere. A Maravar chief in Ramanathapuram told Dumont

(1957a: 7) that there were only eleven Kilai altogether, and despite the discrepancy in absolute numbers my findings support Dumont's view that the list given by Fawcett (1903) is a purely theoretical one. It was actually enumerated in the course of an honorific song praising the caste, and 'real life' seems to be nothing like as elaborate or systematic. In fact, Dumont suggests that the various Kilai have come about through a purely *ad hoc* process of fission, a tendency which he feels is as prevalent within the individual sub-caste as in the context of the caste system as a whole. The same chief told him that, far from the Kottu being a higher-order unit than the Kilai, it was in fact an 'honorific grouping' of *lower* order. One man in TV also claimed that there were two Kottus per Kilai, in agreement with Dumont's report. Data on Kilai and Kottu affiliation in TV do not support the idea that there is any kind of systematic connexion between the two.

The seven Kilais found locally are listed in table 11.2. All the names tally with Fawcett's table (1903), and in fact correspond respectively to number 5, 1, 2, 4, 3, 9 and 6 in that earlier list. In all, my informants named four Kottus, of which only the first two are mentioned by Fawcett. The four are: (a) *milakāy*, 'pepper'; (b) *verrilai*, 'betel leaf'; (c) *mundiri*, 'grape-vine'; (d) *sīrakka*, 'cumin, fennel'.

As to the few correlations of Kottus with Kilais which it proved possible to collect, these were as follows. Kilai (i) in table 11.2 was linked with Kottu (a); Kilai (ii) was variously associated with Kottus (b) and (c); Kilai (iii) with (a) and (d); (iv) with (b), (c) and (d); (v) with (a), (b) and (c); (vi) with (c); no information for Kilai (vii). It is impossible to

Table 11.2 *The pattern of inter-Kilai marriage in Terku Vandanam.*

Wife's Kilai:	(i)	(ii)	(iii)	(iv)	(v)	(vi)	(vii)
Husband's Kilai:							
(i) Maruvidu	–	16	8	2	10	1	0
(ii) Viramuditanki	12	–	7	6	1	0	0
(iii) Setar	8	1	–	1	6	0	1
(iv) Akattiyar	3	3	1	–	0	0	1
(v) Seyankondar	7	2	7	1	–	5	0
(vi) Nattumannar	0	0	0	0	7	–	0
(vii) Alakarpandiyan	0	0	0	0	1	1	–

discern any pattern in this. Most correlations are based on the unsupported testimony of single individuals, and many seemed even at the time to be mere guesses.

Table 11.2 presents in matrix form the distribution of marriage alliances among all the different possible pairs of Kilais in the local sample. Here the sample size is 119, made up of the fifty-eight local marriages and the marriages of the parents of all these people.[11] There is no evidence whatever of any directional bias in these figures (e.g., between 'wife-giver' and 'wife-taker' Kilais), nor is it possible to conclude that there are any exogamous groupings involving more than one Kilai. On the other hand, the rules of Kilai exogamy are scrupulously adhered to, save for a single exception dealt with below.

We saw that only 12.5 per cent of all K.K. Maravar marriages had conformed to the stated urimai preference for the FZDy. On the other hand, thirty-four (59 per cent) of the fifty-eight extant local marriages involved a man being married to a woman of his own F's Kilai. Fawcett (1903) noted that such unions were favoured, and several TV informants spontaneously drew attention to the practice. Clearly, it is *formally* equivalent to FZDy marriage, in that there is a reversal – in this case, a reversal in the Kilai affiliations of the couple – in each generation of the patriline.

Beck (n.d.: 11) has pointed out that among those south Indian castes which place strong stress upon a unilineal principle of descent, the importance of other criteria of marital correctness, such as terminological category, is correspondingly reduced. This seems to be borne out by the data, which show that the degree of conformity to the model of 'restricted exchange' (cf. Lévi-Strauss 1969: 445) is much greater at the level of the Kilai than in purely genealogical terms.

All these inter-Kilai exchanges can easily occur in conformity with the terminological prescription. On the other hand, Beck's generalisation is supported by a distinct tendency to tolerate in practice marriages which are terminologically incorrect, provided that the rule of Kilai exogamy has been obeyed.

Example 1: Kurusami Tevar (T12)[12] married Malaiyammal, his FZDD and *makal* ('daughter'). His wife was therefore not only from the

wrong terminological level but was also a parallel relative. In addition, Kurusami's eB Suppaiya (T13) had already married in accord with the urimai rule. Suppaiya's W is therefore Kurusami's WMZ. Kurusami's marriage is generally agreed (even by him) to have been wrong on all these counts. One result of it is that Malaiyammal and her D use the same kinship terms, at least to their more distant relatives. In practice, Malaiyammal has modified her terms of address to those more in keeping with the fact that she is Kurusami's wife. When I collected terminological data from her, however, she used the other, 'correct' terms, to the astonishment of her daughter, to whom we had to explain these apparent mistakes. In discussing this case, all informants emphasised that the rule of Kilai exogamy had not been broken. Significantly, they went on to draw attention to the fact that both Suppaiya and Kurusami had married into their F's Kilai in accord with the preferred practice.

Example 2: Cellaiya Tevar (T34) married his MBWZ (his *attai*). This too was agreed to be wrong strictly speaking, but again it was justified on the basis of the different Kilai affiliations of the pair. Dumont reports similar unions with terminological 'father's sisters' among other groups of Maravar (1957a: 40).

Example 3: Finally, an example of the opposite state of affairs. In just one case Kilai exogamy had not been observed, although terminologically the marriage was perfectly acceptable. This first became apparent when those most closely involved gave fictitious Kilai affiliations for themselves and their parents, but in such a way as to render their accounts mutually inconsistent. Evidence from more distant relatives made clear what had happened.

These examples demonstrate that terminologically wrong marriages are acknowledged quite openly, whereas breaches of Kilai exogamy are concealed. This is precisely what Beck's argument would lead one to expect.

The sequel to example 1 allows us to confirm another of Beck's observations, namely that a relationship set up as the result of a more recent marriage takes priority over one created by an earlier marriage, should the two not coincide (1972: 226). During my stay in TV, Kurusami took a second wife, the yZ of the first. This naturally appeared to me as a repetition of his 'wrong' marriage with his FZDD, but in this case informants disagreed, pointing out that the WyZ is a prescribed spouse.

Lest the above examples create a false impression, it should be made clear that the vast majority of K.K. Maravar unions *do* conform to the terminological prescription. Indeed, reference has now been made to all Maravar marriages for which this is not the case. In the two villages, over 95 per cent of all marriages conformed to prescriptive requirements.

The rule of Kulateyvam exogamy was also fully observed. There is one instance of a husband and wife sharing the same deity but none in which deity and location are the same for both parties. Genealogical evidence bears out people's statements that there are no systematic or particularly strong connexions with other villages in regard to marital alliances. Sillankulam, some 3–4 miles to the south, has an important agnatic link with TV though, for about half those having TV Kalasami as Kulateyvam reside there.

The requirement that a husband be his wife's senior is, as we saw, built into the terminological prescription, in that senior cross-cousins are distinguished from juniors, only the latter being potential spouses for a male ego. For the sample of fifty-eight K.K. Maravar marriages, the mean age difference between H and W is 5.6 years for all marriages and a little less for both MBDy and FZDy unions. These figures are based on my own census in 1976–7, and one carried out by the Malaria Eradication campaign in 1971. For obvious reasons, given the nature of the terminological prescription, relative seniority is both crucial and precisely known locally. On the other hand, exact ages are of little importance and are given only approximately. The two sets of figures have therefore been averaged wherever there are discrepancies. Of the fifty-eight marriages, the H is indeed older than his W in all but one.[13]

Example 4: Even the solitary exception 'proves the rule'. The man is his wife's senior terminologically, although younger than her in chronological terms. This is in fact another instance bearing out Beck's view that relationships created by recent marriages supersede those existing previously. This one exception involves the second marriage in a 'sister exchange'. As a result of the chronologically prior marriage of his eZ, the man became the eBWB of his eventual bride. Such vicarious seniority was felt sufficient to cancel out what was in any case a very small age difference of less than a year between groom and bride.

The Overall Pattern

So far the aim has been to distinguish as clearly as possible between the three levels of data. In this final section analysis gives way to synthesis. 'Empirical reality' involves the combination of all three levels into a functioning whole, a system which actually works for those living by it. It should at once be added that I do not assume any kind of static or dynamic equilibrium. Moreover, while all marriage systems no doubt serve social functions, that truism does not help us understand how particular systems, in themselves, actually work. In the present case, the system 'functions' in the sense that people do succeed in getting married in ways which are generally agreed to be correct, and do manage to address one another using kin terms which are applied logically and consistently.

Neither the terminological structure nor the marriage rules can therefore be said to be *contradictory*, with respect either to each other or to actual behaviour. At the same time, there are inconsistencies and incongruences, logical lacunae not serious enough to cause the collapse of the system. The extent of this *inconsistency* is explored for the K.K. Maravar case, after which it is argued that, in general, inter-level incongruence is not only inevitable in practice but necessary in theory.

In the first place, the kin terminology of the K.K. Maravar is a symmetric-prescriptive one of the kind somewhat misleadingly described by Needham as 'two line' (1971: *ci*).[14] Its symmetry is quite evident from table 1, in terminological identities such as FG = MGE and MG = FGE for the +1 level, and so on for other levels.[15] As a result, the terminological structure would be perfectly congruent with repeated bilateral cross-cousin marriage – or putting it another way, with a series of sister exchanges – as shown in fig. 11.2. All the genealogical identities depicted in that figure correspond to terminological identities

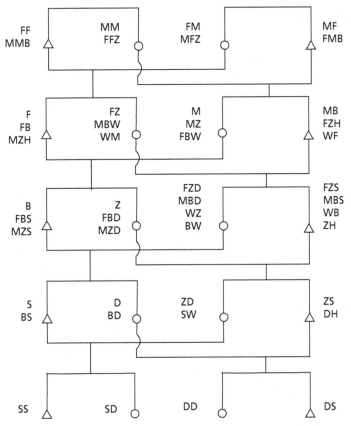

Figure 11.2 *The results of repeated bilateral first cross-cousin marriage (with reference to a male ego).*

included in table 11.1. Moreover, such a system would also be perfectly permissible from the viewpoint of Kilai and Kulateyvam exogamy.

However, a diagram such as fig. 11.2 can be used in several ways, which ought always to be distinguished. First of all, it may represent a real or fictive *genealogy*. Secondly, it may depict the structure of a prescriptive kin *terminology*. Korn (1973) displays a number of terminologies in this way, and 'Dravidian' terminologies have themselves been so displayed in the past. This use seems quite illegitimate. For one thing, it fosters belief in the primacy of genealogically close denotata, or at least implicitly encourages one to visualise terminologies in that way. For another, it provides the terminology with a degree of apparent structural consistency which it does not always possess. Korn is as guilty of ignoring usages which do not fit

her 'genealogical' structures as are the componential analysts (on whom see Good 1978b), as comparison of her tables and figures makes clear. Thirdly, such figures have been used to illustrate and depict the forms of *alliance relations* between groups. Each triangle then represents not a single male but all male members of a single unilineal group, in a given generation. It is not surprising to find Lévi-Strauss (1969: 452) using such diagrams in this way, since it follows naturally from his conflation of categories and rules. For other examples, and cogent criticism of the tendency, see Leach's discussion of matrilateral cross-cousin marriage (1961).

In short, of these behavioural, categorical and jural uses of the diagram, only the first is legitimate, and it is only in that sense that fig. 11.2 is to be taken. This clarifies the fact that fig. 11.2 is by no means the only kind of genealogy which would be consistent with the terminology. The fit would be just as good in situations of universal and repeated marriage with either the patri- or matrilateral first cross-cousin – despite the fact that the terminology, being symmetric, does not distinguish 'wife-givers' from 'wife-takers'. The point is that it is always possible to use rules to make further fine discriminations not inherent in the categories, so long as these rules operate within the framework of categorical boundaries. This point is returned to below.

The Kilai system as depicted by Fawcett seems at first sight to represent a second classificatory framework, as all-embracing in its own way as the kin terminology but – like Australian section systems – group rather than ego-centred. In practice, though, we have seen it to consist merely of an *ad hoc* division into fissionable exogamic groups. Thus while the division into Kilais and Kottus, and for that matter into sharers of the same Kulateyvams, does necessarily involve the use of categorical labels, these are merely vehicles for the expression of rules, or names applied to empirically existing groups. There is no element of prescription here nor, in practice, any consistent, formal logic. These categories do not in themselves form a system. In this respect they resemble kin terms in complex or descriptive terminological systems such as our own or that of northern India.

The most widespread and explicit rules among Maravar are those concerning exogamy and the urimai relationship. These are negative and positive rules, respectively. Taking the negative, exogamic rules first of all, we see that they involve no considerations of symmetry. For that matter, they are not phrased asymmetrically either: rather, symmetry simply does not enter into their formulation. The positive rules, on the other hand, are quite explicitly asymmetric.

In the case of the K.K. Maravar – and most other local sub-castes – a symmetric prescription is coupled with an asymmetric, in this case patrilateral, preference. The two kinds of data therefore raise inconsistent expectations with regard to empirical practice. On the basis of the terminology alone, marriages with MBDy and FZDy ought to be equally frequent, since the two genealogical positions are not distinguished categorically. On the other hand, the rules lead us to expect the latter relative to be married to the exclusion of the former. The terminology does not distinguish MBDy from FZDy, but the rules further sub-divide the category to which both belong, so that they become distinct. A genealogically defined member of the prescribed terminological class, in this case the FZDy, is singled out and made the subject of a preferential rule. This rule does not contradict the distinctions made in the system of categories, but merely makes a further distinction which retains intact all the categorical boundaries in their precise, original forms.

Contradiction would only arise if, say, a rule were to link FZDy with FBDy, while excluding MBDy and MZDy. Here categorical boundaries are broken down and contradiction would be inevitable if people tried to order their lives in conformity to both prescription and preference. So, in a word, preferential rules which further restrict marriage *within* a given prescribed category are acceptable: rules which transgress prescriptive categorical boundaries are not. In this way the terminology sets limits beyond which the rules cannot go. But within these limits, the rules enjoy full autonomy.

So categories and rules yield different, inconsistent expectations with respect to marriage behaviour. To which does the empirical marriage pattern conform more closely? As we saw, marriage behaviour insofar as it affects first cousins only[16] is almost perfectly symmetrical, whether one considers only the local unions or the entire sample. The K.K. Maravar data clearly suggest, therefore, that the symmetric prescription plays a greater part in regulating behaviour than the asymmetric preference.[17] But this is only a single case, and it is interesting to mention the situation among other local sub-castes.

The K.K. Maravar may in this respect usefully be compared with two sub-castes of *āsāri* Artisans living in TV. Both these groups state a quite unambiguous FZDy preference, but differ from the Maravar in allowing eZDy marriage. They contrive, uniquely among local groups, to combine the latter practice with an almost ideal-typical 'Dravidian' kin terminology very like that of the K.K. Maravar.

The Carpenters, first of all, state their urimai preference just as unanimously as the Maravar.

And indeed, in a sample of forty-six marriages, 15.2 per cent prove to have been with the FZDy, another 10.9 per cent with the eZDy, and none at all with the MBDy. This, then, is a situation almost directly opposite to that of the Maravar, one in which the asymmetric rule is observed to something like the maximum extent permitted by the exigencies of demography.

However, the Blacksmiths state their urimai preference even more vehemently, backing it up with several rather confused reasons why MBDy marriage is not merely less preferable but positively to be avoided. Yet in practice, the sample of thirty-four Blacksmith marriages involved *equal* proportions (11.8 per cent.) with FZDy and MBDy, as well as 23.5 per cent. with the eZDy. The total of 47.1 per cent. of marriages with these closest relatives is quite startlingly high; more to the present point is that the behaviour of these Smiths appears to give the lie to a jural preference upon which they insisted with greater passion than any of their neighbours.

So far, the evidence seems to suggest that behaviour is either perfectly symmetrical *vis-à-vis* first cross-cousins, and hence in accord with categorical expectations, or fully asymmetric in conformity to the rules. This is not so, though to illustrate the point it is necessary to turn to a group having the opposite, matrilateral preference, such as the *kōnār* Shepherds. In a sample of eighty-six Konar marriages, 14.0 per cent. were with the MBDy, 3.5 per cent. with the FZDy and 9.3 per cent. with the eZDy. Other examples could be adduced to demonstrate that behaviour may lie anywhere between the two extremes of perfect symmetry and total asymmetry.

It follows, then, that neither the symmetry of the prescriptive kin terminology nor the asymmetry of the preferential rule necessarily determines empirical kinship behaviour. The three levels of data are indeed autonomous.

Individual marriages may therefore be inconsistent with either the prescriptions or preferences of the group concerned (or, conceivably, with both). What happens in such situations? Paradoxically, perhaps, marriages which contravene rules seem more problematic and reprehensible than those going against prescriptions. This seems odd, given that terminological prescriptions are valid *by definition*, whereas preferential rules are merely codes which 'must', 'should' or 'could' be followed but need not be. Rules are by their very nature made to be broken. Yet in fact the situation is quite logical.

All marriages *do* conform to the terminological prescription, if not at the time then at least retrospectively. When two 'strangers', people between whom no previous relation was known, marry, they and their respective families begin immediately to address one another 'as if' the marriage has involved cross-cousins. That, of course, is no more than is to be expected of a prescriptive system. But things go even further here, as Beck's generalisations and the cited examples from TV make clear. Marriages which were 'wrong' at the time become 'right' because the relationships they create supersede those existing beforehand. No marriage can be 'wrong' – in the prescriptive sense – in the long term.

The same opportunity to redefine the situation does not arise in the case of rules. When they are broken the breach is permanent and cannot be reinterpreted retrospectively. For weak rules such as those concerning the urimai partner, disobedience does not matter much. They can, for instance, be overridden when they conflict with other rules or norms such as the desire to marry one's child into as wealthy and respectable a family as possible. However, when a rule is strongly held, and so basic as to pre-empt mere norms and conventions, it will tend not to be broken, and when it is in fact broken, this will be as far as possible concealed. It seems that the exogamic rules *vis-à-vis* Kilais and family deities are of this type. Only one breach was encountered, and as example 3 shows, this was hidden from me by those most affected. Rules, then, differ quantitatively; they become more or less obligatory or coercive. This cannot be said of prescription. A system is either prescriptive or it is not: there are no degrees (cf. Maybury-Lewis 1965: 226).

The position regarding marriageability may be summed up as follows. One can never predict the situation at one level from observations at either or both other levels. The empirical state of affairs at one level is never determined by what happens at another. On the other hand, there is not complete autonomy either.

Certain rules, or forms of behaviour, could not occur because they would directly contradict the system of categories, for example.

It is possible to go further, and say that these remarks do not apply merely to this case but are of universal validity. Inter-level inconsistency is not just inevitable in practice but necessary in principle. Thus rules do not correspond exactly to behaviour but exist in order to regulate it, to set limits upon it. These limits may or may not be observed in particular cases. A rule which was entirely congruent with behaviour would lose its very essence. It would no longer *direct* behaviour and would instead merely *describe* it (cf. Dumont 1972: 311–12). It would be quite superfluous *qua* rule.

Similarly, rules themselves are not simply the inevitable consequences of the categorical system, though they are of course phrased in terms of concepts and distinctions furnished by that system. Again, discrepancies must exist. A rule which merely stated what was already given by the system of classification would be a pure tautology. In the present case, for instance, there would be no point whatever in having a rule such as 'a man should marry his *koḷundiyāḷ*'. That would be tantamount to saying 'a man should marry someone whom he can marry'. Such a rule conveys nothing that is not already true *by definition*.

In this way, Needham's three-level model enables us to carry further the process set in train by Dumont's celebrated aphorism, 'kinship terminologies have not as their function to register groups' (1964: 78). That is, it not only draws attention to the fact that inconsistencies and incongruences between levels exist, but enables these to be codified. Since, as I have argued, inconsistency is not merely inescapable but essential, an analysis which focuses on one level at the expense of the others is bound to give rise to distortion.

NOTES

Fieldwork was carried out in 1976–7 while I was in receipt of an S.S.R.C. Conversion Fellowship; I thank the Staff Research Fund of the University of Durham for further financial support. My assistant Mr Palanimurugapperumal Chettiar contributed to the collection of the data, but responsibility for the analysis offered here is entirely my own.

1   Tamil words are transliterated according to standard conventions on first appearance. Thereafter, diacritical marks and italics are usually omitted. Dictionary definitions come from Fabricius (1972).

2   This being so, 'prescription' is perhaps not the best term to use, as Needham (1972) comments. But the usage has a long history and to change would only cause yet more confusion.

3   In the dualistic view espoused by Dumont (1972: 311), the two analytical levels are 'ideology' and 'behaviour'. He now accepts Needham's further division of 'ideology' into 'rules' and 'categories' (1975: 145n).

4   These issues are discussed more fully in Good (1981), which serves in many ways as a complement to the present article.

5   David is here advancing his own slightly different form of the three-level model.

6   It was generally women who reasoned in this way. This may be because the terminology is harder to apply in an abstract way from their viewpoint, given the 'cross-over' between parallel and cross as between their seniors and juniors.

7   There was one exception to this: the Panchayat President stated that it did not matter if spouses were of the same Kottu, as long as their Kilais were different. But this statement was made minutes after he had read Fawcett's list, in which he and his wife were alleged to be of the same Kottu!

8   The KP Talaiyari is *ex officio* the *pūsāri* (temple priest) at this shrine.

9   This usage is probably not indigenous. Vakuppu means 'class' in the sense of 'school class', and its extension to cover socioeconomic groupings seems to result from a widening of its semantic range to correspond to that of its English equivalent.

10 This is a 'customary' right still exercised in villages but illegal according to the Hindu Marriage Act.

11 Every set of parents was of course counted only once, however many married children they had. This explains why the larger figure is not simply 3 × 58.

12 Men's names include the caste title: this is either the actual name of the caste or, as in the Maravar case, an honorific suffix (*tēvar* means 'lord'). Every household has been

given a code number, to facilitate cross-reference among my various works, and this follows each (disguised) personal name, in brackets.

13 There are no statistically significant differences in the mean or median age discrepancies, as between MBDy, FZDy and other kinds of marriage (*pace* Kodanda Rao 1973: 26).

14 Taken literally, this appellation propagates the idea of 'linearity', a somewhat questionable notion where many peoples in this region are concerned. This is certainly not Needham's intention.

15 G = sibling; E = spouse.

16 It is really only meaningful to speak of symmetry or asymmetry in connexion with *first* cross-cousins. People do not distinguish jurally or categorically between more distant categories of cross-cousin. Moreover, given the convoluted nature of the genealogy, more distant relatives are almost inevitably related to ego both matri- and patrilaterally, though not necessarily equally closely so.

17 If this is so, one might justifiably ask, why bother having the rule in the first place? A partial answer emerges below.

REFERENCES

Aiyappan, A. 1934. Cross-cousin and uncle–niece marriage. *Int. Congr. anthrop. ethnol. Sci.* **1**, 281–2.

Barnes, J. A. 1980. Kinship studies: some impressions of the current state of play. *Man* (N.S.) **15**, 293–303.

Beck, Brenda E. F. n.d. Sister's daughter marriage in south India. Ms.

——1970. The right–left division of south Indian society. *J. Asian Stud.* **29**, 779–98.

——1972. *Peasant society in Konku.* Vancouver: Univ. of British Columbia.

David, Kenneth 1977. Hierarchy and equivalence in Jaffna, north Sri Lanka: normative codes as mediator. In *The new wind: changing identities in south Asia* (ed.) K. David. The Hague: Mouton.

Dumont, Louis 1953. The Dravidian kinship terminology as an expression of marriage. *Man* **53**, 34–9.

——1957a. *Hierarchy and marriage alliance in south Indian kinship.* (Occ. Pap. R. Anthrop. Inst. **12**). London: Royal Anthropological Institute.

——1957b. *Une sous-caste de l'Inde du sud: organisation sociale et religion des Pramalai Kallar.* The Hague: Mouton.

——1963. Distribution of some Maravar subcastes. In *Anthropology on the march* (ed.) Bala Ratnam. Madras: Book Centre.

——1964. Marriage in India, the present state of the question. Postscript to part I. *Contr. Ind. Sociol.* **7**, 77–80.

——1970. *Religion/politics and history in India.* The Hague: Mouton.

——1972. *Homo hierarchicus.* London: Paladin.

——1975. *Dravidien et Kariera: l'alliance de mariage dans l'Inde du sud, et en Australie.* The Hague: Mouton.

Fabricius, J. P. 1972 (1779). *Tamil and English dictionary* (4th edn). Tranquebar: Evangelical Lutheran Mission.

Fawcett, Fred 1903. The Kondaiyamkottai Maravars, a Dravidian tribe of Tinnevelly, southern India. *J. R. Anthrop. Inst.* **33**, 57–65.

Good, Anthony 1978a. Kinship and ritual in a south Indian micro-region. Thesis, Univ. of Durham.

——1978b. The principle of reciprocal sets. *Man* (N.S.) **13**, 128–30.

——1981. Elder sister's daughter marriage in south Asia. *J. Anthrop. Res.* **36**.

Goodenough, Ward H. 1967. Componential analysis. *Science* **156**, 1203–9.

Kadhirvel, S. 1977. *A history of the Maravas, 1700–1802.* Madras: Madras Publishing House.

Khare, R. S. 1977. Prestations and prayers: two homologous systems in northern India. In *The new wind: changing identities in south Asia* (ed.) K. David. The Hague: Mouton.

Kodanda Rao, M. 1973. Rank differences and marriage reciprocity in south India. *Contr. Ind. Sociol.* (N.S.) **7**, 16–35.

Korn, Frances 1973. *Elementary structures revisited: Lévi-Strauss on kinship.* London: Tavistock.

Leach, Edmund R. 1961. *Rethinking anthropology.* London: Athlone Press.

——1964. *Political systems of Highland Burma.* London: Athlone Press.

Lévi-Strauss, Claude 1969. *The elementary structures of kinship.* London: Eyre & Spottiswoode.

Maybury-Lewis, David H. P. 1965. Prescriptive marriage systems. *SWest. J. Anthrop.* **21**, 207–30.

Morgan, Lewis H. 1871. *Systems of consanguinity and affinity of the human family.* Washington: Smithsonian Institute.

Needham, Rodney 1962. *Structure and sentiment.* Chicago: Univ. Press.

—— 1967. Terminology and alliance, II-Mapuche; conclusions. *Sociologus* **17**, 39–53.

—— 1971. Introduction. In *Rethinking kinship and marriage* (ed.) R. Needham (A.S.A. Monogr. **11**). London: Tavistock.

—— 1972. Prescription. *Oceania* **42**, 166–81.

Pate, H. R. 1917. *Madras district gazetteers: Tinnevelly, vol. 1.* Madras: Govt. Press.

Rajayyan, K. 1974. *Rise and fall of the Poligars of Tamilnadu.* Madras: Univ. Press.

Reiniche, Marie-Louise 1978. Statut, fonctions et droits; relations agraires au Tamilnad. *Homme* **18**, 135–66.

Royal Anthropological Institute 1951. *Notes and queries in anthropology* (6th edn). London: Routledge and Kegan Paul.

Scheffler, Harold W. 1977. Kinship and alliance in south India and Australia. *Am. Anthrop.* **79**, 869–82.

—— & Floyd G. Lounsbury 1971. *A study in semantics: the Siriono kinship system.* Englewood Cliffs: Prentice-Hall.

Schneider, David M. 1965. Some muddles in the models, or, how the system really works. In *The relevance of models for social anthropology* (ed.) M. Banton (A.S.A. Monogr. **I**). London: Tavistock.

—— 1968. *American kinship: a cultural account.* Englewood Cliffs: Prentice-Hall.

Thurston, Edgar & K. Rangachari 1909. *Castes and tribes of southern India* (7 vols.). Madras: Govt. Press.

Yalman, Nur 1963. On the purity of women in the castes of Ceylon and Malabar. *J. R. Anthrop. Inst.* **93**, 25–58.

12

Analysis of Purum Affinal Alliance

Rodney Needham

No theory is likely to endure which does not arise directly out of long-continued, intuitive familiarity with the welter of facts which it attempts to order. – HOMANS[1]

Let us now examine the main features of one society with a matrilateral prescription. This will be the Purum of the Indo-Burma border. It has to be admitted that the ethnographic records on this society are not in all respects as comprehensive or reliable as the information available on other societies of the same type, but I choose this society because in certain particulars the ethnography is the most useful for testing Homans and Schneider's argument.

The following account is based on a more extended analysis already published, and therefore includes without further discussion points which I think I have already demonstrated. It also includes certain material which for one reason or another was omitted from the original paper.[2] The bulk of the information comes from the monograph by Das.[3]

I

The Purum are an "Old Kuki" tribe of Manipur, on the eastern border of India. They are of Mongoloid physical stock, and speak a Tibeto-Burman language. In 1932, i.e., in the period from which our information mostly comes, they numbered 303 individuals. They are divided among four villages: there are no non-Purum in these villages, and there are no

Purum in other villages. Marriage is permissible with the Chawte, another Old Kuki tribe with whom the Purum claim a common historical origin, but no cases are reported.

The villages are politically autonomous, each governed by its own council. There is no indigenous centralized government or judiciary. The villages are linked, however, in the first place, by the fact that every clan except one (and this also in the past) is represented in every village. We cannot assert on the evidence available that the villages are related to each other as villages on this basis; but local descent groups in different villages are related by common clanship, and since the component groups are so related it may well be that the villages are politically related also within the descent system.

There are five named, exogamous patrilineal clans, which are further distinguished by personal names traditionally proper to each clan, and by possessing separate sections within each village burial ground. Four of the clans are subdivided into named lineages. The names of these descent groups, and their distribution throughout the three villages for which such information is available, are shown in Table 12.1. Mnemonic letters are appended to the names of the clans and villages, and the lineages are numbered; so that in the following analysis M_3, for example, will stand for

Table 12.1 *Purum Descent Groups*

Clan	Lineage	Village		
		Khulen (Kh)	Tampak (Ta)	Chumbang (Chu)
Kheyang (K)......	1. Julhung	+	+	+
	2. Aihung	....	+	+
Makan (Mk)......	1. Kankung	+	+	+
	2. Makan-te	+	....	....
Marrim (M).......	1. Rimphunchong	+	....	....
	2. Rimkung	+	....	....
	3. Rim-ke-lek	....	+	....
	4. Pilling	....	+	+
Parpa (P).........	....	+	+	+
Thao (T).........	1. Thao-kung	....	+	....
	2. Thao-run	+	....	....
	3. Teyu	....	....	....
	4. Rangshai	+	....	....

Rim-ke-lek lineage of Marrim clan. One lineage of Thao clan (viz., Teyu) died out in 1924, but is retained in the table because it has a place in the argument.

The descent groups are systematically related by ties of prescriptive alliance. The prescribed marriage is with the "mother's brother's daughter," while marriage with the "father's sister's daughter" is strictly forbidden. The rule, however, does not enjoin marriage with the individual matrilateral first cousin, but also covers marriage with a woman from the clan of the mother's brother, i.e., with a woman who does not stand in any particular degree of genealogical relationship. The actual marriage is contracted by a three-year period of bride-service, after which residence is patrilocal.

The relationship terminology (see also Table 12.2) accords with the rule of descent and with the marriage prescription:[4]

1. *pu*   FF, MF, MB, WF, MBS, WB, WBS
2. *pi*   FM, MM, MBW, WM, WBW
3. *pa*   F, FB, MZH
4. *nu*   M, MZ, FBW
5. *ni*   FZ
6. *rang* FZH
7. *ta*   eB, FBSe, MZSe
8. *u*   eZ, FBDe, MZDe
9. *nau*   yB, FBSy, MZSy, yZ, MZDy, MBD, BW, WBD

10. *sar*   Z
11. *mau*   SW
12. *sha*   S, BS, WZS, D, BD, WZD
13. *tu*   FZS, ZH, FZD, ZS, DH, ZD, SS, SD, DSW, DS, SDH, DD.

The equations and distinctions are characteristic. The following, among others, confirm that we are dealing with a lineal descent system:

$$F = FB \qquad FB \neq MB$$
$$M = MZ \qquad FZ \neq MZ$$
$$B = FBS \qquad B \neq MBS$$
$$S = BS \qquad B \neq FZS$$
$$\qquad\qquad\qquad S \neq WBS$$
$$\qquad\qquad\qquad S \neq ZS$$

And these demonstrate the matrilateral prescription:

$$FB = MZH \qquad FZ \neq MBW$$
$$MB = WF \qquad FZH \neq WF$$
$$MBS = WB \qquad MBD \neq FZD$$
$$MBD = BW \qquad WB \neq ZH$$
$$B = MZS, WZH \qquad WBW \neq Z$$
$$FZS = ZH \qquad WBS \neq ZS$$
$$ZS = DH \qquad SW \neq ZD$$
$$S = WZS$$
$$DS = SDH$$

The only point to occasion misgiving is the equation of mother's brother's daughter with

Table 12.2 *Purum Categories of Descent and Alliance*

| | ← | | ← | | ← | |
f.	m.	f.	m.	f.	m.	f.
			pu	pi	pu	pi
	rang	ni	pa	nu	pu	pi
tu	tu	u	tanau	nau	pu	pi
		sar nau	[ego] nau			
tu	tu	sha	sha	nau mau	pu	
tu	tu	tu	tu			

younger sister, which is utterly uncharacteristic of such systems as this.[5] It is understandable that the term may denote brother's wife, and wife's sister after her marriage, for these women may well be addressed by the same terms as are the men to whom they are married, and especially since a woman is incorporated into her husband's group; but there is no ready explanation for this infraction of one of the cardinal rules of matrilateral terminologies, viz., that marriageable women must be distinguished from prohibited women. Yet the ethnographer so clearly and repeatedly gives the particular term for the matrilateral cross-cousin that we may not easily doubt his report. However, another source gives *sar* for "sister," a term common in other Kuki languages, and by this at least the sister is clearly distinguished from the mother's brother's daughter. Also it is only the younger sister who is not so distinguished, while the elder is known by a term (*u*) which is not reported as applicable to the mother's brother's daughter.

The relationships of affinity are not merely ties between individuals or families. Descent groups, whether localized or dispersed, are also related as groups by ties of prescriptive alliance. A descent group may take wives by traditional claim from certain groups but not from others; women are transferred obligatorily in one "direction," and there can be no direct exchange. The total society is divided by the Purum themselves into: (1) lineally related descent groups, (2) wife-giving groups, (3) wife-taking groups; and the fundamental cycle of alliance is exhibited by the specific statement that a wife-taking group may be identical with a wife-giving group of one's own wife-givers.

Members of these three major categories, each of which may comprise one or more descent groups in relation to any particular descent group, are terminologically related in the same way as individuals are related in particular affinal relationships. All the men of a wife-giving group are *pu*, a term of which one of the genealogical specifications is "mother's brother"; and all the men of Ego's generation and below in a wife-taking group are *tu*, one of the specifications of which is "sister's son." Within Ego's own generation all the women of any wife-giving group are *nau(nu)*, one of the genealogical specifications of which is "mother's brother's daughter"; and all those of a wife-taking group are *tu(nu)*, one of the specifications of which is "father's sister's daughter."

Purum society thus exhibits the structural categories and relations of a social system based on prescribed marriage with the "mother's brother's daughter." We may now examine the individual marriages which actually take place and which maintain this system. The information is perfectly clear on the vital point that marriage is not necessarily or even usually with the matrilateral first cousin, but with a classificatory matrilateral cross-cousin. Analysis of the 54 marriages recorded from three villages (Khulen, Tampak, and Changninglong) shows that no fewer than 26 (48.1 per cent) are with women of clans other than that of the mother (Table 12.3). This means that at least this proportion of marriages in this record could not possibly have been with the daughter of the maternal uncle. Furthermore, the proportion is certainly higher, for it is not possible to distinguish in the evidence marriages with the first cousin from marriages with a classificatory relative of the same category in the mother's clan.

This single fact is of the gravest consequence, as we shall see even more clearly later, for Homans and Schneider's theory. Their argument applies specifically and exclusively to marriage with the first cousin. It is conceivable that a theory of sentiments might help to elucidate marriage with such a close relative; but it is not readily conceivable how it could possibly apply to a situation in which nearly half the

Table 12.3   *Marriages outside the Mother's Clan*

	Clan of Wife					Total	Outside Mother's Clan
	K	Mk	M	P	T		
CLAN OF MOTHER K....	3	.....	.....	.....	2	5	2
Mk...	.....	3	.....	1	.....	4	1
M....	6	.....	6	2	.....	14	8
P....	.....	5	2	5	3	15	10
T....	.....	1	2	2	11	16	5
Total......	9	9	10	10	16	54	26

Table 12.4   *Scheme of Alliances*

$$
\begin{array}{rcl}
Mk_2, M_2, M_4, P, T_1, T_2, T_3, T_4 \rightarrow & K_1 \rightarrow & Mk_1, M_1, M_3 \\
Mk_1, Mk_2, M_2, P, T_1, T_4 \rightarrow & K_2 \rightarrow & M_1, M_3, M_4 \\
K_1, M_2, P \rightarrow & Mk_1 \rightarrow & K_2, M_1, M_3, M_4, T_1, T_2, T_3, T_4 \\
K_1, M_1, M_2, M_3, M_4, P \rightarrow & Mk_2 \rightarrow & K_2, T_1, T_2, T_3, T_4 \\
K_1, K_2, Mk_1 \rightarrow & M_1 \rightarrow & Mk_2, P \\
T_1, T_2, T_3 \rightarrow & M_2 \rightarrow & K_1, K_2, Mk_1, Mk_2, P \\
K_1, K_2, Mk_1, T_1, T_2, T_3, T_4 \rightarrow & M_3 \rightarrow & Mk_2, P \\
K_2, Mk_1, T_1, T_2, T_3 \rightarrow & M_4 \rightarrow & K_1, Mk_2, P \\
M_1, M_2, M_3, M_4 \rightarrow & P \rightarrow & K_1, K_2, Mk_1, Mk_2, T_1, T_2 \\
Mk_1, Mk_2, P \rightarrow & T_1 \rightarrow & K_1, K_2, M_2, M_3, M_4 \\
Mk_1, Mk_2, P \rightarrow & T_2 \rightarrow & K_1, M_2, M_3, M_4 \\
Mk_1, Mk_2 \rightarrow & T_3 \rightarrow & K_1, M_2, M_3, M_4 \\
Mk_1, Mk_2 \rightarrow & T_4 \rightarrow & K_1, K_2, M_3
\end{array}
$$

women married come from clans other than that of the mother. How could it ever be thought likely that marriages with all such women should be "sentimentally appropriate" in the way proposed by Homans and Schneider?

Before we expatiate on this point, let us proceed to an examination of the relations between groups established and maintained by such marriages. In Table 12.4 is presented a scheme of alliances between all the component descent groups of Purum society. The groups of reference constitute the center column; the arrows show the direction of transfer of women. Wife-givers are on the left, wife-takers on the right; so that, e.g., K_1 takes wives from Mk_2, from M_2, etc., and gives wives to Mk_1, to M_1, and to M_3. What does this mean in terms of Homans and Schneider's theory? For any man in K_1, every woman in his own genealogical level in every one of the wife-giving groups, viz., $Mk_2, M_2, M_4, P, T_1, T_2, T_3$, and

T_4 is a "mother's brother's daughter." Furthermore, each of these alliance groups may comprise a number of local alliance groups: e.g., the local representatives of Parpa clan in the three villages of Khulen, Tampak, and Changninglong.

If a man is going to visit "the mother's brother" often, as Homans and Schneider say he does, he is going to do an awful lot of walking. But why ever should he? Because, Homans and Schneider tell us, he is "fond" of the mother's brother. To be fond of roughly a third of all the men of his father's generation in the total society seems a promiscuous lavishing of sentiment, but suppose he is? Well, then, we are told, "he will tend to get fond of the daughter." But this, similarly, means being fond of something like one-third of all the women in his own generation, a very expansive affection. Anyway, he is held to have a "sentimental claim" to all these young women, marriage with any one of this large class will be

Table 12.5   *Examples of Alliance Cycles*

1. K_1—M_1—Mk_2—K_2—M_3—P—(K_1)
2. K_1—M_1—Mk_2—K_2—M_4—(K_1)
3. K_1—M_1—Mk_2—K_2—M_4—P—(K_1)
4. K_1—M_1—Mk_2—T_1—(K_1)
5. K_1—M_3—Mk_2—K_2—M_1—P—(K_1)
6. K_1—M_3—Mk_2—K_2—M_4—(K_1)
7. K_1—M_3—Mk_2—T_1—(K_1)
8. K_1—Mk_1—M_1—Mk_2—K_2—M_3—P—(K_1)
9. K_1—Mk_1—M_1—P—(K_1)
10. K_1—Mk_1—M_1—Mk_2—K_2—M_3—P—(K_1)
11. K_1—Mk_1—M_1—Mk_2—T_1—(K_1)
12. K_1—Mk_1—M_3—P—(K_1)
13. K_1—Mk_1—M_4—(K_1)
14. K_1—Mk_2—T_1—(K_1)
15. K_2—M_1—Mk_2—(K_2)
16. K_2—M_1—P—(K_2)
17. M_1—P—Mk_1—(M_1)
18. M_2—Mk_1—T_1—(M_2)
19. M_2—Mk_2—T_1—(M_2)
20. M_3—P—Mk_1—(M_3)

"sentimentally appropriate" – and this implausible tale is the real explanation of the rule of marriage.

The facts so far examined are damaging enough to Homans and Schneider's argument, but we have hardly begun to see the complexity of the social and symbolic systems associated with the rule of marriage. It will be recalled that a defining feature of a system with a matrilateral prescription is the "cycle" of women linking the descent groups into a system, the "*échange généralisé*" of Lévi-Strauss. In the model this is a single cycle (Fig. 12.1); but, as we should expect, the factual situation which this so simply represents is very much more complex. From Table 12.5 we can determine what degree of correspondence there is between the features of the model and those of social reality. There are a large number of cycles to be discerned in it, of which Table 12.5 gives twenty examples. There are many others to be extracted from the scheme of alliances, but these are ample enough to show the large number and the complexity of the affinal ties linking a small number of intermarrying descent groups. Complex though this representation is, it is nevertheless an abstraction from a still more complex reality in terms of local groups. The relation K_1–Mk_1 is a simple relationship between two distinct, named descent

groups; but it has to be remembered – if we are to appreciate more exactly what happens in terms of people on the ground – that K_1 comprises three local descent groups, one in each of the villages in Table 12.1, and that Mk_1 also comprises three territorially separate groups. An analysis of alliance cycles as they in fact link such local groups – which is what a political study of Purum society would ultimately involve – would therefore be far more complex than the situation as I have analyzed it here. In fact, the further we go into the evidence, the more complex in its particulars a social system based on a matrilateral prescription is seen to be – and the more inapt Homans and Schneider's explanation of it.

The reference to a political study brings us finally to the relationships established between villages by the alliances between their component local descent groups. These can be seen from Table 12.6. Out of the fifty-four marriages recorded, eleven (20.3 per cent) have taken place between villages. That is, the autonomous political units of Purum society are also related by the alliances between descent groups which are fundamental to social life.

In sum, so far as the social order is concerned, the same tripartite categorization orders relations between individuals, between descent groups, and between the component local descent groups of the village, and creates ties between the politically independent villages.

II

At this point, let us return to the confrontation of Homans and Schneider's theory with the facts. Here we have a patrilineal society, with patrilocal residence; inheritance and succession are through males exclusively; it is local groups of men who constitute the social and political segments of Purum society between which women are transferred. These groups are allied in the first place by the matrilateral prescription, and their members are denoted by terms which are not genealogically defined designations but are categories defined by descent and alliance.

It should be noted especially that structurally this social classification is exactly congruent with the system diagrammed in Homans and Schneider's Figure 1, save for the fact (which

Table 12.6 *Intervillage Marriages*

		Married into			Total Marriages	Women Married out of Village
	$\rightarrow$	Kh	Ta	Cha		
WOMEN FROM	Kh.....	30	3	1	34	4
	Ta.....	6	10	......	16	6
	Cha.....	1	......	3	4	1
Total.........		37	13	4	54	11

we may now recognize as formally irrelevant) that the Purum system is patrilineal while their figure is matrilineal. More particularly, all the positional equations and distinctions which have been elicited from the Purum terminology are present in Homans and Schneider's diagram also. This diagram is their representation of a system of "matrilateral cross-cousin marriage," in terms of which their argument is premised and to which their theory is intended (however partially or confusedly) to apply. Purum society, then, is precisely a patrilineal instance of this type of system. The only reservation to be registered is that, while the Purum are indeed patripotestal, we are not told what are the sentiments toward the father's sister and the mother's brother, and we therefore do not know whether this is sentimentally a typical instance of Homans and Schneider's "patrilineal complex." The probability is that the Purum configuration of attitudes does conform, but we do not know this for certain. Nor do we know what are the sentiments toward the father's sister's daughter and the mother's brother's daughter. In all other respects, however, Purum ethnography provides an eminently satisfactory case for the empirical testing of Homans and Schneider's theory in its application to matrilateral prescriptive systems. Now this society is patrilineal and its prescription is matrilateral, and it thus supports the correlation in the special hypothesis; but this is not now a very significant issue. What we have constantly to bear in mind in the course of this analysis is the question of whether it is likely that this system may be understood by reference to the sentiments from which, according to Homans and Schneider, the rules of marriage derive.

There are two kinds of relations fundamental to this type of society: (1) between lineally related men; (2) between affines. The corporate group is the lineal descent group, and within it its members are differentiated terminologically according to generation, relative age, and sex; and this is consistent with the differentiation of status normally found essential to the conduct of social life by such a group. On the other hand, the lineal descent group is flanked, as it were, by other such groups with which it is related by alliance – its affines; and, with the exception of one position (viz., *rang*), these groups are not internally differentiated in relation to it. There are *pu*-lines and there are *tu*-lines. These categories include men under one status regardless of their individual attributes of age, genealogical level, rank, or cognatic connection. An alliance group denoted by *pu* is one from which wives are obtained: it is a wife-giving group. An alliance group denoted by *tu* is one to which wives are given: it is a wife-taking group, and marriage with its women is forbidden. Paradigmatically, the second of the two basic kinds of relation, that of alliance, is *pu-tu*.

Now let us look more closely at the connotations of these terms. Wife-givers are denoted by a term (*pu*) which applies also to senior lineal kinsmen; wife-takers are denoted by a term (*tu*) which applies also to the most junior lineal kin (see Table 12.2). These terms in themselves indicate that there is a differentiation of status between affines, and here we approach the content of what so far have been dealt with simply as formal relations. In systems of matrilateral prescriptive alliance it is commonly the case that wife-givers are regarded as superior to wife-takers. The probability now appears that this is the case among the Purum also, and we shall see this confirmed later.

Now, then: the category of woman with whom marriage is prescribed is essentially a daughter or sister of any man (a *pu*) in a wife-giving group. Among these alliance groups there is one to which Ego's mother belonged; within it there is one local alliance group from which she came; and within that group one of the number of men denoted by the term *pu* is the maternal uncle. It is on the basis of this slender circumstance that observers have tended to report that marriage is with the "mother's brother's daughter."

But this particular individual is only one of a large proportion of maritally eligible women belonging to different descent groups, and dispersed over a number of local alliance groups. Similar considerations apply also to the men and women denoted by *tu*, and particularly to the genealogically defined "father's sister's daughter." But these two categories of women are defined, not by genealogical connection but by alliance. It is inaccurate and misleading even to call them the "matrilateral cross-cousin" and "patrilateral cross-cousin." These terms are constructed from the point of view of an individual in a junior generation, whereas alliances are contracted (as is usually the case, and as we shall see is so among the Purum) by members of the senior generation. The relationship contracted is between men in positions to whose definition terms relating to "mother" and "father" are not necessarily relevant. And even from the point of view of Ego in the junior generation, the "matrilateral" cross-cousin whom he marries may well have no connection with his own mother except a terminological one. She may come, that is, from a different descent group (e.g., clan), a different alliance group, a different local alliance group, and a different political and territorial group. Similar considerations apply to the "patrilateral" cross-cousin and to the relation of Ego's father to persons denoted by the term *tu*.

Finally, I wish to emphasize a point which is of quite radical importance, to my mind the most important in this book, viz., that since these categories are those by which other people order their social lives, it is essential when examining a system of prescriptive alliance first of all to make the most intense imaginative effort to think in terms of their classification. This is basically what I mean by "understanding"; but no valid understanding, by contrast, is ever likely to result from genealogical definitions of status, from a purview confined to domestic relationships, or from the pernicious theory of the extension of sentiments.

These considerations bring us back to Homans and Schneider and to the comparison of their argument with the facts as I have presented them. Let me first draw attention to one vital analytical fact, viz., that in this summing-up I started with a consideration of the society as a whole, in factual terms of groups of men; then isolated the fundamental relations which unite these groups into a society; and only gradually particularized to the final point at which individuals were distinguished. This I take to be the characteristic procedure of the social anthropologist. Homans and Schneider, on the contrary, deal with the individual and with his sentimental reactions to other individuals within an extremely narrowly defined family situation; and this approach is determined by the nature of their interest, which is not sociological but psychological. This would not matter, of course, if only it helped us to understand this kind of society. But, far from this being the case, Purum society cannot even be described by the terms and relations of their model. It is not simply that they do not go any further in the analysis of a matrilateral system: from their premises, they cannot.

There is one expedient by which they might try to save their argument, but it is a desperate one. This is by an extreme application of the extension theory. The sentiment associated with the mother's brother, it might be contended, is extended to other men of his local descent group; thence to the men of this generation in all the component groups of his descent group; and thence to such men in all the descent groups which stand in the same alliance relationship to Ego's as that to which his maternal uncle belongs. One would hope, of course, that no social anthropologist today would seriously advance such an argument; but it might just possibly be held that in this process lies the validation of the theory of sentiments. In that case, though, the new formulation would run even more disastrously into the difficulties in the extension theory, and I need not rehearse these. Moreover, we have now seen a hint of yet one more difficulty, viz., that the mother's brother is a member of a superior category (the point may be conceded for the moment: it will be borne out below), and that the conventional attitude towards members of this category in general is likely to be one of respect and distance, not of the affectionate intimacy that the theory demands.

But, all this aside, there is in any case the main question: What would be the analytical advantage in adopting the argument from sentiments? It certainly cannot offer a better understanding of the social classification than that to be gained by apprehending the classification through its own categories and principles; it is irrelevant to the significance of the sociological analysis made so far; and there is no evidence in the ethnography to allow us to believe that it isolates the efficient causes of the "adoption" or maintenance of the marriage rule which defines the social system.

Finally, one more particular point on which Homans and Schneider's theory diverges ruinously from the facts. They maintain that Lévi-Strauss "neglects the degree to which natives depart from the norm in practice, and depart from it they must."[6] One example of such departure, they think, is when a classificatory cross-cousin is married, and the evidence just examined shows that this is quite wrong. But it could still be the case that, for one reason or another, difficulty arises in marrying a woman of the correct category. Must there then be "departure from the norm"? Will a man have to marry a woman of the category of *tu*? The answer, to judge by the common practice in other such societies and particularly by a report from the related Chawte, is that he will not. What typically happens is that a woman is removed from a normally non-marriageable category and adopted into a marriageable one.[7] Her genealogical connection – e.g., as father's sister's daughter – is entirely disregarded, and she is ritually assigned to the appropriate category in the classification which in fact orders social life. This expedient in itself demonstrates the paramountcy of the classification over the factors of genealogy and individual sentiment to which Homans and

Schneider mistakenly attribute such determinative importance.

So much for the main features of the social order, and particularly the descent system and the regulation of marriage to which Homans and Schneider's argument is intended to apply. I now turn to a brief consideration of the symbolic order, where their theory encounters yet more deleterious and invalidating difficulties.

III

Whatever its analytical and empirical complications, a society based on matrilateral alliance is fundamentally a very simple and clearly defined system. It is therefore the more feasible to determine, through a consideration of its symbolic usages, whether or not there are more abstract structural principles underlying both social relations of the sorts we have examined above and other aspects of its culture which are not obviously connected with them. What we seek is in fact (so far as the literature allows) the "total structure" of Purum society. The ethnography on this particular instance of the system is not the most revealing in this respect, but it is possible to glimpse, chiefly in the symbolism of ritual, certain structural features which are radical to Purum society.

A convenient and characteristic point at which to start is the house and its divisions (Fig. 12.1). This is divided lengthwise into two named parts: *phumlil* on the right (looking from a position inside at the back) and *ningan* on the left. The "master of the house" has his bed in the *phumlil* half, near a special post called *chhatra*, and his unmarried sons and daughters sleep near him on the same side. Future sons-in-law (men who live in the house while fulfilling their bride-service) and other young men who pass the nights there as guests (courting the unmarried daughters) sleep in the *ningan* half, near a post called *senajumphi*. At night the *phumlil* is taboo to those outsiders who sleep in the *ningan*, and even married daughters of the house sleep in the *ningan* when they visit their parents' home. The two posts *chhatra* and *senajumphi*, associated respectively with *phumlil* and *ningan*, are of ritual importance. When the house is built they are erected in a fixed order: first *chhatra*, then *senajumphi*; and the stringers which rest

NINGAN   PHUMLIL

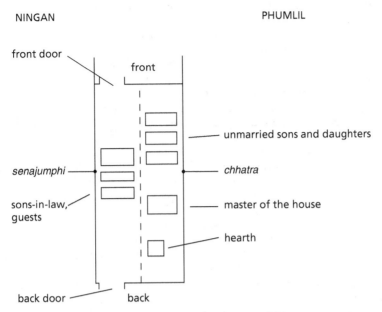

Figure 12.1 *Plan of Purum house. (After Das, 1945, Plate XIX, Fig. 74.)*

on them are also put up in the same order. This order, this ascription of primacy, seems to accord with a difference in status which evidently exists between the two sides of the house, for without doubt the master of the house is of superior status to the sons-in-law who labor for him and to casual young guests. *Phumlil*, we may infer, is superior to *ningan*, and *chhatra* is superior to *senajumphi*. The front door is in what I have designated the "left" (*ningan*) side of the house, and so is the back door. These facts may also be regarded as consistent with the inferred inferior character of this side of the house. The hearth, on the other hand, is in *phumlil*: we know what importance this usually possesses, and we shall see that it is ritually important among the Purum. We may see in this sum of conventional dispositions a division of the house into private and public, family and outsiders, kin and affines, all subsumed under the general characters of superior (*phumlil*) and inferior (*ningan*). Related to this scheme is the probability that the back is superior to the front of the house. In the same way as the stringers are placed right (*phumlil*) first, left (*ningan*) second, so the crossbeam at the back is traditionally set in place first and then the crossbeam at the

front. This in turn is consistent with the facts that the house-owner's bed, the hearth, and the altar of the house-god are all in the back part of the house. These circumstances also confirm the ascription of the designations "right" and "left."

Another context in which the opposition of right and left is seen is the sacrifice of a fowl to the god of the house or the clan. The position of the legs of the bird at the time of death augurs the future of the sacrificers: if the right leg is on top of the left, it augurs well; but if the left is on top of the right it augurs ill. Here, then, right is auspicious, left inauspicious: i.e., right is superior to left. I think it is significant, too, that a sacrificial animal (pig or buffalo) is speared in the right side. This differentiation of value is confirmed by another situation, which clinches the argument with a further correlation. At the name-giving ceremony for a child of either sex, augury is sought in the same way in order to ascertain the child's future. In the case of a boy, a cock is strangled by the priest; and here also if the right is on top of the left leg it is regarded as a good omen, while the reverse forebodes evil. This we readily understand, but now the ritual opposition of right and left is reversed, in a feminine context. In the case of a girl, the ceremony is performed with a hen; and it is if the left leg is on top of the right that the augury is good, while the right on the left forebodes ill. We need not be surprised at this contextual reversal of the symbolism of the legs, nor does it controvert the inference about the general significance of right and left. As we shall see later, it introduces a scheme of oppositions wider than the opposition of the sides, and with which this particular instance of differential interpretation is entirely consistent. The interesting matter at this point is that male is associated with right and female with left.

This brings us back to the divisions of the house. Now *phumlil* is the "masculine" side, associated with the master of the house and with the resident males who are stationary while the women circulate. *Ningan* is certainly the "feminine" side, for the word also denotes all the women of the house, without distinction of generation, after they have been married out of the family and their clan. That is, it denotes women who have been transferred to wife-taking groups. Significantly, as we have seen, daughters who have married out sleep in the *ningan* half when they visit their parents, not in the *phumlil*; so that their status in the alliance system is marked even by the place where they have now to sleep in the house where they were born. This confirms, too, the association of kin with the *phumlil* side, affines with the *ningan* side of the house.

We may now introduce the term *maksa*, which most prominently denotes the husbands of the father's sister, the sister, and the daughter. There is of course the distinct term *rang* for father's sister's husband, while males of the succeeding generations are in any case denoted by the one term *tu*; but the term *maksa* is evidently not redundant. It denotes, not simply members of wife-taking categories, but individual men with whom alliances (by the cession of women to them) have actually been contracted.

The *maksa* are of supreme social and ritual importance to their wife-givers. At a certain prestige-feast it is the *maksa* of the celebrant who ceremonially kills the ox on his behalf, spearing it (significantly) in the right side. At the agricultural festival of Shanghong, each of the village officials performs a rite in connection with the rice and provides rice beer for the villagers; and it is the *maksa* who prepares the beer. At the installation feast of a village official, it is his *maksa* who distributes the rice beer. It is the *maksa* who is in charge of building a new house, not the house-owner; who prepares the rice beer for the feast of formal entry; who ceremonially kindles the first fire in it (cf. the observation above on the symbolic importance of the hearth); and who kills the animals for the feast.

An important ceremony in a child's life – that, in fact, at which his social life begins – is the first hair-cutting, by which he is ritually separated from the ancestral spirits and brought into membership of the lineage group. Rice beer and curried pork are offered to the ancestors, and it is the *maksa* and the *ningan* (their wives) who prepare the offerings. A pig is killed by the *maksa* and is then placed on the veranda with its head pointing east. Not only is the beer made by the *ningan*, but they must fetch the water for it themselves. This means that a *ningan* cannot be helped by women of her natal clan, for whose members the beer is made and to whose ancestors it is offered. The stipulation marks ritually the wife's complete severance from her natal group – she is so assimilated into her husband's group that when she dies she is buried in the cemetery of his clan – and maintains the symbolic separation of the alliance groups. At the feast the *maksa* and *ningan* sit apart from the elders and adult men of the child's descent group, with the young men, women, and children.

At the end of the period of bride-service it is the *maksa* who go to the house of the groom's father, kill a pig provided by him, and prepare a special sort of curry. This they take to the bride's house, with *ningan* bearing containers of rice beer. This party which goes out to bring back the married couple, to transfer the woman physically and finally from her natal group into that with which her marriage creates an alliance, consists of only *maksa* and *ningan* of the husband's group. No member of the clan of the groom's father can go, or can share the presents of meat and beer made at the feast in the house of the bride's father. These items are taboo to the bride and groom themselves, and to all female members who belong by birth to the bride's clan. The *maksa* and *ningan* bring the wife to the house of her husband's father.

At a burial the *maksa* are equally important. They wash the body of their "wife's father," and dress it; one of them spears a pig, and they prepare rice beer. The *ningan* may also bring rice beer with them: this is drunk by the village officials and other guests, but rice beer and other comestibles belonging to the house of the deceased cannot be touched. The *maksa* dig the grave, and four of them carry the corpse to the clan burial ground and bury it. Everything at the funeral is in the hands of the *maksa*: lineal relatives of the deceased take no part.

It is thus evident that in practically every event and institution of both individual and social importance the *maksa* – the actual wife-takers – are not only ritually important but are indispensable. A Purum cannot be socially born, or be married, he cannot make a new house, or assume an office, or approach the gods, he cannot even die, without the aid of his wife-takers.

Let us now look at material prestations and at the extent of their significance. Rice beer and pig-meat are movable economic valuables which are highly prized by the Purum and appear in a variety of contexts. The common character of these contexts, the apparent significance of the transfer of these articles, leads to the inference that we have here symbolic usages which are characteristic of this type of society.

Beer is typically given as an offering to gods and ancestral spirits: viz., at the invocation of a certain deity on entering a new house, the assumption of office by a village official, the ceremony devoted to the deity of the gates, and the invocation of the ancestral spirits at the haircutting ceremony. Pigs are sacrificed to gods and ancestral spirits: viz., to secure release from diseases which particular deities are believed to cause, at the election of the village headman, at the worship of the deity of the gates, at the harvest "thank-offering," to the ancestral spirits at the haircutting ceremony, and at the invocation of the forest deity. Whatever else may be symbolized, it is clear that in these cases beer and pigs are prestations from inferiors to superiors.

With the general character of these items established, we may look at the social relationships in which they also figure. Pigs and rice beer are always given by village officials when they are elected to office; fixed numbers and quantities are given for a village feast by the elected person according to the grade of the position. When a man is honored with a certain feast, he gives three pigs and twenty pots of beer. The set numbers and quantities indicate some symbolic element, but there is no certain evidence in the literature of what the significance may be. But other situations are quite clear. When a man enters his novitiate to become a "medicine-man" he presents his prospective teacher with beer and asks formally for instruction; and when he becomes a master he makes a formal presentation to his teacher of a number of prescribed articles, first among which is rice beer. He shows "respect" to his teacher, and on the latter's death he presents rice beer to his household. Here there is certainly the expression of deference, a prestation from an inferior to a superior.

Fines are the only forms of punishment for delicts and are always levied in beer and pigs. There are other forms of valuables, including cash, with which compensation could be made and economic deprivation inflicted, but beer and pigs are the only permitted forms. In economic terms, the rice with which the beer is made would be an almost equally punitive fine, but it is the beer that has to be given. It is not completely explanatory that pigs and rice are prominent economic valuables in an agricultural society of this sort: the invariant form of the fine and the ban on economic equivalents point to a symbolic significance, which is evidently that of expressing submission, the recognition of inferior status, by a symbolic prestation to a superior.

This leads us to what is structurally the most important context, the relationship between affines. A man wishing to marry his son to a certain girl takes a present of rice beer to the girl's father, begging him not to be "angry," and if the latter agrees to the proposal he drinks it. Here there is a double significance: that of the character of the present; and the fact that it is the wife-taker who pays the visit, humbly acknowledges his inferiority, and makes the proposal which the other may refuse. We know already that at the wedding rice beer is taken from the groom's father and given to the wife's father, together with a pig-meat curry.

Wife-takers, then, give rice beer and pig-meat to their wife-givers, just as do mortals to the gods. There is no indication anywhere in the literature that the reverse might be possible. We have already seen that wife-takers are inferior to wife-givers, and in this transfer of symbolic goods we see this status difference expressed.

We have also seen that, structurally speaking, there is a cycle of women, these supreme "movable valuables" being communicated in one "direction." Opposed to this cycle there is now a cycle of rice beer and pigs going in the opposite direction. That is, there is a division of economic goods (or those which are accorded symbolic significance) into "masculine" and "feminine" goods in contrary cycles. In matrilateral alliance the masculine goods circulate in the opposite direction to that of the women, and feminine goods in the same direction as the women. If we take the rice beer and meat to be masculine goods, what are the Purum equivalents of feminine goods other than the women themselves? There is unfortunately little evidence about gift exchange, but the important fact is clearly stated that when a woman is sent to her husband's house she takes with her one or more of the following articles: cloth, a brass plate, a carrying-basket, a storage-basket for valuables, a chopper, a brass cup, and a loom. If we may assume that the chopper is a domestic utensil proper to a woman's use (the monograph tells us that women use choppers in clearing land, and that it is they who collect firewood), it is satisfyingly clear that all these articles can be regarded as feminine goods and appropriate to the feminine cycle of prestations. Most significantly, we must note the presence of two items – cloth and the loom – which in better-known Indonesian systems of matrilateral alliance are pre-eminently feminine goods.

This division into two classes of goods is not merely a rational extension of the sexual division of labor, for Purum women cultivate and harvest the rice, raise pigs, and manufacture both cloth and beer, i.e., goods which belong to both classes. The goods and their cycles are conventionally opposed in a symbolism which is far wider and more significant, ritually and socially, than the particularities of any one institution or field of activity.

We may now return to the interpretation of the role of the *maksa*. We have seen that there are highly important chains of unilateral transfers of women and goods, which we have called cycles. In one direction there is structurally a circulation of women and certain associated goods in a "feminine cycle," and in the opposite direction there is a circulation of certain other goods in a "masculine cycle." But the importance of the valuables in the masculine cycle must seem rather trivial when compared with the value of women. In fact, however, this cycle includes other values, so that there is more of a "balance" than at first appears. Purum bride-service lasts three years, and we may picture as part of the masculine cycle three-year "units" of masculine labor circulating as prestations in exactly the same way as the more tangible masculine goods. Not only this, but there is a more vital type of prestation – the indispensable ritual services rendered by wife-takers to wife-givers. We may perhaps see, then, in these opposed cycles and classes a balance between two sorts of values, each vital to the total society. If the wife-takers depend on their wife-givers for women and the continuance of their lines, so in a similar fashion wife-givers depend utterly on their wife-takers (*maksa*) for indispensable aid in all the major events of life.

Thus the system is not characterized by the one cycle of the initial model, consisting of a unidirectional circulation of women, important though this is, but by a reciprocal opposition of two cycles, masculine and feminine. There may seem a contradiction in the fact that the superior wife-givers transmit feminine goods, while the inferior wife-takers transmit masculine goods, but I am sure there is not. Wife-takers in other such societies are characterized by the type of goods they receive, and it is they who are associated with the feminine cycle, not the group from which feminine goods issue. Generalizing, we may say that a prestation must be appropriate to the character and status of the receiver, and that a group is associated with those goods which are given to it. Masculine goods are therefore proper to wife-givers, and feminine goods to wife-takers: wife-givers are associated in this way with the (superior) masculine cycle, and wife-takers with the (inferior) feminine cycle.

Table 12.7 *Scheme of Purum Symbolic Classification*

Left	Right
Ningan division	*Phumlil* division
Front	Back
Affines	Kin
Public	Private
Strangers	Family
Wife-takers (*tu, maksa*)	Wife-givers (*pu*)
Inferior	Superior
Female	Male
Below	Above
Inauspicious	Auspicious
Feminine goods	Masculine goods
women	pigs, buffaloes
cloth	rice beer
loom	ritual services
domestic articles	labor (bride-service)
Mortals	Gods, ancestral spirits
Sun	Moon
Earth	Sky
(North)	South
West	East
Bad death	Good death
Even	Odd
Death	Life
Profane	Sacred
Sexual activity	Sexual abstinence
Forest	Village
Famine	Prosperity
Evil spirits, ghosts	Beneficent spirits

But this opposition is itself part of a dualistic system of symbolic classification in which pairs of opposite but complementary terms are analogically related as in the scheme in Table 12.7. To begin with, the oppositions are listed seriatim as they have been elicited in the exposition of the relevant facts; but I have added a number of others which I have not demonstrated. Since I have shown the principles and the pervasive nature of the classification in the major institutions of Purum society, it does not seem necessary to continue the demonstration in this place down to the last particular.

We see here, as elsewhere with prescriptive alliance, a mode of classification by which things, individuals, groups, qualities, values, spatial notions, and other ideas of the most disparate kinds are identically ordered within one system of relations. In particular, I would draw attention to the remarkable concordance and interconnection of social and symbolic structure. In spite of the fact that structurally

there must be three cyclically related lines in the alliance system, the basic scheme of Purum society is not triadic but dyadic. Any given alliance group is wife-taker and therefore inferior to another, but it is also wife-giver and therefore superior to another group in a different context. That is, alliance status is not absolute but relative. The distinction to be appreciated is that between the triadic *system* and its component dyadic *relation*. It is through this mode of relation that the social order concords with the symbolic order.

But in fact, though one may use these distinctive designations for convenience of description and analysis, what one is really dealing with in such a society as this is a classification, a system of categories, which orders both social life and the cosmos. That is, Purum social organization is ideologically part of a cosmological conceptual order and is governed identically by its ruling ideas.

IV

Here, then, we have a structurally typical example of a society prescribing marriage with the "mother's brother's daughter." I would stress, though, that (considerations of ethnographic comprehensiveness aside) it does not exhibit all the kinds of complexity which may be associated with matrilateral alliance. For example, Purum society has no rigid social stratification, and accordingly its descent groups are not ranked; it is not a territorially expansive or politically turbulent society, expressing and confirming political dominance and subjection through the categories of the alliance system; it has no further institutional complications such as moieties; and the population is very small. Yet, in spite of its institutional simplicity, I imagine it will be thought complex enough.

Matrilateral alliance can be regarded as a simple and effective way of creating and maintaining counter-fissive relationships in a segmentary society. We may find it most convenient therefore to characterize this form of society by its marriage prescription, and we have reason to do so since women are the prime movable valuables, and their transmission is in certain respects the most important type of prestation; but this must not distract us from other and contrary cycles of exchange, nor ultimately from the complementary dyadic mode of relation which is fundamental to Purum culture. As Hocart, with his characteristic insight, wrote in 1933 about dual organization, "The system then is not based on marriage, but marriage is regulated by the system."[8] The present system is defined by asymmetry, and the asymmetric rule of marriage is only one particularly prominent instance of this feature.

It is primarily on this point that Homans and Schneider come to grief, though an attentive and unbiased reading of Lévi-Strauss could have led them to see it: "...matrimonial exchange is only a particular case of those forms of multiple exchange which embrace material goods, rights, and persons; these exchanges themselves seem to be interchangeable."[9] It will be recalled that Homans and Schneider charge Lévi-Strauss with an excessively formal analysis, and assert that "the forces he exiled have returned to undo him."[10] But in fact he devotes a whole chapter to the wide range of prestations involved, with the express object of showing that the exchange of women is only one aspect of a "total phenomenon" of exchange; and he specifically denies that he in any way thinks that the exchange or gift of women is the sole means of establishing alliances in simple societies.[11] Although he has to restrict his detailed analyses to the examination of descent systems and rules of marriage (and still ends up with an enormous book), this emphasis on the total character of exchange runs throughout his work and even forms its concluding pages, where he brilliantly relates the marriage systems to other forms of "communication." Homans and Schneider, on the other hand, work with a model which is quite inapt to the study of themes of this scope or societies of this type.

The topic of generality raises two possible objections which might be made, both to Lévi-Strauss's work and to the present analysis, though neither of them really has more than a certain initial plausibility. First, in exchange we are dealing with a universal of human behavior, and it might therefore be thought that an explanation in terms of it is open to the same charge as psychological explanations, viz., that what is completely general cannot account for variant particulars. But it is not just exchange in general that plays such an important part here: it is one particular mode of exchange, *échange généralisé*, conceived as cyclic; and it takes place between groups, and groups of a certain kind, viz., lineal descent groups. Moreover, the notion of "exchange" really does help us to understand this type of marriage rule and social system, as nothing in Homans and Schneider's argument does.

A crucial question, of course, is why marriage with the "father's sister's daughter" is forbidden. By Lévi-Strauss's interpretation, the answer is clear: because it would be quite contrary to the established rules for the communication of women, by which the system is characterized and by which the relative status of the component descent groups of the society is defined. When we pursue the application of this notion of exchange into the analysis of other institutions, as I have done in outline for Purum society, we see that it is not only the exchange of women and the relations between descent groups that is in question, but that one and the same mode of prestation governs economic and religious relationships as well. And not only this, but the relation common to all these social institutions also receives cosmological expression. In other words, marriage with the patrilateral cross-cousin would not be simply an isolated act of wrongdoing, having limited (punitive) consequences just for the two individuals by whom it was perpetrated; but it would constitute an onslaught on the entire complex of identically ordered relationships which are the society, and on the symbolic classification which is its ideological life.

All this we are able to see thanks ultimately to the astonishingly fertile notion of "exchange" as an analytical concept, fashioned for us by Mauss and developed in the field of marriage by Lévi-Strauss. It is true that this is only a mediating concept, and that it alone could not bring the analysis quite to the point of radical understanding that I think we have reached here; but it is an essential notion, and it has done for us what a truly scholarly insight should do – it has made things plain. Would Homans and Schneider be prepared to claim as much now for their own theory? Is all this really to be explained, as they say, by "the Oedipus Complex"?

The second possible objection may be more briefly disposed of. I have tried to demonstrate that the fundamental mode of relation by which this type of society is articulated and through which it is to be understood is that of complementary dualism, and I approached this conclusion by way of the typical differential evaluation of right and left. Now a dualistic categorization of phenomena, and the symbolic opposition of the sides, are so common in history and in societies which we know directly as to appear natural proclivities of the human mind.[12] I think indeed that they are. But is not this part of my analysis, in its turn, analogous therefore to those features of a psychological argument which invalidate the latter? Durkheim has the short answer to this, viz., that a psychological explanation allows everything that is social to escape.[13] But my ultimate recourse to epistemology does the reverse: it permits us to see an instance of matrilateral alliance, in all its institutional aspects, in terms of a relation of complete generality to that society. Moreover, this type of elucidation is, I think, feasible to this degree only in systems of prescriptive alliance, so that the very pragmatic effectiveness of the interpretation is itself a characteristic feature of the type of society in question. None of this is true of an explanation of social phenomena in terms of psychological universals, and certainly not of Homans and Schneider's particular argument.

It all comes down to the matter of understanding what we are trying to understand. I claim that structural analysis, of the sort inaugurated in this field by Lévi-Strauss and developed here in the analysis of a particular society, does give understanding. On the other hand, by thus laying bare the empirical features of matrilateral alliance, with which any theory has to cope, it has become perfectly clear that Homans and Schneider's psychological analysis is based upon a disablingly partial command of the facts. This must be due to a certain extent to the nature of their intellectual interests, and to the type of theory which they had tentatively framed and which they desired to prove; but whether or not these inferences are justified, it is apparent that they did not first comprehend that which they purported to explain. At any rate, it is undeniable that they

have in no way adequately carried out their proclaimed intention to relate the rule of marriage to other institutions;[14] whereas I think the present analysis has done so, and in a completely general fashion.[15]

NOTES

1 Homans, 1942, p. 402.
2 Needham, 1958. A complete analysis, argued without consideration of length and very much amplified, will appear in a future monograph. For another analysis of the same kind, relating to a different culture, see Needham, 1960c.
3 Das, 1945.
4 It may prove interesting to keep the following observation in mind during the course of this chapter: "A disproportionate amount of attention has been given to kinship terminology, largely because it includes the facts about kinship that are most easily collected.... We shall not discuss the different systems of kinship terminology, suspecting that systems which look rather unlike one another may be so because, in effect, a close decision went one way rather than another" (Homans, 1951, p. 223). There could hardly be a remark more revealing of the bias which inspires *Marriage, Authority, and Final Causes*, or so indicative of the roots of its failure.
5 The related Chawte, who may have the same marriage prescription, are reported to make the same equation; but the ethnography on this society is quite unreliable in such respects (Needham, 1960a).
6 Homans and Schneider, 1955, p. 6.
7 Needham, 1960b.
8 Hocart, 1933, p. 258. Cf. Lévi-Strauss, 1949, pp. 129–30.
9 Lévi-Strauss, 1949, pp. 145–46.
10 Homans and Schneider, 1955, p. 59. Cf. "The models may...get too simple, and what Lévi-Strauss discards will live to undo him" (Homans, 1955, p. 136).
11 Lévi-Strauss, 1949, pp. 66–86, 599.
12 Hertz, 1909. Cf. Needham, 1960d.
13 Durkheim, 1901, p. 131.
14 Homans and Schneider, 1955, p. 20. p. 29.
15 This does not at all mean, however, that I think my analysis is finally correct, or that it is the only structural interpretation which might be made.

BIBLIOGRAPHY

Das, Tarak Chandra 1945 *The Purums: An Old Kuki Tribe of Manipur.* Calcutta.

Durkheim, Émile 1901 *Les Règles de la méthode sociologique.* (2d ed.) Paris.

Hertz, Robert 1909 "La prééminence de la main droite: Étude sur la polarité religieuse." *Revue philosophique,* LXVIII, 553–80. (Also in English translation by RODNEY and CLAUDIA NEEDHAM, in *Death and The Right Hand,* London, 1960.)

Hocart, A. M. 1933 *The Progress of Man.* London.

Homans, George Caspar 1942 *English Villagers of the Thirteenth Century.* Cambridge, Mass.

—— 1951 *The Human Group.* London.

—— 1955 Review of de Josselin de Jong, 1952. *American Anthropologist,* LVII, 136–37.

Homans, George C., and Schneider, David M. 1955 *Marriage, Authority, and Final Causes: A Study of Unilateral Cross-Cousin Marriage.* Glencoe, Ill.

Lévi-Strauss, Claude 1949 *Les Structures élémentaires de la Parenté.* Paris.

Needham, Rodney 1958 "A Structural Analysis of Purum Society." *American Anthropologist,* LX, 75–101.

—— 1960a "Chawte Social Structure." *American Anthropologist,* LXII, 236–53.

—— 1960b "Structure and Change in Asymmetric Alliance." *American Anthropologist,* LXII, 499–503.

—— 1960c "Alliance and Classification among the Lamet." *Sociologus,* X, 97–119.

—— 1960d "The Left Hand of the Mugwe: An Analytical Note on the Structure of Meru Symbolism." *Africa,* XXX, 20–33.

13

Tetradic Theory: An Approach to Kinship

N. J. Allen

1. Kinship

1.1. Social anthropology is the collective attempt to come to terms with the diversity of the societies the world has seen.

1.2. One aspect of this diversity is the variety of ways in which societies have elaborated on the biological imperatives to mate and reproduce. *The study of kinship is the study of what societies make of the relations between the sexes and generations.*

1.3. From these relations a society not only makes a kinship system; it makes itself. To merit the name of a society a group must endure, normally by the continuing production of new generations to replace old. Nothing that a society might produce could be more fundamental to it; and the mode of production imposed by biology involves both sexes. Thus kinship is necessarily fundamental among social phenomena.

1.3.1. The production of its new members *constitutes* a society. In contrast, the production or provision of a food supply, which is also a biological imperative and variously elaborated, is merely a *condition* for social continuity; it is not *what we mean* by the continuity.

2. What Sorts of Kinship Phenomena Are Basic to the Theory?

2.1. Societies handle the relations between the sexes and generations in two ways which are logically different: egocentric (relativistic, local, individual) and sociocentric (absolute, global, holistic). The egocentric system pertains to the relatives of an *individual*, ego, the sociocentric to the structure of *society as a whole*.

2.2. Occasionally 'kinship' is used in the narrow sense of 'consanguinity as opposed to affinity'. Ordinary usage associates it most closely with the egocentric system. *But any general theory of kinship must handle sociocentric phenomena as well as egocentric.* (If a society consists of three endogamous hereditary strata, the relations between the sexes and generations are implicated *ipso facto*.)

2.3. From the whole range of kinship phenomena conceived in this way, the theory abstracts the most 'formal', those that provide the framework for the rest.

2.3.1. Sociocentrically, the focus is on social structure or social morphology, and we shall narrow these expressions so as to exclude, especially, considerations of territory. Egocentrically, the focus is on the constitution of the domain of relatives, i.e. on its range and structure, and particularly on kinship terminologies, understood in the narrowest sense.

2.3.2. These formal aspects of kinship are interrelated, offer the greatest scope for rigorous abstract treatment, and have historically been at the centre of the field. If a satisfactory general theory of kinship is possible they must be part of it, and no doubt part of its core. Their relationship to other aspects is scarcely touched on.

3. Conceptual Steps to the Notion of Tetradic Society

3.1. Although the theory grew out of analyses of Tibeto-Burman kinship terminologies and clan organisation, and has been developed by working back and forth between facts and abstractions, it is best *presented* by separating the empirical and theoretical, and concentrating on the latter.

3.2. *The conceptual starting point is the totality* par excellence – *society, endogamous and enduring.* At this point nothing more is specified than that sexual relations stop at the bounds of society, that all new members result from these relations, and that membership of the society is co-extensive with the domain of ego's relatives.

3.3. *The simplest step towards reality is to split the totality into two endomating child-exchanging sociocentric levels* ('generation moieties'). The rules are now that sexual relations are confined to one's own level, and that recruitment is to the level of the grandparents.

3.3.1. The most obvious alternative to 3.3 is to split the totality into patri- or matri-moieties. However, this would be to introduce not only a bifurcation but also a sexual asymmetry.

3.4. The next, and final, step is a second bifurcation: each sociocentric level is split into exogamous sections in such a way that people who are brother and sister to each other belong in the same section. The marriage rule is now 'own level, other section'; but for the recruitment rule there exist two possibilities.

3.4.1. Consider the four grandparents. Symmetry demands that each section contain one male grandparent and one female. FF and FM are married, so must belong in different sections. That leaves FF and MM, i.e. PssP, in one section, PosP in the other. Ego could be recruited to either.

3.4.2. In the former case the line of same-sex ascendants or descendants *oscillates* between two sections, while in the latter it *cycles* round all four. For convenience we shall focus on the oscillatory model. Cf. Figure 13.1.

3.4.3. (We shall ignore some other comparable quadripartite models, for instance, those locating the interlevel division at marriage rather than at birth, and those that make the four components endogamous rather than exogamous.)

3.5. All such models (whose properties remain to be defined) will be called 'tetradic'. The label is used both specifically, as in speaking of 'the focal tetradic model', and generically, to speak of 'tetradic society' (as one might speak of 'feudal society'). Tetradic society is the fundamental concept in the present theory, which is therefore named after it.

4. Some Properties of the Model

4.1. *The focal tetradic model prescribes marriage within a section which includes cross cousins and excludes primary kin; marriage of a male with his M, Z or D is thus precluded.*

4.1.2. If it is stipulated that sexual relations take place only between spouses or potential spouses, the model precludes incest in the sense of sexual

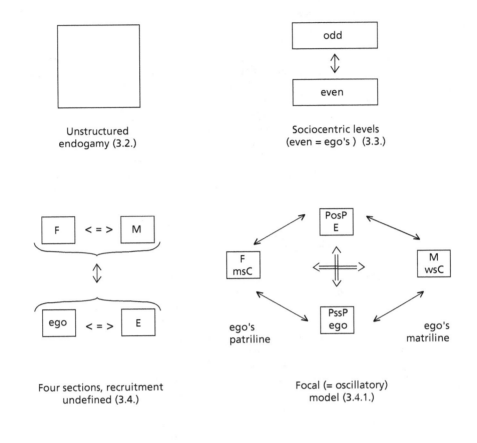

Legend

<   =   >   represents marriage or alliance relations

↕ ↗ ↘   represent child-exchange relations

ms, ws   male ego's, female ego's
ss, os   same-sex, opposite-sex
E   spouse

Figure 13.1   *Conceptual steps leading to the focal tetradic model*

intercourse between primary relatives.

4.2.   This gives the tetradic model a realistic quality absent from the models of 3.2–3.3.1–so much so that if a primate society conformed to the model, one would be confident that the society was a human one. That is

why 3.4. talked of 'marriage' rather than 'mating'.

4.3.   The society posited in 3.2 cannot be split into *two* enduring groups in such a way as automatically to preclude incest in the specified sense. A *four-element* structure is the simplest that can do this.

4.4.   Tetradic models are such elementary logical constructs that anthropologists would have had to invent them even if neither section systems nor cross-cousin marriage had ever been reported.

4.5.   Given a total population of a few hundred, there is no reason of a demographic nature to prevent the rules being adhered to perfectly. (To be sure, real societies seldom obey their rules perfectly; there is nothing to stop the model builder imagining rules to deal with deviants.)

4.6.   Though exceedingly simple compared to attested societies, tetradic models are sufficiently complex to raise worthwhile conceptual problems. Their theoretical significance derives from their position at a threshold along the scale leading from almost vacuous logical simplicity towards unmanageable complication.

4.7.   Their properties derive from human biology, notably from the existence of the two sexes and their necessary co-operation in reproduction (*not* from any a priori interest that may attach to the number four).

5. Tetradic Terminologies

5.1.1. A tetradic society could obey its own marriage and recruitment rules without possessing verbal language (for instance, if section members were distinguished absolutely by body-painting). *A fortiori*, it could function without a kinship terminology.

5.1.2. However, an analyst could not claim to have fully understood it (or to have translated it so as to render it readily understandable to others) without envisaging it egocentrically.

5.1.3. Moreover, the members of a tetradic society could distinguish the sections and follow their rules using *solely* an egocentric, relativistic nomenclature (i.e. kinship terms), in the absence of any absolute nomenclature.

5.2.   *The simplest kinship terminology making the necessary distinctions has four terms.* Each ego classifies relatives into four categories, each category corresponding to one section. Egos in two different sections using the same term are, of course, referring to relatives located (absolutely) in different sections.

5.3.   The otherwise similar four-term terminology presented in *JASO* 1982[1] was unnecessarily indigestible in that it pressed relativism to the limit: the term ego applied to relatives in the odd level was *doubly* relativistic, i.e. relative to the sex as well as to the section of ego.

5.3.1. The focal tetradic society presented here can be characterised from an egocentric point of view as *singly* relativistic. To take account of 3.4.3, one could complete the characterisation by stating that, from both egocentric and sociocentric points of view, the society is not only oscillatory but also 'single-stage' (in that the individual's life-cycle is not bisected at marriage), and 'BZ-merging' (as opposed to 'HW-merging').

5.4.   The categorisation of any kin-type, however remote, can be readily calculated with the aid of Figure 13.2, supplemented by 'the principle of same-sex sibling equivalence'. This states that, whether as alters or as link relatives, ssG are to be treated as indiscriminable. (As an exercise, check that MZSDSWZHMBWM is classified with Z.)

5.5.   The sociocentric structuring of society and the egocentric categorisation of relatives here pattern the same universe using the same dividing lines.

5.6.   *A tetradic society is defined as a quadripartite society which handles the relations between the sexes and generations in such a way that the egocentric and sociocentric systems are co-extensive and isomorphic.*

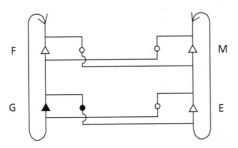

Ego by convention is located in the lower left quadrant. Relatives are categorised with siblings (G), father, mother or spouse, according to their quadrant.
The arrows show the direction of the passage of time. Thus to reach ego's FF, one follows the line from F backwards in time round the outside of the diagram and down to the triangle which already represents a male ego and his ssG.
(The diagram can just as well be drawn with circles replacing triangles and vice versa, in which case the labels M and F must be reversed. The *diagram* would then show a female bias rather than a male one, but the *structure*, the set of relationships represented by the diagram, would be unchanged.)

Figure 13.2   *Genealogical diagram underlying the focal tetradic terminology*

6.   Corollaries and Refinements

6.1.   Sociocentrically, the splitting of the endogamous levels (3.4) affects both levels identically, but egocentrically it does not. The even level is split into ego's own section, which includes parallel cousins, and the section in which the closest cognates are cross cousins; so the split can aptly be called parallel versus cross. As for the odd level, ego is in a sense closer to the section of his or her children, which is also that of his or her ssP, than to the other section; but male ego is closer to one section, female to the other. Thus odd-level relatives can be qualified as parallel or cross only at the cost of neglecting one sex of ego.

6.2.   As presented so far, *tetradic models are wholly symmetrical as between the two sexes.* The term 'descent' is usually, and properly, associated with unilineality, and will always imply it below. Thus the term cannot be applied to tetradic models unless an asymmetry is explicitly introduced.

6.2.1.   In its place, the more general and versatile term 'recruitment' is used to refer to the maintenance of continuity (especially sociocentric) across the gener-

ations. One can speak either of a section recruiting certain of the grandchildren of its members, or of new members of society being recruited to the section of certain grandparents – looking 'downwards' to the future or 'upwards' to the past respectively.

6.2.2.   Where necessary, one can distinguish the sociocentric relation of 'alliance' holding between sections and the egocentric relation of 'marriage' holding between relatives.

6.3.   Out of the rules that constitute a tetradic model, one can theoretically abstract rules of *marriage* bearing on the relations between the sexes and rules of *recruitment* bearing on the relations between the generations; but the separation is artificial, since each type of rule presupposes the operation of the other. *The rules constituting a tetradic society form a single complex, within which marriage and recruitment are of equal significance.*

6.4.   The model prescribes marriage into the section which includes cross cousins, but it does not prescribe cross-cousin marriage, even bilateral. Male ego can marry DD or even, if he wishes, FM.

6.5.   Similarly, the model cannot be im-
          agined as consisting of genealogical
          levels stacked one above another. Sup-
          pose one possesses the complete
          genealogical records of a properly
          functioning tetradic society. If one
          takes a particular genealogical level,
          say +2, and works outwards from a
          lineal relative of ego, say FF, confining
          oneself to intra-generational or 'hori-
          zontal' genealogical links (G, E, PGC,
          CEP), one will eventually reach ego,
          and FFFF, but never FFF or F. *The
          model does not recognise the distinc-
          tion between genealogical levels as
          such; it recognises the distinction be-
          tween even-level relatives and odd-
          level ones.*
6.5.1.   Rather than levels stacked in a pile,
          one can imagine a double helix. The
          two strands represent the two socio-
          centric levels and spiral round an axis
          representing time. The time taken to

complete a single circuit of the axis is
two generations.[2]

7. What Is the Use of Tetradic Models?

7.1.   They can help in refining analytical
          concepts (as in 6).
7.2.   As will be the main theme of the rest
          of the paper, the models can serve as
          the starting point for generating
          models of more complex kinship
          systems. *Tetradic theory is the theory
          that attested kinship systems should
          be set in relation to tetradic models.*
7.2.1.   The relation between a tetradic
          model and an attested kinship system
          has two components: typological
          (conveniently thought of as hori-
          zontal), and ontological, holding
          between different 'levels' of ab-
          straction or concreteness. Cf. Figure
          13.3.

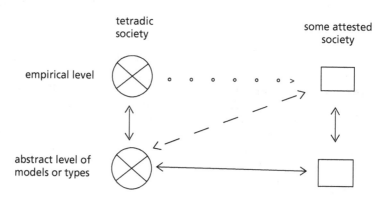

The theory recommends formulating the relation

$\updownarrow$ = reversible analytical operations of abstraction/enrichment.

$\longleftrightarrow$ = reversible analytical operations of typological transfor-

mation (which might be drawn $\longleftrightarrow$ to indicate the divergence
of the egocentric and sociocentric – 8.5.). On the strong interpretation
of the theory, ∘ ∘ ∘ > represents essentially one-way historical processes.

Figure 13.3 *Relations between components of tetradic theory.*

7.2.2. To conceptualize the ontological relation in isolation, imagine a society attempting to realise a tetradic model. It would have to fill out or enrich its formal rules with other rules bearing on residence, divorce, plural marriage, matrimonial choice, forms of address, etc. Given the description of such a society, an analyst could reverse the process of enrichment and abstract the underlying model.

7.2.3. A tetradic model could, of course, be filled out in a variety of ways. The resulting realisations would all have something in common, and from descriptions of them the analyst could abstract what they shared. One might equally well call this the *model* underlying all the realisations, or the *type* of which the realisations were tokens. 'Model' usually implies more precise specification than 'type'.

7.2.4. Types or models generated from tetradic models bear to their realisations the same ontological relation as tetradic models bear to theirs. The ontological relation seems less problematic than the typological, and it is on the latter that we must concentrate in the first instance.

7.3. Tetradic theory can be interpreted in a weak fashion or a strong one. The weak holds merely that it is analytically valuable to look at real kinship systems as if they derived from tetradic models, but remains agnostic on whether they did so. *The strong interpretation holds that attested kinship systems derive historically from ones of tetradic type.*

7.3.1. The weak interpretation could be held alone, but the strong interpretation implies the weak.

7.4. The strong interpretation, which is much the more interesting, might serve to guide research on the relation between prehuman and human society.[3]

7.5. The theory offers a firm base from which to explore the jungle of the specialist literature on kinship. Such an exploration would not only contribute to the historiography of social anthropology, but would also consolidate the theory itself and provide a (much needed) expression of its indebtedness to its predecessors.

7.6. In principle, the theory might guide reflection on kinship phenomena other than the strictly formal (e.g. prescribed sentiments[4]), and on non-kinship phenomena relatable to kinship ones.

7.6.1. For instance, in so far as society is an aspect of the cosmos, and in so far as religion is an attempt to apprehend what gives continuity to the cosmos, the theory could have a bearing on religion. (Supernaturals are commonly associated with components of social structure, or with the functions performed by such components.[5])

7.7. If the theory is taken seriously, it must have a bearing on general theoretical positions within anthropology. For instance, as regards structuralism, one thing it suggests is that the binary oppositions favoured by that approach may sometimes be fragments of or derivative from more complex four-element structures.

7.8. However, applications 7.4–7.7 lie outside the scope of this paper.

8. How Can the Focal Tetradic Model Be Used to Generate Other Models (7.2.)?

8.1. The model is subjected to stepwise transformations, each of which can be regarded as instantaneous and complete (in contrast, of course, to *historical* transformations – 15.2.1.).

8.2. The number of transformations theoretically conceivable is indefinite – a powerful enough magic wand can change anything into anything else. The transformations likely to prove *instructive* will be as follows: (i) they will produce more or less familiar models, i.e. idealisations approximating to attested kinship systems; (ii) they will be reasonably simple in themselves, from a logical point of view; (iii) they will be such as could be realised by reasonably plausible historical processes.

8.3. In formulating transformations, it is unnecessary to specify every detail. It is sufficient to generate *types* (7.2.2–3.).

8.4. *The majority of the more familiar types can be generated by a single series of transformations*, each acting on the result of its predecessor. (This finding results from trial and error, rather than from any a priori leaning towards unilineal evolutionary theory.)

8.5. Tetradic society is characterised by the perfect overlap and isomorphism of the egocentric and sociocentric systems, but the perfect fit disappears as soon as one leaves tetradic models, and the further one moves away from them, the more the two branches draw apart. They are best followed separately in the first instance.

9. Egocentric Branch: Properties of the Focal Tetradic Terminology

9.1. The terminology covers the whole of society, and not only its members within living memory, but *all* members, from the indefinite past to the indefinite future; its range is truly total. This makes the society 'closed', in a strong sense.

9.2. Each term covers a homogeneous category. The genealogical distance separating ego from an alter is irrelevant, and to stipulate that a category 'centred' on a focal specification would be to detract from its perfect congruence with a component of social structure, and hence to change the character of the terminology as a whole.

9.3. The 'formal' semantic structure of a terminology consists in the discriminations and equations that it makes. In a model terminology these will fall into clear-cut types. The focal terminology makes three types of discrimination, one structurally insignificant type of equation, and three important types of equation.

9.4. The three types of discrimination separate relatives belonging to (i) different sociocentric levels, (ii) different even-level sections, (iii) different odd-level sections (cf. 6.1.). One may refer to the one 'vertical' and the two 'horizontal' discriminations.

9.5. Step 5.2. equated male and female members of a section; but nothing fundamental changes if we introduce the discrimination of sexes (a suffix marking one sex would suffice).

9.6. *The three important types of equation are as follows:*

9.6.1. Alternate generation equations (like $Z = FFZ$) equate kin-types belonging within a single section but removed from each other by two generations. (It is convenient to include under the heading equations such as $FF = SS$ where the number of generations separating two kin-types is a multiple of two.)

9.6.2. Prescriptive equations (like $MBD = W$) equate same-generation relatives who are represented by a single symbol in a genealogical diagram showing prescribed cross-cousin marriage. (Figure 13.2 can be counted as such a *diagram*, in spite of 6.4. Prescriptive equations include not only cognate-affine ones but also cognate-cognate and affine-affine ones.)

9.6.3. Classificatory equations (like $F = FB$, $S = msBS$) equate kin-types by using the principle of same-sex sibling equivalence (5.4.).

10. Egocentric Branch: The Three Major Recognised Types

10.1 Tetradic terminologies, which have not been attested empirically or recognised theoretically, can be called type 1. *Types II–IV are generated by replacing the three major types of equation by three new types of discrimination.*

10.2.1. Type II are the conventional prescriptive terminologies; they make prescriptive equations (9.6.2.), but the diagrams they are related to lack the 'vertical cycles' shown by the lines with arrows passing round the outside of Figure 13.2. (In practice, the conventional diagrams usually show a 'stack' of five genealogical levels.)

10.2.2. Type II is generated from type I by eliminating the alternate generation equations. Since *adjacent* genealogical levels are already discriminated, to discriminate *alternate* ones is to distribute relatives into a stack of genealogical levels (cf. 6.5.). This has radical effects, both 'horizontal' and 'vertical'.

10.2.3. The prescribed category is no longer sociocentric as well as egocentric. It is no longer an enduring component of society with a constant inflow of new members. Unlike a sociocentric level, a genealogical level eventually dies out. If marriages were strictly confined to a genealogical level, instances would necessarily arise when the last-born member of a genealogical level could not find a spouse. If one takes account of demography (not merely of genealogical diagrams), *the only societies which can obey perfectly a rule prescribing marriage with an egocentric category of relatives are those in which the category is also sociocentric.* Tetradic societies are workable (4.5.) in a sense that non-tetradic societies with positive marriage rules are not. The latter *must* sometimes 'fudge' their marriage rules.

10.2.4. The temporal range of the terminology is restricted. It could only continue to cover the indefinite past and future (9.1.) by inventing indefinite numbers of new terms for the 'unfolded' remoter levels. Being excluded from the field of the terminology, distant ancestors are no longer relatives of ego *in the same sense* as members of close genealogical levels.

(Perhaps the relation might rather be felt as religious.)

10.3. Type III terminologies are classificatory but non-prescriptive. They are generated from type II by eliminating the prescriptive equations, most obviously by systematically discriminating cognates and affines.

10.3.1. Although theoretically it may not be absolutely necessary, we may reasonably stipulate that the range of the terminology is no longer co-extensive with society (understood more or less synchronically). This creates an implicit category of contemporary members of society who are not relatives. (One supposes that ego might feel towards them a sense of 'ethnic' identification or solidarity, with political implications.)

10.4. Type IV terminologies are non-classificatory, i.e. descriptive. They are generated from type III by eliminating the classificatory equations, i.e. by systematically discriminating those previously equated on the basis of the ssG equivalence principle. Type IV terminologies are necessarily limited to covering a range of kin-types removed from ego by only a relatively small number of genealogical steps.

10.4.1. (If such a terminology is used by a society having endogamous sub-divisions, the effect of the limitation is to create for ego an implicit category of potential-but-not-actual relatives, towards whom he might feel yet a third type of identification, based perhaps on common life-style or economic expectations.)

11. Egocentric Branch: Elaborations

11.1. The majority of generally recognised terminological types can be related to types II–IV. The main exception is the generational ('Hawaiian') type, which in addition to using the principle of ssG equivalence treats osG as equivalent when they are link relatives.

11.2.   Types I–IV can be refined to give constructs having any desired degree of specificity. We consider only one subdivision per type.

11.2.1. Closely related to tetradic terminologies are terminologies which retain the egocentric-sociocentric isomorphism but divide the universe into a *multiple* of four categories (this number assumes that males and females within a category are not discriminated). For instance, eight categories can be arranged two-by-two in four sociocentric levels, or four apiece in two levels as with the Aranda.

11.2.2. Type II can be divided into symmetrical and asymmetrical, as is conventional.

11.2.3. Type III may show 'skewing', i.e. it may override the vertical tetradic discrimination by making the Crow–Omaha equation of cross cousins on the one side with +1 cognates, on the other side with −1; or it may not.

11.2.4. Type IV may wholly lack equations; or it may make 'counter-tetradic' equations, like FBS = FZS or FB = MB, which override the horizontal tetradic discriminations (even-level and odd-level respectively) – as in English.

11.3.   A type I terminology takes account neither of genealogical distance (9.2.) nor of genealogical level (as distinct from sociocentric level). In a type IV terminology genealogical concepts are fundamental, and sometimes a one-to-one relationship exists between kinship terms and genealogical formulae. The importance given to genealogy by types II and III is intermediate, and they can be envisaged, as it were, from either side.

11.3.1. If the analyst's conceptual starting-point is type IV, ego is envisaged as surrounded by concentric circles of relatives, primary, secondary and tertiary, at increasing degrees of genealogical distance. Classificatory equations then appear as the result of kinship terms *extending* their meanings outwards from the closest, focal meaning, and prescriptive equations appear as the result of eliminating the terms rendered redundant by superimposing cognates and affines. In so far as one is interested merely in translation between European kinship categories and exotic ones, this approach is not necessarily valueless.

11.3.2. However, tetradic theory naturally recommends starting conceptually with type I, and envisaging the other types as resulting from *contraction*. The general trend is *from* focus on the totality *towards* focus on the individual ego.

11.3.3. The model-builder can leave unspecified the extent to which categories in the intermediate types II and III may be conceived of by ego as polarised (between the genealogically closest kin type and remoter types), rather than as homogeneous in the sense of 9.2.

12. Sociocentric Branch: Generalities

12.1.   For our model-building purposes, *social structure can be defined as the mode of division of a whole endogamous society on the basis of kinship.*

12.2.   Some societies, especially nowadays, lack a social structure in this sense, and to generate corresponding models one must include in the theory a transformation deleting non-egocentric internal dividing lines.

12.3.   Whereas there is little incentive to generate models in which two kinship terminologies co-exist, there is no objection to models in which a plurality of social structures co-exist, either subsuming or cross-cutting each other.

12.4.   As with the egocentric branch (8.2–4), the types or models an analyst is most likely to want can be generated in essentials with a reasonable degree of economy and historical plausibility by starting from tetradic models.

13. Sociocentric Branch: Major Transformations

13.1. In tetradic society one sociocentric dividing line separates parents *en bloc* from their children, while the other splits up spouses, including an ego's parents. (Following 9.4, one has to call the P/C divide 'vertical'; but although it pertains to a 'vertical' relationship, the line is most naturally *pictured* horizontally.)

13.1.1. By eliminating first the P/C divide, then the E/E divide as well, one distinguishes three major types of social structure. In terms of recruitment, child-exchanging structures locate children in the component of *neither* parent, while descent-based ones locate them in that of *one* parent; structures based on endogamous groups recruit bilaterally and locate children in the component of *both* parents. In terms of alliance, the three types (i) put E, F, M and ego into equally separate components, (ii) keep E and ego in separate components while putting ego in the natal component of one parent (E may or may not be in the natal component of the other), (iii) put all four in the same component.

13.2. To move from exogamous tetradic sections to exogamous descent groups, one must merge the children's section with the section of one or other parent. The following seem the most obvious transformational paths.

13.2.1. If each odd-level section merges with one even-level section, the result is descent moieties (patri- or matri-).

13.2.2. By moving to an eight-element Aranda-type model (11.2.1) before merging sections (or 'sub-sections') of adjacent levels, one can generate a four-clan model with symmetrical exchange.

13.2.3. If, before the merging, one moves to an eight-element model with asymmetrical exchange between subsections, one can generate a four-clan model with asymmetrical exchange.

13.2.4. In both four-clan models the clans are arranged in exogamous pairs. One can therefore recognise two levels of organisation or segmentation: binary into moieties, quadripartite into clans.

13.3. All these sociostructural models possess a quality of rigidity resulting from (i) a fixed number of exogamous components (at most eight), (ii) a fixed number of levels of organisation (at most three), (iii) fixed alliance relations (symmetrical or not) between components. To generate models applying to a wider range of descent-based societies, one must eliminate the rigidity.

13.4. A plausible way to do this is to increase the number of components. If the society remains reproductively bounded, the new units must be formed by segmenting preexisting ones. By segmenting and resegmenting, one can generate models with an indefinite number of units arranged in an indefinite number of levels of segmentation.

13.4.1. Whenever a unit is segmented, the model-builder can stipulate the fate of the original unsegmented component. The latter may be eliminated from the model so that the resultant units are no more closely interrelated than any other pair of units of the same level of segmentation; or it may be retained as a component of the model on the superordinate level of segmentation. If it is retained it may remain exogamous; or the new segments may be defined as the maximal exogamous units.

13.4.2. Further flexibility can be introduced by eliminating fixed alliance relations. The model-builder again enjoys considerable freedom to stipulate how and at what point this shall come about.

13.4.3. These operations generate sociostructural models in which the relations between generations are handled by the rule of unilineal descent and the relations between sexes by rules of descent-group exogamy. The descent groups may or may not show more than one level of segmentation. The rules of exogamy may apply to the descent groups of more than one of ego's grandparents (Crow–Omaha models), or only to ego's own descent group.

13.5. *The final major step is to segregate descent groups into endogamous sets.* Once such 'endo-recruiting' components have been constituted, the descent groups may be deleted.

13.5.1. Theoretically, each endogamous component might be equally valued, but the models will come closer to empirical societies if the components are ranked. (Empirically, higher rank might be represented by greater honour, power, wealth, purity, etc., but formal models must abstract from such particular values. The highest ranking element would be the one closest to representing the whole.)

13.5.2. All the social structures considered so far have consisted of components which are sharply bounded, in the sense that every member of society belongs unambiguously in one component or another, or at least in the sense that this applies to one sex. Such structures can be called segmentary or 'partitional'. (Where there is any risk of confusion, one must distinguish this concept from the narrower notion of segmentation on a multiplicity of levels, as in 13.4.)

13.5.3. To generate a model of a class-based society, one must replace sharp boundaries by statistical ones. In the limit, even the notion of statistically separable strata can be replaced by a continuum of ranked positions with a statistical tendency for members of a nuclear family to cluster around a point on the continuum. This would no longer be a social structure in the sense of 12.1.

14. Relations Between the Egocentric and the Sociocentric

14.1. Corresponding more or less to the types set up independently for the two branches, one may distinguish the following situations: (i) perfect isomorphism; (ii) approximate isomorphism; (iii) egocentric domain covers at least one component of social structure but not all of them; (iv) egocentric domain is included within one component.

14.2. In the perfectly isomorphic tetradic models, the systematic equation of alternate genealogical levels correlates with socio-structural components which endure by recruiting grandchildren, not children; and the lateral symmetry of the terminology corresponds to the symmetry between the sexes, in particular to the lack of lineality.

14.3. The conventional genealogical diagrams which underlie prescriptive *terminologies* (10.2.1) can also represent *social structures* consisting of descent groups in enduring alliance relationships. For the sake of clarity the two interpretations of the diagrams should be distinguished, but the very possibility of ambiguity expresses the approximate isomorphism which characterises kinship systems based on conventional (= non-tetradic) elementary structures.

14.3.1. ('Elementary structures', in whatever forms they may be *realised*, are best understood as *being* the abstract relations expressed in genealogical diagrams representing cross-cousin marriage [cf. 9.6.2]. Tetradic structures, as exemplified in Figure 13.2, are more elementary than conventional elementary structures and can be termed the only *truly* elementary structures.)

14.4. With the loss of prescriptive equations and of the corresponding alliance relations, the scope for egocentric–sociocentric isomorphism decreases, but Crow–Omaha models attempt, as it were, to salvage what they can. The terminology covers the descent groups not only of ego but also (at whatever level of segmentation) of some of his non-lineal cognates (13.4.3), reflecting the lineality of these groups in its vertical equations (11.2.3).

14.4.1. Other type III terminologies can retain a degree of isomorphism by making some egocentric category boundaries coincide with group boundaries – for instance, by limiting 'classificatory father' to covering +1 males *within the patriclan*. Except in certain cases of double descent, this would preclude application of the principle of ssG equivalence to both sexes *to the same extent*.

14.5. The elimination of classificatory equations and of descent groups are parallel operations. With this step, one eliminates the possibility of the egocentric and sociocentric systems sharing internal dividing lines, and there is nothing left of the original isomorphism.

14.5.1. (In an absolute sense, one now sees a return to the symmetry between the sexes that was characteristic of tetradic models. Sociocentrically, the symmetry is seen in the bilateral recruitment rule, and egocentrically in the elimination of the asymmetry mentioned in 11.2.3 and 14.4.1; also, where they occur, in counter-tetradic equations such as FB = MB. However, where this form of symmetry *disregards* the difference between the sexes, the tetradic form recognises the difference while avoiding differential *weighting* of one or other sex.)

15. In Conclusion

15.1. This paper has offered an *approach*; within its framework there is indefinite scope for elaboration. In principle, one could readily build into the models other formal kinship phenomena such as relative-age discriminations, double descent, hypergamy and age sets (not to mention matters like territory and property which are often related to kinship).

15.1.1. How would such elaborated models fit into Figure 13.3? The abstract level there does not consist simply of a single sequence of types for each branch, for we have already suggested a choice of paths leading from four sections to four clans (13.2) and, at least by implication (11.1), one or more side branches leading to Hawaiian terminologies. Thus one possibility would be to locate additional phenomena in models situated on the same conceptual level or plane as the others.

15.1.2. Alternatively, one might envisage levels of abstraction intermediate between the two as shown in Figure 13.3. On these would be located types and models more 'filled out', closer to concrete realities, than those considered so far.

15.2. This paper has concentrated on the lower horizontal arrow in Figure 13.3 at the expense of the vertical and the upper horizontal arrows. The vertical arrows represent two things: (i) statically, the gap between a model and its realisation (for instance, between an elementary structure (14.3.1) and a society in which cross-cousin marriage is present in some sense, perhaps merely as a preference); (ii) dynamically, the gap between analytical transformations and historical processes. (Henceforth, we can ignore the weak interpretation of tetradic theory, which declines the challenge of history and simply abstains from comment on ii.)

15.2.1. Whereas the transformations take place instantaneously and completely on the conscious decision of an analyst manipulating models in a vacuum, the gradual, incomplete, overlapping historical processes take place under local impulses unclear to those involved, in societies which interact, which may be multilingual, which migrate and invade each other. Nonetheless, the transformations can serve as *models* of historical processes; and the step leading from tetradic to non-tetradic structures is intended to be as *real* as the concept of the Neolithic Revolution.

15.3.   Thus the central problem for the strong interpretation lies in the upper horizontal arrow in Figure 13.3. Before attempting to justify the arrow empirically, one would have to be clear about its significance.

15.3.1. Tetradic theory is in certain senses evolutionary, but evolutionism is by no means a single package (such as might reasonably be rejected *en bloc*).

15.3.2. In particular, if tetradic theory can be described as 'unilineal' at all, it is so only in a very qualified sense. Although the theory proposes a single starting-point, a sort of Big Bang for human society, it is not committed to forecasting an end-point. It is happy to recognise side-branches and multiple rightward paths. It does not exclude either leap-frogging or leftward regression; indeed it expects both of these to occur, as a result of influences between societies. Above all, *it does not suppose that real societies can be fitted into clear-cut stages or ranked unambiguously along a single scale of distance from tetradic models.*

15.3.3. The fundamental reason for this (in addition to the parallel paths and side-branches) is that the unilineal stages one can stipulate on the level of types and models do not survive on the empirical level. In real societies, formal aspects of the kinship system will occasionally conform quite well to a single type, but generally they will present a mixture of features related to several types. Supposing one were determined to set up a single scale of distance from tetradic models, procedures would have to be devised for balancing progressiveness in one respect with conservatism

in another; but such procedures could not escape being arbitrary. There is no possibility of a logically based *quantitative* left–right scale.

15.3.4. Admittedly, one can sometimes make more or less *intuitive* estimates of the relative global position of real societies along such a hypothetical scale. The kinship system of the nineteenth-century Kariera stands closer to tetradic models than does the system of the modern West. But the purpose of the theory is not to facilitate such 'league-table' judgements, which have little point, but to understand kinship systems within a world-historical perspective.

15.3.5. This orientation can be contrasted with certain brands of a priori anti-evolutionism, for instance, the view which is sometimes expressed that societies 'choose' their kinship systems from the range of logical possibilities. This is unrealistic and misleading. The most that societies do is adapt the systems they inherit, and their options are far from unlimited.

15.4.   The central claim of tetradic theory is that (in so far as changes can be conceived in such left–right terms) *endogenous historical change has always led AWAY from tetradic society.* For instance, the theory proposes that since the emergence of tetradic society, some time in prehistory, equations of the three main types (9.6) have regularly been broken down but have never been invented; apparent exceptions will be due to complex socio-linguistic interactions (e.g. sub-strata).

15.4.1. The theory also suggests that, in so far as it is meaningful to speak of typological transitions in the context of historical systems, they are likely to occur in a certain order. For instance, a terminology which at a given time conforms to type II is unlikely to go on to eliminate all its classificatory equations while retaining all its prescriptive ones.

15.5   These claims and suggestions must, of course, be tested empirically. The relevant materials are dispersed and in need of careful evaluation, but their volume is considerable. The methods of history and of ethnohistory (studies of tribes documented over longish periods) must be supplemented by comparative methods, both those based on language families and those of the lexical evolutionists.[6] Evolutionary theories are sometimes dismissed as speculative and untestable, but the second charge at least does not apply here.

15.5.1. Particular attention should be given to empirical cases which appear to show leftward changes.

15.5.2. Some other possible lines of exploration, which might add weight to the theory, were suggested in 7.4–7.

15.6.   However, before a theory can be justified, tested or used, it has to be stated.

NOTES

1   N. J. Allen, 'A Dance of Relatives', *Journal of the Anthropological Society of Oxford*, Vol. XII, no. 2 (1981), pp. 139–46.

2   See N. J. Allen, 'Assimilation of Alternate Generations', *Journal of the Anthropological Society of Oxford*, Vol. XX, no. 1 (1989), pp. 44–55.

3   N. J. Allen, 'Effervescence and the Origins of Human Society', in N. J. Allen, *Categories and Classifications: Maussian Reflections on the Social*, Oxford: Berghahn, 2000.

4   Cf. 'Dance', p. 140.

5   Cf. 'Dance', p. 145.

6   Cf. N. J. Allen, Review of Cecil H. Brown, *Language and Living Things: Uniformities in Folk Classification and Naming*, in *JASO*, Vol. XV, no. 2 (1984), pp. 169–72, at pp. 171–2; idem, 'The Evolution of Kinship Terminologies', *Lingua*, Vol. LXXVII (1989), pp. 173–85; and 'The Prehistory of Dravidian-type Terminologies' in M. Godelier, T. R. Trautmann, and F. E. Tjon Sie Fat (eds.), *Transformation of Kinship*, Washington: Smithsonian Institution Press, 1998.

Part II

Kinship as Culture, Process, and Agency

Section 1 The Demise and Revival of Kinship

Introduction

Linda Stone

This second part of the reader covers the contemporary period of kinship studies, from the 1970s to the present. In this period kinship moves away from its focus on social organization to an emphasis on cultural symbols and meanings. In its later reformulations, kinship study incorporates ideas of social process and human agency, reflecting broader trends in anthropological theory.

In and through these shifts, the contemporary era saw both the demise and the rebirth of kinship in anthropology, as covered in the articles of this section. The demise was to a great extent instigated by David Schneider, who charged that the anthropological concept of kinship was based on Eurocentric[1] notions of biological reproduction. As the work of David Schneider was so instrumental in the falling away and, indirectly, the revival of kinship, his life and contributions are discussed in some detail here.

Based on Schneider's ideas, kinship began its revival in feminist anthropology where it was closely linked with gender, followed by subsequent attempts to reformulate kinship. By the mid-1990s a new kind of kinship had emerged – one less Eurocentric, using more open and flexible concepts. Kinship was further revitalized through its focus on novel topics such as the New Reproductive Technologies, gay and lesbian kinship, and new family forms resulting from rising rates of divorce, remarriage, and recent trends in adoption. Kinship moved also into the area of political economy, in line with wider concerns in anthropology with social inequality, power, and history. These new directions for kinship studies are covered in the final section of the reader.

David Schneider and the Demise of Kinship

In 1972 David M. Schneider, then Professor at the University of Chicago and already prominent, dropped a bomb on the field of anthropology. Schneider's bomb was nearly lethal for kinship studies: it spread shrapnel outward into other areas of anthropological inquiry, and its powerful echoes are still reverberating today. This bomb is summed up in Schneider's now famous pronouncement that kinship "does not exist in any culture known to man" (1972: 59, article reproduced here). He declared that kinship – the very soul of anthropology, the subject that Robin Fox (1967: 10) had said was to anthropology what the nude was to art – was thus a "non-subject."

To be sure, Schneider's view was not entirely novel; Rodney Needham (1971), for example, had expressed a similar opinion. Needham held that kinship components – for example, marriage and incest rules – were too ethnographically variable for any meaningful cross-cultural comparisons or generalizations to be made. Unlike Schneider, however, Needham did not advocate that kinship be abandoned in anthropology, but argued instead for the development of more rigorous conceptual tools for cross-cultural comparison. While Schneider's denunciation of kinship was influential in the United States, Needham's less radical critique was probably more influential in Britain in the 1970s and 1980s.

There were also other forces behind the demise of kinship. One was a growing feeling among anthropologists that kinship concepts had become too abstract, rigid, and formal to apply in any meaningful way to real societies. Another problem was that by the 1960s, so much of kinship had been focused on unraveling so-called "primitive" societies, as opposed to "advanced" ones (ones less entangled in kinship structures), whereas anthropology was becoming more critical of these ethnocentric dichotomies (Stone 2001; see also Peletz 1995). In addition, among other intellectual shifts, anthropology was moving away from a central question that kinship studies had addressed – how societies remain stable and integrated – to new questions about social inequality and conflict (Carsten 2000a). But in and through these changes, Schneider played a particularly powerful role in furthering kinship's demise, making kinship very nearly a non-subject in anthropology for over twenty years.

Schneider's own life took some twists and turns that may be related to his anarchistic role in anthropology (Kuper 1999: 31–32). He was born in 1918 in Brooklyn, New York. His parents were Eastern European Jewish immigrants and active communists, and when Schneider was six they had another boy. Schneider (1995: 41–42) reported in one of his interviews that this event caused him such anxiety that he began to perform poorly in school. His parents then sent him to a boarding school, which, he recalled, "hurt me very badly. I felt I had been rejected; I felt I was unwanted" (1995: 42).

In 1936 Schneider entered Cornell University to study agricultural bacteriology, a perhaps ill-advised choice since he did not master his chemistry and math courses. He did better in his social science classes, and under the influence of Lauriston Sharp, he switched to anthropology, eventually receiving his MA in 1941. He next moved to Yale, where he entered but soon dropped out of the doctoral program in anthropology and thereafter was drafted into military service during World War II. His short stint at Yale was in part due to his intellectual and personal conflicts with George Peter Murdock (Schneider 1995: 34). But, while brief, this phase at Yale would prove significant for him because it was during this time that he met some key thinkers – most notably Margaret Mead, who facilitated his post-war move to Harvard in 1946, from where he received his Ph.D. Schneider conducted his dissertation fieldwork on Yap in Polynesia, producing a study of Yapese kinship. At Harvard he came under the influence of sociologist Talcott Parsons, whose ideas of culture were perhaps the greatest single influence on Schneider's work.

Schneider held a number of academic positions, ending up at the University of Chicago in 1960. In 1982 he moved to Santa Cruz, California, where he died in 1995 at age 77. It was during his time in Chicago and Santa Cruz that he produced his two most important books, *American Kinship: A Cultural Account* (1980 [originally 1968]) and *A Critique of the Study of Kinship* (1984). The latter intellectually enlarged and re-detonated his 1972 bomb.

Adam Kuper (1999: 122) characterized Schneider as "a maverick, a trickster, something of a trouble maker, out to shock the orthodox, never at peace with his colleagues or with himself." Such reactions to Schneider seem to have been commonplace. Raymond Fogelson, a newly hired anthropologist at the University of Chicago in 1965, described his interactions with the department chair, Schneider, as follows:

> He made me nervous. On the one hand he could be generous and supportive and flash his not inconsiderable charm; when in his paranoid mode, on the other hand, he could be vindictive, mean-spirited, destructive and self-destructive. ... If he invited me to his house and presented me with a potted plant, a book, or some other seemingly gratuitous gift, I left wondering what he had done behind my back. ... Faculty meetings with David ... could devolve into emotionally draining identity struggles. ... In thinking about and writing this chapter, these feelings of nervous apprehension return. (2001: 33)

Along with these kinds of characterizations, many also find that Schneider's work was sometimes contradictory (Feinberg 2001: 19) or muddled (Kuper 1999: 135), or charge that he ignored his own data (Fogelson 2001: 36, which Schneider [1995: 211] admitted). Yet no one denies that Schneider transformed anthropological kinship. It was largely through David Schneider that anthropologists moved from a focus on kinship in relation to social organization, to a rejection of that focus and onward to a new kinship, one reformulated around culture, human agency, and process. Most of the articles in this section of the reader in some way reflect the impact of and reaction to Schneider's bomb. And anthropologists are still mulling over Schneider today, as seen for example in the recent volume by Richard Feinberg and Martin Ottenheimer, *The Cultural Analysis of Kinship: The Legacy of David M. Schneider* (2001).

Critical to all Schneider's work on kinship is his definition of culture, which he spells out in some detail in the article reprinted here. Along with Clifford Geertz, Schneider was a leading figure in American symbolic anthropology, a theoretical framework in which culture is understood as a people's shared symbols and meanings. Within this framework, Schneider's approach to culture is notable for two characteristics: his definition of culture is particularly narrow, and his approach to culture is strongly relativistic. Drawing from Talcott Parsons (1966), Schneider defined culture as analytically separate from social organization, norms, or actual human behavior. In addition, and in line with a dominant current in anthropology at the University of Chicago in his day, Schneider sharply separated culture from human biology.

As he makes clear in the article reproduced here, Schneider was exclusively interested in a society's basic categories and premises about life, through which its members interpret and make sense of their world. Thus his severing of kinship from social organization follows from his focus on and definition of culture. He did not deny that "social organization" exists. Nor did he deny that aspects of culture are related to social organization or behavior; he only insisted that these layers of human life be kept analytically distinct. Since he saw himself as a *cultural* anthropologist, he was exclusively interested in the cultural layer. Social organization could be left to others, namely to sociologists. His (1980) exploration of American kinship, discussed below, is an attempt to discover and analyze kinship purely in cultural terms.

Like many of his colleagues, Schneider followed American cultural relativism, a position that can be traced back to Franz Boas. Cultural relativity stresses the importance of understanding each culture on its own terms, or from within. An outside anthropologist needs then to approach another culture not through his or her own culturally biased perspectives but through the native peoples' own terms, categories, and concepts. These indigenous categories or concepts are in anthropology sometimes described as "emic," as contrasted with "etic" categories, or the external, analytical categories used by anthropologists to describe and compare cultures. Many anthropologists found the emic/etic distinction useful because it gave them a common set of analytical tools through which to talk about culture, while it also drew attention to the potentially unique ways that each culture might interpret the world. Schneider, however, took cultural relativity a bit further than most and rejected the distinction between emic and etic (Feinberg 2001:18). He saw that so-called etic anthropological categories and concepts could in fact stem from the anthropologist's own (emic) culture, and so be culturally biased. Studying another culture through these categories, then, might be no better than interpreting another culture through one's own culturally biased emic categories. Schneider's brand of cultural relativity is important to his denunciation of the anthropological category of "kinship" because he saw "kinship" as a Eurocentric cultural construct, not a universally valid etic concept, that anthropologists were merely imposing on other cultures.

Schneider took cultural relativity further than most in another way as well. He held that not only are a culture's symbols arbitrary (there is no necessary connection between a symbol and what it symbolizes), but also a symbol's referents (the things or ideas it stands for) do not exist as an external reality but are themselves culturally constructed (Kuper 1999: 133).[2] Thus expanding the realms of what can be viewed as cultural construction, Schneider's point foreshadows a later development in feminist anthropology, discussed below. This idea that culture constructs reality (as opposed to the idea that external realities shape cultural constructions, or to the idea that cultures perceive and interpret external realities in different ways) was later referred to as cultural "constructivism."

The view that a culture can only be understood from within, on its own terms, tends to discourage cross-cultural comparison or generalizations. Yet, as seen in his 1972 article, Schneider apparently was not against cross-cultural comparison, only against anthropologists comparing apples and oranges, or comparing what in one culture is not perceived as the same phenomenon in another culture (Feinberg 2001: 10–11). Theoretically, once a few cultures are studied in a thoroughly emic fashion, those cultures' symbols and meanings could be compared, or an anthropologist could compare the symbols and meanings of a new culture with those of his or her own. Schneider did not say, however, what the point of such an exercise would be (other than, of course, to reveal which cultural concepts are or are not comparable across cultures).

Reflecting Schneider's particular views of culture was his study of American kinship, his first major contribution to anthropology. This study was based on interviews, conducted by a team of assistants, with slightly over one hundred informants, white middle-class residents of Chicago, about their kinship terminology and attitudes toward their relatives. With this study Schneider sought to reveal the categories, meanings, and symbols through which Americans understand their own kinship relationships and in the process to show "that kinship is a cultural system, not a set of biological relationships" (Feinberg 2001: 8). Americans very much use the notion of biological reproduction to construct their kinship, but they do so symbolically, according to Schneider.

The result of this study was an analysis of kinship in America that posited two underlying cultural "orders" – the order of nature and the order of law – through which Americans construct their kinship. The "order of nature" refers to kinship based on the natural facts of procreation, resulting in kin based on "shared biogenetic substance." The "order of law" refers to a human refinement of raw nature, that is, legalized or customized kinship, ties based on, for example, marriage and adoption. The order of law is governed not by natural facts of procreation but rather by "a code for conduct" characterized by love, a sentiment that Schneider translated as "enduring, diffuse solidarity."[3] These two orders produce three classes of American kin: (1) kin in nature alone (for example the "natural child" or illegitimate child); (2) kin in law alone (husbands and wives, in-laws, an adopted child); and (3) kin in nature and in law, or kin one traces simultaneously through both ties of blood and marriages (or on codes for conduct). The later class of kin Schneider claimed to be the "truest" relatives to Americans, the real class of what Americans call and understand to be their "blood relatives": "[T]he blood relative, related in nature and by law, brings together the best of nature modified by human reason; he is thus the relative in the truest and most highly valued sense" (Schneider 1980: 110).

Schneider further claimed that at the core of American kinship was the cultural concept of love. Love is the symbol of American kinship and, further, serving as a symbol of love is sexual intercourse between husband and wife.[4] Sexual intercourse between husband and wife expresses love and not mere carnal lust (or animal nature; there is a great deal in Schneider's work about an American cultural opposition between nature and culture and Americans' need to transcend nature through culture). It is also the rarefied sexual intercourse between husband and wife that produces "true blood relatives," children, who are themselves a symbol of the love between husband and wife and who link the husband and wife together by virtue of their sharing biogenetic substance with both parents. In the American family there are two types of love – that between husband and wife (conjugal love) and that between parents and children and between siblings (cognatic love). The first is erotic and the second is decidedly not so.

While *American Kinship* was very influential, it also met with criticism and continues to do so. Wallace (1969) complained, among other things, about Schneider's depiction of "love" in American culture. Scheffler (1976) disputed the validity of Schneider's American cultural "orders" based on American kinship terminology. Schneider had said that his portrait of American kinship basically held, with minor variations, among different class and ethnic groups in America, but Sylvia Yanagisako (1978) showed that his analysis did not apply to ethnic minorities, in particular Japanese Americans (see also Wallace 1969: 106). Kuper

(1999: 135) objected to Schneider's convoluted discussion of love, sex, and kinship as all somehow symbolizing each other: "With the best will in the world, there is no way to sort out this confusion between symbol and concept. Schneider is culpably content with a mélange in which signifier and symbolized are hopelessly muddled."[5]

By his 1972 article Schneider had taken a new turn with respect to American kinship: he declared that kinship does not really exist as a distinct cultural domain in American culture. Following on an earlier (1969) article, he claimed that what he had seen as distinctive features of American kinship (namely the ideas about shared substance and a code for conduct, or sentiments of solidarity) are also at work in American ideas about nationality and religion. Therefore kinship is not a culturally distinct domain in America. Feinberg (1979, 2001) criticizes this position, saying that it violated Schneider's own dictum that the native view is the ultimate authority. Since Americans do have terms like "kin" and "kinship" and clear ideas about what they mean, it follows that, "by Schneider's criteria, kinship *must* be a distinct domain in America. If his distinctive features are incapable of differentiating kinship from nationality and religion, it shows not the absence of kinship but a defect in his analysis – he must be mistaken in his identification of distinctive features" (2001: 12–13, emphasis his).

As Feinberg points out, Schneider used his 1972 denial of American kinship in the following way: "since kinship is an English word, and since anthropologists from Morgan onward have been involved in studying what they termed kinship, if it were to exist in any culture it should exist in ours" (Feinberg 2001: 9). Since it does not, Schneider could then make his famous statement in this same article that kinship does not exist in any known culture. In the 1972 article presented here, Schneider moves from the lack of kinship as a cultural domain in America[6] to make his larger case against kinship in anthropology, spelling out the flaws in the thinking of anthropologists from Morgan through Lévi-Strauss in rooting kinship one way or another in biological reproduction. At length he attacks the work of many anthropologists reviewed in Part I of this reader. Even granted that anthropologists had all along understood that some "kinship" was "social" – for example, fictive kinship and adoptions – they still assumed that *genealogical* connections were everywhere what kinship is all about, or as Schneider put it, they assumed a universality to genealogy, a concept itself inseparable from notions of biology. In his second major book, *A Critique of the Study of Kinship*, Schneider more explicitly claims that the anthropologists' mistake in constructing their concept of kinship is based on their Eurocentric assumptions. That kinship is a matter of biological connections is simply not true of other peoples, who might very well construct what looks to anthropologists like "kinship" along lines of shared residence, feeding or other nurture, rituals, or what have you. Anthropologists, then, had constructed their idea of kinship on the assumption that the culturally specific notion that "Blood Is Thicker Than Water" is universal. They had then invalidly imposed this assumption on other cultures. In his book Schneider even denounced his own former work on Yapese kinship. What he had seen before as a patrilineal descent construct was an illusion that resulted from his indoctrination as an anthropologist. Furthermore, the Yapese, he claimed, did not have an idea of biological fatherhood but rather believed that children were produced by ghosts. Thus, taking seriously the emics of a culture, one could not posit that "kinship" is a cross-culturally valid domain. The key for Schneider was to show that biological connections were crucial to the anthropologists' concept of kinship, and that "Robbed of its grounding in biology, kinship is nothing" (1984: 112).

Schneider's bomb, especially the 1984 version, fell at a precipitous time in anthropological thought. The 1980s were a time when anthropologists were becoming acutely sensitive to misrepresentations of "the Other," or the "crisis of representation" (Marcus and Fischer 1986). It was a time of severe anthropological self-criticism and a period of growth in postmodernism. Schneider himself claimed that what he had said of anthropological "kinship" could just as well be said of "religion," "politics," and so on and, indeed, the scrutiny of anthropological concepts for implicit ethnocentrism was taking place in other quarters. Many were questioning the legitimacy of a metacultural "science" of any kind. Schneider was a part of this postmodern movement and his brand of strong cultural relativity was welcomed by many.

In later years, Schneider's "symbols and meanings" approach to culture continued to influence kinship studies in the sense that researchers focused on uncovering people's own terms and conceptions of their own relationships. However, there developed a growing dissatisfaction with Schneider's narrow view of culture that severed it from behavior and social organization or social structure. Later anthropologists then sought to connect kinship ideology with practice (Böck and Rao 2000), or to the uses to which human actors put kinship (Schweitzer 2000a). This movement did not reunite kinship with social organization in the old sense of looking at how kinship constituted the social organization of a particular cultural group; rather, later researchers sought to see how people use local ideas and practices of kinship to reinforce or challenge structures within their own society. The emphasis shifted away from seeing kinship as a social system to focusing on individual strategies or agency (willful action), with respect to local conceptions of kinship (Schweitzer 2000b: 9).

Finally, from a contemporary perspective, Schneider seems to have naively depicted culture as integrated, coherent, and shared (Peletz 1995: 347). Since his time, anthropologists have emphasized conflict and ambiguity within "symbols and meanings" and have come to see culture as "multi-vocal" and contested among individuals and groups.

While Schneider was deconstructing kinship, a new challenge to traditional kinship in anthropology was being developed by Claude Lévi-Strauss, whose application of structuralism to kinship is reviewed in Part I of this reader. In his later writings, Lévi-Strauss (1983, 1987) developed the concept of "house societies," which has ever since intrigued many anthropologists. To Lévi-Strauss, house societies are those in which persons are grouped into corporate estates, or "houses," that perpetuate themselves through the transmission of their names, titles, privileges, and wealth through real or imagined lines of descent. People of house societies have an emic understanding of their houses in this sense and perceive their own identity and their relationship with others in terms of their houses. Actual membership in houses can follow simultaneously any number of different paths – descent (matrilineal or patrilineal), marriage (endogamous or exogamous), through fictive kinship, adoption, or other means of incorporating assorted persons.

The concept of house societies shows a number of parallels with other currents of contemporary kinship in anthropology as discussed in previous sections. For one thing, it separates "kinship" relationships from relationships rooted in biological connections (Gillespie 2000: 26). The house concept also easily matches with native, emic, terms (Carsten and Hugh-Jones 1995: 20). In addition, it opens a way to view kinship construction as a process operating through strategic actions. Houses rise, fall, and otherwise transform themselves as persons act strategically to advance their interests (Carsten and Hugh-Jones 1995: 36–42). The concept also blurs the ethno-centric distinction between the primitive "other" and "complex," literate societies (Gillespie 2000: 26). In addition, house societies are understood to be historically situated. Finally, the concept of house society reflects later currents in post-Schneiderian kinship in that it ties kinship back to social organization. Indeed, the house is understood as the central feature of social organization in house societies (Carsten and Hugh-Jones 1995).

The Extension into Feminist Anthropology

While Schneider's writings were largely destructive of kinship studies, his earlier work on American kinship and cultural analysis did inspire a richer, more emically oriented look at kinship and, in the process, gender. An example of this is Anna Meigs's study (1984, 1989) of the Hua of the Eastern Highlands in Papua New Guinea. Meigs discusses how the Hua conception of individuals' kinship positions are not fixed for all time by acts of birth, as in the American cultural context discussed by Schneider (1980), but are rather fluid and processual. Hua kinship proceeds through the transfer of *nu* (vital substance), which includes bodily emis-sions or products (e.g., sweat, semen, footprints, shadows), bodily substances (e.g., hair, nails) and products of one's labor, particularly food that one produces, pre-pares, or serves. To the Hua, kin are persons who share *nu*. Common residence alone will establish transfers of *nu* and therefore kinship between people. In addition, parents establish kinship with children, not just through ideas of insemination or through acts of birth but through transfers of *nu* to their children before and after birth. Meigs also shows how *nu*, in association with concepts about personal "pollution," operates to define gender, which, like kinship, is fluid and processual rather than static and set for all time. For example, over the life course, restrictions on *nu* transfers change for women; as a result, their pollution decreases and they become "like men." After menopause and after the birth of three or more children, a woman is formally initiated into the Hua men's house.

Schneider's later ideas moved more directly into feminist anthropology largely through the work of Sylvia Yanagisako and Janet Collier at Stanford University (1987; article reproduced here). Their article opens with a history of feminist anthropology, a history they feel has been plagued by the persistent appearance of certain analytical dichotomies – nature/culture, domestic/public and production/reproduction – that have been used to account for various gender constructions and inequalities cross-culturally. All of these dichotomies are flawed, they argue, because they are all themselves grounded in the notion of natural biological differ-ences in male and female reproduction. Thus they are all ultimately based on Western cultural conceptions of gender.

These authors then draw parallels between kinship studies and gender studies in anthropology to make the central point of their paper: just as the anthropologists' concept of "kinship" had been loaded with Western cultural assumptions about biological connections, so too the study of "gender" had been distorted by culturally biased assumptions of male and female biological differences in reproduction. Other cultures do not perceive male/ female sexual difference and reproduction in this way. They sought, then, to do for "gender" what Schneider had done for "kinship." They argued that the emics of "male," "female," "human reproduction," and so on must be investigated separately for each culture, just as Schneider had argued that each culture must be investigated separately in terms of its own emic conceptions of human relationships.

In taking this position, Yanagisako and Collier were challenging an earlier view of "gender" in anthropology that contrasted it to "sex." "Sex" had referred to the universal biological or anatomical differences between males and females whereas "gender" had referred to the culturally specific interpretation and evaluation of those differences (Shapiro 1981). Yanagisako and Collier were saying that this earlier view mistakenly universalized a Western cultural construction of "sex," or sexual difference.

With this, Yanagisako and Collier shoved biology even further away from gender than it already had been shoved in feminist thought. Earlier feminists had fought against "biological determinism" in relation to gender, or ideas that rooted inequalities between men and women in biology or sexual difference. In their view these ideas only served to "naturalize" gender inequality, that is, make the inequality appear perfectly natural and therefore inevitable (see also Yanagisako and Delaney 1995). But seeing "gender" alone as a cultural construction, leaving an etic biology lingering in the background, still left the door open to a biological "naturalizing" of gender differences. Seeing biologically defined sexual differences between men and women as themselves cultural constructions more firmly closed the door.

Unlike Schneider in relation to kinship, Yanagisako and Collier did not declare "gender" a non-subject, nor did they discourage further studies of gender. And, in sharp contrast to kinship studies, gender studies flourished after their publication of *Gender and Kinship*. In fact, what they did do was to suggest that "kinship" and "gender" should be studied together, as indicated by the subtitle of their book, *Essays toward a Unified Analysis*. They argued that kinship and gender had been two discrete fields of study. At the same time, both of these fields of study had been rooted in Western cultural folk conceptions of the biology of sexual reproduction. Therefore the two fields of study actually constitute "a single field that has not succeeded in freeing itself from notions about natural differences between people" (1987: 15).

A criticism could be raised here. The anthropologists' rooting of kinship and gender in biological reproduction has in both cases been a mistake because, according to Yanagisako and Collier, this rooting is a Western cultural conception. Should kinship and gender, then, be joined together because they have shared the same error within anthropology (Stone 2001: 18n)? Yanagisako and Collier go on to say that "Although the two [kinship and gender] are mutually constituted in *our* society, this does not mean that they are linked in the same way in all societies" (1987: 34). But if they are not, would it not be in error for anthropologists to link them, to approach them as "mutually constituted" from the outset? Would this not be an ethnocentric imposition of *our* "mutually constituted" cultural categories (or, worse, of anthropology's mistakes) on other cultures?

In the last part of their paper, Yanagisako and Collier outline a new approach to the study of gender, one first and foremost purged of the premise that any biological facts themselves create particular social conditions or have particular cultural meanings. Their opening premise is that all social systems are inherently systems of inequality (not necessarily or in every respect entailing a gender inequality). From this they devise an "analytical program" that covers the cultural analysis of meaning, the development of "systemic models of inequality," and that incorporates historical analysis. In the cultural analysis of their program they follow Schneider's "symbols and meanings" approach to culture. But in their interest in identifying structures of inequality for their "systemic models" they depart from Schneider, who sought to focus only on a cultural realm, independent of social structures. Here Yanagisako and Collier's ideas reflect the more contemporary view, following Pierre Bourdieu (1977), of social and cultural life emerging from the dynamic interaction between structures and people's actions.

On the whole the response to Yanagisako and Collier's ideas within feminist anthropology has been very positive, although their position has not been everywhere adopted (e.g., Stone 2000: 4, Parkin 1997: 3). One important critique of the Yanagisako–Collier proposal has come from Harold Scheffler (1991, reproduced here). Scheffler (1973) has consistently maintained that kinship is universally a matter of genealogy though not of biology. He held a mother–child genealogical connection to be universal and a father–child genealogical connection to be likely universal as well. From these basic links, other genealogical relationships are drawn in various ways in different cultures. For Scheffler, like Schneider, Yanagisako, and Collier, emic conceptions are important, but not because they will demonstrate the fallacy of universalizing Euro-American conceptions of biology as a basis for kinship. It is rather because it is through their own folk-cultural theory of human reproduction that particular cultures will construct their ideas of genealogical connections. For Scheffler, emic ideas of sex and reproduction are important as a basis for genealogy; it is irrelevant whether any actual kin are in fact biologically related or not.

In the article reproduced here, Scheffler claims that the Yanagisako–Collier position does not work as a feminist resistance to the naturalization of gender inequality. By closing the door on biology, their position prevents them from dealing with many real questions pertinent to gender or gender inequality. There are, in his view, certain biologically rooted patterns of human life (he refers, for example, to women giving birth to children and women forming primary bonds with dependent children) that do impact gender; if these relationships between biology and social life are ignored or discounted, we can make no headway in either understanding or changing them. Scheffler also charges that while Yanagisako and Collier's "radical constructivism" moves away from biologically essentializing women, it only takes them to a cultural essentialization of women instead. He also claims that their project to explore kinship/gender emically in each culture "on its own terms" is impossible, since any attempt to study another culture is inherently comparative and theory-laden. Yanagisako and Collier, however, did acknowledge in their paper that comparison is inevitable in attempts to understand other cultures.

One positive aspect of Yanagisako and Collier's work has been that, as with Schneider before them, their ideas encouraged a new look at kinship/gender from the ground up, taking local conceptions about men, women, sexual difference, and human reproduction into account. Their work has led to ethnographies of emic views of sexual difference and of how these views relate to kinship (see, for example,

Strathern 1988, Böck and Rao 2000). Additional work in kinship and gender has shown how cultural ideas about procreation may rationalize patriarchal social orders. For example, Carol Delaney (1991) has analyzed the implications of a procreative metaphor of a generative male "seed" implanted in a passive female "soil" found in certain monotheistic traditions that emphasize a male God as world creator.

Rescuing Kinship

Another response to Schneider's attack on kinship in anthropology has been the attempt, in the words of Janet Carsten (1995: 224, reproduced here), to "rescue kinship from its post-Schneiderian demise." Carsten tried to do this by replacing "kinship" with the broader term "relatedness," a term that allows us to move away from the Western ideas concerning kinship in terms of biological connection. Carsten agreed with Schneider that kinship studies in anthropology were biased by Euro-American cultural conceptions and that other peoples (e.g., the Malay people of her study) do not necessarily construct their "kinship" (or relatedness) in comparable terms. She insisted, following Schneider, that the study of other people's social worlds must begin with their terms and conceptions. In addition, Carsten went beyond Schneider to question the validity of the distinction between "social" and "biological" kinship, a distinction crucial to the older anthropological concept of kinship but which, she claims, Schneider himself took for granted. As a result, his only choice was to abandon the concept of "kinship," since it could not validly be applied cross-culturally. As an alternative to this, Carsten abandoned the social/biological distinction, which then freed her to explore Malay notions of "relatedness." Instead of asking, do Malays have kinship by our (anthropological) definition, she asks, what, in terms of a broader, more open and flexible category of "relatedness" *do* they have?

There is of course a problem with abandoning the term kinship and using "relatedness" instead. Schneider (1984) himself had pointed out that trying to broaden the concept of "kinship" would result in destroying it as a distinct domain. The concept would then have no boundaries and we would be unable to distinguish "kin" from neighbors, friends, co-workers, and so on. On Carsten's attempt to broaden kinship, Ladislav Holy wrote:

> Replacing the concept of kinship with that of relatedness thus amounts in practice to a semiotic solution of the difficulties involved in the definition of kinship. But renaming a phenomenon does not solve the problems involved in its conceptualization. If we insist on talking about relatedness rather than kinship, we will soon be debating what we mean by relatedness as we have been for decades what we mean by kinship. (1996: 168)

In the introduction to her later edited book, *Cultures of Relatedness* (2000b), Carsten admits that broadening the concept of kinship does not solve the problem. In defense of her use of "relatedness" and in response to Holy she writes:

> Readers will perceive that "relatedness" offers no neat solutions for the comparative endeavor – merely that its use has enabled me to suspend one set of assumptions, and to bracket off a particular nexus of problems, in order to frame the questions differently. "Relatedness" makes possible comparisons between Inupiat and English or Nuer ways of being related without relying on an arbitrary distinction between biology and culture, and without presupposing what constitutes kinship. (2000b: 5)

Although "relatedness" does not solve the Schneiderian problem of kinship, Carsten has succeeded in making a significant contribution to the rescuing of kinship from its post-Schneiderian demise. In the article reproduced here, she details the emic terms and perceptions of relatedness among Malays on the island of Langkawi (see also Carsten 1997). This is a lucid account of how Malay constructions of their relatedness operate through food, acts of feeding, and sharing of house and hearth space. She demonstrates the fluid nature of Malay relatedness and the lack of meaning to any distinction between "social" and "biological" kinship in the Malay cultural context. Carsten's work is also significant in that it shows Malay relatedness as *process*. One is not born into a kinship position, but rather relatedness emerges through time, through, for example, the process of receiving and giving food.

Along with kinship as process, Carsten also discusses Malay conceptions of personhood as fluid and mutable. Her work and that of others has revealed that these kinds of fluid conceptions of personhood contrast with a more bounded conception of personhood in the Western world. These non-Western conceptions have been called "partible persons" or "dividuals" (Holy 1996, Strathern 1992, Marriott 1976). In the West, persons are considered discrete, "skin-bound" (Holy 1996: 157) entities, separated off from one another, their physical nature independent of their relations with others. In a cultural conception of partible persons or dividuals, by contrast, persons are formed through relationships with others and give, as it were, parts of themselves to others in a process that produces others. Thus permeable bodies and selves are conduits for the transmission, sharing, and exchange of assorted substances (food, bodily emissions, etc.), the circulation of which can be constructive of relatedness. In this view, cultural conceptions of relatedness are inseparable from cultural conceptions of personhood. Carsten's discussion of fluid, mutable personhood and fluid, mutable relatedness in Langkawi has helped to expose the image of bounded persons and static, immutable kin statuses to be culturally specific to the Western world and not necessarily shared elsewhere.

In "rescuing" kinship from the Schneiderian demise, Carsten sought not only to advance emic studies of relatedness, but also to make possible the cross-cultural study of relatedness. Her edited book, *Cultures of Relatedness* (2000a), shows cross-cultural comparisons in terms of, for example, kinship as process and performance and kinship established through everyday practices. She also demonstrates the cross-cultural inapplicability of a distinction between biological and social kinship.

There have been other attempts to reformulate "kinship" in such a way that escapes Euro-American cultural biases yet allows for comparison. Kathey-Lee Galvin (2001), for instance, took Schneider's "order of nature" and "order of law" from American culture, broadened each of these and constructed a framework for cross-cultural comparisons. She used this model to compare the Malay kinship of Carsten's study with Steven Parish's (1994) description of kinship among the Newar of Nepal and Mary Weismantel's (1995) account of adoption among the Zumbagua in Ecuador. In Galvin's model, the transmission of biogenetic substance is only one of several possible processes within an "Order of Sharing."

By the mid-1990s, kinship studies had fully incorporated the idea of kinship as social process and kinship constructed through human action or agency. Agency becomes even more salient in the "new kinship" discussed in the final section of the reader.

NOTES

1   Several authors referred to in this section use terms like "Eurocentric," "Euro-American," and "Western" to refer loosely to cultural concepts and modes of thought prevalent or historically rooted in Europe and other areas primarily settled by Europeans, such as the United States and Australia. These categories are imprecise and problematical. "Euro-American" or "Western" culture has no precise geographical boundaries, and within Europe and the United States, there is significant cultural variation such that generalization about cultural concepts is not always warranted. In addition, these terms can suggest stereotypical dichotomies between, for example, the West and the Orient, leading to further imprecision and misunderstanding of cultural contrast and variation. Nevertheless, and with these problems in mind, these terms have been useful in pointing out how some concepts in anthropology may be ethnocentric and thus not validly applicable cross-culturally.

2   It is not entirely clear how far Schneider took his relativity or what he thought of scientific biology. On the one hand, in his earlier (1965) article on the topic he clearly did not claim that biology does not exist or that it is a relative cultural construction (see also Feinberg 2001: 15). On the other hand, as Kuper (1999: 146–147) points out, the clear tendency of Schneider's position is in the direction of claiming that biology (and all of science) is merely ethnoscience (see also Feinberg 2001: 18).

3   By "diffuse" in the phrase "enduring, diffuse solidarity," Schneider probably meant that the feeling of solidarity among kin is wide-ranging, not specific to any particular issue or set of circumstances. For discussion of the limitations of translating love in America as "enduring, diffuse solidarity" see Kuper (1999: 135–136).

4   At the time Schneider was writing, he, like most scholars, did not consider the cultural implications of gay/lesbian relationships.

5   To these criticisms one might also add that while Americans might anticipate "enduring, diffuse solidarity" in the order-of-law relationships between husband and wife and between parents and an adopted child, they probably do not culturally anticipate such love between a person and his or her spouse's parents, their in-laws. These relationships may be based on some sort of "code for conduct," but that code is itself governed as much by notions of tension and divisiveness as by enduring diffuse solidarity.

6   Schneider may have continued to believe that kinship is not a distinct cultural domain in Euro-America, but the cultural existence of kinship in Euro-America was crucial to *A Critique of the Study of Kinship*. Here Schneider said that were the world ethnographically put to the test, it is likely that kinship would turn out to be "a special custom distinctive of European culture, an interesting oddity" (1984: 201). And it was on the basis of that cultural oddity that Schneider made his charges of ethnocentrism in anthropological kinship.

REFERENCES

Böck, Monica, and Aparna Rao, eds., 2000 Culture, Creation and Procreation: Concepts of Kinship in South Asian Practice. New York and Oxford: Berghahn Books.

Bourdieu, Pierre, 1977 Outline of a Theory of Practice. Cambridge: Cambridge University Press.

Carsten, Janet, 1995 The Substance of Kinship and the Heat of the Hearth: Feeding, Personhood, and Relatedness among Malayans in Pulau Langkawi. American Ethnologist 22(2): 223–242.

—— 1997 The Heat of the Hearth: The Process of Kinship in a Malay Fishing Community. Oxford: Clarendon Press.

—— ed., 2000a Cultures of Relatedness: New Approaches to the Study of Kinship. Cambridge: Cambridge University Press.

—— 2000b Introduction: Cultures of Relatedness. *In* Cultures of Relatedness: New Approaches to the Study of Kinship. Janet Carsten, ed. pp. 1–36. Cambridge: Cambridge University Press.

Carsten, Janet, and Steven Hugh-Jones, eds., 1995 About the House: Lévi-Strauss and Beyond. Cambridge: Cambridge University Press.

Delaney, Carol, 1991 The Seed and the Soil: Gender and Cosmology in Turkish Village Society. Berkeley: University of California Press.

Feinberg, Richard 1979 Schneider's Symbolic Culture Theory: An Appraisal. Current Anthropology 20(3): 541–549.

—— 2001 Introduction: Schneider's Cultural Analysis of Kinship and Its Implications for Anthropological Relativism. *In* The Cultural Analysis of Kinship: The Legacy of David M. Schneider. Richard Feinberg and Martin Ottenheimer, eds. pp. 1–31. Urbana and Chicago: University of Illinois Press.

Feinberg, Richard, and Martin Ottenheimer, eds., 2001 The Cultural Analysis of Kinship: The Legacy of David M. Schneider. Urbana and Chicago: University of Illinois Press.

Fogelson, Raymond D., 2001 Schneider Confronts Coponential Analysis. *In* The Cultural Analysis of Kinship: The Legacy of David M. Schneider. Richard Feinberg and Martin Ottenheimer, eds. pp. 33–45. Urbana and Chicago: University of Illinois Press.

Fox, Robin, 1967 Kinship and Marriage: An Anthropological Perspective. Cambridge: Cambridge University Press.

Galvin, Kathey-Lee, 2001 Schneider Revisited: Sharing and Ratification in the Construction of Kinship. *In* New Directions in Anthropological Kinship. Linda Stone, ed. pp. 109–124. Lanham, MD: Rowman & Littlefield.

Gillespie, Susan D., 2000 Lévi-Strauss: Maison and Société à Maisons. *In* Beyond Kinship: Social and Material Reproduction in House Societies. Rosemary A. Joyce and Susan D. Gillespie, eds. pp. 22–52. Philadelphia: University of Pennsylvania Press.

Holy, Ladislav, 1996 Anthropological Perspectives on Kinship. London and Chicago: Pluto Press.

Kuper, Adam, 1999 Culture: the Anthropologists' Account. Cambridge, MA: Harvard University Press.

Lévi-Strauss, Claude, 1983 The Way of the Masks. S. Modelski, trans. London: Jonathan Cape.

—— 1987 Anthropology and Myth: Lectures 1951–1982. Oxford: Blackwell.

Marcus, George E., and Michael M. J. Fischer, 1986 Anthropology as Cultural Critique: An Experimental Movement in the Human Sciences. Chicago: University of Chicago Press.

Marriott, McKim, 1976 Hindu Transactions: Diversity without Dualism. *In* Transactions in Meaning. Bruce Kapferer, ed. Philadelphia: ISHI Publications.

Meigs, Anna S., 1984 Food, Sex, and Pollution: A New Guinea Religion. New Brunswick: Rutgers University Press.

—— 1989 The Cultural Construction of Reproduction and Its Relationship to Kinship and Gender (New Guinea Highlands). *In* Culture, Kin and Cognition: Essays in Honor of Ward H. Goodenough. Mac Marshall and John L. Caughey, eds. pp. 33–42. Special publication of the American Anthropological Association, No. 25, Washington, DC: American Anthropological Association.

Needham, Rodney, 1971 Introduction. *In* Rethinking Kinship and Marriage. Rodney Needham, ed. London: Tavistock.

Parish, Steven M., 1994 Moral Knowing in a Hindu Sacred City. New York: Columbia University Press.

Parkin, Robert, 1997 Kinship: An Introduction to Basic Concepts. Oxford: Blackwell.

Parsons, Talcott, 1966 Societies: Evolutionary and Comparative Perspectives. Englewood Cliffs, NJ: Prentice-Hall.

Peletz, Michael G., 1995 Kinship Studies in Late Twentieth-Century Anthropology. Annual Review of Anthropology 24: 343–372.

Scheffler, Harold W., 1973 Kinship, Descent, and Alliance. *In* Handbook of Social and Cultural Anthropology. John J. Honigman, ed. pp. 747–793. Berkeley: University of California Press.

—— 1976 The "Meaning" of Kinship in American Culture: Another View. *In* Meaning in Anthropology. Keith H. Basso and Henry A. Selby, eds. pp. 57–91. Albuquerque: University of New Mexico Press.

—— 1991 Sexism and Naturalism in the Study of Kinship. *In* Gender at the Crossroads of Knowledge: Feminist Anthropology in the Postmodern Era. Micaela di Leonardo, ed. pp. 361–382. Berkeley: University of California Press.

Schneider, David M. 1965 Kinship and Biology. *In* Aspects of the Analysis of Family Structure. Ashley J. Coale, Loyd A. Fallers, Marion J. Levy, Jr., David M. Schneider, and Silvan S. Thomas, eds. pp. 83–101. Princeton, NJ: Princeton University Press.

—— 1969 Kinship, Nationality and Religion in American Culture: Toward a Definition of Kinship. *In* Forms of Symbolic Action. Robert F. Spencer, ed. pp. 116–125. Seattle: University of Washington Press.

—— 1972 What Is Kinship All About? *In* Kinship Studies in the Morgan Centennial Year. Priscilla Reining, ed. pp. 32–63. Washington, DC: Anthropological Society of Washington.

—— 1980 [1968] American Kinship: A Cultural Account. Chicago: University of Chicago Press.

—— 1984 A Critique of the Study of Kinship. Ann Arbor: University of Michigan Press.

—— 1995 Schneider on Schneider: The Conversion of the Jews and Other Anthropological Stories by David Schneider, as Told to Richard Handler. Durham NC: Duke University Press.

Schweitzer, Peter P., ed., 2000a Dividends of Kinship: Meanings and Uses of Social Relatedness. London and New York: Routledge.

—— 2000b Introduction. *In* Dividends of Kinship: Meanings and Uses of Social Relatedness. Peter P. Schweitzer, ed. pp. 1–32. London and New York: Routledge.

Shapiro, Judith, 1981 Anthropology and the Study of Gender. Soundings: An Interdisciplinary Journal 64(4): 446–465.

Stone, Linda, 2000 Kinship and Gender: An Introduction. 2nd edition. Boulder, CO: Westview Press.

—— 2001 Introduction: Theoretical Implications of New Directions in Anthropological Kinship. *In* New Directions in Anthropological Kinship. Linda Stone, ed. pp. 1–20. Lanham, MD: Rowman & Littlefield.

Strathern, Marilyn, 1988 The Gender of the Gift: Problems with Women and Problems with Society in Melanesia. Berkeley: University of California Press.

—— 1992 After Nature: English Kinship in the Late Twentieth Century. Cambridge: Cambridge University Press.

Wallace, Anthony F. C., 1969 Review of American Kinship: A Cultural Account by David Schneider. American Anthropologist 71(1): 100–106.

Weismantel, Mary, 1995 Making Kin: Kinship Theory and Zumbagua Adoptions. American Ethnologist 22(4): 685–709.

Yanagisako, Sylvia J., 1978 Variance in American Kinship: Implications for Cultural Analysis. American Ethnologist 5(1): 15–29.

Yanagisako, Sylvia J., and Janet F. Collier, 1987 Towards a Unified Analysis of Gender and
    Kinship. *In* Gender and Kinship: Essays towards a Unified Analysis. Jane F. Collier and
    Sylvia J. Yanagisako, eds. pp. 14–50. Stanford: Stanford University Press.
Yanagisako, Sylvia J., and Carol Delaney, eds. 1995 Naturalizing Power: Essays in Feminist
    Cultural Analysis. New York: Routledge.

14

What Is Kinship All About?

David M. Schneider

We are here to celebrate the centenary of Morgan's *Systems*, and the topic I have chosen for this occasion is "What Is Kinship All About." Let us look at the one who began it all and ask what he thought kinship was all about.[1]

I need not remind you that Morgan was concerned to discover the history and origin of the Indians of North America. He believed that he could reconstruct their history and locate their origins by their manner of classifying kinsmen. He argued that it was not the words or the language that could be taken as reliable indices but rather the mode of classification regardless of the words or language used.

Morgan's reasoning was that if the system of relationship of consanguinity should be found to be the same among all the Indians of America and should also be shown to be the same as those from India, then it would follow that the Indians of America brought that system with them from Asia. Why? Because it is "a system which is transmitted with the blood" (1871:4). By "blood" Morgan meant precisely what we mean: genetics and biology. He says elsewhere in the book: "In the systems of relationship of the great families of mankind, some of the oldest memorials of human thought and experience are deposited and preserved. They have been handed down as transmitted systems through the channels of the blood, from the earliest ages of man's existence upon the earth; but revealing certain definite and pro-gressive changes with the growth of man's experience in the ages of barbarism" (1871:vi).

What did the mode of classification show? How did it come about? What did it reflect? Morgan's answer was: *The actual biological facts as these were known or knowable, given the state of knowledge of the group on the one hand and the state of marriage and sexual relationship on the other, at the time the classification first was established.*

In Morgan's own words:

The family relationships are as ancient as the *family.* They exist in virtue of the law of derivation, which is expressed by the perpetuation of the species through the marriage relation. A system of consanguinity which is founded upon a community of blood, is but the formal expression and recognition of these relationships. Around every person there is a circle or group of kindred of which such person is the center, and the Ego, from whom the degree of the relationship is reckoned and to whom the relationship itself returns. Above him are his father and mother and their ascendants, below him are his children and their descendants; while on either side are his brothers and sisters and their descendants and the brothers and sisters of his father and of his mother and their descendants as well as a much greater number of collateral relatives descended from common ancestors still more remote. To him they are nearer in degree than other individuals of the nation at large. A formal arrangement of the more immediate blood kindred into lines of descent, with the adoption of some method to distinguish one relative from another and to express the value of the relationship, would be one of the earliest acts of human intelligence [1871:10].

And so Morgan called the *descriptive system* a "natural system" precisely "because it is founded upon a correct appreciation of the distinction between the lineal and several collateral lines and of the perpetual divergence of the latter from the former. Each relationship is thus specialized and separated from every other in such a manner as to decrease its nearness and diminish its value according to the degree of distance of each person from the central Ego" (1871:142–143). Conversely, the *classificatory system*, as it is used among American Indians and others, Morgan said, is contrary to the nature of descents, confounding relationships which are distinct, separating those which are similar, and diverting the streams of the blood from the collateral channels into the lineal. Where, for the descriptive system, knowledge of the lines of parentage is necessary to determine the classification, just the opposite is true for the classificatory system; a knowledge of parentage is quite unnecessary. It is impossible to explain its origin on the assumption of the existence of the family founded upon marriage between single pairs; but it may be explained with some degree of probability on the assumption of the antecedent existence of a series of customs and institutions, one reformatory of the other, commencing with promiscuous intercourse and ending with the establishment of the family, as now constituted, resting on marriage between single pairs (paraphrased from 1871:143).

It will prove useful for us to keep two parts of Morgan's paradigm distinct from each other. One is the mode of classification itself. The other is the manner in which the mode of classification can be established, that is, by means of the analysis of the kinship terminology.

Morgan's paradigm states that the mode of classification of kinsmen derives from the knowledge of how people are actually genetically or biologically related to each other. This knowledge in turn depends on their form of marriage. Hence for Morgan, as for others

since, marriage is the central institution of kinship. Implicit in this part of Morgan's paradigm is the premise that marriage consists of a sexual relationship between male and female. It is the processes of biological reproduction that make the married pair the parents of their biological offspring and the offspring of such a mated pair are siblings. The links which are recognized or marked in the mode of classification of kinsmen are the biological or genetic links among these people as these may be known, which in turn depend on the mode of marriage. Thus, by taking one male and one female in the abstract and tracing their siblings, their parents, their offspring, and the parents, siblings, offspring, and spouse of each of these, it is possible to create a genealogical grid, as it is called today; the particular classification of kin which a particular people use can be mapped on this grid and compared with other classifications which other people use by comparing the differently partitioned grids. The classification, in turn, can be derived from which positions on the genealogy are grouped together and which positions are distinguished.

... [I]t seemed obvious to Morgan that the mode of classification could be read directly from the kinship terminology; that is, those positions on the genealogical grid which were grouped together under one kinship term could be distinguished from those positions on the genealogical grid grouped under a different kinship term and so on. Hence kinship terminology was *the* key to the mode of classification and in fact, practically the only key, since the kinship terms meant (either only or primarily) specific relationships of blood or marriage. The taxonomy, then, was derived from no other source than the kinship terminology.

What was kinship all about for Morgan, then? Kinship was about the way in which a people grouped and classified themselves as compared with the real, true, biological facts of consanguinity and affinity. The facts of consanguinity mean those persons who are related by biological descent from the same ancestor. The facts of affinity are the facts of marriage, and marriage means the sexual, reproductive relationship between male and female.

McLennan took issue with Morgan on one specific score, and his argument is easy to misunderstand if one does not observe it closely.

"The ... mistake, or rather I should say error, was to have so lightly assumed the system to be a system of blood-ties" (1886:269).

For the following reasons I think that assumption was an error:–(1) it is apparent, on the slightest inspection of Mr. Morgan's tables, that 'son' and 'daughter', in the classificatory system, do not mean son or daughter 'begotten by' or 'born to'; that 'brother' and 'sister' are terms which do not imply connection by descent from the same mother or father; and that 'mother' does not mean the bearing mother. From the analogies of the case, we must believe that 'father' does mean the begetting father. ... These facts surely ought to have strongly suggested that the classificatory system cannot be a system of blood-ties at all... [1886:270]. (2) That the classificatory system is a system of mutual salutations merely, appears from many of its peculiar features. For one thing, the names for relationship are framed for use in address. They want generality [McLennan 1886:270, 273].

This, then, is what McLennan said KINSHIP TERMS were all about; they were courtesies and modes of address, of mutual salutation.

But did McLennan differ with Morgan on what 'KINSHIP' was all about? Not a bit!

all, or almost all, the peoples using a form of the classificatory system have, besides, some well-defined system of blood-ties – the system which traces blood-ties through women only, or some other. It is inconceivable that any people should have at the same time two entirely different systems of *blood* relationship. And it may be confidently affirmed that in every case it is the system which is unquestionably a system of blood-ties, and not the classificatory system, that alone is of practical force – which regulated succession, for instance, to honours or estates. ... What duties or rights are affected by the 'relationships' comprised of the classificatory system? Absolutely none. They are barren of consequences, except indeed as comprising a code of courtesies and ceremonial addresses in social intercourse [McLennan 1886:270–273].

For McLennan as well as for Morgan, 'kinship' was about marriage, about the facts of procreation and conception, about blood-ties and genetic relationships as they could be known or were knowable, about the ties that arise out of the biological facts of human reproduction; for McLennan, rights and duties, succession and estates followed blood-ties, not kinship terms. For both Morgan and McLennan, marriage meant a sexual relationship between male and female; consanguinity meant descent from the same ancestor. These are the only two components that are necessary for the construction of a genealogy, that is, for the construction of the analytic apparatus needed to describe any particular mode of classification or kinship system and to compare it with any other system.[2]

Ever since Morgan's *Systems*, anthropologists have followed this basic paradigm in its essential outline and have continued to argue about the meaning of kinship terms as well. For many since then, like Durkheim and Rivers, the notions of paternity and maternity and blood connection had to be taken in their social and not in their biological meanings; indeed, their social and their actual biological senses did not always accord with each other too well. Sometimes these biological relationships are either presumptive, fictive, errors of fact based on ignorance, or putative rather than empirically demonstrable. But this hardly alters the fact that it is the system of what are socially defined as the biological facts of reproduction that 'kinship' is all about. That there are rights and duties, statuses and roles, and interpersonal relationships of different complexions associated with the genealogically defined 'kinship' relationships has always been agreed; but the two have been kept quite distinct and held to be inherently distinguishable so that the defining feature, the definition of a 'kinship' relationship as against any other kind of relationship, has always been the biological aspect, whether treated as pure biology or as the social definition of what biology is. Indeed, the prevailing view since Morgan has been that the fictive or presumptive or undemonstrable biological relationship, the social aspect itself, is modeled after, or is a metaphorical extension of, or is a social accretion to, the defining and fundamental biological relationship. Thus for instance adoption is not ruled outside the 'kinship' system but is understandable as a kind of 'kinship' relationship precisely in terms of the fact that it is modeled after the biological relationship. Without the biological relationship, in this view, adoption makes absolutely no sense. Hence even if it is in its social aspects, and even if it is as a social relationship that anthropologists are concerned with it, the real, actual, and true facts of biology as they concern human reproduction remain the base and the defining feature of 'kinship.'[3]

A variant of this view, which is not fundamentally different from it is the position that the genealogical grid itself, can be treated as the defining feature, regardless of how the specific genealogical relationships themselves may be defined and even when they are not defined in biological terms at all. Thus whatever the theory of procreation may be for a given people, it is the fact that a system of genealogical-like relations can be mapped out and partitioned into categories, each systematically related to the other which is the crucial and defining feature of 'kinship.' Yet however different this position may seem to be at first glance it boils down to the fact that a parent–child relationship – however that may be defined procreatively – obtains which implies a sibling relationship which implies a sexual relationship between parents, and so on, which creates the genealogy. By definition, of course, no genealogy is formed or can be formed from the exchange of morning greetings or salutations, nor can a genealogical grid be constructed from material other than some set of premises about the nature of human reproduction.

The two sides of 'kinship,' the biological model (whether real or presumptive, putative or fictive) and the social relationship (the rights, duties, privileges, roles, and statuses) stand in a hierarchical relationship to each other, for the biological defines the system to which the social is attached, and is thus logically prior to the latter. If two relationships are precisely the same except for one single feature, that one is the 'kinship' relationship where some biological relationship prevails or is presumed to prevail, and the other one, lacking this feature, is not. It is possible to hold that the genealogical grid can be distinct from all other aspects of 'kinship' and that the boundaries of the system are those defined by the grid. These boundaries, for some but not for all, include the putative or metaphoric extensions of the genealogical grid. [...]

The position I have argued both in print and in person is that Morgan's paradigm is wrong and that no matter how elegantly it has been revised, amended, altered, embellished, or tightened up, it does not do what it purports to do. I take it that Lounsbury and Goodenough in the United States follow that paradigm, as well as Lévi-Strauss in France, Leach and Needham in England, and many others. I do not mean this as an exhaustive list of followers of Morgan's kinship work, but only to suggest that it holds a position of preeminence in the anthropological world today. Neither do I mean to suggest that the work of Goodenough and Lounsbury or any of these men is in any sense identical except that they all follow Morgan's use of the genealogical grid as the basic analytic tool and they all remain wedded to Morgan's definition of what 'kinship' is all about.

My criticism of Morgan's paradigm is plainly contained in the alternative strategy I have followed. I have tried here to show its utility and productivity given my aims, objectives, and analytic procedures.

I

There is general agreement among all of us, followers of Morgan as well as others, that a classification of kinsmen does not exhaust the 'kinship' system by any means. Where we differ is in how we handle this fact. The position which follows from Morgan's paradigm, which Lounsbury, Goodenough, Lévi-Strauss, Leach, Needham, and the many others whom I should mention take, is that the kin classification can be treated as a distinct, separate, and autonomous part of the 'kinship' system, however it may be related to a larger system. Just as some anthropologists believe that the phonemic system can be analyzed apart from grammar and syntax in language, so these anthropologists also feel that the kin classification can be analyzed apart from the rest of the 'kinship' system. My own position is that an accurate account of the kin classification in a cultural sense (see below) cannot be given without taking the whole 'kinship' system into account.

The second major part of the strategy I have followed is to ask what, in each and every instance, the definition of the domain of 'kin-ship' may be for each and every culture I study. I do not assume that this domain is defined *a priori* by the bio-genetic premises of the genea-logically defined grid. In other words, where the followers of Morgan take it as a matter of definition that the invariant points of reference provided by the facts of sexual intercourse, conception, pregnancy, and parturition consti-tute the domain of 'kinship,' I treat this as an open, empirical question. Of what primitive elements, I ask in each and every case, is the cultural system composed? It is this question which on the one hand enables me to ask what 'kinship' is all about, while on the other hand it seems to deprive me of an externally based, systematically usable comparative frame. I shall return to this point below.

The second major aspect of the strategy I have used follows directly from, and is required by, the third, which is the use of a different, narrower, and I think sharper and more power-ful concept of culture than has been traditional in anthropology. Briefly, I start with concrete, observable patterns of behavior and abstract from it a level of material which has usually been called 'norms.' The normative system consists in the rules and regulations which an actor should follow if his behavior is to be accepted by his community or his society as proper. These are the "how-to-do-it" rules, as Goodenough has recently put it (1970). They should on no account be confused with the patterns of behavior which people actually per-form. It is the rule "thou shalt not steal" that is the norm, not the fact that many people do not steal; it is the rule that a middle-class father should earn the money to support his family, not the fact that many actually do.

The next step is to abstract from the norma-tive system what, following Parsons, I have called the 'cultural system' (Parsons 1966, 1971). This consists in the system of symbols and meanings embedded in the normative system but which is a quite distinct aspect of it and can easily be abstracted from it. By sym-bols and meanings I mean the basic premises which a culture posits for life: what its units consist in; how those units are defined and differentiated; how they form an integrated order or classification; how the world is struc-tured; in what parts it consists and on what

premises it is conceived to exist, the categories and classifications of the various domains of the world of man and how they relate one with another, and the world that man sees himself living in. Where the normative system, the how-to-do-it rules and regulations, is Ego-centered and particularly appropriate to deci-sion-making or interaction models of analysis, culture is system-centered and appears to be more static and 'given,' and far less processual (but only in contrast with the normative system of course; culture has its own processes and its own rules of change and movement). Culture takes man's position *vis-à-vis* the world rather than *a* man's position on how to get along in the world as it is given; it asks "Of what does this world consist?" where the normative level asks, "Given the world to be made up in the way it is, how does a man proceed to act in it?" Culture concerns the stage, the stage setting, and the cast of characters; the normative system consists in the stage directions for the actors and how the actors should play their parts on the stage that is so set.

This is not to say that the cultural and nor-mative level are unconnected. The cultural level contains implications for the general dir-ections in which normative patterns of action ought to take place, but it does not spell them out in the detail which the normative patterns themselves provide. The cultural premise that "there are two kinds of relatives, relatives by blood and relatives by marriage," does not tell how a man should treat his relatives by mar-riage. Yet once it is known that there are these two categories, how each is defined, and the values attached to each, general directions of action are laid out already even if they are not sufficient to provide a precise template for how-to-do-it. By the same token, the cultural premises allow a wide range of possibilities and alternatives in the normative rules.[4]

This conception of culture is far more narrow and, I think, far more precise than those generally in use in anthropology today. Furthermore, it is explicitly tied into a wider social theory rather than linked in a loose, ad hoc way to a variety of eclectically given and not always internally consistent theories. This conception of culture and the social theory of which it is a part yields a considerably smaller, more concentrated, and homogeneous body of materials abstracted as culture than many other definitions.

This leads to the final point in this introductory section. What 'kinship' is all about is considered here only in its cultural aspects; it is 'kinship' at a cultural level as here defined. I am explicitly *not* speaking of 'kinship' at a psychological level. Nor am I speaking of it as a system for the organization of social groups, that is, not at the social system, social organizational or social structural level, for these are, by my definitions, *not* the same as the cultural system. The cultural level is focused on the fundamental system of symbols and meanings which inform and give shape to the normative level of action.

This theory, like every other theory, is easily transformable into a series of questions which are put to the data. It assumes that every concrete act, or system of action, has a cultural component, a social system component, a psychological component, and so on. Thus the question I am asking, which follows directly from this theory, is: What are the underlying symbols and their meanings in this particular segment of concrete action and how do they form a single, coherent, interrelated system of symbols and meanings? If that question cannot be answered satisfactorily, there must be something wrong with my theory. If I can answer the question, it may at least show that the theory can be applied, even if it is not enlightening. I have followed this theory, however, not because it is merely applicable but because I think that it is enlightening and that we learn much from it.

Many other fruitful and useful questions can be asked about the same segment of concrete action using the same social theory. For instance, one can ask about the motivations entailed in that action. Or one may ask the history of that segment of action. A relatively common question in anthropology is sometimes called a comparative, functional question.[5]

The crux of the issue, then, is what is being compared. If we ask how any particular cultural system is constructed, for instance, we ask what units it contains, how they are defined in that culture, how they are differentiated and articulated as symbols and meanings; but if we pose a question taken from outside any particular socio-cultural system, this is different

from the cultural question. For instance, it is a functional prerequisite to the maintenance of any society to regulate sexual behavior, since unregulated sexual behavior is a source of disruption. We can then ask of each socio-cultural system or society, "How do they do it?" The boundaries of sex and of the different regulatory mechanisms are defined in terms of their relevance to the question and are related only loosely to the boundaries which the society itself embodies in its cultural constructs. We may ask, for whatever reason, how the processes of human reproduction are ordered in different societies, and a study of certain aspects of their 'kinship' system will of course be included; but the particular cultural constructs which obtain within that society are cut off or are included at points determined by the relevance of that material to the question being posed and asked in a comparative framework from outside the bounds of the particular culture.

A cultural question is by definition a question of from what units this particular socio-cultural system is constructed, of how those units are defined and articulated, and of how those units form a meaningful whole. It is not true that such a question necessarily yields material which is unique, distinctive, and cannot be compared from one society to another. Quite the contrary. The systems of symbols and meanings of different cultures can be compared as easily as systems of human reproduction can be compared from one society to another.

I do not mean to play semantic games here or to beg fundamental questions; but if culture consists in the system of symbols and meanings of a particular society, and if a social system consists in the manner in which social units are organized for various social purposes, then comparative operations of the former are cross-cultural comparisons while, by definition, comparative operations of the latter are not cross-*cultural* comparisons but rather cross-*social* comparisons, that is, comparisons of social organization, social systems, or social structures. The key definitional difference lies between the concepts of society and culture, between modes of organization of action systems and systems of symbols and meanings.

I am concerned with questions of cross-cultural comparison and questions having to do with the analysis of particular cultures, not social systems.

II

What happens if this analytic strategy is used on a particular 'kinship' system? Does it tell us anything usefully new or different about that system or about the nature of 'kinship'?

I have tried to do this for the American 'kinship' system. Since much of this material already has been published (1968, 1969: 116–125, 1970:88–90), I will merely touch on the points which bear directly on the task at hand.

What anthropologists have heretofore regarded as THE domain of 'kinship' in American culture turns out to be only one part of a larger domain, made up of two different parts. The domain we have traditionally called 'kinship' is Ego-centered, consisting of a network of related *persons*, such as mother, father, brother, etc. It is not hard to see that this domain is constructed out of many different kinds of components from many different systems. Thus each unit in the system, such as 'mother' or 'father,' is defined first by what might be called a pure 'kinship' component, second by an age or generation component, third by a sex-role component, fourth by a class component, and by other components of other kinds as well. Hence I have called this the 'conglomerate' system or the 'conglomerate' level of the system.

To understand the second part we must go a step further. We can, by using a level of contrast which is not generally employed in 'kinship' analysis, abstract the 'kinship' component alone and in its pure form from the conglomerate system. We do so by asking what the distinctive features are which define the person as a kinsman as against a non-kinsman.[6] When we do this, it becomes apparent at the level of the 'pure' system that the distinctive features or the defining features (1968:22, 41 ff.) or the primitive and irreducible elements are, first, shared bio-genetic substance and, second, a code for conduct which I have characterized as diffuse, enduring solidarity. These two elements combine to yield three major categories of kin; when both elements occur together the category of blood relative is formed; when the code for conduct element occurs alone and

without the shared bio-genetic substance element the category of relatives-in-law or relatives by marriage is formed; and, finally, when the shared bio-genetic substance is present alone the category of relatives in nature is formed. Hence at the pure kinship level the so-called 'kinship terms' do not play a classificatory role.[7]

If we consider the pure 'kinship' system alone, we can see that the distinctive features by which it is defined are parts of two much wider and more general categories of American culture. That is easy to see when we remember that blood relatives are considered to be related in nature and that they are parts of the natural order of things as defined in American culture. Their second distinctive feature, the code for conduct, is simply part of that much wider category called the *order of law*, defined in opposition to the *order of nature*. This is the order imposed by man on nature, the order defined in American culture as consisting in rules, regulations, customs, traditions, and so forth which man, with the aid of human reason, creates. The limited domain of law in the juridical sense is only one part of this wider domain; and when we understand how much a part of the same domain they are, we have explained in some significant degree why relatives 'by marriage' are also called relatives 'in law.'

At the pure level, then, part of what anthropologists have traditionally been calling 'kinship' seems to be defined in American culture as an indistinguishable part of these two much wider and more general cultural categories, the order of nature and the order of law.

If we now consider the domains of religion and nationality[8] and analyze them as we have analyzed 'kinship,' a rather interesting fact emerges. We again distinguish the pure system from the conglomerate system. The conglomerate system of nationality consists in the entire federal and state systems; the legislative, judicial, and executive branches of government; the two Houses of Congress; the different states and their organization, and so forth. But to abstract the pure system we simply ask, What makes a person a citizen? What are the distinctive features which define a person's nationality? He is either born an American or he is – and the word is of course quite significant – naturalized. Once again we find that the distinctive features are shared substance (being born American) and a code for conduct which enjoins diffuse, enduring solidarity: being a loyal American, loving one's country, and, in President Kennedy's felicitous phrase, "Ask not what your country can do for you. Ask rather what you can do for your country." The same is true, as I have tried to show elsewhere, for religion, where the conglomerate level includes the organization of the church and so forth; but what makes a member of the church is, once again, shared substance and a special code for conduct which can be characterized as diffuse, enduring solidarity (1969). [...]

If the conglomerate level consists in units made up of elements from different pure systems, then the question arises of how the different components relate with each other in the conglomerate unit. Are they simply added together? Do they form some special configuration?

The answer to these questions seems to be that at the level of the person, each pure component receives *further* specification of its content, defined now with reference to how a person should act, and this further specification derives from the total context or the interaction of all of the defining components.

Let me try to explain this by going back to the so-called 'kinship' component once more. The 'kinship' component says that persons are related either by shared bio-genetic substance, a shared code for conduct, or by both. But at the level of the person something called 'distance' comes into play, so that the question is no longer shared or not shared but of how much is shared. If the shared elements are now conceived in terms of magnitudes, then class factors, personal factors, and a variety of other considerations permit it to be cut off at various points and at various times and under various circumstances and for various purposes at the option of the actor himself. Hence the common observation in both America and England that some people will actually trace blood connections to people, whom they then say they do not count among their relatives or kinsmen. They simply say, "Yes, they are my blood relatives, I suppose, but I don't consider them relatives; they are too far away" or words to that effect.

In sum, the difference between the pure system and the conglomerate system lies in their orientations. The conglomerate system is oriented toward action, toward telling people how to behave, toward telling people how-to-do-it under ideal circumstances. It is thus much closer to the normative system. The pure system, however, is oriented toward the state-of-being, toward How Things Are. It is in the transition from How Things Are and How Things Ought To Be to the domain of If That Is So, How Then Should One Act that the pure systems come together to form the conglomerate systems for action.

At this point the question of just what is 'kinship' all about or how the domain of 'kinship' is to be defined must be raised. If, on the one hand, the broad categories of the order of nature and the order of law contain as special instances the two major components which are distinctive features out of which the categories of kin are formed, and if, on the other hand, at the level of the pure system, the 'kinship' system, the nationality system, and the religious system cannot be distinguished from one another in terms of their defining features, what justification is there for calling this system either a 'kinship' or a 'religious' or a 'nationality' system? They are, culturally speaking or with respect to their distinctive features, all exactly the same thing.

And if it is true that at the level of the conglomerate system it is not possible to say that the 'kinship' component is dominant and modifies the sex-role component, or the other way around, but only that each retains its integrity in the configuration, while a new, emergent level is formed, then it is equally problematic as to what, for comparative analytic purposes, any particular conglomerate system should be called. That is, if it is a 'kinship' plus sex-role plus age-role plus class, system, why call it a 'kinship' system? Or, for that matter, why call it a sex-role system? Is there one good reason why a particular bundle of components should be characterized by only one of its components rather than by another?

There is ONE good reason and that is when, in the particular culture we are studying, it is done that way. I can think of no other good reason.

This turns out to be the case in American culture. As in modern Western European culture in general, there are clear-cut, formal divisions which are called in that culture itself 'institutions.' These institutions refer precisely to the conglomerate level – the 'family' is one, the 'church' is another (it may also be called 'religion'), the 'state' is a third, and so on.

Hence if our term 'kinship' is synonymous with that institution as it is defined in American culture, sometimes called 'family,' then 'kinship' is indeed a valid cultural unit which is actually found in American culture, and it is found so that its defining features are *at the cultural level* to be identical with those of religion and nationality while it is found to be very clearly differentiated from those other units at the conglomerate level and in its normative aspects. Nor should it be forgotten that, however 'kinship,' nationality, and religion are differentiated at the conglomerate, organizational level, the very same distinctive features which define all three as cultural domains are themselves an integral part of the orders of nature and law. That is, we have simply not explored the entire universe of American culture and so we cannot as yet say what other units should fall into the same cultural category with 'kinship,' nationality, and religion or, to put it in the other way, whatever other categories exhaust the domains of the order of nature and law. Thus there are grounds for accepting Parsons' suggestion that education ought to be considered along with kinship, religion, and the moral community (nationality) as part of a single cultural entity. My purpose here, however, is not to introduce a new element but to remind the reader that we have approached American culture rather as the blind men approached the elephant. Even if we have discovered that a leg is linked to the body, we have not gone much further and cannot claim to have examined American cultural categories exhaustively. This is a very important point to which I shall return.

In introducing the terms *pure* and *conglomerate* I confine their meaning to the cultural level and speak only of cultural components. It is clear that the pure level is confined to the cultural level alone. The conglomerate level should be understood as the cultural elements embedded in the normative system and the way in which they are embedded in that system as well as the way in which they are articulated to the social system components at the normative level. The normative level thus includes more than those cultural elements in it. It follows therefore that the conglomerate level and the normative system are at the same level of abstraction, but that the notion of conglomerate is simply the identification of the cultural elements in their matrix of the normative system.

To move to the pure cultural level, then, is to abstract distinct cultural domains apart from and regardless of the normative matrix in which they are found. Thus one normative matrix containing certain cultural elements may be an institutionally distinct family system in modern Western European society, but the pure cultural domain is quite different as I have tried to show, and the same cultural elements can be found in a variety of other differentiated normative systems as well (such as religion, the moral community, etc.). To distinguish the conglomerate level, then, is simply to locate the cultural elements in their place in the normative system and to be able to analyze them in relation to each other and to the normative system which contains them.

Let me conclude this section by repeating that as anthropologists we can study different cultures or we can study different social systems. If we study different cultures we do not do the same thing as when we study different social systems. When we study different cultures we study different conceptual schemes for what life is and how it should be lived, we study different symbolic and meaningful systems. We do not study the different ways in which different theoretically defined functions are actually or ideally carried out. There is thus a major difference between cultural anthropology and what has been called, following British usage (and quite correctly, too) social anthropology or comparative sociology. I take my task to be the study of culture and identify myself as a cultural anthropologist (although I will be the first to admit that this has not always been so).

Given this definition of the task, we can proceed. Even if 'kinship' is culturally segregated as a domain at one level of American culture – the conglomerate or normative level – it is not culturally segregated as a distinct domain in most of the cultures we encounter outside the Western European culture area. Quite the contrary. The vast majority of other cultures we know do not have culturally differentiated domains of the sort which occur in Western European or American culture.

But note clearly what I am trying to say. I do not mean that we must cease to observe domestic arrangements in different societies; I do not mean that we cannot ask how a people order their relationships between men and women or between a woman and the child she bears; I do not mean that we cannot go out and ask for the theories of procreation which a particular people hold. We can do all of these things and more and have learned much from such questions. I mean only that such questions of organization, or social organization, or social structure should not be confused with or identified with questions about the nature, the structure, or the content of either particular cultures or of culture in general. Because domestic arrangements can be an analytic category which may not correspond to anything as it is defined as a cultural category in a particular culture, the relationship between a woman and the child she bears may be an analytic category which we erect for various reasons, but it may or it may not correspond to any particular cultural category in a particular culture; theories of procreation may be an analytic or functional category which we invent but which may or may not have one or another cultural counterpart in a particular culture, or be incorporated indistinguishably into one or another cultural scheme in a particular culture. It may indeed be true that some culture does have, as a cultural category, 'domestic units,' but that needs to be shown empirically, not assumed so simply on one theoretical ground or another.

There is one final point. I have said that the American 'kinship' system has two distinctive features, shared bio-genetic substance and diffuse, enduring solidarity. I have said elsewhere that these derive from the master symbol of coitus and that each is a facet of this act. The last few pages of my book, *American Kinship*, make the point that the biological elements have symbolic significance. They constitute an integrated set of symbols in the sense that they are a model for how life, in certain of its aspects, is constituted and should be lived. The symbols are 'biological' in the sense that the culturally given definition of the symbol system is that it is derived from the facts of biology as a process of nature itself. But it is fundamental to our understanding that we appreciate that these biological elements are symbols and that their symbolic referents are not biology as a natural process at all.[9]

Now one may well ask if in a somewhat roundabout way I am not saying here what Morgan and his followers have always said, for they too stressed genealogy as a biologically defined network, and descent can easily be seen as shared bio-genetic substance, the whole being treated in its social rather than in its biological aspects. I think that I am saying something quite different. First, although what appear to be biological elements seem to be present in both Morgan's analysis and mine, we treat those elements in very different ways. I insist that these 'biological' elements have primarily symbolic significance and that their meaning is not biology at all. Morgan and his followers have insisted that it is the biological elements of human reproduction as they are scientifically demonstrable in nature which are directly reflected in 'kinship' and that it is these facts which people have slowly, over time, learned to recognize more or less accurately and then give further social value. For Morgan the matter stopped there; but for many of his followers, like Rivers, Malinowski, and some of our contemporaries, the biological elements need not rest on the scientifically determined or actual facts of nature but merely on whatever the natives believe to be the facts of human reproduction. Thus whatever their theory of procreation, it is the fact that these are believed to be true facts of nature and it is therefore in terms of these biological, or hypothetical facts of nature, that 'kinship' is defined.

Whether it is the true facts of human reproduction or only those which the natives happen to believe to be true, human reproduction in its biological aspects plays the fundamental role for Morgan as well as for the functionalists who follow him. For both, the socio-cultural position of 'kinship' is similar. For Morgan, it was an achievement of great evolutionary significance when the classificatory system gave way to the descriptive system, for it showed not only that man had achieved the most advanced form of the family but had also achieved an advanced level of knowledge, for the descriptive system was "founded upon correct appreciation of the distinction between lineal and several collateral lines of perpetual divergence of the latter from the former" (1871:142). "A formal arrangement of the more immediate blood kindred into lines of descent, with the adoption of some method to distinguish one relative from another and to express the value of the relationship, would be one of the earliest acts of human intelligence" (1871:10).

For the 'functionalists' of Malinowski's school the situation was not much different except that the evolutionary material was excised with gusto. 'Kinship' was the social recognition of biological facts, and the presence and function of a socio-cultural system of 'kinship' was explicable and understandable precisely on the ground that these facts constitute elements in the external environment with which man must cope directly as well as indirectly and to which he must adapt. His way of coping with them and adapting to them is, by definition, the 'kinship' system. The family, a part of the 'kinship' system, was seen by Malinowski as, among other things, one way of maintaining order in the sexual sphere, for it provided rules and regulations governing sexual relations and these, when obeyed, were orderly and permitted man to proceed with his life in an orderly fashion and without disruptions and the chaos that would be attendant on unregulated sexuality.

As I have already indicated, I too am a functionalist and I too have a functional explanation to offer, though it is somewhat different from Malinowski's or his co-workers'.

No one can disagree that man must cope with the facts of life and the facts of nature, whether he knows what these facts are scientifically or has only erroneous beliefs. It can be demonstrated easily that the question of how man copes with the facts of human reproduction is answered only in part, and in very small part at that, by the 'kinship' system. But that is not the main point here at all. The main point here is that that is a social system question, a sociological question. It is a question of how roles are defined and articulated into a set of patterns for action which adapt man to the facts of his environment.

A different functional question centers on the cultural rather than the social system level. That question has to do with the system of symbols and meanings which the so-called 'kinship' system embodies, with what the boundaries of that sub-system of symbols and meanings are and whether they stretch beyond the 'kinship' system or only fall within a portion of it. The functional question at the cultural level, then, is what that system of symbols and meanings consists in and, once that is answered, what part it plays in the total socio-cultural system. [...]

III

In section I, I drew a distinction between culture and social or normative system and said that this distinction had an important place in a wider social theory, essentially Parsonian in conception.

The fundamental point of section II was that at the cultural or symbolic level, 'kinship,' religion, nationality (pending a full clarification and revision of this term), and possibly education as well are identical, although they are quite different in their social system or social organizational aspects.

In sections I and II, I emphasized that the question asked of the data is different, depending on whether it is a cultural question or a social system or social organizational question.

The next problem, and the problem of this section, is the old one of how comparison can be conducted on a cultural level if it is assumed that each and every culture may be uniquely constituted. How can one compare wholly different things?

In part, the answer to this question has been given in the discussion of the differences between culture and social system. The units of any particular culture are defined distinctively within that culture. By definition, they cannot be imposed from outside. It follows, therefore, from the definitions and the theory used here, that there is and can be only one cultural question, the question of what its particular system of symbols and meanings consist in.

We must start, of course, as adults who have lived in our own society and been socialized in our own culture before we even imagine any others. Thus we start by asking that question and answering it for our own culture, which always serves as a base-line for cross-cultural comparison. Without some comprehension, however botched, distorted, biased, and infused with value judgments and wishful thinking, both good and bad, our own culture always remains the base-line for all other questions and comparisons. In part, this is because the experience of our own culture is the only experience which is deep and subtle enough to comprehend in cultural terms, for the cultural aspects of action are particularly subtle, sometimes particularly difficult to comprehend partly because they are symbols not treated usually as symbols but as true facts. So it is difficult at times to convince an American that blood as a fluid has nothing in it which causes ties to be deep and strong. So, too, many aspects of culture are unconscious and are not part of an explicit scheme of things.

A more fundamental reason for the fact that our own culture is always implicitly or explicitly, immediately or remotely, the base-line for comparison and comprehension is that that is what anthropology is all about. It is an attempt to understand ourselves as human beings by using anthropology as the mirror for man. By seeing ourselves against the contrast of others and by seeing others in contrast with ourselves, we learn about ourselves and about mankind.

It is unnecessary to raise the old problem of how it is possible for two things to be compared as wholes when each is wholly unique. We are spared this burden by the fact that the basis for comparison is given by our definition of culture as a system of symbols and meanings. Symbols and meanings can be compared just as easily as modes of family organization, the roles of seniors to juniors, or the methods of agriculture. The comparative base is given therefore by the theoretical stipulation of what it is we are trying to abstract from each system and from the fact that we can indeed systematically abstract the system of symbols and meanings for each society. Hence the key to the comparative problem is in locating the symbolic elements from a careful analysis of the units which the culture itself defines. We do not say, "Let's look at the lineages," we ask instead what units this culture postulates, and the

answer may have nothing whatever to do with lineages. We must then follow these symbolic elements throughout the particular culture, wherever they may lead and in whatever forms they may be found. In short, framing a question is the first step. It must then be answered for our own culture as an hypothesis. One then takes those cultural constructs and asks if any other culture has anything like it or not, how they differ, where and in what way, and where they appear to be the same. [. . .]

Let me conclude and summarize by returning to Morgan and company. I think it is quite clear that this is *not* in fact what Morgan and his followers have actually done. Their cultural categories do *not* come from a previously analyzed culture at all, but are composed of ad hoc elements which derive from social system questions, functional questions, and from (in Morgan's case especially) evolutionary considerations, all of which are quite foreign to any particular culture. Morgan did *not* use the cultural system of American 'kinship' as the model for his comparative analysis because as I have shown in *American Kinship*, the genealogical grid which Morgan used is not part of that system. Morgan is quite clear that what he took to be the comparative model as the many quotes cited at the outset of this paper show, is the genealogically defined or biologically defined network. By using the genealogically defined grid Morgan and his followers have protected themselves from finding out what the true units of American 'kinship' in a cultural sense are and what their distinctive features actually are. In other words, they have not dealt with American 'kinship' as a cultural system but have simply assumed that their model caught or contained some part of it.

I have affirmed repeatedly that the genealogically defined grid is not appropriately applied to American 'kinship' for three reasons. First, it does not in fact correspond to the cultural units of which the American 'kinship' system is actually made up, nor to the distinctive features in terms of which these cultural units are defined, unless, of course, the results of the research presented in *American Kinship* are largely in error. Second, the genealogically defined grid is tied to the false assumption that it is possible to discover the classification of kinsmen without taking into account the rest of the 'kinship' system, particularly the system of roles and patterns *for* behavior as well as the wider cultural context in which the 'kinship' system is situated. Third, as McLennan was first to point out and as only a few since have maintained, is the false assumption that the so-called 'kinship terms' are either the sole avenue through which the classification of kin can be established or constitute a major or decisive body of evidence on that problem.

One might raise the question of whether, perhaps, the American 'kinship' system is unique in that it is the only one in the world where the genealogical grid is inappropriate for cultural comparison. I am sure that you will agree that this does not seem to be so. I can assure the reader that from my own work on Yap, the Mescalero Apache, and the Zuni . . . the genea-logically defined grid does not fit these cultures either. I would suggest that the Nuer cannot be fitted to a genealogical grid, nor most of the Eskimo systems we have adequate information on.

The important point is that the genealogic-ally defined grid is the only analytic device that has been applied to most of the systems which anthropologists have studied. There has been almost no systematic attempt to study the question without employing this device. To put it simply, it is about time that we tested some other hypotheses. [. . .]

IV

We are ready now to deal with the question which is the title of this paper: What Is Kinship All About?

The answer is simple and self-evident by now. 'Kinship' is an analytic category which has been prevalent in anthropology since Morgan first invented it. *In the way in which Morgan and his followers have used it, it does not corres-pond to any cultural category known to man.* The closest thing to it is the Western European category of 'family,' but if I am correct in my analysis even that is not close. From the begin-ning of this paper I have put the word 'kinship' in quotes, in order to affirm that it is a theoret-ical notion in the mind of the anthropologist which has no discernible cultural referent in fact.

I have consciously misused the term 'kinship' simply as a way of beginning the discussion. But it is no longer necessary to misuse the words; now we can use them correctly. 'Kinship' is what Morgan's, Goodenough's, Lounsbury's, Lévi-Strauss', Leach's and Need-ham's (among others) analytic schemes are all about, but they have no known referent in any known culture *except* at the conglomerate level of Western European culture, as in America. To speak precisely, the title of my book, *American Kinship*, is a misnomer. I really did not deal extensively with 'kinship' at the conglomerate level nor did I intend to; in the pure culture level there is no such thing as 'kinship.' Hence my use of the term 'pure kinship level' is wrong, too, which I have tried to suggest by the use of quotes around the word. The level is the pure culture level as defined by certain symbols.

Let me conclude this section on a simple note. For a while anthropologists used to write papers about Totemism as if it were a concrete or conceptual entity that had an actual, existential counterpart in the cultures of the Australian aborigines, among others. Goldenweiser and others then demolished that notion and showed that totemism simply did not exist as a useful analytic category pre-cisely because it had no corresponding referent in any of the cultures with which it was alleged to be associated. It became, then, a non-subject. In due course Lévi-Strauss wrote a book about that non-subject, in which he first explained that it was a non-subject and there-fore could not be the subject of the book, for it did not exist outside the minds of those who invented it and believed it, and these were an-thropologists, not the natives they wrote about. The 'matrilineal complex' suffered the same fate in the hands of Lowie.

In my view, 'kinship' is like totemism, matri-archy, and the 'matrilineal complex.' It is a non-subject. It exists in the minds of anthro-pologists but not in the cultures they study. If you like to think that I have devoted a good part of my intellectual life to the industrious study of a non-subject, you are more than wel-come to do so. If you think that I have now talked myself out of a subject for study you are quite right, too. But that is not the whole story. I have talked myself out of studying 'kinship' as if it were a distinct, discrete, isolable sub-system of every and any culture. What I have learned and have tried to convey here is that in the study of culture one must proceed in a very different way.

When I started to study American 'kinship' I went to households to talk with the inhabitants about how those who were living there were related to each other and to others who were not living there. I systematically collected genealogies at the very outset. When I began to discover that their concepts were somewhat different from those which traditional 'kinship' studies led me to expect, I followed their concepts and their definitions and the formulation of the cultural domains of their actions, depending as well on my own experience over the past years here in America, on Yap, and among the Mescalero Apache. Once that was done, and it was not easy for me to do it systematically, I could see that there was no such thing as 'kinship,' except as it existed as a set of *a priori* theoretical assumptions in the mind of the anthropologist.

One must take the native's own categories, the native's units, the native's organization, and articulation of those categories and follow their definitions, their symbolic and meaningful divisions wherever they may lead. When they lead across the lines of 'kinship' into politics, economics, education, ritual, and religion, one must follow them there and include those areas within the domains which the particular culture has laid out. One does not stop at the anthropologist's arbitrarily defined domains of 'kinship,' 'religion,' 'ritual,' and 'age-sets,' etc., but instead draws a picture of the structure of a culture by means of the categories and congeries of units which the culture defines as its parts; one interrelates these in terms which, in that particular culture are symbolically defined as identical, drawing distinctions among parts which that culture itself defines as different by their different symbolic definition and designation.

Proceeding this way, a somewhat different analysis emerges than when one asks questions about the social system or the social organization. Yet the two systems, as I have said all along, articulate and are related to each other. Ultimately the study of culture can no more be isolated from all other sub-systems of a society

than the study of its social system, although this is the way we have been proceeding in the past, largely neglecting or omitting the study of culture or relegating the idea of culture to the kinds of hats the natives wear or, correspondingly, to the level of arts and crafts it has achieved. [...]

V

I will try to briefly summarize this paper and what I take to be its major points, and add one point in conclusion.

Theory suggests that it may be useful to systematically and rigorously distinguish culture from social system, defining culture rather narrowly as a system of symbols and meanings. When this view of culture is applied to what have ordinarily been treated as 'kinship' systems, new material emerges because a new question has been asked about it. Instead of the classic question which is at the social system level of How Does This Society Organize to Accomplish Certain Tasks (establish alliances, maintain control over territory, provide for inheritance and succession, hold and transmit property, etc.), a cultural question is asked: namely, what are the units, how are they defined in the native culture itself, how does it postulate their interconnections, their mode of differentiation, by what symbolic devices do they define the units and their relationship, and what meanings do these have?

I tried to give an example, briefly condensed from published literature, of what happens when a particular 'kinship' system is analyzed in this way, using my own work on American 'kinship,' and I think I was able to show that some rather new and different results emerged.

One of the lessons derived from this study of American 'kinship' was that the very same symbols defined 'kinship,' nationality, and religion at the cultural level and that, if this were so, then all of these – with the possible addition of the educational system in American culture – could be included in one single cultural unit or domain. Hence there need be – there could be – no grounds for distinguishing the 'kinship' system from the 'religious' system, from the 'nationality' system, from the 'educational' system at the cultural level.

Further, where the bio-genetic elements, the elements of conception and parturition were taken simply as defining elements or were treated as states of affairs with which every society must cope in one way or another, the alternate strategy of study which I commended yielded the suggestion that these defining elements of 'blood,' of one flesh and blood, of bio-genetic identity could be understood as symbols which stood for social relationships of diffuse, enduring solidarity. That is, the biological elements which previous theories took as merely defining features, 'givens' in the state of affairs, could be understood better as symbols for kinds of social relationships, and probably these did not derive from, not stand for, the biological material they purported to order functionally. Indeed, at many points the scientific facts sharply contradicted the cultural facts about biology; but the fact that the scientific facts had little or no discernible effect on changing the cultural facts seemed good evidence for concluding that the bio-genetic elements in American kinship were primarily symbolic of something else and hardly relevant to biology as a natural or actual state of affairs.

The next step in the argument was simply to generalize from that fact. 'Kinship,' from the time of Morgan, had been defined in terms of consanguinity and affinity, that is, by an *a priori* set of criteria, and studied with respect to the organization of its elements for discharging certain functions. If 'kinship' is studied at the cultural level, however, then it is apparent that 'kinship' is an artifact of the anthropologists' analytic apparatus and has no concrete counterpart in the cultures of any of the societies we studied.

Hence the conclusion that 'kinship,' like totemism, the matrilineal complex, and matriarchy, is a non-subject, since it does not exist in any culture known to man.

I then tried briefly to show that even those who seemed to have broken with the Morgan tradition – Rivers, Leach, Needham, and Lévi-Strauss – were still ensnared in that tradition either by their commitment to genealogical criteria in the definition of kinship or by their commitment to the positing of questions purely at the social system or social organizational level, or both. I used Lounsbury and Good-

enough as examples of those who were without question squarely in the tradition of Morgan.

And finally, embedded here and there in the paper is the plea to try, for a change, another approach to kinship, another set of hypotheses, to ask another question and see what the pay-off might be. We have asked these functionally defined, social organizational questions of kinship exclusively since the 1870's. There is no need to stop asking those questions for they are good, productive, legitimate questions. I only urge that we ask a different kind of question, a cultural question, as well.

In conclusion, if the argument of this paper has any merit, it follows that it will no longer be possible to study 'kinship' or religion or economics or politics, etc., as distinct cultural systems, for in each case the definition of each of these domains has been in social system or sociological and not cultural terms. This has been the classic Weberian approach,[10] where the basic frame of reference is the institution, socially or sociologically defined, and the two different questions, one organizational and the other cultural, are then put to the data. (Indeed, one of the favorite Weberian questions of recent times has been of the effect of religious organization and its cultural aspects on the development of the economic system.) The result of this Weberian approach is a fragmentation of the cultural material into artificial segments which remain unlinked and unlinkable. It is not possible to relate the cultural aspects of the religious system to the cultural aspects of the 'kinship,' political, or economic system without extraordinary skill and good luck, if it is possible at all.

If the argument I have presented here is followed out logically it will be necessary to treat the whole culture as a single cultural system, following out its different segments and its different divisions and domains as these are defined and differentiated by the symbolic system itself.

It follows from the irreducibility of the cultural to the social systems, or vice versa, that this examination of the cultural system as a whole, apart from its social system aspects, is necessarily undertaken independently of any examination of the social system, at least in its initial phases. Ultimately, of course, as the Parsonian theory of action makes so clear, these all come together and are mutually inter-dependent parts of any concrete system of action, but they are analytically distinct. As no one system can be reduced to any other each system therefore has an integrity of its own which must be respected by the analytic procedures used.

It is precisely this failure to distinguish the social system aspects from the cultural aspects and the primary analytic emphasis on the social system to the neglect of the cultural that has led us – the descendants and followers of Morgan – into such untenable conclusions as I have tried to deal with here – that because in some sense genealogy and procreation and conception are 'really out there as indisputable and unavoidable facts of life' it is and it must be the material out of which kinship systems are made.

To my mind it will no longer be acceptable to consider 'religion as a cultural system' any more than it would be acceptable to consider 'kinship as a cultural system' or 'politics as a cultural system.' Each culture must be approached apart from its institutional segments, its social organizational segments, or its social structural segments, and from a purely cultural perspective. Once the cultural system as a whole is outlined – at least in its more or less broad outline, with its major symbolic features defined and the links between them roughly established – then, and only then, can such questions be usefully raised as, for instance, the role of the culture of a given society on its economic development, its religious organization, or its political system. But I would stress the importance of undertaking cultural analyses which are truly and clearly independent of the sociological analyses and uncontaminated by them. This is not the place to elaborate this last point but only to make clear that if the analysis of this paper has any merit, then the independent study of the culture of a society as a whole culture must be undertaken apart from and uncontaminated by the study of its social system.

NOTES

1   I would like to acknowledge with gratitude the helpfulness and the many useful suggestions of Dr. Priscilla Reining, the fact that

Mr. James A. Boon was kind enough to read the first draft of this paper when my health prevented me from doing so, for Mr. Boon's many useful suggestions and criticisms, as well as those of Mr. Carlos Dabezies, and for the long and useful letters on the first draft of this manuscript written me by Mr. Michael Silverstein, Dr. Paul Kay, Dr. Roy d'Andrade, Dr. Edmund Leach, Professor Claude Lévi-Strauss, Dr. Ward H. Goodenough, and Dr. Judith Shapiro. In addition, I would mention again my seminar on Culture Theory of spring, 1971, the students in the Department of Anthropology who heard and discussed the first version of this paper, making many helpful suggestions, and the students at the University of Minnesota who also listened patiently and made acute and perceptive observations and suggestions which I have incorporated without further, more specific acknowledgment.

2   Unless, of course, one takes the position that marriage is necessarily entailed in the notion of descent and therefore all that is needed is one single component, parenthood.

3   One of the best contemporary statements of this position is contained in two papers by Ernest Gellner, 1957 and 1960.

4   Parenthetically, I should note that the cultural system can be abstracted either from the normative system or directly from the level of observable behavior, for it is a distinct aspect of each. Methodologically the situation may be such that it is easier to abstract the cultural material from the normative system, and I think that this is often true. Furthermore, it is a useful methodological device to treat the normative system and the system of observed behavior as relatively independent sources of material – they cannot be completely independent, of course – so that the cultural material abstracted from the normative system can be checked against the cultural material abstracted from the patterns of concrete behavior. If these two sources do not yield the same cultural material, the analyst is alerted to the fact that he has a problem on his hands, for if every cultural premise is embedded in the normative system, and the normative system plays a role, though by no means the only or even the decisive role, in concrete action, then the cultural aspect ought to appear in both and not only in one area. Finally, it should be noted that some parts of

the cultural system are constructs of the observer which deal with implicit, covert, or unconscious categories while others can be formulated directly from the natives' own, explicit model itself. For further discussion of these points see my "American Kinship" (1968), especially Chapter One.

5 All questions are really functional. When the question deals with the relations between the parts under given conditions it is a structural question. When it deals with the relations between parts taken over a period of time and with reference to their change and interaction, then the question is processual. Hence the popular term 'structural-functional' is a fundamental misunderstanding as well as a misnomer. Since all questions are functional, some structural, and some processual, then all questions are either functional-structural or functional-processual, and it is a mistake to call a kind of theory 'structural-functional.' See Parsons (1970) on this point.

6 I cannot think of a single work on 'kinship' which has systematically done this. Instead, the assumption is made that consanguinity and affinity define 'kinship' and, therefore, if a bond of either sort can be shown to obtain, then by definition those are kinsmen. This is a good example of the difference between asking a social from a cultural question. The externally given criterion, a definition of 'kinship' taken from outside the culture, is used rather than a definition of 'kinship' elicited from inside the culture itself.

7 The fundamental reference here is Schneider (1970); see also Schneider (1965). Note the discussion of McLennan above as well. The point is fundamental, since the assumption has been widespread if not universal since Morgan that the mode of classification of kin is embodied in the kinship terminology and can be derived from no other source. As I have suggested (Schneider 1968, ch. 2, 5), there are other, more reliable as well as valid ways of deriving the classification of kin than by the use of kinship terms. I am obliged to Michael Silverstein for pointing out to me that I had failed to make this point clear in earlier drafts of this paper.

8 I am roughly summarizing Schneider (1969) here. There is, however, a fundamental error in that paper which I want to acknowledge here but which I cannot correct fully since there is hardly space in which to do so. First,

let me acknowledge that my seminar in Culture Theory in the spring of 1971 drove home to me the fact that there was an error involved in this formulation; second, that Talcott Parsons also pointed out the error and that the solution emerged in conversations with him during that same period. The problem is that birth in a country is not quite comparable to birth by a mother in American culture. The word birth is the same but two different meanings seem to be implied. Second, nationality is really a modern invention and the presumption implicit in most of the work I have done on American kinship is that these are fundamental cultural categories of long standing and considerable stability. That the concept of nationality seems to fit so easily does suggest I am not far off the target. The solution seems to be to treat the third element in the triad not as nationality but as something like Durkheim's 'moral community,' the group sharing the same cultural system constituting one society. This may at certain levels be a nation, at others but a region of a nation or a smaller unit, or at certain levels supra-national with an ethnic or racial or religious reference, as the Jews and Moslems and the Buddhists or Christians at certain levels constitute such a moral community. The second aspect of the solution centers on series of symbolic equations between birth, blood, and land or place or locality. It is the analog in some instances of the "Where Ya From?" questions which strangers sometimes ask of each other; but I must forego spelling out the ways in which common blood and common soil or land are treated as equivalent under certain conditions in America. I hope to be able to publish a correction of this in the near future but until then will leave things stand here as originally presented.

9 It is even a moot question as to whether the symbols derive from the facts of nature and the facts of biology as these can be demonstrated scientifically. What is indisputable is that the symbols are formed of elements which in native culture are defined as biological, particularly as aspects of the reproductive process. What is disputable is whether they in fact derive from, or mirror, or are models formed after the scientific facts of biology. I do not think that they are, but this is a subject best left to another time.

10 Of which C. Geertz (1966) is a clear
     example. Schneider (1968) also starts from
     such an institutional beginning but does not
     attempt to relate the cultural and social
     system aspects, only to isolate the cultural
     aspects.

References Cited

Geertz, C. 1966 Religion as a Cultural System. *In*
     Anthropological Approaches to the Study of
     Religion. ASA Monographs 3:1–49.
Gellner, E. 1957 Ideal Language and Kinship
     Structure. Philosophy of Science 24:235–242.
—— 1960 The Concept of Kinship. Philosophy of
     Science 27:187–204.
Goodenough, W. H. 1970 Description and Com-
     parison in Cultural Anthropology. Chicago:
     Aldine.
McLennan, J. F. 1886 Studies in Ancient History.
     Comprising a Reprint of Primitive Marriage.
     London and New York: Macmillan.
Morgan, L. H. 1871 Systems of Consanguinity
     and Affinity of the Human Family. Washington:
     Smithsonian Institution. Vol. 17 of the Smithso-
     nian Contributions to Knowledge. (First printed
     1870.)
Parsons, T. 1966 Societies. Englewood Cliffs:
     Prentice-Hall.
—— 1970 Some Problems of General Theory
     in Sociology. *In* Theoretical Sociology.
J. C. McKinney and E. A. Tiryakian, Eds.
     New York: Crofts.
—— 1971 The System of Modern Societies.
     Englewood Cliffs: Prentice-Hall.
Schneider, D. M. 1965a Kinship and Biology. *In*
     Aspects of the Analysis of Family Structure.
     A. J. Coale et al., Eds. Princeton: Princeton
     University Press. pp. 83–101.
—— 1965b American Kin Terms and Terms for
     Kinsmen: A Critique of Goodenough's
     Componential Analysis of Yankee Kinship Ter-
     minology. *In* Formal Semantic Analysis.
     E. A. Hammel, Ed. American Anthropologist
     67(5, pt. 2):288–308.
—— 1965c The Content of Kinship. Man 108:
     122–123.
—— 1965d Some Muddles in the Models: Or,
     How the System Really Works. *In* The Rele-
     vance of Models for Social Anthropology.
     London: Tavistock. pp. 25–85.
—— 1968 American Kinship: A Cultural Ac-
     count. Englewood Cliffs: Prentice-Hall.
—— 1969 Kinship, Nationality and Religion. *In*
     Forms of Symbolic Action. V. Turner, Ed. Pro-
     ceedings of the 1969 Annual Spring Meeting
     of the American Ethnological Society.
     pp. 116–125.
—— 1970 What Should Be Included in a Vocabu-
     lary of Kinship Terms? Proceedings of the VIII
     International Congress of Anthropological and
     Ethnological Sciences, Tokyo 2:88–90.

15

Toward a Unified Analysis of Gender and Kinship

Sylvia Junko Yanagisako and Jane Fishburne Collier

This essay attempts to draw together and advance the theoretical contribution that feminist rethinking of gender has made to our understanding of both gender and kinship. Our answer to the question of what a feminist perspective has to offer the study of gender and kinship is that, above all, it can generate new puzzles and, thereby, make possible new answers.

A productive first step in rethinking any subject is to make what once seemed apparent cry out for explanation. Anthropologists inspired by the women's movement in the late 1960's took such a step when they questioned whether male dominance was a cross-cultural universal and if so, why (Rosaldo and Lamphere 1974; Reiter 1975; Friedl 1975). By asking what explained sexual inequality, they rejected it as an unchangeable, natural fact and redefined it as a social fact.[1] A second step entailed questioning the homogeneity of the categories "male" and "female" themselves and investigating their diverse social meanings among different societies (Rosaldo and Atkinson 1975; Ortner and Whitehead 1981; Strathern 1981a). Once we recognized that these categories are defined in different ways in specific societies, we no longer took them as a priori, universal categories upon which particular relations of gender hierarchy are constructed. Instead, the social and cultural processes by which these categories are constituted came to be seen as one and the same as those creating inequality between men and women.

In this essay, we suggest that the next puzzle we must generate and then solve is the *difference* between men and women. Rather than taking for granted that "male" and "female" are two natural categories of human beings whose relations are everywhere structured by their difference, we ask whether this is indeed the case in each society we study and, if so, what specific social and cultural processes cause men and women to *appear* different from each other. Although we do not deny that biological differences exist between men and women (just as they do among men and among women), our analytic strategy is to question whether these differences are the universal basis for the cultural categories "male" and "female." In other words, we argue against the notion that cross-cultural variations in gender categories and inequalities are merely diverse elaborations and extensions of the same natural fact.

We begin our essay with a critical review of a number of analytical dichotomies that have guided much of the literature on gender in anthropology and related disciplines for the past decade, and we conclude that they assume that gender is everywhere rooted in the same difference. Our point is that, in doing so, these dichotomies take for granted what they should explain. In the second section of this essay, we discuss commonalities between the assumptions underlying these dichotomies and the assumptions that have dominated kinship studies in anthropology since their beginnings in the nineteenth century. We argue that gender and kinship have been defined as fields of study by our folk conception of the same thing, namely, the biological facts of sexual reproduction. Consequently, what have been conceptualized as two discrete fields of study constitute a single field that has not succeeded in freeing itself from notions about natural differences between people. In the final section of the essay, we propose a multifaceted strategy for transcending the analytical categories and dichotomies that have dominated past studies of kinship and gender. Because the analytical program we suggest requires study of culturally constructed social inequalities, we begin with a critique of the concept of "egalitarian society." We then suggest an analytical program that entails explicating the dynamic cultural systems of meanings through which different kinds of historically specific systems of inequality are realized and transformed.

Questioning Analytical Dichotomies in the Study of Gender

In questioning analytical dichotomies, we first examine those of "nature/culture" (Ortner 1974), "domestic/public" (Rosaldo 1974), and "reproduction/production" (see Harris and Young 1981). Each of these has been said to structure relations between men and women in all societies and, therefore, to offer a universal explanation of sexual inequality. Whereas the dichotomies of domestic/public and nature/culture are more in line with structuralist perspectives, the distinction between reproduction and production has emerged from a functionalist-Marxist perspective.

Second, we examine implicit dichotomies between women's and men's consciousnesses. Scholars (for example, Rohrlich-Leavitt, Sykes, and Weatherford 1975; Weiner 1976) seeking to correct the androcentric bias in ethnographic accounts by advocating attention to "women's point of view" have posited a distinction between men's and women's perspectives of social relationships. Arguing that most anthropological monographs reflected men's views of how their system worked, they sug-

gested we correct this bias by including women's accounts of social and cultural institutions in our ethnographies. In contrast, Sherry Ortner and Harriet Whitehead (1981) have more recently proposed a focus on male prestige systems, not as a way of correcting male bias, but as a way of understanding the cultural construction of gender. These latter authors, however, share with the former the notion that men and women – as unitary and opposed categories – have different views of how their mutual system works.

Domestic/public and nature/culture

Ortner and Whitehead propose that the nature/culture and domestic/public oppositions, along with the distinction between self-interest and the social good identified by Marilyn Strathern (1981b), derive from the same sociological insight: "that the sphere of social activity predominantly associated with males encompasses the sphere predominantly associated with females and is, for that reason, culturally accorded higher value" (1981: 7–8). The emphasis placed on any one of these specific contrasts, they suggest, depends upon the theoretical interests of the analyst and the empirically observed "idiom" of a particular culture; however, "all could be present without inconsistency; all are in a sense transformations of one another" (1981:8).

Since these dichotomies were first presented a little over ten years ago as explanations of universal sexual asymmetry, both the domestic/public dichotomy proposed by Michelle Rosaldo (1974) and the nature/culture opposition proposed by Sherry Ortner (1974) have come under considerable criticism. Ortner's hypothesis that the symbolic association of a lesser valued "nature" with females and of a more highly valued, transcendent "culture" with males is the basis for the universal devaluation of females has been most persuasively and thoroughly criticized in Carol MacCormack and Marilyn Strathern's volume *Nature, Culture, and Gender* (1980). In their introduction to this collection of essays, MacCormack and Strathern pose the crucial question, When can we usefully translate a symbolic opposition found in another culture into one found in ours? Together the case studies in their volume argue that our nature/culture opposition does not do justice to the range of symbolic configurations of gender meanings found in other societies. [. . .]

[Maurice] Bloch and [Jean] Bloch's historical analysis of the changing usage of "nature" as a category for challenging the prevailing cultural order in eighteenth-century France (1980) reveals a particularly crucial dimension that is missed by the claim for a universal nature/culture opposition – a synchronic dimension that permits change. Like all universal structural oppositions, this one necessarily flattens dynamic transformations of meanings into static structural sameness. Consequently, it tends to impede the elucidation of the historical processes through which systems of meanings change.

This absence of a historical dynamic is closely tied to another problem inherent in the claim for a universal symbolic opposition. This is the problem of conceptualizing symbolic systems as if they exist apart from social action. Only if we construed symbolic systems as having a structure independent of social action could we claim that a symbolic opposition of gender categories is universal without claiming that a system of gender relations is universal. Such a view is the result of too dichotomized a vision of ideas and action. [. . .]

Whereas the nature/culture opposition draws on a Lévi-Straussian symbolic-structuralist perspective, the domestic/public opposition is more in line with a structural-functionalist perspective of the sort that has prevailed in the field of kinship studies. Michelle Rosaldo first construed the domestic/public opposition as the "basis of a structural framework" necessary to explain the general identification of women with domestic life and men with public life and the consequent universal, cross-cultural asymmetry in the evaluation of the sexes. At the core of this identification of women with domestic life lay their role as mothers: "Women become absorbed primarily in domestic activities because of their role as mothers. Their economic and political activities are constrained by the responsibilities of childcare and the focus of their emotions and attentions is particularistic and directed toward children and the home" (Rosaldo 1974: 24).

Although she did not initially draw a link between the domestic/public opposition and the distinction between the domestic domain and the politico-jural domain, which had long been employed in kinship studies (Fortes 1958, 1969), Rosaldo later (1980) acknowledged that link and its problematic theoretical implications (Yanagisako 1979). She came to share Rayna Reiter's (1975) view of the domestic/public opposition as an ideological product of our society and a legacy of our Victorian heritage that "cast the sexes in dichotomous and contrastive terms" (Rosaldo 1980: 404). [. . .]

The a priori definition of the domestic domain by the mother–child relation is inextricably linked with the troubling analytical problems arising from its claim for universality. These are shared by the nature/culture opposition. As Karen Sacks (1976, 1979), Eleanor Leacock (1978), and Alice Schlegel (1977) have argued convincingly, those writers who assert the universality of sexual asymmetry encourage the search for biological causes, even though such writers explicitly emphasize social processes. In their contributions to *Woman, Culture, and Society*, Rosaldo and Ortner both proposed social causes for universal sexual asymmetry, as did Nancy Chodorow in her contribution to the 1974 book, but each author focused on the social construction of a biological "fact": women's capacity to bear and nurse infants. The obvious conclusion is that biological motherhood "explains" the universal devaluation of women. As Rosaldo herself later noted, a focus on universals makes us "victims of a conceptual tradition that discovers 'essence' in the natural characteristics" that distinguish the sexes, "and then declares that women's present lot derives from what, 'in essence,' women are" (1980: 401).

In summary, we suggest that Ortner and Whitehead's claim that the domestic/public and nature/culture oppositions are transformations of each other is valid (1981:7–8), although not because these oppositions summarize, each in a way more suited to the theoretical interests of a particular analyst or the cultural idiom of a particular society, a universal structure of gender relations. Rather, domestic/public and nature/culture, like the reproduction/production distinction we discuss below, are variations of an analytical dichotomy that takes for granted what we think should be explained.

Reproduction/production

In the last decade, several writers (for example, Eisenstein 1979; Benería and Sen 1981; Harris and Young 1981), attempting to develop a Marxist theory of gender while at the same time bringing a feminist perspective to Marxist theory, have argued for the need to develop a theory of relations of reproduction. Olivia Harris and Kate Young (1981: 110) note that the proliferation of studies in Marxist literature centered on the concept of reproduction reflects not only feminist concern with the status of women but, among other things, the concern of some Marxists to "break conclusively with economistic versions of a Marxism which places too great an emphasis on the forces of production" (see, for example, Hindness and Hirst 1975; Friedman 1976). Women have been cast as the "means of reproduction" in several Marxist discussions of the control of labor and its reproduction in both capitalist and precapitalist societies.

Claude Meillassoux's (1981) evolutionary theory of the domestic community is perhaps the most ambitious of these works in its attempt to build an analysis of the family into a Marxist analysis of imperialism. For Meillassoux, control over the labor of individual human beings is more important than control over the means of production in defining the relations of production in agricultural societies where productive forces are not highly developed. The reproduction of the domestic community of these societies is contingent upon the reproduction of human beings and, consequently, upon control over women, whom Meillassoux views as the means of that reproduction. In capitalist societies, on the other hand, capital is unable itself to reproduce the labor power necessary for social reproduction. Therefore, it must rely on both precapitalist modes of production, such as exist in Third World countries, and on the family – in particular, women's work in it, in industrial society – as the means of reproduction of labor power.

Feminists have strongly criticized two inextricably linked aspects of Meillassoux's theory: his analytical treatment of women and his concept of reproduction. They challenge his view of women solely as "reproducers" and his neglect of their productive activities (Harris and Young 1981; O'Laughlin 1977), which blind him to the ways in which the social constraints placed on women's productive activities, as well as the control placed on their reproductive activities, structure their oppression. They point to the ironic lack of attention to what is commonly called "domestic work" in a book dedicated to the analysis of reproduction.

These limitations in Meillassoux's work can be largely traced to the considerable ambiguity surrounding his use of the term reproduction, which conflates biological reproduction with the reproduction of the social system. For Meillassoux, kinship is the institution which at once regulates the function of the reproduction of human beings and the reproduction of the entire social formation (Meillassoux 1981: xi). This functionalist perspective also underlies his assumption – one common in much of the anthropological literature – that precapitalist societies are in static equilibrium. Thus, despite his interest in the evolution of social forms, Meillassoux ends up with a Marxist version of teleological functionalism in which "all modes exist to reproduce themselves" (Harris and Young 1981: 115).

Unfortunately, many critics attempting to compensate for Meillassoux's inattention to "domestic work" have employed a concept of reproduction similar to his. As a consequence, their work has also been characterized by conceptual confusion. These writers take as their starting point Engels's formulation of the distinction between reproduction and production. In contrast to Marx (1967: 566), who used these terms to describe a unitary social process, Engels tended to treat production and reproduction as two distinct, although coordinated, aspects of the process of social production: "This again, is of a twofold character: on the one side the production of the means of existence, of food, clothing, and shelter and the tools necessary for that reproduction; on the other side the production of human beings themselves, the propagation of the species" (1972: 71).

It is not surprising that Engels's formulation would receive so much recent attention from

Marxist-feminist social scientists, as it is one of the few early Marxist statements offering an explicit approach to gender. Much of the literature on the subject of women and capitalist development, for example, employs this distinction. In their 1981 critique of Ester Boserup's neoclassical, comparative study of the role of women in economic development (1970), the economists Lourdes Benería and Gita Sen argue that we should attend to the role of reproduction in determining women's position in society. They rightly fault Boserup for her distinction between "economic activity" and "domestic work," which results in her excluding such activities as food processing – largely a female activity – from her description of economic activity in agricultural societies. Their concept of reproduction, however, proves more a liability than an asset. They define reproduction as not only biological reproduction and daily maintenance of the labor force but also social reproduction, that is, the perpetuation of social systems (Benería and Sen 1981: 290). Yet, in their analysis of the ways in which the status of women has changed with economic transformations, reproduction is reduced to "domestic work." Accordingly, when they discuss industrial society, they equate "housework" with reproductive work and assume the household is the focal point of all sorts of reproduction (Benería and Sen 1981:293, 291). [...]

[A]uthors who draw upon Engels's distinction between production and reproduction... locate the construction of gender relations – and, consequently, women's subordination – in the reproductive process. The productive process, regardless of the particular mode of production it comprises, is conceptualized as theoretically independent of gender considerations. Like the notion that relations of reproduction are more homogeneous and unchanging than relations of production, this line of thought grants the two spheres of activities an analytical autonomy that seems unjustified.

What lies behind the willingness of so many authors to overlook the conceptual ambiguity and confusion of the reproduction/production distinction and to remain committed to its usefulness for understanding gender relations? Behind this distinction, we suggest, is a symbolically meaningful and institutionally experienced opposition that our own culture draws between the production of people and the production of things. [...]

In this folk model, which informs much of the social scientific writing on reproduction and production, the two categories are construed as functionally differentiated spheres of activity that stand in a means/end relation to each other. Our experience in our own society is that work in production earns money, and money is the means by which the family can be maintained and, therefore, reproduced. At the same time, the reverse holds: the family and its reproduction of people through love and sexual procreation are the means by which labor – and thus the productive system of society – is reproduced. Although we realize that wage work, money, and factories do not exist in many of the societies we study, we impose our own institutional divisions and culturally meaningful categories onto them by positing the universal existence of functionally differentiated spheres of activity. In our folk model, we contrast the following pairs, each linked, respectively, to the productive and reproductive spheres:

material goods	people
technology	biology
male or gender neutral	female or gendered
wage work	nonwage work
factory	family
money	love

A means/end relation between the family and capitalism has prevailed in Western sociological thought, not only in the writings of Marxist functionalists but in those of structural-functionalist theorists as well. In Talcott Parsons's theory of the family in capitalist-industrial society (Parsons and Bales 1955), the particular form of the family helps to reproduce the "economic system" by permitting the social and geographic mobility required by an open-class, universalistic, achievement-based occupational system while still providing for the socialization of children and nurturance of adults. In sum, both Parsonian structural-functionalist theory and Marxist-functionalist theory posit a means/end relationship between what they construe as the reproductive and productive spheres of capitalist-industrial society.

At the bottom of the analytical confusion surrounding the reproduction/production dichotomy is a circularity similar to that which has plagued the domestic/public distinction. Like the former analytical opposition, it leads us back to reinventing, in a new form, the same dualism we were trying to escape.

Women's consciousness/men's consciousness

One of the first changes called for by feminist scholars in the social sciences was the correction of androcentric views that had paid little attention not only to women's activities and roles but also to their views of social relationships and cultural practices. This feminist challenge was useful in calling into question seemingly natural social units. Among the social units taken for granted were the "families" that anthropologists continued to discover everywhere as long as they confounded genealogically defined relationships with particular kinds of culturally meaningful, social relationships (Yanagisako 1979; Collier, Rosaldo, and Yanagisako 1982). The feminist questioning (for example, Collier 1974; Lamphere 1974; Harris 1981; Wolf 1972) of the assumed unity of families, households, and other sorts of domestic groups denaturalized these units by asking whether their members had the same or different views, interests, and strategies. The recognition of the diversity and, in some cases, the conflict of interests among the members of supposedly solidary groups opened the way to a richer understanding of the dynamics of these groups (for example, Wolf 1972; Yanagisako 1985) and their interaction with other social units.

At the same time, we have come to realize that correcting the androcentrism of the past without reproducing its conceptual error in inverted form requires considerable rethinking of our notions of culture and ideology. We appear to have left behind naive claims (for example, Rohrlich-Leavitt, Sykes, and Weatherford 1975) that female anthropologists intuitively understand the subjective experience of their female informants simply by dint of their sex. Likewise, we have rejected claims for a universal "woman's point of view" or a universal "womanhood." Marilyn Strathern has

argued convincingly that "it is to mistake symbol for index to imagine that what Trobrianders make out of women identifies something essential about *womankind*. We merely learn, surely, how it is that cultures constitute themselves" (1981a:671). Furthermore, we cannot assume that *within* a society there is a unitary "woman's point of view" that crosscuts significant differences in, for example, age, household position, or social class.

Despite this skepticism about the existence of a unitary "woman's point of view" in any society, the notion that there is a unitary "man's point of view" appears more resilient (for example, Ardener 1972). Because men are socially dominant over women, it is tempting to treat the cultural system of a society as a product of their values and beliefs and to assume that it is shared by most, if not all, of them. This assumption is implicit in the concept of a "male prestige system," which Ortner and Whitehead (1981) have proposed for understanding, among other things, the connections between gender and kinship.

Ortner and Whitehead suggest that in all societies the most important structures for the cultural construction of gender are the "structures of prestige." Moreover, because some form of male dominance operates in every society, "the cultural construction of sex and gender tends everywhere to be stamped by the prestige considerations of socially dominant male actors" (Ortner and Whitehead 1981: 12). "Women's perspectives are to a great extent constrained and conditioned by the dominant ideology. The analysis of the dominant ideology must thus precede, or at least encompass, the analysis of the perspective of women" (Ortner and Whitehead 1981:x). In the above quotations, Ortner and Whitehead assume that men's perspectives are not also constrained and conditioned by the dominant ideology. Instead, in the case of men, ideology and the perspectives of social actors are conflated. This, of course, assumes a priori that men and women have distinctly different perspectives, including different ideas about prestige relations. [. . .]

[C]onfusion [results from] equating the dominant ideology with men's point of view. Even in those hypothetical cases where men as a whole are socially dominant over women as a whole and share the same values, beliefs, and goals, it seems a mistake to construe their perspective as more encompassing of the larger cultural system than women's perspective. For, like women's views, men's views are constrained and conditioned by the particular forms of their relations with others. The men and women in a particular society may construe women's ideas and experience as more restricted than that of men, and this may be reflected in the appearance that men have certain kinds of knowledge that women do not. But, this appearance does not justify the analytical incorporation of women's views in a supposedly more inclusive male ideology. Our task, rather, should be to make apparent the social and cultural processes that create such appearances.

In the end, the concept of "male prestige system" tends to replicate the problems inherent in the domestic/public dichotomy. Because it too rests on the notion of an encompassing male sphere and an encompassed female one, it assumes that "domestic life" is "insulated from the wider social sphere" (although its degree of insulation may vary) and that "domestic life" is concerned with "gender relations" and "child socialization." [...]

Pierre Bourdieu's (1977) notion of "embodiment" offers a useful framework to counter the notion of conservative domestic spheres, detached from the public world of struggle and change. Domestic life, for Bourdieu, is not insulated from the wider social sphere. Rather, he argues that both gender relations and child socialization take place in a socially structured world. He writes that, for the child, "the awakening of consciousness of sexual identity and the incorporation of the dispositions associated with a determinate social definition of the social functions incumbent on men and women come hand in hand with the adoption of a socially defined vision of the sexual division of labor" (1977: 93). Bourdieu's framework thus suggests that gender relations and child socialization – far from being insulated from changes in "meanings, values, and categorical relations" – are implicated in those changes. [...]

The reemergence of a form of the domestic/public dichotomy in the concept of "male prestige systems" brings us full circle and poses, in a particularly dramatic way, the question of why we keep reinventing this dichotomy or transformations of it, such as reproduction/production. If, as we have argued, these oppositions assume the difference we should be trying to explain, why do we find them so compelling? Why do they seem, as Rosaldo (1980) claimed even when she argued against using domestic/public as an analytic device, so "telling"?

The answer, we suggest, lies in our own cultural conception of gender and its assumption of a natural difference between women and men. To arrive at an understanding of that conception, however, requires that we first review some recent insights in kinship studies. As we will demonstrate, there are striking similarities between muddles in kinship studies and those that we have just discussed in gender studies. Kinship and gender, moreover, are held together by more than a common set of methodological and conceptual problems. They constitute, by our very definition of them, a single topic of study.

The Mutual Constitution of Gender and Kinship

Both "gender" and "kinship" studies have been concerned with understanding the rights and duties that order relations between people defined by difference. Both begin by taking "difference" for granted and treating it as a presocial fact. Although social constructions are built on it, the difference itself is not viewed as a social construction. The fundamental units of gender – males and females – and the fundamental units of kinship – the genealogical grid – are both viewed as existing outside of and beyond culture. In this section, we consider David M. Schneider's critique of the biological model that pervades and constrains kinship studies in order to suggest a parallel critique of gender studies.

Kinship and the biological "facts" of sexual reproduction

Among kinship theorists, Schneider (1964, 1968, 1972, 1984) has been the most consistent in refusing to take for granted what others have, namely, that the fundamental units of kinship are everywhere genealogical relationships. In his cultural analysis of American kinship (1968), Schneider first demonstrated that our particular folk conceptions of kinship lie behind our assumption of the universality of the genealogical grid. By explicating the symbolic system through which Americans construct genealogical relationships, Schneider denaturalized kinship and displayed its cultural foundations.

Most recently, in his 1984 critical review of the history of kinship studies, Schneider argues that, for anthropologists, kinship has always been rooted in biology because, by our own definition, it is about relationships based in sexual reproduction. When we undertake studies of kinship in other societies, we feel compelled to start from some common place, and that place has always been sexual reproduction. We do not ask what relationships are involved in the reproduction of humans in particular societies. Instead, we assume that the primary reproductive relationship in all societies is the relationship between a man and a woman characterized by sexual intercourse and its physiological consequences of pregnancy and parturition. The only time we bother to ask questions about reproduction is when we discover that the natives do not draw the same connections we do between these events, as in the case of the Trobriand Islanders, or when we discover that the natives permit marriages between people with the same genital equipment, as among the Nuer or Lovedu. In other words, we assume that of all the activities in which people participate, the ones that create human offspring are heterosexual intercourse, pregnancy, and parturition. Together these constitute the biological process upon which we presume culture builds such social relationships as marriage, filiation, and coparenthood.

The one major modification in kinship studies since the middle of the nineteenth century, according to Schneider, was the shift from an emphasis on the social *recognition* of the biological bonds arising out of the process of procreation to an emphasis on the sociocultural *characteristics* of the relations mapped onto those bonds (Schneider 1984:54). Since this shift, kinship theorists have been adamant that they view marriage, parenthood, and all other kinship relationships as social relationships and not biological ones. Schneider argues convincingly, however, that for all the claims these writers make that they are speaking of social paters and social maters and not genitors and genetrixes, they have biological parenthood in mind all the time. This point is perhaps no more clearly illustrated than in the following statement by Fortes, quoted by Schneider: "The *facts* of sex, procreation, and the rearing of offspring constitute only the universal raw material of kinship systems" (Fortes 1949:345, italics ours). For Fortes, as for the other kinship theorists reviewed by Schneider, these *facts* are unambiguously construed as *natural* ones.

Although it is apparent that heterosexual intercourse, pregnancy, and parturition are involved in human reproduction, it is also apparent that producing humans entails more than this. M. Bridget O'Laughlin (1977) put it very succinctly when she wrote, "Human reproduction is never simply a matter of conception and birth." There is a wide range of activities in which people participate besides heterosexual intercourse and parturition that contribute to the birth of viable babies and to their development into adults. These activities, in turn, involve and are organized by a number of relationships other than those of parenthood and marriage. Given the wide range of human activities and relationships that can be viewed as contributing to the production of human beings, why do we focus on only a few of them as the universal basis of kinship? Why do we construe these few activities and relationships as natural facts, rather than investigating the ways in which they are, like all social facts, culturally constructed? The answer Schneider has proposed is that our theory of kinship is simultaneously a folk theory of biological reproduction.

Gender and the biological "facts" of sexual reproduction

Schneider's insight that kinship is by definition about sexual procreation leads us to realize that assumptions about gender lie at the core of kinship studies. Moreover, not only are ideas about gender central to analyses of kinship, but ideas about kinship are central to analyses of gender. Because both gender and kinship have been defined as topics of study by our conception of the same thing, namely, sexual procreation, we cannot think about one without thinking about the other. In short, these two fields of studies are mutually constituted.

Gender assumptions pervade notions about the *facts* of sexual reproduction commonplace in the kinship literature. Much of what is written about atoms of kinship (Lévi-Strauss 1949), the axiom of prescriptive altruism (Fortes 1958; Fortes 1969), the universality of the family (Fox 1967), and the centrality of the mother–child bond (Goodenough 1970) is rooted in assumptions about the natural characteristics of women and men and their natural roles in sexual procreation. The standard units of our genealogies, after all, are circles and triangles about which we assume a number of things. Above all, we take for granted that they represent two naturally different categories of people and that the natural difference between them is the basis of human reproduction and, therefore, kinship. Harold Scheffler's (1974: 749) statement that "the foundation of any kinship system consists in the folk-cultural theory designed to account for the fact that women give birth to children" reveals that, for him, kinship is everywhere about the same biological fact. Although he recognizes that there are a variety of ways in which this "fact" may be accounted for in different societies, Scheffler, like most kinship theorists, assumes certain social consequences follow necessarily from it, including that biological motherhood is everywhere the core of the social relationship of motherhood (Scheffler 1970).[2]

Likewise, the literature on gender is sensitive to the many ways in which pregnancy and childbirth are conceptualized and valued in different societies and to the different ways in which the activities surrounding them can be socially organized. But, the conviction that the biological *difference* in the roles of women and men in sexual reproduction lies at the core of the cultural organization of gender persists in comparative analyses. As we argued in the previous section, the analytical oppositions of domestic/public, nature/culture, and reproduction/production all begin with this assumption of difference. Like kinship theorists, moreover, analysts of gender have assumed that specific social consequences necessarily follow from this difference between men and women. For example, the assumption that women *bear* the greater burden and responsibility for human reproduction pervades gender studies, in particular those works employing a reproduction/production distinction. Yet, this notion often appears to be more a metaphorical extension of our emphasis on the fact that women *bear* children than a conclusion based on systematic comparison of the contribution of men and women to human reproduction. In other words, the fact that women bear children and men do not is interpreted as creating a universal relation of human reproduction. Accordingly, we have been much slower to question the purported universals of the reproductive relations of men and women than we have been to question the purported universals of their productive relations. For example, as we have shown, in the literature on women and capitalist development, women's natural burden in reproduction is viewed as constraining their role in production, rather than seen as itself shaped by historical changes in the organization of production.

The centrality of sexual reproduction in the definition of gender is reflected in the distinction between sex and gender that has become a convention in much of the feminist literature. Judith Shapiro summarizes the distinction between the terms as follows:

[T]hey serve a useful analytic purpose in contrasting a set of biological facts with a set of cultural facts. Were I to be scrupulous in my use of terms, I would use the term "sex" only when I was speaking of biological differences between males and females, and use "gender" whenever I was referring to the social, cultural, psychological constructs that are *imposed upon these biological differences*[. . .] (1981: 449, italics ours).

The attempt to separate the study of gender categories from the biological facts to which they are seen to be universally connected mirrors the attempt of kinship theorists reviewed by Schneider (1984) to separate the study of kinship from the same biological facts. Like the latter attempt, this one seems doomed to fail, because it too starts from a definition of its subject matter that is rooted in those biological facts. It is impossible, of course, to know what gender or kinship would mean if they are to be entirely disconnected from sex and biological reproduction. We have no choice but to begin our investigations of others with our own concepts. But, we can unpack the cultural assumptions embodied in them, which limit our capacity to understand social systems informed by other cultural assumptions.

Although gender and kinship studies start from what are construed as the same biological facts of sexual reproduction, they might appear to be headed in different analytical directions: kinship to the social character of genealogical relations and gender to the social character of male–female relations (and even to male–male relations and female–female relations). How-ever, because both build their explanations of the social rights and duties and the relations of equality and inequality among people on these presumably natural characteristics, both retain the legacy of their beginnings in notions about *the same natural differences* between people. Consequently, what have been conceptualized as two discrete, if interconnected, fields of study constitute a single field.

Our realization of the unitary constitution of gender and kinship as topics of study should make us wary of treating them as distinct analytical problems. As Schneider (1984: 175) points out, part of the "conventional wisdom of kinship" has been the idea that kinship forms a system that can be treated as a distinct institution or domain. Like "economics," "politics," and "religion," kinship has been posited as one of the fundamental building blocks of society by anthropologists (Schneider 1984: 181).[3] At the same time, neither should we assume that in all societies kinship creates gender or that gender creates kinship. Although the two may be mutually constituted as topics of study by *our* society, this does not mean they are linked in the same way in all societies. Instead, as we shall suggest below, we should seek rather than assume knowledge of the socially significant domains of relations in any particular society and what constitutes them. Having rejected the notion that there are presocial, universal domains of social relations, such as a domestic domain and a public domain, a kinship domain and a political domain, we must ask what symbolic and social

processes make these domains appear self-evident, and perhaps even "natural," fields of activity in any society.

Transcending Dichotomies: A Focus on Social Wholes

Understanding the folk model of human reproduction underlying the analytical categories and dichotomies – explicit and implicit – that have dominated both gender and kinship studies is the first step toward transcending them. The next step is to move beyond the dichotomies by focusing on social wholes. Instead of asking how the categories of "male" and "female" are endowed with culturally specific characters, thus taking the difference between them for granted, we need to ask how particular societies define difference. Instead of asking how rights and obligations are mapped onto kinship bonds, thus assuming the genealogical grid, we need to ask how specific societies recognize claims and allocate responsibilities. Our ability to understand social wholes, however, is limited by another analytic concept – that of "egalitarian society" – which, as used by many feminists and Marxists, once again bears the legacy of our folk notion of difference.

Questioning the concept of "egalitarian society"

Anthropologists have used the concept of "egalitarian society" in two, somewhat contradictory, ways. Morton Fried coined the term to denote a particular form of organizing inequality. Given his assumption that "equality is a social impossibility" (1967: 26), he defines an "egalitarian society" as "one in which there are as many positions of prestige in any given age-sex grade as there are persons capable of filling them" (1967: 33). Not all people achieve valued positions. Fried, for example, writes that men in such societies "display a considerable drive to achieve parity, or at least to establish a status that announces 'don't fool with me'" (1967: 79). He thus reveals that some men fail, whereas women and youths never have a chance to "achieve parity." Given that Fried focuses on the organization of inequality, his usage of the term "egalitarian society" is misleading.

In contrast to Fried, many Marxist and feminist scholars use the concept of "egalitarian society" to denote societies in which people are indeed "equal" in the sense that they do not exhibit the class and gender inequalities characteristic of ancient societies and modern capitalism. These scholars define egalitarian societies less in terms of features they possess than in terms of features they lack. In arguing that the gender and class inequalities familiar to us today and from accounts of the past are the product of specific historical processes, these scholars suggest, usually by default, that the organization of gender and production in nonclass societies is not produced by history. Consequently, the social categories in nonclass societies are seen as reflecting "natural" human propensities, given particular environmental conditions (Jaggar 1983: 70). [. . .]

Feminists arguing against the universality of sexual asymmetry are presently the most active proponents of the concept of egalitarian society. Not only do they believe that such societies once existed, but they consider the concept our most effective rhetorical strategy for establishing that biology is not destiny (Sacks 1976; Sacks 1979; Leacock 1978; Schlegel 1977; Caulfield 1981). They argue that assertions of universal sexual asymmetry – such as those by Rosaldo (1974), Ortner (1974), and Friedl (1975) – legitimize a search for biological causes. Consequently, to posit the existence of sexually egalitarian societies is to obviate such a search before it begins.

Eleanor Leacock, in an important article positing the existence of sexually egalitarian societies (1978), argues that Western observers have failed to recognize such societies because their ability to understand egalitarian socioeconomic relations is hindered by concepts derived from the hierarchical structure of capitalism.[. . .] In particular, Leacock criticizes our tendency to interpret a sexual division of labor as hierarchical – our inability to imagine that men and women who do different things might be "separate but equal" (1978: 248).

In seeking to counter anthropological accounts portraying women in band societies as subordinate to men, Leacock suggests that men and women were equally "autonomous." Men and women may have engaged in different activities, but women "held decision making

power over their own lives and activities to the same extent that men did over theirs" (1978: 247). Leacock writes that she prefers "the term 'autonomy' to 'equality,' for equality connotes rights and opportunity specific to class society and confuses similarity with equity." (1978: 247).

Substituting "autonomy" for "equality," however, does not free Leacock from the problems inherent in using concepts based on the hierarchical structure of our own society. "Autonomy," as used in our cultural system, is not a neutral term. As Sandra Wallman observes, in Western social science, "behavioral differences between men and women have generally been attributed *either* to natural, and therefore, essential differences in biology, physiology, genetics *or* to cultural, and therefore non-essential impositions, the fortuitous demands and/or accidents of a social system and the dialectics of history and/or the human mind" (1978: 21, italics hers). In other words, our folk system posits that behavioral differences not explained by culture must be due to nature, and vice versa. As a result, by claiming a freedom from outside constraints, "autonomy" inevitably invokes notions of biological destiny.

Leacock surely did not intend to portray women in band societies as acting out their biological natures when they engaged in women's work. But by failing to treat "men" and "women" as cultural constructs and in accepting the difference in their activities, Leacock suggests this position by default (see Strathern 1978; Atkinson 1982). Leacock's notion of "autonomy" can be read in two ways, but neither avoids the implication of biological destiny. If we interpret her statement that women "held decision making power over their own lives and activities" to mean that women could decide what they wanted to do, then we are faced with the question of why women all decided to do women's tasks rather than doing what men did. Why did women not decide, like good Marxists, "to hunt in the morning, fish in the afternoon, rear cattle in the evening, [and] criticize after dinner" (Marx and Engels 1970: 53)? The obvious answer, given Leacock's failure to investigate the social and cultural factors shaping women's decisions, is that women "naturally" wanted to do women's tasks, just as men "naturally" wanted to do men's tasks. If we adopt an alternative reading of Leacock's statement and conclude that women "held decision making power over their own lives and activities" *only* "to the same extent that men did over theirs," we are left with the question of what it means to "have decision making power" over one's own life. In this reading, women and men appear equally constrained to take up only sex-appropriate tasks. But the social and symbolic practices through which they are constrained are not discussed, suggesting, again by default, a "natural" division of labor by sex.

In summary, however useful the concept of "egalitarian society" may be for denaturalizing gender in class societies, it raises many of the problems we encountered in our discussion of the analytic dichotomies of domestic/public, nature/culture, and reproduction/production. By positing a past Eden in which women and men were "autonomous," we assume precultural, natural differences as the bases for the sexual division of labor.

Analyzing social wholes: meanings, models, and history

Given our tendency to reinvent the analytic dichotomies that limit our ability to understand gender in our own and other societies, we need an explicit strategy for transcending them. The one we propose in this final section of the paper rests on the premise that there are no "facts," biological or material, that have social consequences and cultural meanings in and of themselves. Sexual intercourse, pregnancy, and parturition are cultural facts, whose form, consequences, and meanings are socially constructed in any society, as are mothering, fathering, judging, ruling, and talking with the gods. Similarly, there are no material "facts" that can be treated as precultural givens. The consequences and meanings of force are socially constructed, as are those of the means of production or the resources upon which people depend for their living.

Just as we reject analytic dichotomies, so we reject analytic domains. We do not assume the existence of a gender system based on natural differences in sexual reproduction, a kinship system based on the genealogical grid, a polity based on force, or an economy based on the

production and distribution of needed resources. Rather than take for granted that societies are constituted of functionally based institutional domains, we propose to investigate the social and symbolic processes by which human actions within particular social worlds come to have consequences and meanings, including their apparent organization into seemingly "natural" social domains.

We begin with the premise that social systems are, by definition, systems of inequality. This premise has three immediate advantages. First, it conforms to common usage. By most definitions, a society is a system of social relationships and values. Values entail evaluation. Consequently, a society is a system of social relationships in which all things and actions are not equal. As Ralf Dahrendorf (1968) notes, values inevitably create inequalities by ensuring rewards for those who live up to valued ideals and punishments for those who, for one reason or another, fail to do so. Every society has a "prestige structure," as Ortner and Whitehead (1981) presume. A system of values, however, is not "male," and in analyzing any particular society, we must ask why people appear to hold the values they do.

Second, the premise that all societies are systems of inequality forces us to separate the frequently confused concepts of equality (the state of being equal) and justice (moral rightness). By presuming that all societies are systems of inequality, we are forced to separate the study of our own and other people's cultural systems of evaluation from considerations of whether or not such systems meet our standards of honor and fairness.

Finally, the premise that all societies are systems of inequality frees us from having to imagine a world without socially created inequities. We therefore avoid having to assume social consequences for "natural" differences. If we assume that all societies are systems of inequality, then we, as social scientists, are forced to explain not the existence of inequality itself but rather why it takes the qualitatively different forms it does.

In defining "egalitarian society" out of existence, however, we do not propose a return to the hypothesis of women's universal subordination. Rather, the premise that all societies are systems of inequality forces us to specify what we mean by inequality in each particular case. Instead of asking how "natural" differences acquire cultural meanings and social consequences (a strategy that dooms us to reinventing our analytic dichotomies), a presumption of inequality forces us to ask why some attributes and characteristics of people are culturally recognized and differentially evaluated when others are not. This requires us to begin any analysis by asking, What are a society's cultural values? And what social processes organize the distribution of prestige, power, and privilege? We may find that in some societies neither cultural values nor social processes discriminate between the sexes (that is, a nongendered system of inequality). But this conclusion must follow from an analysis of how inequality is organized.

Given our premise that social systems are systems of inequality, we propose an analytical program with three facets. These facets are arranged not in order of theoretical importance but in the sequence we feel they should be employed in any particular analysis. Some researchers, depending on the particular question or type of society that is the topic of study, may find another sequence preferable or may choose to focus on one facet more than the others. But, we suggest, no attempt to analyze social wholes can proceed very far without employing all three.

The cultural analysis of meaning. The first facet of our program entails an analysis of cultural systems of meanings. Specifically, we must begin by explicating the cultural meanings people realize through their practice of social relationships. Rather than assume that the fundamental units of gender and kinship in every society are defined by the difference between males and females in sexual reproduction, we ask what are the socially meaningful categories people employ and encounter in specific social contexts and what symbols and meanings underlie them. Just as Schneider (1968) questioned, rather than took for granted, the meanings of blood, love, and sexual intercourse in American kinship and their influence on the construction of categories of relatives, so we have to question the meanings of genes, love, sexual intercourse, power, independence, and whatever else plays into the symbolic construc-

tion of categories of people in any particular society. [. . .] By attending to the public discourses through which people describe, interpret, evaluate, make claims about, and attempt to influence relationships and events, we can extract the relatively stable symbols and meanings people employ in everyday life.

These symbols and meanings, as will be stressed in the next section on systemic models of social inequality, are always evaluative. As such, they encode particular distributions of prestige, power, and privilege. However, because they are realized through social practice, they are not static. As will become apparent when we discuss the importance of historical analysis, we do not assume cultural systems of meaning to be timeless, self-perpetuating structures of "tradition." Yet, even when the meanings of core symbols are changing, we can tease apart their different meanings in particular contexts and, thereby, better understand the symbolic processes involved in social change (Yanagisako 1985).

Once we have investigated the various ways in which difference is conceptualized in other societies – including whether and how sex and reproduction play into the construction of differences that make a difference – we can return to examine the biological model that defines gender in our own society. In other words, just as our questioning of the domestic/public dichotomy as the structural basis for relations between men and women in other societies has encouraged us to question its analytical usefulness for our own society, so we can ask what a conception of gender as rooted in biological difference does and does not explain about relations between men and women in our society. Having recognized our model of biological difference as a particular cultural mode of thinking about relations between people, we should be able to question the "biological facts" of sex themselves. We expect that our questioning of the presumably biological core of gender will eventually lead to the rejection of any dichotomy between sex and gender as biological and cultural facts and will open up the way for an analysis of the symbolic and social processes by which both are constructed in relation to each other.

The cultural analysis of meaning, however, cannot be isolated from the analysis of patterns of action. We do not view systems of meaning as ideational determinants of social organization or as solutions to universal problems of meaning and order. Rather, we conceptualize the interrelated, but not necessarily consistent, meanings of social events and relationships as both shaping and being shaped by practice. Our refusal to dichotomize material relationships and meanings or to grant one or the other analytic priority derives from our conceptualization of practice and ideas as aspects of a single process.

Systemic models of inequality. Ideas and actions are aspects of a single dialectical process, and we understand this process by focusing on how inequality is organized. Because we assume that cultural conceptions are voiced in contexts in which, among other things, people make claims, provide explanations, try to influence action, and celebrate the qualities they use when creating relationships, we understand cultural conceptions by focusing on what claims may be made, what things explained, what actions influenced, and what relationships forged. In order to understand what people talk about, we must ask what people may want or fear. And so we must understand how inequality is organized in any particular society.

The second facet of our analytical strategy thus requires the construction of systemic models of inequality. These models are of a particular type. Following Bourdieu (1977), we analyze a social system not by positing an unseen, timeless structure but rather by asking how ordinary people, pursuing their own subjective ends, realize the structures of inequality that constrain their possibilities. This is why the first facet of our strategy requires an analysis of the commonsense meanings available to people for monitoring and interpreting their own and others' actions. But this analysis of meaning must be followed by an analysis of the structures that people realize through their actions. Because we understand the commonsense meanings available to people not by positing an unseen, timeless culture but rather by exploring how people's understandings of the world are shaped by their structured experiences, we must move back and forth between an analysis of how structures shape

people's experience and an analysis of how people, through their actions, realize structures.

Although a systemic model of inequality may be constructed for any society, developing a typology of models aids in the analysis of particular cases. In the end, as we will discuss in the next section, each society must be analyzed in its own, historically specific terms, but a set of ideal typic models helps us to see connections we might otherwise miss. All attempts to understand other cultures are, by their nature, comparative. It is impossible to describe a particular, unique way of life without explicitly or implicitly comparing it to another – usually the analyst's own society or the society of the language the analyst is using. Since comparison is inevitable, it seems more productive to have a set of models available for thinking about similarities and contrasts than to have but ourselves as a single implicit or explicit standard of comparison. [...]

In seeking to develop such models, however, we do not view either technology or socially organized access to productive resources as determining traits (see Collier and Rosaldo 1981: 318; Collier n.d.). Given our assumption that no biological or material "fact" has social consequences in and of itself, we cannot begin by assuming the determining character of either the forces or relations of production. We therefore do not classify societies according to technologies – such as foraging, horticulture, agriculture, pastoralism, and industry (for example, Martin and Voorhies 1975) – or according to social relations governing access to resources – such as egalitarian, ranked, and stratified (Etienne and Leacock 1980) or communal, corporate kin, and class (Sacks 1979).

An example of the kind of model of inequality we are proposing is Janet Collier and Michelle Rosaldo's ideal typic model of "brideservice" societies (1981). The classification scheme employed in this essay and others (Collier 1984; Collier n.d.) uses marriage transaction terms – brideservice, equal or standard bridewealth, and unequal or variable bridewealth – as labels for systemic models, treating marriage transactions not as determinants of social organization or ideas but rather as moments when practice and meaning are negotiated together. Marriage negotiations are moments of "systemic reproduction" in those societies in which "kinship" appears to organize people's rights and obligations relative to others. Societies with different bases of organization will have different moments of "systemic reproduction." [. . .]

Although models provide conceptual tools for analyzing social and cultural systems, they, like the cultural analysis of meaning, are but one facet of our strategy. If our aim is to understand real people, model building can never be an end in itself. Because models are necessarily abstract, to the degree that we succeed in building a systemic model, we cease to illuminate the particularities of any given historical society. It is not, as has often been claimed, that systemic models of the sort we are proposing are inherently static. Because these models rest on the assumption that social structures are realized and cultural conceptions voiced by people pursuing their own subjective ends in social worlds of inequality, competition, and conflict, the potential for change is inherent in every action. Systemic models appear static, however, because they are designed to answer the unstated question of why societies appear to change as little as they do given the constant possibility of change. Models thus tend to reveal how those in power use their power to preserve their positions of privilege.

Historical analysis. The third facet of our analytical strategy is motivated by our belief that change is possible in all social systems, regardless of their particular configuration of inequality. We thus need an explicit strategy to counterbalance the emphasis on social reproduction in our systemic models, so that we can see how social systems change and, at the same time, better understand the processes that enable them to remain relatively stable over time. A historical analysis that interprets current ideas and practices within the context of the unfolding sequence of action and meaning that has led to them provides this balance. Such an analysis broadens the temporal range of our analysis of social wholes by asking how their connection with the past constrains and shapes their dynamics in the present, whether that connection is one of relative continuity or of radical disjunction. In other words, whereas historical analysis is of critical importance for

understanding societies and communities that are undergoing dramatic transformations (for example, Yanagisako 1985; Collier 1986), it is of no less importance for understanding societies characterized by seeming social and cultural continuity (R. Rosaldo 1980). For, given that change is inherent in social action, the reproduction of social systems requires no less explanation than does their transformation.

The kind of historical approach we are proposing will enrich our cultural analysis of meaning by broadening the range of symbols, meanings, and practices to which we relate concepts of value and difference. Our proposal to link historical analysis with symbolic analysis rests on the premise that we cannot comprehend present discourse and action without understanding their relation to past discourse and action (Yanagisako 1985). The relevant context of specific cultural elements, such as "marriage," "mother," "blood," or "semen," is not limited to current practices and meanings, but includes past practices and their symbolic meanings. For example, the meanings of "equality," "duty," and "love" in the conjugal relationship may be shaped by the past character of conjugal relationships as well as their present ones and by the way in which past and present are symbolically linked. Likewise, the meaning of "agnatic" ties at any one period may be shaped by the uses to which such ties were previously put. All these analyses argue that we must know the dialectical, historical processes through which practices and meanings have unfolded if we are to understand how they operate in the present.

Similarly, grounding our analysis of social wholes and fashioning our systemic models of inequality within particular historical sequences will enable us to see how the dynamics of past actions and ideas have created structures in the present. Relationships suggested by our systemic models can be tested in a dynamic context and, if necessary, modified or refined. By taking such a historical perspective on the constitution of social wholes, we avoid assuming that present systems of inequality are the timeless products of identical pasts; instead, we question whether and how these systems developed out of dissimilar pasts. We can see how aspects of ideas and practices, which in our systemic models seem to reinforce and reproduce each other, also undermine and de-stabilize each other.

A historical perspective also highlights the interaction of ideas and practices as dialectical, ongoing processes and so avoids the teleo-logical bent of those models that seek a single determinant, whether material or ideational, for social reproduction. [...]

Finally, to return to the beginning of this essay, historical analysis can help us to tran-scend the analytical dichotomies and domains that we have argued have plagued gender and kinship studies. Historical studies reveal how seemingly universal, timeless domains of social structure are created and transformed in par-ticular times and places.

Conclusion

At the beginning of this essay, we suggested that feminism's next contribution to the study of gender and kinship should be to question the difference between women and men. We do not doubt that men and women are different, just as individuals differ, generations differ, races differ, and so forth. Rather, we question whether the particular biological difference in reproductive function that our culture defines as the basis of difference between males and females, and so treats as the basis of their rela-tionship, is used by other societies to constitute the cultural categories of male and female.

Past feminist questions have led to the opening up of new areas for investigation, even as such investigations have raised new prob-lems and questions. By doubting the common assumption that sex and age are "natural" bases for the differential allocation of social rights and duties, feminist scholars paved the way for studies of the social processes that granted men prestige and authority over women and children. Yet feminists' attempts to provide social explanations for perceived universal sexual asymmetry used the analytic dichoto-mies of domestic/public and nature/culture that themselves became problematic.

Doubts concerning the analytic utility and cultural universality of these dichotomies led, in turn, to studies of the social and cultural processes by which the categories of masculin-ity and femininity are constituted in particular times and places. Yet, as we have suggested,

some of these studies raised a new set of ques-tions. Attempts to replace the inherently gen-dered dichotomies of domestic/public and nature/culture with the distinction between re-production and production, and the positing of "male prestige systems," have revealed our ten-dency to rediscover gendered dichotomies. Similarly, attempts to argue that men and women have not everywhere and at all times been unequal have given rise to the concept of "egalitarian society," a concept that, if not complemented by a cultural analysis of person-hood, implies, by default, a "natural" basis for sexual divisions of labor.

Now, we suggest, our problem of continually rediscovering gendered categories can be over-come by calling into question the universality of our cultural assumptions about the differ-ence between males and females. Both gender and kinship studies, we suggest, have foun-dered on the unquestioned assumption that the biologically given difference in the roles of men and women in sexual reproduction lies at the core of the cultural organization of gender, even as it constitutes the genealogical grid at the core of kinship studies. Only by calling this assumption into question can we begin to ask how other cultures might understand the dif-ference between women and men, and simul-taneously make possible studies of how our own culture comes to focus on coitus and par-turition as *the* moments constituting masculin-ity and femininity.

It is not enough to question the universality and analytic utility of our implicit assumptions about sex differences. Rather, we need specific strategies to help us overcome our tendency to reinvent gendered analytic dichotomies. In this essay, we have argued for the need to analyze social wholes and have proposed a three-faceted approach to this project: the explica-tion of cultural meanings, the construction of models specifying the dialectical relationship between practice and ideas in the constitution of social inequalities, and the historical analy-sis of continuities and changes.

The commitment to analyzing social wholes is one we share with all the contributors to the original volume. Not everyone might agree with our questioning of the difference between women and men, or with our three-faceted approach to analyzing social wholes, for we formulated both notions after the conference. Nevertheless, we believe that this volume provides a good illustration of the insights to be gained from a commitment to holistic analysis.

Finally, we have no illusions that the strategy we propose will resolve all the issues we have raised. We know that we, too, can never be free from the folk models of our own culture, and that in questioning some folk concepts we privilege others. We expect that the studies we hope to generate by questioning the difference between women and men will, in time, reveal their own problematic assumptions. These will generate new questions that will, in turn, give rise to new strategies and new solutions.

NOTES

1 Although we recognize that some anthropologists questioned the universality of Western concepts of gender before the late 1960's, we begin with the 1960's women's movement because it inspired the arguments we discuss in this paper.

2 It is noteworthy that motherhood is the locus of many assumptions in feminist writing as well as in the nonfeminist kinship literature. However, in the feminist literature, the emphasis is more on the ways in which mothering constrains and structures women's lives and psyches (for example, Chodorow 1978), whereas in the nonfeminist kinship literature (for example, Fortes 1969; Goodenough 1970; Scheffler 1974), the emphasis is on the positive affect and bond that maternal nurturance creates in domestic relationships.

3 Schneider attributes this to the mid-nineteenth-century attempt by anthropologists to establish the history or development of civilization as this was embodied in European culture, and to the notion that development proceeded from the simple to the complex, from the undifferentiated to the differentiated. To the extent that kinship, economics, politics, and religion were undifferentiated, a society was "primitive," "simple," or "simpler."

REFERENCES

Ardener, Edwin. 1972. "Belief and the Problem of Women." In J. LaFontaine, ed., *The Interpretation of Ritual*. London.

Atkinson, Jane Monnig. 1982. "Review Essay: Anthropology." *Signs: Journal of Women in Culture and Society* 8, no. 2:236–58.

Benería, Lourdes, and Gita Sen. 1981. "Accumulation, Reproduction, and Women's Role in Economic Development: Boserup Revisited." *Signs: Journal of Women in Culture and Society* 7, no. 2:279–98.

Bloch, Maurice, and Jean H. Bloch. 1980. "Woman and the Dialectics of Nature in Eighteenth-Century French Thought." In Carol MacCormack and Marilyn Strathern, eds., *Nature, Culture and Gender*. Cambridge, Eng.

Boserup, Ester. 1970. *Woman's Role in Economic Development*. New York.

Bourdieu, Pierre. 1977. *Outline of a Theory of Practice*. Cambridge, Eng.

Caulfield, Mina Davis. 1981. "Equality, Sex, and Mode of Production." In Gerald Berreman, ed., *Social Inequality*. New York.

Chodorow, Nancy. 1974. "Family Structure and Feminine Personality." In Michelle Zimbalist Rosaldo and Louise Lamphere, eds., *Woman, Culture, and Society*. Stanford, Calif.

——. 1978. *The Reproduction of Mothering: Psychoanalysis and the Sociology of Gender*. Berkeley, Calif.

Collier, Jane F. 1974. "Women in Politics." In Michelle Zimbalist Rosaldo and Louise Lamphere, eds., *Woman, Culture, and Society*. Stanford, Calif.

——. 1984. "Two Models of Social Control in Simple Societies." In Donald Black, ed., *Toward a General Theory of Social Control, Vol. 2: Selected Problems*. New York.

——. 1986. "From Mary to Modern Woman: The Material Basis of Marianismo and Its Transformation in a Spanish Village." *American Ethnologist* 13, no. 1:100–107.

——. N.d. *Marriage and Inequality in Classless Societies*. Stanford, Calif. In press.

——, and Michelle Z. Rosaldo. 1981. "Politics and Gender in Simple Societies." In Sherry B. Ortner and Harriet Whitehead, eds., *Sexual Meanings: The Cultural Construction of Gender and Sexuality*. Cambridge, Eng.

——, Michelle Z. Rosaldo, and Sylvia Yanagisako. 1982. "Is There a Family? New Anthropological

Views." In Barrie Thorne, ed., with Marilyn Yalom, *Rethinking the Family: Some Feminist Questions*. New York.

Dahrendorf, Ralf. 1968. *Essays in the Theory of Society*. Stanford, Calif.

Eisenstein, Zillah. 1979. *Capitalist Patriarchy and the Case for Socialist Feminism*. New York.

Engels, Friedrich. 1972. *The Origin of the Family, Private Property, and the State*. New York.

Etienne, Mona, and Eleanor Leacock, eds. 1980. *Women and Colonization: Anthropological Perspectives*. New York.

Fortes, Meyer. 1949. *The Web of Kinship Among the Tallensi*. London.

———. 1958. "Introduction." In Jack R. Goody, ed., *The Developmental Cycle in Domestic Groups*. Cambridge, Eng.

———. 1969. *Kinship and the Social Order*. Chicago.

Fox, Robin. 1967. *Kinship and Marriage*. Middlesex, Eng.

Fried, Morton. 1967. *The Evolution of Political Society*. New York.

Friedl, Ernestine. 1975. *Women and Men: An Anthropologist's View*. New York.

Friedman, Jonathan. 1976. "Marxist Theory and Systems of Total Reproduction." *Critique of Anthropology* 7:3–16.

Goodenough, Ward H. 1970. *Description and Comparison in Cultural Anthropology*. Chicago.

Harris, Olivia. 1981. "Households as Natural Units." In Kate Young et al., eds., *Of Marriage and the Market: Women's Subordination in International Perspective*. London.

———, and Kate Young. 1981. "Engendered Structures: Some Problems in the Analysis of Reproduction." In Joel S. Kahn and Joseph R. Llobera, eds., *The Anthropology of Pre-Capitalist Societies*. Atlantic Highlands, N.J.

Hindness, B., and P. Hirst. 1975. *Pre-Capitalist Modes of Production*. London.

Jaggar, Alison M. 1983. *Feminist Politics and Human Nature*. Totowa, N.J.

Lamphere, Louise L. 1974. "Strategies, Cooperation, and Conflict Among Women in Domestic Groups." In Michelle Zimbalist Rosaldo and Louise Lamphere, eds., *Woman, Culture, and Society*. Stanford, Calif.

Leacock, Eleanor. 1978. "Women's Status in Egalitarian Society: Implications for Social Evolution." *Current Anthropology* 19, no. 2: 247–75.

Lévi-Strauss, Claude. 1949. *The Elementary Structures of Kinship*. Boston.

MacCormack, Carol, and Marilyn Strathern, eds. 1980. *Nature, Culture and Gender*. Cambridge, Eng.

Martin, M. Kay, and Barbara Voorhies. 1975. *Female of the Species*. New York.

Marx, Karl. 1967. *Capital*. Vol. 3. New York.

———, and Friedrich Engels. 1970. *The German Ideology*. Ed. C.J. Arthur. New York.

Meillassoux, Claude. 1981. *Maidens, Meal, and Money: Capitalism and the Domestic Community*. Cambridge, Eng.

O'Laughlin, M. Bridget. 1977. "Production and Reproduction: Meillassoux's *Femmes, Greniers, et Capitaux*." *Critique of Anthropology* 8: 3–32.

Ortner, Sherry B. 1974. "Is Female to Male as Nature Is to Culture?" In Michelle Zimbalist Rosaldo and Louise Lamphere, eds., *Woman, Culture, and Society*. Stanford, Calif.

———, and Harriet Whitehead. 1981. "Introduction: Accounting for Sexual Meanings." In Sherry B. Ortner and Harriet Whitehead, eds., *Sexual Meanings: The Cultural Construction of Gender and Sexuality*. Cambridge, Eng.

Parsons, Talcott, and Robert F. Bales. 1955. *Family, Socialization, and the Interaction Process*. Glencoe, Ill.

Reiter, Rayna. 1975. "Men and Women in the South of France: Public and Private Domains." In Rayna Rapp Reiter, ed., *Toward an Anthropology of Women*. New York.

Rohrlich-Leavitt, Ruby, Barbara Sykes, and Elizabeth Weatherford. 1975. "Aboriginal woman: Male and Female Anthropological Perspectives." In Rayna Rapp Reiter, ed., *Toward an Anthropology of Women*. New York.

Rosaldo, Michelle Zimbalist. 1974. "Woman, Culture, and Society: A Theoretical Overview." In Michelle Zimbalist Rosaldo and Louise Lamphere, eds., *Woman, Culture, and Society*. Stanford, Calif.

———. 1980. "The Use and Abuse of Anthropology: Reflections on Feminism and Cross-Cultural Understanding." *Signs: Journal of Women in Culture and Society 5*, no. 3:389–417.

———, and Jane M. Atkinson. 1975. "Man the Hunter and Woman." In R. Willis, ed., *The Interpretation of Symbolism*. London.

———, and Louise Lamphere. 1974. "Introduction." In Michelle Zimbalist Rosaldo and Louise Lamphere, eds., *Woman, Culture, and Society*. Stanford, Calif.

Rosaldo, Renato. 1980. *Ilongot Headhunting 1883–1974: A Study in Society and History.* Stanford, Calif.

Sacks, Karen. 1976. "State Bias and Women's Status." *American Anthropologist* 78:565–69.

———. 1979. *Sisters and Wives.* Westport, Conn.

Scheffler, Harold. 1970. "Kinship and Adoption in the Northern New Hebrides." In Vern Carroll, ed., *Adoption in Eastern Oceania.* Honolulu.

———. 1974. "Kinship, Descent, and Alliance." In J.J. Honigman, ed., *Handbook of Social and Cultural Anthropology.* Chicago.

Schlegel, Alice. 1977. "Toward a Theory of Sexual Stratification." In Alice Schlegel, ed., *Sexual Stratification.* New York.

Schneider, David M. 1964. "The Nature of Kinship." *Man* 64:180–81.

———. 1968. *American Kinship: A Cultural Account.* Englewood Cliffs, N.J.

———. 1972. "What Is Kinship All About?" In Priscilla Reining, ed., *Kinship Studies in the Morgan Centennial Year.* Washington, D.C.

———. 1984. *A Critique of the Study of Kinship.* Ann Arbor, Mich.

Shapiro, Judith. 1981. "Anthropology and the Study of Gender." *Soundings: An Interdisciplinary Journal* 64, no. 4:446–65.

Strathern, Marilyn. 1978. "Comment on Leacock (1978)." *Current Anthropology* 19, no. 2:267.

———. 1981a. "Culture in a Netbag: The Manufacture of a Subdiscipline in Anthropology." *Man* 16:665–88.

———. 1981b. "Self-Interest and the Social Good: Some Implications of Hagen Gender Imagery." In Sherry B. Ortner and Harriet Whitehead, eds., *Sexual Meanings: The Cultural Construction of Gender and Sexuality.* Cambridge, Eng.

Wallman, Sandra. 1978. "Epistemologies of Sex." In L. Tiger and H. Fowler, eds., *Female Hierarchies.* Chicago.

Weiner, Annette. 1976. *Women of Value, Men of Renown: New Perspectives on Trobriand Exchange.* Austin, Tex.

Wolf, Margery. 1972. *Women and the Family in Rural Taiwan.* Stanford, Calif.

Yanagisako, Sylvia Junko. 1979. "Family and Household: The Analysis of Domestic Groups." *Annual Review of Anthropology* 8:161–205.

———. 1985. *Transforming the Past: Tradition and Kinship Among Japanese Americans.* Stanford, Calif.

16

Sexism and Naturalism in the Study of Kinship

Harold W. Scheffler

I

Empirical studies of and theory about kinship, marriage, and family are among the major foci of feminist criticism and reconstruction, not only in anthropology, but also in sociology, history, and other disciplines. That is because sexist notions are especially likely to find their way into discussions of such topics, and they are likely to be represented as immutable "facts of nature" with which each society must somehow come to terms. Such facts are commonly said to include pronounced differences in body size and in physical strength between men and women; the physical handicaps and vulnerabilities that women suffer when pregnant; the prolonged dependence of their infants on them; and, as a consequence, a strong tendency for adult males and females to form durable mating pairs in which the woman and her offspring are dependent on and, in general, subordinate to the man. All of that, it is commonly maintained, accounts not only for the near universality of the nuclear or elementary family, but also for the more general subordination of women and children to adult males.

Because these contentions would naturalize inequitable features of gender relations in our own social order and make them appear inevitable, feminists have contested them in various ways.[1] This essay is a commentary on one such response: the strange alliance of some feminists (anthropologists and others) with the antikin-ship school in symbolic anthropology – an alliance by means of which those feminists seek not only to denaturalize and deuniversalize but also to deconstruct or dismantle the categories[2] "kinship," "marriage," and "family" and, with them, the putative natural and universal subordination of women and children to men. Foremost in this school are Jane Collier and Sylvia Yanagisako, who take this stance in their introduction to the 1987 feminist anthropological anthology *Gender and Kinship*. The arguments and analyses of the kinship dismantlers are, I argue, an insecure basis on which to found a feminist resistance to the naturalization of male dominance.

II

In 1891 the British scholar Edward Westermarck concluded his encyclopedic study *The History of Human Marriage* with this observation:

> The history of human marriage is the history of a relation in which women have been gradually triumphing over the passions, the prejudices, and the selfish interests of men. (559)

Westermarck believed that the dominant tendency in that history had been "the extension of the wife's rights." He pointed out that in his own society the wife was "no longer the husband's property," and he characterized it as "the modern idea" that "marriage is, or should be, a contract on the footing of perfect equality between the sexes." Eighty years later, an American anthropologist, Ward Goodenough (1970a, 1970b), proposed to discuss marriage as though it had no history.[3] As a necessary preliminary, he argued, to construction of a definition of "kinship" for purposes of cross-cultural comparison, Goodenough defined "marriage" as a transaction and resulting contractual relation in which a person or set of persons establishes a continuing and exclusive right of sexual access to a woman and in which that woman is eligible to bear children (Goodenough 1970a: 6–17; Goodenough 1970b).

A few years later, Micaela di Leonardo (1979) objected that this definition is deeply sexist. It treats women only as objects of rights and ignores their rights as wives, which in many ethnographic instances (including a number cited by Goodenough) are no less extensive than the rights of men as husbands.[4] Goodenough might have replied that his definition does not preclude the possibility that the wife may herself be given an exclusive sexual right in relation to the husband, and he did note that typically each party acquires rights and duties of other kinds in relation to the other party. But, as he saw it, those other rights and duties are much too variable from one society to another to permit use of them in a generally applicable definition of marriage. In other words, Goodenough's definition of marriage is not so much reductionist as it is minimalist. But even so it *is* sexist. The claim that it is necessary to define "marriage" in Goodenough's asymmetrical fashion rests on the presumption that, if there is an asymmetry in the marital relation, it will favor the male party (or his surrogate). That presumption rests in turn on the conviction that there is in "human nature" (another timeless entity) a "universal tendency to a division of labor by sex and [a] universal tendency to male dominance of women and children" (Goodenough 1970a: 11–12, 18).

In proposing to define marriage in this asymmetrical fashion, and as a preliminary to formulation of a universally applicable definition of "kinship," Goodenough was indulging in a long-established anthropological practice.[5] At least since the founding of modern anthropology in the 1860s, most scholars have regarded it as self-evident that, for purposes of cross-

cultural comparison, "kinship" cannot be defined independently of marriage. The principal difficulty has been the apparent necessity to define the key concepts "maternity" and "paternity" in somewhat different ways, with the latter based on the former and on the additional concept "marriage."

In our own culture, kinship consists in relationship by birth to a woman, or maternity, and relationship by birth to a man, or paternity, and it has seemed wholly obvious that "maternity," so defined, but not "paternity," will be found in each and every culture. The received ethnographic and epistemological wisdom has been that maternity is plainly observable (in the form of pregnancy and parturition) and is therefore a highly probable concept; it is also necessary because the prolonged physical dependency of the human infant makes it compelling for species survival that each infant be suckled and reared by its mother and that she should have the right and duty to do that. In contrast, paternity has not been regarded as a directly observable relation but as one that is only tenuously inferable. The consequence (or so it is reasoned) is that in those societies where "the relationship between sexual intercourse and pregnancy is unknown," no one is presumed to have a genitor or a direct male contributor to his or her being; and in many more societies although some concept of "genitor" is present, the notorious difficulty of knowing with certainty who is the genitor of any particular child has had the result that the identity of the genitor is largely if not wholly discounted for social purposes.

For all that, however, it has not been generally accepted that a society can get by without a concept of paternity or a functional analogue of it. As Bronislaw Malinowski, one of the founding fathers of modern social anthropology, put it in his 1930 essay "Parenthood – The Basis of Social Structure," it is a

most important moral and legal rule [he gave it the name "the principle of legitimacy"] . . . that no child should be brought into the world without a man – and one man at that – assuming the role of sociological father, that is, guardian and protector, the male link between the child and the rest of the community. (Malinowski 1930 [1963]: 63)

Making ignorance of or uncertainty about paternity no excuse for not having at least a "social father," Malinowski and other anthropologists have argued that, in general, and not only where there is "ignorance of physical paternity," it is *not* being the begetter that makes a man socially the "father" of a child; it is instead the marriage of that man to the mother of that child. In the words of A. R. Radcliffe-Brown (1950: 4), "Social fatherhood is usually determined by marriage." Malinowski at least was not merely generalizing about human social practice; he was also hypothesizing a natural origin for his "principle of legitimacy" in the presumed natural debilitations of women and their offspring, both of whom therefore require adult male guardians and protectors.

In Goodenough's updated version of this theory, "derives from" replaces "determined by," and human beings are attributed a natural propensity for heterosexual pair bonding; jealous and possessive adult males compete for sexual access to females and for control over their labor and that of their offspring; and that competition is, as it must be, socially regulated. The prototypical way of meeting this functional requisite of social order is said to be via the institution of marriage, and "marriage" itself is defined (for this theoretical purpose) as the attribution to an adult male of exclusive sexual rights in relation to a particular female, which rights typically underpin various other rights in relation to her and her offspring.[6] Goodenough argues that "marriage" must be defined in that way because "jural fatherhood" cannot be defined in a way that is broadly applicable except in terms of the rights that a man has in relation to the offspring of his wife, irrespective of their actual paternity (if known).

This version of "the nature of kinship" has always been resisted, and not only because it would naturalize the patriarchal nuclear family and the sexual double standard. One of the longest-standing objections is that it assumes ethnocentrically that "kinship," so defined, is and must be a ubiquitous component of human social orders, and it does so in the face of substantial evidence to the contrary. It has been argued repeatedly since the 1860s that the ethnographically so-called kinship concepts

and institutions of many societies are *not* rooted in local theories of procreation and are *not* responses to what David Schneider (1972) has called "the problem of reproduction." The ethnographically so-called kinship terms of many if not most languages are not expressions of egocentric genealogical reference but are expressions of some other semantic kind or kinds; and, instead of being described as kinship terms, they ought to be described as "social category" or "jural category" or "relationship" terms. They only appear to be kinship terms because of certain superficial and purely formal similarities between the categories they designate and Western kinship concepts.[7]

Anthropologists who take this second position acknowledge that relationship by birth is a condition, even a sufficient condition, for inclusion in "relationship" categories, but they deny that it is *the* necessary and sufficient condition or, in some sense, the "most important" condition. Indeed, some have gone so far as to argue that even Western kinship concepts are not exclusively or even chiefly about relationship by birth, and neither are they designed to cope with or to adapt to "the problem of reproduction." According to Schneider (1972: 47), although our own (American) "symbols of kinship" are phrased in terms of consanguinity ("blood relationship"), they really "mean or stand for [relations of] diffuse, enduring solidarity," and their function is "to provide a meaningful social order."[8]

Although Collier and Yanagisako (1987: 30) contend that Schneider has "denaturalized kinship" and has shown that "the fundamental units of kinship" are not always, if ever, "genealogical relationships," what he and others have actually tried to do is to "decenter" relationship by birth, that is, to deprive it of the structural primacy attributed to it in numerous ethnographic accounts of other social and cultural orders. Indeed, Schneider himself once wrote that, try as he would, even he could not "make biology and sexual intercourse go away," because, he said, "All known kinship systems use biological relationship and/or sexual intercourse in the cultural specification of what kinship is" (1965: 97, 98). In other words, relationship by birth *is* a criterion (*even a sufficient condition*) for inclusion in the various categories ethnographically described as kin categories (otherwise, why describe them as *kin* categories to begin with?), but it is not anywhere the only criterion or even culturally the somehow "most important" criterion. But, even so, Schneider and others now claim that what they have shown is that "kinship," as commonly defined by anthropologists, simply does not exist; it is merely an anthropological fiction which they have dismantled. More accurately, the claim is that there are no such things as cultural categories that are wholly and solely genealogically constituted; genealogical relationship or relationship by birth is nowhere the necessary and sufficient condition but is a merely sufficient condition, for inclusion in any so-called kin class.

As already noted, this rather extreme relativistic – we would now say "social constructivist" – view is not all new. Something more or less like it has long enjoyed a degree of popularity among liberal social reformers, feminist and nonfeminist, who contend that the character of our social relations is not given in nature, that those relations are largely if not wholly conventional, and therefore that different systems of social relations are not indicative of differences in biological constitution. It has seemed necessary to establish that so as to establish also "the psychological unity of [hu]mankind," despite the patent diversity of cultures, and to establish the noninevitability of discriminatory gender relations and practices. Via that argument anthropology has been a major contributor to liberal humanism (Fee 1973; Stocking 1987). Kinship has figured prominently in those debates precisely because it has seemed self-evident to many people that it is, as John Barnes (1973: 64) once put it, that "aspect of culture with the closest links to the natural world." Therefore, if it could be shown not only that kinship practices vary from place to place and time to time but also that concepts of kinship are not universal, that there can be genuine human societies without them, it would (seem to) follow by implication that our social relations in general are not rooted in nature but are purely conventional. To suggest otherwise was and still is construable as undermining the (political) cause by undermining the claim that we have made ourselves what we are and we can, if we wish, make ourselves different and better than we are.

But the arguments of the kinship dismantlers do not really address the issue of naturalism and, therefore, they are largely silent on the issue of sexism as well. Because that criticism of kinship theory leaves its naturalistic and sexist elements standing where it found them, those elements may reappear, and they have in fact reappeared, in some feminist attempts to theorize kinship – albeit not as natural but as culturally constituted relations, and with a positive rather than a negative valuation. After expanding on these remarks, I discuss the possibility of formulating a more satisfactory conception of kinship for purposes of cross-cultural comparison.

III

Refutation of the naturalistic and sexist assumptions of the standard theory of kinship has never been on the agenda of the kinship dismantlers. From the outset, those theorists have called for a self-contained cultural-anthropological project that would render those assumptions largely if not wholly irrelevant. Building on a Parsonian distinction between social system and cultural system, and, taking a radically relativistic methodological stance, they insist that the first and most essential ethnographic task is to understand and then to describe each culture, as the saying goes, "in its own terms." They are especially worried about the possibility that, if we suppose that "recognition of kinship" is a functional requisite for coping with or adapting to the natural facts of biparental reproduction and the physical dependency of infants, we will dispose ourselves to find kinship everywhere we look and even where it does not exist. As David Schneider (1972: 46) once put it, "No one can disagree that man [*sic*] must cope with the facts of life and the facts of nature, whether or not he knows what those facts are scientifically or has only erroneous beliefs." What we must disagree with, he says, is the presumption that it is necessary to have a kinship system with which to do that coping. He claims that careful, unbiased ethnographic research has shown that many societies do lack kinship concepts and institutions, and that many so-called kinship concepts and institutions are not designed to cope with or to adapt to "the problem of reproduction."[9]

Following Schneider, Collier and Yanagisako (1987: 42) go further in the social-constructionist direction. They assert:

> [h]aving recognized our [own Western folk] model of biological difference as a particular cultural mode of thinking about relations between people, we should be able to question the "biological facts" of sex themselves.

They expect that such a "questioning of the presumably biological core of gender" will lead, eventually, to "rejection of any dichotomy between sex and gender as biological and cultural facts." The question, "What, if not a kinship system, is the local means for coping with the natural facts of bisexual reproduction and the dependency of infants?" is thus left unanswered and even unasked. It is *set aside* in favor of getting on with the purely cultural and self-contained project of analyzing and describing each culture (and more specifically its construction of gender) "in its own terms."

That, however, is an impossible project. The difficulty is not only the most obvious one, that ethnographic analysis and description are theory-laden activities. It is also that ethnographic inquiry begins and ends as a theory-laden act of comparison. In the course of it we try to detect in the speech and actions of another people concepts and practices that are analogous to those we know from our own social experience or from other ethnographic studies. Our initial hypotheses about such analogies may well require modification as we go along, but they can be replaced only by other, if more complex and sophisticated, hypotheses of the same general kind. We can and should continually interrogate our own culture's constructions of gender, kinship, and reproduction through cross-cultural comparison; but there is no way to abandon such constructions altogether, for when reporting the results of our observations and analyses in some scholarly language, we must again, explicitly or implicitly, compare the concepts and practices of one people with those of our own and other societies.[10] Finally, a purely culturalogical approach divorces our considerations of our own and other societies' cultural constructions of gender and kinship from the corporeal realities of our ongoing inhabitation of the planet. As feminists we should seek to transform the study of human biology, not to turn our backs on it.

So, the contention that most if not all reports of the existence of kinship concepts and institutions are biased by ethnocentrism boils down to a complaint that the process of comparison has been foreshortened, that an initial hypothesis has been put insufficiently to the test. We are told that evidence for that claim is contained in certain facts that ethnographers often report but refrain from incorporating systematically into their analyses. By far the most common observation of that kind is that it is often reported of expressions described as kinship terms that they are used not only in reference to persons presumed to be related by birth but also in reference to persons *not* presumed to be related in that way. Therefore, it is argued, an expression such as Trobriand *tama* "cannot mean 'father'"; because its reference is not exclusively to one's presumed genitor, it must mean something else. If it is suggested that, like English *father, tama* is polysemous – that it has two or more related meanings or even kinds of meaning – the reply is that it is unwarranted to say that. What it is warranted to say, we are told, is that "the category *tama*" happens to include the person who is one's presumed genitor, but that that is not sufficient reason to gloss *tama* as "father" or to say it is a kinship term.[11]

That argument turns, however, on a theoretically naive conflation of terms and categories (words and meanings, signifiers and signifieds), as in phrases like "the category *tama*," incautious use of which commonly leads to the supposition that the task is to "define the term (or the category) *tama*," rather than to define the perhaps several categories that *tama* designates and to specify the logical-structural relations between them. In that way polysemy[12] is made virtually invisible, and the way is opened for freewheeling invention of "exotic" cultures and of reinventions of our own (as in Schneider 1968).

Consider, for example, how such a set of assumptions directs us to interpret practice in American English whereby a child may be taught to address or even to refer in the third person to a close male friend of a parent as *uncle* so-and-so. We would be constrained to argue that *uncle* is not, after all, a kinship term, or at least not only a kinship term; to believe that "the category 'uncle'" is not genealogically defined or constituted; and that it is not necessary, and perhaps not even sufficient, to be related by birth to someone in order to be classified as a kinsperson or relative of that person. We must take into account, however, that to address or otherwise refer to a parent's male friend as *uncle* so-and-so is not at all the same thing as classifying him as a relative or even as a particular kind of relative (in this case as an "uncle"). Also, although a person may assert of a parent's friend who is spoken of as *uncle* so-and-so that he is not in fact that person's uncle or relative or kinsman, the same may not properly be said of that person's parent's brother. That shows, of course, that we have to deal with two distinctly different uses and meanings of *uncle*, one of which *is* a kin-classifying usage, the other not. The same thing is shown by the fact that the use of *uncle* in reference to a parent's male friend is *not* complemented by the use of *nephew* or *niece* in reference to the children of one's close friends, although in the domain of kin classification it is a mere truism that a child of a sibling is a nephew or a niece. In short, there is no category "uncle" that is partly genealogically and partly "socially" defined. However we may wish to describe the other, asymmetrical use of *uncle*, it cannot fairly be used as evidence that egocentric, genealogically constituted categories simply do not exist, either in English or in any other language.

Although these points have been made repeatedly in other contexts,[13] many ethnographers continue to hold radical social-constructionist notions concerning kinship and gender. Most recently, in a collection of anthropological essays on gender (and not incidentally, kinship), J. Weiner (1987: 262) reports that among the Foi of the Southern Highlands of Papua-New Guinea, when men migrate into a community to "live together" and "eat together" with men born into it "they [all] consider themselves 'brothers' in the widest sense of the term." He adds: "'relationship' or 'kinship' in this sense is an automatic consequence of long-term coresidence and the sharing it implies for the Foi." It is significant that Weiner does *not* report the Foi expression he glosses as "relationship" or "kinship," and neither does

he show that the Foi themselves describe a "brother" by coresidence, as well as a "brother" by birth, as a "relative" or "kinsman." Once again, it seems, cultural categories have been violated ethnographically via methods widely proclaimed virtually to guarantee authenticity.

A slightly different argument against genealogically based kinship derives from the Victorian anthropological contention that expressions such as Trobriand or Fijian *tama* "cannot mean 'father'" because they are used not only in reference to one's presumed genitor but also in reference to his brothers and male cousins, and, indeed, in reference to all men of more or less his age who are comembers with him of some social group usually designated a clan, whether or not it is possible to demonstrate via a pedigree that they are related genealogically to one's father. Thus, *tama* is not a kinship term but is a "social category" term, one that signifies something like "man of my father's group and of more or less his age." There is, however, ample evidence not only for the metaphoric use of kinship terms (as in the uses of *uncle* discussed above) but also for polysemy within the domain of kin classification. As (for example) in the difference between English *father* and *stepfather*, so also in many other languages kinship terms often occur in unmarked/marked pairs, and that is a sure sign of polysemy. Fijian *tama* or "father" has the complementary marked forms *tama-levu* for father's elder brother and *tama-lailai* for father's younger brother. Those forms are definitive evidence that "father" is the structurally primary or logically most basic sense of *tama*.[14] It has to be noticed also that the definition usually proffered as the only or structurally basic one – that is, "man of my father's group ..." – is logically based on and presupposes the category "father." That renders "father" the structurally most basic sense of the expression, and "man of my father's group ..." a structurally derivative sense.

The semantic-theoretical foundations of the arguments of the antikinship school are not only simplistic and seriously misleading. They also routinely muddle up questions that must be kept quite distinct because the answers to them require at least partially different kinds of data. Questions about synchronic-structural relations get mixed up, confused with, and answered as though they were questions about historical or diachronic relations; and questions about logical relations get mixed up, confused with, and answered as though they were questions about the "mental states" of single social persons.[15]

Thus, when feminist and nonfeminist anthropologists take the anti- or no-kinship line, some of them in reaction to sociobiological attempts to naturalize our social relations as kin of one another and as males and females, they do nothing to refute them. For example: in their essay "'Explanations' of Male Dominance," Stephanie Coontz and Peta Henderson (1986: 6) seek to discredit sociobiological accounts of gender, and to do so they cite Marshall Sahlins's *The Use and Abuse of Biology* (1976). He has shown, they say, that in societies "based on kinship as an organizing principle," it is "expediency rather than actual blood relationship" that dictates the form of interaction between individuals. Sahlins's point was, however, the rather different one, that kinship conduct – the social relations between persons who account themselves kin of one another – cannot be explained by appeal to some sort of universal reproductive and genetic rationality, any more than it can be by appeal to a crude, presocial notion of "expediency." He sought to turn the arguments of the sociobiologists on their heads, as it were, by showing that it is not even recognition of one another as kin, much less simply being genetically related, that governs how people interact; instead, it is often because they agree voluntarily to interact in a certain way that they then recognize one another as "kin." As he put it, "The relation between the recognition of kinship and an appropriate mode of action is often reciprocal" (Sahlins 1976: 26). Thus depriving a complex, multilayered cultural reality of most of its detail, the ethnographer or theorist is bound to end up arguing that what passes for kinship elsewhere is not at all the same kind of thing as what passes for kinship at home. But turning that line against the naturalizers of kinship *conduct* is bound to be futile when it is recognized, as it was by Sahlins, that relationship by birth is typically a sufficient, even if not also a necessary, condition for inclusion in a so-called kin class and for designation by a so-called kinship term. As my colleague Alison

Richard has pointed out to me, sociobiological theory does not require that *all* persons treated socially as close kin should be also genetically close kin. It requires only that at least 51 percent are, and it is highly probable that in most societies that condition is more than fulfilled. Surely, also, the common use of kinship terms metaphorically to establish kinlike social relations between nonkin (which is what Sahlins was writing about) is testimony *for*, rather than against, the case of the sociobiologists.[16]

Wholly "culturalizing" kinship not only leaves us vulnerable to socio-biological arguments; it also opens the door to feminist essentialism. In the place of Universal Woman the Natural Reproducer and Nurturer, bound by her physical disabilities and by her helpless infant to her naturally dominant and legally superordinate mate, some feminist anthropologists have substituted Universal Woman the Culturally Constituted Reproducer not only of dependent infants, but also of social persons and even of whole systems of social relations (Yeatman 1983, 1984; A. Weiner 1976, 1978, 1979, 1980). In some accounts she appears as The Controller of Reproduction, almost to the exclusion of men. This theme is especially strong in the work of A. Weiner (1976, 1978, 1979, 1980), which shows a pronounced tendency to objectify as the essence of womanness the "biological *and* cultural regenerative powers that women possess" and that men are continually expending their power "in attempts to assume and incorporate" (Weiner 1976: 235–236; but cf. Strathern 1981, 1987). Expectably, when the question is raised, why Universal Woman should be culturally constituted in that way, the answer is likely to revert to the fact that it is women, and not men, who bear and rear infants. Thus, the difference between this account and the more standard masculinist-anthropological account becomes one of value. Woman's Body, instead of being a burden and a handicap that must be compensated for by "male dominance" over women and children, becomes in this construction a natural resource that she does, or certainly can, "control," and thus also a potential source of power in women's relations with men. But women's much touted "control over reproduction" appears to amount to nothing more than women's ability to bear offspring.[17] How can it be that in the absence of the necessary technology and the freedom legally to use it, having no choice but to bear children or to do without heterosexual intercourse constitutes having control over reproduction? And, in fact, Woman the Moral Mother has been and still is a potent symbol for both popular feminism and antifeminism in the West.

Janet Sayers (1982), Alice Echols (1984), Marilyn Strathern (1981), and others have already pointed out that reconstituting the essence of Woman culturally is bound to turn out to be just another way of constituting her naturally – this time in opposition, rather than in relation, to Man. It reproduces our own dominant cultural assumptions about women, albeit with a different valuation. At this juncture, the issue becomes not "Are we going to tolerate sexism in theory construction?" but "Must we flee sexism only to be landed with feminist essentialism?" The answer must and can be a definite "No!" because there is a more moderate, both naturalistic and social-constructionist, but also nonsexist alternative.

IV

I noted earlier that in trying to understand another culture we always begin by trying to detect in the speech and actions of a people concepts and practices that are similar to ones we know from our own native social experience or from other ethnographic studies. In the matter of "kinship," because it is so defined in their own cultures, anthropologists have looked for concepts of interpersonal relationship established via processes of reproduction; they have looked for some "recognition" that heterosexual intercourse is a necessary (though perhaps not also sufficient) part of that process; and, thus, for "recognition" that each person has both a male and a female contributor (via the process of reproduction as locally conceived) to his or her being. Ethnographers have never had any qualms about supposing that, because childbirth is a plainly observable event, relationship by birth to a woman is a "known fact" in any society, as it is in their own, and no one has ever reported the existence of a society from which a concept of maternity is absent. Even if the local conception and evaluation is that a woman merely carries

and nurtures *in utero* a being that a man placed there via sexual intercourse with her, ethnographers have not been disposed to talk about "ignorance of maternity" (or even of physical, biological, or physiological maternity). But the positivist-empiricist epistemology that makes maternity seem obvious and a concept of maternity seem inevitable, also makes paternity seem just the opposite, and it has, as a consequence, seemed entirely plausible that there are (or were) many societies in which "ignorance of paternity" *is* the state of affairs; or, if a concept of paternity is present, that being the genitor of a child counts for little or nothing socially because of the notorious difficulty of knowing with certainty who the genitor of any particular child really is. It is not without significance for this discussion of sexism in the theory of kinship that anthropologists have usually attributed that difficulty to, as Westermarck (1891: 113) put it, "adultery on the woman's side." All that has had the further rather curious consequence that the criteria for "having a concept of paternity" have been typically far more stringent than the criteria for "having a concept of maternity." That in turn has led to the conversion of a seemingly plausible state of affairs into an "actual" state of affairs.

One of the positive features of the social-constructionist orientation in contemporary anthropology is that it does at least try to dispense with that epistemology and to treat the concepts of other cultures as positive knowledge, and *not* as just so many more or less "erroneous beliefs" or manifestations of "savage nescience" of one thing or another (see Schneider 1965 for a useful discussion of some of these issues). It forces us to see that local concepts of "maternity" (female reproductive contribution) are no less *cultural* constructs than are local concepts of "paternity" (male reproductive contribution); and, as I have already shown in some detail in other contexts (Scheffler 1970; 1973: 748–756; 1978: 5–13), it enables us to see that concepts of the latter kind are no less common than are those of the former kind.[18] Moreover, it is simply not true that genitors not wed to the mothers of their offspring are typically devoid of rights and duties in relation to their offspring.[19] Appearances to the contrary have been ethnographically and theoretically created and sustained by ignoring moral and sentimentally sanctioned rights and duties in favor of legally sanctioned ones and by mistaking what counts as *legal* evidence for paternity with the nature of the relationship itself (see references in n. 19).

There is, then, no need for the concept of the purely "social father"; it is an anthropological red herring, and we will get by much better without it. That is just as well because it has been the apparent necessity to institute that concept that has led also to the ahistorical and sexist definition of marriage as rooted, like maternity, in presumed timeless, natural, biological facts, especially in a presumed tendency for men to "dominate" women and their offspring, and for their own good.

We can now define "kinship" for purposes of cross-cultural comparison as culturally postulated "relationship by birth to an ego or propositus," and we can generalize that, wherever we find it, it is "bilaterally" constituted. We can do that without presupposing that postulation (*not* "recognition") of kinship is a cultural universal and is a functional requisite of a recognizably human social order. Nevertheless, the ubiquity of that kind of cultural form does suggest that there has been, all along, some sociological wisdom in the suspicion that you won't have to look very hard to find culturally constituted kinship wherever you find human beings. After all, it does not follow from its being perhaps ethnocentric from the outset that a suspicion *is* wrong. Assuming, then, that kinship constructs are ubiquitous, it becomes an interesting question why they are.

As soon as we ask that question radical social-constructionism (at least of the "symbolic anthropology" kind) becomes useless, because it is not an explanatory but only a methodological paradigm. For the radical social-constructionist whose purpose is to understand and to describe each culture "in its own terms," that question is an irrelevant "social system question," one about "how roles are defined and articulated into a set of patterns for action which adapt *man* to the facts of his environment" (Schneider 1972: 47, emphasis added). Indeed, as N. Redclift (1987: 125) has noted, what is strikingly and most deliberately *absent* from this perspective is "any idea that sexuality or sexual divisions are a relevant, or problematic,

aspect of kinship"; and that, as she goes on to remark, entails that many of the most contentious and difficult questions feminists need and want to raise about kinship and its relations with gender cannot even be asked.

Collier and Yanagisako's (1987: 7, 15, 29) claim to the contrary that the "domains" of "gender and kinship are mutually constituted" or are "one field," because both center on folk conceptions or theories about human reproduction, is not a tenable reply. On the one hand, it is contrary to Schneider's insistence that "kinship" does *not* center on, although it does include, concepts of bisexual reproduction; and were it not for that insistence there would be very little to differentiate his views, which Collier and Yanagisako wish to adopt, from those of most other anthropologists. On the other hand, it must be admitted that "gender" and "kinship" are related categories that are central to related fields or topics of study, and relations between social relations of gender and of kinship are urgently in need of further theorization and empirical research – as Collier and Yanagisako (1987) and Redclift (1987) strongly stress. But "mutual constitution" begs the question and prevents us from attending to this intellectual task.

In contrast to kinship deconstructionism, the standard theory of kinship is explanatory in intent. What is wrong with it is not its attempt to explain the ubiquity of kinship concepts and practices by positing certain, as Clyde Kluckhohn once put it, "invariant points of reference supplied by the biological [and] psychological...givens of human life" (cited in Goodenough 1970a: 2). It is, after all, one of those "givens" that humans *do* reproduce bisexually and *do* produce helpless offspring who *do* require physical and psychological nurturance for many years. The real defect in the standard theory is that it constructs some of those "givens" in a blatantly sexist fashion and then uses them to constitute the ethnographic facts to be explained.

To acknowledge that, because of our evolutionary history, we humans are disposed to form fairly durable heterosexual mating pairs, the members of which cooperate in, among other things, the rearing of their offspring, is not to say also that the only "natural" form of human sexuality is heterosexuality and that homoerotic attraction and interaction are perversely contrary to nature. R. W. Connell (1987: 72) and others have already pointed out that widely diverse social-sexual arrangements are consistent with the occurrence of more than enough heterosexual intercourse to reproduce species. To do that, it is hardly necessary for humans to be innately and exclusively heterosexual in erotic orientation. Also, primate studies have shown that <u>playful homo-erotic attraction and interaction are common in various species</u>, are a powerful socializing force, and are among the ways in which adolescent animals learn sexual and other social behaviors (see e.g. Lancaster 1979; Hrdy and Whitten 1986; Smuts 1986*a*, 1986*b*).

V

The long-standing anthropological debate about the nature of kinship has been all along not only an intellectual but also a moral and political controversy. Early on it had no direct feminist voice, although as shown by the final sentence of Westermarck's *The History of Human Marriage* (which I quoted at the outset), feminist voices were being heard and, to some extent, even attended to. Now that feminists are in a much better position to have a direct voice, we are well advised not to indulge in or to poach off the arguments of the kinship dismantlers, but to direct our critical attention, as many of us already have, to the naturalness of that vaguely defined syndrome "male dominance" and of a social division of labor that has infants dependent primarily on their mothers and their mothers on their mates or husbands.[20] It is all too easy, though, in the social contexts in which anthropology is practiced, to get seduced into thinking that, if we grant the radical social-constructionist premise that it is culture that constitutes what is "real" for any society (as per Yeatman 1983), we are relieved of the necessity to do that.

Anthropology is often represented as a liberal-humanitarian voice that speaks for the "other," and to the extent that we do that we have a strong interest in assimilating that "other" to ourselves and, in the process, to a common humanity equally entitled to the same human rights. In the past that effort took the form of a search for the elements of "the psycho-logical unity of [hu]mankind" or for "the universal categories of culture," one of which was "kinship." Nowadays, the tendency is to define "Man" as "The Culture-Maker" whose creative capacities, including the possibility of self-definition, are virtually unbounded. Although this stance may appear to serve the feminist cause, it also makes us all the more susceptible to being pulled in the opposite direction. Barbara Lloyd (1976) has shown how the ideal, statistical-experimental, scientific method leads to a tendency to treat only findings of difference as "real results," with the consequence that findings of similarities between males and females are often treated as no findings at all. Although anthropology is not that kind of science, we have a similar problem.

Because our discipline operates in the context of late-capitalist, consumption-oriented society, we have a strong interest in maintaining, even producing, cross-cultural difference, that of *creating* the "other" as an esoteric and exotic object, not merely of disinterested knowledge, but of commodity exchange and consumption. Just as each year's Ford must be made to appear not only different from but also new, better, and improved in comparison with last year's if the Ford Motor Company is to survive in the marketplace, so also must culture *x* be made to appear different from other cultures in general if the ethnographer is to make his or her mark in anthropology *as a trade*. As a consequence, hardly a year goes by without the appearance of yet another New Theory of Culture that stresses its symbolic constitution and dissociates it from the taint of anything natural or even material; or of yet another New Theory of Women's Status that would conventionalize the whole thing; or, even more frequently, of yet another claim that culture *x* lacks that, sometimes alleged, most "basic" of all human social institutions, "kinship" itself. What all those enterprises have in common is that they would deprive us of any dimensions of human, cross-cultural similarity, other than our symbol-creating capacity, by reference to which cross-cultural differences may be ordered and understood. They would, thereby, open the way for virtually endless commodity differentiation unconstrained by even the most minimal standards of intellectual or social value.

Surely, though, all human social orders have it in common that they have come to terms culturally with the biological givens that women bear children and need the assistance of men to engender them; and it does seem to be a cross-cultural social reality that, however varying the patterns, both women and men contribute to the rearing of dependent children. Kathleen Gough (1975: 75), Janet Sayers (1982: 191), and many others have already pointed out that feminists need not fear to acknowledge these patterns and, indeed, must do so as a preliminary to showing also that historically it has not always entailed the subordination of women to men and, certainly, it need not do so in the future.

NOTES

1   See e.g., the essays by Leibowitz, Slocum, and Gough, all in Reiter (1975); Dahlberg (1981), Harding (1987).

2   For the purposes of this chapter, and in general, it is vitally important not to conflate words and the categories or concepts they designate. Accordingly, in references to a word that word is italicized (e.g., *marriage*), and in references to a category or concept the word is put in double quotes (e.g., "marriage").

3   For many feminists the classic treatment of the history of marriage, family, and kinship is F. Engels's (1884) *The Origin of the Family, Private Property, and the State*. Some feminist surveys and criticisms are Gough (1975), Collier, Rosaldo, and Yanagisako (1982), Sayers, Evans, and Redclift (1987).

4   Additional relevant ethnographic accounts include Nash (1974, 1978a, 1978b, 1981, 1987) and Bell (1980, 1983, 1987).

5   In addition to the one discussed below, we might question also the presumption, hardly unique to Goodenough, that it is either necessary or wise *for any purpose* to attempt to devise a universally applicable definition of "marriage." An alternative strategy, which cannot be elaborated on here, would be to settle for a category of marriage-like cultural categories and social institutions. Of course, the same goes for "kinship" and "family."

6   I have here simplified Goodenough's definition of marriage by omitting from it the possibility that the party who acquires the

relevant rights in relation to a particular woman may be someone other than an adult male. Doing that is not critical for the argument being developed here.

7   For the details on the anti-kinship side, see Schneider (1972, 1984), Needham (1971), Barnard and Good (1984); on the other side see Scheffler (1972), Scheffler and Lounsbury (1971), where the argument presented is critically quite different from Schneider's (1984) representation of it.

8   For Schneider's full "cultural" analysis of American kinship see Schneider (1968). The "second edition" of 1983 differs only in the addition of brief replies to a few critics; they deal with *none* of the issues mentioned here or in Scheffler (1976).

9   Because of the severity and persistence of Schneider's condemnation of what he represents as rampant ethnocentrism in the study of kinship in the past, it is only fair to note that the general outlines and many of the details of his own reanalysis of "American kinship" (Schneider 1968) have been reproduced by two dozen or more of his students and other young anthropologists influenced by him and his students in their studies of cultures scattered all around the world, though mainly in South Asia and Oceania. Is it ethnocentrism or something else that has produced this remarkable series of results?

10   The same general points are made also in Barnes (1973) and Horton (1982: 203), and they are rapidly becoming commonplace in the burgeoning literature focusing on ethnographies as texts (e.g. Asad 1986).

11   For fuller representation of this view see Hocart (1935) and Leach (1958). The Hocart essay, despite some major logical flaws (see Scheffler 1972) is often cited as authoritative and conclusive by Louis Dumont and his followers. Westermark (1891: 88–89) also took this position, but he thought he had to in order to refute claims that relationship terminologies can be used to deduce archaic forms of social organization and, especially, of marriage.

12   Polysemy is the condition wherein an expression designates two or more related categories, one being derived (logically and usually, though not necessarily, temporally) from another. It contrasts most directly with homonymy, the condition wherein an expression designates two or more categories,

but there is no relation of derivation between them (as in *bare* = uncovered, and *bear* = the animal, words having the same pronunciation but wholly unrelated meanings). See also Scheffler and Lounsbury (1972: 6–12).

13 Scheffler (1972, 1973, 1976), Scheffler and Lounsbury (1972).

14 The relevant Fijian data are in Sahlins (1962). For more general discussions of markedness relations in systems of kin classification see Scheffler (1984, 1987).

15 For an example of the first confusion see again Hocart (1935); and for an example of the second confusion see Hirschfeld (1986). Both kinds of confusion are dealt with in Scheffler and Lounsbury (1972, esp. chaps. 1 and 7), also Scheffler (1972).

16 It ought to be a matter for serious scholarly concern that the logical fallacies that underpin the arguments of the antikinship school in modern cultural anthropology are filtering into gender studies more generally, where they are sometimes made foundational to ambitious claims. Consider Kessler and McKenna's (1978: 38) claim that in some North American Indian societies "gender role" rather than genital anatomy determined "gender attribution" or classification as a male or a female. (They sometimes qualify the "determined" with "sometimes.") Their "ethnomethodological" argument is intended to liberate gender from any biological basis; to show that it is instead a "social accomplishment"; and to show that a system of two genders is by no means inevitable. They acknowledge, however, that "gender role" is definable only as conduct or behavior normative for a member of one or the other genital-sex class (in their terms, gender category) and that assignment to one or the other sex class is typically at birth and *not* dependent on any conduct or behavior on the part of the person being classified. Because, logically, categories must be defined or constituted by criteria independent of the normative implications of inclusion in those categories, certain forms of conduct cannot be both criteria for and normative implications of inclusion in one and the same category. It must be that Kessler and McKenna are dealing with situations in which some men (less often women) are per-

mitted to act, in some degree, as *though* they were women (or men), and may be spoken of as though they were women (or men), or as anomalous "he-she" or "she-he." Ethnographic data cited by Kessler and McKenna, and more recently summarized or revealed in Williams (1986), provide definitive evidence that such persons were not regarded as having somehow moved from one sex (or in Kessler and McKenna's terms, gender) category to the other, but were only metaphorically "women" (or "men"). It is only to be expected that Kessler and McKenna cannot in the end produce any linguistic data to demonstrate that the so-called *berdache* are treated in any language as a genuine third gender. In any event, a third gender would be just another gender straightjacket, hardly an open door leading out of Kessler and McKenna's prison house of gender.

17 A. Weiner frequently asserts that Trobriand women control reproduction of the *dala* or lineage. Of course, women do, with the cooperation of men, reproduce human beings, and it does deserve to be stressed, as Weiner does, that what is produced are not mere corporeal entities but are social persons. One of the features with which any Trobriander is born is an identity as a member of a dala (lineage), and he/she necessarily shares that identity with his/her mother. That is because the constitutive rule of the dala kind of group is that being an offspring of a female member is the necessary and sufficient condition for inclusion in her group. Such a rule gives neither the mother nor anyone else any powers of choice or decision in the matter of group affiliation and, thus, no "control" over either individual or lineage reproduction (or, we might more accurately say, perpetuation), except, again, in the instance of the woman who refrains from heterosexual intercourse and thus from getting pregnant. For a general discussion of such rules of group affiliation see Scheffler (1986).

18 In one of those contexts (Scheffler 1973: 749), and still too much under the influence of the epistemology of which I am here being critical, I wrote: "the foundation of any kinship system consists in a folk-cultural theory designed to account for the fact that women give birth to children, i.e., a theory of human reproduction." Collier and Yanagisako

(1987: 32) misrepresent this as a claim that "kinship is everywhere about the same biological fact," although (following Schneider 1965) I had already cautioned against representing folk concepts which posit genealogical relationship or relationship by birth as "biological" concepts or knowledge. They object also to what they say is my assumption that "biological motherhood is everywhere the core of the social relationship of motherhood." I have done no more, however, than to argue that the very existence of "social relations of motherhood" is contingent on the prior existence of the category "mother" (i.e., female reproductive agent of ...) and to point out the logical and technical-linguistic errors of the claim (insisted on by Schneider [1968] and by Collier and Yanagisako) that one and the same category named "mother" may have "alternate" genealogical and behavioral distinctive features.

19 Yet so entrenched is this view in academic anthropology that one historian (Trautmann 1981: 60) has asserted that "consanguinity and affinity are related as chicken and egg," exactly as though it were an irrefutable ethnographic fact that relations of consanguinity (especially of paternity) created out of wedlock nowhere count as kinship and are everywhere wholly discounted for any and all social purposes. Modern ethnographic evidence is wholly to the contrary (see e.g. Evans-Pritchard 1945; Fortes 1949; Scheffler 1970; and for a summary Scheffler 1973: 751–756).

20 There are, of course, innumerable essays and books that attack that naturalization and that vagueness. Among them I have benefited from Rosaldo (1980), Sayers (1982), Leacock (1981), Coward (1983), Hartsock (1985), Tabet (1982), Harding (1987), and Connell (1987).

BIBLIOGRAPHY

Asad, T. 1986. The concept of cultural translation in British social anthropology. In *Writing culture: The poetics and politics of ethnography*. J. Clifford and G. Marcus, eds., 141–164. Berkeley, Los Angeles, London: University of California Press.

Barnard, A., and A. Good. 1984. *Research practices in the study of kinship*. London: Academic Press.

Barnes, J. A. 1973. Genetrix: genitor:: nature: culture? In *The character of kinship*. J. Goody, ed., 61–74. London: Cambridge University Press.

Bell, Dianne. 1980. Desert politics: Choices in the marriage market. In *Women and colonization*. M. Etienne and E. Leacock, eds., 239–269. New York: Praeger.

——. 1983. *Daughters of the dreaming*. Sydney: Allen and Unwin.

——. 1987. The politics of separation. In *Dealing with inequality: Analyzing gender relations in Melanesia and beyond*. M. Strathern, ed., 112–129. London: Cambridge University Press.

Collier, Jane, Michelle Rosaldo, and Sylvia Yanagisako, 1982. Is there a family? New anthropological views. In *Rethinking the family: Some feminist questions*. B. Thorne and M. Yalom, eds., 25–39. New York: Longman.

Collier, Jane, and Sylvia Yanagisako, eds. 1987. *Gender and kinship: Essays toward a unified analysis*. Stanford: Stanford University Press.

Connell, R. W. 1987. *Gender and power*. Stanford: Stanford University Press.

Coontz, S., and P. Henderson, eds. 1986. *Women's work, men's property: The origins of gender and class*. London: Verso.

Coward, R. 1983. *Patriarchal precedents*. London: Routledge.

Dahlberg, F., ed. 1981. *Woman the gatherer*. New Haven: Yale University Press.

di Leonardo, M. 1979. Methodology and the misinterpretation of women's status in kinship studies. *American Ethnologist* 6: 627–637.

Echols, A. 1984. The taming of the id: Feminist sexual politics. In *Pleasure and danger: Exploring female sexuality*. C. Vance, ed., 50–72. Boston: Routledge & Kegan Paul.

Engels, Frederick. 1972 (1884). *The origin of the family, private property, and the state*. Edited by Eleanor Leacock. New York: International Publishers.

Evans-Pritchard, E. E. 1945. *Some aspects of marriage and the family among the Nuer*. Rhodes-Livingstone Papers, no. 11.

Fee, E. 1973. The sexual politics of Victorian social anthropology. *Feminist Studies* I: 23–29.

Fortes, M. 1949. *The web of kinship among the Tallensi*. London: Cambridge University Press.

Goodenough, W. 1970a. *Description and comparison in cultural anthropology*. Chicago: Aldine.

———. 1970b. Epilogue: Transactions in parenthood. In *Adoption in Eastern Oceania*. V. Carroll, ed., 391–410. Honolulu: University of Hawaii Press.

Gough, K. 1975. The origin of the family. In *Toward an anthropology of women*. R. R. Rapp, ed., 51–76. New York: Monthly Review Press.

Harding, S. 1987. The politics of the natural: The case of sex differences. In *Sexuality and medicine*. E. E. Shlep, ed., I: 185–203. Dordrecht: D. Reidel.

Hartsock, N. 1985. *Money, sex, and power*. Boston: Northeastern University Press.

Hirschfeld, E. 1986. Kinship and cognition: Genealogy and the meaning of kinship terms. *Current Anthropology* 27: 217–242.

Hocart, Arthur M. 1935. Kinship systems. *Anthropos* 32: 545–551.

Horton, Robin. 1982. Tradition and modernity revisited. In *Rationality and relativism*. M. Hollis, ed., 201–260. Cambridge: MIT Press.

Hrdy, S., and P. Whitten. 1986. Patterning of sexual activity. In *Primate societies*. B. Smuts et al., eds., 370–384. Chicago: University of Chicago Press.

Kessler, S., and W. McKenna. 1978. *Gender: An ethnomethodological approach*. New York: Wiley.

Lancaster, J. 1979. Sex and gender in evolutionary perspective. In *Human sexuality*. H. A. Katchadourian, ed., 51–79. Berkeley, Los Angeles, London: University of California Press.

Leach, E. R. 1958. Concerning Trobriand clans and the kinship category *tabu*. In *The developmental cycle in domestic groups*. J. Goody, ed., 120–145. London: Cambridge University Press.

Leacock, E. 1981. *Myths of male dominance*. New York: Monthly Review Press.

Leibowitz, Lila. 1975. Perspectives on the evolution of sex differences. In *Toward an anthropology of women*. R. R. Rapp, ed., 20–35. New York: Monthly Review Press.

Lloyd, B. 1976. Social responsibility and research on sex differences. In *Exploring sex differences*. B. Lloyd and J. Archer, eds., 1–23. London: Academic Press.

Malinowski, Bronislaw. 1930 (1963). Parenthood – The basis of social structure. In *Sex, culture and myth* (Collected essays of Bronislaw Malinowski). Pp. 42–88. New York: Harcourt, Brace, and World.

Nash, J. 1974. *Matriliny and modernization: The Nagovisi of South Bougainville*. New Guinea Research Bulletin No. 55. Canberra: Australian National University Press.

———. 1978a. A note on groomprice. *American Anthropologist* 80: 106–108.

———. 1978b. Women and power in Nagovisi society. *Journal de la société des Océanistes* 58 (34): 119–126.

———. 1981. Sex, money, and the status of women in aboriginal South Bougainville. *American Ethnologist* 8: 107–126.

———. 1987. Gender attributes and equality: Men's strength and women's talk among the Nagovisi. In *Dealing with inequality: Analyzing gender relations in Melanesia and beyond*. M. Strathern, ed., 150–173. London: Cambridge University Press.

Needham, R. 1971. Remarks on the analysis of kinship and marriage. In *Rethinking kinship and marriage*. R. Needham, ed., 1–34. London: Tavistock.

Radcliffe-Brown, A. R. 1950. Introduction. In *African systems of kinship and marriage*. A. R. Radcliffe-Brown, ed., 1–85. London: Oxford University Press.

Redclift, N. 1987. Rights in women: Kinship, culture, and materialism. In *Engels revisited: New feminist essays*. J. Sayers, M. Evans, and N. Redclift. eds., 111–143. London: Tavistock.

Reiter, R. R., ed. 1975. *Toward an anthropology of women*. New York: Monthly Review Press.

Rosaldo, M. 1980. The use and abuse of anthropology: Reflections on feminism and cross-cultural understanding. *Signs* 5: 389–417.

Sahlins, M. 1962. *Moala: Culture and nature on a Fijian island*. Ann Arbor: University of Michigan Press.

———. 1976. *The use and abuse of biology*. Ann Arbor: University of Michigan Press.

Sayers, J. 1982. *Biological politics: Feminist and anti-feminist perspectives*. London: Tavistock.

Sayers, J., M. Evans, and N. Redclift, eds. 1987. *Engels revisited: New feminist essays*. London: Tavistock.

Scheffler, H. W. 1970. Kinship and adoption in the northern New Hebrides. In *Adoption in Eastern Oceania*. V. Carroll, ed., 68–89. Honolulu: University of Hawaii Press.

———. 1972. Kinship semantics. *Annual Review of Anthropology* 1: 309–328.

——. 1973. Kinship, descent, and alliance. In *Handbook of social and cultural anthropology.* J. Honigmann, ed., 747–793. Chicago: Rand McNally.

——. 1976. Kinship in American culture: Another view. In *Meaning in Anthropology.* K. Basso and H. Selby, eds., 57–91. Albuquerque: University of New Mexico Press.

——. 1978. *Australian Kin Classification.* Cambridge: Cambridge University Press.

——. 1984. Markedness and extensions: The Tamil case. *Man* 19: 557–574.

——. 1986. The descent of rights and the descent of persons. *American Anthropologist* 88: 339–350.

——. 1987. Markedness in systems of kin classification. *Journal of Anthropological Research* 43: 203–221.

Scheffler, H. W., and F. G. Lounsbury. 1972. *A study in structural semantics: The Siriono kinship system.* Englewood Cliffs, N.J.: Prentice-Hall.

Schneider, D. M. 1965. Kinship and biology. In *Aspects of the analysis of family structure.* A. J. Coale, ed., 83–101. Princeton: Princeton University Press.

——. 1968. *American kinship: A cultural account.* Englewood Cliffs, N.J.: Prentice-Hall.

——. 1972. What is kinship all about? In *Kinship studies in the Morgan centennial year.* P. Reining, ed., 32–63. Washington, D.C.: Anthropological Society of Washington.

——. 1984. *A critique of the theory of kinship.* Ann Arbor: University of Michigan Press.

Slocum, S. 1975. Woman the gatherer: Male bias in anthropology. In *Toward an anthropology of women.* R. R. Rapp, ed., 36–50. New York: Monthly Review Press.

Smuts, B. 1986a. Sexual competition and mate choice. In *Primate societies.* B. Smuts, et al., eds., 385–399. Chicago: University of Chicago Press.

——. 1986b. Gender, aggression and influence. In *Primate societies.* B. Smuts, et al., eds., 400–412. Chicago: University of Chicago Press.

Stocking, G. 1987. *Victorian anthropology.* New York: Free Press.

Strathern, M. 1981. Culture in a netbag: The manufacture of a subdiscipline in anthropology. *Man* 16: 665–688.

——. 1987. Conclusion. In *Dealing with inequality: Analyzing gender relations in Melanesia and beyond.* M. Strathern, ed., 278–302. Cambridge: Cambridge University Press.

Tabet, P. 1982. Hands, tools, and weapons. *Feminist Issues* 2: 3–62.

Trautmann, T. R. 1981. *Dravidian kinship.* London: Cambridge University Press.

Weiner, A. 1976. *Women of value: Men of renown.* Austin: University of Texas Press.

——. 1978. The reproductive model in Trobriand society. *Mankind* 11: 175–186.

——. 1979. Trobriand kinship from another view: The reproductive power of women and men. *Man* 14: 328–348.

——. 1980. Reproduction: A replacement for reciprocity. *American Ethnologist* 7: 71–85.

Weiner, J. F. 1987. Diseases of the soul: sickness, agency, and the men's cult among the Foi of New Guinea. In *Dealing with inequality: Analyzing gender relations in Melanesia and beyond.* Marilyn Strathern, ed., 255–277. Cambridge: Cambridge University Press.

Westermarck, E. W. 1891. *The history of human marriage.* London: Macmillan.

Williams, W. L. 1986. *The spirit and the flesh: Sexual diversity in American Indian culture.* Boston: Beacon Press.

Yeatman, A. 1983. The procreative model: The social ontological bases of gender-kinship systems. *Social Analysis* 14: 3–30.

——. 1984. A rejoinder (to comments on Yeatman 1983). *Social Analysis* 16: 26–43.

17

The Substance of Kinship and the Heat of the Hearth: Feeding, Personhood, and Relatedness among Malays in Pulau Langkawi

Janet Carsten

This article describes how, for Malays on the island of Langkawi, feeding (in the sense of receiving as well as giving nourishment) is a vital component in the long process of becoming a person and participating fully in social relations. The process begins with conception and birth; it continues through feeding and through growing and living together in the house; it involves marriage and the birth of new children; and it is only in a limited sense completed when adult men and women become grandparents. For these Malays kinship itself is a process of becoming.

During the 18 months of my initial stay in Langkawi, and for four months on a subsequent visit, I lived in one house with a Malay family, eating with its members and participating in household activities on a daily basis. I thus gained a particularly intimate picture of life inside houses. My own experience of "becoming kin" lies behind some of what I present here, but it is also another kind of story that I must tell elsewhere.

Most of the material I present is derived from conversations I had with middle-aged and older women (including one traditional midwife) whom I knew well in the village where I did my fieldwork. Like all such material it is thus "slanted" in a particular way.

Although men might put matters somewhat differently, nothing I know about this village leads me to suspect that they would deny the information I present. They might add more. But then women too differ among themselves over how they see the matters I discuss (their views are often complementary rather than contradictory). What I present here would not seem strange to most of the villagers I know. Of course, my account is incomplete, but I do not take completeness to be a proper aim for an anthropologist.

I also refer to published material on other areas of Malaysia, collected at different times by different ethnographers. The beliefs and practices I describe vary both regionally and over time – in some places I note such variation. Like other ethnographers, however, I have also been struck by a certain consistency in the cultural logic I describe. I hope I have not overemphasized the degree of coherence or consistency, since my aim is to convey the processual and transformative potential of Malay culture.

My argument may be placed in the general context of an analysis of kinship that begins from native categories. I take for granted that the meaning of "kinship" cannot be assumed a priori. I use the term "relatedness" to indicate indigenous ways of acting out and conceptualizing relations between people, as distinct from notions derived from anthropological theory. Ways of living and thinking about relatedness in Langkawi lead me to stress a processual view of personhood and kinship. It is through living and consuming together in houses that people become complete persons – that is, kin. The core substance of kinship in local perceptions is blood, and the major contribution to blood is food. Blood is always mutable and fluid – as is kinship itself.

James Fox has remarked that "it is true for the Austronesian world that one's social identity is not given at birth" (1987: 174). He contrasts this with the image given by classical monographs on Africa in which identity seems to be defined at birth by a structural position in a lineage. The material presented here bears out Fox's emphasis on the fluidity of identity in Austronesia. Further, it suggests that it is not just a newborn child whose identity is unfixed (an assumption that is certainly not confined to Austronesian cultures) but that this fluidity of identity continues to a quite remarkable degree into adulthood. In Langkawi birth itself merely begins the process of becoming a person, a process that continues with feeding and living together in houses. Food creates both persons in a physical sense and the substance – blood – by which they are related to each other. Personhood, relatedness, and feeding are intimately connected. To unravel these connections it is necessary to understand the nature and mutability of substance and the way conception, birth, living in houses, and death are connected through the theme of substance.

Fox's remarks address "social" identity. Schneider underscores how in both anthropological analysis and Western notions

> kinship has to do with the reproduction of human beings and the relations between human beings that are the concomitants of reproduction. The reproduction of human beings is formulated as a sexual and biological process. [1984:188]

Both indigenous Western ideas and the analysis of kinship assume that social aspects of a relationship can be separated from, or added to, a biological substratum.

> [S]exual reproduction creates biological links between persons and these have important qualities apart from any social or cultural attributes which may be attached to them. Indeed, the social and cultural attributes, though considered the primary subject matter of anthropologists, and of particular concern to social scientists, are nevertheless derivative of, and of lesser determinate significance than the biological relations. These biological relations have special qualities; they create and constitute bonds, ties, solidary relations proportional to the biological closeness of the kin (though the correlation between the strength of the tie and the closeness of the kin may not be perfect beyond primary kin). These are considered to be natural ties inherent in the human condition, distinct from the social or cultural. [Schneider 1984:188]

Schneider gives a trenchant critique of the way that anthropologists since Morgan have applied these ideas, derived from Western notions, to the analysis of kinship in other cultures. He convincingly shows that not all societies have something called "kinship" defined in these terms, and this is the basis of his thoroughgoing rejection of the category "kinship" in anthropological analysis. The material I present on notions of relatedness in Langkawi supports much of Schneider's argument. In these ideas kinship is not always derived from procreation. I would nevertheless seek to rescue kinship from its post-Schneiderian demise. Although Schneider gives a convincing critique of the way kinship has been defined in anthropological analysis and the way it has been studied cross-culturally, he does not suggest that it might be possible to get beyond the criticisms he makes except by abandoning the comparative use of kinship as an analytic category.[1]

On the basis of ideas about relatedness in Langkawi, I suggest a more flexible definition of kinship. Instead of asking, as Schneider does, "Given this definition of kinship, do these particular people have it or do they not?" (1984:200), I attempt to show, first, how people in Langkawi define and construct their notions of relatedness, and then what values and meanings they give these notions. On the basis of these local notions, I show how the separation of the "social" from the "biological," which Schneider has shown to be at the heart of the historical definition of kinship in anthropology, is culturally specific. Recently, Ingold (1991:360–365) has argued that this distinction is both culturally constructed and peculiar to Western thought: it is difficult to find any comparable division for many non-Western people. The distinction is certainly less than useful in understanding relatedness as Malays in Langkawi understand it.

In the conclusion of this article I suggest how the Malay understandings not only challenge traditional anthropological definitions of kinship but also how they offer the possibility of getting beyond Schneider's critique and of re-defining kinship in a more flexible and open way. The merging of levels, the elusiveness of boundaries within indigenous ideas, is a central theme of this article. Boundaries between people and what they consume – food – or between people and the structures in which they live – houses – may be less clear than we tend to assume. In the Malay case houses and food are not merely inanimate entities. Both houses and food share many qualities with the people they contain or nourish; the boundaries between the container and the contained are at some levels unclear.

Of course, it is impossible to cover the whole range of relations and their symbolic associations within the confines of a short article. Here I focus strictly on notions about substance and the way it is acquired through feeding. My intent is to show how bodily substance is not something with which Malays are simply born and that remains forever unchanged, and to show how it gradually accrues and changes throughout life, as persons participate in relationships. First, however, it is necessary to emphasize the centrality of houses, women, and siblingship to Malay kinship and the way these are symbolically linked together. Siblingship, houses, and hearths are in fact central to the way shared substance is conceived.

Houses, Hearths, Women, and Siblings

The house has a fundamental structural significance for Malays, as it does in many Southeast Asian societies. Some implications of this emphasis on the house in Southeast Asia have been explored by Lévi-Strauss (1984), among

others.[2] To underline the fact that houses constitute a central feature of social organization in these societies, Lévi-Strauss has used the term "sociétés à maison," house-based societies. While some of the features of Lévi-Strauss's model of the "house-based society" do not apply to Pulau Langkawi (see Carsten 1987a, 1995), his suggestions that the house is both an important indigenous category and that many Southeast Asian societies can be analyzed in terms of the house are fertile ones.

Perhaps the most important principle embodied by the house in Langkawi is that of unity and resistance to division. Household unity is reflected in the spatial arrangements of the house, which show a minimum of division. In particular, houses never have more than one hearth, *dapur*. However many couples reside together in one house, they always cook and eat full meals together; rice is a main constituent of these meals. To eat such meals in other houses is much frowned upon, and children from an early age are taught to return home for full rice meals. This commensality is a prime focus of what it means to be of one household.

Houses in Langkawi are strongly associated with women. In the first place this is because women spend much of their time there, while men are absent during most of the day on fishing trips, in the coffee shops, or at the mosque. The association between women and houses, however, should not be construed as merely symptomatic of their absence from another, "public" domain. Women are particularly and positively associated with the focal space of the house, the *dapur*, a term that is used for the hearth, the kitchen, and the main living area of the house.[3] It is in the dapur that women perform the activities that are central to the reproduction of the house and its members: here food is cooked and eaten, and here women spend a great deal of their daytime work and leisure hours.

People in Langkawi make explicit the association between women and houses when they say that while a widowed woman may live in a house by herself, a widowed man may not. A house without a woman living in it is not a proper house because it does not have a "mother of the house," *ibu rumah*. The association is also asserted symbolically. When houses are built, the senior woman to reside there, the "mother of the house," must hold the central post, *tiang seri*, as it is erected. This post is the abode of the house spirit, *semangat rumah*, who is also female. Houses are decorated and adorned just as women are, and this is another aspect of the way houses are conceived as female.

Houses are also strongly associated with children. New houses are never established until a couple has at least one child, and this is part of an enormous emphasis on children in marriage. The unity of the house, which I mentioned above, is also conceived in terms of siblingship. As McKinley (1981) has emphasized, siblingship is the most elaborated relation in Malay kinship, a relation from which all others may be said to derive.[4] In Langkawi distantly related people who are asked to explain how they are connected will always express their link in terms of a sibling bond between ancestors.[5] Many spirits appear in stories and myths as siblings, and in these cases their parentage is always unknown.

The importance of siblingship in other areas of Malaysia has also been underlined by Banks (1983:141–142) for mainland Kedah, and by Peletz (1988) for the "matrilineal" Malays of Negeri Sembilan. In Langkawi, as elsewhere, siblings are expected to render aid to each other and to remain close throughout life; this is especially evident in the warm, affectionate relations that occur between adult sisters. The relation between brothers is much more attenuated: while they adhere to the same ideal of sibling solidarity, brothers tend to avoid close cooperation in adult life (see also Carsten 1989, 1990; McKinley 1981:337–339; Peletz 1988:29, 40–41). Older brothers often have affectionate relations with younger sisters, and this has a structural significance in that it provides a model for the relation between husband and wife. Normatively a married couple should use the terms "older brother" and "younger sister" to address each other (although they may avoid this in practice); these terms capture the ideal of affection, equality, and respect on which marriage should be based. The modeling of marriage on siblingship means that affinity has a special status as it is always in the process of being transformed into consanguinity (see Carsten 1991; McKinley 1981:348–354).

Siblings are conceived as a more or less indivisible set, and this principle is expressed in naming systems for siblings that emphasize their similarity and completeness (see Carsten 1987b:143–191; McKinley 1981). If an in-marrying husband disrupts the natural order of the sibling group by marrying a woman whose older brother or sister is still unwed, he is said to "step over the threshold," *langkah bendul*. This phrase implies that the husband in such cases is viewed as violating the integrity of the house itself, and he incurs a ritual fine.

The association between a set of siblings and the house in which they originate is made ritually at the time of birth. Each child belongs to a set of "birth siblings" whose existence precedes birth. The child and the placenta, *uri*, are conceptualized as "two siblings," *dua beradik*. When a child is born, the uri – conceived as the younger sibling – is washed by the midwife and placed in a woven basket together with various ritual objects. It is then buried by the father on the grounds of the house-compound in a manner that recalls the burial of human corpses in the graveyard outside the village. The placenta sibling can cause sickness and mood changes in the child.[6] What I would stress here is the way that the sibling set, in this ritual, is anchored to the house.

Siblingship thus asserts itself in the womb before birth and continues to influence a person's fortunes throughout life. The uterus may be considered the siblings' first house,[7] and the placenta sibling can be considered as the child's first commensal relation. Co-eating, which is constitutive of kinship, begins before birth. Houses occupied after birth merely create a weaker form of siblingship than that created in the womb. The very notion of personhood can be said to involve the relation of commensal siblingship since even an only child – highly undesired – has its placenta sibling. Although individuals may lack or be separated from human siblings, they are still part of sibling sets whose other members closely affect their well-being.

Notions of the person reflect the fundamental importance of siblingship in another way. Each person is said to have a life spirit or essence, *semangat*. The semangat is not, however, confined to people – animals and plants, for example, have a semangat too. The most important semangat are those of people, rice, houses, and boats. The semangat, then, is considered a vital principle of things that are valued. Each house, person, and boat only has one semangat, whose unity is highly ambivalent. The semangat is said to be one of seven siblings, but the seven members of this set do not have any independent existence. They are seven in number, but only one is active. It is as if they formed a kind of sevenfold unity. And this unity is perceived in terms of the sibling relation. Endicott, who draws on various sources, many of them published at the beginning of this century, discusses how

> the vital principle permeates the whole of the physical world, and its division into *sěmangat* is an integral part of the division of matter into significant discrete "things". On the conceptual plane, the *sěmangat* contributes to the object's identity, preventing it being merged into another concept, and this is expressed in physical terms as the function of the *sěmangat* to guide the actions and preserve the boundaries of the body. ... Each *sěmangat* is naturally differentiated and defined to the same degree as its body. [1970:63]

The person is thus both individual and multiple. Each body is the container of a sibling set. The semangat of the person is part of a seven member set, which may be likened to the parts of the body. Persons and their bodies have a multiple identity, and this is conceived in terms of the relation of siblingship. The human sibling set is closely associated with the house that gives it life, and the notion of semangat makes clear an association between the life-stuff of persons, houses, and siblings.[8]

Houses, hearths, feeding, women, and sibling sets are all intimately bound up with each other and with the way kinship is lived and conceptualized in Langkawi. These connections emerge more clearly through an examination of how substance derives from feeding.

Feeding and Shared Substance

Feeding is said to begin in the womb. In its first house the child is nourished by its mother's blood. After birth, the milk fed to a baby from its mother's breast is believed to derive from the mother's blood. People say that "blood becomes milk," *darah jadi susu*. The mother's milk is immensely important to a child's physical and emotional development and to the child's connection with its mother. Children who are not breast-fed supposedly become ill; they may also fail to "recognize" their mothers.

Milk feeding also defines the prime category of incestuous relations: kin who have drunk milk from the breast of the same woman may not marry. This is an Islamic prohibition, but one that seems to gain additional salience for Malays because of the particular way it fits into notions that otherwise might not be considered in religious terms. Given local concepts of kinship, it is particularly important that this category of incestuous relations, prohibited in Islam, be primarily constituted by siblings.

The salience of a prohibition on marriage between milk siblings is rendered greater by the fact that many children spend a considerable part of their childhood in houses other than their maternal ones. The frequency of formal and informal fostering arrangements (see Carsten 1991) substantially increases the possibility that a child may drink the milk of a woman who is not its birth mother. It is this possibility that gives this definition of incest its particular fascination and horror. It is quite easy to imagine that a child who has been casually put on the breast of a neighbor or distant kinswoman might later marry her child. This ever-present threat looms large in the minds of villagers and runs through their discourse on incest. Women often described to me how in the past one might easily have given a child a breast to comfort it, but that now this is not done.[9] If two of the children a woman had breast-fed later married each other, she would bear responsibility for the incest.

The substance that kin are said to share derives in a large part from their shared consumption of milk as babies. Milk feeding also makes reference to blood since, as I mentioned earlier, human milk is believed to be produced from blood circulating in the body. In these notions the blood shared through consumption of milk is, of course, only that of the mother or the woman from whose body the milk comes. Shared blood is shared female substance; it is never paternal blood. In the context of widespread fostering arrangements of different kinds, co-feeding can create shared blood, shared substance, and kinship. People in Langkawi say, "If you drink the same milk you become kin," *kalau makan sama susu, jadi adik-beradik*. "You become one blood, one flesh," *jadi satu darah, satu daging*.

Ideas about incest have a number of important implications that apply to feeding more generally. Blood itself is said to be created in the body from food, and the prime food for Malay is cooked rice. *Darah, daging mari pada nasi*, "Blood, flesh come from cooked rice," people say. Those who do not eat rice become "dry," *kering*. Such individuals have no "blood," and of them it is said, "All that remains is bones," *tinggal tulang sahaja*.

Eating rice and eating a meal are synonymous in Malay perception. Food is rice – the defining component of a proper meal. The day-to-day sharing of rice meals cooked in the same hearth (which is a definitive activity for those who live in the same house) thus also implies shared substance, albeit in a weaker sense than for milk siblings. There exists a continuum between rice (food), milk, and blood. The sharing of any or all of these connotes having substance in common, hence being related.[10] Traditionally, after being given the mother's breast a child was ritually fed cooked rice and banana because "cooked rice becomes blood too," *nasi jadi darah juga*. A baby's body is cold at birth and, since breast milk – like blood – is hot, the baby becomes heated through breast-feeding. After this the baby can consume rice with its kin in the way that is constitutive of relations within one house.

Just as relatedness is thought of in terms of a continuum – one is more or less distantly related, and only rarely are the related categorically opposed to the unrelated – we find a parallel in the realm of substance and feeding. Mothers and their offspring and full siblings are most closely related, having blood in common. In fact, the blood of siblings is identical. I was once told that when someone is ill and requires a blood transfusion, they must be given the blood of nonrelatives rather than the blood of a sibling. If the blood requires changing, then that of a sibling would have no effect because it is the same as one's own. More distant than full siblings, but still close enough for marriage to be incestuous, are those, like foster siblings, who have drunk the same milk. Those raised in one house who have shared meals with each other on a daily basis could technically marry. They are very unlikely to do so, however, because this would carry connotations of incest.

If milk and blood are the prime sources of shared substance, it would seem to follow that transfusions of blood might be problematic in terms of incest. When I asked about the implications of receiving blood during operations in hospital, villagers seemed rather perplexed and worried. Generally, they referred me to those experts who they thought might know the answer, but their own creativity eventually supplied an answer (in accord with the logic of local notions of kinship): donated blood does not carry the potentiality of incest because it is not eaten (*bukan makan, bubuh, tambuh*, "it is not eaten, it is put there, added"). I was told only *eating* the blood could render relations potentially incestuous.

It is important to emphasize the way that this axis of relatedness operates through women. Blood, milk, and rice meals derive from women, and all denote commonality and similarity. Blood, milk, and food are more than a source of physical strength. The emotional tie children have with their mother is thought to be particularly strong, because mothers are the source of shared substance. Shared substance gives emotions and words a special effectiveness. Love for one's mother derives from being breast-fed: as people say, *makan susu badan, kasih ke ibu lagi*, "drinking milk from her body, you love a mother more." If a baby is given away it should first be given its mother's milk. If it does not at least taste this milk it will not recognize its mother. It is because children share blood with their mother that a mother's curse is thought to be especially powerful.[11]

The mother's milk is thus the source both of shared substance and of the strong emotional bond between mother and child. It enables the child to recognize its mother. It is in this sense the enabling substance of kinship. If a mother dies before giving her child her milk, then, before it leaves the house, the child should be given water cooked in the house hearth. This is the only possible substitute for the mother's milk. It implies that the hearth itself is a source of shared substance, of attachment to the house and its occupants.

Women and hearths can produce kinship in another way. When children are fostered they are said to take on the character traits and the physical attributes of those who raise them. They come to resemble them, in the same way that children often resemble their birth parents (see Carsten 1991).[12] These speculations "at the margins" of normal occurrence – when a child is fostered, when a mother dies, when blood is given in transfusion – show very clearly that notions of shared substance to which blood and milk are central are also very much bound up with ideas about shared consumption, feeding, and the house hearth.

I have described a continuity between the relatedness of a mother and child or full siblings who are thought to share bodily substance, which in turn is partly derived from procreation, and those who are considered to share substance because they live in one house and eat rice meals together. These ideas show very clearly that kinship in Langkawi cannot be defined solely in terms of procreation, but also that it may be difficult to distinguish ties we would consider "biological" because they are derived from procreation from those we think of as "social" because they derive from commensality. These notions challenge us to rethink the conventional distinction between the biological and the social that Schneider has shown to be at the heart of anthropological definitions of kinship. I will return to this question in the conclusion.

That blood and milk should be central to ideas about bodily substance is not particularly surprising. But the fact that substance is conceptualized in terms of food cooked in the dapur means that food and the heat of the house hearth have a particular importance. This is vividly reflected in notions about conception and childbirth. It is to these ideas that I will now turn.

Conception, Birth, and Feeding[13]

According to Malays in Langkawi children are created from the seed, *benih*, of their father and the blood, *darah*, of their mother. The father's seed comes from the fluid in the backbone, *air tulang belakan*. The seed spends 40 days inside the body of the father. The first, 15th, and 30th days of the month are the "days on which the seed falls," *hari jatuh benih*. The seed then "descends to the mother," *turun ke ibu*, where it mixes with the menstrual blood. It only has to mix with the blood of the mother once in order to conceive. The seed is then nourished in the mother's womb from her blood. People say that the blood of the mother becomes the child. And blood, as we have seen, is transformed food.

Both sex and conception are associated with heat and with blood. Marriage involves a process of heating that may be counteracted by ritual means. Massard (1980:359) reports that the absorption of heating food leads to a surplus of sexual energy. In Langkawi, a couple that has consummated its marriage may be described as "cooked," *masak* (a term that also means "ripe" or "mature" and can have sexual connotations in all usages). Before consummation the man and woman are said to be "raw," *mantah*.[14] Once women are old, after menopause, they "have no blood," *darah t'ada*, and they cannot conceive. I was told by the village midwife that male infertility results from a lack of seed, for which there is no cure. Since female infertility is attributed to problems of the blood, it is perceived as alterable – as are other aspects of blood.[15]

Another middle-aged woman told me that infertility in women can be caused by "a thing," *benda*, in the uterus that "eats the seed," *makan benih*. It bores a hole in the uterus so that the blood escapes, and, since it is the blood that "grows the child," *membesar anak*, the fetus cannot survive in its absence. The boring of this hole causes bad pains just before menstruation. Severe menstrual pains are therefore associated with infertility. Such problems are potentially curable, however, through the consumption of medicine and proper food.

Menstruation, sex, and pregnancy are times of body heating. For conception to take place the body must be hot and healthy, *badan hangat, sihat*. It is the "blood of menstruation" that "becomes the child," *darah haidh jadi anak*. Menstrual blood is thus a potential child, and a good flow is a sign of fertility. At the end of the sixth month of pregnancy, according to Endicott (1970:65, citing Annandale and Robinson 1903:93–94), the fetus receives a *nyawa*, soul or "life-breath," and "becomes a person," *jadi orang*, having previously been part of its mother's blood. In Langkawi it is at this point that the services of the village midwife, *bidan*, are secured by the husband's mother, and it is also from this time on, Malays believe, the fetus can sustain life. At this point in a woman's first pregnancy the midwife performs a ritual "bathing of the stomach," *mandi perut*, of the pregnant mother, and a small feast is held to ensure a safe and easy delivery.

During the delivery itself the semangat of the child is believed to come into existence at the moment when the umbilical cord is cut by the midwife. The semangat is said to "come of itself," *jadi sendiri* (Endicott 1970:51, citing Annandale and Robinson 1903:97). It has no existence before this moment.[16] The midwife must cut the umbilical cord with a special bamboo knife rather than a metal one, because metal frightens spirits (in this case the semangat), and that would cause sickness in the child. Generally, if the semangat leaves the body a person is thought to become vulnerable to intrusion by spirits (see Endicott 1970:51). It is the semangat that maintains the boundaries of the body. At the moment when the umbilical cord is cut, the child is also given a name by the midwife. (Names are often changed later, however, and this can be linked to the fluidity of identity.) At the point that the child is physically detached from the body of its mother, it gains the components of its independent identity: a name and a semangat, a life force and a bounded body.

The rituals following childbirth are elaborate and complex (see Laderman 1983:174–207 and Skeat 1900:333–348 for fuller descriptions of birth rites among Malays elsewhere). I will only give a partial account here, focusing on how such rites were conducted at the time of my fieldwork in Langkawi. Briefly, the rites reflect a concern to protect the participant's body from the dangers of invasion by spirits that may cause sickness and infertility. Such spirits are thought to enter through the extremities of the body. Babies are swaddled during the first weeks of life, and an iron object may be kept near them because babies are particularly vulnerable to loss of the semangat and attack by spirits. Such spirits are presumably attracted by the "dirt of childbirth" *kotor beranak*,

which is removed through ritually shaving and bathing the child.[17] These ideas imply that the child, who is still strongly attached to its mother, is not yet properly bounded. Although the newborn receives considerable ritual attention, the baby's mother is the subject of greater attention. By focusing on the mother in the ensuing discussion I aim to amplify further how fertility and becoming a person are assured through the consumption of proper food and through the heat of the hearth.

During the 44-day period of postpartum taboos, *pantang beranak*, both the child and its mother are confined to the house and, particularly, to the dapur. One aspect of this period of restrictions is especially striking – the continued application of heat to the mother. Immediately after the birth and for some days following, she bathes in hot water inside the house, whereas normal bathing is done at the well with cold water.[18] Most importantly, throughout the period of postchildbirth prohibitions, she must not consume foods that are considered to be "cooling."[19] All Malay foods are classified according to their "heating" and "cooling" properties, and women are extremely careful to consume the correct types of food at this time. They spend many happy hours discussing the heating properties of different foods.

The most explicit postpartum ritual is the traditional practice of heating the mother on a platform, *gerai* or *salaian*, beneath which a dapur (fireplace, hearth) is constructed by the midwife. Skeat describes the process:

> The fire (*api saleian*) is always lighted by the Bidan, and must never be allowed to go out for the whole of the 44 days. To light it the Bidan should take a brand from the house-fire (*api dapor*), and when it is once properly kindled, nothing must be cooked at it, or the child will suffer. [1900:342, n.2][20]

This heating is no longer performed in Langkawi, although many middle-aged women described to me how it had been done when they gave birth. The platform was built in the dapur, kitchen, of the house. The fire underneath it was lit by the midwife from the house hearth, *dapur masak*. Oil was rubbed into a woman's back and she leaned her back against the gerai so that she became properly heated from behind. Women say their "body was cooked," *masak badan*, "cooked inside," *masak didalam*.

Today, postpartum women still apply to their stomachs a stone, *batu tungku*, which has been "cooked in the hearth," *masak dalam dapur*, and then wrapped in cloth (see Gimlette 1971[1939]:245; Laderman 1983:176; Skeat 1900:343). In the past, I was told, more heat was applied frequently and with greater force. The stone was used until the skin became blackened, the prohibitions more strictly observed, hot medicines were used, cold food not eaten at all, and, supposedly as a result, women were more healthy.

It is evident that the process of heating involved in the postchildbirth rituals is designed to counteract the cooling effect of giving birth, a cooling particularly associated with excessive bleeding (Laderman 1983:41). The hot blood lost in childbirth cools the body excessively, rendering it vulnerable to the effects of the consumption of cooling foods.

Both the midwife and other women expressed their belief that if the postpartum proscriptions were not observed the mother would become sick. In particular, they feared that women would become afflicted with *sakit meroyan*, translated by Gimlette (1971:167) as "diseases after childbirth."[21] In Langkawi I was told sakit meroyan means that the "blood is cold," *darah sejuk*, so that it could not flow. The consumption of cold foods during the period of postpartum prohibitions could lead to various kinds of sakit meroyan. These included *kudis meroyan*, skin disease; *gila meroyan*, meroyan madness; *sakit kancing gigi*, lockjaw; *demam*, fever; *bisa*, blood poisoning; bleeding; swelling of the blood vessels; and *keras*, in which the body goes hard and stiff like a plank, preventing speech.[22] Women in Langkawi also spoke of "wind" entering and "rising," *naik angin*, up the body.[23]

Women's principal fears are of bleeding, *darah turun*, and that the "uterus might swell," *sarong anak kembang*, after childbirth. During pregnancy, women say, the uterus swells; after birth it becomes loose and there is a danger that it might prolapse. During labor itself, however, it is considered healthy to bleed a lot, because the body becomes *bisa*, septic, poisoned, unless the blood of childbirth is ex-

pelled. This blood is considered to be dirty, *kotor*, and must leave the mother's body so that her body may become light, *ringan*. The flow should then dry up, and the blood vessels of the uterus and stomach should shrink, *kecut*. *Meroyan* is a general sickness following childbirth that takes many forms. Women say there are 44 different kinds of sickness, and their origin invariably lies in the blood. The blood is sick, *sakit darah*. "Meroyan comes from blood that isn't good," *nak jadi meroyan dari darah tak elok*.

The beliefs surrounding meroyan sickness show a deep concern with the boundaries of the body. In some contexts the meroyan is likened to an external malevolent spirit, *hantu* (it is "a kind of spirit," *jenis hantu*), but it is also described as "a kind of blood," *jenis darah*. According to one midwife, the origin of meroyan is postpartum women, within their blood. Blood that is not good is said to descend back, *turun balik* (i.e., does not flow out of the body). She told me that a spirit, hantu, is different, it is not inside women. Whereas meroyan is a sickness inside the body, *sakit dalam badan*, a hantu is from outside, *dari luar*.[24]

Metal implements such as scissors, betel nut cutters, or a nail in the hair are taken to the well by women who have recently given birth to guard against invisible spirits prone to attack postpartum women. Such spirits want to eat women's blood. Especially feared at this time is Langsuir, a vampire spirit of a woman who died in childbirth. She has a hole in her back and very long hair that covers it. She lives in trees in the jungle and especially likes the blood of women who have just given birth. She can take any form, animal or human, but often appears as a beautiful woman. She may be rendered harmless by plugging the hole in her back with a nail or other metal object; she is then immobilized so that she cannot fly.

This nexus of ideas about blood and heat is applied not only to women's health and fertility but also to men's. All Malay boys are circumcised according to Islamic rites and for religious reasons. Circumcision is also strongly linked in local terms to marriage and male reproduction. This is clear in the timing of the ritual, its form, and in men's comments on it. The food taboos imposed on boys after circumcision bear a strong resemblance to postpartum taboos: in both cases there is a restriction on the intake of "cooling" foods (see Laderman 1983:63; Massard 1978:148), although the restrictions applied to boys after circumcision last only until the wound is healed. I was told that cold food would lead to swelling; *angin*, wind, might enter the wound preventing it from healing. Once again this is linked to a control of bleeding and concern that the wound should heal rapidly. While these regulations are less restrictive than postpartum taboos, and are taken less seriously, the connection between the two states is evident to villagers.[25]

Both sex and pregnancy imply "overheating"; at marriage and during pregnancy there is an attempt to keep cool. Excessive heating in these states leads to abortion, miscarriage, and infertility, perceived in terms of uncontrolled bleeding. In contrast, childbirth implies "overcooling"; women have to be reheated, and this process is closely associated with the consumption of appropriate food, with the hearth, and with fire used for cooking. In meroyan sickness it would seem that overcooling or overheating of the mother – both caused by the ingestion of cold foods or by wind entering the body – results either in the retention of bad blood, or in excessive bleeding. In practice, the two effects are equivalent, as Lévi-Strauss has observed in a South American context:

> [Women] are perpetually threatened – and the whole world with and through them – by the two possibilities...: their periodic rhythm could slow down and halt the flow of events, or it could accelerate and plunge the world into chaos. It is equally conceivable that women might cease to menstruate and bear children, or they might bleed continuously and give birth haphazardly. [1978:506]

Marriage, circumcision, and childbirth are all symbolically and ritually associated. In childbirth and circumcision the regulated bleeding of women and men is linked to their proper fertility and to the reproduction of the house (see Massard 1978:148). In both cases this is assured through feeding and the heat of the dapur. It is the dapur that both equilibrates the heat of the body through the provision of food of appropriate heat and controls the flow

of blood leaving the body.[26] The centrality of the dapur to processes that might be considered as much "biological" as "social" once again underscores the difficulty of distinguishing the two as separate spheres in the case of Pulau Langkawi.

Both the symptoms of meroyan sickness and its various causes can also be read as a subtle speculation on bodily boundaries. The origins of the disease are in fact at once external and internal: childbirth itself, the ingestion of food, wind, and blood that is retained instead of being released, becoming poisoned. The typical symptoms are also suggestive: lockjaw, skin disease, bleeding, and fever. The body's boundaries seem to become either too permeable or too rigid. Meroyan sickness can be thought of as both similar to and dissimilar from spirit possession. It is at once internal and external in causation and effect. Appropriately, after childbirth, when the body's boundaries have opened to produce another body from within, normal health in the mother is restored through the reassertion of these boundaries. The boundaries of the baby are equally problematic: the child is liable to lose its semangat and to be penetrated by spirits.

The Substance of Death

If life, blood, and fertility are associated with heat, it is not at all surprising to find that death should be associated with cold. The apparent obviousness of this connection should not prevent us, however, from trying to understand its meaning as fully as possible. That people in Langkawi make this association in an extremely emphatic way suggests that its meaning is both more central and more complex than might be assumed. "Death is *really* feeling cold," *mati, rasa sejuk sunggu*, I was told. "If there is heat, it's all right, there's still life," *kalau hangat, t'apa ada lagi nyawa*. Death was described as a state of coldness and stiffness, and a feeling of extreme coldness could be interpreted as a sign of imminent death. But there was more to it than that.

"At the time of death the soul leaves the body and all the blood flows out," *masa dia mati, cabut nyawa, darah terbit*. The blood leaves the body but humans cannot see this. "There is no blood at all in the body," *t'ada darah langsung dalam badan.* The dead become bones and empty blood vessels without flesh or blood. If a person dies in the house, the blood from the corpse is believed to flow everywhere and become mixed with all the food in the house. "Everything becomes soaked in blood," *darah basah apa-apa.* Consequently, nothing that has been in a house at the time of a death may be eaten. Neither already cooked food nor raw products such as betel quids or water stored in the house can be consumed at this time. Most importantly, no food may be cooked in the house from the time immediately before a death until after the burial has taken place. Meals may be prepared on a fire made outside the house or in other houses, and must be consumed elsewhere.

After the corpse has been buried according to the Muslim rites, the floor of the house is washed and food can once again be eaten normally. Death, then, negates the life of the house and of its hearth. A house with death in it cannot simultaneously produce food and life. There is no cooking and no feeding. Death involves the loss of the substance of life – the blood, derived, as we have seen, from women.

Violent death by accident or intention has other implications. I was told several stories of murder in which it is clear that the taking of life affected the murderer as dramatically as the victim. A murderer became weak, powerless, and frightened; in this state the murderer was thus liable to be caught. The only way to prevent this was to drink the blood – life substance – of the victim. By performing the act of a vampire spirit, the murderer became "like a spirit," *macam hantu.* The act of drinking blood lent the murderer superhuman powers, and particularly the ability to appear and disappear at will and to evade pursuers. In this way the killer became brave, *berani,* and powerful, *kuasa.* Given all the attributes of a spirit but the substance of a human, the murderer was considered doubly alive, supersubstanced.[27]

The murderer, then, was faced with two possibilities: either to be consumed by the victim's substance or to be empowered by consuming it. Once again the notion of feeding is crucial. It is the act of feeding that confers power. The equation of murderers with vampires makes clear that this feeding is in every way negatively construed. Feeding on blood is the negation of feeding on rice cooked in the house hearth: it is death dealing rather than life giving; it negates human ties rather than producing them.[28]

Hearths, Feeding, and Substance: The Process of Becoming Related

I have described how the house in Langkawi is a "female" structure, but that it also "contains" the notion of siblingship. Women and siblingship have been shown to lie in equal measure at the core of the house as a domain of meaning. I have described the house as an expanded hearth, and it is in the *dapur* that the most important reproductive activities are carried out, notably, cooking, eating, and childbirth.[29]

I have given an extended discussion of notions of substance. These are subtle and complex. At their heart lie ideas about blood. Kin share blood, but the degree to which this is true varies. Siblings, and mothers and their children – all of whom share substance to a high degree – are most closely related. This is why the affective ties between a mother and her children, and between siblings, are said to be particularly strong. Blood is not simply a substance with which one is born – it is continuously produced and transformed from food that is eaten. Endicott (1970:82, 85) has suggested that blood, having a quality intermediate between organized physical bodies and undifferentiated matter, derives its power from its potential for being organized. Blood is a potential child.

Milk, too, has a particular significance in these ideas about substance and relatedness, since it is both a bodily substance and food to be consumed. It may be understood as the enabling substance of kinship: a source of emotional and physical connectedness. But relatedness is not so simple. To a lesser degree, food cooked on the natal hearth has the same qualities as milk. Through the day-to-day sharing of meals cooked in the same hearth, those who live together in one house come to have substance in common. From this point of view, eating such meals in other houses has negative implications, and children are strongly discouraged from doing so. Eating meals in other houses implies a dispersal of intimate substance to other houses.

This argument implies that husband and wife also eventually come to share substance. While I have heard no direct statements to this effect, it seems to me entirely in accord with the logic of marriage, which, as described above, is itself modeled on siblingship. As they become more familiar with each other, the relationship of a married couple recalls many aspects of that between older brother and younger sister. In this sense, as McKinley (1981) has argued, Malay marriage can be thought of in processual terms as converting "strangers" and "affines" into "kin."

In a culture in which people often move to different houses, these ideas gain further salience. The frequency of divorce, and temporary or more permanent fostering, lend an enormous force to the idea that living and eating together is one way of coming to share substance. This has further significance, however, in the historical context of demographic mobility characteristic of Langkawi. Feeding is one way in which strangers and outsiders can begin their incorporation into a village community, a process that continues with fostering and marriage. The converse process means that if close kin move to the mainland or to other villages in Langkawi and cease to interact (either because of geographic distance or quarrels) their kinship and that of their descendants effectively lapses.[30]

There are other important implications to the notions I have described. The long process of becoming – acquiring substance – is one that to a very great degree occurs through the actions and bodies of women. Children are produced from their mothers' blood; their mothers' milk may activate or create kinship. The food cooked in the hearth by women not only nourishes physically, it creates emotional ties and is central to the process of becoming related. The dapur is the transforming center of the house, producing life and ensuring the process of kinship.

The material I have presented has another theme: the notion of boundary. Boundaries are sometimes asserted, but they are always tantalizingly elusive. Blood, milk, and rice are similar and convertible into each other, but also different from each other. Houses, likewise, have boundaries within them, but these are systematically negated. The house spirit, who may be said to embody the house, is herself one of seven siblings, although only one of these is active and the degree to which these siblings have separate identities is ambiguous.

These same ideas are echoed in notions of the person. Each individual is part of a sibling set, and these ties are conceived as being more or less unbreakable. Individuals' identities are always bound up with those of their siblings. The semangat of the person, like that of the house, is one of seven siblings. Once again the precise identity of and relationship between the different members of this set is unclear. One might say that persons and houses are simultaneously individual and multiple, just as a human sibling set has both a single and a multiple identity. Although they grow up in one house, after marriage siblings eventually come to be embodied in different houses.

These ideas suggest a subtle and complex speculation on ideas about boundaries. We are confronted with the possibility of boundedness only to see it recede before us. Childbirth, when one body literally produces another from within, brings these concerns to the fore. The boundedness and permeability of both the baby's and the mother's body at this time are especially problematic. Bodies are simultaneously bounded and porous. In some respects it seems hard to say where one person stops and another begins. The person contains the core of relatedness, which is siblingship. What is true for people is also true for houses, and in exactly the same way. If the house is envisaged as a female body, it is also clear that the body is in another way a house, containing other bodies.[31] Like bodies, houses have single and multiple identities that are envisaged in terms of siblingship.

Conclusion: Toward a Redefinition of Kinship

In the introduction to this article I mention Fox's remarks on the fluidity of social identity in Austronesia. Certainly, the material I present here bears out his thesis. My argument, however, goes further. It is clear that not only is "social" identity in Langkawi unfixed, but "physical" identity, a person's substance, is also continuously acquired and alterable. Identity and substance are mutable, fluid, and closely connected.[32] Thus the ideas I describe lead me to question the division – as assumed by Schneider (and perhaps also implicit in Fox's comments) – between the "biological" and the "social," between kinship as a biological, genetic, instant, and permanent relationship, and social identity as fluid. In Langkawi, ideas about relatedness are expressed in terms of procreation, feeding, and the acquisition of substance, and are not predicated on any clear distinction between "facts of biology" (like birth) and "facts of sociality" (like commensality).

For Schneider, the analytical significance of defining kinship in these terms lies in the universality presupposed:

> The Doctrine of the Genealogical Unity of Mankind is a necessary corollary of the way in which kinship is defined (as reproduction) and the way in which reproduction is understood (as a biological process following sexual intercourse), and the fact that "Blood Is Thicker Than Water" for all human beings (the third axiom). If motherhood differed from one society to another, if there were no universal aspects to fatherhood, there could be no standard genealogy against which to plot cultural variants. [1984:195]

Schneider, partly by using his Yapese material, explicitly challenges the idea that procreation is everywhere accorded the same high value as in Western cultures. Although he traces the separation of the "biological" and the "social" in the anthropological study of kinship, however, his own analysis simultaneously (and implicitly) relies on their analytical separation. The distinction itself is not explicitly challenged.

> The second axiom, that kinship, by definition, has to do with human reproduction and that this is a biological process entailing sexual relations, *fails not by reason of its definition*, but rather because of the associated assumptions. These are that kinship is everywhere and always a culturally distinct, distinguishable, and highly valued entity. That is, the fact of engendering another human being . . . is always a culturally distinct construct and is always given a high cultural value. [1984:198; emphasis added]

Schneider is correct to challenge these corollaries: it is because the meaning and centrality of procreation are assumed a priori by most anthropologists that the culturally specific meaning and value of kinship cannot be discovered (see Schneider 1984:199). For Schneider, the category of kinship has no cross-cultural value because its definition is bound up in Western notions. The only solution is to abandon the category completely or to set a more limited agenda: "Given this definition of kinship, do these particular people have it or do they not?" (1984:200).

Schneider does not, however, specifically propose that we abandon the equally "Western," and logically prior, distinction of the biological from the social on which the definition of kinship as a biological process rests. Indeed, while analyzing the way earlier anthropologists have applied this distinction, his own argument appears simultaneously to rely on it (Schneider 1984:95–112). Thus in his conclusion, Schneider argues,

> Blood Is Thicker Than Water is not only axiomatic in studies of kinship, it is a fundamental axiom of European culture. Even if this axiom were true as a biological fact, . . . the point remains that culture, even if it were to do no more than recognize biological facts, still adds something to those facts. The problem remains of just what the sociocultural aspects are, of what meaning is added, of where and how that meaning, as a meaning rather than as a biological fact, articulates with other meanings. [1984:199]

At issue here is the way Schneider speaks of culture as somehow superimposed upon, and adding to, prior biological facts.

Like Schneider (1984:95), I would argue that the relationship between "physical" and "social" kinship is central to the way kinship has been defined by anthropologists. It is only after biological and social ties have been distinguished from each other that kinship can be defined in terms of biology, and accorded a special value; conversely, the "social" – whether as separable aspect of kinship or as something opposed to it – comes to have an implicit "merely" attached to it.

Given our current *definition* of kinship, which Schneider shows to be thoroughly imbued with Western notions, he suggests that we might attempt to discover the culturally variable *meanings* attributed to ideas surrounding procreation. Following this argument, I would suggest that since both the definition *and* the meaning of kinship are culturally variable, we cannot apply a universal definition of kinship to which procreation is central. But – and here I part company with Schneider – this does not mean that we cannot compare both how people conceive of relatedness and the meaning they attribute to it. Schneider rejects a cross-cultural definition of kinship in terms of procreation because procreation may not be central in some cultures. He accepts that other kinds of relationship, which do not derive (or are not perceived as deriving) from procreative ties, may be important; but for Schneider these are necessarily "social" rather than "biological" facts and therefore not kinship within our present definitions.

For Schneider (1984:200–201) the central question is: Given our definition of kinship, do other people have it, and what value and meaning do they give it? I would suggest, by contrast, that the central question should be: how do the people we study define and construct their notions of relatedness and what values and meaning do they give them? It seems to me that we would do better to use the term "kinship" to characterize the relatedness that people act and feel. In this way we may arrive at a new and more flexible approach to the study of kinship in anthropology.

Ideas about relatedness in Langkawi show how culturally specific is the separation of the "social" from the "biological" and the reduction of the latter to sexual reproduction.[33] In Langkawi relatedness is derived both from acts of procreation and from living and eating together. It makes little sense in indigenous terms to label some of these activities as social and others as biological. I certainly never heard Langkawi people do so. It is clear that the important relationships of kinship involve what we would regard as both. If blood, which is the stuff of kinship and to some extent of personhood, is acquired during gestation in the uterus and, after birth, in the house through feeding with others as people in Langkawi assert, is it, then, biological or social? The impossibility of answering this question merely underlines the unsatisfactory nature of the distinction.

Instead, the Malay fascination with boundaries, the subtle way in which distinctions are made only to be erased, may lead us in turn to question and refine the way in which, as anthropologists, we use dichotomies such as that between the biological and the social as analytical tools. If Malay thought on these subjects seems in many respects more subtle than our own, perhaps it is because kinship for Malays is part of a process of speculation as well as a process of becoming.

NOTES

1 My criticisms of Schneider are "friendly" in the sense that I am in broad sympathy with his endeavor and that I agree with, and draw on, much of the argument of his important book without necessarily accepting his conclusions. (I agree particularly with his attack on the procreative model in kinship and his situating of anthropological definitions within Euro-American notions.) In contrast, Yeatman (1983) has presented an argument in favor of the procreative model in kinship, and Scheffler (1991) has criticized Schneider partly for the relativism of his analysis and its lack of explanatory power. Scheffler would keep a universal definition of kinship as a category for cross-cultural comparison but once again his definition is in terms of procreation (1991:373). Like Schneider, I would argue that such a definition does not apply cross-culturally.

2 See also Barraud 1979; Carsten and Hugh-Jones 1995; Errington 1987, 1989; Lévi-Strauss 1979, 1983; Macdonald 1987; and Waterson 1987, 1990 for a discussion of house-based societies in Southeast Asia.

3 I have argued elsewhere (Carsten 1987a) that houses in Langkawi can be seen as expanded hearths.

4 Space does not allow me to elaborate on all the complex associations of siblingship here; in what follows I highlight certain features that are particularly relevant to the present discussion. Elsewhere I explore other aspects of this topic in more detail (Carsten 1987b, 1989, 1990, 1991), as do the authors cited in the text. For the significance of siblingship in Oceania see Marshall 1981.

5   It is significant in this context that migration is very important to the demographic history of Langkawi. Many villagers have described to me how their ancestors came to the island together with siblings.

6   Similar beliefs and practices have been recorded widely elsewhere in Southeast Asia and can be related to a complex cosmology that has been explored by Headley 1983, 1987a, 1987b. See Laderman 1983 and Massard 1985 for a description of these rites in the Malaysian states of Terengganu and Pahang respectively, and see Geertz 1961:89 for Java. In most of the recorded cases, however, the placenta seems to be considered the *older* sibling of the child. One woman in Langkawi told me that whether the placenta sibling is considered older or younger than the child depends on whether age is calculated by time of formation (in which case the placenta is older) or by time of birth (in which case the child is older).

7   See Headley 1987a. This idea is particularly powerful in the case of twins. It is notable that cross-sex twins seem to exercise a particular fascination for the more hierarchical Southeast Asian societies in terms of incest and marriage (see Boon 1977:138–40, 201–202 and Errington 1987). McKinley (1975:226) suggests that once a child begins to be able to socialize in the house it no longer needs to interact with its placenta sibling, from whom it becomes progressively detached.

8   See Endicott (1970:38–39, 41, 50, 63) on the fragmented and unitary nature of the semangat, which he does not, however, discuss in terms of siblingship. Barraud (1990:218, 223) discusses the notion of *mat inya* in Tanebar-Evav in terms strikingly similar to the terms I use in discussing the semangat. The mat inya is a kind of sevenfold life essence of things that have social value.

9   The reference to the past is meant to imply that the villagers had been less aware of the connotations of milk feeding in Islam in the past than they were at the time of my fieldwork.

10 As far as I know, the idea that the shared consumption of food creates a weak form of siblingship is not an Islamic one.

11 Babies are regularly bottle-fed with powdered milk as a supplement to breast milk, but I know of no case where bottle-feeding replaced breast-feeding entirely. While I would expect the impossibility of breast-feeding at all to be quite problematic, there is no indication that supplementary bottle-feeding causes any concern or that it has similar connotations to breast-feeding. Fresh cow's milk is not available in the village.

12 The daily sharing of rice meals defines members of one household. While those who live together are generally close kin, there are important exceptions that are normally thought of in terms of fostering (Carsten 1991). My own experience of living in one house and eating with a family on a daily basis was also one of being fostered, of "incorporation" and of "becoming kin."

13 Some of the material used here was presented in an earlier form in a paper specifically on childbirth (see Carsten 1992).

14 In contrast, Laderman (1983:74) reports in her material on Terengganu that conception occurs when both parents are in a "cool" state. This may be a regional variation, or it may be that while sex produces and requires heat, *jatuh benih*, "dropping of the seed" requires coolness. However, it is clear that in Terengganu heat is believed to have a powerful effect on pregnancy: "hot" medicines have abortifacient and/or contraceptive qualities (Laderman 1983:78–79). "The fetus is considered to be a clot of blood in the early stages, and hot medicine is thought to liquefy the blood, and to make the womb uncongenial for the child" (1983:78). "Hot" foods are avoided during pregnancy in order to control bleeding (1983:82).

15 Ideas about menstrual pollution are not very elaborate in Langkawi. Women may not pray or have sex at this time, and may cause ill fortune to a fishing trip. Elsewhere in Malaysia, Laderman (1983:73) also notes that a scanty menstrual flow is not considered healthy, and that, while sex during menstruation is religiously prohibited, it is also believed to restore potency to a man (1983:74).

16 Interestingly, Endicott (1970:37–38) notes that Cuisinier (1951:207–208) states that a mother gives part of her soul material to her baby.

17 Laderman reports that spirits "are attracted by the sweet smell of the blood of parturition

and the lochia of the puerperium"
(1983:201).

18   Laderman (1983:175) refers to "hot" leaves
added to this water.

19   The categorization of foods according to
their intrinsic "heating" and "cooling" properties is discussed at length by Laderman
(1983:35–72). She discusses postpartum
food restrictions in detail (1983:183–188).
See also Massard 1983:262–268.

20   Together with Laderman (1983:181) I
would argue that use of the terms "roasting"
and "roasting bed" by Skeat (1900:
342–343) and others for these practices is
misleading, and "heating" is more appropriate. What is aimed at is a *regaining* of *lost*
heat through a more gentle warming than
"roasting" implies, that is, a reassertion of
the body's equilibrium not an objective rise
in temperature; see also Massard 1978.

21   Gimlette states that *meroyan* is derived from
royan, "to run, or discharge, of a sore,"
particularly used for "abnormal uterine dis-
charges following childbirth" (1971:167).
He continues, "the causal agent is referred
to as *angin meroyan* (*angin*, wind)"
(1971:167). See also Laderman 1983:98,
201–202.

22   An anonymous reviewer of this article suggested that the symptom of losing speech
makes this condition the inverse of *latah*, in
which women's speech becomes uncontrolled and usually obscene. The suggestion
that various conditions affecting women's
speech (including spirit possession) be
looked at in relation to each other merits
further research.

23   See Laderman 1983:58–60 on angin, glossed
as "temperament." A build up of angin in the
body destroys the balance among the four
elements – earth, air, fire, and water – and
causes sickness.

24   Laderman discusses how sakit meroyan is
caused by the "Hantu Meroyan" that "arises
from the afterbirth, the blood and the amni-
otic fluid" (1983:201).

25   Wilkinson (1957:49) describes a rite performed at circumcision, involving coconuts
rolled over the boy, that strongly recalls that
traditionally undergone by women in the
seventh month of pregnancy.

26   See also Gimlette (1971:49, 245) on heat of
the dapur applied directly to the bukang root
in the treatment of loss of male virility. That

a state of heat may have political implications is suggested by Zainal-Abidin bin
Ahmad (1947) and Laderman (1981), who
note that the Malay ruler's coolness balances
the destructive heat of war, anger, dissent,
and nature that threaten the body politic.
The sultan embodies coolness, which ensures the prosperity of the kingdom.

27   These notions about the power of blood can
be related to Endicott's discussion of the
Malay concept of *badi* (Endicott 1970:
66–86). The badi can be thought of as a
harmful expression of disturbed blood – it
arises from the blood – and, in the case of a
murdered person, it is the badi that makes
this blood especially potent (1970:72). The
badi can eventually become an independent
spirit, which in the case of a murdered
person is likely to be especially powerful
and malicious (1970:73–74). In the case of
a woman who dies in childbirth, it is the
badi that reanimates her body as a vampire
spirit (1970:72). Endicott points out that
vampires, familiar spirits, and badi all
share an intimate connection with human
blood.

28   Once again I am indebted to an anonymous
reviewer for the suggestion that the female
vampire spirit, Langsuir, who attacks
women after childbirth and herself died in
childbirth, can be thought of as the spirit of
"pure alienated kinship." Her untimely
death cuts off the normal process of feeding
and making kinship between mother and
child. The sucking of blood from her victims
is the inversion of the social feeding that
should have occurred had Langsuir not
died in childbirth.

29   Sexual intercourse normally occurs, in privacy, in a couple's sleeping area inside houses.
This is either situated in the main living area,
dapur, or the optional formal room, *ibu
rumah*, or in a small sleeping room, *bilek*,
partitioned off one of these rooms.

30   The implications of this, in a society where
divorce followed by relocation of one or
other spouse is a frequent occurrence, are
intriguing and merit further research. Relations between a divorced father and his children are in fact quite variable, depending
partly on how far away the father lives
from his children.

31   This idea has been explored by Headley
(1987a) for Java. He describes how

the body physically houses siblings during gestation.

32 Fluidity of identity has also been described, if in somewhat different terms, for Melanesia (see, for example, Strathern 1988). Elsewhere in the Austronesian world, Astuti (1995) gives a beautiful example of how the Vezo of Madagascar continuously acquire identity. She explores the implications of this for notions of ethnicity.

33 Our own rather narrow definition of "biology," in which reproduction is separated from nutrition and is seen chiefly as a matter of genetic transmission rather than generation, appears to date from the mid-19th century (see Ingold 1990:209–211; 1991: 359 on the conflation of biology and genetics). In this view the individual is more or less determined at conception, but it is notable that in both the popular and the scholarly culture of early modern Europe the characteristics of a wet nurse were thought to pass to the children she fed because breast-feeding was part of a long process, intrauterine and extrauterine, by which a new individual was generated (see Marvick 1974; Ross 1974).

REFERENCES CITED

Annandale, Nelson, and Herbert C. Robinson 1903 Fasciculi Malayenses: Anthropological and Zoological Results of an Expedition to Perak and the Siamese States, 1901–1902. Anthropology, 1. London: University of Liverpool Press.

Astuti, Rita 1995 The Vezo Are Not a Kind of People: Identity, Difference, and "Ethnicity" among a Fishing People of Western Madagascar. American Ethnologist 22(3): 464–482.

Banks, David J. 1983 Malay Kinship. Philadelphia: Institute for the Study of Human Issues.

Barraud, Cecile 1979 Tanebar-Evav: Une société de maisons tournée vers le large. (Tanebar-Evav: A Society of Houses Turned toward the Open Sea.) Paris: Cambridge University Press.

—— 1990 Kei Society and the Person: An Approach through Childbirth and Funerary Rituals. Ethnos 3–4:214–231.

Boon, James 1977 The Anthropological Romance of Bali 1597–1972. Cambridge: Cambridge University Press.

Carsten, Janet 1987a Analogues or Opposites: Household and Community in Pulau Langkawi, Malaysia. In De la hutte au palais: Sociétés "à maison" en Asie du Sud-Est insulaire. (From the Hut to the Palace: House Societies in Insular Southeast Asia.) Charles Macdonald, ed. Pp. 153–168. Paris: Editions du CNRS.

—— 1987b Women, Kinship and Community in a Malay Fishing Village on Pulau Langkawi, Kedah, Malaysia. Unpublished Ph.D. dissertation, University of London.

—— 1989 Cooking Money: Gender and the Symbolic Transformation of Means of Exchange in a Malay Fishing Community. In Money and the Morality of Exchange. Jonathan P. Parry and Maurice Bloch, eds. Pp. 117–141. Cambridge: Cambridge University Press.

—— 1990 Women, Men, and the Long and the Short Term of Inheritance in Langkawi, Malaysia. Bijdragen tot de Taal-, Land- en Volkenkunde 146:270–288.

—— 1991 Children in Between: Fostering and the Process of Kinship on Pulau Langkawi, Malaysia. Man 26:425–443.

—— 1992 The Process of Childbirth and Becoming Related among Malays on Pulau Langkawi. In Coming into Existence: Birth and Metaphors of Birth. Göran Aijmer, ed. Pp. 20–46. Gothenburg: Institute for Advanced Studies in Social Anthropology.

—— 1995 Houses in Langkawi: Stable Structures or Mobile Homes? In About the House: Lévi-Strauss and Beyond. Janet Carsten and Stephen Hugh-Jones, eds. Cambridge: Cambridge University Press.

Carsten, Janet, and Stephen Hugh-Jones, eds. 1995 About the House: Lévi-Strauss and Beyond. Cambridge: Cambridge University Press.

Cuisinier, Jeanne 1951 Sumangat: L'âme et son culte en Indochine et en Indonésie. (Sumangat: The Soul and Its Cult in Indochina and Indonesia.) Paris: Gallimard.

Endicott, Kirk M. 1970 An Analysis of Malay Magic. Kuala Lumpur, Malaysia: Oxford University Press.

Errington, Shelly 1987 Incestuous Twins and the House Societies of Southeast Asia. Cultural Anthropology 2:403–444.

—— 1989 Meaning and Power in a Southeast Asian Realm. Princeton: Princeton University Press.

Fox, James J. 1987 The House as a Type of Social Organisation on the Island of Roti. In De la hutte au palais: Sociétés "à maison" en Asie du Sud-Est insulaire. (From the Hut to the Palace: House Societies in Insular Southeast Asia.) Charles Macdonald, ed. Pp. 171–178. Paris: Editions du CNRS.

Geertz, Hildred 1961 The Javanese Family: A Study of Kinship and Socialization. Glencoe, IL: Free Press.

Gimlette, John D. 1971[1939] A Dictionary of Malayan Medicine. Kuala Lumpur, Malaysia: Oxford University Press.

Headley, Stephen 1983 Houses in Java: The Missing Kin. Unpublished paper presented to the Seminar on Cognation and Social Organization in Southeast Asia. University of Amsterdam.

—— 1987a The Body as a House in Javanese Society. In De la hutte au palais: Sociétés "à maison" en Asie du Sud-Est insulaire. (From the Hut to the Palace: House Societies in Insular Southeast Asia.) Charles Macdonald, ed. Pp. 133–152. Paris: Editions du CNRS.

—— 1987b The Idiom of Siblingship: One Definition of "House" Societies in Southeast Asia. In De la hutte au palais: Sociétés "à maison" en Asie du Sud-Est insulaire. (From the Hut to the Palace: House Societies in Insular Southeast Asia.) Charles Macdonald, ed. Pp. 209–218. Paris: Editions du CNRS.

Ingold, Tim 1990 An Anthropologist Looks at Biology. Man (N.S.) 26:208–229.

—— 1991 Becoming Persons: Consciousness and Sociality in Human Evolution. Cultural Dynamics 4:355–378.

Laderman, Carol 1981 Symbolic and Empirical Reality: A New Approach to the Analysis of Food Avoidances. American Ethnologist 8:468–493.

—— 1983 Wives and Midwives: Childbirth and Nutrition in Rural Malaysia. Berkeley: University of California Press.

Lévi-Strauss, Claude 1978 The Origin of Table Manners. Introduction to a Science of Mythology, 3. John and Doreen Weightman, trans. London: Jonathan Cape.

—— 1979 La voie des masques. (The Way of the Masks.) Paris: Plon.

—— 1983 Histoire et ethnologie. (History and Ethnology.) Annales 38:1217–1231.

—— 1984 Paroles Données. (Anthropology and Myth: Lectures 1951–1982.) Paris: Plon.

Macdonald, Charles, ed. 1987 De la hutte au palais: Sociétés "à maison" en Asie du Sud-Est insulaire. (From the Hut to the Palace: House

Societies in Insular Southeast Asia.) Paris: Editions du CNRS.

Marshall, Mac, ed. 1981 Siblingship in Oceania: Studies in the Meaning of Kin Relations. ASAO Monographs, 8. Lanham, MD: University Press of America.

Marvick, Elizabeth W. 1974 Nature versus Nurture: Patterns and Trends in Seventeenth-Century French Childrearing. In The History of Childhood. Lloyd de Mause, ed. Pp. 259–301. London: Souvenir Press.

Massard, Josiane 1978 Un retour à la simplicité: L'alimentation de la jeune accouchée en Malaisie. (A Return to Simplicity: Feeding of Postpartum Women in Malaysia.) Asemi 9:141–150.

—— 1980 "Les moineaux avec les moineaux..." Rapport des Malais au monde animale. ("The Sparrows with the Sparrows..." Malay Relations with the Animal World.) Asemi 11:349–363.

—— 1985 The New-Born Malay Child: A Multiple Identity Being. Journal of the Malaysian Branch of the Royal Asiatic Society 58(2):71–84.

McKinley, Robert 1975 A Knife Cutting Water: Child Transfers and Siblingship among Urban Malays. Unpublished Ph.D. dissertation, University of Michigan.

—— 1981 Cain and Abel on the Malay Peninsula. In Siblingship in Oceania: Studies in the Meaning of Kin Relations. Mac Marshall, ed. Pp. 335–387. ASAO Monographs, 8. Lanham, MD: University Press of America.

Peletz, Michael G. 1988 A Share of the Harvest: Kinship, Property and Social History among the Malays of Rembau. Berkeley: University of California Press.

Ross, James B. 1974 The Middle-Class in Urban Italy, Fourteenth to Early Sixteenth Century. In The History of Childhood. Lloyd de Mause, ed. Pp. 183–228. London: Souvenir Press.

Scheffler, Howard W. 1991 Sexism and Naturalism in the Study of Kinship. In Gender at the Crossroads of Knowledge: Feminist Anthropology in the Postmodern Era. M. di Leonardo, ed. Pp. 361–382. Berkeley: University of California Press.

Schneider, David M. 1984 A Critique of the Study of Kinship. Ann Arbor: University of Michigan Press.

Skeat, Walter W. 1900 Malay Magic: An Introduction to the Folklore and Popular Religion of the Malay Peninsula. London: Macmillan.

Strathern, Marilyn 1988 The Gender of the Gift. Berkeley: University of California Press.

Waterson, Roxana 1987 The Ideology and Terminology of Kinship among the Sa'dan Toraja. Bijdragen tot de Taal-, Land- en Volkenkunde 143:87–112.

——1990 The Living House: An Anthropology of Architecture in Southeast Asia. Singapore: Oxford University Press.

Wilkinson, R. J. 1957 Papers on Malay Customs and Beliefs. Journal of the Malay Branch of the Royal Asiatic Society 30(4):1–79.

Yeatman, Anna 1983 The Procreative Model: The Social Ontological Bases of the Gender-Kinship System. Social Analysis 14:3–30.

Zainal-Abidin bin Ahmad 1947 The Various Significations of the Malay Word *Sejok*. Journal of the Malay Branch of the Royal Asiatic Society 20(2):40–44.

Section 2 Contemporary Directions in Kinship

Introduction

Linda Stone

Kinship not only survived Schneider, it gradually began to revitalize. Starting with the end of the 1990s, many new texts and edited books on kinship began to appear (e.g., Holy 1996; Maynes et al. 1996; Parkin 1997; Pasternak, Ember, and Ember 1997; Böck and Rao 2000; Carsten 2000a; Schweitzer 2000a; Stone 2000, 2001a; Feinberg and Ottenheimer 2001; Franklin and McKinnon 2001). Even Schneider (1995: 193) remarked that kinship had "risen from its ashes." Louise Lamphere (2001:21) wrote that kinship never really disappeared but was rather transformed, largely through approaches in feminist anthropology and political economy. And perhaps it would have been difficult for anthropologists to entirely let kinship go, given its longstanding importance to anthropology theory (Holy 1996:165) and its central place in many societies anthropologists study (Parkin 1997: ix).

But there were two other forces at work in the revival of kinship. One was that over the long haul Schneider's work itself had more of a liberating than a destructive impact on kinship. Schneider in effect had freed kinship from biology, making it less Eurocentric and especially appealing to feminists. His deconstruction of the field had also freed kinship and its standard concepts from strict definitions and formal relationships, allowing kinship to then absorb influences brewing elsewhere in anthropology – influences such as a new emphasis on social process and human agency, attention to historical context, interests in political economy and social inequality, and intersections between gender, ethnicity, and class (Stone 2001b).

A second influence was that over the 20-year post-Schneider hiatus during which kinship was little discussed or taught, kinship, marriage, and the family were undergoing profound transformations in Europe and the United States. Rising rates of divorce, the growth of single-parent households, gay and lesbian movements, and advances in New Reproductive Technologies (NRTs) were transforming European and North American society. Some of these new social developments were themselves challenging older, more "biologized" cultural conceptions of kinship in the West, and post-Schneiderian kinship was now prepared to analyze these developments. As a result, many anthropologists are now actively studying these transformations, largely in Europe and America but also elsewhere, through more flexible and culturally sensitive approaches to kinship.

We saw in the previous section that the issue of biology and its relationship with kinship was a key one in the demise and revival of kinship. This issue continues as kinship studies take new directions. While post-Schneiderian kinship has increasingly dismissed biology, a growing current in the field of anthropology is attempting to connect biology to kinship through evolutionary frameworks.

New Reproductive Technologies

The NRTs – surrogate motherhood, artificial insemination, in vitro fertilization (IVF), and combinations thereof – potentially fracture Western concepts of kinship. For example, in the case of contract surrogacy with donor eggs from a third party and conception through IVF, we can distinguish a legal mother, a genetic mother, and a birth mother. Which one is now the "real" mother, or in what sense should we understand motherhood to be shared?

There is by now a substantial anthropological literature dealing with kinship in relation to the NRTs (see especially Ginsburg and Rapp 1991, 1995; Strathern 1992a, 1992b; Edwards et al. 1999; Ragoné 1994; Franklin 1997; Franklin and Ragoné 1998). The work of Marilyn Strathern (1992a), who was among the first in Britain to show the influence of Schneider (Schweitzer 2000b: 5), has been particularly influential. With reference to England, Strathern argued that the effect of the NRTs and the extension of consumer choice to the area of human reproduction was to "destabilize" nature in the English worldview. In effect the availability and use of the NRTs forced the perception of kinship as social construction and as choice. In Strathern's view, in this Euro-American cultural context "nature" can no longer be seen as independent of cultural construction, and kinship can no longer be seen as resting on a "nature" independent of this construction.[1]

While new constructions of kinship are occurring in European and American society and in this process choice is playing a larger role, there is at the same time a counter-current drawing Americans, at least, back to biogenetic conceptions of kinship. This is the new genetics and what Finkler (2001) has called the "medicalization of family and kinship" in America. The new genetics concerns the tremendous advances in research on genetic inheritance, which now promise to alleviate disease and extend human life. More and more diseases are being shown to have a genetic basis, and more and more people are being drawn into their genetic family histories as a means to promote their health or confront their risk factors for specific diseases. As the new genetics very clearly defines "kinship" and "family" biogenetically, it simultaneously reflects and promotes a culturally more traditional American conception of kinship as shared and transmitted biogenetic substance. Finkler shows how this new "medicalization" of family and kinship is reflected in the popular media and affects the everyday experiences of people who learn about their genetic propensity toward specific diseases.

What we may be seeing, then, along with a destabilization of nature and the emergence of choice in kinship is a tension between kinship as choice and social construction and the older cultural conception of kinship as rooted in biological reproduction. A pioneer study of the NRTs that reflects these tensions was Helena Ragoné's investigation of surrogate motherhood in the United States. A chapter of her book, *Surrogate Motherhood: Conception in the Heart* (1994), is reproduced here. Among Ragoné's most interesting findings is the interplay between the old biology and a new sense of choice in kinship constructions among those participating in reproduction through surrogacy. On the one hand, infertile women who seek a surrogate emphasize their positive role, their agency and will, in the creation of the child, one woman phrasing this reproductive process as her own "conception in the heart." On the other hand there is in surrogacy arrangements a strain to replicate, as far as possible, a more orthodox American kinship and family construction. Thus (in "open" surrogacy programs, where participants know one another and interact) the legal mother-to-be and the surrogate form a close bond, with the former participating in the surrogate's experience of pregnancy and birth. If he was the sperm donor, the husband's role is accordingly downplayed. Since he has a biological connection to the child, his parental status is secure and his further active participation might underline his wife's inferior position. Also, since the surrogate is carrying his child, there are disturbing parallels with adultery.

The work of Susan Kahn in Israel challenges Strathern's idea that the NRTs "necessarily displace a culture's foundational assumptions about kinship" (Kahn 2000: 159). The chapter of her book, *Reproducing Jews: A Cultural Analysis of Assisted Reproduction in Israel* (2000), presented here, discusses sperm processing, egg donation, and IVF at an Israeli fertility clinic. The issue of ovum-related technologies of reproduction has particular importance in Israel where Jewish identity is understood to be transmitted matrilineally and to confer citizenship. While clearly these NRTs are raising profound questions about the origin and transmission of Jewishness, Kahn shows how these NRTs are also being made to bend to the force of culture, to traditional conceptions of religious identity and kinship, in the discourse of Israeli rabbis.

Israel is a particularly interesting case for the NRTs. Not only does it provide culturally unique issues concerning kinship and religious transmission, but in addition Israel is culturally and politically pro-natalist. For orthodox women, procreation is not only a right but also a religious duty. Given the strong cultural interest in fertility, it is no surprise that in the mid-1990s there were more fertility clinics per capita in Israel than in any other country. Israel is at the cutting edge of research on and application of these technologies; its clinics draw patients from all over Europe and elsewhere in the Middle East. And all the NRTs are subsidized by the Israeli national health insurance. Indeed, "every Israeli, regardless of religion or marital status, is eligible for unlimited rounds of in-vitro fertilization treatment free of charge, up to the birth of two live children" (Kahn 2000: 2).

In addition to the intense interest in motherhood in the Israeli Jewish context, Kahn's book also discusses fatherhood and the challenges to Jewish tradition that the NRTs bring. Here she focuses on rabbinical arguments about the appropriate uses of artificial insemination for orthodox married couples where the husband is infertile. Orthodox Jewish couples undergo fertility treatment only through the guidance of their rabbi and many will only undergo treatment at special medical facilities under the strict supervision of trained supervisors who monitor all procedures "to ensure that there is no untoward mixing of sperm, eggs, or embryos" (2000: 89). In this context there are a number of intriguing issues. For example, adultery, forbidden in orthodox Judaism, is defined as sexual intercourse between a married Jewish woman and a man other than her husband. Then comes the question, does artificial insemination constitute adultery? Or, "can a Jewish man be permitted to donate sperm for a married Jewish woman other than his wife? And if so, what is the status of the child so conceived?" (Kahn 2000: 95). The concern is great because if artificial insemination *is* adultery, the woman is henceforth prohibited from sexual relations with her husband and the resulting child is considered a *mamzer* (child of an illicit union who is therefore not marriageable).

There are also questions about whether or not a child conceived in this way has a father at all. As a result of the NRTs, rabbis now debate whether Jewish fatherhood is contingent upon a man's sexual intercourse with the mother or upon genetic connection with the child. Because of the importance of these issues in orthodox Judaism, many rabbis discourage orthodox Jewish couples from using third-party Jewish sperm for artificial insemination and encourage the use of non-Jewish donor sperm instead. Yet other rabbis consider this alternative to be an abomination that pollutes Jewishness. What Kahn sees in all these debates is that the NRTs in Israel are responsive to their particular cultural context; they do not necessarily favor choice as in other Euro-American contexts, nor do they necessarily favor genetic relatedness. Rabbinical discourse aims to regulate and define the meaning of the NRTs in accordance with traditional culture.

New Families

In the United States, the tension between biology and choice is also seen in some studies of the new gay and lesbian kinship and family constructions, for example in the article by Corinne Hayden (1995) reproduced here. Hayden reviews the earlier major work in lesbian/gay kinship by Kath Weston (1991) and lesbian motherhood by Ellen Lewin (1993) in terms of how biology is in some contexts denounced and in others made central to the construction of kinship. Hayden then moves to discuss some novel ways through which lesbian co-mothers create their own new families and mutual ties to children. For example, one partner may perform the insemination of the birth mother, or the lesbian co-mothers may both become impregnated by the same donor sperm, creating a biogenetic tie between their children. These people are using biology to construct kinship but are doing so in ways that are in the very process reformulating biology and undermining it as the only factor in kinship creation. What Hayden concludes is that while biology is not being displaced as a symbol in lesbian co-motherhood, it no longer operates as a "natural" taken-for-granted basis of kinship. It becomes explicit, and in this way lesbian co-motherhood strategies confirm Strathern's (1992a) idea that new technologies and strategies of reproduction are destabilizing nature in the construction of Euro-American kinship.

New trends in adoption are also reformulating kinship in the United States (Modell 1994, 2001a, 2001b), while high rates of divorce and remarriage are producing new family forms and kinship concerns in North American society (Stacey 1990; Jacobson, Liem, and Weiss 2001; Johnson 1989). Bob Simpson (1994) shows how divorce and remarriage are also transforming the family in Britain. Simpson refers to the complex social arrangements following divorce and remarriage as the "unclear" family, as opposed to the "nuclear" family of bureaucratic, political, and intellectual imagination in Britain.

Families are possibly nowhere more "unclear" than in the contemporary American soap opera, the subject of Linda Stone's paper. This paper contrasts American soaps of the early 1970s, as studied by Susan Bean (1976), with contemporary soaps to ask, "Has the World Turned?" (from the name of the soap, *As the World Turns*). The answer is yes. American soaps abound with new family forms through divorce and remarriage, adoptions, and novel, intentional families. They appear obsessed with kinship and replete with tensions between biology and choice. Using plotlines and dialogues from two popular shows, the paper shows how soap-opera characters struggle to discover, contest, denounce, and manipulate biological relatedness in their construction of kinship. With reference to Schneider's early study of American kinship, Stone offers a reformulated model of American soap-opera kinship where choice emerges as a new "order," but an order insufficient in itself to create "real" kinship.

Political Economy

Since the 1970s and 1980s, issues of power and inequality have loomed in anthropology, inspiring a trend that has led kinship studies more fully into the realm of the political economy. Current research focuses on interactions between kinship and the state (Goody 1990) and on kinship in relation to political struggles, national identity, and transnational forces (Ginsburg and Rapp 1991, 1995). Those interested in power and inequality found both American cultural anthropology and British structural-functionalism inadequate as a theoretical framework (Lamphere 2001: 21), leading to a renewal of materialist and Marxist approaches and historical analyses (for example Bloch 1975, Meillassoux 1981). In terms of kinship studies, these trends also brought about a renewed link between kinship and socioeconomic structures in ever-widening contexts spanning household economies, national policies, and a transnational or global political economy (Ginsburg and Rapp 1995).

The paper included here by Hua Han shows some of these trends. Her study focuses on mode of production to account for variations in kinship and gender in two rural communities in northern China. Han follows a distinction between "petty capitalist mode of production" and "tributary mode of production" that Hill Gates (1996) uses to analyze variations in kinship, gender, and family life through the broad sweep of Chinese history. Han finds that this same distinction also applies to micro-level village studies in the contemporary post-Mao era where economic changes are impacting Chinese families and, especially, women's domestic choices and economic opportunities. As throughout the history of China, both petty capitalist and tributary modes of production operate in villages in the contemporary period of economic "reform," but in some communities one mode dominates over the other. Where the petty capitalist mode of production is dominant, women are less constrained by traditional kinship norms and have greater flexibility in post-marital residence. At the same time, this mode of production results in some economic discrimination against women. Han also discusses the effects of the Chinese one-child-one-family policy, and how variations in the mode of production account for its very different reception in the two communities of her study.

Back To Biology

Schneider sought to sever cultural anthropology not only from studies of social organization but also from biological anthropology. Connections between biology and culture in any case had been discredited through their associations with racism in the nineteenth century and both racism and sexism in the twentieth. In the view of some anthropologists, however, these associations are not inevitable and the questions about human adaptations that can be addressed by evolutionary biology are not irrelevant to cultural anthropology. As a result, in some anthropological quarters biology is moving back into kinship, although not quite in the way to which Schneider objected. Gone are the days when anthropologists assume that people the world over construct their kinship in terms of presumed biological links. What we see is the re-entry of biology, not as a universal factor *of* kinship construction, but as a potential universal factor (and not the only factor) *behind* human kinship construction and behavior.

Here the important concepts are those developed in neoevolutionary theory, including kin selection, inclusive fitness, parental investment, and reciprocal altruism (see Glossary). Behind all of these is the Darwinian notion that living organisms "seek" (not necessarily consciously, of course) to maximize their fitness, or reproductive success. These concepts have for long been applied to studies of primate kinship (Silk 2001). For human kinship, Robin Fox (Tiger and Fox 1971; Fox 1980, 1989) developed a comparative ethological approach that studies human society from the much broader context of mammalian and primate adaptations, and which treats "the 'cultural' status of social relationships as problematical" (Fox 1997: 209). This approach sees human kinship systems as primarily frameworks for mating and allocation of people to groups. More recently, evolutionary anthropologists, a minority group within social or cultural anthropology, study the extent to which human behavior toward presumed kin (however emically defined), human kinship systems, and cultural ideas about kinship reflect the operation of evolutionary forces in human populations and individuals (e.g., van den Berghe 1979; for a review of these approaches see Hewlett 2001).

Nearly thirty years separate the publication of the two articles by Robin Fox (1975) and by Maurice Bloch and Dan Sperber (2002) reprinted here. During this interval anthropology, kinship studies, and biological approaches to culture have all changed considerably. Yet both of these articles strive to make the same point, namely that human culture is not completely detached from human biological evolution. Both criticize the dominant views of culture of their respective times (the "superorganic" in the case of Fox and "cultural constructivism" in the case of Bloch and Sperber) for their presumption of this detachment or "freedom" of culture.

Though following neoevolutionary theory, neither article supports what was earlier known as sociobiology, which posited that much of human behavior is a direct expression of human genes. Fox, himself critical of sociobiology (1997), refers rather to "evolved behavioral propensities" in the human species, while Bloch and Sperber speak of evolved human "psychological dispositions."

Fox's article looks at human kinship systems in relation to primate kinship. Human kinship systems, in his view, consist of "alliance" (which establishes who can marry whom) and "descent" (which "defines who belongs to what category or how any category is related to any other category") (1975: 11). What Fox finds is that both "alliance" (as mating arrangements) and "descent" (kin groups) exist in primate kinship but never together in the same system; their combination in one system was a uniquely human development. In human kinship systems alliance and descent are not only combined, they are interlocked: the system of descent defines who can marry whom. From an evolutionary perspective, Fox's analysis is insightful and highly original.

Since the publication of Fox's article, primatologists have made subsequent discoveries about primate mating practices and kinship behavior. One is that females in what Fox calls "one-male groups" do mate with outside males (Small 1993: 76–77) and sometimes switch groups (Abegglen 1984). Another is that some "one-male" groups of hamadryas baboons (who already exhibit "alliance") may be also organized into larger groupings ("clans") that display "descent" through males, thus combining "alliance" and "descent" in one primate kinship system (Rodseth et al. 1991; for Fox's response to this see Fox 1991; 1997: 218–220). Fox says in his article here that such a finding would only strengthen his argument that human kinship is not purely cultural.

Fox does not in this article address why or how human groups came to combine alliance with descent in their kinship systems. But in his other work (1980) he ties this development to the emergence of big game hunting in the human species. Here he is on less firm ground and is more speculative, if imaginative. Big game hunting, he says, brought about a division of labor by sex, with men hunting and women gathering, and a trade of meat for vegetable food. Securing and trading food demanded a new kind of social organization that put "alliance" and "descent" together. In this process women with children became dependent on males for provision of protein from meat, leading them to grant men authority over the allocation of women for mating, at least officially. Needless to say, this evolutionary scenario has been criticized by feminist anthropologists (see, for example, Stone 2000: 48–52; Mageo and Stone 2003).

The selection that closes this volume reflects a new acceptance of some evolutionary approaches within kinship studies. Here, Maurice Bloch and Dan Sperber (2002) take up an old issue within anthropology – the mother's brother controversy. This controversy concerns the ethnographically widespread avunculate, or special relationship between a man and his sister's child and the different theories that have been used to account for it in patrilineal societies. Following a review of this controversy (see also Fox 1997[2]), they offer a new interpretation of the avunculate in terms of concepts developed in evolutionary anthropology.

Bloch and Sperber begin by showing their agreement with Schneider: biological connections are not universally the basis for "kinship" constructions. But, they argue, an acceptance of the kinship critique formulated by Schneider and his followers does not mean that biological factors must be abandoned in the explanation of these cultural constructions. In their view, cultural representations are not "free-floating," detached from any natural factors. They criticize a "radically relativistic constructivism" for threatening to destroy not just kinship but "the very idea of the possibility of anthropology." They draw attention to the clear existence of at least some cross-cultural regularities, the avunculate being one, and the legitimacy of seeking anthropological explanations for these regularities.

In terms of the avunculate, Bloch and Sperber revive but modify the theories of Meyer Fortes and Jack Goody. Both Fortes and Goody, in somewhat different ways, connected the avunculate with the idea that all human beings actually trace kinship bilaterally even if they live in a unilineal system. However, if they live in a patrilineal system, that system will favor inheritance, or the transmission of resources, in one line only, or patrilineally. As this goes against natural impulses, a special favoring of a man's sister's children in a patrilineal system acts as a compensatory device, allowing resources to actually flow bilaterally. The mistake of Fortes and Goody, according to Bloch and Sperber, was to assume that people naturally act in terms of their presumed biological relationships. However, it could be the case that on account of an evolved psychological disposition to favor kin bilaterally (following kin selection theory), certain cultural forms, such as the avunculate, are in fact likely to develop, spread, and stabilize in patrilineal systems. People follow their cultural constructions (not their own intuitively understood biological links), but those cultural constructions themselves may reflect underlying evolved human tendencies.

Bloch and Sperber use an "epidemiological" approach that sees culture as shared information, the spread and stability of which is influenced by a number of factors, evolved psychological dispositions being only one. Evolved dispositions can affect the probability of the spread and stabilization of cultural expressions, but they do not deterministically bring them about. Many local and historical factors also operate in any population, so that an avunculate in patrilineal societies is not inevitable and its form not everywhere the same where it occurs. Thus, evolved human dispositions do not directly cause particular cultural phenomena, but can lie behind some cultural phenomena, being generally more attractive and more resilient than others.

Clearly, kinship in anthropology has had a long and rich, if sometimes tortured, history. Now, in the opening of the twenty-first century, kinship, if not quite to anthropology what the nude is to art, is once again at the center of research and theory. Stripped of its grounding in Eurocentric notions of biological reproduction, kinship has absorbed and now reflects the broader theoretical currents and contemporary areas of concern in anthropology, especially including interests in gender, personhood, social identities, and relationships as process, human agency in interaction with social structures, inequalities of power, and the impact of national and transnational political economies on local experiences. From Schneider's contributions the field has in general retained an emphasis on the importance of local, emic cultural constructions. However, Schneider's own narrow view of culture has been supplanted with a concern for linking cultural ideas and symbols with social action, or practice. Gone too is Schneider's notion of culture as shared, integrated, and coherent in favor of a new understanding of culture as multi-vocal, contested, and negotiated. Finally, kinship studies are now central to a number of topics in anthropology, such as gender, NRTs, gay and lesbian studies, and transformations of families. NRTs and family transformations are particularly salient in Europe and North America, but it is predictable that kinship studies will expand to explore these topics in other contexts.

As ever, kinship in anthropology is also the site of debates. We are in fact still debating what "kinship" really is, the extent to which cross-cultural comparisons of kinship are valid, whether or to what extent genealogical connections are universally drawn, and whether or in what sense kinship can be understood in relation to human biology.

NOTES

1   Strathern (1992a) took her idea further to discuss the destabilization of knowledge itself. NRTs challenge the cultural view that knowledge rests on an independent "nature" out

there, to be discovered (for further discussion of Strathern's idea see Carsten 2000b: 8–10 and Franklin 2001).

2 Although not reviewed by Bloch and Sperber, Fox (1997) also advanced a theory for the avunculate. In his analysis, the use of the brother–sister bond (rather than or in addition to the husband–wife bond) for parental purposes is an option available to human societies generally. There are variations in the extent to which it is so used, if at all, depending on circumstances. Matrilineal societies contain a built-in avunculate, but patrilineal societies can also make use of the brother–sister tie for parental purposes. Since this possibility exists, "the *probability* of the avunculate's cropping up in one form or another is quite high" (1997: 212, emphasis his).

REFERENCES

Abegglen, J. J., 1984 On Socialization in Hamadryas Baboons. Cranbury, NJ: Associated University Press.

Bean, Susan, 1976 Soap Operas: Sagas of American Kinship. *In* The American Dimension. W. Arens and Susan Monague, eds. New York: Alfred Press.

Bloch, Maurice, ed., 1975 Marxist Analyses and Social Anthropology. New York: John Wiley.

Bloch, Maurice, and Dan Sperber 2002: Kinship and evolved psychological dispositions: the mother's brother controversy reconsidered. Current Anthropology 43 (5): 723–734.

Böck, Monica, and Aparna Rao, eds., 2000 Culture, Creation and Procreation: Concepts of Kinship in South Asian Practice. New York and Oxford: Berghahn Books.

Carsten, Janet, ed., 2000a Cultures of Relatedness: New Approaches to the Study of Kinship. Cambridge: Cambridge University Press.

——2000b Introduction: Cultures of Relatedness. *In* Cultures of Relatedness: New Approaches to the Study of Kinship. Janet Carsten, ed. pp. 1–36. Cambridge: Cambridge University Press.

Edwards, Jeannette, Sarah Franklin, Eric Hirsch, Frances Price, and Marilyn Strathern, 1999 Technologies of Procreation: Kinship in the Age of Assisted Conception. London and New York: Routledge.

Feinberg, Richard, and Martin Ottenheimer, eds., 2001 The Cultural Analysis of Kinship: The Legacy of David M. Schneider. Urbana and Chicago: University of Illinois Press.

Finkler, Kaja, 2001 The Kin in the Gene: The Medicalization of Family and Kinship in America. Current Anthropology 42 (22): 235–249.

Fox, Robin, 1975 Primate Kin and Human Kinship. *In* Biosocial Anthropology. Robin Fox, ed. pp. 9–35. New York: John Wiley.

——1980 The Red Lamp of Incest. New York: Dutton.

——1989 The Search for Society: Quest for a Biosocial Science and Morality. New Brunswick, NJ: Rutgers University Press.

——1991 Reply to Rodseth et al., The Human Community as a Primate Society. Current Anthropology 32 (3): 242–243.

——1997 Sisters' Sons and Monkey's Uncles: Six Theories in Search of an Avunculate. *In* Reproduction and Succession: Studies in Anthropology, Law, and Society, pp. 191–232. New Brunswick and London: Transaction Publishers.

Franklin, Sarah, 1997 Embodied Progress: A Cultural Account of Assisted Conception. London: Routledge.

——2001 Biologization Revisited: Kinship Theory in the Context of the New Biologies. *In* Relative Values: Reconfiguring Kinship Studies. Sarah Franklin and Susan McKinnon, eds. Durham, NC: Duke University Press, 302–325.

Franklin, Sarah, and Susan McKinnon, eds. 2001 Relative Values: Reconfiguring Kinship Studies. Durham, NC: Duke University Press.

Franklin, Sarah, and Helena Ragoné, eds. 1998 Reproducing Reproduction: Kinship, Power, Technological Innovation. Philadelphia: University of Pennsylvania Press.

Gates, Hill, 1996 China's Motor: A Thousand Years of Petty Capitalism. Ithaca, NY: Cornell University Press.

Ginsburg, Faye, and Rayna Rapp, 1991 The Politics of Reproduction. Annual Review of Anthropology 20: 311–343.

——eds., 1995 Conceiving the New World Order: The Global Politics of Reproduction. Berkeley and Los Angeles: University of California Press.

Goody, Jack, 1990 The Oriental, the Ancient, and the Primitive: Systems of Marriage and the Family in the Pre-industrial Societies of Eurasia. New York: Cambridge University Press.

Hayden, Corinne P., 1995. Gender, Genetics, Generation: Reformulating Biology in Lesbian Kinship. Cultural Anthropology 10(1): 41–63.

Hewlett, Barry S., 2001 Neoevolutionary Approaches to Human Kinship. In New Directions in Anthropological Kinship. Linda Stone, ed. pp. 93–108. Lanham, MD: Rowman & Littlefield.

Holy, Ladislav, 1996 Anthropological Perspectives on Kinship. London and Chicago: Pluto Press.

Jacobson, David, Joan H. Liem, and Robert S. Weiss, 2001 Parenting from Separate Households: A Cultural Perspective. In New Directions in Anthropological Kinship. Linda Stone, ed. pp. 229–245. Lanham, MD: Rowman & Littlefield.

Johnson, Colleen Leahy, 1989 In-law Relationships in the American Kinship System: The Impact of Divorce and Remarriage. American Ethnologist 16(1): 87–99.

Kahn, Susan Martha, 2000 Reproducing Jews: A Cultural Account of Assisted Conception in Israel. Durham, NC and London: Duke University Press.

Lamphere, Louise, 2001 Whatever Happened to Kinship Studies? Reflections of a Feminist Anthropologist. In New Directions in Anthropological Kinship. Linda Stone, ed. pp. 21–47. Lanham, MD: Rowman & Littlefield.

Lewin, Ellen, 1993 Lesbian Mothers. Ithaca, NY: Cornell University Press.

Mageo, Jeannette Maria, and Linda Stone, 2003 Screen Images and Sexual Agency in Science and Social Science. Studies in Gender and Sexuality, in press.

Maynes, Mary Jo, Ann Waltner, Birgitte Soland, and Ulrite Strasser, eds. 1996 Gender, Kinship, Power: A Comparative and Interdisciplinary History. New York: Routledge.

Meillassoux, Claude, 1981 Maidens, Meals and Money: Capitalism and the Domestic Community. Cambridge: Cambridge University Press.

Modell, Judith S., 1994 Kinship with Strangers: Adoption and Interpretations of Kinship in American Culture. Berkeley: University of California Press.

——2001a A Sealed and Secret Kinship: Policies and Practices in American Adoption. New York: Berghahn Books.

——2001b Open Adoption: Extending Families, Exchanging Facts. In New Directions in Anthropological Kinship. Linda Stone, ed. pp. 246–263. Lanham, MD: Rowman & Littlefield.

Parkin, Robert, 1997 Kinship: An Introduction to Basic Concepts. Oxford: Blackwell.

Pasternak, Burton, Carol R. Ember, and Melvin Ember, 1997 Sex, Gender and Kinship: A Cross-Cultural Perspective. Upper Saddle River, NJ: Prentice Hall.

Ragoné, Helena, 1994 Surrogate Motherhood: Conception in the Heart. Boulder, CO: Westview Press.

Rodseth, Lars, Richard W. Wrangham, Alisa M. Harrigan, and Barbara B. Smuts, 1991 The Human Community as a Primate Society. Current Anthropology 32(3): 221–241.

Schneider, David M., 1995 Schneider on Schneider: The Conversion of the Jews and Other Anthropological Stories by David Schneider, as Told to Richard Handler. Durham, NC: Duke University Press.

Schweitzer, Peter P., ed., 2000a Dividends of Kinship: Meanings and Uses of Social Related-ness. London and New York: Routledge.

——2000b Introduction. *In* Dividends of Kinship: Meanings and Uses of Social Relatedness. Peter P. Schweitzer, ed. pp. 1–32. London and New York: Routledge.

Silk, Joan B., 2001 Ties That Bond: The Role of Kinship in Primate Societies. *In* New Directions in Anthropological Kinship. Linda Stone, ed. pp. 71–92. Lanham, MD: Rowman & Littlefield.

Simpson, Bob, 1994 Bringing the 'Unclear' Family into Focus: Divorce and Re-marriage in Contemporary Britain. Man 29: 831–851.

Small, Meredith, 1993 Female Choices. Ithaca, NY: Cornell University Press.

Stacey, Judith, 1990 Brave New Families: Stories of Domestic Upheaval in Late Twentieth-century America. New York: Basic Books.

Stone, Linda, 2000 Kinship and Gender: An Introduction. 2nd edition. Boulder, CO: Westview Press.

——ed., 2001a New Directions in Anthropological Kinship. Lanham, MD: Rowman & Littlefield.

——2001b Introduction: Theoretical Implications of New Directions in Anthropological Kinship. *In* New Directions in Anthropological Kinship. Linda Stone, ed. pp. 1–20. Lanham, MD: Rowman & Littlefield.

Strathern, Marilyn, 1992a After Nature: English Kinship in the Late Twentieth Century. Cambridge: Cambridge University Press.

——1992b Reproducing the Future: Essays on Anthropology, Kinship and the New Repro-ductive Technologies. Manchester: Manchester University Press.

Tiger, Lionel, and Robin Fox, 1971 The Imperial Animal. New York: Holt, Rinehart & Winston.

van den Berghe, Pierre L., 1979 Human Family Systems: An Evolutionary View. Prospect Heights, IL: Waveland Press.

Weston, Kath, 1991 Families We Choose: Lesbians, Gays, Kinship. New York: Columbia University Press.

18

Surrogate Motherhood and American Kinship

Helena Ragoné

At the bright center is the individual. And radiating out from him or her is the family, the essential unit of closeness and of love. For it's the family that communicates to our children, to the twenty-first century, our culture, our religious faith, our traditions and history. – **George Bush, Republican presidential nomination acceptance speech, 1989**

Beginning with the earliest theorists such as Lewis Henry Morgan, Emile Durkheim, and Alfred Radcliffe-Brown and continuing with the work of contemporary theorists such as David Schneider, Marilyn Strathern, Jane Collier, Rayna Rapp, and Sylvia Yanagisako, kinship theory has been considered one of the principal areas of study in anthropology. Nevertheless, precise definitions as to what constitutes kinship have been hotly contested throughout the history of the discipline. In view of surrogate motherhood and other medical advances in the area of assisted reproduction, changes in kinship ideology were declared by some to be inevitable,[1] yet in spite of these advances, the central symbols of American kinship ideology have remained unchanged. Assisted reproduction and surrogate motherhood, in particular, introduce numerous questions and issues about the meaning of kinship for participants. As we have seen, programs, surrogates, and couples highlight those aspects of surrogacy that are most consistent with American kinship ideology, deemphasizing those aspects that are not congruent with this ideology. Thus, although the means of achieving relatedness may have changed, the rigorous emphasis on the family and on the biogenetic basis of American kinship remains essentially unchanged.

It can be said, then, that surrogate motherhood is consistent with American kinship ideology in the sense that biogenetic relatedness is achieved (for the father) and that the birth of the child transforms the couple into a family. But although biogenetic relatedness is one of the most important aspects of the surrogate arrangement and is its goal, biogenetic relatedness must be deemphasized during the insemination process and throughout the pregnancy in order to highlight, or place in the foreground, those elements of the relationship that are held to be consonant with American kinship ideology and with "traditional" reproduction. In the interest of achieving these goals, motherhood is reconceptualized as being composed of two separable components: social motherhood and biological motherhood. Social motherhood is, in this configuration, defined as comprising intentionality, choice, and nurturance[2] and is regarded as more important than biological motherhood. This view serves two important functions. First, it deemphasizes the blood tie between the surrogate and the child; and second, it deemphasizes the surrogate's tie to the father vis-à-vis the child. Thus the traditional symbol of unity between the surrogate and the father, created by the child, is circumvented, along with any lingering (if unfounded) connotations of adultery. As we will see, once the child is born and the relationship between the couple and surrogate is effectively terminated, certain elements of the kinship system are permitted to reassert themselves. This can happen only after those kinship elements (e.g., the primacy of the father/child blood tie and the symbolic unity of the couple as it is expressed through or represented by the child) no longer pose a threat to the relationship between the couple and surrogate. As the following analysis will reveal, surrogate motherhood, in spite of its potentially disruptive elements, is being accommodated by the participants under the rubric of preexisting kinship structures and ideology.

Historically there have been three profound shifts in the Western conceptualization of the categories of conception, reproduction, and parenthood. The first shift occurred in response to the separation of intercourse from reproduction through birth control (Snowden, Mitchell, and Snowden 1983); Andrews suggested that this change might have paved the way for surrogacy in the 1980s (1984:xiii). The second shift occurred in response to the fragmentation of the unity of reproduction wherein it has become possible for pregnancy to occur without necessarily having been "preceded by sexual intercourse" (Snowden, Mitchell, and Snowden 1983:5). The third shift occurred in response to further advances in reproductive medicine wherein the "organic unity of fetus and mother can no longer be assumed" (Martin 1987:20). Not until the emergence of reproductive medicine did the fragmentation of motherhood become a possibility; and now, what was once the "single figure of the mother is dispersed among several potential figures, as the functions of maternal procreation – aspects of her physical parenthood – become dispersed" (Strathern 1991:32).

With the advent of gestational surrogacy, surrogate motherhood, however, not only separates reproduction from sexual intercourse, but it also separates motherhood from pregnancy, creating three discernible categories of motherhood where there was previously only one. These three categories created by surrogacy are (1) the biological mother, the woman who contributes the ovum (the woman whom we have traditionally assumed to be the "real mother"); (2) the gestational mother, the woman who gestates the embryo but bears no genetic relationship to the child; and (3) the social mother, the woman who nurtures the child.

Two of these categories can be readily accounted for in American kinship ideology: The biological mother occupies a position similar to that of a woman who places her child up for adoption, although the intentionality is clearly different in each case. A surrogate intentionally conceives a child for the purpose of surrendering that child to its biological father and his wife; she thus creates a "wanted child," who is, however, wanted by someone other than herself. The social mother is similar to an adoptive mother in that her relationship to the child exists not in nature, but in law alone (Schneider 1968). However, the intentionality of the participants makes social motherhood, in the case of surrogacy, different from adoption in that the child is fathered by the adoptive mother's husband during their current relationship, not in a prior relationship, as in the case of a stepchild.

The gestational mother's position is less clear, for her relationship to the child does not occur strictly either in nature or in law, that is, it is neither "code for conduct" nor "substance" (Schneider 1968), at least as that relationship has tended to be defined. How then is the gestational mother to be accounted for? Should a gestational surrogate's maternal rights be "modeled on the law of paternity, where proof of genetic parentage establishes...parentage, or...on the nine month experience of pregnancy as establishing the preponderant interest of...parentage" (Hull 1990:152)?

Some theorists have advanced the argument that the definition of biological motherhood might well be expanded to include the entire process of pregnancy because, they argue, the fetus would not be able to develop or survive without the womb provided by the gestational mother. The authors of both the Glover and the Warnock reports are of the opinion that the gestational mother has a "biological link" to the child (Glover 1990; Warnock 1984). It should be noted, however, that the decision to place gestational surrogacy within the realm of "nature," as both the Glover and the Warnock reports do, runs counter to the logic of the motivations expressed by women who choose gestational surrogacy over traditional surrogacy – to carry a child that is "not related" to her – as well as the intentionality of the commissioning couples. It should be added that to call a gestational surrogate, a woman who bears no genetic relationship to the child, the "mother" contradicts the importance of the blood tie as articulated in Euro-American kinship ideology. Gestation, once a biological given, has, in view of the changes wrought by reproductive technologies, become "culturally ambiguous" (Strathern 1992:27), but whether Euro-American cultural definitions of biogenetic relatedness will be modified by the phenomenon of gestational surrogacy remains unclear. Will those definitions, in the British case, come to emphasize biological relatedness rather than biogenetic relatedness so as to account for the fact that the gestational surrogate provides the physiological/biological environment for the embryo/fetus/child, as the Warnock report has attempted to do? Will the issue be circumvented in the United States through an emphasis on the genetic component of parenthood, characterizing the gestational surrogate as the vessel through which another couple's child is born, as is currently the case among gestational surrogates and commissioning couples?[3]

Both Britain's Warnock Report and the Australian Waller Committee concluded that "when a child is born to a woman following donation of another's egg the woman giving birth should, for all purposes, be regarded in law as the mother of that child" (Shalev 1989:117). For some theorists, the question posed by this decision is why the law should be differentially applied to a gestational surrogate when a sperm donor, for example, bears neither legal rights nor legal duties toward the child and is not regarded as the father of that child (Shalev 1989:117).[4]

The New Jersey Supreme Court's (NJSC) decision concerning the Baby M case illustrates some of the problems inherent not only with surrogate motherhood but with the surrogate contract as well. For example, although the court awarded custody to the father (William

Stern), it also awarded the surrogate, the biological mother (Mary Beth Whitehead), visitation rights. That decision relied upon the basic tenets of American kinship, namely, the enduring solidarity created by the blood tie, rather than upon the original intentionality of the parties or on the terms of their contractual agreement.[5] Legal decisions surrounding surrogate motherhood have as a general rule tended to mirror kinship ideology, as the Baby M case demonstrates. The contract was, however, declared "unenforceable" since the court reasoned that a woman could not make a binding pre-birth contract because she would not know how she felt until after the birth. Some legal experts concluded that the decision was a biologically deterministic one, that the "refusal to acknowledge the legal validity of surrogacy agreements implies that women are not competent, by virtue of their biological sex, to act as rational moral agents regarding their reproductive actions" (Shalev 1989:11).

The decision of the NJSC to give the surrogate visitation rights is understood by some to be a reiteration of essentialist ideas about gender: "The biological argument, thus perverted, has been so compelling, so strong, and so oppressive to women for so long, that feminists should invoke it (if at all) only with supreme caution, and with total consciousness of its cultural history, and therefore, of its potential consequences. Otherwise, the danger that the argument may be turned against them is obvious and grave" (Dolgin 1990:103).

Furthermore, it can be reasoned that the law contradicts itself when it states that a sperm donor can legally decide to disavow any moral, legal, or social rights to a fetus before its birth but a surrogate cannot do the same (Shalev 1989). It is important to bear in mind that one of the principal reasons the surrogate solution is chosen by the commissioning couples is precisely that it provides a partial biogenetic remedy (in the case of traditional surrogacy) or a complete biogenetic remedy to childlessness (in the case of gestational surrogacy).

In June 1993, the California Supreme Court upheld the decisions of both the lower court and the court of appeals with respect to the surrogate contract. In *Anna Johnson v. Mark and Crispina Calvert*, Case #SO 23721, the supreme court ruled that gestational surrogacy contracts are enforceable and not at odds with prevailing public policy. Specifically, Justice Edward Penelli wrote: "It is not the role of the judiciary to inhibit the use of reproductive technology when the Legislature has not seen fit to do so. Any such effort would raise serious questions in light of the fundamental nature of the rights of procreation and privacy."

This dispersing, or fragmentation, of motherhood as a by-product of reproductive technologies has resulted in the "claims of one kind of biological mother against other kinds of biological and nonbiological mothers" (Strathern 1991:32). In the California case cited, the gestational surrogate and the commissioning couple both filed custody suits. Under California law, both of the women could, however, claim maternal rights: Johnson, by virtue of being the woman who gave birth to the child; and Calvert, who donated the ovum, because she is the child's genetic mother. In rendering their decision, however, the court in a sense circumvented this issue of relatedness and focused instead upon the intent of the parties as the ultimate and decisive factor in determining parenthood. In addition the court concluded that compensation to the surrogate is understood not as the NJSC ruled – as baby selling or selling the rights to her child – but rather as payment for her services, for gestation and labor, not for relinquishing her parental rights. As we will see, the issue of intent, specifically, the intentionality of the participants, is of fundamental significance to them. There is little doubt that the California Supreme Court's decision will have far-reaching implications for commercial surrogate motherhood in the United States.[6]

The fact that the surrogate allows herself to be intentionally inseminated for the purpose of conceiving, bearing, and parting with a child calls for a reevaluation of biologically deterministic models, which have tended to inform cultural definitions and expectations about the perceived bond between mother and fetus and mother and child. Surrogate motherhood thus calls for a reconsideration of the inviolability of the chain of events between marriage, procreation, and motherhood.[7]

What follows is an analysis of the strategies utilized by both couples and surrogates to emphasize those aspects of surrogate motherhood that are most consistent with American kinship ideology, notably, the importance of family, biogenetic relatedness, and nurturance. I will also analyze the ways that the couples and surrogates skirt those aspects that depart from the basic tenets, in particular, how participants in the surrogate mother process have attempted to modify definitions of family, kinship, and relatedness in order to resolve the numerous tensions and ambiguities created by surrogacy within the context of the American kinship system. Included for the purposes of comparison is a longitudinal British study, covering the years from 1940 to 1980, of couples choosing donor insemination, or DI (where the semen of a man other than the husband is used for insemination), a process that poses many of the same dilemmas experienced by participants in the surrogacy arrangement. DI places the husband, who is not the child's biological father, in the same structural position as surrogacy places the wife and is thus the closest available parallel to surrogacy.[8]

Surrogate Motherhood and Donor Insemination

Surrogacy and DI pose several dilemmas for the participants in that both require that a married couple who would under "traditional" circumstances procreate on their own behalf (within their relationship) go outside of their marriage and enlist the services of a third party in order to conceive a child. Both methods are invoked because of the infertility of one partner. In surrogacy arrangements the couple employs the services of a woman to whom they usually bear no relationship in order to conceive a child who will be biologically related to the husband. Couples who choose surrogacy and couples who choose DI offer the same explanation for their choice: to have a child who is genetically related to at least one member of the couple (their other choices being to remain childless or to adopt a child who bears no genetic relationship to either of them). This motivation mirrors the emphasis on the primacy and importance of the blood tie in Euro-American kinship. However, third-party reproduction and the genetic inequity of the arrangement (the fact that only one of them will be genetically linked to the child) require that various strategies be devised to correct for the perceived imbalance in the relationship.

Initially, as we have seen, many husbands view surrogacy as undesirable and express instead a preference for continuing to pursue infertility treatments or adopting a child. They feel that adoption (in which the child is not genetically related to either wife or husband) will allow them to "start out equally." DI wives are similarly aware that their husbands "might have reason to feel excluded and jealous" (Snowden, Mitchell, and Snowden 1983:85). Husbands involved in surrogate arrangements and wives involved in DI are thus cognizant of the inequity of a relationship in which one partner will be considered the "real," that is, the biological, parent whereas the other partner will be considered a parent in law only, not in both nature and law.

DI couples and surrogate couples employ various strategies to remedy these problems. If one considers the widely held belief that a married couple without children "does not quite make a family" (Schneider 1968:33) and the belief that having children is a "natural and normal thing to do" (Snowden, Mitchell, and Snowden 1983:126), it is not, in the final analysis, difficult to understand what motivates infertile couples to stretch the limits of Euro-American kinship in order to have a child. What unites these couples and solidifies their marriage is their quest for a child.[9]

Some researchers have concluded that "couples without children. ... are likely to have unsatisfied needs for giving and receiving affection and for making enduring relationships" (Tizard 1977:2). Thus, even though surrogacy and donor insemination may be regarded as being at symbolic and structural odds with traditional reproduction, the very fact of their childlessness has already made these couples feel "inadequate and stigmatized" (Snowden, Mitchell, and Snowden 1983:125; Miall 1985; Lasker and Borg 1987; Sandelowski and Jones 1986); therefore they are ready to employ nontraditional methods to attain traditional ends. The importance of being able to have children in the lives of these couples is illustrated by the degree of adversity they undergo, first in response to their infertility and childlessness, and later

because of their willingness to partake of and grapple with the stigma associated with assisted reproduction.

The definition of a family as two adults with a child or children remains a "powerful normative influence, despite the increasing prevalence of alternative life choices" (Kuchner and Porcino 1988:262). With DI, the stigma is specifically associated with the need to employ an extramarital solution in order to acquire donor semen, which casts doubt upon the husband's "manhood" (Snowden, Mitchell, and Snowden 1983:128): There has long been an association between male infertility and impotence, though the two are not necessarily linked (Humphrey and Humphrey 1988). Sex-role stereotyping, which assigns to males the role of "initiators," thus defining infertile men as "powerless" or passive, and as unable to undertake successfully that which is considered "appropriate masculine behavior" (Snowden, Mitchell, and Snowden 1983:132), exacerbates the situation. The lack of medical knowledge and effective treatment programs (Snowden, Mitchell, and Snowden 1983:121) further contributes to the stigma attaching to male infertility. Although sex-role stereotyping may heighten the stigma associated with male infertility, it may also lessen the stigma associated with female infertility in that the characteristics associated with infertility, such as powerlessness, are more readily considered part of the spectrum of "appropriate feminine behavior" (Snowden, Mitchell, and Snowden 1983:142). This theory is supported in part by the fact that many women with infertile husbands who participate in DI allow others to believe that it is they rather than their husbands who are infertile (Snowden, Mitchell, and Snowden 1983:132). This is a protective strategy to shield men from potential embarrassment or ridicule. Perhaps even more important, it is also a means by which the wife compensates for the fact that the resultant child will be biologically related to her and not to her husband. In addition, when a DI wife feigns infertility, she is aware that any stigma associated with her infertility will be removed once she becomes pregnant, that her infertility can thus be understood as a transient form of infertility, whereas his would not be so understood.

The medical profession as well often routinely shifts the onus of infertility onto the wife, as revealed in an American Medical Association (AMA) statement to the 1979 Ethics Advisory Board to the Department of Health, Education, and Welfare: DI was described as a procedure that "enabled women to bear children and overcome natural impediments to conception and frustration of a basic biological drive" (as quoted in Shalev 1989:107). That statement quite clearly resorts to biologically deterministic and gender-specific ideas, as no mention is made of the fact that DI also allows an infertile man to become a father, albeit a social one. Throughout the history of donor insemination, physicians have paid particular attention to the "psychology of the childless woman," reasoning that a woman's "full psychic role hinged on motherhood, whereas a man's reproductive propensity was secondary to other spheres of social activity" (Shalev 1989:66–67).

For couples who participate in the surrogacy process, the husband's "manhood" is not in question since he is not infertile; it is the wife who bears the brunt of the infertility stigma. It appears that the pain these women experience is related to feelings of inadequacy, loss, and guilt – of not being able to, as several women expressed it, "give my husband a child," which again is understood to result from the cultural significance of children in the Euro-American definition of family. Interestingly enough, the feelings expressed by English men who have been diagnosed as infertile are not dissimilar to the feelings expressed by American women who have been diagnosed as infertile; for example, one infertile man stated that he felt "incomplete" (Snowden, Mitchell, and Snowden 1983:135).

But there is another dimension of infertility that affects women and men differentially not only on a personal level but also on a social and economic one. The director of the Allen program, a psychologist with a practice primarily composed of infertile couples, reported that infertility and the prospect of childlessness affected men and women differentially, with women experiencing a greater degree of psychological difficulty. In one study of couples experiencing infertility, 50 percent of the women and 15 percent of the men viewed their infertility as the most stressful of life experiences (Freeman et al. 1985). The Allen director attributed this difference to the widely held belief that a man's self-image is more closely related to his career, and also that he derives more satisfaction from his career than does a woman. The Allen director viewed this as resulting from biological differences between women and men, namely, the importance of pregnancy and birth in a woman's life cycle. Her theory, like many of the theories that assess the differential impact of infertility on women and men, resorts to biologically deterministic models and tends to give short shrift to the social, cultural, and economic factors that affect the ways in which women and men come to define themselves.

Although there are in fact real differences in the effect that infertility produces on women and men (the subject is beyond the scope of this study), there is no doubt that the importance of children for both DI couples and couples choosing surrogacy can be understood to unite them in a profound way (although the wife's pain is often emphasized, quite likely because it is considered more culturally appropriate to the female role). The following quotations have been excerpted from letters written by couples choosing surrogacy to their state legislature in response to a then-pending bill to criminalize commercial surrogacy:

Dear Legislature:

As the male half of an infertile couple, I can testify to the misery and anguish that not being able to bear a child in the conventional way brings.

In a short letter such as this, it's not possible to demonstrate the pain and suffering that infertility causes. Words can't describe the feelings you have when you see the most important person in your life, your wife, break down and cry at the sight of a pregnant woman. Worse yet, to be awakened from a deep sleep by the crying of your spouse, because she feels that she has failed you by not providing the most essential and basic of human needs – a child. (Husband with an infertile wife, 1989)

Dear Legislature:

As an infertile woman the pain, suffering, and anguish I have suffered over the years has been almost unbearable. Everyone around me has babies, all my friends, all my relatives and I can't have one. Every aspect of life resolves around babies, whether I am watching TV, reading magazines, books, walking down the street; everything and everywhere I am reminded that I cannot do the most natural thing, bear a child. The cruelty of the situation has at times almost destroyed me.

Last year for the very first time I found hope. With an IVF surrogate I could have a biological child of my own. The joy this has brought me is indescribable. With the help of a surrogate I could at last give my husband what he rightfully deserves, a biological baby of our own. (Infertile woman, 1989)

Dear Legislature:
Take a moment and think of the things you value most. For most of us our family comes close to the top of this list. Infertile couples know the emptiness and pain of a life without a family of their own. (Infertile couple, 1989)

Dear Legislature:
Please don't deny us our biological lineage. Surrogate parenting is our only hope to preserve it. We are law-abiding citizens and all we want is the opportunity to have a baby. If we are unable to conceive a biological child, thousands of years of family evolution and lineage will end. It's not fair to deny us this most fundamental and essential need.

Also please don't deny surrogate mothers the opportunity to give the ultimate gift. Life.

Yes, the alternative is adoption. And yes, we will take advantage of this wonderful possibility. It's just that the very core of our existence is tied up in having a biological child. Please don't deny us this chance. (Infertile couple, 1989)

Children, of course, also represent different things to different individuals; they may be viewed as a "public proclamation of sexual maturity," "family continuity," a way to resolve "issues of one's identity in relationship to parents," a way to have "someone to love who will love in return," as providing a "purpose for work and life," or as someone who will care for you later in life (Kuchner and Porcino 1988:262–263). For some couples the

need to bear a biological child is related to the desire to perpetuate their "biological lineage"; as we saw, one of these couples stated that without surrogacy "thousands of years of family evolution and lineage will end." The belief that the couple without children does not properly constitute a family is underscored by the statement that "infertile couples know the emptiness and pain of a life without a family of their own." Children are thus symbolically representative of the love and unity of a couple (Schneider 1968), and the quest to have children can be understood as these couples' effort to provide their marriage with the one crucial element that is perceived to be missing.

With DI, the social contradiction stems from the fact that the child has two fathers, and with surrogacy, the child has two mothers. DI fathers resolve this dilemma by "rationally concluding that the role of genitor is unimportant compared with that of the nurturing father" (Snowden, Mitchell, and Snowden 1983:141). These men thus stress the "social reality. ...and minimize the genetic reality" (Snowden, Mitchell, and Snowden 1983:141) and in this way emphasize the importance of nurture over nature. They also receive reinforcement for this position once the child begins (as it undoubtedly will) to exhibit certain mannerisms and characteristics identical with or similar to their own. This phenomenon prompted one – not unrepresentative – father to speculate that perhaps the child was after all his own biological child. As he expressed it, "I keep thinking perhaps he is mine" (Snowden, Mitchell, and Snowden 1983:141). It may in fact be less problematic for DI fathers to conclude that nurture is more important than biology since "whether men like to admit it or not," there "has always been. ...a certain degree of paternal uncertainty" (Caplan 1990:100).

Prior to the emergence of reproductive technologies, the "figure of the mother provided a natural model for the social construction of the 'natural' facts" (Strathern 1991:5). In the past, motherhood was always understood as a unified experience, combining social and biological aspects into one, unlike fatherhood, in which the father acquired a "double identity"; but with the separation of the social and biological elements, motherhood has, in the context of surrogacy, also taken on this double identity (Strathern 1991:4–5). Surrogate motherhood thus produces the "maternal counterpart to the double identity of the father, certain in one mode and uncertain in another" (Strathern 1991:4).

Fathers, Surrogates, and Adoptive Mothers

Other parallels between surrogacy and DI, aside from the fact that both seek to remedy childlessness, include the fact that both arrangements transgress the "sexual norms of . . . society" in that a "child is being conceived outside the marriage bond and this carries with it connotations of adultery and illegitimacy" (Snowden, Mitchell, and Snowden 1983:127). IVF candidates often view surrogacy and donor insemination as problematic and undesirable because both methods introduce a third party, a "blood tie to a third person and, by implication, extramarital sex," whereas IVF does not symbolically "separate having children from sex" (Modell 1989:134). Thus IVF couples are more likely to attempt adoption than to enlist the services of a surrogate or a sperm donor (Modell 1989:134). IVF leaves intact the "conventional experiences of pregnancy, birth and parenthood" (Modell 1989:134), and participants view IVF as "natural" in that the "pregnancy and birth [are] themselves natural processes . . . comparable to traditional reproduction" (Sandelowski 1991:38). IVF is understood by the participants as a reproductive technology that falls safely "within the boundaries of natural conception" (Sandelowski 1991:39). The association of surrogate motherhood with adultery is illustrated by one Brookside program surrogate's comment: "The general public think I went to bed with the father; people consider this adultery because of lack of knowledge. The public needs to be educated" (*San Diego Tribune*, 1986).

[S]tudies on surrogate motherhood have for the most part tended to characterize the couples' motivations as fairly straightforward: to have a child that is biologically related to at least one member of the couple (Glover 1990). Although genetic relatedness is clearly one of the primary motivations for couples choosing surrogate motherhood, it is a simplification to assert this without also acknowledging the extent to which surrogacy contradicts a number of cultural norms and taking note of the ensuing difficulties encountered by couples, not the least of which is that it involves procreation outside of marriage. Despite the simplicity of the initial motivation of the couple, the fact that this can only be achieved by employing the services of a woman other than the husband's wife raises a host of dilemmas. Fathers and adoptive mothers each develop different strategies to resolve the problems posed by surrogate motherhood. Their disparate concerns stem not only from the biogenetic relationship the father bears to the child and the adoptive mother's lack of such a relationship but also from the differential pressure of having to negotiate the landscape of this novel terrain. Wives and husbands who pursue a surrogate remedy to their childlessness must therefore resolve certain of the inherent tensions that the surrogate arrangement creates; and although they are each faced with different issues, the strategies of both are designed to deemphasize those aspects of the surrogate relationship that are at odds with the basic tenets of American kinship ideology.

For the father, the principal dilemma posed by surrogate motherhood is that a woman other than his wife will be the "mother" of his child. The following quotes by fathers illustrate the not inconsiderable amount of ambiguity created by surrogate motherhood. They also reveal the degree to which the programs' attempts sometimes fall short of their desired goals and objectives, if only temporarily, when those objectives collide with some of the central features of American kinship ideology. For example, Tom, who shared seventeen years of infertility with his wife and who was initially opposed to surrogacy, said:

Yes, the whole thing was at first rather strange. I thought to myself, here she [surrogate] is carrying my baby. Isn't she supposed to be my wife?

Ed, a forty-five-year-old professor who was initially concerned about the exploitation of surrogates by programs and couples, explained:

I felt weird about another woman carrying my child, but as we all got to know one another, it didn't seem weird; it seemed strangely comfortable after a while.

Richard, the software engineer who had wanted to find a surrogate that he and his wife would like as friends, said:

> Seeing Jane [the surrogate] in him [his son], it's literally a part of herself she gave, that's fairly profound. I developed an appreciation of the magnitude of what she did and the inappropriateness of approaching this as a business relationship. It didn't seem like such a big thing initially for another woman to carry my baby, a little awkward in not knowing how to relate to her and not wanting to interfere with her relationship with her husband. But after Tommy was born I can see Jane in his appearance and I had a feeling it was a strange thing we did not to have a relationship with Jane. But it's wearing off and I'm not struck so much with [the idea that] I've got a piece of Jane here.

The concern and confusion of husbands are reflected in questions such as Tom's, "Isn't she supposed to be my wife?" Their ambivalence underscores the continued symbolic centrality of sexual intercourse and procreation in American kinship, both of which continue to symbolize unity and love (Schneider 1968). The father's relationship to the surrogate, although it is strictly noncoital, is altered by the fact that it produces what was always the product of a sexual union until the recent past, namely, a child. Feelings of "awkwardness" and very practical concerns over how to relate to both the surrogate and the surrogate's husband stem from the fact that the father/surrogate relationship may be considered a form of adultery by others. In one case, a father, James, when speaking about the surrogate's husband, expressed his confusion in the following manner:

> I really empathize with Mark [the surrogate's husband]. I really don't understand how he could let his wife have another man's child. I know I couldn't. It's not just her [surrogate] you are affecting.

Richard expressed a similar feeling:

> I felt...a little awkward in not...wanting to interfere with her relationship with her husband.

For some, the surrogate mother is understood less as a "substitute mother" than as a "substitute spouse, who carries a child for a man whose wife is infertile" (Robertson 1990:157), and for others the surrogate serves the husband as a "symbolic sexual replacement" (Glover 1990:67). As we have seen, even though the connection between sexual intercourse and reproduction has been severed by technology, the two remain linked.

Although the relationship between the husband and the surrogate is devoid of romantic love and sexual intercourse, it nevertheless produces a child, and therefore that relationship collects those symbolic associations. As one father, Richard, when reflecting upon the surrogate's role, said:

> I realize now that what Jane gave was a part of herself, that's fairly profound.

Thus the child serves as a point of connection between the surrogate and the husband in the same way it would normally provide a bridge between the wife and husband. Richard's statement reflects the enduring quality of the blood tie, a relationship that can never be severed in American kinship ideology because blood is "culturally defined as being an objective fact of nature" (Schneider 1968:24). It is therefore impossible for a person to have an ex-blood relative, an ex-mother, ex-father, or ex-sibling (Schneider 1968:24). Besides, of course, the fact that blood is understood as "a shared bodily substance," there is also the "connection between ideas of blood...and ideas of genes" (Strathern and Franklin 1993:20). Fathers cannot help but acknowledge this connection and comment upon it, and neither can surrogates and adoptive mothers (as we will see).

In addition to concerns about their relationship to the surrogate vis-à-vis the child, fathers are aware that the child produced from their surrogate union is biologically theirs and that their wives bear no such tie. The husband gains his inclusivity in the surrogate arrangement through his biological contribution: He is the genitor and the pater, but it is the surrogate, not his wife, who is the genetrix. As previously discussed, it is not uncommon for husbands to express concern over the possibility that their wives may feel "excluded" from this relationship. Thus surrogacy blurs, obscures, and in some sense redefines normative ideas about spousal relationships and their corresponding boundaries because couples have chosen to seek an extra-conjugal solution to facilitate the conception of their child. On the one hand, the father must grapple with confusion about his relationship to their surrogate, and on the other, the adoptive mother must resolve her feelings of inadequacy connected with being infertile. She must also come to terms with the fact that unlike her husband and her surrogate, she shares no biological relationship to the child.

One of the primary strategies employed by couples and surrogates to address these concerns is to deemphasize the husband's relationship to the surrogate. That is because it is the surrogate/father relationship that raises the specter of adultery, or more accurately of temporary polyandry and temporary polygyny. Couples also downplay the significance of the father's biological link to the child. They focus instead upon the relationship or bond that develops between the adoptive mother and the surrogate mother, and this emphasis is facilitated in several ways. Surrogate and adoptive mother view each other's participation in the process and the ensuing bond that develops between them as central to the process.

As noted earlier, one of the most frequently stated motivations offered by women who are considering becoming surrogates is a desire to help an infertile woman have a child, and the relationship that develops between the surrogate and the adoptive mother in open programs is often very close. Surrogates commonly express what can be described as a woman-focused view, a view that they often elaborate upon in their descriptions of their relationship to the adoptive mothers. For example, one surrogate, Mary, whose adoptive mother gave her a heart-shaped necklace to commemorate the birth of the child, said:

I feel a sisterhood to all women of the world. I am doing this for her, looking to see her holding the baby.

Celeste, who compared herself and other surrogates to "people who want to climb Mt. Everest," said:

The whole miracle of birth would be lost if she [the adoptive mother] wasn't there. If women don't experience birth or their children being born, they would be alienated and would be breeders.

These quotes reveal a strong belief on the part of surrogates that their primary and very crucial task is to provide an infertile woman with a child. The adoptive mother and father of the child attempt to resolve the inherent tensions created by surrogacy, in particular, the extent to which it rearranges boundaries, sometimes blurring boundaries between pregnancy and motherhood, genetic relatedness and affectional bonds. Meanwhile, the surrogate's role in achieving these goals is, as we have seen, essential.

From the perspective of both the surrogate and the adoptive mother, it is the surrogate's procreative role and the relationship that develops between surrogate and adoptive mother that make the surrogacy arrangement "special." Women, surrogates reason, would be "alienated" if their role in reproduction and the surrogacy process were viewed as secondary to the procreative role of the father; in such a situation, women would be reduced to "breeders" and motherhood rendered profane. This position mirrors and provides a response to anti-surrogacy theories, which tend to view surrogate motherhood and the other forms of commodification of life as creating a class of breeders. By focusing upon her relationship to the adoptive mother, in particular, to the idea that she is giving the adoptive mother a child, the surrogate shifts the emphasis away from her relationship to the father vis-à-vis the child and from the perception that she will be "giving the baby away." Her relationship with the adoptive mother places the surrogate's actions in a more socially acceptable light. It is interesting to note that this bond reestablishes the unity of the experience of birth by joining or uniting the two women in their efforts and purpose.

Reproduction is characterized by both surrogates and adoptive mothers as "women's business." An additional reason that both the surrogate and the adoptive mother focus on reproduction as the domain of women is that their relationship serves to deemphasize the technological or impersonal elements of surrogacy while highlighting the human element; it also provides a counterpoint to the belief that surrogate motherhood creates in surrogates a sense of alienation from their own bodies, their own pregnancies, and the children they produce. The symbiotic terms used by both surrogates and adoptive mothers to refer to their relationship are of particular interest. Here again, just as motherhood is described by surrogates and adoptive mothers as being composed of two roles or parts, social and biological, a sense of self or identity is here represented as also able to be shared. As one adoptive mother, Lucy, a nurse, expressed the relationship:

> She [the surrogate] represented that part of me that couldn't have a child.

Celeste, a surrogate, summed up the feeling shared by many surrogates when she stated:

> She [the adoptive mother] was emotionally pregnant and *I was just physically pregnant.* [Emphasis mine]

One surrogate described her adoptive mother as being "every bit as pregnant as I was," conveying the sense of shared pregnancy or pregnancy by proxy. Thus pregnancy, like motherhood, is redefined as composed of parts or elements that can be separated and shared by women. When pregnancy and birth are defined as women's business, the father's role is intentionally demoted to a secondary position in the relational triangle. In the interest of assisting this process, the surrogate consistently devalues her own biological contribution and link to the child. In this way, participants focus upon the folk theory of reproduction, which is made possible by the fact that even though in the realm of scientific knowledge, women are acknowledged to be co-creators, "in Europe and America, the knowledge that women are...co-creators... has not been encompassed symbolically. Symbols change slowly and the two levels of discourse are hardly ever brought into conjunction" (Delaney 1986:509). In the "dominant folk theory of procreation in the West," paternity in particular has been defined as the "power to create and engender life" (Delaney 1986:510), whereas maternity has come to mean "giving nurturance and giving birth" (Delaney 1986:495). Surrogates therefore emphasize the importance of nurturance and consistently define that aspect of motherhood as a choice that one can either elect to make or elect not to make. The emphasis on nurturance is readily embraced by the surrogate and adoptive

mother since "one of the central notions in the modern American construct of the family is that of nurturance" (Collier, Rosaldo, and Yanagisako 1982:34).

One of the most pronounced differences between DI and surrogacy is that DI allows the wife to experience pregnancy while also allowing her husband to be involved in the process from the moment of conception, whereas with surrogacy it is the surrogate who experiences the pregnancy firsthand in that she is "genetically, physically, psychologically and socially involved in the creation and development of the growing child in a way that no male semen donor ever is" (Snowden, Mitchell, and Snowden 1983:17). [S]urrogates dismiss or devalue their own biological contribution in order to emphasize the importance of the social, or the nurturant, role played by the adoptive mother. The desire and ability of surrogates and adoptive mother to separate social motherhood from biological motherhood is understood to be a reworking of the nature/culture dichotomy.

One of the primary strategies employed by the adoptive mother in order to resolve her lack of genetic relatedness to the child is her use of the idea of intentionality. One adoptive mother (Cybil, who is quoted below) described it as conception in the heart, that is, the belief that in the final analysis it was her desire to have a child that brought the surrogate arrangement into being and therefore produced a child. Since the adoptive mother is incapable of giving biological birth, both the adoptive mother and the surrogate focus not on biological relatedness, not on biological birth, and not on the scientific model of women as co-creators, but rather on the idea of intentionality. This position is reinforced by adoptive mothers, as the following quote from Cybil, a full-time mother, reveals:

> Ann is my baby, she was conceived in my heart before she was conceived in Lisa's body.

By saying that the child was "conceived in my heart," the adoptive mother was focusing upon her own mythical conception of the child rather than the genetrix role played by the surrogate, reasoning that her role took precedence over the surrogate's genetrix role since it was her desire for a child that facilitated the surrogate's pregnancy. Motherhood is thus redefined as an important social role in order to avoid the problematic aspect of the surrogate's biogenetic relationship to the child and the adoptive mother's lack of such a link.

The adoptive mother's position is strengthened by the surrogate who dissociates herself from her pregnancy and from the child by echoing her sentiments, for example, "If it wasn't for this couple, I wouldn't be pregnant," or "It's their baby," or "She was every bit as pregnant as I was." By focusing on the mythical conception or on the amount of love they are able to bestow upon the child, adoptive mothers are able to view their participation in the process as essential. The words of an adoptive mother, Susan, illustrate this belief that the child was created by love:

Someday my unborn child will know that he or she was created from the very special love of three people.

This idea of intentionality or "choice" is of great importance to surrogates, whose use of the term suggests that they may have been influenced by feminist arguments that a woman has the right to choose what to do with her body, in particular, to make her own decisions with respect to sexual relations, birth control, or abortion. In any case, surrogates believe that motherhood is composed of two separable components: the biological process, conception, pregnancy, and delivery; and the social process, intentionality, love, and nurturance. They reason that a woman can choose to nurture, that is, to accept the role of social mother, or can reject that role. The surrogate's reasons for articulating this are twofold: This emphasis on social mothering helps the adoptive mother in that it allows her to fully experience her mythical conception and her pseudo-pregnancy; and it benefits the surrogate by eliminating any suggestion of illegitimacy and adultery and in this way normalizes the situation from her perspective as well. When we consider that the surrogate is conceiving a child for another couple, outside of her own marriage, we can see that a surrogate's efforts to deny that the child is hers cast her actions in a less stigmatizing light for herself, her husband, and her family. In addition, the surrogate is

being paid by the couple to forfeit the child; it would be at odds with the goal of making the experience a positive and fulfilling one for the couple if she were to call attention to her biological relationship to the child or to emphasize her bond with the father. The decision on the part of the surrogate to intentionally conceive a child that she will not mother is, in American culture, anathema to cultural definitions of motherhood. However, by focusing on nurturance as a choice, surrogates and adoptive mothers highlight one of the most acceptable and central cultural embodiments of motherhood and thus shift the focus away from the anomalous quality of the surrogate's actions, her decision to "give her baby away." Surrogates go to great lengths to define nurturance and to highlight its importance, as illustrated by their pronouncements about the specialness of the children they are creating.[10]

The bond that develops between the surrogate and the adoptive mother is necessary for two reasons: It merges the adoptive mother and surrogate into one in order to maintain the unity of experience (or erase boundaries), and it also establishes and maintains boundaries as needed between the surrogate and the father. The majority of surrogates are married (85 percent), as are the majority of couples who engage the services of a surrogate (98 percent). Thus, if the surrogate were to focus her affections and attention on the father rather than the wife, thereby forming a primary attachment and bond with him, she would threaten not only her own marriage but also the couple's marriage. The surrogate therefore focuses upon the adoptive mother and the adoptive mother focuses upon the surrogate in order to avert this potential problem by anticipating and circumventing it. What surrogates, couples, and programs attempt to create is a new sense of order and appropriate relations and boundaries by directing their attention to the sanctity of motherhood as illustrated by the surrogate and adoptive mother bond. Celeste, a surrogate, expressed this idea of shared motherhood and the special relational bond it creates:

Mother's Day is going to be special to both of us, we are kind of like sisters.

The way in which surrogates and adoptive mothers interact can also be seen as an extension of women's roles as the sustainers of social connections, since traditionally "women... maintain the primary bonds with relatives" (Farber 1971:74; Di Leonardi 1987).

Once the adoptive mother and surrogate have bonded with each other, forming an emotional attachment, two things are accomplished. First, the focus of the relational triangle is shifted away from the surrogate and the father and onto the adoptive mother's new role as someone who is experiencing what I call a "pseudo-pregnancy." This pseudo-pregnancy also allows the adoptive mother to begin to bond with the child while it is in utero. The idea of a pseudo-pregnancy is reinforced by her attendance at doctor's appointments, obstetrical exams, checkups, birthing classes, and related appointments. (It should be noted that although the pseudo-pregnancy usually remains just that, a role-playing imaginary construct, it can lead to difficulties such as those described in the case of the adoptive mother who was simulating her own pregnancy, with plans to allow others to believe that the child was her own biological child.) The pseudo-pregnancy of the adoptive mother thus affords her access into the dyad between her husband and the surrogate not only by transforming the dyad into a triad but also by designating the adoptive mother as the central player.

Although the adoptive mother's pseudo-pregnancy and emotional conception of the child results in many personal rewards for her, it also serves to obscure any lingering connotations of adultery and illegitimacy. Besides fulfilling the adoptive mother's needs to feel included in the triad, the pseudo-pregnancy provides her husband an opportunity to return his focus to his wife's role (as wife and mother). This minimizes for him the confusion created by the fact that the surrogate is carrying his child and is literally "the mother of his child." The child, of course, remains a symbol of unity, a reminder of the husband's and surrogate's noncoital, yet reproductive, union.

The adoptive mother's entry into the dyad through emotionality and role-playing serves to normalize the relationship and to neutralize any remaining ambivalence created by the surrogacy arrangement. Her role thus mitigates the confusion or fear that her husband may be experiencing. It also serves to lessen the cen-

trality and importance of his biological contribution and his biological link to their surrogate vis-à-vis the child. When Cybil, an adoptive mother, said, for example, "Ann is my baby, she was conceived in my heart before she was conceived in Lisa's [the surrogate's] body," she was reiterating and emphasizing the importance of the child's emotional conception. Without that conception (or desire for a child), there would in fact be no child: thus the emphasis placed upon its being a "wanted child." In this sense, the husband's role is a biological/genetic one and the adoptive mother's role is an emotional one. Although I do not intend to suggest that there is no emotional attachment on the father's part, it should be noted that his emotionality originates in and is predicated upon his biological role and contribution. Just as the adoptive mother views the child as the product of her emotional conception, the surrogate focuses upon the adoptive mother's desire for the child so that although the adoptive mother's husband may have facilitated the creation of the child, his role is reduced to that of a secondary figure, a situation that is less threatening and more comfortable for all parties concerned.

All the participants in the surrogate motherhood arrangement deemphasize the importance of biological relatedness as it pertains to women and emphasize motherhood as nurturance so that the adoptive mother's inability to give birth, or her inability to become a genetrix, to become both wife and mother, is made to seem insignificant. The adoptive mother's situation is reformulated so that she is not only a wife in that she has a sexual relationship with her husband but she is also, through surrogacy, a mother because her desire for a child brought that child into existence and because she nurtures the child.

One case in which programs were unsuccessful in their attempts to restructure the bonds between participants offers an illustration of the sometimes tenuous nature of the surrogacy triad and the importance of maintaining the appropriate boundaries within it. One of the fathers interviewed said that he developed a closer relationship to their surrogate than did his wife.

In this case, the fact that the father believed he was closer than his wife to their surrogate (though it should be noted his wife thought that she was closer to their surrogate) reveals what can occur when the adoptive mother is not firmly established as a central figure. During the course of the interview, Bruce, a thirty-eight-year-old real-estate broker, who considered surrogacy his "salvation," said:

I would be prepared to pay her [surrogate] another fee so that she would not have a child for someone else. It's something so special, to do it for one couple, and if she did it for another couple, she would be too much of a baby machine.

He then added:

You [interviewer] didn't ask me, but I wouldn't do it with another surrogate.

Bruce's description of his relationship to his surrogate could be characterized as spouselike in that he alluded to issues of fidelity and commitment. His willingness to pay his surrogate not to have a child for another infertile couple suggests that if she were to do so, he would consider her action a form of betrayal similar to adultery. The fact that Bruce would not wish to have a child with another surrogate implies a pledge of fidelity of the kind involved in a marriage vow, a pledge that he would like to take and have his surrogate take as well and for which he would be willing to remunerate her. He also appeared to suggest that his surrogate's reputation was somehow connected to his own when he said that if she were to have another child for a different couple, she would become "too much of a baby machine." Although surrogacy does in fact separate sexual intercourse from conception and pregnancy from motherhood, there remains, as Bruce's remarks suggest, the biological tie established between the father and the surrogate through the birth of the child.

For some adoptive mothers, however, the importance of the blood tie, with all of its attendant symbolic meanings, cannot be completely resolved through the mythic conception (pseudo-pregnancy) or through the reassuring knowledge that the child will know only the adoptive mother as its mother. One adoptive mother, Melissa, who was initially apprehensive, or "scared," about surrogacy and who had undergone four unsuccessful in vitro attempts, stated the problem in this way:

I think of him [child] as Joe's side of the family. I wish he had some traits of my family. I'll always feel that way.

The fact that Melissa is not able to see herself in the child although she is able to identify her husband's and his family's genetic "traits" in the child intensifies her feeling of exclusion and reminds her that she does not have a biogenetic tie to the child, that her relationship exists solely in law and not in both nature and in law, as it does for her husband. Thus, in spite of the emphasis placed by programs, couples, and surrogates on nurturance, the primacy of the blood relationship in American culture and the idea that it creates a "state of almost mystical commonality and identity" (Schneider 1968:25) remains a forceful influence.

Another adoptive mother, Karen, the executive who went to the library to research surrogacy, expressed her feelings this way:

There are times when I see my husband with him and I'm a little sad because they are carbon copies and I know he can't see me in him.

Although the motivation to pursue a surrogate solution to childlessness is always determined to an extent by the desire to attain biogenetic relatedness, in the final analysis, the attainment of that biogenetic link "simultaneously promotes the severance of that link for other individuals" (Overall 1987:150), most notably for the adoptive mother (and, with DI, for the adoptive father). The lingering and resurgent importance of that biogenetic link once the child has been born is illustrated by the following quote by Susan, an adoptive mother:

There are times, many times, I think who is this child? I still have moments, I flash on Betty [the surrogate], she is a significant part of Chris's [the child's] life.

Such statements reflect the belief that it is impossible for a blood relative, in this case, the surrogate, to become an ex-mother, in spite of the efforts of the programs to facilitate the demise of that relationship, and to alter the couple's and surrogate's perceptions about what relatedness means.

The ideal of having a child who is biologically related to both the wife and the husband, which can be fully realized with gestational surrogacy, cannot be achieved with traditional surrogacy. It is theorized that when continued advances in IVF technology are translated into higher success rates, more couples (if physiologically capable) will select gestational surrogacy for the simple reason that it most closely approximates traditional reproduction without introducing any of the potentially sensitive problems that traditional surrogacy raises. In gestational surrogacy most of the elements of American kinship remain intact: IVF transforms the wife into the genetrix and the husband into the genitor and provides a child who is biologically related to both wife and husband and is thus a symbol of the couple's love and marriage bond.[11] Gestational surrogacy is similar to Insemination by Husband (IH) in that it does not challenge the underlying tenets of the biogenetic basis of American kinship ideology. The tendency of couples pursuing IVF to "incorporate conceptive technology within the boundaries of natural conception" (Sandelowski 1991:39) is accomplished by focusing not upon fertilization (which occurs in a petri dish and represents a departure from traditional reproduction) but rather upon the genetic and gestational components of IVF (Sandelowski 1991:38), which are consistent with traditional reproduction. As might have been expected, couples choosing gestational surrogacy emphasize their roles as genetrix and genitor; when asked if they consider the child theirs, they emphatically respond, "She *is* ours!"

Thus far, egg banks have been used primarily by women whose infertility is related to their inability to produce a viable ovum but who are nonetheless able to sustain a pregnancy. In 1991, I theorized that with the proliferation of "egg banks," some couples after initially considering traditional surrogacy would prefer to select an anonymous egg donor, not in the interest of equalizing the relationship between the husband and wife per se, but rather because it weakens the surrogate's claim to the child (Ragoné 1991), and as of 1994, directors report that this is occurring.

Because of the emphasis these couples place on having a child who is biologically related to at least one of them, it was initially perplexing to learn that less than 2 percent of couples choose to have a paternity test performed on the child once it has been born (an option offered to all couples). According to the contract, the couple is not required to accept the child until a paternity test is performed – if requested – to verify that the child is in fact the husband's child. This degree of confidence is surprising in view of the fact that some paternal doubt is always present. Insemination is most often conducted in a physician's office, but some programs permit home insemination, which makes the process more susceptible to error, at least from a symbolic point of view, in that the formal setting and structure provided by the presence of a physician is removed. Additionally, in more practical terms, both the use of frozen semen and the practice of shipping fresh semen when the surrogate and father are separated by geographical distance introduce the possibility of mix-ups. Another and perhaps more important factor that introduces doubt is the possibility that the surrogate did not abstain from intercourse with her husband, as agreed upon in the contract. In one case, a paternity test was performed when a disabled child was born to the surrogate and a dispute arose over the discontinuation of life-sustaining treatments. The surrogate's husband was determined to be the father of the child, a material breach of the contract. Although errors such as these are not unheard of in the surrogate industry, they do not for the most part appear to cause undue concern for the couples. When asked about paternity testing, wives frequently respond in this fashion, "We knew she was ours from the minute we saw her," or "We decided that it really didn't matter; he was ours no matter what."

These statements, even though they may initially appear to contradict the stated purpose of pursuing a partial biogenetic solution to childlessness, can upon further study be understood to fulfill two important functions. From the wife's perspective, an element of doubt as to the child's paternity introduces a variable that equalizes the issue of relatedness. The husband, as we have seen, is aware that he has a decisive advantage over his wife as evident in the frequently expressed initial preference for adoption or continued infertility treatments; thus a slight element of doubt about the child's paternity redresses the imbalance from his perspective as well. However, biogenetic relatedness remains a preoccupation with most couples, as seen in instances where a couple desires to have a second surrogate child: The norm is to reengage the services of the original surrogate if she is willing. The primary reason offered for this preference is that the child will have a full sibling, rather than the half-sibling that would be produced if another surrogate were selected. Surrogates frequently discuss their hopes that their couple will decide to have a second child so that they can give the child "a brother or sister." The surrogate's rationale in these cases is the same as that of the couple, to provide the family with genetic continuity. It should be noted that there are many more surrogates willing to have a second child for their couple than there are couples interested in having a second child. Most couples cite either age or financial constraints as obstacles to having a second child.

Because surrogacy is a relatively new phenomenon and little studied, its effects on children and the family are not known. There are, however, more extensive data on donor insemination and its effects upon the children produced thereby. Because of the close parallels between DI and surrogacy, some of these data may shed light on the future of surrogate children and their parents with respect to their personal relationships. Since a great deal of secrecy continues to surround the issue of DI, it is not surprising that according to the studies done on this subject, the majority of DI participants have not told their children about their origins (Snowden, Mitchell, and Snowden 1983). But in cases in which they have been told, DI children appeared to be "enjoying life and happy to be alive," knowing that they "owed their existence to AID [artificial insemination by donor]. They were pleased to feel that their parents had wanted a child so badly and that they were that child which fulfilled their parents' wishes" (Snowden, Mitchell, and Snowden 1983:98).

Furthermore, it was found that when DI children were informed of the circumstances of their origins, that knowledge, rather than damaging their relationship to their parents, appeared to enhance it (Snowden, Mitchell, and Snowden 1983:123). Nor was the experience of being told of their origins found to be "particularly traumatic" (Snowden, Mitchell,

and Snowden 1983:123). The reasons for this appear to be that, unlike adopted children, who must come to terms with having been "abandoned by their natural mother...an AID child is above all else, a wanted child and has no experience of rejection" (Snowden, Mitchell, and Snowden 1983:123).

Whether the same experience will hold true for surrogate children is presently unknown, although surrogate children share the experience of being "wanted" children and may therefore share in the positive feelings of DI children. However, unlike the surrogate child, the DI child has a biological mother who is also its social mother; whereas the surrogate child might be perceived as having lost her/his biological mother.

Although almost all of the couples who choose surrogacy and enroll in open programs anticipate informing their child of its origins, couples who select closed programs may not be so forthcoming. Studies on adopted children reveal that "adoptees have a healthy curiosity about their origins and a need for a full personal history in order to complete their sense of self" (Humphrey and Humphrey 1988:111). It has been shown that secrecy, in the case of DI, "whilst ostensibly being maintained for the sake of the child, is closely bound up with the concept of stigma" (Snowden, Mitchell, and Snowden 1983:121) and is "reminiscent of the practice followed by adoptive parents" (when parents do not tell a traditionally adopted child that he/she has been adopted) about which it has been concluded that "emotional energy spent on denial and concealment is better expended in facing and resolving the inherent problems" (Snowden, Mitchell, and Snowden 1983:147).

The authors of the DI study concluded that parents should be assisted with information about "how best to set about the practical task of telling their children in practical terms" (Snowden, Mitchell, and Snowden 1983:123) of their origins. In the open programs both couples and surrogates avail themselves of what is commonly referred to as the "broken tummy" theory to explain to their children their birth origins. Surrogates explain to their children that they are having a child for their couple because the adoptive mother's "tummy is broken" and that the baby belongs not to the surrogate and her family but to the couple.[12] In turn, the couple is instructed to tell their child that its mother's tummy is broken and that that is why a surrogate had to give birth to him or her. Within the open surrogate programs, the broken tummy story has gained overwhelming acceptance by industry personnel, adoptive couples, and surrogates alike. Fifteen out of the seventeen individuals interviewed, or about 88 percent, planned to use (or did use) this explanation. Parents involved in the surrogacy process frequently express concern about the proper age at which to tell their children because although they have been advised by open programs to share this information, no specific guidelines accompany the suggestion.

When Tom, one of the fathers I interviewed, for example, told me that he thought it might be best to let his son believe that he had been adopted until he had reached adulthood, his wife, who had overheard that part of the conversation, promptly poked her head into the room to say: "Absolutely not. He will be told the truth from the beginning." Some couples are very forthcoming, telling all their friends and even acquaintances of their surrogacy plans, whereas others tell primarily family members, allowing neighbors and acquaintances to believe that the child is adopted. Almost 65 percent, or eleven, of the couples interviewed from the open programs intended to tell their child of its origins before she/he reached adulthood. For these couples, the point at issue is the appropriate time at which to tell the child. Many couples expressed the belief that the moment the child expresses curiosity about the subject is the proper time to introduce the subject.

Couples are in the position of having to invent, almost independently, their own methods of informing the child about her/his origins. The strategy of one adoptive mother, a member of the staff at the Brookside program, whose surrogate was her own biological sister, is a good example. In telling her child about her origins, she combined the words "mother" and "aunt" to create the term "mattie," the kinship term her daughter now uses for the woman who is both her biological mother and her aunt. In addition to creating origin stories and new kinship terms, couples often create symbolic rituals or invent new ways to honor their relationship to their surrogate, such as the pre-

viously mentioned joint celebration of Mother's Day. For example, when Betty, the surrogate whose own father offered to pay her not to become a surrogate, told her couple, Susan and Ken, about the ritual she "created" after her own son's birth, in which she buried the placenta in her yard and then planted a fruit tree on that site, they decided to reenact the ritual with "Chris's [surrogate child's] placenta," planting a second fruit tree in Betty's yard to commemorate the event. Another couple named their child after their surrogate, thereby incorporating her name into their family history. Another surrogate, Carolyn, who described surrogacy as the "ultimate way to give," was invited to participate as a birth coach for her adoptive mother, when the adoptive mother herself became pregnant (through the use of GIFT). As Carolyn explained the sense of equal exchange and shared experience:

I was her coach; I was there for the C-section and I took the movies this time!

In summary, assisted reproductive techniques such as surrogacy, which are designed to redress the problem of infertility and resulting childlessness, do introduce numerous structural and symbolic questions as well as more practical issues such as the proper time to inform a child of her or his origins. On the simplest level, surrogacy assists the infertile by helping them to overcome their childlessness; however, as we have seen, it also introduces potential problems, for example, by providing a biogenetic link for only one parent and excluding the other parent.

From the couple's perspective, surrogacy is conceptualized not as a radical departure from tradition but as an attempt to achieve a traditional and acceptable end: to have a child who is biologically related to at least one of them, in this case, the father. This idea is consistent with the emphasis on the primacy of the blood tie in American kinship ideology and the importance of family. Thus, although biogenetic relatedness is the initial motivation for, and the ultimate goal of, surrogacy and the facet of surrogacy that makes it consistent with the biogenetic basis of American kinship ideology, such relatedness must be deemphasized, even devalued, by all the participants in order to make surrogacy consistent with American cultural values about appropriate relations between wives and husbands.

I have attempted to illustrate that surrogates' stated motivations for choosing surrogate motherhood represent but one aspect of a whole complex of motivations; thus although surrogates clearly do, as they say, enjoy being pregnant, take pleasure in being able to help an infertile couple start a family of their own, and value the remuneration they receive, there are other equally, if not more, compelling reasons motivating this unique group of women to become surrogate mothers. In addition to broadening the understanding of the motivations of the couples who choose to pursue a surrogate solution, I hope to have illuminated the complexity of their deliberative process and eventual accommodation of surrogacy as an aspect of their lives.

As we have seen, surrogates as a group tend to highlight only those aspects of surrogacy that are consistent with traditional reproduction. They emphasize, for example, the importance of family, motherhood, and nurturance. Like the couples, they deemphasize those aspects of the surrogate relationship that represent a departure from traditionally held beliefs surrounding motherhood, reproduction, and the family. Interspersed, however, with surrogates' assertions that surrogate motherhood is merely an extension of their conventional female roles as mothers are frequent interjections about the unique, exciting, and special nature of what they are doing.

It is not surprising, in view of their socialization, their life experiences, and their somewhat limited choices, that surrogates claim that it is their love of children, pregnancy, and family and a desire to help others that motivate them to become surrogates. To do otherwise would be to acknowledge that there may be inconsistencies within and areas of conflict between their traditional female roles as wives, mothers, and homemakers and their newfound public personae as surrogate mothers.

In conclusion, it can be said that all the participants involved in the surrogacy process wish to attain traditional ends and are therefore willing to set aside their reservations about the means by which parenthood is attained. Cloaking surrogacy in tradition, they attempt to circumvent some of the thornier issues raised by the surrogacy process, and in this way, programs and participants pick and choose among American cultural values about family, parenthood, and reproduction, now choosing biological relatedness, now nurture, as it suits their needs.

NOTES

1 See, for example, Chris Shore's conclusion that "our most basic assumptions about parenthood, procreation, conception, and the family are about to undergo a radical transformation" (Shore 1992:301).

2 See, for example, the ways in which nurturance is understood to be on the one hand a "source of moral authority for female action" and on the other hand a way of confining women to the "unappreciated tasks of caring for dependent people" (Ginsburg 1987:627).

3 As part of this definitional matrix, it seems likely that a restriction or ban on commercial surrogacy will produce differences in definition.

4 In terms of the time and biological processes invested, sperm donation and pregnancy cannot be equated; however, the issue of an individual's right to decide how and in what way she or he chooses to use her or his reproductive resources is an area of commonality between the two.

5 The fact that Mary Beth Whitehead sought custody of the child may have been an indiation that she had preexisting marital difficulties.

6 I want to expressly thank William Handel for sharing with me his interpretation of this recent decision and for keeping me apprised of this and other legal decisions.

7 The "dominant procreation story" in the United States is one in which "pregnancy necessarily results in childbirth and motherhood, preferably within marriage" (Ginsburg 1987:623).

8 Clearly there are differences between the United States and Britain that inform the responses to surrogate motherhood, illustrated by the British ban on commercial surrogacy, but I believe that the shared importance of the blood tie unites American and British couples who are pursuing surrogate motherhood. I also found the motivation of British couples pursuing DI and American couples pursuing

surrogate motherhood strikingly similar and worthy of comparison, as are the ways in which they attempt to reconcile the lack of a biogenetic tie for one of the partners.

9   In Britain, for example, the idea of children as "strengthening the infertile couple" would, as the Warnock report concluded, be undermined if a surrogate were to want custody of the child (Cannell 1990:674).

10 As revealed in both pro-choice and pro-life narratives, nurturance is "embraced" and viewed as "both natural to women and the basis of their cultural authority" (Ginsburg 1987:629).

11 In 1988–1990, when the bulk of this research was conducted, gestational surrogacy constituted less than 5 percent of the Brookside program's arrangements. [T]he rate had increased to 50 percent by the time I revisited the program in 1992 and again in 1994 and was also reported to be 50 percent at the Wick program. Although I had predicted an increase in the rates of gestational surrogacy in 1989 (see Ragoné 1991), I did not anticipate an increase of this magnitude in such a short period of time. This change is deserving of further study.

12 Although surrogates (both traditional and IVF) deny or minimize their biological connection to the child, all the traditional surrogates interviewed (who had their own children) had told or planned to tell their children that the surrogate child was their half-sibling.

REFERENCES

Andrews, Lori. 1984. *New Conceptions: A Consumer's Guide to the Newest Infertility Treatments.* New York: Ballantine.

Cannell, Fanella. 1990. "Concepts of Parenthood: The Warnock Report, The Gillick Debate and Modern Myths." *American Ethnologist* 17(4):667–686.

Caplan, Arthur. 1990. "The Ethics of In Vitro Fertilization." In *Ethical Issues in the New Reproductive Technologies*, ed. R. Hall. Belmont, Calif.: Wadsworth Publishing.

Collier, Jane, Michelle Rosaldo, and Sylvia Yanagisako. 1982. "Is There a Family?" In *Rethinking the Family*, ed. B. Thorne and M. Yalom. New York: Longman.

Delaney, Carol. 1986. "The Meaning of Paternity and the Virgin Birth Debate." *Man* 24(3):497–513.

Di Leonardi, M. 1987. "The Female World of Cards and Holidays: Women, Families and the Work of Kinship." *Signs* 12(3):440–453.

Dolgin, Janet. 1990. "Status and Contract in Feminist Legal Theory of the Family: A Reply to Bartlett." *Women's Rights Law Reporter* 12(2):103–113.

Farber, Bernard. 1971. *Kinship and Class: A Midwestern Study.* New York: Basic Books.

Freeman, Ellen, et al. 1985. "Psychological Evaluation and Support in a Program of In Vitro Fertilization and Embryo Transfer." *Fertility and Sterility* 43(1):48–53.

Ginsburg, Faye. 1987. "Procreation Stories: Reproduction, Nurturance and Procreation in Life Narratives of Abortion Activists." *American Ethnologist* 14(4):623–636.

Glover, Jonathan. 1990. *Ethics of New Reproductive Technologies: The Glover Report to the European Commission.* DeKalb: Northern Illinois University Press.

Hull, Richard. 1990. Gestational Surrogacy and Surrogate Motherhood." In *Ethical Issues in the New Reproductive Technologies*, ed. R. Hull. Belmont, Calif.: Wadsworth Publishers.

Humphrey, Michael, and Heather Humphrey. 1988. *Families with a Difference: Varieties of Surrogate Parenthood.* London: Routledge & Kegan Paul.

Kuchner, Jean, and Jane Porcino. 1988. "Delayed Motherhood." In *The Different Faces of Motherhood*, ed. B. Birns and D. Hay. New York: Plenum Press.

Lasker, Judith, and Borg, Susan. 1987. *In Search of Parenthood: Coping with Infertility and High-Tech Conception.* Boston: Beacon Press.

Martin, Emily. 1987. *The Woman in the Body: A Cultural Analysis of Reproduction.* Boston: Beacon Press.

Miall, Charlene. 1985. "Perceptions of Informal Sanctioning and the Stigma of Involuntary Childlessness." *Deviant Behavior* 6:383–403.

Modell, Judith. 1989. "Last Chance Babies: Interpretations of Parenthood in an In Vitro Fertilization Program." *Medical Anthropology Quarterly* 3:124–138.

Overall, Christine. 1987. *Ethics and Human Reproduction: A Feminist Analysis.* Boston: Allen and Unwin.

Ragoné, Helena. 1991. "Surrogate Motherhood in America." Ph.D. dissertation. Brown University, Providence, R.I.

Robertson, John. 1990. "Surrogate Mothers, Not So Novel After All." In *Ethical Issues in the New Reproductive Technologies*, ed. R. Hull. Belmont, Calif.: Wadsworth Publishers.

Sandelowski, Margarete. 1991. "Compelled to Try: The Never-Enough Quality of Conceptive Technology." *Medical Anthropology Quarterly* 5(1):29–47.

Sandelowski, Margarete, and Linda Jones. 1986. "Social Exchanges of Infertile Women." *Issues in Mental Health Nursing* 8:173–189.

San Diego Tribune. 1986. "Surrogate Mothers: Not All Regret or Renege on the Delicate Pact." December 26.

Schneider, David. 1968. *American Kinship: A Cultural Account.* Englewood Cliffs, N.J.: Prentice-Hall.

Shalev, Carmel. 1989. *Birth Power: The Case for Surrogacy.* New Haven: Yale University Press.

Shore, Chris. 1992. "Virgin Births and Sterile Debates: Anthropology and the New Reproductive Technologies." *Current Anthropology* 33(3):295–314.

Snowden, R., G. Mitchell, and E. Snowden. 1983. *Artificial Reproduction: A Social Investigation.* London: Allen and Unwin.

Strathern, Marilyn. 1991. "The Pursuit of Certainty: Investigating Kinship in the Late Twentieth Century." Paper presented at the American Anthropology Association Meeting, Chicago, Illinois.

—— 1992. *Reproducing the Future.* New York: Routledge.

Strathern, Marilyn, and Sarah Franklin. 1993. "Kinship and the New Genetic Technologies: An Assessment of Existing Anthropological Research." A Report compiled for the Commission of the European Communities Medical Research Division (DG-XII) Human Genome Analysis Programme.

Tizard, Barbara. 1977. *Adoption: A Second Chance.* New York: Free Press.

Warnock, Mary. 1984. *The Warnock Report: Report of the Committee of Inquiry into Human Fertilisation and Embryology.* London: Her Majesty's Stationery Office.

19

Eggs and Wombs: The Origins of Jewishness

Susan Martha Kahn

The next time I see you, I want to see an embryo in your womb. – An Israeli ultrasound technician to an Israeli woman seeking to get pregnant through in-vitro fertilization

In this chapter I focus on eggs and wombs as the determinants of maternal, religious, and national identity in Israel. There is a direct correlation between the social construction of motherhood and the social reproduction of the nation, for when the dominant religious culture provides the conceptual groundwork for kinship, as it does in Israel, and when this same religious culture determines identity matrilineally, as Judaism does, then eggs and wombs are not only the variables that determine maternal and religious identity, they are the variables that determine citizenship as well; for Israel is a nation-state where the positive determination of Jewish identity automatically confers citizenship.

The origins of maternality become complicated with the advent of ovum-related technologies. By forcing the biological roles of maternality to fragment into genetic and gestational components, ovum-related technologies force a conceptual fragmentation of maternality as well. As soon as eggs can be surgically removed from one woman's ovaries and transferred into another woman's womb, unprecedented reproductive possibilities are created. Traditional beliefs about the origins of motherhood are thereby challenged, creating Halakhic [pertaining to the legal part of Talmudic literature] dilemmas for contemporary rabbis who must scramble to develop conceptual and practical strategies

for determining where maternity is located: in the genetic substance of the egg? In the gestational environment of the womb? Or perhaps in both? The restrictions regarding the appropriate pathways of exchange for ova and the consequences for beliefs about maternity are the subject of ongoing rabbinic contestation, and appropriate policies regarding ovum donation have not yet been definitively formalized.

In the first section of this chapter, I describe an Israeli fertility clinic in which sperm is processed and eggs are surgically extracted from women's ovaries and reimplanted in women's wombs as embryos. Here I contextualize the practice of reproductive technology in Israel by focusing on the specific ways that the Halakhic imagination of women's bodies exerts a practical impact on clinical protocol. I hope this vivid ethnographic description of the medical and laboratory procedures in which eggs and wombs are the operable variables will make them more conspicuous subjects of analysis in the second section of the chapter. In the second section, I analyze the interpretive dilemmas facing contemporary rabbis as they attempt to understand the Halakhic problems posed by ovum-related technologies. These rabbis explicitly consider eggs and wombs as independent entities with various contingent statuses and identities. I examine the construction of maternity in a context where the technological expertise of fertility doctors and the conceptual categories of orthodox rabbis are understood as dynamically juxtaposed. Rabbinic debates about eggs and wombs are not simply theoretical, nor do their consequences only reverberate conceptually. These debates, and their outcomes, explicitly determine the appropriate rules for the appropriate conception of new Jewish citizens.

To be sure, the conceptual fragmentation of women's bodies into eggs and wombs is clearly problematic. It threatens to dehumanize women and to promote an attitude that views their bodies as detachable parts that can be combined and recombined in order to create legitimate maternity according to rabbinic specifications. Indeed, the egg-related procedures that I describe have been the subject of much feminist analysis and critique, for in these procedures women's bodies are routinely anesthetized, surgically invaded, and otherwise intruded upon, all in the name of conceiving children (Corea 1987; Stanworth 1987; Spallone 1989; Raymond 1993). However, a feminist critique of these procedures, while highly instructive, is not my focus here.[1] I am more interested in how these egg-related procedures challenge rabbinic and folk-cultural understandings of maternity.

The Setting: A Jerusalem Fertility Clinic

I conducted fieldwork in a small religious hospital in Jerusalem where most of the patients were either ultraorthodox Jews or religious Muslims, though secular Jews and Christian Palestinians also went there for treatment. What made this hospital "religious" was that all treatments and procedures that took place in the hospital were performed with careful consideration of Jewish law. The hospital's amenities were quite basic: there was no gift shop, no patient lounge, no cafeteria. The waiting room for the women's clinic was an uncarpeted hallway with chairs lined up along the walls and a bookcase full of prayer books in the corner. In the women's ward, there were five or six beds per room.

I spent several months in the fertility unit, which is part of the Department of Obstetrics and Gynecology. There were two different fertility laboratories in the hospital. In the first, the lab workers accept sperm samples from people undergoing fertility treatment; they check sperm for motility and mobility (spermogram) and process sperm for inseminations (swim-up, Percol wash, etc.). In the second, which was located next to the operating room in the women's ward, they perform in-vitro fertilization and micromanipulation; they also prepare gametes, zygotes, and embryos for surgical and intravaginal insertion into the womb. There were two incubators in this laboratory to store embryos until they were transferred into women's wombs. Toward the end of my fieldwork a new freezer arrived, which allows them to freeze embryos at the hospital as well.

There were four principal lab workers who rotated between the labs. All were secular Jewish women, a fact that will become important as we learn more about the working conditions in this clinic.

Because this was a hospital where treatments and procedures were performed with careful consideration of Halakha, often under the auspices of particular rabbis, only married couples with fertility problems were eligible for treatment; unmarried women were not accepted for treatment. Moreover, all the fertility procedures were monitored by *maschgichot*, or Halakhic inspectors, who watch each procedure to make sure that there is no untoward mixing of sperm and eggs.

The maschgichot were ultraorthodox women who were paid a nominal hourly sum to sit in the lab and supervise the lab workers as they process the incoming sperm and eggs. A maschgicha was required to be present in each lab whenever any sperm or eggs were being processed. [. . .]

In this clinic there were five principal maschgichot who rotated shifts; all but one were older orthodox women who had many children and grandchildren of their own; the fifth was a younger woman who was married without children. At various stages of my research, each of them asked me detailed questions about what I was studying, and they seemed to take a keen interest in the ethical and religious questions that these technologies raised. Their job, however, was rather simple. As one maschgicha put it: "We make sure that

Lichtenberg and Silberstein don't get mixed up." Meaning, of course, that they make sure that Lichtenberg's sperm and Silberstein's sperm do not get accidentally mixed up by the lab worker who may inadvertently use the same syringe, pipette, or catheter to handle sperm as she transfers it between test tube and petri dish. For if Lichtenberg's wife's egg was inadvertently fertilized with Silberstein's sperm, and the resulting embryo was implanted in Lichtenberg's wife for gestation and parturition, then Lichtenberg's wife would give birth to Silberstein's baby. This would obviously give rise to numerous social, ethical, and Halakhic questions. The maschgichot, then, are keenly aware of the larger implications of their work. Indeed, one of them told me that what she does is "holy work" and is more important than what the doctors and lab workers do to achieve pregnancy.

I was very impressed with how well the maschgichot seem to get along with the lab workers, considering the fact that the maschgichot literally peer over the lab workers' shoulders all day long. Amazingly, there seemed to be little animosity bred from what would seem to be an annoyance; on the contrary, one lab worker said she felt there was a need for supervision. "Four eyes are always better than two," she said, "and we also don't want to make any mistakes." Over many months, I observed only one professionally related altercation between a maschgicha and a lab worker, when an impatient client demanded that his sperm be processed quickly, and the lab worker complied, even though there was no maschgicha present in the lab to monitor the procedure.

The maschgichot often spoke Yiddish among themselves, as is common for many Ashkenazi ultraorthodox Jews. One maschgicha always kissed the mezuzah as she walked in and out of the laboratory. She liked to tell me how all of this technology would only work if God Almighty wanted it to work. Another maschgicha told me, quoting the *Talmud*, that there are three partners in the creation of a child: Father, Mother, and God. I jokingly added the names of the lab workers to her list, and she replied seriously: "They are not partners, they are only envoys" (*Hem lo shutafim, hem rak shlichim!*).

That the maschgichot and the lab workers were all women seemed to create a common,

albeit limited, realm of conversation that revolved around shared family and domestic concerns like children's birthdays, weddings, brits [naming ceremonies], food, recipes, haircoloring, or diets. Although these discussions formed the constant backdrop to the rather extraordinary procedures that were taking place, the lab workers and the maschgichot did occasionally engage in more theoretical discussions about current events, politics, or religion. At the base of their shared working lives was an overlap of interests: both the lab workers and the maschgichot wanted infertile people to conceive children. Their mutual interest in this outcome was apparent every time we heard that one of the patients had gotten pregnant or given birth. Daily news in the lab consisted of who had gotten pregnant or who had not, and everyone seemed to share the pleasure or the despair of the news equally, and equally personally. When one of the patients in fertility treatment would give birth, they would all say: "Mazel Tov! One of 'ours' gave birth!" Indeed, when one woman gave birth to twins at the age of forty-two, after twenty-two years of infertility, all the maschgichot and all the lab workers went to the nursery to see "our babies."

One could argue that the matrix of relationships that exists in these fertility laboratories can be imagined as a fictive kin network, for it is within these relationships that conception occurs. The social practice of assisting reproduction creates an intimacy between the lab workers and the maschgichot in which the social pressure to achieve legitimate conception overwhelms the ideological and religious differences between the participants.

The positive working relationships and easy coexistence between the secular lab workers and the religious maschgichot was also indicative of the ways medicine and religion were structurally enmeshed at this hospital. One of the most striking examples of this intersection was manifest in the fertility clinic's patient flowcharts, where next to the spaces for recording hormonal treatments, blood tests, temperature readings, and ultrasound results, there was a space for recording the date of immersion in the *mikveh* (ritual bath). Immersion terminates the woman's status as niddah, rendering her ritually pure and thus able to engage in sexual relations with her husband. This state of ritual purity is also a crucial Halakhic prerequisite to conception, so it becomes important for the timing of inseminations and embryo transfer procedures. Recording the date of immersion thus becomes an integral part of the medical considerations in fertility treatment.

The influence of Halakhic concerns on medical protocol was similarly manifest in the prescriptive use of perforated condoms, which allowed patients to collect sperm for analysis while symbolically fulfilling the commandment to be fruitful and multiply. Clearly, the practice of medicine at this hospital was everywhere dependent on and determined by the interpretative framework of traditional Judaism.

In the Operating Room

To observe procedures in the operating room, I was given a pair of blue surgical scrubs, a gauze hat for my hair, and plastic shoe coverings for my sandals. I was allowed to roam freely in and out of the operating rooms, and once it became known that I was interested in observing procedures, the doctors often made a point of alerting me to upcoming operations.

When I began the fieldwork, I spontaneously identified with the anesthetized patients whose bodies were being slit, probed, suctioned, and sewn up. Gradually, I began to identify more with the doctors and nurses, who approached their tasks with dispassionate and pragmatic efficiency. The switch in identifications was important because it enabled me to endure surgical procedures that were often not only visually disquieting, they were clearly emotionally debilitating to the patients, with whom I often spoke before and after their procedures.

I observed a range of operations during my fieldwork, from cesarean sections to laparoscopies to zygote intrafallopian transfers and various other procedures. After they got used to seeing me in the operating room during various operations, the surgical staff began to ask me to help during some of the more routine procedures, like the oocyte pick-up. I would carry vials of ovarian fluid from the operating room to the lab, or help wheel patients in and out on gurneys. I was happy to help, though the patients would often ask me questions as if I were a doctor or a nurse, which made me somewhat uncomfortable.

The Oocyte Pick-Up

In an oocyte pick-up, ova are surgically extracted from a woman's hormonally hyperstimulated ovaries. The operation is a necessary prelude to in-vitro fertilization and micromanipulation and lasts approximately thirty minutes. It is an outpatient procedure; no major incisions are made in the woman's body, and recovery is usually rapid.[2] At the clinic I observed this procedure innumerable times. There were always three medical professionals present: the doctor who performs the procedure, the anesthesiologist, who anesthetizes the patient, and the nurse, who sets everything up and carries the ovum-bearing vials from the operating room to the laboratory (unless she has her hands full, in which case this task is performed by the visiting anthropologist).

During the oocyte pick-up, the patient is fully anesthetized and lies on her back with her feet in stirrups, as in a gynecological exam. The procedure takes place in a darkened operating room, since eggs are sensitive to light. The doctor begins by inserting a phallus-shaped ultrasound probe into the patient's vagina. Attached to this probe is a hollow aspirating needle that the doctor uses to pierce the egg-bearing ovarian follicles; the aspirating needle must pass through the walls of the vagina to reach the ovary, which produces some minor bleeding. [...]

There are three standard forms of embryo transfer: gamete intrafallopian transfer (GIFT), zygote intrafallopian transfer (ZIFT), or intravaginal embryo transfer. The first two are surgical procedures, the third is not. To be sure, a host of considerations determine what kind of embryo transfer will be most effective, depending on the nature of the patient's infertility and the quality of her reproductive genetic material. For instance, a patient with blocked fallopian tubes would be unlikely to benefit from the ZIFT procedure, which involves the surgical implantation of zygotes into the fallopian tube with the expectation that the resulting embryo will drop down through the fallopian tube into the uterus. [...]

One of the most interesting aspects of the oocyte pick-ups I observed was that "Jewishness" was manifest in the way the medical procedure itself was performed. The doctor in charge explained to me how she performs an oocyte pick-up in such a way as to avoid rendering the woman a niddah as a result of the procedure. For if in the course of surgically denuding ovarian follicles of their eggs, the doctor inadvertently causes bleeding from the uterus, the woman could technically be considered niddah, defined Halakhically as a woman who is bleeding from the uterus.[3] A woman in niddah is considered to be ritually unclean for purposes of conception, and she may not conceive a child until she stops bleeding, observes seven "clean" days when she refrains from sexual contact, and immerses in a ritual bath. Thus, if while undergoing an oocyte pick-up a woman bleeds from the uterus, some rabbis would say that she is forbidden from receiving the subsequent embryo transfer two days later, for the resulting child could be considered a ben-niddah (a child of niddah) with all the associated stigma.[4]

There is a vast rabbinic literature that discusses the various sources, causes, and consequences of women's uterine and vaginal bleeding. A full examination of these Halakhic issues and the various determinants of niddah is beyond the scope of this discussion.[5] Suffice it to say that despite the lack of consensus in the rabbinic world on whether surgical procedures that cause uterine bleeding can render a woman a niddah, the Halakhic concerns are substantial enough that surgical protocol has been designed to circumvent any possibility that a woman undergoing an oocyte pick-up or other surgical procedure would be considered ritually impure and therefore ineligible for the subsequent embryo transfer.

The doctor who performs oocyte pick-ups explained to me that she avoids extracting eggs that are positioned in such a way as to require her to pierce the uterine wall with the oocyte pick-up needle, even if this means that she has to forego extracting an egg or two. She will only retrieve eggs that she can reach by inserting the needle through the walls of the vagina and into the ovary, since vaginal and ovarian bleeding are not considered to trigger the status of niddah. Strategic and ethical complications are presented in cases in which the ovary is positioned awkwardly behind the uterus in a way that would require the doctor to pierce the uterus to gain access to the ovary. If a woman has undergone hormonal hyperstimulation specifically to have her oocytes removed, should they not be removed simply because there's a chance that removing them would cause uterine bleeding? Are the medical risks incurred by the ovarian hyperstimulation enough to justify the extraction of eggs in a way that may cause the woman to become ritually impure? In other words, are the medical risks associated with oocyte pick-up sufficient to warrant a more lenient definition of niddah, if it would allow the woman to get pregnant?

These decisions are made on a case-by-case basis by the doctor, the patient, and the patient's rabbi. The doctor tells the patient if there has been uterine bleeding during the oocyte pick-up, the patient may then tell her rabbi, and the rabbi will then determine whether or not the patient is permitted to undergo subsequent embryo transfer without her child being considered a ben-niddah.

Obviously, there is considerable room for playing with boundaries here; a doctor who is under administrative pressure to increase the number of IVF pregnancies in his or her unit may be less forthcoming about the source of bleeding during IVF procedures if he believes that his patients will get pregnant as a result of the procedure. A patient who has been undergoing extended fertility treatment may be less likely to volunteer information to her rabbi that may negatively impact her treatment. And a rabbi may choose to grant a *heter*, or special rabbinic permission, for a woman to receive treatment who has been suffering unduly from childlessness, even if the medical procedures have caused some form of uterine bleeding. What is interesting here is that traditional Halakhic ideas about purity and impurity based on rabbinic understandings of bleeding from the uterus are explicitly translated into surgical protocol.

The oocyte pick-up is not the only procedure that the doctor performs with the practical intent of observing the laws of niddah. When the patient is not undergoing in-vitro fertilization and is simply receiving artificial insemination with her husband's sperm, the doctor often performs two inseminations, one immediately before and one immediately following ovulation. There are two primary forms of insemination: intracervical insemination, in which the sperm is inserted in a catheter and placed at the mouth of the cervix; and intra-uterine insemination, in which the sperm is introduced through the cervix and into the uterus. The second form of insemination often produces some form of uterine bleeding. Thus, if the doctor thinks that the second insemin-ation is going to be more successful, based on her assessment of the ultrasound imagery of the follicle, she will be careful to make the first insemination intracervical as opposed to intra-uterine. That way, the uterus is less likely to bleed, and the patient will be "clean" for the second insemination. If she thinks the first in-semination will be more successful, she will do an intrauterine insemination, and if any uterine bleeding occurs she will tell the patient, and the patient may then ask her rabbi, who may or may not grant permission for the woman to undergo a second insemination.[6]

The doctors performing these procedures are often secular and have had to learn the practical indications of niddah in order to work with ultraorthodox patients. The doctor who runs the clinic explained that she had to become expert at determining whether bleeding incurred during these procedures originated in the uterus, the cervix, or the vagina, because the patient trusts her to tell her where the bleeding is coming from. Then, if the patient has a question about whether or not she is in niddah, she can go and ask her rabbi. In sum, it is the doctor's responsi-bility to tell the patient if there is uterine bleed-ing, it is the patient's responsibility to tell her rabbi, and it is the rabbi's responsibility to deter-mine whether or not this makes the woman in-eligible for subsequent fertilization.

Fertilization

The oocyte pick-up procedure does not end in the operating room. The actual isolation and fertilization of the oocytes occurs in the labora-tory. The nurse brings the vials of egg-bearing ovarian fluid from the operating room into the lab and gives them to the waiting lab workers. The lab workers then pour out the blood-colored, egg-bearing fluid into petri dishes and check it for eggs by swirling the petri dishes around under the microscope. When

the lab worker locates an egg (which is identi-fied as a small round shadow inside a little cloud of biological material) she sucks it into a pipette and transfers it into another petri dish, which she puts into the incubator until the sperm is processed for fertilization. The maschgicha is present, of course, and she watches to make sure the lab worker does not inadvertently use a pipette or a syringe from a previous procedure, which may carry traces of someone else's reproductive genetic material. The oocyte pick-up does not require constant monitoring; it is the subsequent fertilization that must be carefully watched, for that is when sperm may be inadvertently mixed up. During an oocyte pick-up, the maschgicha just makes sure that the petri dishes are correctly marked with the patient's name. [...]

The method of fertilization has been predeter-mined by the doctor, depending on several factors, including the number of eggs retrieved in the oocyte pick-up, the age of the woman, and, most importantly, the quality of the hus-band's sperm. Either the eggs are fertilized "in-vitro," which means that sperm is placed on the individual egg with a syringe, or the eggs are fertilized through micromanipulation, whereby one individual sperm is isolated and inserted into an egg under a high-power microscope. [...]

After the eggs have been fertilized with sperm they are placed in the incubator.

The Morning After

Twenty-four hours after the eggs and sperm have been combined, through either in-vitro or micromanipulation, they are removed from the incubator and examined under the microscope; successful fertilization is determined according to whether a dividing cell is visible. This day-old dividing cell, or zygote, can be surgically intro-duced into a woman's fallopian tube through "zygote intrafallopian transfer" (ZIFT). A detailed description of one particular ZIFT oper-ation is illuminating for what it reveals about the day-to-day functioning of an Israeli fertility lab as well as the public culture in which con-ception and impregnation takes place.

It is the day before the national elections, so the city is buzzing with preelection propaganda. "Netanyahu is good for the Jews" is the latest slogan, and when I arrive in the morning the lab workers and the maschgichot are debating whether or not it is racist. I arrived in the lab late, about 10 A.M. and thought I had missed all the interesting procedures, but it turned out I had arrived just in time for a ZIFT on a forty-four-year-old woman. I first stopped into the lab and greeted Netta, the lab worker, and Bracha, the maschgicha, who were respectively preparing and watching some of the ten intrauterine inseminations they had done that day. I walked over to the operating room, past the ultraorthodox patients sitting outside in the sunshine, past the bookcase full of prayer books and psalm books that stands in the hallway, and went into the second laboratory, which they call the ICSI (intracytoplasmic sperm injection) room, for this is where they do micromanipulation. Pnina, another lab worker, was doing micromanipulation on some eggs that had been extracted in an earlier oocyte pick-up while lab workers Idit and Beatrice looked on. Suri, the maschgicha, was saying psalms in the corner, her surgical gauze cap falling off the blonde wig she wore in order to keep her hair modestly concealed, as is customary for ultraorthodox women. They told me there was a ZIFT going on, so I quickly went and put on my surgical scrubs.

When I entered the operating room, the patient was lying on the table, anesthetized, and Dr. Benjamin was waving her sterilized hands in the air to dry them before she put on her operating gloves. Dr. Elchanan was there, as were two nurses, a Russian woman anesthesiologist, and a tall assistant whose job seemed to consist of moving equipment around. I stood at the head of the operating table and watched as Dr. Elchanan slathered brown sterilizing liquid over the patient's abdomen. They were talking politics as they prepared for the operation. One nurse said the country would go to hell if Bibi (Netanyahu) was not elected; Dr. Benjamin countered with some pro-Labor statement; the anesthesiologist chimed in with her theory about the peace process, until finally Dr. Benjamin said: "Okay, enough, let's get started!"

The ZIFT is performed using a laparoscope. First, Dr. Benjamin inserted a hollow needle through a small incision in the patient's belly button. Then she inserted a tube into the needle, through which she pumped carbon dioxide in order to expand the abdominal cavity. She then took an instrument I called the "puncher," which is a long steel tube that has a rotating blade in the middle, squeezed the belly button, aimed the puncher, and jabbed it quickly down through the belly button, making a larger incision. She inserted a surgical video camera, which is like an eye on the end of a flexible metal tube, through the hole she had made in the belly button and peered around at the patient's innards. The image from the video camera was simultaneously projected on a television screen. The uterus and other internal organs appeared all reddish, yellowish, and shiny; Dr. Benjamin pointed at a reservoir of blood sloshing around one of the ovaries, which she said had been caused by the oocyte pick-up the day before.

Once she became visually acclimated to the caverns and slopes inside this woman's body, she made another incision, this time lower, about two inches below the belly button. Looking at the TV screen I could see the top wall of the abdominal cavity get depressed, then depressed again as the doctor tried to jab the scalpel through the abdominal wall. As I saw the doctor's arm slip suddenly down out of the corner of my eye, I saw the knife simultaneously enter into the abdominal cavity on the television screen. [. . .]

Dr. Elchanan inserted metal tongs through the lower incision and began fishing around for the fallopian tube, which was hidden behind the bulge of the uterus. She grasped the fallopian tube with the tongs and gently pulled it out from behind the uterus. She then picked at the fallopian tube with the tongs until the fleshy, free-floating end of it was exposed; it looked like a mushy, wet lily. Once she located this part of the fallopian tube, Dr. Benjamin called for Idit and Beatrice (the workers from the lab) to bring in the embryos. Idit had already positioned the embryos in a long, thin, and pliable embryo-transfer catheter. Beatrice brought the embryo-transfer catheter from the lab and stood next to the operating table. She and Dr. Benjamin then fed the embryo-transfer catheter through the hollow rod that was inserted into the lower abdominal incision (the tongs had been removed) and down into the mushy end of the fallopian tube. Dr. Benjamin then released the embryos into the fallopian tube and withdrew the embryo-transfer catheter. The ZIFT was completed. Dr. Elchanan quickly withdrew the hollow tube from the lower incision and the video camera from the higher incision, and began to sew up the patient.

Dr. Benjamin yelled to me in the middle of this ZIFT procedure: "Sue, is it nice? We're making her a mother!" With this comment, Dr. Benjamin made the connection literal between the medical realm of the operating room and the symbolic realm of kinship. She made explicit what was implicit, that this technology created a new way to make mothers, a new origin myth, as it were, for the beginning of motherhood. Mothers are now something that doctors make women into, as if the surgical implantation of zygotes into the fished-out end of a fallopian tube is now how mothers are formed. The technological creation of motherhood is what Dr. Benjamin was drawing my attention to here. "Is it nice?" she asked me, somewhat proudly.

Two Mornings after the Oocyte Pick-Up

Forty-eight hours after the fertilization, the dividing cell is no longer considered a zygote, but an embryo, and may be introduced into the woman's womb intravaginally through an embryo-transfer catheter. On one slow Friday, Dr. Benjamin brought a patient clad in her surgical gown into the lab before the embryo transfer and said, "Devorah wants to see her children." So one of the lab workers opened up the incubator, pulled out a few petri dishes with the patient's name on them, and showed them to her. Then Devorah walked into the operating room, lay down on the operating table, and waited to have her "children" inserted into her uterus.

This kind of intravaginal embryo transfer was performed without any anesthetic, just like a pelvic exam. The most commonly used catheter for this procedure is called the "tom-cat" catheter, a small plastic tube attached to the end of a special syringe. The lab worker uses the syringe to suck the two-day-old embryos out of the petri dish and into the catheter. The nurse brings the syringe with the embryo-bearing catheter attached to it into the operating room and gives it to the doctor. The doctor places the catheter into the woman's vagina, up through her cervix into her uterus and releases the embryos. [. . .]

The embryo transfer takes two seconds if all goes well, and there are no complications. The nurse yells the patient's name into the lab, the maschgicha checks and makes sure that the lab workers are preparing the catheter with the right woman's embryos, the nurse brings the catheter to the doctor, and then the doctor simply places the catheter inside the woman's womb and releases the embryos. No sexual connotations, no fanfare, just impregnation. The doctor wishes the patient good luck, the nurse wheels the patient back to the ward, where she lies in bed for a few hours, hoping the embryos "take." I often chatted with the patients as they lay there waiting to "conceive," as it were. Many had been through the procedure multiple times. We would chat about their treatment cycles, how much pain they were in, or what they were having for dinner.

Ovum-Related Technologies: Halakhic Concerns

The Halakhic questions raised by ovum-related technologies are similar to those raised by artificial insemination, and there is a similar distinction between questions concerning treatments in which the couples' own reproductive genetic material is at issue and questions concerning treatments in which donated reproductive genetic material is used.

The rabbis' central concern in cases of ovum donation is: Who is the mother? The woman who donates the egg, or the woman who carries the pregnancy and gives birth? These are important questions in a kinship system that determines religious identity matrilineally, and even more so in Israel, where the positive determination of Jewish religious identity automatically confers citizenship.

The Halakhic problem here stems from the fact that ova were not thought to exist in the traditional rabbinic imagination, and there are therefore no clear precedents for deciding this question.[7] Rabbinic arguments about the appropriate use of ovum donation are therefore arguments about interpretation. Yet on what basis is the discovered "fact" of the existence of ova to be interpreted? The problem is that the texts that rabbis look to as Halakhic precedents regarding ovum donation do not explicitly contain the objects of knowledge (ova) that must be interpreted. In an interpretive framework for which legal analysis depends on conceptual grounding in traditional texts, it is difficult to construct an interpretation of an entity that was not known to exist in those texts.

In light of this interpretive dilemma, some rabbis advocate an appropriation of biogenetic understandings of maternity as a legitimate guide for rabbinic opinion. To these rabbis, it is legitimate to decide that maternity is derived from the genetic substance of the ova.[8]

Others argue that it is the woman who carries the pregnancy and gives birth who should be considered the mother, following the traditional dictum that while paternity is established at conception, maternity is established at birth.[9] This interpretation suggests that maternity should be determined at parturition. Still others argue that a child born as the result of ovum donation should be considered to have two mothers, one biological and one gestational.[10] Finally, some rabbis suggest that any child conceived with an egg extracted from an ovary, fertilized in-vitro, and reimplanted in a womb should be considered to have no mother at all.[11] No rabbinic consensus on these questions has yet been reached, though the majority opinion holds that the woman who gestates the child and gives birth should be considered the Halakhic mother.

Some rabbis have developed particularly novel explanations of these issues.[12] For example, Rabbi Ezra Bick (1993) advocates discarding the biological model, in which men and women are understood to contribute genetic material equally to an embryo, and in its place resurrecting what he calls "the agricultural model," in which conception occurs when men sow the seeds in women's fertile soil.[13] In this model the roles of men and women are not parallel but complementary; men are the active donators of reproductive material and women are the passive receptors of it. According to Bick, the determinant of maternal identity is

"the ground from which a human being springs," which he reasons to mean that the gestational mother is the Halakhic mother.

In another example of contemporary Halakhic innovation, Rabbi J. David Bleich suggests a different way of using Talmudic agricultural analogies to understand where maternal identity is located. Bleich suggests that ovum donation can be understood as a parallel to agricultural cases in which there is continued growth and development of grain, trees, or vegetables after uprooting, reimplantation, or grafting onto older species. In these cases Bleich suggests:

> If this analysis of these Talmudic questions is accepted as correct, the question of maternal identity of progeny born as the result of in-vitro fertilization of a donated ovum may be regarded as analogous. Maternal identity is established in the first instance by the production of the gamete. The question is whether that determination is also dispositive with regard to the identity of the fetus whose later physical development is attributable to the gestational host or whether the identity of the developing fetus is derived from its nurturer, viz. the host mother, in which case the child could be regarded as having two mothers just as, for example, a single grain of wheat may be in part "pre-omeric" and "post-omeric." Since the Gemara leaves the basic issue unresolved and, accordingly, rules that the stringencies of both possible identities must be applied, a child born of in-vitro fertilization, on the basis of this analogy, would to all intents and purposes be regarded as having two mothers. (1991: 87)

Bleich's interpretation, while suggestive and compelling, does not resolve questions concerning the Jewish identity of a child who, for example, is conceived with a non-Jewish egg but gestated within a Jewish womb, or who is conceived with a Jewish egg and gestated in a non-Jewish womb. According to Bleich, such a child would have two mothers, but it is still unclear which mother confers Jewishness.

This Halakhic crisis, whereby the determination of maternity has been so profoundly destabilized by the advent of ovum-related technologies, will undoubtedly continue to reverberate in Israel with unpredictable social consequences. It has not prevented the practice of ovum donation, however; the drive to reproduce, and the technological potential presented by ovum donation, seems to have superseded any desire to await conclusive rabbinic rulings on the subject, even among the ultraorthodox population. To be sure, as with artificial insemination, ultraorthodox Jews follow the opinions of different rabbis in this matter, and some rabbis are much more lenient than others when it comes to ovum donation.

Moreover, rabbinic disagreements over the determination of maternal identity in cases of ovum donation have not slowed the secular rush to create regulations that legislate the appropriate uses of ovum donation.[14] Nor have these disagreements and Halakhic ambiguities prevented Israeli Jews, both religious and secular, from using the eggs of non-Jewish women to create Jewish babies.[15]

I asked Aryeh, the office manager of PUAH [Poriyoot ve'Refuah Alpi hattalakah, an organization that offers advice about fertility treatment according to Jewish law], about the use of donated non-Jewish eggs to conceive Jewish children. He explained that for those rabbis who believe that maternal identity is determined at parturition, a Jewish woman can give birth to a Jewish baby even if the baby is conceived with a non-Jewish egg. Other rabbis, who believe in the genetic basis for maternal identity, suggest that a child born of a non-Jewish egg to a Jewish mother needs to be converted to "sanctify the people of Israel."[16]

I then asked Aryeh whether women in Israel were using donated non-Jewish eggs to get pregnant. He explained:

Yes, it is happening every day, though it is a *mahkloket* [rabbinic dispute]. I should take you to Herzliya to see all the non-Jewish eggs women are using. [Eggs] from Arabs, or from Turkish women and other women who come here for treatment. You see, it is ILLEGAL in Israel to sell an egg. Because it is an operation and no doctor wants to authorize an operation that is not necessary, that is just to sell the egg. So women who are undergoing treatment are asked if they will donate eggs; I could show you one hundred people on the waiting list.

Aryeh mentioned that non-Jewish eggs also enter the Israeli ova marketplace via the many foreign women from Turkey, Europe, and the United States who come to private Israeli fertility clinics, like the one in Herzliya, in order to receive treatment. These women come to Israel because the reproductive services available are on the international cutting edge of infertility research and development. In addition, fertility treatment is often cheaper in Israel than in other countries. These non-Jewish foreign women, like Jewish and non-Jewish Israeli women, are routinely asked to donate any surplus ova "harvested" during their own fertility treatments. To be sure, the exchange of ova is not unidirectional. Non-Jewish Israeli and foreign women who receive treatment in Israeli fertility clinics also receive donated ova from Jewish women. Christian Palestinian women who undergo fertility treatment are also potential sources for, and recipients of, ova, although religious restrictions prohibit Muslim women from donating or receiving ova, as we will see below.[17]

In 1999 Israeli newspapers reported that Israeli doctors were setting up a fertility clinic in Cyprus to meet this demand for ova and to circumvent Israeli regulations against buying and selling eggs for profit. In the Israeli-run Cyprus clinic, women from Russia and other countries would be flown to Cyprus, paid to have their ova harvested, and then flown out; infertile Israelis and other nationals who are prepared to purchase ova wait in Cyprus and buy these freshly harvested ova (*Ha'aretz*, 16 February 1999).

It is important to understand that the Israeli ova marketplace is a competitive one. There is an enormous shortage of ova and a long list of women waiting for a donation, not unlike the predicament of those waiting for organ donations. A prominent lawyer in Jerusalem explained that the fact that there is such a critical shortage of ova was one reason that the ministry of health regulations allow unmarried women access to fertility treatment. To enlarge the pool of available ova, which by law can only be extracted from women undergoing treatment themselves, unmarried women were allowed access to fertility treatment so that their unused eggs, harvested to solve their own infertility, could enter the ova marketplace, provided they consent to donate extra eggs harvested in their own treatments. Aryeh explains the demand for eggs from unmarried women: "The most ideal situation is to have eggs from an unmarried Jewish woman (not necessarily single, but widowed or divorced as well). But it is better to use a non-Jewish egg than a married Jewish woman's egg."

The eggs of unmarried Jewish women are considered the most desirable eggs for donation to married Jewish women for two reasons: (1) there is a widespread social preference for eggs that are considered to be genetically "Jewish"; (2) eggs that come from unmarried Jewish women are often preferred because they circumvent the Halakhic problem of gestating an embryo that is the result of an adulterous combination of a married Jewish woman's donated egg and the sperm of a Jewish man who is not the egg donor's husband. As we saw in the rabbinic discussions of artificial insemination in the previous chapter, such a child could be considered a mamzer, with all the associated stigma.

It would seem, then, that a Jewish egg does not just carry the religious identity of the woman who produces it, it contains her marital status as well, and as her marital status changes, so does the status of her eggs. The rabbinic imagination would thus appear to have very innovative ways for thinking about the status of ova, for if a married woman is divorced or widowed her eggs simultaneously seem to lose their status as married for purposes of determining whether an adulterous union of sperm and egg has occurred.

Two Egg Stories

The practice of egg donation in Israel seemed to have curious and unpredictable dimensions. Though I did not conduct in-depth ethnographic interviews on this subject, I conclude this section with two particularly unusual conversations about egg donation I recorded, one with a fertility specialist and one with a religious woman undergoing IVF treatment.

The Doctor In an interview with the head of one of the fertility clinics in Israel, I asked how he decides to ask a woman for an egg donation.

I only do it if the conditions are right, if we've harvested over fifteen eggs in her oocyte re-

trieval and if she's under thirty-five years old, so that the risks for her are less. I only ask if she's a secular or Sephardi Jew or if she's Christian; I don't ask if she's religious Ashkenazi or Muslim, since they are specifically forbidden from donating for religious reasons. Also, I only ask in cases in which it will not lower a patient's own chances of getting pregnant. I tell her not to feel any pressure or threat, but if she wants to help another woman who needs an egg, she can do it. I take off all the reasons to feel pressured and tell them that it is fine to say no.

It is totally anonymous, the other woman won't know it is she who gave the egg, and she won't know if there is a pregnancy. I will tell the woman who donates if there is a fertilization, because this is important if there is a problem of male-factor infertility with her husband; at least she will know if her eggs are fertilizable and good.

I then asked how long it takes to receive an egg donation at his clinic.

There is a waiting list of over a year until you are eligible for one donation. If that donation does not lead to pregnancy, you are put back on the end of the list. When there is money involved, at Herzliya for example, it can take only two–three months. When ova become available, women on the waiting list are called. Who receives the ovum donation depends on who has been waiting the longest, whose husband is at home to come in and fertilize the ovum, and simply who is in the right place at the right time. Again, for ultraorthodox women, constraints are much more explicit. They may only receive ova from donors that are deemed legitimate by their rabbis.

I was interested to know whether egg donors receive any form of monetary compensation at his hospital.

Not at this clinic. In Herzliya, where there is money involved, they get some form of compensation, like a reduced rate on their next round of fertility treatment. Here, they just get to know that they helped another woman, and they also get to know if their eggs were successfully fertilized, which can be important knowledge for their own treatment.

I concluded by asking how many egg donations he successfully performs per year.

Only four or five. Also, you have to understand that ICSI [intracytoplasmic sperm injection] has cut down on the number substantially. Because in problems of male-factor infertility before ICSI, there would only be enough sperm to fertilize five or six eggs, the rest would be thrown away, so you could say to the woman: "The excess eggs are going to be thrown away, would you consider donating them." But now with ICSI, if you have seventeen eggs, you can certainly find seventeen live sperm to inject in them. And then you can freeze the embryos. So the motivation to give is less, because instead of donating them or throwing them away, now you can keep them frozen as embryos for yourself.[18]

It would seem that at his clinic, only secular Jewish women, Sephardic Jews, and Christian Palestinians are asked to donate eggs. Muslim women and religious Ashkenazi women are forbidden from donating their ova for religious reasons, though they may be eligible to receive egg donations under the specific guidance of their respective religious authorities.[19] Potential egg recipients are informed of the ethnic and religious identity of the egg donor and may refuse to accept an egg donation from a woman on those bases, or based on her marital status, depending on how her rabbi, priest, or sheikh rules on ovum donation. Moreover, the doctor made it clear that he only asks for eggs from women under thirty-five, since younger women generally produce more and better quality eggs than older women. These practices were in no way unique but seemed to reflect the standard procedure for asking for egg donations at Israeli fertility clinics. They are extraordinary not just because they reveal a sophisticated understanding of the different religious attitudes toward the appropriate use of third-party donor material but because they reflect the pragmatic assimilation and integration of these differences into standard medical practice.

The Patient An additional account of the practice of egg donation, this time from the patient's perspective, reveals similarly unusual and irregular features of this experience in Israel. This story was told to me by a woman I met in the waiting room of one of the large fertility clinics in Tel Aviv.

The doctor told me I needed an egg donation. So we registered for one in August. This entailed sitting with the egg donation clerk and telling her what we wanted in an egg donor. We told her we wanted a short woman of Hungarian/Byelorussian origin, cute and smart. Like me. She wrote down our preferences: short, brown eyes, brown hair, Ashkenazi, and asked me for a photograph. I sent her a letter with the photograph and in the letter I wrote: "Dear X, enclosed please find a photograph as you requested. I see you as the matchmaker between me and the woman who will donate her eggs in order to help us create children in the future (with the help of God). I bless you to choose this woman with wisdom, understanding, and truth. You are doing very important work. Sincerely. . . . "

That was it except for the fact that the doctor encouraged us to bribe her with chocolates in order to get a donation faster. So my husband and I went and bought a square of chocolate that said "Toda" (thank you) on it. We also [bought] a box of nice fancy chocolates, which we decided to give her in the event that I got pregnant. Since then the chocolates have become something of a joke between us.

Insofar as the questions about the birth mother, she told us that if I got pregnant, I would receive all the information about the birth mother. The egg donor would also be informed that I became pregnant so that she will know about her own fertility. If we both have children (God willing) then we will be informed about that, too.

I took estrogen tablets for two months without any phone calls telling us to come in. Finally, on the twenty-first day of the third month she called and told us to come in that night. We called PUAH and requested a maschgicha to meet us there, you had to order a maschgicha there, it was a secular hospital and they weren't part of the regular staff. The maschgicha was a nice woman named Bracha, she is Hasidic and lives in Petach Tikva.

She met us at the clinic, they handed us the condom and instructed us in how to use it properly. Bracha waited until we returned from our conjugal relations, took the sperm and carried it to the laboratory and gave it to the technician. She stood there and watched to make sure that no other man's sperm snuck in with ours.

We went home and waited. The next day we called and were told that we had four fertilized embryos growing away. We returned on Sunday, again with Bracha present, to unlock the precious embryos from the secured strong-box where they were stored. She gave them to the nurse to carry into the room where the insertion took place. The doctor was totally matter of fact and relaxed. I lay on my back for an hour, and then we went home. Two weeks later I took the test and I was pregnant; I was thrilled. But then I had a miscarriage. It has been a long road. Finally, we came to see the doctor here, and it turns out I don't necessarily need an egg donation. So now they took some eggs out of me and hopefully this time it will work.

Clearly, the social practice of egg donation in Israel is not governed by strict regulations. These dynamics will become even more pronounced [as elsewhere], in which we will see how far ovum entrepreneurs are willing to go to make these valuable procreative objects available. The intense market demand for ova in Israel, fueled by the overwhelming desire to have children, creates complex dilemmas for both infertile and fertile Israeli women.

Conclusion

Ovum-related technologies bring into sharp relief a question central to the conceptualization of kinship: Where do mothers come from? From surgical procedures? From the genetic material in ova? From the gestational experience of carrying a fetus? From the act of parturition? In a kinship system that determines religious identity matrilineally, and in a country that confers citizenship based on religious identity, these questions become even more profound: where does Jewish identity, the primary substance of Israeli citizenship, come from? Is it embedded in bodily substance? Or is it created in gestational environment? Does the incorporation of non-Jewish reproductive material into the bodies of Jews change the meaning of being an Israeli? Or of being a Jew? One would think that what goes into making the body is what goes into making the body politic. In this chapter, I have attempted to illustrate how reproductive technology makes these questions simultaneously explicit in the medical, Halakhic and political realms and how the answers overlap, collide, and remain unanswerable.

Even though ovum-related technologies provoke deep questions about the origin of Jewishness, the rush to utilize these technologies surges forward in Israel. Contemporary rabbis remain confident that proper exegesis of traditional texts will yield cogent answers to current and future reproductive dilemmas. For example, J. David Bleich (1991: 95) points to the Talmudic discussion in the Gemara, Tractate *Niddah* 23b in which the Talmudic rabbis presciently discuss how to determine the identity of a human embryo gestated in and born from an animal womb. Bleich observes that this text may function as a precedent for determining the identity of a human being born from an animal womb, a technological innovation that he acknowledges may soon become a real possibility.[20] The rabbinic questions here were (and may be): Is a human being born from an animal womb a person? Or is such a creature an artificial person, a *"golem."* The Talmudic rabbis debated these and other related questions that were once wildly hypothetical and yet now may become pragmatic: if a genetically human creature is born to a kosher animal, can it be slaughtered and eaten? Or the converse, if an animal-like creature is born to a Jewish woman, is such a creature a Jew, since it was gestated in and born from a Jewish womb? Based on rabbinic discussions of these questions, arguments are made that a being's identity should *not* be determined by its distinguishing *physical* characteristics, characteristics that today we would consider to be manifestations of its genetic substance, but should be determined by the identity of the being in which it was gestated and from which it was born.[21]

Bleich argues that to circumvent such questions, contemporary rabbis must begin to recognize genetic substance as a codeterminant of identity, together with the traditional determinant parturition. He argues that a strict adherence to parturition as the sole determinant of identity will create these and other serious interpretive problems as reproductive technology advances.

Bleich is not alone in expressing rabbinic caution and concern about the appropriate uses of these technologies, nor is he alone in making cogent, Talmudically based arguments for reshaping Jewish kinship thinking in light of them. He is in the minority, however, in advocating for genetic and gestational codeterminants of maternity; the majority of contemporary rabbinic decisors continue to adhere to the traditional notion that parturition from a Jewish woman must be the sole determinant of Jewishness.

Though traditional Jewish texts contain a rich variety of relational and reproductive metaphors, one must wonder if these technologies may one day provoke a conceptual crisis where the Halakhic tools for thinking about relatedness are finally called into question, where the Talmudic precedents for establishing Jewishness are ultimately revealed as anachronistic, and where the technologies for creating persons are acknowledged as truly novel and without metaphorical resonance in the traditional sources.

NOTES

1 I address these issues in another context: see Kahn 2000.
2 Some women recovered more slowly. Some said they felt significant cramping for a few days after the oocyte pick-up, in addition to nausea and exhaustion. Moreover, the operation and associated hormonal treatments are not without their considerable risks. In 1987 a woman named Rivi Ben Ari died in Tel Aviv following Pergonal treatments, which are often a prelude to the oocyte retrieval (Solomon 1991: 102–4).
3 See *Talmud Bavli Niddah* 17b and *Shulkhan Arukh, Yoreh De'ah* 183: 1.
4 The principal Halakhic source that contemporary rabbis interpret in relation to this question is the thirteenth-century *P'sak Halakha* (ruling) of Rav Peretz of Corbeil.
5 For a fuller discussion of these issues in the context of fertility treatments see Grazi 1994. In his chapter "Diagnostic Evaluations," Grazi explains the differences between a niddah and a *zavah*; the former is defined as "a woman who experiences vaginal bleeding from the uterus during her expected menstrual period, and a *zavah* is a woman who

experiences bleeding at times other than her expected period" (80). Both statuses render a woman ritually "unclean," though the period of uncleanliness differs. Grazi makes clear that bleeding produced "from a wound" incurred during diagnostic procedures in gynecological exams and fertility tests falls under a different Halakhic category: *makkah*. There is considerable rabbinic disagreement as to what constitutes a wound and how you can determine whether the source of bleeding is a wound or menstruation.

6 For a full discussion of the problems associated with artificial insemination and embryo transfer during the niddah period see Green 1984.
7 Rabbi J. David Bleich explains: "An organism that can be seen only by means of a magnifying glass or under a microscope is an organism of which Jewish law takes no notice.... (Hence) when the developing (human) organism is still sub-visual, the law takes no cognizance of its existence." See Bleich 1986: 144.
8 See Halperin 1988.
9 Rav Zalman Goldberg (1987) explains: "Rav Yosef Engel (Bet Otzar, 'Av') argues that there is a legal distinction between maternity and paternity. Paternity is determined at conception, as stated in the Talmud. Maternity, however, depends on birth and not on conception. He bases this distinction on a comment of Rashi (Meg. 13). The Gemara states that Queen Esther's father died when she was conceived and her mother died when she was born. Rashi explains that the statement is based on the verse '...and when her father and mother were dead' (Esther 2, 7). It previously states that '...she had neither father nor mother.' The redundancy teaches us that: 'she did not have a father or mother even one day. When she was conceived her father died, hence she did not have a father from the time that he was eligible to be considered a father. When she was born, her mother died; hence (her mother) was not eligible to be considered a mother.' We see here that there is a difference between maternity and paternity. The reason is that the father is irrelevant to the birth; hence his relationship is necessarily dependent on his role in conception. Maternity, however, is determined by the birth, since the mother gives birth to the baby. ...it follows that birth is the determinant of maternity...

the possibility exists, however, that birth is not the sole determinant of maternity." See also discussions of Midrashic sources regarding the intrauterine transfer of Dinah from the womb of Rachel to Leah, and the transfer of Joseph from the womb of Leah to Rachel as a model for understanding parturition as the determinant of maternity (Bleich 1983: 92–93); Rav Ezra Bick's discussion of this issue (Bick 1987); Gemara, *Yevamot* 97b, for the Halakhic source that indicates parturition is the determinant of maternity; and Bleich 1994.

10 See Bleich 1991.

11 Rav Waldenburg, *Tzits Eliezer* (in Hebrew), 15: 45, as reprinted in *Sefer Assia*, 5, Jerusalem 5746; R. Gershuni, *Kol Zafayikh*, Jerusalem 5740, as reprinted in Bleich 1991.

12 For a fuller discussion of the various rabbinic opinions on the determination of maternal identity see Bleich 1979, 1983, 1991. – 1981. Bleich, "Survey of Recent Halakhic Periodical Literature" in *Tradition*, 19(4).

13 Interestingly, this agricultural model of conception, known anthropologically as the "monogenetic theory of procreation," has been well documented among other Middle Eastern peoples and could be understood as one of the most compelling kinship myths indigenous to the region (Delaney 1991; Inhorn 1994).

14 For example, Regulation (4) of the ministry of health regulations (1987) provides: "Eggs shall be taken from women only for whom the following conditions exist: 1) The patient is involved in medical treatment as the result of fertility problems. 2) A responsible doctor determines that the removal of eggs will advance this treatment." Regulation (12b) states: "An egg which was taken from a woman for donation will be implanted in another woman only if she gave her consent to the donation."

15 For a fuller discussion on the religious status of children born to Jewish women from non-Jewish eggs see Bleich 1991.

16 See Bleich 1991. Bleich also provides an interesting discussion of rabbinic attitudes toward conversion of a child in utero in response to the question: could a Jewish woman carrying an embryo conceived with a non-Jewish egg immerse in a ritual bath and thereby convert the child in utero? (1991: 88–89).

17 For more information about Islamic rules concerning the new reproductive technologies see Inhorn 1994.

18 Many women I spoke to, all Jewish Israelis, have made it clear that though it is not an easy decision, they agreed to donate eggs because they wanted to help alleviate someone else's childlessness, a form of suffering they know all too well.

19 See Marcia Inhorn (1994) on Islamic law and the use of third-party donor material in infertility treatment.

20 See Klass 1996.

21 See also *Talmud Bavli Hullin* 79a, for a Talmudic discussion that favors determining species by descent.

BIBLIOGRAPHY

Bick, Ezra. 1987. "Maternity in Fetal Transplants." In *Crossroads: Halakha and the Modern World*. Alon Shvut-Gush Etzion: Zomet, 79–85.

——. 1993. "Ovum Donations: A Rabbinic Conceptual Model of Maternity." *Tradition* 28(1): 28–46.

Bleich, J. David. 1979. *Contemporary Halakhic Problems*. Vol. 1. New York: Yeshiva University Press.

——. 1983. *Contemporary Halakhic Problems*. Vol. 2. New York: Yeshiva University Press.

——. 1986. "Ethical Concerns in Artificial Procreation: A Jewish Perspective," *Publications de l'Académie du Royaume du Maroc, vol. X: Problèmes d'éthiques Engendrés par les Nouvelles Maîtrises de la Procréation Humaine*: 144.

——. 1991. "In-Vitro Fertilization: Questions of Maternal Identity and Conversion." *Tradition* 25(4): 82–102.

——. 1994. "Maternal Identity Revisited." *Tradition* 28(2): 52–57.

Corea, Gena, et al. 1987. *Man-Made Women*. Indianapolis: Indiana University Press.

Delaney, Carol. 1991. *The Seed and the Soil: Gender and Cosmology in Turkish Village Society*. Berkeley: University of California Press.

Goldberg, Rav Zalman N. 1987. "Maternity in Fetal Transplants." In *Crossroads: Halakha and the Modern World*. Zomet: Alon Shvut-Gush Etzion.

Grazi, Richard. 1994. *Be Fruitful and Multiply: Fertility Therapy and the Jewish Tradition*. Jerusalem: Genesis Press.

Green, Joseph. 1984. "Artificial Insemination in Particular Cases of Infertility (in Hebrew). *Assia* 10(32): 17–29.

Halperin, Mordechai. 1988. "In-Vitro Fertilization, Embryo, Transfer, and Embryo Freezing." *Jewish Medical Ethics* 1(1): 25–30.

Inhorn, Marcia. 1994. *Quest for Conception: Gender, Infertility, and Egyptian Medical Traditions.* Philadelphia: University of Pennsylvania Press.

Kahn, Susan Martha. 2000. "Rabbis and Reproduction: The Social Uses of New Reproductive Technologies among Ultraorthodox Jews in Israel." In *Interpreting Fertility*, edited by Marcia Inhorn and Frank Van Balen. Berkeley: University of California Press.

Klass, Perry. 1996. "The Artificial Womb Is Born." *New York Times Magazine*, 29 September.

Raymond, Janice. 1993. *Women as Wombs.* San Francisco: Harper.

Solomon, Alison. 1991. "Anything for a Baby: Reproductive Technology in Israel." In *Calling the Equality Bluff*, edited by Barbara Svirsky and Marilyn Safir. New York: Pergamon.

Spallone, Patricia. 1989. *Beyond Conception: The New Politics of Reproduction.* Granby, Mass.: Bergin and Garvey.

Stanworth, Michelle, ed. 1987. *Reproductive Technologies: Gender, Motherhood, and Medicine.* Cambridge: Cambridge University Press.

20

Gender, Genetics, and Generation: Reformulating Biology in Lesbian Kinship

Corinne P. Hayden

The complicated historical relationship be-tween ideas about homosexuality and concepts of "the family" in American culture makes the idea of gay and lesbian families – "chosen" or "created" – a provocative one in the study of American kinship. Insofar as lesbians and gay men have been ideologically excluded from the realm of kinship in American culture (Weston 1991:4–6), it is perhaps not surprising that claims to the legitimacy of gay and lesbian family configurations are often articulated *and* contested in terms of their perceived differ-ence from (or similarity to) normative ideolo-gies of "the American family." In her pivotal work, *Families We Choose* (1991), Kath Wes-ton argues for the *distinctiveness* of a certain configuration of gay and lesbian kinship in which biological ties are decentered and choice, or love, becomes the defining feature of kin relationships. For Weston, gay and les-bian chosen families are neither derivative of, nor substitutes for, "straight," biological fam-ilies; rather, they are distinctive in their own right (1991:210). Ellen Lewin takes a markedly different approach to the value of distinctive-ness in her recent book, *Lesbian Mothers* (1993). By her own account exceeding the goal of her earlier work on maternal custody strategies – showing that lesbian mothers are "just as good" as heterosexual mothers – Lewin finds that "motherhood" in American culture constitutes a defining feature of womanhood that indeed supersedes the "difference" of les-bian identity (1993:3). In this reading, there is nothing particularly unique about the ways in which lesbian mothers negotiate relatedness and relationships.

Though they are not explicitly foregrounded in such terms, I would argue that these two pivotal ethnographies together suggest that "biology," broadly conceived, is a crucial axis around which claims to the "distinctiveness" of gay and lesbian kinship revolve. Thus the rela-tive centrality of biology in gay and lesbian families might be seen to signal a corollary assimilation into, or departure from, "trad-itional" forms of American kinship. In this logic, the argument would read as follows: when biological ties are displaced (as in Wes-ton's work), claims to distinctiveness can be made; where biological ties are central (espe-cially in the case of motherhood), claims to difference lose their relevance or legitimacy.

I want to disrupt the flow of this argument on several levels. To that end, this article is an exploration of the ways in which many lesbian mothers employ notions of biology, in the con-text of donor insemination, to articulate their own sense of uniquely lesbian kinship. I offer, then, an ethnographic reading of specific kinds of claims I have encountered in recent lesbian-feminist writings, newspaper articles, court cases, and informal conversations. I must stress that these particular articulations of lesbian familial desire in no way offer a "representative" stance on parenting within lesbian and gay communities.[1] On the one hand, the question of whether or not to become a parent has a long and complicated history for many gay men and lesbians; for lesbians in particular, the centrality of motherhood to American cultural narratives of womanhood has long made mothering a particularly potent site of contestation. Current articulations of the radical potential of lesbian families must be placed within the context of continuing debates over reproductive "choice" – and the choice *not* to mother – within various lesbian and feminist communities.[2]

On the other hand, for lesbians and gay men who are parents, the two-parent "intentional" family (Lewin 1993) is obviously not the only model. Lesbians and gay men have children through previous heterosexual relationships; they adopt children; they are single parents or raise children with several co-parents. Moreover, gay and lesbian parenting families have long existed, and certainly predate the current interest in "alternative" families. I focus specifically on lesbians who create families through donor insemination not because they are a defining model for lesbian kinship (if there could be such a thing) but rather because of the particular ways in which biology is made both explicit and mutable in these visions of a "distinct" family configuration.[3] Moreover, these claims to a uniquely lesbian kinship often challenge the (heterosexual) gender configuration that is foundational to American cultural notions of kinship. These articulations of lesbian families thus provide a context in which to continue important theoretical discussions of the relationship among gender, sexuality, and kinship (see Collier and Yanagisako 1987; Rubin 1975; Weston 1991).

I want to follow Marilyn Strathern in resisting the temptation to argue for wholly novel conceptual developments in ideas about kinship, though I do hope to retain space for imagining how "images pressed into new service acquire new meanings" (Strathern 1992b:15). Such an approach assumes from the outset that there is nothing "truly new" under the sun; at the same time, the continual back and forth between "new" and "old" ideas allows for the possibility of reformulating existing symbols in creative and meaningful ways.

Taking on "American Kinship"

The claim to a distinctive gay and lesbian kinship elicits questions about the elasticity of American kinship as a symbolic system and implies the possibility of transforming the dominant model of American kinship. Such moves call for a clarification of exactly what *kind(s)* of kinship one has in mind and how one chooses to define dominant, transformative, or derivative versions of American kinship. Though it has been challenged on many fronts, the foundational model of American kinship laid out by David Schneider (1980[1968]) more than 25 years ago remains an enduring one. Discussions of gay and lesbian kinship, and arguments about its sameness (and therefore derivative nature) or difference (implying the potential for transformation), continue to resonate with the terms that Schneider set forth in 1968. American kinship, he argued, is a symbolic system resting on the two contrasting but mutually dependent elements of blood (shared biogenetic substance) and love (a code for conduct both legitimating the creation of blood ties and governing the behavior of those who are related by blood). Characterizing Americans' (and American anthropologists') understanding of kinship as a "folk theory of biological reproduction," Schneider declared the *symbol* of (hetero)sexual intercourse – mediating and mediated by blood and marriage – as central to American kinship (1980[1968]:37–38).

Not surprisingly, this premise has been made problematic by lesbians and gay men, who have been symbolically excluded from the realm of kinship. The supposed exclusion from, and threat to, family that marks gay men and lesbians has amounted to a virtual denial of their cultural citizenship, as Weston has noted (1991:4–6). Indeed, one has only to glance at the most basic manifestations of homophobia in the United States to grasp their foundation on the interdependent web of kinship, sexuality, gender, and procreation. Exemplified by the pseudo-evolutionary theory that homosexuals must *recruit* progeny because they cannot reproduce themselves, this particular version of the "threat to family" argument highlights the ways in which heterosexuality, gender, and kinship are mutually constituted.[4]

The perceived centrality of procreative sexuality to the stability of "the family" underlies such familiar statements as, "I have a problem with homosexuals who flaunt what they're doing... before the public in an effort to destroy and break down family life.... The family creates. Homosexuals only cause trouble. They can't create anything" (Glasgow quoted in Green 1991:1–2). It is likewise this notion of creativity that figures so strongly in claims to the legitimacy of gay and lesbian families, with or without children. At stake in such contests over creativity is the meaning of sexual intercourse in American kinship and, subsequently, the ways in which blood and love are privileged as defining features of families. Weston notes the ways in which chosen families complicate "traditional" notions of blood and love: "Familial ties between persons of the same sex that may be erotic *but are not grounded in biology or procreation* do not fit any tidy division of kinship into relations of blood and marriage" (1991:3, emphasis added). Weston's work focuses on families of friends and lovers – "chosen families" that challenge the sanctity of blood and marriage as the sole determinants of legitimate kin ties.

Although these chosen families bring up crucial questions about kinship *without* biological connections (or without the *expectation* of creating biological kin through procreation),[5] quite different questions arise in the creation of lesbian and gay parenting families in which biology, via procreation, reenters the picture. Using Weston's work as a foundation for exploring lesbian and gay critiques of the central premises of American kinship, I will focus below on the complicated intersections of biological procreation and lesbian kinship. I am interested not simply in the assertion that biology *is* mobilized in articulations of "uniquely" lesbian family configurations; my concern lies more in the ways in which the symbol of biology is unpacked, dispersed, and distributed within these configurations.[6] In this way, certain articulations of lesbian kinship provide important

ground on which to theorize biology as a symbol that is continually refigured within the contested symbolic field(s) of American kinship.

Love Makes a Family[7]

Weston implicates chosen families in an explicit challenge to the dominant model of American kinship and its foundation in procreation and biological ties. In *Families We Choose*, she writes,

The very notion of gay families asserts that people who claim nonprocreative sexual identities... can lay claim to family ties of their own. ... Theirs has not been a proposal to number gay families among variations in "American kinship," but a more comprehensive attack on the privilege accorded to a biogenetically grounded mode of determining what relationships will *count* as kinship. [1991:35, emphasis in original]

The families to which Weston refers are families forged out of ties to friends and lovers. United by choice and love, not by biological ties or the expectation of creating such, these families clearly set themselves apart from the dominant model of American kinship and its maxim that "blood is thicker than water." Without denying that blood ties "work" (Strathern 1992b), chosen families nonetheless level a profound critique at the *centrality* in American kinship of heterosexual, procreative relationships and the biogenetic ties that arise from these relationships.

Weston clearly believes that chosen families are neither imitative nor derivative of the dominant model of American kinship. Rather, she argues that they constitute a distinctive form of kinship, contrastive rather than analogous to straight kinship (Weston 1991:211).[8] Still, she maintains that choice cannot be read as license to create a family structure unfettered by conventional notions of kinship. Situating chosen families within the bounded symbolic universe of American kinship, Weston's analysis posits a continuum in which gay, chosen families have emerged in explicit opposition to, but coexisting with, straight, biological families. Thus the very idea of chosen families becomes meaningful only in the context of the cultural belief in the power of blood ties (Weston 1991:211).

There is another dimension to chosen families' position within the dominant symbolic matrix of American kinship. In her review of *Families We Choose*, Strathern writes that perhaps *the* fundamental critique enacted through chosen families is that they "make explicit the fact that there was always a choice as to whether or not biology is made the foundation of relationships" (1992b:3). This, indeed, is one of Schneider's central points throughout *American Kinship:* though Americans believe that blood determines family, there is and always has been a necessary element of choice in the degree to which blood ties become "relationships" in any given family (not to mention the ways in which blood ties are conceived in the first place) (Schneider 1980[1968]:62–63; see also Strathern 1981).

Schneider's and Strathern's reminders of the centrality of choice in heterosexual kinship dislodge biology from its privileged place in that model; they assert unequivocally that there is much more at work in the creation of kinship in American culture than a fervent belief in the self-evidence of blood ties might allow. In the context of lesbian and gay kinship, this displacement of biology as *the* central and defining feature of family connotes a challenge to the direct, exclusive correlation that is assumed between heterosexual procreation and the production of kin ties.

In Strathern's analysis, chosen families challenge the privilege enjoyed by straight kinship by shifting the emphasis from blood to choice *on two levels* – explicitly, through their own chosen families, and implicitly, by suggesting that despite its supposed basis in the "facts of nature," straight, blood-based kinship is itself a construction. As the focus of this article now turns to lesbian motherhood, Strathern's point bears elaboration. The creation of lesbian and gay families with children cannot be discussed in exactly the same terms as chosen families, since each indexes somewhat different notions of biology. Where chosen families may *decentralize* biology, lesbian families' explicit mobilization of biological ties challenges the notion of biology as a *singular* category through which kin ties are reckoned. Far from depleting its symbolic capital, the dispersal of the biological tie seems here to highlight its elasticity within the symbolic matrix of American kinship.

Gender and Kinship

While the chosen families of lesbians and gay men may forge new ground in kinship divorced from procreation, lesbian co-parenting families engender a slightly different set of symbolic renegotiations, since the presence of procreation refigures the blood/choice dichotomy. Does biological reproduction ground kinship "back" in biology, thereby negating the "progress" achieved by chosen families? Does lesbian sex itself create kinship different from that mediated by heterosexual sex? Does a child with two mothers come from a different kind of kinship arrangement than a child with one mother and/or one father? As these questions suggest, sex and gender, in the context of a procreative family, become central elements of contestation in efforts to define the place of lesbian families in American kinship.

Many feminist anthropologists, in critique of Schneider, contend that "the American Kinship System" does not exist apart from its constituent elements of gender, age, ethnicity, race, or class, among other things (Collier and Yanagisako 1987; Delaney and Yanagisako, in press; McKinnon 1992; Strathern 1992a). For Schneider, these mediating factors do not inhabit the realm of "pure culture." Collier and Yanagisako (1987) have argued that the split between the "cultural" realm of kinship and the "mediating factor" of gender is illusory, at least in American culture. Kinship and gender are mutually constituted, they write, because both categories are based on the same ideas of biological difference. Gender assumptions about the facts of sexual reproduction pervade kinship theory, just as sexual reproduction is central to the definition of gender (Collier and Yanagisako 1987:23–34). Thus even a separation of the two on a "purely analytical" level, as Schneider enjoins, becomes problematic.[9]

Further, categories such as gender, age, class, and so on, produce structural distinctions that mediate relationships within families; to talk about any of them, therefore, means to talk about power. Schneider's insistence on separating gender from kinship has, by extension, opened him up to criticisms that his model ignores issues of power and inequality (Delaney and Yanagisako, in press; McKinnon

1992). Delaney and Yanagisako write, "Schneider did not address the question of how inequality is embedded in cultural systems, in part because he did not follow out the logic of the specificity of symbols and instead made abstractions of them" (1995:3). Standing firm in the position that symbolic analysis of kinship – kept separate from gender, age, power, and so on – goes only so far as blood and love, Schneider ensures the stability of his model of kinship. For, in these fairly abstract terms, a "transformation" in kinship would necessitate a complete departure from the blood-love (or blood-choice) symbolic matrix. Thus, for example, chosen families as described by Weston cannot claim distinctiveness because they remain enmeshed within the tension between blood and love. A more contextualized, power-conscious analysis such as that enjoined by Delaney, Yanagisako, McKinnon, and Strathern allows for the stability of Schneider's symbolic *universe* while leaving room for reconfigurations of the meanings of these symbols.

Power and Parenthood

The centrality of power and gender to American kinship is particularly illuminated by lesbian families in which both parents are explicitly considered mothers. These families potentially unsettle the "dominant" vision of American kinship in several ways, perhaps most significantly in their challenge to ideas about gendered hierarchy and parenthood. For women with a clear and gendered agenda for lesbian motherhood, its promise is deeply bound to the existence of a second female parent, who is neither downplayed nor de-gendered. She is not a father substitute, nor is she a gender-neutral parent; she is clearly another mother. Resonating with a legacy of feminist and lesbian-feminist writings on "compulsory heterosexuality" (most notably, of course, Adrienne Rich's [1984] article by that name), such understandings of the radical potential of lesbian motherhood are offered in criticism of – and as an alternative to – the institutionalized gender inequities seen to inhere in heterosexuality.

There is a dual implication to this oppositional construction of parental roles. First, embracing rather than contesting the image of motherhood as a distinctly female, nurturant enterprise, the benefits of the family are construed in terms of a doubling of maternal love and support. In the feminist volume *Politics of the Heart: A Lesbian Parenting Anthology*, one contributor writes, "I'm not opposed to fathers, but I do believe every baby should have at least two mothers" (Washburne 1987: 144–145). Another notes that "when straight mothers find out my son has two moms, they are actually envious on some level; there are two people doing the job they often do alone" (Hill 1987:118).

Second, more than the "convenience" of double motherhood, claims to the distinctiveness of lesbian co-parenting rest heavily on a critique of the power relationships that many of these women associate with heterosexual families. Such understandings of lesbian parenting allege, on the one hand, that heterosexuality contains built-in power inequities; by contrast, lesbian mothers claim to offer gender equality and therefore parental equality. Counteracting the accusations that same-sex relationships are, by definition, pathological (and therefore detrimental to children's development), many mental health professionals and theorists contend that the gender configurations of gay and lesbian relationships are indeed as healthy as, if not healthier than, those of their straight counterparts.[10] Contributing to this compensatory project is psychologist Margaret Nichols, who writes,

> In my experience, far too many heterosexual relationships become bogged down in the mire of sex-role conflicts and never transcend these conflicts to a point where both partners see each other as full human beings. I do not mean to imply that lesbian and gay relationships are without conflict, simply that the conflicts...are certainly much less likely to exhibit the vast power differentials that can be found in many heterosexual relationships. [1987:102]

If the absence of gender *difference* is portrayed as a positive attribute, then the gendering of both partners as *female* is seen to multiply the benefits exponentially. Suzanne Cusick writes that a lesbian relationship is

> a relationship based on non-power – that is, a relationship in which a porous boundary

exists at all moments between she who seems to have the power and she who doesn't, allowing for a flow of power in both directions. *No one in the relationship is formed to be the power figure, though all can play at it.* [1991: 10, emphasis added]

De-eroticizing this last point for a moment, the thesis of equal or fluid power – given the premise of non-power – forms the basis of a politicized view of the potential for difference in certain lesbian co-parenting families. Thus, bearing and raising a child in a lesbian household is understood as a tool for "radical motherhood" to combat "heteromothering" (Cooper 1987:223); a "unique opportunity in history to raise children in a home with two parents with potentially equal power" (Polikoff 1987: 329); or, on the other side of the coin, perhaps creates a perverse environment in which men and women do not "adhere to their roles" (Polikoff 1990:560).

Further, as Cusick's erotic gender equation amply suggests, gender roles within kinship are inextricably linked to the act and symbol of sex itself. Schneider contends that sexual intercourse is a central symbol in American kinship because it is through sex (or the symbol thereof) that blood ties are created and family relationships mediated:

Sexual intercourse (the act of procreation) is the symbol which provides the distinctive features in terms of which both the members of the family as relatives and the family as a culture unit are defined and differentiated. [1980 (1968):31]

He continues, "Father is the genitor, mother the genetrix of the child which is their offspring.... Husband and wife are lovers and the child is the product of their love as well as the object of their love" (1980[1968]:43). In these terms, lesbian parents do not fit easily into American kinship. Genetrix and genitor are not interchangeable; to replace one with the other is dramatically to change the character of the union between parents. The union between man and woman (as husband and wife) is one imbued with deep symbolic meaning in American culture, not the least of which is, as Schneider says, the means through which family relationships are created and differentiated.

Strathern notes that this symbolic union is also deeply imbued with gendered relations of power:

In ... Euro-American formulations, male and female parents are differently placed with respect to parenthood: *an equal union is also an asymmetric pairing....* The relationship of the sexual act to conception is not, therefore, simply a technical one. It serves to reproduce parenthood as the perceived outcome of a union in which the parties are distinguished by gender. Apart from anything else, it thus plays a *conceptually* significant part in procreation. [1992a:4, emphasis added]

In an analysis conscious of gender and power relations, a family mediated by lesbian sex arguably makes kinship look different than a family "unified" through the sexual relationship between mother and father. Strathern clearly implicates sexual intercourse in the symbolic reproduction of structural gender relations. For those invested in a feminist reworking of parental roles, the unity symbolized by lesbian lovers as mothers reproduces a different gender and power configuration through which the lesbian family is organized. To follow the logic of Collier and Yanagisako's argument that gender and kinship are mutually constituted, this particular understanding of lesbian kinship carves out its own place along the spectrum of American kinships *precisely because* it refigures the alignment of gender and power roles which have traditionally marked the American family.

All Lesbian Mothers Do Not Create Equally

As might be expected, this somewhat utopian, egalitarian vision of lesbian kinship runs into trouble in the face of a legal structure that retains its historic commitment to the equation of blood ties with family. The promise that some women see in lesbian families – the opportunity to raise children in an environment of gender equality – is often thrown into disarray when one partner bears a child. Having children through donor insemination automatically introduces its own asymmetry into the relationship among lesbian parents and child. The "birth mother" has a validated and immediately recognizable relationship with her child, while her partner (as neither a biological parent nor a legally recognized spouse) is doubly excluded from the realm of kinship. Her marginality is expressed in the dearth of established, much less positive, terms for the role of the "co-mother." Often represented as the proverbial "lack," she is the "nonbiological mother," the "nonbirth mother," the "other mother" (Riley 1988:89).

This structural inequality is perceived to have profound repercussions for the dynamics of lesbian families. Psychologist Sally Crawford writes,

> When the relationship between parents is unrecognized . . . then no matter how defined the system may be internally, ex-lovers, ex-husbands, and members of the couple's family of origin can often walk in and walk out at will, as though the family unit does not exist. [1987:203]

One mother notes, "If the family structure is not reflected legally, then our families are distorted, they're not supported, and we're not able to function fully as the families we are" (Keen 1991:8)

While both mothers may talk of the ways their family is distorted by the lack of legal recognition, co-mother and birth mother often express significantly different concerns. Toni Tortorilla writes,

> There is no readily definable slot [for nonbiological parents in a lesbian or gay relationship]. The parameters of society's vision are stretched by our very existence. . . . And yet, though standing outside the protection and sanction of the system, many adults still choose to enter into a parental role with the children of their lovers. They commit time and energy to loving, nurturing, and supporting these children while risking the changes which could lead to separation from those whose lives they nourished and formed. It is a risk the biological parent often minimizes or fails to recognize in her own need for support with childrearing. [1987: 174]

Another woman writes of feeling like a fraud "if I act like he's my baby. I'm afraid someone will ask me about labor or my husband or something. I have to keep telling myself he *is* my baby and he will be perceived that way

because it's the truth" (Gray 1987:136, emphasis in original).

Though not articulated as frequently, there is a flip side to this imbalance, which one woman terms "The Comother's Choice." She writes,

> Kathleen is angry that I have [a choice]. . . . My doubts – "I don't know if I can do my writing and be in This Situation" – all point to the imbalance between us. She can't choose anymore. . . . Andrew is the new life. That's not the choice I made. That's the choice of the biological mother. I chose parenting without complete sacrifice. [Gray 1987:137]

The dilemmas engendered by the absence of a biological tie between a child and co-mother illuminate the centrality of blood ties to the dispensation of familial rights and obligations in American kinship. The element of choice in these families simultaneously heightens the sense of "risk," "creativity," and freedom from "complete sacrifice" for the nonbiological partner. The myriad ways in which lesbian mothers attempt to legitimize their family structures by rectifying this asymmetry, symbolically and legally, demonstrate the complexity with which the symbol of the blood tie retains its salience even in the midst of an explicit challenge to certain "traditional" notions of American kinship.

Blood and Other Fluid Symbols

In contrast to the attempts by chosen families to decentralize biology in kinship, many gay and lesbian co-parenting families often attempt to create equality between parents precisely by establishing a figurative or literal sharing of blood between the nonbiological mother and her child. Whether calling up the metaphor of shared blood ties or creating a more direct genetic link between co-mother and child, these families employ biology as an important symbol that can be articulated and embodied in a number of ways.

In the recent case *Alison D. v. Virginia M.* (552 N.Y.S.2d 321), in which the co-mother petitioned for a hearing for visitation rights after she and her partner separated, one *Amici Curiae* brief (Gay and Lesbian Parents Coalition et al. 1990) delineated explicit actions generally taken by co-parents to indicate their intention to enter into a fully functioning parental role with their children. The brief cites actions that imply a desire to maintain an equal relationship between parents vis-à-vis the child. These actions include combining or hyphenating the co-parents' names to form the child's surname, "a practice which identifies the child with both co-parents," and having the child call both parents names that reflect equal parental obligations, as in "Daddy Wayne and Daddy Sol," or "Momma G and Momma D" (Gay and Lesbian Parents Coalition et al. 1990:29–31). Further, they often "manifest their equal roles as parents by having the parents and siblings – *on both sides* – participate as aunts, uncles, and grandparents" (Gay and Lesbian Parents Coalition et al. 1990:31, emphasis added). Kinship terms thus become one medium through which gay and lesbian co-parenting families declare equal claims, for both parents, to a legitimate relationship with their children. These relationships and their assertion of familial love clearly infer blood ties (and the rights and obligations that accompany blood relations) among children, parents, and extended family.

The mobilization of kinship terms is part of an overall display of "deliberateness," a symbolic flag that signals partners' commitment to forming a "real" family. As the *Amici* brief states, "The acts and declarations of co-parents leave little doubt that they intend to assume all the obligations of parenthood, including financial support, on a permanent basis" (Gay and Lesbian Parents Coalition et al. 1990:29). Part of the determination of intent to form a family is, arguably, co-parents' extensive deliberation over the decision to have a child: "These couples take the act of parenting very seriously" (Gay and Lesbian Parents Coalition et al. 1990:29).

This strategy leads to an intriguing attempt to locate the metaphor of biological, *generative* power in the co-parent. Claiming that co-parents engage in a *joint* decision to raise a child, the *Amici* brief argues that lesbians and gay men claim an active role, both figuratively and literally, in the creation of the child:

It is because *both* co-parents wish to act as parents that a child is brought into their home. The non-biological co-parent is thus partly re-sponsible for the child's presence in the home, *or even for the child's very existence.* ...The non-biological co-[mother] typically participates in every step of the ... pregnancy to the fullest extent possible. [Gay and Lesbian Parents Coalition et al. 1990:32, emphasis added]

By asserting the co-parent's responsibility for the existence of the child, gay and lesbian parents make clear their investment in the central relationship between procreation and unity within the family. On one level, such a declaration of procreative agency is equally significant for both gay men and lesbians, given the context of a cultural logic in which gay and lesbian relationships are deemed illegitimate because of their figurative impotence/sterility.

Further, the appropriation of generative power specifically by a lesbian co-parent places her squarely in the realm of (male) authorship. She grounds her claim to chosen motherhood in the image of agency and biological creativity – an image that has defined American cultural conceptions of the male contribution to procreation. As Carol Delaney (1986) has argued, the cultural narrative of paternity as authorship positions the male contribution as central and irreplaceable to the identity of the product of conception. Thus paternity "has meant the primary and creative role" (Delaney 1986:502). Despite a general sense that men and women contribute equally to the genetic makeup of their progeny, this symbolic asymmetry persists (Delaney 1986; Rothman 1989). Thus the woman is not a co-creator but a provider of a nurturant environment; "female receptivity" is glorified at the expense of "female creativity" (Delaney 1986:495).[11]

Lesbian co-mothers who take on a generative role in the conception of their children claim space for female creativity. In so doing, the co-mother does not attempt to become male; rather, she carves out a distinctive but recognizable place in the birth of her child.[12] Nancy Zook and Rachel Hallenback write of their experience performing donor insemination at home:

The jar [of semen] was handed over, hugs exchanged, and he was on his way. With Nancy's hips on pillows at a forty-five degree-angle, Rachel, taking a quick breath, inserted the

semen into Nancy's vagina with a sterile syringe.... Rachel's participation in conception
was crucial to us, as this was to be her child
as well. [1987:90]

By impregnating Nancy, Rachel becomes
intimately connected with the act of conception in a way that challenges the dichotomy
between (female) gestation/receptivity and
(male) authorship/agency.

Central to this transformed reading of generative power is the "uncertainty" of the physical bond of paternity. Generation becomes less
a genetic concept than a kinetic one; it is less an
issue of the *ownership* of biogenetic substance
than one of placing this substance in motion, of
being responsible for starting off the "unseen
process unfolding in Nancy's body" (Zook and
Hallenback 1987:90). Rachel's claim to generative power and the sharing of her identity
with the child's thus constitutes a powerful
reworking of the idea of genetic authorship.
The act of begetting is separated from authorship; shared parenthood can be demonstrated
through active participation in the process,
without necessarily laying claim to a genetic
relationship as well.[13]

Where such claims to female creativity can
remove the sperm donor's genetic contribution
from the picture, other strategies unreservedly
embrace the underlying American cultural
understanding of genetics as a defining feature
of personhood, an indicator of health and personality, a blueprint for appearance and disposition. Thus some lesbian co-mothers use
donor insemination in ways that more directly
establish biogenetic ties *within* the family. In
cases where each woman bears a child, the
same donor is sometimes used so that the children will be related (Gay and Lesbian Parents
Coalition et al. 1990:30–31). This tactic is
often utilized not only by women who want a
consistent "male presence" for their children
but also by those who desire an anonymous
donor while retaining genetic connections
within the family (Hill 1987:112). One couple
interviewed in *Politics of the Heart* (1987) al-
ternated donors to make the identity of the
father unclear, only to decide later that they
wanted to identify him in response to their
daughter's fascination with a friend's father.
The mothers imply that the father, if known,

will become the donor for the next child,
though they do not envision that he will have
a relationship with the children (Hill
1987:111).[14] In such instances, the donor
gains significance within the family, not
through his direct involvement as a person
who is a "relative" (Schneider 1980 [1968]),
but rather through his ability to provide the
substance that will ensure biogenetic continuity between offspring. Biogenetic substance
itself becomes the object of importance, separate from the identity of the donor.

Biology here is abstracted and dispersed in a
way that challenges the cultural assumption of
the primacy of the male seed (Delaney 1986).
Though lesbians may take great care in choosing a donor, the act of insemination, by eliminating direct physical contact, is often seen to
minimize the man's role *as a gendered individual* in conception. The focus is then not on the
person of the donor, but rather on semen,
"making the procreative pair (if any) woman
plus sperm, gendered person plus gender signifier" (Weston 1991:171).

Weston suggests that lesbians are somewhat
unique in creating a distinction between male
personhood, on the one hand, and the male's
physical contribution to conception, on the
other; such a distinction does not seem to be
an inevitable consequence of the technology
itself (1991:171). She cites a 1989 study
indicating that married heterosexual women
associated insemination with adultery and
extramarital sex, and believed that insemination would allow an unwanted third party
into their marriage relationship. The lesbians
surveyed by Weston (1991:171), in contrast,
did not view insemination as a substitution
for something that would otherwise have
come from their sexual partners; their link to
the donor was patently nonsexual. This dis-
juncture allows the nonbiological mother to
take on a parenting role without the danger of
displacing another (male) individual who is
also a parent; she *is* the other parent. Though
genetic continuity is powerful as an abstracted,
disembodied signifier of family, it is also
employed as a literal signifier for kinship and
love in a more "connected" or "owned" sense
(Laqueur 1990:212). A couple may choose a
donor whose physical characteristics in some
way resemble those of the co-mother, suggest-

ing again the sharing of substance and the re-production of her image. Or, the brother of the nonbiological parent-to-be may be the donor, giving both women a biogenetic link to the child. Thus, when the donor possesses desirable traits (i.e., a genetic relationship with, or physical resemblance to, the co-mother), lesbian mothers may choose to incorporate those traits into their notions of family. Genetic continuity, whether literal or implied, becomes an integral resource in such attempts to bring a certain unity to lesbian parenting families.

Finally, in the most old-fashioned sense of biogenetic relatedness, the donor might be incorporated into the family, whether as a gendered individual (the proverbial "male presence") or as a co-parent. Of course, such relationships are not always simple matters of unilateral choice. On the one hand, they can be complicated by donors' contestatory attempts to secure paternity and parental rights; on the other hand, not uncommonly, lesbian mothers may rethink their initial decision on the matter and attempt to create a more (or less) involved relationship with the donor than they had originally planned.

As the myriad examples above suggest, lesbian mothers' strategies to gain symbolic legitimation for their families (in the context of donor insemination) effectively disperse the "biological connection" as it has been conceived in American kinship. Insemination is perceived to give lesbian parents space to negotiate the degree to which a donor's sperm is imbued with (or disabused of) distinctive features of identity. In many cases, the mobility of disembodied sperm allows the deployment of genetic ties in the service of unifying lesbian families. Thus genetic substance *itself* can become the referent for relatedness (as when the same anonymous donor is used so that the children will be related); a donor may be chosen on the basis of features that he shares with the "nonbiological" mother, thereby implying a biogenetic connection between her and the child; or the donor, by virtue of his biogenetic connection to the child, can be incorporated into the family configuration. On the one hand, these moves reify the importance of genetic continuity in the construction of kin relations; however, insofar as they allow for varying gradations of the separation of genetic

substance from its "owner," they disrupt the cultural narrative of paternity as authorship. But, again, just as genetic ties retain their appeal (in dispersed form), so too does this notion of authorship persist though it is reinscribed here with a different kind of gender/genetic symbolism. Within the logistics of insemination, the *act* of begetting can be separated from the ownership of genetic substance. Here, a kinetic reading of generation, of bringing into being, supersedes genetic connection as the privileged signifier of relatedness.

The notion of biological relatedness in this context takes on an excess of meanings. One effect of this excess is that biogenetic connection explicitly becomes a contingent, rather than immutable, feature of relatedness. Yet, as is apparent above, its contingency does not signal trivialization. Instead, the creative lengths to which many lesbian mothers go to inscribe their families with genetic continuity speak eloquently to the tremendous, continued salience of biological relatedness.

Reformulating the "Single" Mother

The enterprising mobilization of genetic/kinetic relatedness in these visions of lesbian kinship often calls up an arguably "old-fashioned" notion of motherhood as the quintessential fulfillment of womanhood (see Lewin 1993). Indeed, as I noted earlier, the very distinctiveness of lesbian families is often predicated on the fact that they offer a multiplication of femaleness; it is perhaps not entirely surprising that the cultural narrative of motherhood as the ultimate expression of female identity often finds its way into these claims. This, arguably, is the central paradox that arises in casting lesbian motherhood as "unique"; just as the gender configuration of lesbian co-parenting families promises an ostensibly different model of parenthood, the supposed naturalness, and therefore universality, of motherhood both highlights and undermines that uniqueness. Thus the virtues of lesbian families are articulated in terms of the virtue of having not just two parents, but two *mothers*; at the same time, motherhood can eclipse the difference encoded in a lesbian identity. Thus, as one woman notes, "even when someone knows I am a lesbian my motherhood makes me seem normal" (Polikoff 1987:53).

Lewin's work (1993) is particularly instructive regarding the ways in which motherhood can become the core of identity for heterosexual and lesbian mothers alike. Quite apart from my focus here, her concern is with single mothers. Arguably, the challenges of single parenthood magnify the centrality of motherhood to the identities of the women Lewin describes. Lesbians who enter into motherhood with one or more co-parents confront slightly different demands, including negotiating the place of the so-called nonbiological mother within the family configuration. It is here, in the space occupied by this "other mother," that the radical potential of lesbian co-parenting is often envisioned.[15]

How then does the "naturalness" of motherhood intersect with negotiations of nonbiological motherhood in lesbian family configurations? Quite in line with conventional American cultural constructions of maternity and paternity, it is the perceived singularity or unitariness of biological motherhood that might be seen, in the first place, to impel the mobilization of genetic continuity (associated with paternity) in creating a biogenetic connection for the "nonbiological" mother. For, unlike paternity, which is understood in terms of alienable relationships and mobile biogenetic substance, maternity is understood to be less easily dispersed (see Barnes 1973). If it is "inconceivable to Euro-Americans that a child could be born motherless" (Strathern 1992a:12), it has been equally inconceivable that a child could have two biological mothers – thus the troubling legal and symbolic asymmetry between the biological mother and her partner. Of course, current possibilities for "assisted reproduction" – especially in vitro fertilization and surrogate motherhood – are fragmenting, in popular and legal views, the supposedly self-evident idea of real, biological motherhood.[16] In the context of these reproductive technologies, maternity has become thinkable in tripartite form, divvied up among genetic mother, birth mother, and social mother. Awareness of such possibilities informs what is sometimes imagined as the obvious and "perfect" option for lesbian families: one woman could contribute the genetic material, and her partner could become the gestational/

birth mother. The implied self-evidence of this techno-fantasy of distributed maternity suggests the degree to which biology is operative, in the imaginings of some women, even as it is dispersed. More commonly practiced on this front is a kind of dual motherhood, in which each mother gives birth. If the same donor is used, the children will be related to each other. To complete this particular circle of biological and legal unification, it is becoming increasingly common for courts to grant lesbian partners the right to adopt each other's (biological) children.[17]

In one sense, this move does little to unsettle the supposed unitariness of maternity. Yet there is an important slippage implied here between "maternity" and "motherhood." Maternity, I suggest, signals the epitome of embodied relationality – that is, gestation and birth – whereas motherhood connotes both this physical relationship *and* a gendered, naturalized code for conduct. This biologized desire to mother is expressed quite nicely in the euphemism of the maternal instinct. I would argue that the so-called naturalness of motherhood – not only as a biological relationship but also as a supposedly nurturing, explicitly feminine propensity – in some ways makes intelligible the notion of the two-mother family. Implied here is a latent split between the "natural" and the "biological"; if biological motherhood can renaturalize a lesbian's womanhood, so too, I would suggest, does the mothering performed by a so-called nonbirth mother become intelligible as natural in the name of women's propensity "to mother."[18] While I do not want to make too much of this (rather speculative) point, I consider it an important element within the amalgamation of ideas that both makes sense of and asserts dissonances in the notion of a family composed of mothers – who are lovers – and their children.

Conclusion

Underlying this entire discussion, as I noted at the beginning of this article, is a persistent cultural narrative denying the naturalness of lesbian and gay sexuality quite explicitly because it is perceived to be inherently nonprocreative. As a key context from which these lesbian procreative families emerge, this narrative lends a complex oppositionality to many lesbians' mobilization of the "naturalness" of motherhood, as well as to their desire to endow co-parenting families with biogenetic continuity. When put into service in the name of creating a uniquely lesbian kinship configuration, these "old" ideas of what constitutes relatedness are both made explicit and reformulated.

The so-called core symbols of American kinship, blood and love, are mediated here by very different unifying symbols (and gender/power configurations) than the central emblem of (hetero)sexual intercourse described by Schneider. On the one hand, lesbian sex provides a different model for love partly, to build on Strathern's (1992a:4) argument, by reproducing a gender configuration that is seen to promise gender equality rather than asymmetry. At the same time, the symbol of blood, also inscribed as biogenetic substance or biological relatedness, is deployed to give unity to families that are marked both by proscribed gender relations *and* the particular asymmetries of biological and nonbiological motherhood.

In the process, these lesbian mothers simultaneously affirm the importance of blood as a symbol and challenge the American cultural assumption that biology is a self-evident, singular fact and *the* natural baseline on which kinship is built. Biology is not understood here to stand on its own as a defining feature of kin, nor does biogenetic connection retain any single, transparent meaning. The dominant idea of American kinship as Schneider describes it posits a belief in the genetic tie as a baseline, elaborated into a relationship through certain kinds of behavior. In the negotiations of lesbian motherhood discussed above, the creation of blood ties – varying in kind and degree – instead becomes an indicator (if not enhancement) of parent-like behavior. The baseline then becomes the co-mothers' generative agency, broadly conceived. Central to this subtle reformulation of the blood/love symbolic hierarchy is a disruption of the once taken-for-granted matrix of paternity, authorship, generation, and genetic substance. As the perceived meanings of these notions of blood and code, authorship and agency, are made contingent rather than self-evident, these lesbian mothers set forth quite complex notions

of what constitutes both distinctiveness and unity in the creation of their kin ties.

As the symbol of the blood tie is both embraced and dispersed within certain lesbian families, so too does the dichotomy between straight biological families and gay and lesbian chosen families become muddied. Rather than trying to determine which understanding of gay and lesbian kinship promises a more radical critique of American kinship, I have been concerned here with drawing out some of the ways in which the so-called core symbols of kinship – the ideas that define what constitutes relatedness – are reworked and recontextualized. As reproductive and genetic technologies continue to proliferate, blood and love will surely continue to be (re)inscribed in notions of relatedness, in often predictable but perhaps also surprising ways. The ways in which lesbians and gay men negotiate such reinscriptions make explicit not only the contingency of these symbols but also – equally important in theorizing kinship – the dynamic, mutual construction of gender, generation, kinship, and sexuality.

NOTES

1   I thank Ellen Lewin for her helpful comments on this subject. The question of representativeness is here, as ever, not a simple one. First, my intention is to examine certain articulations of distinctiveness; I do not claim to represent a "critical mass" of lesbian families. I recognize also that access to reproductive technologies (though donor insemination is one of the most low-tech practices on the menu) is a key foundation for the visions of lesbian motherhood discussed in this paper. Access inevitably raises questions of class, as well as race; the creation of lesbian families through insemination is, arguably, an option most available to a largely white, middle-class clientele. Though insemination can certainly take place without the intervention of sperm banks or health care providers (as attested to by the legendary turkey-baster joke), laws protecting women from donors' paternity suits encourage the institutionalization of such arrangements. Thus a California statute on insemination protects married couples from "any claim of paternity by any outsider,"

regardless of physician involvement, while "unmarried" women are provided such protection only if they broker their insemination through a physician (*Jhordan C. v. Mary K.* 1986). The implication is that although access to sperm banks is not necessary to the creation of these families, it is certainly made desirable in terms of maintaining their legal integrity. And insofar as many lesbians choose gay male friends as donors, the specter of HIV transmission also contributes to increasing medical intervention in the insemination process.

2   For a rich contextualization of the recent "lesbian baby boom" vis-à-vis ongoing lesbian and feminist debates on motherhood, see Pollack and Vaughn's anthology, *Politics of the Heart* (1987). Jan Clausen, for example, writes,

> Most interesting and most painful is a totally irrational feeling of betrayal: I thought other lesbians were with me in the decision not to give birth, in that defiance of our expected womanly role – and now here these new lesbian mothers go, showing me up, *proving* that the fact that I'm a dyke is no excuse for my failure to have a baby. [1987:338]

See also Lewin (1993:14) for a discussion of the heightened salience, for lesbians, of the narrative of motherhood as an "achievement." Paralleling shifts in American cultural notions of gender and reproduction, the notion of achieved motherhood indexes the complexities with which women's assertions of autonomy and individualism circulate within existing narratives of conventional femininity (see Ginsburg 1990 and Ginsburg and Tsing 1990:7).

3   See Marilyn Strathern, *Reproducing the Future* (1992), for a discussion of the ways in which new reproductive technologies provide a context for making the "natural" mutable.

4   Several pivotal feminist works speak to this argument for the mutually instituted categories of heterosexuality, gender, and kinship, including Collier and Yanagisako's *Gender and Kinship: Essays Toward a Unified Analysis* (1987), Rich's "Compulsory Heterosexuality" (1984), and Rubin's "The Traffic in Women" (1975).

5   I use the phrase "expectation of creating biological kin" in anticipation of the question of

how same-sex couples (which are only one facet of chosen families) differ from heterosexual couples without children in terms of their relation to blood and choice. Expectation here is a simplified reference to the complicated cultural belief in the interdependence of heterosexual marriage, biological procreation, and social reproduction. Legal scholar Hannah Schwarzschild quotes a 1971 Minnesota decision denying same-sex couples the right to marry:

> The state's refusal to grant a [marriage] license ... is based upon the state's recognition that our society as a whole views marriage as the appropriate and desirable forum for procreation and the rearing of children.... [I]t is apparent that no same-sex couple offers the possibility of the birth of children by their union. Thus the refusal of the state to authorize same-sex marriage results from such impossibility of reproduction. [Schwarzschild 1988:116]

In this logic, all heterosexual couples conceptually have the potential to beget and raise offspring; whether or not they can or choose to is irrelevant to the defenders of the primacy of heterosexual marriage. Chosen families, whether composed of friends or lovers, or both, take on this assigned nonprocreative identity and challenge its implications for their place in kinship. Thus the contestation emerges in their claim that kinship can exist beyond blood and marriage, both of which assume procreative relations as their central referent.

6   See Biddick 1993, Spillers 1987, and Strathern 1991 for perspectives on dispersed kinship and distributed maternity.

7   A popular bumper sticker sold in many lesbian and gay bookstores.

8   This point is highlighted in Strathern's review of *Families We Choose* (1993:196).

9   Personal communication with David Schneider, August 13, 1992.

10 See, for example, psychologist Charlotte Patterson's landmark review article, "Children of Lesbian and Gay Parents" (1992).

11 Among those who make sperm their business, the assumption that the male role in conception is *the* creative one remains strong. Beautifully articulating the 19th-century vision of sperm as the "purest ex-

tract of blood" and the "sum and representation of its bearer" (Barker-Benfield 1974:49), the director of a California sperm bank distributed T-shirts with a picture of swimming sperm, captioned "Future People" (Rothman 1989:35).

12 The association of a nonbiological parent with the creative, generative aspect of conception also appeared in a 1985 custody case in slightly macabre form. In *Karin T. v. Michael T.* (1985), the two parties had been married, had given birth to two children through donor insemination, and Michael T. had signed the birth certificate as Karin T.'s husband. Upon their separation, Michael T. claimed to be exempt from child support. The grounds? Michael T. was actually a woman who presented herself to the world as a man. She argued that she should not have to pay child support because she was "a woman who was not biologically or legally related to the children." Given the usual legal response to such situations, Michael T. could reasonably expect to get away with such an allegation. But judicial interpretation is full of surprises: the court rejected her argument. "Defining parent as 'one who procreates, begets, or brings forth offspring,' the Court determined that Michael T.'s actions 'certainly brought forth these offspring *as if done biologically*'" (1985:784, emphasis added). This remarkable opinion is not the watershed lesbian and gay parents might hope for; the court clearly aims *not* to establish lesbian and gay co-parents' claim to children but rather to punish Michael T. for gender fraud. The court's assertion that she had an active part in bringing forth the children is apparently predicated on her appropriation of the male role, since she played "husband" by seeking out "men's work." In the interest of punishment, the court becomes curiously complicit in this game of gender-switching.

13 This idea of generativity is in no way limited to articulations of lesbian and gay kinship. See, for example, Helena Ragoné's (1994) work on surrogacy, where the intent to conceive signals an act of generation. I am also reminded of international patent laws regarding biotechnological manipulation of DNA; legal ownership of genetic substance is not determined in terms of its original "source" but rather in terms of the party responsible for manipulating and replicating the DNA. Here, and in concert with other developments in the enterprising management of life itself, the act of replication or manipulation itself becomes the moment of authorship. Such developments suggest intriguing intersections among notions of reproduction, ownership, and (kinetic?) intervention. For discussions of replication, authorship, and ownership, see Lury 1993; see also Sarah Franklin's notions of auto-paternity in "Romancing the Helix" (1995).

14 Alternating donors is similar to the practice, used by some heterosexual couples, of having sexual intercourse immediately after the woman is inseminated. The scientific uncertainty of the paternal bond enables the couple to entertain the possibility that, if the woman does become pregnant, her (thought-to-be-sterile) husband is the father. Uncertainty here is used to fictionalize the identity of one specific father, whereas for lesbians, uncertainty can help perpetuate anonymity.

15 This is not to argue that couples are more radical than single mothers but merely to point out that the challenges facing co-parents are different than those facing single mothers; the implication is that the particular challenges of co-parenting also open up space for creating uniquely "lesbian" families. Of course, the location of radical potential in the second parent effects a somewhat ironic inversion of the argument that the valuation of the "mating pair" is a decisively conservative move (see Ettelbrick 1992). I am indebted to Anna Tsing for this insight.

16 For a discussion of negotiations of "natural" parenthood within surrogacy arrangements, see Ragoné 1994. For a discussion of anxieties surrounding the relationships engendered via surrogate motherhood and other technologies of reproduction, see Gallagher 1993 and Franklin 1993.

17 See, for example, Keen 1991, Sullivan 1992, *The New York Times* 1993. Of course, the legitimation of lesbian parental relationships conferred by these joint adoptions is by no means a new legal standard; Sharon Bottoms and April Wade, a lesbian couple in Virginia, recently had their child taken from them on the basis of their "immoral" relationship.

Without assuming too much coherence in the rationale informing these particular decisions, it is impossible to dismiss the significance of class here. Of the three successful cases cited above, one couple consists of two physicians, another of a physician and a Ph.D. In contrast, Sharon Bottoms and April Wade are characterized in court and in the press as working class. Their unfitness as parents – as charged by Sharon Bottoms' mother, Kay – rests not only on their lesbianism but also on the "instability" of their working-class home (see Kelly 1993).

18 Arguably, women's appropriation of generativity is also made intelligible in terms of the naturalness of maternal desire. Again, see Ragoné 1994 for a discussion of the generative potential of intent. The other side of this logic, of course, is that the decision not to mother is often used to demonize women as unnatural. In addition to the vast literature on abortion in the United States, see Tsing 1990.

REFERENCES CITED

Barker-Benfield, Ben 1972 The Spermatic Economy: A Nineteenth-Century View of Sexuality. Feminist Studies 1(1):45–74.

Barnes, John A. 1973 Genetrix : Genitor : Nature : Culture? In The Character of Kinship. Jack Goody, ed. Pp. 61–73. Cambridge: Cambridge University Press.

Biddick, Kathleen 1993 Stranded Histories: Feminist Allegories of Artificial Life. Research in Philosophy and Technology 13:165–182.

Clausen, Jan 1987 To Live outside the Law You Must Be Honest: A Flommy Looks at Lesbian Parenting. In Politics of the Heart: A Lesbian Parenting Anthology. Sandra Pollack and Jeanne Vaughn, eds. Pp. 333–342. Ithaca, NY: Firebrand Books.

Collier, Jane Fishburne, and Sylvia Junko Yanagisako, eds. 1987 Gender and Kinship: Essays Toward a Unified Analysis. Stanford, CA: Stanford University Press.

Cooper, Baba 1987 The Radical Potential in Lesbian Mothering of Daughters. In Politics of the Heart: A Lesbian Parenting Anthology. Sandra Pollack and Jeanne Vaughn, eds. Pp. 233–240. Ithaca, NY: Firebrand Books.

Crawford, Sally 1987 Lesbian Families: Psychosocial Stress and the Family-Building Process. In Lesbian Psychologies. Boston Lesbian Psychologies Collective, ed. Pp. 195–214. Urbana and Chicago: University of Illinois Press.

Cusick, Suzanne 1991 On a Lesbian Relationship to Music: A Serious Effort Not to Think Straight. Paper presented at the Feminist Theory and Music Conference, Minneapolis, MN.

Delaney, Carol 1986 The Meaning of Paternity and the Virgin Birth Debate. Man (n.s.) 21:494–513.

Delaney, Carol, and Sylvia Junko Yanagisako, eds. 1995 Naturalizing Power: Essays in Feminist Cultural Analysis. New York: Routledge.

Ettelbrick, Paula 1992 Since When Is Marriage a Path to Liberation? In Lesbian and Gay Marriage: Private Commitments, Public Ceremonies. Suzanne Sherman, ed. Pp. 20–26. Philadelphia: Temple University Press.

Franklin, Sarah 1993 Making Representations: The Parliamentary Debate on the Human Fertilization and Embryology Act. In Technologies of Procreation: Kinship in the Context of the New Reproductive Technologies. Jeanette Edwards, Sarah Franklin, Eric Hirsch, Frances Price, and Marilyn Strathern, eds. Pp. 96–131. Manchester: Manchester University Press.

——1995 Romancing the Helix. In Romance Revisited. Jackie Stacey and Lynne Pearce, eds. London: Falmer Press.

Gallagher, Janet 1993 Eggs, Embryos and Fetuses: Anxiety and the Law. Paper presented at Conceiving Pregnancy/Creating Mothers: Perspectives on Maternal/Fetal Relations Conference, March 26–27, University of Virginia, Charlottesville.

Gay and Lesbian Parents Coalition et al. 1990 Brief Amici Curiae. New York Court of Appeals, In the Matter of the Application of Alison D. Submitted by Janet E. Schomer and Susan R. Keith.

Ginsburg, Faye 1990 The Word-Made Flesh: The Disembodiment of Gender in the Abortion Debate. In Uncertain Terms: Negotiating Gender in American Culture. Faye Ginsburg and Anna Lowenhaupt Tsing, eds. Pp. 59–75. Boston: Beacon Press.

Ginsburg, Faye, and Anna Lowenhaupt Tsing 1990 Introduction. In Uncertain Terms: Negotiating Gender in American Culture. Faye Ginsburg and Anna Lowenhaupt Tsing, eds. Pp. 1–16. Boston: Beacon Press.

Gray, Pamela 1987 The Other Mother: Lesbian Co-Mother's Journal. In Politics of the Heart:

A Lesbian Parenting Anthology. Sandra Pollack and Jeanne Vaughn, eds. Pp. 133–139. Ithaca, NY: Firebrand Books.

Green, Leonard 1991 Anti-Gay ABC Laws Challenged. Our Own Community Press October: 1–2.

Hill, Kate 1987 Mothers by Insemination. *In* Politics of the Heart: A Lesbian Parenting Anthology. Sandra Pollack and Jeanne Vaughn, eds. Pp. 111–119. Ithaca, NY: Firebrand Books.

Jhordan C. v. Mary K. 1986 224 Cal. Rptp. 530 (Cal. App. 1 Dist. 1986).

Karin T. v. Michael T. 1985 484 N.Y.S. 2d 780 (Fam. Ct. 1985).

Keen, Lisa 1991 D.C. Lesbians Become the First to Adopt Each Other's Children. The Washington Blade, September 13:1, 8.

Kelly, Deborah 1993 Mother Said Unfit in Appeal of Custody: Grandmother Cites More Than Lesbianism. Richmond Times-Dispatch, December 9:B1.

Laqueur, Thomas 1990 The Facts of Fatherhood. *In* Conflicts in Feminism. Marianne Hirsch and Evelyn Fox Keller, eds. Pp. 205–221. New York: Routledge.

Lewin, Ellen 1993 Lesbian Mothers: Accounts of Gender in American Culture. Ithaca, NY: Cornell University Press.

Lury, Celia 1993 Cultural Rights: Technology, Legality and Personality. London and New York: Routledge.

McKinnon, Susan 1992 American Kinship/American Incest. Paper presented at the 91st Annual Meeting of the American Anthropological Association, San Francisco.

The New York Times 1993 Court Grants Parental Right to Lesbian Mother and Lover. September 12:42.

Nichols, Margaret 1987 Lesbian Sexuality: Issues and Developing Theory. *In* Lesbian Psychologies. Boston Lesbian Psychologies Collective, ed. Pp. 97–125. Urbana and Chicago: University of Illinois Press.

Patterson, Charlotte 1992 Children of Lesbian and Gay Parents. Child Development 63(5):1025–1042.

Polikoff, Nancy D. 1987 Lesbians Choosing Children: The Personal is Political. *In* Politics of the Heart: A Lesbian Parenting Anthology. Sandra Pollack and Jeanne Vaughn, eds. Pp. 48–54. Ithaca, NY: Firebrand Books.

——1990 This Child Does Have Two Mothers: Redefining Parenthood to Meet the Needs of Children in Lesbian-Mother and Other Non-traditional Families. Georgetown Law Journal 78(3):459–575.

Pollack, Sandra, and Jeanne Vaughn, eds. 1987 Politics of the Heart: A Lesbian Parenting Anthology. Ithaca, NY: Firebrand Books.

Ragoné, Helena 1994 Surrogate Motherhood: Conception in the Heart. Boulder: Westview Press.

Rich, Adrienne 1984 Compulsory Heterosexuality and Lesbian Existence. *In* Powers of Desire: The Politics of Sexuality. Ann Snitow, Christine Stansell, and Sharon Thompson, eds. Pp. 177–205. New York: Monthly Review Press.

Riley, Claire 1988 American Kinship: A Lesbian Account. Feminist Issues 8(2): 74–94.

Rothman, Barbara Katz 1989 Recreating Motherhood: Ideology and Technology in a Patriarchal Society. New York: W. W. Norton.

Rubin, Gayle 1975 The Traffic in Women: Notes on the "Political Economy" of Sex. *In* Toward an Anthropology of Women. Rayna Reiter, ed. Pp. 157–210. New York: Monthly Review Press.

Schneider, David M. 1980[1968] American Kinship: A Cultural Account. 2nd ed. Chicago: University of Chicago Press.

Schwarzschild, Hannah 1988 Same-Sex Marriage and Constitutional Privacy: Moral Threat and Legal Anomaly. Berkeley Women's Law Journal 4:94–127.

Spillers, Hortense 1987 Mama's Baby, Papa's Maybe: An American Grammar Book. Diacritics 17(2):65–81.

Strathern, Marilyn 1981 Kinship at the Core: An Anthropology of Elmdon, a Village in North-West Essex in the Nineteen-Sixties. Cambridge: Cambridge University Press.

——1991 Displacing Knowledge: Technology and the Consequences for Kinship. Paper presented at Fulbright Colloquium, The Social Consequences of Life and Death Under High Technology Medicine, London.

——1992a Gender: A Question of Comparison. Lecture, University of Vienna, May 23.

——1992b Reproducing the Future. Anthropology, Kinship, and the New Reproductive Technologies. New York: Routledge.

——1993 Review of K. Weston, Families We Choose: Lesbians, Gays, Kinship. Man (n.s.) 28(1):195–196.

Sullivan, Ronald 1992 Judge Allows for Adoption by Lesbian. The New York Times, January 31:B1, B3.

Tortorilla, Toni 1987 On a Creative Edge. *In* Politics of the Heart: A Lesbian Parenting

Anthology. Sandra Pollack and Jeanne Vaughn, eds. Pp. 168–174. Ithaca, NY: Firebrand Books.

Tsing, Anna Lowenhaupt 1990 Monster Stories: Women Charged with Perinatal Endangerment. *In* Uncertain Terms: Negotiating Gender in American Culture. Faye Ginsburg and Anna Tsing, eds. Pp. 282–299. Boston: Beacon Press.

Washburne, Carolyn Knott 1987 Happy Birthday from Your Other Mom. *In* Politics of the Heart: A Lesbian Parenting Anthology. Sandra Pollack and Jeanne Vaughn, eds. Pp. 142–145. Ithaca, NY: Firebrand Books.

Weston, Kath 1991 Families We Choose. New York: Columbia University Press.

Zook, Nancy, and Rachel Hallenback 1987 Lesbian Coparenting: Creating Connections. *In* Politics of the Heart: A Lesbian Parenting Anthology. Sandra Pollack and Jeanne Vaughn, eds. Pp. 89–99. Ithaca, NY: Firebrand Books.

21

Has the World Turned? Kinship and Family in the Contemporary American Soap Opera

Linda Stone

The small suburban communities of the American soap opera represent highly unusual populations. In soap communities, most of the people are wealthy and very stylishly dressed at all times. Occupationally, there is an unusually high proportion of doctors and lawyers among them. Though most of the people, women and men, work outside the home, they enjoy great freedom of movement and are rarely actually *at* work. Yet for some reason they almost never go outside, confining themselves largely to living rooms, bedrooms, and restaurants. They become involved in complicated tangles of love and deception. They are accident-prone, and, often as a result of those accidents, suffer extraordinarily high rates of amnesia. But perhaps what distinguishes soap communities more than anything else from any real community in the United States is their convoluted kinship connections and, indeed, their utter obsession with kinship. Figures 21.1 and 21.2 show kinship connections among characters on two popular soaps, *One Life to Live* and *All My Children*. A glance at these figures demonstrates that in terms of kinship, these communities rival the so-called kinship-based societies that were once central in the work of anthropologists seeking to comprehend the exotic, tribal Other.

Convoluted soap opera kinship does not reflect social life in suburban America, no more than do the innumerable cases of kidnappings and temporary amnesia now common in American soaps. Rather, it is through exaggeration and extremity, through sometimes overdrawn characters and often bizarre plots that soaps play upon American cultural concerns and in the process serve as a commentary on them. Kinship is writ large in soaps, and it is between these lines that we can discern some cultural ideas behind the current reformulation of kinship and changes in family formation now taking place in middle-class American society.

This paper analyzes kinship in contemporary soaps in terms of concepts David Schneider (1968) developed for the study of American kinship in the 1960s. Particular attention is paid to Schneider's idea that biological relationships, or the sharing of "biogenetic substance," is at the core of American cultural constructions of kinship and central to an ideal American middle-class family of husband and wife living with their own biological children. Much has changed in "real" middle-class American kinship and family forms since Schneider's work. In real life many American middle-class households consist of single mothers with children, divorced and remarried couples, and assorted "blended" families of stepchildren and step-siblings (Stone 2001). In real life, we also have reports of reworkings of

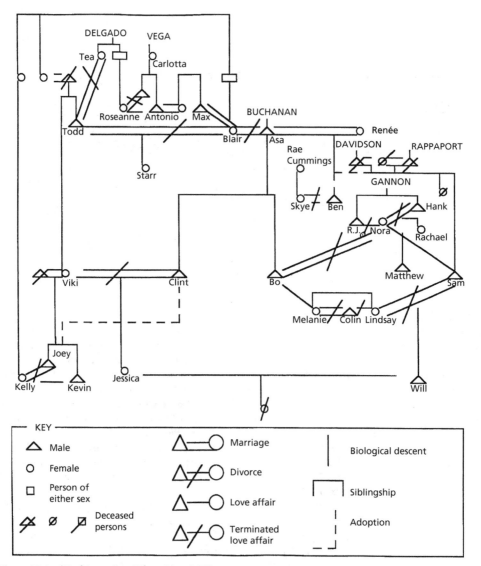

Figure 21.1 *Kinship on One* Life to Live, *2000*

American notions of kinship and family in the wake of new reproductive technologies (Ragoné 1994), among lesbian and gay couples (Weston 1991, Lewin 1993), and in cases of "open" adoption (Modell 2001).

In real life, the issue of what constitutes kinship and family has been undergoing redefinition, beginning at the margins of society or in novel situations. It is often through popular culture that marginal ideas and behavior move to the center, and in this process popular culture can become both a force in and a reflector of culture change (Mageo 1996). I suggest that contemporary soap operas have become a popular playing field of culture change for American kinship.

The questions I address in this paper are: What are contemporary soap operas expressing about family formation and kinship construction? How far away, if at all, have they moved from Schneider's idea of an American "biogenetic" kinship and the ideal nuclear

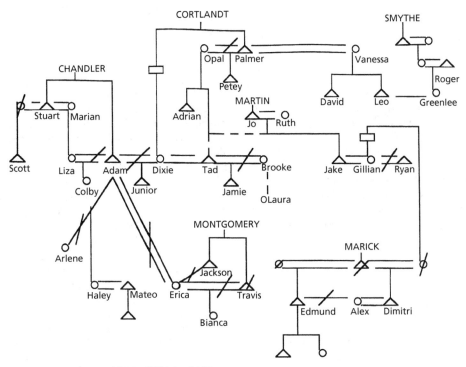

Figure 21.2 *Kinship on* All My Children, *2000*

family? I conclude that biology remains at the core of soap opera kinship, but with some new twists. Biology clearly defines kinship in soaps; but it is now manipulated in some novel ways. At the same time biogenetic kinship is also fiercely contested, even denounced, and it is rivaled by a new dimension of kinship construction – individual choice, or will. The paper is based on my study of the two soaps depicted in figures 21.1 and 21.2 – *One Life to Live* and *All My Children* – over the year 2000.

Before moving on to soap opera kinship, however, a few words about the soap genre are in order. Soaps began in America as radio serials in the 1930s. Many of the programs were sponsored by soap-powder companies, hence the name "soap operas." Soaps moved into TV in the 1950s (the first being *The Guiding Light*, which still airs).

Soaps are serials depicting everyday life (however bizarre the plotlines may be) among a set of characters. Their plots are potentially without end, or closure of any kind, as opposed to series, where the characters also remain constant but each episode follows a self-contained

story (Chandler 2002). Like the related genre of melodrama, soaps exhibit strong emotions and extreme, unlikely situations. They are often analyzed as a form of feminine narrative or style (Modleski 1982; Warhol 1998; Chandler 2002) on account of their lack of closure in favor of generating constant anticipation of what will happen next; a focus on dialogue rather than action; inclusion of multiple, complex, intertwined plots and multiple moral perspectives, as opposed to a lineal plotline with a single hero and one clear moral statement.

Soaps are watched by millions of Americans every day. The vast majority (over ninety percent in the 1980s [Modleski 1982]) are women. Soaps traditionally targeted women (Warhol 1998), particularly the at-home, middle-class housewife. Judging by today's soap ads alone (which largely advertise cosmetics, feminine hygiene products, birth control pills, women's health aids, diapers, and children's' medicines), it is clear that soaps are continuing to target women, especially women with young children. Today, possibly as a result of more women working outside of the home and a consequent fall in ratings, soaps are deliberately seeking a more diversified audience. The decline in ratings has been steady and significant over the last 50 years. In the 1950s and 1960s, the top-rated soaps could each boast that 10–15 percent of TV households were tuned in to their shows; by 1966–7, the percentage fell to 7 for the top-rated soaps (Waggett 1997:626–642).

Needless to say, soaps change with the times, reflecting trends in fashion, social issues, women's roles, and so on. But one characteristic of soap operas has remained constant: on soaps, men and women, regardless of their occupation, ethnicity, and sexual orientation, regardless of their evil cunning or their virtue, are defined first and foremost in relation to romance and marriage, kinship and family.

Schneiderian Kinship and Soaps of Times Past

David Schneider distinguished between what he called the "order of nature" and the "order of law" in relation to American kinship. The order of nature is "the way things are in nature … .It is the 'facts of life' as they really exist" (1980:26). Blood relatives partake of the order of nature. Opposed to this is the order of law, which is "modified by man and consists of rules and regulations, customs and traditions" (1980:27). Relations by or through marriage or adoption fall under the order of law. These relationships are governed not by nature but by a "code for conduct," by which Schneider

meant a culturally acknowledged proper way of behaving in the relationship.

From these two orders, Schneider derived three classes of relatives: (1) relatives in nature alone, (2) relatives in law alone, and (3) relatives in nature and in law. In the first category is the link between a genitor or genetrix and the "natural" or illegitimate child. In the second category – relatives in law alone – are spouses, in-law relationships and step or foster relationships. The last category encompasses the most important relatives, those found in nature and in law – namely consanguineal relatives whose connections come about through legitimate births. Schneider considered these last to be the true "blood relatives" in America, relatives who are endowed with special meaning and importance (see figure 21.3). As he put it: "[T]he blood relative, related in nature and by law, brings together the best of nature modified by human reason; he is thus the relative in the truest and most highly valued sense" (1980:110).

Schneider saw the American family as built on another "fact of nature" – namely, sexual intercourse between husband and wife. Between husband and wife sexual intercourse is a "natural fact" but it is also culturally refined: Sexual intercourse should be exclusive (adultery is wrong), and it should be an expression of love (culture), rather than mere carnal lust (nature). At the same time it is the sexual intercourse between husband and wife that creates the ties of shared biogenetic substance between parents and children. Children are culturally viewed as an expression of the love between husband and wife: "For the child brings

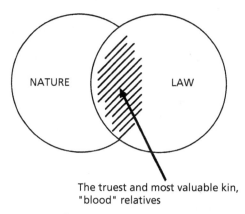

The truest and most valuable kin, "blood" relatives

Figure 21.3 *Schneider's American Kinship*

together and unifies in one person the different biogenetic substances of both parents" (1980:40).

Schneider also held that Americans have a very specific idea of *the* family: "'The family' is a cultural unit which contains a husband and wife who are the mother and father of their child or children" (1980:33). This family is considered to be thoroughly natural and rooted in nature, but it also partakes of law (or culture) – the husband and wife must be legally married and their creation of children through sexual intercourse is an expression of love.

Schneider is well remembered for drawing out that American kinship, encapsulated in the phrase *related by blood,* is kinship through shared biogenetic substance. "[K]inship is whatever the biogenetic relationship is" (1980:23). It was this biogenetic conception of kinship that Schneider held was not cross-culturally universal but peculiar to Euro-American culture (1984). That "blood is thicker than water" is an American cultural construction. In American kinship, he emphasized, relations in law alone can be terminated, but ties of nature cannot be severed. Schneider also showed how American kinship terminology reinforces the importance of "blood" or biogenetics. For example, modifiers such as "step" and "foster" are added to basic kin terms such as "brother," "son," etc., to sharply distinguish non-blood kin from blood kin. Similarly, modifiers such as "half" are attached to "brother" and "sister" to indicate a lesser degree of consanguinity.

American soap opera families in the 1970s mirrored Schneider's ideas perfectly. Soap opera characters strove to achieve the family ideal: a man and woman married and in love, living with their own biological children who are expressions of their love. A subplot might begin with the ideal but then see it dissolve: the children would turn out not to be the biological offspring of the husband after all; the husband or wife might inexplicably fall in love with someone other than his or her spouse; a married couple in love perhaps could not have their own biological children. In Susan Bean's (1976) analysis, soap operas were a continual tearing-down and then re-creating of the ideal, over and over again. In the 1970s it was possible to analyze soap opera kinship fully in

terms of Schneider's order of nature and order of law, and *the* family as consisting of husband, wife, and their biological children.

In contemporary soaps, constructions of kinship and the family have undergone a transformation. A division of kin into an order of nature and an order of law, with the "truest" and most highly valued kin being those who partake of both orders, no longer applies. Illegitimate children are no longer marginalized or valued less than legitimate ones. *The* family no longer consists of a husband and wife living with their own biological children. Today's soaps are enmeshed in a whole new dimension of kinship and family construction: human choice or will. Indeed choice, though insufficient by itself to create kinship, is so crucial that not even relationships in nature and by law can count as true kinship without it. Biological connection or shared biogenetic substance is still definitive of kinship in soaps; but both the order of nature and the order of law must now contend with an order of choice. The result is that many kinship relationships on soaps are unstable and under negotiation. Also interesting is that soap-opera characters rarely ever use modifiers like "step," "foster," and "half" to refer to their kinship relationships. Their kinship is consistently constructed and negotiated in bold, basic terms.

Soap Opera Kinship

One Life to Live (OLTL) is set in Llanview, a suburb of Philadelphia. As with many soaps these days, it centers on two feuding kinship groups – in this case the Buchanans and the Davidson-Rappaports. Innumerable marriages, divorces, love affairs, and disputed paternities have linked the two groups in a history of struggle, conflict, and divided loyalties. Heading the Buchanans is the would-be patriarch, Asa Buchanan, wealthy businessperson, cantankerous, and often evil in his manipulations of others' lives. Central to the Davidson-Rappaport side are Sam, a lawyer, and his "half-brother" Ben Davidson, a doctor. They are not actually biological brothers, although this was unknown to them for many years.

For Asa Buchanan nothing is more important than "family," yet he forever loses the loyalty of his kin by his very actions intended to cement them together under his rule and against the Davidson-Rappaports. Asa is quite clear about what true kinship is. For him, a biological connection, or blood, is crucial. In one of his many tirades about the importance of blood, he remarked: "it takes a lot more than the same last name to be a father. It takes the same blood running through your veins" (OLTL, 5/23/00). But biology alone is not enough; true kinship depends on proper behavior. A real son, for example, is a biological descendant who shows loyalty to Asa. Here we see a "code for conduct" detached from law and applied to the "making real" of kinship in nature. *All My Children* (AMC) takes place in Pine Valley, a suburban area not far from New York City. The feuding kin groups are the Martins and the Chandlers, again with many thorny interconnections between them. Somewhat similar in position to Asa Buchanan is Adam Chandler – wealthy, powerful, and manipulative.

On both these soaps we can uncover constructions of kinship and the family, as we see

many characters' multifaceted encounters with biogenetic connections: they search for them, they contest them, they throw them into their love triangles, and they "create" them in some remarkable ways.

The struggle to find biology

Several characters on OLTL (see figure 21.4) are embarked on a quest to find their true biological kin. For some this is a quest for self-definition; for others a yearning for connection and love that only links with real biological kin can provide. One woman, Rae Cummings, herself adopted and recently reunited with her own long-lost mother, had an illegitimate child who was stolen from her at birth. In her ardent wish to now find this child, the matter of its illegitimacy is irrelevant to her. She searches all over Llanview for her child, assisted by her boyfriend, Detective John Sykes. John is quite sympathetic to issues of lost parents and children since he was himself

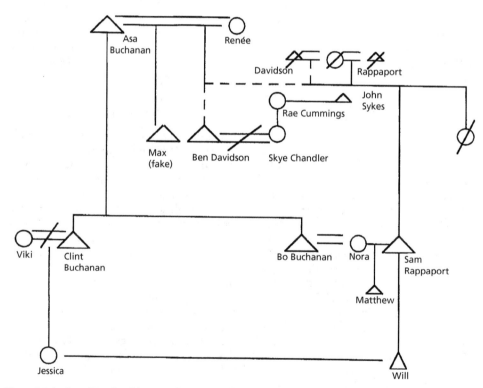

Figure 21.4 *Searching for, faking, and contesting biology on One Life to Live*

adopted and has never found his real parents. He tells a friend that if you don't know who you came from, you never know who you really are. Eventually Rae learns that her lost child is Skye Chandler (adopted daughter of Adam Chandler on AMC).

Another case is Renée, a former madam, recently married to Asa Buchanan. Much earlier in life they conceived a son that Renée gave up for adoption (not wishing to raise him in a brothel) and whose existence was long unknown to Asa. When Renée finally told Asa of the existence of their son, he was ecstatic. That this son was "in nature alone" and not also in law was as irrelevant to him, as was the illegitimacy of Rae's child to her. Renée and Asa then set out to find their now grown son. One conniving rogue, Max Holden, seeking to be heir to Asa's vast wealth, managed to pass himself off as Asa and Renée's long-lost son. This worked for a while and everyone was happy. Then Renée discovered that Max had tricked them (faking DNA tests) and was not really her son at all. Yet she sided with Max and hid this news from Asa. Luckily for Max, Renée feared that knowledge of the truth would destroy Asa, who, along with a risky heart condition, had thoroughly alienated his other children and their descendants, leaving him isolated. While Asa is left believing that Max is his son, the two grow close. Max actually sees Asa as a father and so is emotionally as well as financially motivated to sustain the relationship. He does everything to show loyalty to Asa who then rewards Max with fatherly love. Asa frequently refers to Max as his "only real son," the only one who behaves as a son should.

Meanwhile Renée's private search for her real son goes on. Like Asa, Renée sees the biological connection as paramount: "He was a part of me. He came from me. My heart made his heart. My blood made his blood, and that makes him my real son" (OLTL 5/22/00), she remarks to Max. Actually *we* know who her real son is: Ben Davidson. Ben knows this too and would like to tell Renée, since he truly loves and admires her. Alas, he cannot. To admit that Renée is his mother is to acknowledge that Asa is his father – Asa, wicked archenemy of Ben's adoptive family, the man responsible for the prison sentence of his

"nephew," Will. Asa in turn despises Ben, whom he sees as the worst member of the enemy Davidson-Rappaport line. What a shock it is then when he learns that Ben, of all people, is his biological son and Max a fake! Asa decides that as Max faked his sonship, he will be punished by himself losing a son. So to exact revenge on Max, Asa marries one of Max's ex-wives and legally adopts Max's son of that union.

Contesting Biology

Figure 21.4 also shows a few characters on OLTL who denounce particular biological kinship connections altogether. Perhaps most alienated from Asa is Jessica, Asa's granddaughter through his son, Clint. Not approving of Jessica's boyfriend, Will Rappaport, a member of the enemy camp, Asa connived to have Will falsely accused of embezzlement and face a term in prison. Infuriated, Jessica denounces kinship to Asa, telling him: "You are *not* my grandfather" (OLTL 5/17/00). Notice that Jessica does not say, for example, "You are a bad grandfather" or "I will never speak to you again," which would suggest mere estrangement, but rather she disclaims kinship altogether in spite of her relation to Asa in both nature and in law.

We find similar cases of denying biology on AMC (see Figure 21.5). Vanessa, for example, an unfit mother if ever there was one, is denounced by both her sons, David and Leo. David denounced her long ago because he believed she was responsible for the suicide of his biological father. Leo denounced her because, after murdering her lover, she was willing to see Leo charged with the crime rather than confess her own guilt. "I do not *have* a mother"; says Leo to a friend, "as far as I'm concerned she's a non-person" (AMC 6/5/00).

On AMC another unfit mother, Arlene, is denounced by her daughter, Haley. Arlene is an incurable alcoholic and conniving gold digger. Haley recalls her childhood with Arlene with bitterness. She herself became an alcoholic, but, unlike Arlene, is in successful recovery. Although Arlene seeks Haley's love, Haley repeatedly and emphatically tells her, "You are not my mother." Arlene violates the "code for conduct" for motherhood and so fails to win

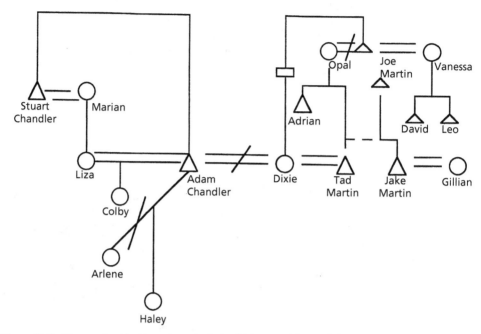

Figure 21.5 *Denouncing kinship and manipulating biology on* All My Children

Haley's recognition of their kinship. Yet, on the very few occasions when Arlene does something good or right, Haley in fact softens. On these occasions she actually refers to Arlene with the kinship term, "mother" rather than the personal name, Arlene, that she normally uses. At these times their kinship appears negotiable. If only Arlene could figure out how to behave properly more often, she could in fact reestablish kinship with Haley.

Haley's biological father is Adam Chandler, a major character on AMC. Adam has a twin brother, Stuart. The two are opposites: Adam is conniving and manipulative; Stuart is simple but good-hearted and brings out the best in everyone. But their biological connection is so strong that they can hardly live without one another. They often refer to their close biological connection, their identical DNA. They know each other's thoughts and sense when the other is in danger or pain. Adam tells Stuart, "You and I are brothers. We are brothers forever. We have the same DNA" (AMC 3/17/00).

Yet even this closest of biogenetic-sharing kinship is denounced by Stuart when he learns of the treacherous act Adam carried out against Stuart's beloved wife, Marian (Adam had ar-

ranged for Marian to be photographed in a compromising position with another man so that Stuart would leave her). When Stuart learns the truth he tells Adam, "I could never hate my brother. The fact is I *do* hate you. I *hate* you! So we can't be brothers anymore. We just never gonna be brothers again" (AMC 3/17/00). The denunciation of this brotherhood is very destructive: Stuart wanders around in a daze, is hit by a car, suffers total amnesia, disappears, and is presumed to be dead. Adam self-destructs and severs his ties with everyone.

Intertwined with the cases of persons searching for lost biological kin and denouncing others are a series of people who actually know "who they really are" in terms of their biological connections, but desperately seek kinship in other directions. They struggle to contest the importance of biology; they wish they could claim kinship through their sheer will and choice.

One case from OLTL is Ben Davidson, who wishes he were a real half-brother to Sam Rappaport. Ben and Sam were raised together, believing themselves to be real brothers and establishing brotherly love. In fact, Ben was adopted by Sam's parents. It was only recently, in advanced adulthood, that Ben discovered they are not biologically related after all. Eventually, and in great agony, he tells Sam the truth. In this case, choice, combined with "law" and "code for conduct," triumphs. Ben and Sam accept the biological truth yet still consider themselves to be real brothers. In a reversal of Asa's statements about the significance of "blood," Ben tells a friend about his adoptive family members, "They're my family. . . . I don't care whose blood is running through my veins" (OLTL 5/16/00). Later he remarks to Sam, "Let me tell you something: Blood doesn't make a family" (OLTL 7/17/00).

Another case on OLTL is Kelly, a woman recently married to one of Asa's grandsons (through adoption; see figure 21.1), and whose own mother was mentally ill. She sought desperately to be Rae Cummings's long-lost biological daughter. Knowing this was extremely unlikely, she nevertheless insisted that she and Rae have a blood test. The test showed that the two could not be mother and daughter. With great emotion and amid tears, they realize they cannot establish true kinship. "Well, it would have been nice," Kelly says sadly to Rae (OLTL 7/16/00). In contrast to Ben and Sam, this kinship link, supported by nothing other than choice, fails under the blast of biological truth.

Yet even as many characters contest biological connections, they are in fact haunted by biogenetic substance, which leads them into ambivalence and contradiction. Ben struggles with the terrible knowledge that Asa's blood runs through his veins. However much he discounts the importance of blood in some scenes, in other scenes, he, like John Sykes, equates biology with personal identity, who we really are. He asks one of Asa's biological sons, Bo Buchanan (who does not know that Ben is Asa's son and therefore his own half-brother), "How do you expect people to respect you, to love you, when they know who you came from, who you really are?" (OLTL 5/18/00). Finally confiding his disreputable paternity to his girlfriend, Viki, Ben asks, "But now that you know who I really am, can you still love me?" (OLTL 5/22/00).

Another case is Bo Buchanan himself, Llanview's police commissioner. Bo talks to his friend Hank Gannon, a district attorney, about blood ties. He refers to another of Asa's biological sons, his own brother Clint. Clint had once been married to Viki and had then adopted her two sons, Kevin and Joey, by a previous marriage. Bo says to Hank:

> To Asa love is loyalty. Blood ties above everything else. Oh, this blood thing! Doesn't matter anyway. Look at Clint. He doesn't share one drop of blood with Joey or Kevin. [But] they worship him and vice versa. I think this whole blood tie business is a bunch of bull. (OLTL 5/24/00)

Yet in nearly the next scene, Bo talks of the importance of knowing the biological paternity of a child, Matthew, who might be his. Matthew is the son of Nora, Bo's ex-wife. He was born when Nora and Bo were still married, but for a long time on OLTL it was uncertain whether he was Bo's biological child or the child of Sam Rappaport, Nora's lover (the latest DNA test shows Sam to be the father). After denouncing the importance of blood ties to Hank, Bo tells an ex-girlfriend, "I want to know if Matthew's my son" (OLTL 5/24/00). Soon thereafter he demands that a new DNA test be conducted.

Biology in the love triangles

As though searching for lost biological kin and fighting against one's true biological connections were not causing enough problems on daytime shows, these soaps further complicate life by mingling kin in love triangles. Nearly every love triangle, the very stuff of soap operas, romantically involves two kin with the same woman or man. In the past Asa and his son Bo were involved with several of the same women. Max, while passing himself off as Asa's son, was married to Blair, Asa's ex-wife. Kelly was married to Joey but in love with his brother, Kevin. And previously Joey had an affair with Kelly's aunt! AMC is also replete with cases of two kin caught in a romantic triangle. In years past Marian and Liza, who are mother and daughter, were simultaneously involved with Tad Martin. Erika Kane, who has had eight husbands on AMC, was earlier involved with two brothers, Travis and Jackson Montgomery. Recently Alex Duvane was married to Dimitri but, when she thought that Dimitri was dead, became involved with his brother, Edmund. This set of circumstances recapitulated a previous scenario whereby Dimitri had an affair with Edmund's now deceased wife, Maria.

Perhaps most intriguing is the tangle of relationships shown in figure 21.6. Nora used to be married to Hank Gannon but had an affair with his brother, R.J., which led to her divorce from Hank. Nora is later happily married to Bo, but believes (unwisely as it turns out) that he is infertile. Wishing to give him a son, she asks her friend Sam to impregnate her. She gives birth to Matthew, but when Bo finds out what Nora did, he divorces her. After divorcing Nora, Bo had an affair with Lindsay (Sam's ex-wife) and almost married her. When his relationship with Lindsay was over, he began an affair with her sister, Melanie, then married to Colin, who earlier had an affair with Lindsay.

How will these people ever sort all of this out? Perhaps they never will, but one way in which they are trying to do so is through biological reproduction. This brings us to another dimension of biology in soap operas. Biological connection is not only searched for or fought against, it can be strategically used.

Using biology

Many soap characters positively use biology to get what they want, usually love, sometimes also money. Kelly tries to save her marriage to Joey by getting pregnant, even though she loves Joey's brother, Kevin; Max's wife, Blair, tries to get pregnant to hold onto Max. These are old tactics, long familiar to soaps. But today there are new strategies. One interesting case on OLTL is that of Lindsay Rappaport (figure 21.6). Lindsay is a beautiful woman who runs an art gallery. Often jealous and vindictive, she apparently lacks all scruples and moral sense; yet despite her incredible, wicked manipulations, it is clear that deep down inside, all she needs is love. And she is desperately in love with Bo. Her attempts to win Bo nearly always involve reproduction of some kind. She was pregnant with his child when he was about to marry her, but by the time she announced this fact, she had told so many other lies that Bo canceled their wedding. Later she miscarried. Her enemy is Nora, Bo's ex-wife who helped destroy Lindsay's earlier marriage to Sam, and for whom Bo may "still have feelings."

As noted, for a long time on OLTL it was known that either Bo or Sam could be the

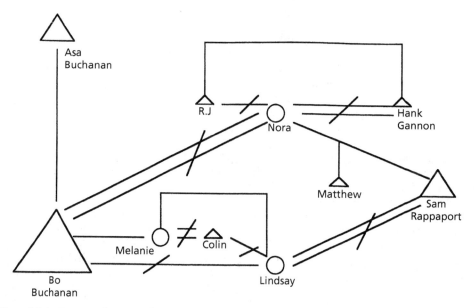

Figure 21.6 *Strategically manipulating biology on* One Life to Live

father of Nora's son, Matthew, since Nora, when still married to Bo, was sleeping with both Bo and Sam. Eventually, to decide the matter, Bo and Sam decided to have a DNA test. At this point Lindsay figured that if Bo turned out to be the father, he and Nora might reunite. So, she bribed a lab technician to make sure the results of the test showed Sam (her own ex-husband) to be Matthew's father. But then, feeling guilty, she decided to call it off. Unfortunately she couldn't reach the lab technician, who had skipped town after taking her money. She had left him voice-mails urging him not to fake the tests. But did he? Linsday didn't know, and neither did we. The tests showed Sam to be the father, but was he?

Later, Nora disappeared, having apparently died in a train wreck. She was not actually dead but everyone thought she was. This was great for Lindsay who saw a clear road to Bo, now free of Nora. But Bo resisted her. Now Lindsay had another idea: what if Bo really *were* the father of the now motherless Matthew? Bo would be delighted to have a son *and* he would want a "mother" for his child. She tried then to entrap Bo through her potential step-motherhood. So she confessed her previous bribery, reopening the question of Matthew's paternity, leading Bo to demand another DNA test. And on top of that, Lindsay discovered Nora and arranged to have her kidnapped, keeping her away from both Bo and Matthew!

AMC also shows an interesting case of stra-tegically manipulating biology. At one point, Adam Chandler and his wife, Liza, were married but separated. Liza wanted to have a child, but not by Adam. She asked a friend and former lover, Jake, to donate sperm to insemin-ate her. Jake complied and was excited that he would be the biological father of the child. But Adam sneaked into the clinic and substituted his sperm for Jake's. When Liza went in for impregnation, Adam became the real father to Liza's daughter, Colby. This act was referred to as a case of "biological rape" by Dixie, one of Adam's many ex-wives. When the truth of all this came out, Liza was furious, Jake was des-troyed, but Adam now had a link to Lisa, whom he loved and wanted back, through Colby.

The Family

A notable pattern on both OLTL and AMC is that a nuclear family of husband and wife in love and living together with their own bio-logical children is now exceedingly rare and by all accounts no longer an ideal or an expect-ation. An ideal match today on AMC is Tad Martin's marriage to Dixie. They live with Dixie's child, Junior, biological son of Adam Chandler, and Jamie, Tad's son with his previ-ous wife, Brooke (see figure 21.7). Tad shares custody of Jamie with Brooke, an arrangement with which everyone is happy. He is an ideal stepfather to Junior, even though Junior's father, Adam Chandler, is Tad's sworn enemy. And Dixie is an ideal stepmother to Jamie. In this family there are biological connections with children, but these are not shared between husband and wife. On today's soaps, this is as good as it gets. Tad and Dixie are happy to have created a family and they do not long to create biogenetic children together.

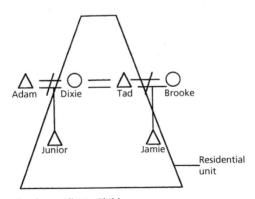

Figure 21.7   *A happy soap family on* All My Children

Already noted on AMC is the case of Liza and Jake, previously lovers, who agreed to reproduce through artificial insemination and then share custody of the child. Liza wanted a child, but not by her husband, Adam. Jake just wanted a child to whom he could be a father. Later he married Gillian, hoping she could be the child's part-time stepmother. This novel, intentionally created split family was only thwarted by Adam, who switched his sperm with Jake's. In the end, biology determined fatherhood; no one questions that Adam is the child's real father. But it is significant that the intention of the other people involved was to share a child over two households without marriage of the mother and father.

Discussion

Kinship on OLTL and AMC shows the centrality of biological connection, or shared biogenetic substance, but it also resonates with choice and deliberation. In addition, biogenetic kinship fails to stand on its own, even when biogenetic kin are also related in law. Schneider (1980) wrote that in American kinship, relationships by law can be terminated but ties of shared biogenetic substance cannot be severed. Yet Jessica, David, Leo, Haley, and Stuart have all emphatically denounced kinship to specific biological kin. They have not merely claimed estrangement from their kin; they have denied the kinship in spite of the biological tie.

Schneider also wrote that relatives in nature and in law are the "truest blood relatives" and the most highly valued kin. This appears to no longer be the case in soap opera kinship. The strength and "truth" of kinship ties are unaffected by the many cases of illegitimate births and family reformation through divorce and remarriage that occur on the two soaps discussed here. And while legal relationships recede in importance, individual choice and mutual commitment loom large in the construction of what Schneider considered the essence of American "blood" kinship, a sentiment of "diffuse enduring solidarity."

Figure 21.8 is a model of soap opera kinship, following from Schneider's idea of American cultural "orders." Here we see three potentially overlapping orders: nature, law, and choice. This does not, as it would in Schneiderian fashion, lead to six classes of kin; rather the "rule" seems to be that any one order is insufficient in itself to create real kinship but that any order that overlaps with the mutual choice of the participants *can* create real kinship.

On OLTL we see many cases of wished for but unrealizable kinship, relationships that exist "in choice alone." Thus Rae and Kelly wish to be mother and daughter but know they can never be real mother and daughter for their choice lacks overlap with either law or nature. By contrast, Ben and Sam are brothers by law as well as by choice. Their brotherhood survives the knowledge that they

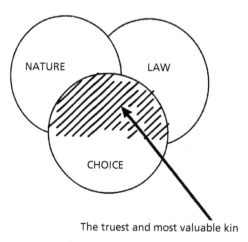

The truest and most valuable kin

Figure 21.8 *The cultural construction of soap-opera kinship*

are not biological kin. Max wishes to be Asa's son, but realizes he cannot be so by choice alone. Hence he fakes a biological tie. And Asa, believing the faked biological tie, chooses to be Max's father since Max strictly adheres to the code for conduct that sanctifies his sonship. Though Asa believes Max to have been a child in nature alone, Max becomes, for a time, *his* "truest" blood relative, his "only real son."

In soap opera kinship biological connection remains pivotal. But whereas blood may still be thicker than water, it is now considerably thickened not by law, but by mutual choice. Like relationships in law, those by blood are capable of being severed and depend on a "code for conduct" rather than "natural facts" for their perpetuation. By extension, "the family" is more open, fluid, a creative act, itself more fully based in choice and codes for conduct than rooted in the biological reproduction of husband and wife. Finally, the illegitimate child is no longer devalued.

The world *has* turned in the American soap opera. Soaps in the 1970s showed the breaking-down and reconstruction of an ideal nuclear family of husband and wife in love and living with their biogenetic children. In those days kinship was more fully constructed in biogenetic terms and the ideal was to combine relationships in nature with those in law. Soaps of the early twenty-first century show a similar fascination with biology but also creative strategies and counter-strategies that construct kinship through combining choice with either law or nature.

The contemporary soap opera has picked up the theme of reworking kinship seen first at the margins of society and has moved it to center stage. In the process soaps are reflecting a broader reworking of kinship in American society. They work through outlandish biogenetic manipulation (faking DNA, switching DNA, switching sperm), through extreme violations of kinship codes for conduct, through characters' desperate quests to find their biogenetic ancestors and descendants, and through their counter-struggles to create kinship by choice and determination. In the very process of enlarging kinship on our daytime screens, soap operas are commenting upon the dynamics of its reformulation in American society.

REFERENCES

Bean, Susan S., 1976 Soap Operas: Sagas of American Kinship. *In* The American Dimension. W. Arens and Susan Monague, eds. New York: Alfred Press.

Chandler, Daniel, 2002 The TV Soap Opera Genre and its Viewers. http:www.aber.ac.uk/media/Modules/TF33120/soaps.html

Lewin, Ellen, 1993 Lesbian Mothers. Ithaca, NY: Cornell University Press.

Mageo, Jeanette-Marie, 1996 Samoa, on the Wilde Side: Male Transvestism, Oscar Wilde and Liminality in Making Gender. Ethos 24(4), 588–627.

Modell, Judith S., 2001 Open Adoption: Extending Families, Exchanging Facts. *In* New Directions in Anthropological Kinship. Linda Stone, ed. Lanham, MD: Roman & Littlefield.

Modleski, Tania, 1982 Loving with a Vengeance: Mass Produced Fantasies for Women. Hamden, CT: Archon.

Ragoné, Helena, 1994 Surrogate Motherhood: Conception in the Heart. Boulder: Westview Press.

Schneider, David M., 1980 [1968] American Kinship: A Cultural Acount. Chicago: University of Chicago Press.

——1984 A Critique of the Study of Kinship. Ann Arbor: University of Michigan Press.

Stone, Linda, 2001 Kinship and Gender: An Introduction. Boulder, CO: Westview Press.

Waggett, Gerard J., 1997 The Soap Opera Encyclopedia. New York: HarperCollins.

Warhol, Robyn R., 1998 Feminine Intensities: Soap Opera Viewing as a Technology of Gender. Genders 28, 1–15.

Weston, Kath, 1991 Families We Choose: Lesbians, Gays, Kinship. New York: Columbia University Press.

22

Kinship, Gender, and Mode of Production in Post-Mao China: Variations in Two Northern Villages

Hua Han

Economic changes in post-Mao China have had tremendous impact on Chinese families over the past two decades (Davis and Harrell 1993). With respect to these changes, anthropologists have engaged in a debate over whether the transformation of the rural economy from a collective mode to a household-based responsibility system has improved or deteriorated gender equality in rural China (Andors 1983; Judd 1994; Stacey 1983; Wolf 1985). Using the Marxist concept of the mode of production, this paper sheds light on this issue through a comparison of economy, kinship, and gender in two rural communities. As I will show, the issue is too complex to answer with a simple "better or worse" judgment.

Marxist and feminist anthropologists have sought to explain gender inequality through examining women's and men's roles in relation to modes of production. Eleanor Leacock (1978) contends that women are autonomous in hunting and gathering societies, because they not only make economic contributions but also control the conditions of production and the dispensation of the goods they produce. Through a comparison of women's positions in four precolonial African societies, Karen Sacks (1979, 1974) shows that in nonclass societies, in which both men and women are involved solely in production for use, women as well as men have an adult social status. By contrast, in a class society, where men are mostly engaged in production for exchange and women are confined to production for domestic use, women do not have social adulthood and their roles are limited to "wifely wards." More importantly, women's lack of adult status through participation in social production leads to their domestication and subordination to men. This paper provides ethnographic data from contemporary China to discuss how gender relations and modes of production are dynamically interrelated in the current context of the economic transformation of this region. Moreover, my paper shows how the mode of production affects gender not only through specifying women's roles in production, but also through its connection to kinship. Like Maurice Bloch (1975), I use the mode of production to account for variations in kinship patterns in areas that are otherwise culturally similar. I then draw out the implications of these variations for gender.

Baifu and Nanyi

Located about 30 kilometers to the north of Beijing in Changping District, Baifu is a rural village with a population of 2,040. Under the administration of the Baifu brigade there are five relatively independent economic units consisting of two communal farms and three work teams. I chose one of the two farms, which I call P farm, as the focus group for my study. This farm has 450 people registered in 150 households (132 stem and 18 nuclear). In Baifu, this farm is considered very successful in economic development and it is well known for providing 80 yuan (US $9.6) as a monthly pension to elder villagers and for providing free grain to both old villagers and young children. In Baifu, sources of household income vary and may include state jobs, wage labor, agriculture, family business, and the monthly pension provided by the two communal farms.

I was interested in studying P farm because it has maintained a collective mode of production, which is uncommon for the political economy in post-Mao China. Since 1978, the Chinese government has initiated rural economic reforms to transfer the collective mode of production to the de-collective household-based responsibility system, in which households are units of production and state authority has minimal control over the usage of land and labor. Against the reform policies, however, the collective mode of production remains popular throughout the Changping region. For instance, my second research site, Nanyi village, did not adopt household-based production until 1998, further confirming my impression that the household-based responsibility system has not been as widely implemented in this area as elsewhere. At the same time, there is variation between the two villages of my study in that Baifu is significantly more decentralized than Nanyi. I wanted, then, to explore how the political economy in the past two decades might have shaped kinship and transformed gender accordingly within these two villages.

Since the 1980s, in Baifu, farming has receded in importance in the village economy and the most lucrative enterprise has been land rental. Located in the vicinity of Beijing and merely two kilometers from the capital of Changping District, Baifu is an ideal location for small and medium-sized businesses and industries to find cheap housing and rent factory buildings. Running through the western border of the village, the recently renovated Beijing–Thirteen Ming Tombs highway facilitates travel between downtown Beijing and Changping,

shortening travel time to 45 minutes (one way). Each of the five economic units in Baifu has rented some of the village farmland to migrants who use the land to develop pine nurseries. In addition to individual migrants, state, collective, and private enterprises have also rented land from the village.

The village of Nanyi lies about eight kilometers to the south of Baifu. The Beijing–Thirteen Ming Tombs highway also runs through Nanyi, cutting the village into two parts, with residential areas in the east and most farming fields and village factories in the west. Like Baifu, Nanyi is under the administration of Changping District. However, in comparison to Baifu, Nanyi is more urban, as shown in the dramatic shrinkage of farmland and a large increase of non-agricultural residents and migrants in the village in the past 50 years.[1]

As in Baifu, the majority of the households in Nanyi do not depend on farming for income. In addition to family enterprises,[2] sources of household income come mainly from state jobs and wage labor in non-agricultural sectors, such as service, industries, transportation, and construction. However, there are more households in Nanyi that receive income from non-agricultural sources than in Baifu. While in Baifu 33 percent of the 70 households in my survey have sources of income from state jobs or state retirements, in Nanyi, the percentage increases to nearly 50. Having started in the early 1980s, some state industries helped create more non-agricultural jobs in the village by assisting Nanyi to develop its own village industries. And in 2000, out of 1,865 rural residents, only four local women were farming.

The importance of these and other differences between Baifu and Nanyi, and their effects on people's lives, is further explored in the following discussion of kinship and gender in relation to the petty capitalist mode of production (PCMP) and the tributary mode of production (TMP). Developed by Hill Gates (1993, 1996), the concept of these two modes of production and, more importantly, the dialectical relationships between them, provide a Marxist-oriented framework for my study of kinship and gender in Baifu and Nanyi in the post-Mao rural political economy.

Petty Capitalist and Tributary Modes of Production

Having first bloomed in the early Song period (960–1127), the petty capitalist mode of production (PCMP) is a system of commodity production by kin corporations which can be households, groups of agnates, patrilineage members, or simply a conjugal family consisting of a husband and his wife (Gates 1996: 7). No matter what form, patri-corporations own and control production resources.

Petty capitalists produce commodities for market exchange more than for use. Although it is capitalist-like in that it is profit-driven and involves production for exchange rather than for use, the PCMP is not capitalism. In PCMP, wealth is often accumulated but it does not trigger the transition to capitalism due to the intervention of the tributary mode of production (TMP) from the state. In Western capitalist production, by contrast, state intervention is minimal, therefore wealth can be easily accumulated through the exploitation of wage laborers. Petty capitalists exploit others not only by means of wage labor (as capitalists do), but also by hierarchical relationships embedded in kinship and gender systems (Gates 1996: 3) and hence, the PCMP has great implications for kinship behaviors and the positions of women and men.

While petty capitalists are deft at using market mechanisms to gain profits, the TMP depends on non-market mechanisms such as tribute and appropriation of goods and services to extract surplus from petty capitalists. And according to Gates, the confrontation between the two modes of production and therefore between the petty capitalists and tributary classes (state officials) was the real driving force of Chinese culture. In her words,

> The motor of China's history was the petty-capitalist tendency toward accumulation unrelentingly harnessed by tributary might, turned to tributary rather than capitalist purposes .... Although Chinese who benefited primarily from the tributary mode resisted Western capitalism as long as possible, those who benefited from petty capitalism embraced the new commerce and industry, often in flagrant contravention of ruling-class wishes. (1996: 8)

Petty Capitalist Kinship and Tributary Kinship

Created by human history and cultural variations, kinship responds to economic and political changes (Maynes et al. 1996; Lamphere 1987). The petty capitalist mode of production and the tributary mode of production create correspondingly two different kinship systems – the petty capitalist kinship and the tributary kinship systems (Gates 1996, 1993). Also referred to as the idealized traditional kinship in China, the tributary mode of kinship is constructed on orthodox Confucian ideologies and strict social hierarchies. In addition, tributary kinship has more legal protection from the state. In those Chinese societies where the TMP is more salient and dominant, individual and family behaviors are more constrained by regulative kinship norms, such as the "cycle of yang" – an assumed long-term reciprocal relationship – which constructs obligations between family members and sometimes between non-kin as well. In tributary kinship, a woman is dutiful for bearing male offspring for her husband's patriline. In short, tributary kinship, created in the context of the TMP, perpetuates orthodox kinship norms and behaviors.

Anthropological studies of China have paid much attention to the elements of tributary kinship. Topics such as the patrilineage, ancestor worship, and the dynamics of extended families frequently pioneered anthropological literature on China (Freedman 1958, 1966, 1970; A. Wolf 1974; M. Wolf 1968). More recently, Charles Stafford (2000) reinterpreted the mutual obligations between parents and children as defined by Confucianism in terms of a culture of "relatedness." Ann Walter (1996) analyzed how the importance of the continuity of the patriline in Chinese kinship legitimized the practice of adoption and concubinage in late imperial China.

Traditional Chinese gender as displayed by tributary kinship has been readily interpreted along the lines of female subordination. The notorious practice of foot binding has been seen as a token of the extremely low status of Chinese women in traditional China. Other indicators of gender imbalances shaped by tributary kinship may include the exclusion of women from ritual activities and the practice of minor marriages, widespread in Taiwan (A. Wolf 1974; M. Wolf 1972).[3] Anthropologists who specialize in East Asian studies have become accustomed to seeing, analyzing, studying, and teaching Chinese society in the framework of the tributary tradition.[4]

However, beneath the dominant tributary kinship lies the less orthodox and less repressive petty capitalist kinship system. It is constructed around the patri-corporations in which male agnates organize household production together. Similar to tributary kinship, petty capitalist kinship stresses age and gender hierarchies. Yet, in contrast to tributary kinship, petty capitalist kinship is not only defined by "blood and bones" (in other words, by the norms of patrilineal descent), but also by "contracts and market transactions" (Gates 1993: 256). Equipped with a profit-gaining morality, commercial incentives, and contractual relationships, petty capitalist kinship has "egalitarian tendencies" (Gates 1996: 12), allowing more aberrant kinship and gender behaviors.

For instance, a female petty capitalist shop-owner's economic power and ownership of the means of production may empower her to bargain for birth limitations. She may consider her duty to bear children a "contingent" one that depends on her mother-in-law's willingness to help with child-care. Here, clearly, in petty capitalist kinship, "money and children are interchangeable contributions" (Gates 1993: 257). And a Chinese daughter-in-law obeys the mother-in-law not only because of the latter's senior positions in a kin hierarchy, but also on the basis of the precise contribution of child-care that the mother-in-law will provide (Gates 1993: 258). In Chinese kinship, the expedient relations always exist side by side with regulative norms and cultural ideology. One good example is what Margery Wolf described as the uterine family, which is largely based upon a mother's calculation for returns (care and status in her old age) through her investments in creating strong, loving bonds with her sons.[5]

Gates's proposal of examining China's social formation in a framework of the interaction between the petty capitalist mode of production and the tributary mode of production pro-

vides an analytical tool for understanding kinship and gender in the current mixed political economy in rural China. In the past two decades, many anthropologists have engaged in a debate over whether the transformation of rural economy from a collective mode to a household-based responsibility system has restored the pre-Mao traditional cultural norms and so hindered gender equality (Andors 1983; Judd 1994; Stacey 1983; Wolf 1985).

Instead of seeking to answer whether traditional cultural practices and Confucian morality have been restored in post-Mao China, this paper argues that so called traditionalism and orthodox Confucian ideology have always co-resided with aberrant and heterodox moralities. Traditionalism was never completely wiped out by Maoism and the expedient or instrumental human relationships operating through gift exchange (Yan 1996) were not just recently reconstructed in the reform period. Today, what we observe as traditional cultural elements have been incorporated into contemporary socioeconomic formations (Siu 1989), and what people are practicing in the post-reform era is historically contingent to the revolutionary time (Liu 2000). Once in a while orthodox behaviors confined by traditionalism may be subsumed by other heterodox elements, never having disappeared, even during high socialism. Like salt and pepper, these other elements are part of the basic ingredients of a flavorful Chinese culture. Therefore, to understand the positions of men and women in Chinese society, it is necessary to embrace diversities and include variances that differ in time and space.

This paper expands Gates's framework from the late imperialist time to the current situation and from an emphasis on macro societies to micro societies. As indicated by Gates herself, her attempt to understand China in the framework of the interplay of the petty capitalist mode of production and the tributary mode of production is "suggestive rather than definitive" (Gates 1996: 10). And built upon the macro analyses of Chinese social and economic history, Gates's approach seeks to outline "structural regularities," but not to examine historical and regional particulars. This paper, however, by focusing on the transformation of local political economy as well as its influences on kinship and gender in two villages in the past two decades, argues that Gates's approach also applies to micro studies of rural communities in a given historical context, namely post-Mao rural China.

Petty Capitalist Production in Baifu

The post-Mao histories of the political economies in Baifu and Nanyi share similarities yet differ in many respects. Neither of them followed the neat trajectory designed by Deng Xiaoping, namely changing from the collective mode of production to the household-based responsibility system. They did, nevertheless, gradually decentralize their economic and political configurations to some degree, at the same time retaining some elements of the collectives. In these two villages, collective authorities remain in control of families and people's lives. Household registration, birth control, and village housing regulations are a few examples of the remaining power of village authorities. Yet, between the two villages, Baifu is more decentralized and petty capitalist whereas Nanyi is more pro-collective and tributary.

In Baifu economic organizations are decentralized from the brigade and organized into five independent sub-units – three production teams and two collective farms. P farm is a perfect example for illustrating how petty capitalist production is organized in this local setting. At first glance, the economic production of the farm may appear collective and thus seemingly tributary. Organized as a communal farm, it conducts agricultural production collectively. As during the collective period of the people's commune, its 19 full-time workers go to work every day, 8 hours a day, 7 days a week. Together, they run the entire agricultural production and do some sporadic industrial work as well. They produce corn, soybean, wheat, and vegetables and provide free grain to young children and both free grain and monthly allowances to elder residents. No matter how hard they work, most women workers are paid 12 yuan a day whereas men are paid 15 yuan a day, echoing the gender-based workpoint system used during collective times. However, by and large, P farm does not replicate the tributary mode of production. Instead, its economy has many characteristics of

the petty capitalist mode of production. Its economic structure resembles the patri-corporation in which the farm manager – Zhang – functions like a household head who makes economic and managerial decisions crucial to the whole farm.

With a background in engineering and working experience in a state factory, Zhang has tried to develop industries within P farm. Several years ago, he wanted to set up a production line to produce recyclable plates and bowls made from corn stalks. He said that the Railway Transportation Ministry of China had agreed to use the plates and bowls on trains. And since the farm grew corn, it would be very easy and cheap to supply corn stalks. Although it seemed to be very promising, the project was not implemented. Due to the high level of chemical accumulation in corn stalks from using fertilizers, the plates and bowls were not safe to use.

In winter 2000, Zhang started another business project – making and selling furnaces. He decided to invest 150,000 yuan in this project, hoping that at the price of 800 yuan each, the furnace business would make money. His male workers and several hired temporary workers were brought together to work on this project. By the end of the year, about 200 furnaces were made yet only a few had been sold. So, it was not likely that the farm would be able to make money from the furnace business either.

Trials and failures were painful yet the farm, or I should say Zhang, was learning from the mistakes. He told me that for the year 2001, to guarantee some profit, he planned to lease 400 out of a total 500 *mu* of land. He wanted to keep only 100 *mu* for farming, which would produce grain for the state quota and food. Toward the end of my fieldwork, I learned that a local sawblade factory, which has been paying P farm 120,000 yuan a year for using land, may relocate in the near future.[6] If this happens, it will be unclear as to how long the farm and its collective mode of production will be able to survive. Like a household head who protects the welfare of the entire family in case of crises, the manager of P farm has to make tough decisions.

Some workers of the P farm are agnatic kinsmen. For instance, three workers are brothers of a *Han* patrilineage whose wives also work on the farm. In addition, a woman worker is a distant niece of the manager. Although not all the workers are related in patrilineal kinship, they do share the same local residency and identify themselves with the territory-based rural community. Like the *danwei* (work unit) to city people, P farm forms an important element in local workers' identity.[7] In addition to being a resident of Baifu village, a member of the *Han* or *Liu* lineage, or the wife of a local man, a worker on the farm is also *nongchang de*, literately translated as "someone belonging to (P) farm." This sense of belonging reinforces the enclosed and familial production relations in the PCMP, which is not only shaped by market transactions but also framed by the notions and structures of kinship.

The role of kinship in production is so crucial that the manager of the farm could not refuse a female worker's request to employ her retired husband on the farm as well. As a household is obligated to raise children and support seniors, the farm fulfills its "kinship" duties by providing allowances and grain to children and elders. By contrast, economic relations with outsiders who contract farmland are purely contractual and mainly based on market transactions. And lastly, the economic relationship between P farm and the state mimics that between households of the imperial period and the tributary officials. Like households in imperial China that paid tribute to officials in the terms of tax, and free grain and services, P farm is obligated to pay an annual agricultural tax of 8,800 yuan on top of fulfilling its state grain quota.

On the farm, the familial and contractual production relations of the petty capitalist production constantly interplay. While economic production is confined by the concerns of kinship, the motivation to make profits, fulfill contracts, and win in market transactions greatly involve the farm in calculating costs and benefits. To reduce the cost of production and therefore keep the economy profitable, most female workers are paid less than their male counterparts. Implicit in this gendered wage system is the consideration that for the benefit of the whole farm, women's interests can be sacrificed.

Recently, the farm has been contemplating the replacement of most of its agricultural production with land rental in order to bring more profits and avoid facing the financial difficulties caused by lower grain prices. If implemented, there will be an extra labor force created, which will become less important to the farm. Will the workers be laid off? According to the principles of petty capitalist production, they will be. If this is the case, then women will probably be affected the most since mostly women are engaged in farming. Women, according to kinship rules, are outsiders, and being involved in petty capitalist production, they "are especially likely to be commodicized" (Gates 1993: 256). The demand to make profits legitimizes market behaviors, even those apparently sexist behaviors.

Tributary Mode of Production in Nanyi

The political economies of Baifu and Nanyi are operated by social and political organizations at different levels. In Baifu, economic production has decentralized to production teams or farms over which the brigade has little control. By contrast, the power and authority of the village committee in Nanyi has by no means collapsed. Since the economic reform, there have been criticisms about the village committees losing power over community affairs as a result of decentralizing the rural political economy. The term, *kongke cun*, which literately means "empty shell village," is used to refer to those villages in which the power of the village authority has been removed. Represented by Zhaojiahe, a rural village in Xin Liu's ethnography, in these villages social life has become like a sheet of loose sand, so disunited that along with the removal of local authority, a sense of communality and the coherent codes that guide social behavior have also disappeared (Liu 2000: 182). To avoid having its shell emptied, the local village authority in Nanyi has been holding its collective political and economic organizations together tightly and strictly enforcing village rules and regulations.

Different from Baifu's petty capitalist production organized by corporate-like entities, the political economy in Nanyi reveals many characteristics of the tributary mode of production. In Baifu, should a household want to *baodi*, lease land and conduct household-based farming, a contract must be signed between the household and the production team to which it belongs. In Nanyi, however, if a household wants to *baodi*, a contract has to be endorsed by the village authority. Another example is that in Nanyi, birth control is supervised by the village *jisheng ban* – the birth control office. In *jisheng ban*, a woman, who also sits on the village committee, directly controls the implementation of the one-child-one-family policy in the whole village. Her specialization and responsibility is only in birth control. In Baifu, by contrast, the responsibilities for the implementation of the one-child-one-family policy are dispersed to production teams or farms. Usually, a woman accountant/cashier is also in charge of birth control.

The long history of the development of state industries in Nanyi, the loss of farmland to industries, and the shrinkage of agricultural production in the past 20 years have all lessened the impacts of rural economic reforms. Industries have been playing a significant role in the village economy and virtually only those people who could not find other jobs farmed.[8] Because people did not depend on or like farming anyway, rural economic reform advocating the change from collective agriculture to the household responsibility system did not seem very relevant and necessary to the villagers. And it made more sense for the village to keep agricultural production collective. Even after the responsibility system was finally adopted in 1998, collective behaviors and moralities have not faded away.

The most important room in the office building of the village committee is the Communist Party room where crucial issues are discussed and decisions are made. Inside the room, the large party flag that covers the whole front wall along with pictures of Marx, Engels, Stalin, Lenin, and Mao, which neatly hang on the rear wall, cannot help but show that Maoism and Communism still play a central role in the village's life. In that room, I was introduced by the party secretary (a middle-aged man) to the female committee members who later assisted me throughout my research. It was also in this room that the village chief, a capable woman in her late forties, organized the village women's *yangge* dance team[9] to participate in the district parade in Changping. To liven up their looks and spirits, the dancers, many of them grandmothers, put makeup on each other before the "eyes" of the great Communist Party leaders. Teasing, laughter, excitement, nervousness, pride, and a sense of mission filled the party room.

In Nanyi, clashing with and contradicting the growing market-driven morality in the post-Mao era, the socialist mentality still hangs on firmly and colors villagers' political and economic lives, as shown in the story of four village women. In their late forties or early fifties, these four women are the only local villagers who have been farming since 1998. On the one hand, motivated by the market mentality of making more money, they wanted their rent payment exempted. On the other hand, they believed in a collective morality and wished the brigade would find them easier and more profitable non-agricultural jobs so they could quit farming. Three years ago, for three days, they went to talk to the village committee, asking for other jobs or for the postponement of their rental payment for the farming land. Unfortunately, their attempts did not get them new jobs and they had to continue to pay rent, which largely reduced their annual income.

The relationship between the four Nanyi women who farm and the village authority also parallels the conflicting relationship between the petty capitalists and the tributary officials. As the direct producers of their products and the tenants of the village,[10] these women are motivated to increase their productivity and eventually increase profit. However, locked in by contracts, they are obligated to provide their products and services for the village whether or not they make a profit. The village, playing a dominant role in the relationship, limits their accumulation of profit by controlling finance and levying rent.[11] Officially, gender discrimination is strongly discouraged, as shown in the equal pay for female and male workers in Nanyi village enterprises. The village committee is very proud of having a woman as village chief and a woman as vice party secretary. In addition, three other women assigned by the village committee serve as the managers of three village enterprises. However, the experiences of the four local woman farmers seem to indicate another and less desirable reality.

In many ways, the present government in China continues the tributary pattern developed during the Ming and Qing periods. State and village officials were endorsed with enormous economic, administrative, and ideological powers that they could use to "contain, manipulate, and benefit from private markets" (Gates 1996: 21). The confrontation between the four women and the village committee, accelerated by the women's petition three years ago, verifies that there are, indeed, conflicts of interest between the village and these four women that have arisen from the two differing modes of production. Like the "talented" and "opportunist" petty capitalists in imperial China, who sought niches through which to challenge their "tributary opposites" (Gates 1996: 275), the four courageous women of Nanyi tried to increase their benefits by engaging in a long yet peaceful petition to remove their rent. Their petition reminds me of the fine ethnographic film – *Small Happiness* – in which a group of young girls, who were employees of a village factory, went on strike in order to improve their work conditions. By hiding out together, the girls successfully challenged the manager, a senior kinsman (Hinton and Gordon 1984). However, in the case of the four women of Nanyi, things did not improve as a result of their petition. In 1999, after paying rent, their combined income decreased by 12,000 yuan and they expected a further loss in 2000.

Now, as in the past, the petty capitalist mode of production and the tributary mode of production do not occur in pure form, but, as illustrated by the case of Baifu and Nanyi, are always interacting together. In Baifu, although the petty capitalist mode of production is stronger, it is by no means exclusive; in Nanyi, the tributary mode of production is more dominant, though constantly challenged by the petty capitalist mode of production. How, then, does the dominance of the tributary mode of production in Nanyi and the stronger petty capitalist mode of production in Baifu, or more accurately, the articulation between the two modes of production, shape kinship and shed light on gender? What are the similarities and differences between kinship/gender systems in Baifu and Nanyi?

Kinship and Gender in Baifu and Nanyi

In both Baifu and Nanyi, at the core of kinship lies patrilineal descent, and "the power of patrilines" defines cultural norms and social behaviors (Stone 2000: 63–112), including, of course, ideas about the roles that women and men ought to play in the family and in society. My interviews with village women reveal that women in both villages assume most of the household work. And in both villages, patrilocal residence is still the pattern, village exogamy is widely practiced, filial piety is valued, and orthodox kinship ideologies remain to regulate female sexual behavior. For example, *bufafang*, a sexual taboo which forbids a married woman to have sexual intercourse in her natal home, is practiced in both villages. Cases of uxorilocal marriages are rare in both villages and are reserved for families who do not have sons or have practical concerns which make uxorilocal marriage necessary. In Baifu and Nanyi, adoption is also rare. Finally, families in both Baifu and Nanyi practice dowry, which may include furniture, household electronic equipment, and money. Bride price is not required in either Baifu or Nanyi, yet the groom's parents are responsible for providing housing for the new couple.

The above kinship aspects shared by Baifu and Nanyi reflect the ways that petty capitalist kinship and the tributary kinship relate to each other in the two villages. No matter how commodicized a place is, its petty capitalist kinship is articulated by the principles of tributary kinship. In other words, while in Baifu the petty capitalist kinship allows for more creative, flexible, and less traditional social behavior, its creativity is capped by tributary kinship, which sets the basic principles and norms for the whole society. Therefore, though Baifu has a dominant petty capitalist production and a more flexible petty capitalist kinship, the core of its kinship – patrilineal descent and patrilocality – is unchanged. Moreover, the principles of tributary kinship not only shape kinship behaviors but also define cultural notions and beliefs about kinship and gender. Thus in Baifu a woman who has undertaken two uxorilocal marriages is ridiculed and in Nanyi, kinsmen and the village authority think that local brides staying in the village after marriage endangers men's housing rights, as shown in later discussions.

While Baifu and Nanyi share similarities in their kinship systems, there are two aspects in their kinship and cultural practices that distinguish them. First, although families in both Baifu and Nanyi follow patrilocal residence, the regulation of postmarital residence in Nanyi is stricter than that of Baifu. In addition, in comparison to women in Nanyi, women in Baifu appear to be more relaxed about the one-child policy and more willing to limit their reproduction to one child. These two differences reflect greater petty capitalist influences on kinship in Baifu and stronger influences of tributary kinship in Nanyi.

For P farm in Baifu, the petty capitalist mode of production defines a mode of kinship in which human behavior, relationships, and even women may be commodicized. At the same time, however, it also creates more flexible and heterodox kinship behaviors which allow women to have more leeway. We know that most societies with patrilineal kinship also practice patrilocal residence where a bride moves in with or close to the groom's kin (Stone 2000: 71). In China, the patrilocal residence rule is further legitimized by the *hukou* system – household registration – invented by the communist government in the early 1950s. Together, the rule of patrilocal residence as shaped by patrilineal kinship and the *hukou* system regulated by the Chinese state bring about a residential pattern that village women have followed for years. If married to a man who has a rural *hukou* and is from another village, the local bride ought to move herself as well as her *hukou* to her husband's village.

Recently, the household registration rule in Baifu has been loosened up. To take advantage of good transportation and a more prosperous economy, many local outmarrying brides have deliberately kept their *hukou* in Baifu, which would be virtually impossible to do in other villages such as Nanyi (discussed below). Although patrilocal residence remains the norm in the village, the women's ability to retain *hukou* in their natal village gives them more leeway in case of divorce, in arranging their children's education, and so on. In short, it broadens the spectrum of women's personal choices.

By contrast, the dominant tributary mode of production in Nanyi constructs a more orthodox kinship system that is deeply rooted in territory. Like many traditional rural communities in China, the village of Nanyi is largely constructed by the rules of village exogamy and patrilocal residence, "which created territorial groupings of men who are lineally related and women who are usually either married in or preparing to marry out" (Judd 1992: 354). And Chinese kinship and gender can be brought together "in addressing questions posed by the apparently patrilineal and effectively androcentric character of emergent forms of social organization controlling land resources" (1992: 338). For men, rights over property such as land and housing are so important that without these rights, the men lose their territorial foundations in the community and their roots in patrilineal kinship. For them, houses are not just shelters, but also tokens of patrilineal membership. In their minds, houses are linked with agnatic rights, familial duties, kin ties, marriage, family, children, and even death.[12]

Industrialization in Nanyi has increased intermarriage between local women from Nanyi and locally resident state workers who have city household registrations (all state workers are allowed city registration). As a result, many Nanyi women do not move out of the village after marriage. In fact, among the 25 women I interviewed, 20 of the women's husbands have city *hukou*. And among these 20 women, 8 are natives of Nanyi. These local brides/wives are able to keep their *hukou* in Nanyi after marriage. Not only do they have legitimate rights to live in the village, they also have rights to claim land and build houses in the village, and indeed, many women have done so. The unusually large number of local women living in Nanyi after marriage has become a threat to local kinsmen who consider themselves to be more eligible permanent residents of the village.

To reduce the housing shortage and limit the number of local women staying in the village after marriage, the village authority in Nanyi added a monetary constraint (a large fee) on the already confining patrilocal residence and the *hukou* regulation. In Nanyi, if a rural bride marries out to a rural man in another village, she has no other choice but to move her household registration and herself to her husband's village. If she decides not to move her household registration, she is required to pay a large fee. This residential rule and its influences on marriage and women are illustrated in the following case study.

The Case of Xiu's Marriage

Xiu was born in 1969. Her mother is a native of Nanyi and married a construction worker who has a city *hukou*. Following the *hukou* regulations, Xiu's *hukou* was registered in Nanyi as a rural resident. She was married in 1994 to Qiang, a young man from a rural village in Haidian District. Before her marriage, she was introduced to another young fellow who had a city *hukou*. In Nanyi and its vicinity, the development of state industries and non-agricultural economy has increased the number of urban folks who work and live in the area as well as the number of intermarriages between local rural brides and city grooms. This type of intermarriage is considered ideal and is admired by local parents who eagerly want to change their daughter's rural status.

While marrying a city man is marrying up for a rural bride and is highly hoped for by her kin, the groom's kin are likely to oppose it. When Xiu's mother learned that the urban man's parents opposed the relationship, she advised Xiu to pull out. She reasoned that if the marriage took place Xiu would be looked down upon and mistreated by her in-laws.

When Xiu was dating her future husband, Xiu's mother was not happy because he had a rural *hukou*. However, luckily, his father was about to retire from a state factory located in Nanyi and he could take his father's position and become a state worker after his father left. In so doing, he would be able to change his rural *hukou* to city *hukou* (state workers are issued a city *hukou* automatically) and things would be settled. Eventually, Xiu's mother did approve the marriage but asked Xiu's future husband to change his *hukou* within six months. The change took longer, however. At the time of marriage, Xiu's husband still had a rural *hukou* so that Xiu had to move her *hukou* to her husband's village. She told me that at first she was thinking about keeping her *hukou*

in Nanyi and registering her child's *hukou* there as well because the conditions of the economy, transportation, and schools in Nanyi are much better than in her husband's village. Since her husband was going to work in the factory anyway, it would be more convenient for them to live in Nanyi. Also, staying closer to her parents would make childbirth and nursing easier since her mother could help her at any time.

However, due to the village residential regulation, which is reinforced by a large fee, Xiu could not keep her *hukou* in Nanyi. She then moved her *hukou* to her husband's village, where she delivered her son and lived for three years. Finally Xiu's husband got his *hukou* changed from rural to city and the residential rule does not apply anymore. Xiu's parents and brother bought a five-room house for the couple in Nanyi and eventually they moved back to Nanyi.

Chinese marriage is "a process of negotiation and a mirror of social change" (Liu 2000: 26). Constrained by the village residential rule that prevents local women who took village exogamous marriages from staying in Nanyi, Xiu's marriage went through negotiations between the patrilineally formed kin groups, represented by the village authority, the groom's kin, and the bride's kin. It reveals the impacts of both patrilineal kinship and state *hukou* regulations on women and marriage practices. Unlike daughters in Baifu who can retain their household registration in Baifu after marriage, local women in Nanyi are not only obliged by traditional patrilocal residence but also forced by the state *hukou* system to move their *hukou* outside of the village. Worst of all, they are pushed by the village to do so through the payment of a large fee should they seek to do otherwise. While largely compelled by the ethics of patrilineal kinship, this fee is also perpetuated by the local and regional political economy in Nanyi, and in return it reinforces the power of tributary kinship in the village by adding to it more orthodox and legal regulations.

Xiu's marriage reflects the social changes triggered by the transitions in Nanyi's political economy. The village residential rule arose out of the problem of housing shortages for local kinsmen, which is caused by multiple socioeconomic factors such as the increase of the local and migrant population, loss of village land, and marketization.

Designed by the village authority to protect the interests and rights of patrilineal kinsmen, the strict monetarily regulated residential rule in Nanyi further consolidates the tributary kinship system that is supported by the collective moralities and the tributary mode of production. This shows that orthodox and traditional norms embedded in tributary kinship define how villagers and families behave. Unlike in Baifu, where the petty capitalist mode of production has a stronger impact on the local kinship system and therefore allows for more heterodox kinship behavior, here in Nanyi, the petty capitalist mode of production is subordinate to the tributary mode of production and thereby tributary kinship prevails. In addition, although in Nanyi, the Maoist ideology of gender equality is advocated by the village authority, as shown in the equal pay of female and male workers in village industries, the collective political and economic structures in some cases can actually reinforce the extreme androcentrism of the tributary mode of kinship.

The One-Child-One-Family Policy

In addition to the differences in postmarital residence, tributary kinship in Nanyi and the more direct control of the village authority in the village political economy generate stricter regulations on family reproduction. Although the birth quota is limited to one in both Baifu and Nanyi, the one-child-one-family policy is more accepted and supported by village women in Baifu than in Nanyi.

During my first meeting with the village committee in Nanyi, I already felt as though there might be some resistance from villagers toward the one-child-one-family policy. In that meeting, I introduced myself, explained my field project, and tried to seek help from all the women members of the village committee. To obtain approval from the committee for me to conduct research in Nanyi, I also provided a copy of my questionnaire and explained the questions I would be asking to interviewees. One question was,

– Who decided which birth control method for you to use?

a. wife b. husband c. birth control personnel d. doctor

As I was reading the question, the birth control officer stopped me. She suggested I omit this question and explained that if I asked it, the only answer I would get from interviewees would be "C." I would receive lots of complaints that it was only the village birth control office and its personnel who ask women to get an IUD. I followed her suggestion and excluded this question from the questionnaire.

I am not sure whether I would have indeed only received "Cs" on that question. Yet the concern of the birth control officer shows the difficulties of implementing the one-child-one-family policy in Nanyi. Although, as in Baifu, there has been only one case of birth control violation in Nanyi, limiting women's fertility to one was not an easy task. From the officer's suggestion, I saw the pressure she has from her job. More importantly, I felt the resentment that many local villagers have toward the one-child policy and birth control personnel. If having only one child in each family had already become a cultural norm and was willingly accepted and followed by families in Nanyi, it would be unnecessary for birth control personnel to organize village women to install IUDs, for the village women would have it done themselves, as many women in Baifu have done. The village authority in Nanyi does seem to have close and strict control over reproduction.

There is a written village birth control regulation listing rules and procedures that families and the village must follow in various situations. The regulation also includes many rules that are specifically designed to supervise the birth control of migrants living in the village and villagers who are absent temporarily. For instance, the village birth control office sends notices of needed gynecological exams to village women who are married for more than three months and for some reason not living in Nanyi. These women are required to return for the exam within ten days of receiving the notice. If they do not return and are without reasonable explanation as to why, the village will stop giving them all village benefits. Additionally, if they violate birth control regulations while absent, they will receive more severe punishment.

In comparison to birth control regulations in Nanyi, birth control regulations in Baifu are less strict and less detailed. For example, there are no regulations written for local women who are temporarily absent. They are not required to return to take a gynecological exam. In fact, regulations in Baifu are made by the Machikou township and apply uniformly to all the villages within the township. Birth control regulations in Nanyi, by contrast, are adapted and redesigned to fit the local conditions of Nanyi.

In Baifu, having only one child has become a norm among many families. The birth control officer, who is also the accountant of P farm, says that her job of supervising birth control is very easy. She does not have to persuade women to limit their fertility to one because they do not want to have a second child anyway. Very often, women comment that it is useless and time-consuming to raise children.

The one-child policy was not implemented in Baifu until the early 1980s. However, I interviewed a woman who could have had her second child in 1979 but decided to have an abortion. She is known as a capable woman and is praised by many villagers. Her first child, a son, was born in 1974. Her husband, a carpenter, is the only son in his family. I asked her the reasons for having the abortion. She told me that she had a full-time wage labor job when she was pregnant, and she did not want to waste her time bringing up another child. In the trade-off between job/income and reproduction, she chose the former. She proposed the abortion and her husband and parents-in-law did not oppose it.

In Baifu, while women's reproduction is obviously regulated by the national one-child-one-family policy, within the family women have relatively autonomous control over their reproduction. Several women went ahead and had abortions during their second pregnancies without first consulting their husbands. They said that abortion was not their husband's business. Moreover, they said they could not have more than one child anyway because of the one-child policy, so that it made no difference to talk to the husbands about it.

Women's different reactions to the one-child policy in Baifu and Nanyi not only echo the kinship systems in the villages, they are also derivative of the different production relations in PCMP and TMP, which consistently shape social and interpersonal relations in the villages. The PCMP in Baifu is organized and operated by small and patri-corporation-like units, like the P farm. In PCMP, production relations are influenced not only by a profit-driven mentality but also by strong sentiments of kinship. Very often, workers are kinsmen or are related to others through kinsmen, and the relationships between them are likely to be close and personal. The birth control officer on P farm works and interacts with other village women every day, allowing her to know and understand the anxiety and needs of other women. The close personal relations between the birth control officer and other women, as constructed by the petty capitalistic familial/small-scale mode of production, help ease women's hostility and resentment toward the one-child policy and the person who implements it – the birth control officer. By contrast, in Nanyi's tributary mode of production, production relations are less familial and more collective and official. As a result, social relations are more distant and less personal than in Baifu. In Nanyi, women's reproduction is strictly monitored by the village authority and its birth control officer. Like the state officials in the tributary mode of production during the imperial period, the birth control officer in Nanyi stands only for the village authority and thus seems to be authoritarian and distant to villagers.

Although the one-child-one-family policy has been implemented in China for over two decades, anthropological studies on how the policy impacts rural families, kinship, and gender status are limited and mostly focused on local resistance and the victimization of Chinese women. However, the effects of the one-child policy, as indicated by the differences between people's attitude toward the policy in Baifu and Nanyi, are much more complex and profound than that. It especially has changed many aspects of Chinese kinship and hence reshaped Chinese gender.

For one thing, in Baifu and Nanyi's local kinship systems, uxorilocal marriage is a secondary form of marriage and is not preferred by families. *Bufafang*, which I briefly referred to earlier, is a sexual taboo that forbids women to have sexual intercourse in their natal home. It arose largely from people associating the idea of a woman having sex in her natal home with the structure of uxorilocal marriage. But with women's fertility having been limited to one child, uxorilocal marriages will likely increase, since families that do not have sons may wish to arrange uxorilocal marriages for their daughters in order to secure care in their old age. This increase in uxorilocal marriages may dispel the negative attitude toward *bufafang* and thereby may lessen the sexual constraints of *bufafang* on women (Han 2002).

Also, my study shows that in Baifu and Nanyi, women assume the double burden of work and child-care. The decrease in women's fertility triggered by the one-child-one-family policy reduces women's double burden and so increases their economic and educational opportunities. Additionally, the one-child policy has great impact on family composition and the household developmental cycle. Due to the one-child policy, the number of siblings in many families is reduced to one. This shortens the serial household development cycle, which is largely determined by the number of children a family may have. The decrease in the number of siblings and the shortened cycle of household division may also increase the possibility of grandmothering and therefore allow young mothers to return to work sooner after childbirth. Thus, whether women wish to limit their fertility or not, the one-child policy is lessening women's domestic burdens and increasing their extra-domestic opportunities.

Conclusion

The petty capitalist mode of production in Baifu and the tributary mode of production in Nanyi have led to some variations in local kinship systems and kinship behaviors. In Baifu, the dominant petty capitalist production leads to a petty capitalist kinship, which creates and allows for more flexible and creative kinship behavior, as demonstrated by the permission given to marrying-out women to retain their household registration in Baifu and the ease of implementing birth limitation in the village. In Nanyi, however, the more dominant tributary production and tighter

control of the village authority generate a tributary kinship in which behaviors are more constrained by traditional kinship norms. As a result, the one-child-one-family policy is strictly implemented in Nanyi and the kinship norm of patrilocal residence is not only encouraged, but is also further strengthened by a local regulation enforced by a large fee. In comparison to women in Baifu, local women in Nanyi have more limited personal choices of postmarital residence.

The differences between the political economies of Baifu and Nanyi and their effects on kinship and gender systems demonstrates that the dynamic interaction between the petty capitalist mode of production and the tributary mode of production does apply to micro studies of Chinese rural communities. Because of the various displays of the two modes of production in the reform era, the formation of kinship patterns in any given community are ever changing and differ from patterns in other communities. As a result, gender patterns in the post-Mao rural communities have become diversified.

While many Western anthropologists (Stacey 1983; Wolf 1985; Andors 1983) have argued that the rural economic transition has jeopardized the liberation of Chinese women and that the household-based production has reinforced the patriarchal social order in rural China, voices coming from China seem to disagree. Gao Xiaoxian (1994) contends that rural economic reforms provide equal opportunities to both Chinese women and men and that household-based production, especially the development of family enterprises, has reduced the boundary between the economic contributions of women and men. In addition, "market mechanisms have provided a relatively equal competitive arena, compelling some women to rely on their own ability, courage, and insight to become policymakers and managers" (Gao Xiaoxian 1994: 86). Women's participation in family enterprises has modified traditional values and inspired rural women's self-improvement. She continues,

Male peasants recognize women's competence and authority in the home, discuss important issues with their wives, subsidize their daughters' school attendance, and are beginning to help with household chores. The degree of male–female equality has clearly changed. (1994: 88)

What Gao Xiaoxian has argued seems to confirm the egalitarian tendencies of the petty capitalist mode of production. So, between Gao Xiaoxian and those Western anthropologists who believe that China's economic reforms endanger gender equality, who is (are) closer to reality? Although pursuing a definite answer is a strong impulse, very often realities are too complicated to do so. Indeed, my study shows that even between Baifu and Nanyi, it is very hard to generalize regarding in which village women and men are more equal. In the two villages, the positions of women and men correspond to a different interplay between petty capitalist production and tributary production. Assisted by the Maoist ideology of gender equality and the firm control of the village authority, women and men get equal pay in village enterprises in Nanyi. In Baifu, influenced by a profit-driven morality and shaped by the kinship-based formation of petty capitalist production, women workers on P farm are paid less than men. Yet, this does not mean that in Nanyi, women and men are equal in all respects whereas in Baifu women are discriminated against, as demonstrated by the different village rules of postmarital residence, which allow women more flexibility in Baifu.

In March 2002, I visited Baifu and Nanyi again. Nanyi does not seem to have changed greatly, except that one of the four women who farm had suffered from a stroke so that only three local women are still farming. However, on P farm in Baifu village, as I expected, more economic changes had taken place in 2001, reflecting the creativity and flexibility in the farm's petty capitalist mode of production. After the sawblade factory had moved away, P farm found a new business partner who wanted to rent land and buildings from P farm for a production line, which produces boxed plastic forks, knives, and spoons for export. Currently, more than sixty young migrants are hired as cheap labor to work on the production line. The farm not only rents factory buildings but also provides dormitories and dining services for these young laborers. The rent generates an annual net income of 150,000 yuan

(US$ 17,857) for P farm. Unlike its petty capitalist economy two years ago, P farm's current economic production has become more capitalist-like. Not only is P farm making profits from renting land to the plastic utensils business, but several agnates (two women and one man) of P farm's manager have also invested in it. On P farm, they are the only investors in this business, not because they have enough money to do so, but due to their agnatic ties to Zhang, the manager of the farm. Their direct investments and therefore greater potential to gain benefits from the business demonstrate that for P farm, the roles of kinship in forming petty capitalist production have been further strengthened. While as investors both the female and male relatives of the manager are able to make more money from the new production, other workers who are not related to the manager in kinship are left out.

What had developed on P farm in 2001 extends and supports my analyses in that the economy of P farm resembles the petty capitalist mode of production, which can, without the effective control of the tributary government, quickly develop into Western capitalism. In 2000, P farm depended mostly on renting land to the sawblade factory for profits; now several privileged associates of P farm are actually investing in and running the business. In so doing, they have become the owners of a joint enterprise, which is making profits by using cheap labor. Here comes an interesting question – has P farm transformed its economy from petty capitalism to Western-style capitalism? I would say it has not yet, but may do so if it stops fulfilling its kinship obligations by no longer providing free grain and the 80 yuan monthly pension to old people and young children. In any event, in comparison to the political economy two years ago, current economic production on P farm has definitely become more capitalist-like.

It is difficult to make generalizations regarding village political economy, kinship, family life, and gender status for all Chinese villages. However, my return visit to the two villages in March 2002 leads me to wonder how long the tributary mode of production and tributary kinship will remain in China's political economy. The further developed petty capitalist production in Baifu suggests

that the Western-style capitalist market economy may overtake the petty capitalist mode of
production and become the dominant political
economy in many rural villages. Until then,
China's political economy will remain diversified and Chinese gender will continue to be
shaped by the dialectical relations between
petty capitalist kinship and tributary kinship.

NOTES

1 In the past 50 years, agricultural land has
   decreased from 5,483 *mu* in the 1950s to
   1,200 *mu* in 2000, while the number of non-
   agricultural residents has increased from zero
   to 1,503. And in 2000, there were 876 temporary migrant residents who had moved here
   since the 1980s.

2 The largest family enterprise in Nanyi is a
   restaurant, run by a young couple in the village. It is said that the restaurant makes about
   500,000 yuan (US$ 59,524) each year.

3 In minor marriages, a baby girl was adopted
   into a family as the family's future daughter-
   in-law. She and her future husband were
   raised together in the same household.

4 I cannot be excused either. I include several
   lectures on Confucianism, the New Year Sacrifice, bound feet, etc., in my Gender and
   Culture class.

5 The uterine family is built around a mother
   and her son(s), in which the mother cultivates
   close and loving ties to her sons carefully over
   years. In return, the mother expects emotional
   and financial support from her sons once they
   grow up. More importantly, the strong and
   close ties between a mother and her sons help
   secure her positions in both her husband's
   family and her son's future family, in which
   another woman, the son's wife, might likely
   become a threat to her power and interests.

6 During my short visit in spring 2002, I found
   that the sawblade factory has indeed re-
   located.

7 It does not, however, provide physical and
   institutional walls for people's lives, as *danwei* did for urban people in the Maoist era
   (Harrell 2001).

8 Industrialization in Nanyi has shifted the occupational choices of the local residents away
   from agriculture. In the village, unlike their
   parents, young adults and couples in their
   thirties and early forties have never farmed.

9 Yangge is a folk dance popular in rural
   northern China.

10 Skinner argues that in the household respon-
    sibility system, "family farms have been
    reborn as tenants of the landholding produc-
    tion team" (1985: 406).

11 Although I am not certain as to how much
    village financial control may affect the final
    profits of the four women, their lack of in-
    volvement and control in financial and ac-
    counting activities definitely constrains their
    ability to expand.

12 A married son living with parents under the
    same roof usually assumes both obligations
    and rights. In comparison to his siblings, he
    takes on more responsibility in caring for old
    parents, yet usually he has the right to in-
    herit his parents' house.

REFERENCES

Andors, Phyllis, 1983 The Unfinished Liberation
  of Chinese Women, 1949–1980. Bloomington:
  Indiana University Press.
Bloch, Maurice, 1975 Property and the End of
  Affinity. *In* Marxist Analyses and Social An-
  thropology. Maurice Bloch, ed. London:
  Malaby Press.
Davis, Deborah, and Stevan Harrell eds., 1993
  Chinese Families in the Post-Mao Era. Berkeley:
  University of California Press.
Freedman, Maurice, 1958 Lineage Organization
  in Southeastern China. London: Athlone Press.
—— 1966 Chinese Lineage and Society: Fukien
  and Kwangtung. London: Athlone Press.
—— 1970 Ritual Aspects of Chinese Kinship and
  Marriage. *In* Family and Kinship in Chinese
  Society. Maurice Freedman, ed. Stanford: Stan-
  ford University Press.
Gao Xiaoxian, 1994 China's Modernization and
  Changes in the Social Status of Rural Women.
  In Engendering China: Women, Culture,
  and the State. Christina K. Gilmartin, Gail
  Hershatter, Lisa Rofel, and Tyrene White,
  (eds.) Cambridge: Harvard University Press.
—— 1993 Cultural Support for Birth Limitation
  among Urban Capital-owning Women. *In*
  Chinese Families in the Post-Mao Era.
  Deborah Davis and Stevan Harrell, eds. Berke-
  ley: University of California Press.
—— 1996 China's Motor: A Thousand Years of
  Petty Capitalism. Ithaca: Cornell University
  Press.

Han, Hua, 2002 Sexuality and Uxorilocal Marriage in Rural North China, unpublished manuscript.

Harrell, Stevan, 2001 The Anthropology of Reform and the Reform of Anthropology: Anthropological Narratives of Recovery and Progress in China. *Annual Review of Anthropology* 30: 139–161.

Hinton, Carma, and Richard Gordon, 1984 Small Happiness. Wayne: New Day Films.

Judd, Ellen, 1992 Land Divided, Land United. China Quarterly 130: 338–356.

——1994 Gender and Power in Rural North China. Stanford: Stanford University Press.

Lamphere, Louise, 1987 From Working Daughters to Working Mothers: Immigrant Women in a New England Industrial Community. Ithaca: Cornell University Press.

Leacock, Eleanor, 1978 Women's Status in Egalitarian Society: Implications for Social Evolution. *Current Anthropology* 19(2): 247–275.

Liu, Xin, 2000 In One's Own Shadow: An Ethnographic Account of the Condition of Postreform Rural China. Berkeley: University of California Press.

Maynes, Mary Jo, Ann Waltner, Birgitte Soland, and Ulrite Strasser, eds., 1996 Gender, Kinship, Power: A Comparative and Interdisciplinary History. New York: Routledge.

Sacks, Karen, 1974 Engels Revisited: Women, the Organization of Production, and Private Property. *In* Women, Culture, and Society. Michelle Zimbalist Rosaldo and Louise Lamphere, eds. Stanford: Stanford University Press.

——1979 Sisters and Wives: The Past and Future of Sexual Equality. Westport: Greenwood Press.

Siu, Helen, 1989 Agents and Victims in South China: Accomplices in Rural Revolution. New Haven: Yale University Press.

Skinner, William G., 1985 Rural Marketing in China: Repression and Revival. *China Quarterly* 103: 393–399.

Stacey, Judith, 1983 Patriarchy and Socialist Revolution in China. Berkeley: University of California Press.

Stafford, Charles, 2000 Chinese Patriliny and the Cycles of Yang and Laiwang. *In* Cultures of Relatedness: New Approaches to the Study of Kinship. Janet Carsten, ed. Cambridge: Cambridge University Press.

Stone, Linda, 2000 Kinship and Gender: An Introduction. Boulder: Westview Press.

Walter, Ann, 1996 Kinship between the Lines: The Patriline, the Concubine and the Adopted Son in Late Imperial China. *In* Gender, Kinship, Power: A Comparative and Interdisciplinary History. Mary Jo Maynes, Ann Waltner, Birgitte Soland, and Ulrite Strasser, eds. New York: Routledge.

Wolf, Arthur, 1974 Religion and Ritual in Chinese Society. Stanford: Stanford University Press.

Wolf, Margery, 1968 The House of Lim: A Study of a Chinese Farm Family. Englewood Cliffs: Prentice-Hall.

——1972 Women and Family in Rural Taiwan. Stanford: Stanford University Press.

——1985 Revolution Postponed: Women in Contemporary China. Stanford: Stanford University Press.

Yan, Yunxiang, 1996 The Flow of Gifts: Reciprocity and Social Networks in a Chinese Village. Stanford: Stanford University Press.

23

Primate Kin and Human Kinship

Robin Fox

Introduction

One of the main differences between the bio-social approach in social anthropology, and what might be characterized as the superorganic approach, is that scholars interested in the phylogeny of behaviour have to take as problematical the relation of cultural to natural factors. Those who espouse the dominant superorganic theory treat 'culture' as a self-evident category of 'non-genetic' behaviour: mostly, they see culture as 'intrusive' into 'nature'. Thus, the incest taboo, or kinship systems themselves, are seen as rule-governed and, hence, free products of the human imagination which are imposed on 'natural' tendencies. In the extreme form of this doctrine human behaviour is 99 per cent 'cultural' whereas animal behaviour is 99 per cent 'genetic'. Thus, animal breeding systems are genetic, while human kinship systems are cultural, and so on. The biosocial approach does not deny that culture can intrude into or impose itself upon nature, but (a) it regards this as a problem not a dogma, and seeks to establish of any widespread human institutional or behavioural pattern whether or not it is intrusive or simply an amplification or elaboration of 'natural' tendencies; (b) in its most extreme form (e.g. in Tiger and Fox 1971) it regards the issue as phony since 'culture' is simply the species-specific behaviour of a particular primate, and must be explained on the same principles as the evolved behaviour of any other primate. Here we will take the 'weak' view and simply ask to what extent human kinship systems are cultural intrusions and to what extent they are a natural product of the evolved behavioural propensities of the particular primate species *Homo sapiens* (or even of the genus *Homo*, since it is likely that *H. erectus* had them – at least there is no good reason why it should not). A full demonstration of the thesis proposed here would take us into subjects like the evolution of cranial capacity and its relation to sexual selection which I have dealt with at length elsewhere (Fox 1967a; 1972). Here I will be concerned with presenting evidence for a simple point: that our primate cousins have 'kinship systems' which contain the elements of human kinship systems, but that no other primate combines elements in the way that we do. In other words, there is little in our systems that is not found in 'nature' (and, therefore, there is no reason to suppose that it is 'unnatural' to us), but nowhere in nature is our system found in its entirely. The elements are common: the combination is unique. My contention is, therefore, that it is to the combination of elements that we must look for clues to the uniqueness of human systems, not to the elements themselves.

This is not the same as the approach that says humans have *rules* and this is what makes the difference. I take for granted that we have rules since we are an animal that makes rules;

the real question is do the rules represent more than a 'labelling' procedure for behaviour that would occur anyway? It seems to be Bischof's conclusion on the incest taboo that the taboos and rules indeed label 'natural' tendencies, and also that while all these tendencies exist in nature the human combination is unique. My conclusions about kinship, therefore, match his about incest. Of course, in the same way, there will be a variety of different styles and content to rules, varying with the cultural experience, ecology, and history of different peoples. (Much the same is true of other primates, as it happens.) But the contention here is that even in the absence of cultural rules and the logic of human imagination there would be kinship systems anyway, and that much of the rule-making and imaginative logic is simply (or complexly) playing games with a quite elaborate raw material. To those for whom kinship is a matter of categories this must be mystifying. But categories simply mean that linguistic labelling is possible, and that hence, with communication operating in another dimension than gesture and face-to-face contact, greater elaboration of the basic system is possible. In the absence of language, if a group of animals shows a tendency to treat certain classes of relatives differently from others, then it has invented categories even if these are not linguistically labelled. Discriminatory behaviour creates 'category systems' which, while more limited than linguistic systems, operate in much the same way. Thus, in a linguistic system I might act in a specific way towards a relative because he is recognized by his label; in a non-linguistic system I act towards him in a specific way because he is recognized by some other mark of distinction: his proximity to, or preferential treatment by, 'mother' for example.

Without labouring this point further, I will state that the problem here is to ask (a) what are the characteristics of kin relationships among primates; (b) how do these differ from the most rudimentary of human kinship systems; (c) wherein lies the crucial difference?

Previous attempts to answer this last question have concentrated on such things as (a) development of a 'pair bond' in man; (b) origin of 'families' in man and particularly 'nuclear families'; (c) the repression of unregulated sex in favour of regularized mating; (d) the reduction of hormonal control over behaviour permitting non-seasonal mating – etc. These probably all miss the point. They do not take into account either the complexity of primate kinship systems, or the true differentiating feature – exchange of mates. [. . .]

We know a great deal about primates which can tell us what is behaviourally available to our order in general and, therefore, what must have been available by way of a behavioural repertoire to our ancestors. We also know that there must have been a gradual transition – 'hominization' process – in which cultural and somatic features evolved together and in a feedback interaction. 'Early man' then, in this sense, was less like modern man gone wild than like a primate tamed. And even if we cannot deduce accurately the kinship systems of early man from those of the most primitive humans, we can do something better – we can distil the essence of kinship systems on the basis of comparative knowledge and find the elements of such systems that are logically, and hence in all probability chronologically, the 'elementary forms of kinship'. How we put all this information on primates, hominid evolution, and human kinship together is another question; for the moment let us establish this elementary pattern and work from there.

I will simply make a bald assertion clearly derived in part from Lévi-Strauss but also obvious in all my own work: the two elementary functions of human kinship systems are what I will call, borrowing somewhat recklessly from the jargon of social anthropology, descent and alliance. Descent defines who belongs to what category or how any category is related to any other category. In other words, kin are 'grouped' and the grouping of people in this way, the deciding of who belongs with whom, etc., I am calling descent for convenience. Alliance refers to the allocation of mates. In all human kinship systems people have assigned mates, and the system determines who can mate with whom – crudely who gets whom, who is allied with whom. Whatever else, in other words, a kinship system may or may not do, it has to do these two things: establish who belongs to what group (descent) and who can or must mate with whom (alliance). So, at its most basic, what I am saying is that if we had a heterosexual group of human beings, even without a language and cultural traditions, they would group themselves on a kinship basis, and they would allocate mates among themselves. They need not even do this according to 'rules' initially. All that we need assume is that they would find a 'means' to do this – that their behaviour would tend in this direction and that a social system would emerge on this basis.

My contention about non-human primate systems is simply this: both elements – descent and alliance – are present, but never in the same system. The uniqueness of the human system, therefore, lies not in inventing something new, but in the combination of these two elements so that the mode of descent itself determines the nature of the allocation of mates: in other words, exogamy. I am by no means the first person to say that the essence of human kinship is exogamy – it is a great tradition, and I dedicate this essay to the memory of John Ferguson McLennan – but I may have found a new way of getting at the nature of this uniqueness.

Types of Social System

Very roughly we can distinguish old-world non-human primate social structures on the basis of the number of adult males in the group. The two 'types' that emerge are (a) one-male groups and (b) multi-male groups. I am including primates with 'nuclear families' in the one-male group category. The family of one adult male and one adult female with dependent offspring can be seen simply as a limiting case of the one-male group, which otherwise involves the 'polygynous' family with one adult male, several adult females, and again the dependent offspring. Species with nuclear family organization do not seem to combine these families into larger herds or bands (e.g. the gibbon and many prosimians). The nuclear family system seems basically territorial, with dispersion of dependent offspring. The polygynous or harem species, on the other hand, do often combine, and while the families remain distinct breeding units they unite into larger herds for protection, sleeping, etc. When this happens (as with e.g. hamadryas baboons, gelada, etc.) the herd structure includes not only polygynous families but the 'peripheralized' younger males who have yet to acquire harems of their own.

This total herd structure comes then to resemble in some ways the multi-male system (found in many species of baboon and macaque) where the 'families' do not exist, where there are several males in the group, and where the breeding system is on a 'consort' basis with brief breeding encounters between the more dominant males and oestrus females. Again the younger males are 'peripheralized', but instead of having to collect harems they have to work their way back into the 'centre' of the system so that they too may breed. The multi-male systems differ in the extent to which they are dominated by a central male who is their focus of attention (mostly the open-country species) or alternatively dominated by the older males generally without a 'principal breeder'. The difference is purely one of degree. Among savanna baboons, for example, there tends to be a dominant animal who can also dominate the breeding process by having first choice of females in oestrus; but in a large group there will always be several females in heat and several large males consorting with them. Among forest-dwelling chimpanzees – a multi-male group type – there is again a dominant male, but he is less likely to dominate breeding. But even here older and more dominant animals form consort relationships with females in oestrus, and younger males are relatively peripheralized. The differences have been much overdrawn. Chimpanzees and common baboons, for example, are, in being 'multi-male' types, much more like each other than either is like the hamadryas or gelada baboons with their 'one-male' systems.

What all these systems have in common is a threefold division of the larger group into (a) adult males (b) females and young (c) peripheral males. We can look at any primate social system, including our own, in terms of the 'accommodations' made between these three blocks.

The One-Male Group

The one-male group has not had as much attention as its multi-male counterpart. The early work of Washburn and DeVore [1961] brought the latter into scientific and public attention, and most speculation about human origins rested heavily on the multi-male evidence. [. . .]

This structure was originally thought to be associated with the dry savanna and desert ecologies (Crook and Gartlan 1966), but the cercopithecine, langur, and colobus data suggest that forest species might also prefer it. However, there is a difference. The forest species tend to prefer relatively solitary families, while the savanna and desert species (with the exception of the patas monkey) prefer to encapsulate the harem group in a larger herd. Assuming the forest mode of existence to be more basic, it is easy to see how, when a species moved out into the open desert environment, it would amalgamate for protection. [. . .]

The data we now have show that a social system based on one-male groups is characteristic of the following species: *Cercopithecus ascanius*; *C. campbelli*; *C. cephus*; *C. diana*; *C. erythrotis*; *C. l'hoesti*; *C. mitis*; *C. mona*; *C. nictitans*; *C. patas*; *C. pogonias*; *C. preussi*; *Colobus badius*; *Papio hamadryas*; *Theropithecus gelada*; *Presbytis johni*; *P. pileatus*; (*C. mitis*, Omar and DeVos 1971; on *P. johni*, Poirier 1970).

The basic unit is the polygynous family. This unit exists only as long as the male exists. The 'sons' of the male, at about one year of age, become peripheralized. How they acquire harems differs. Among hamadryas baboons, for example, an older male may take on an 'apprentice' – a younger male who comes to be tolerated more and more until he enters the group and eventually takes it over on the older male's death. Alternatively, the young males kidnap young females whom they 'mother' and who eventually become part of the harem. Either way, the 'father' of this avowedly patriarchal system is not in any sense succeeded by his 'sons'. There is a constant forming and breaking-up of the family units. Daughters may stay with the family but they may also be kidnapped into other families. If a male dies his mates are reallocated. The only group that persists over time is the herd itself. And, in some species, e.g. the patas monkey, there is no herd. Among some langurs, groups of peripheralized males will invade a one-male group, drive out the patriarch, and fight among themselves.

Eventually, one will emerge as the new leader of the harem (Sugiyama & Parathasanathy 1969). There are many variations. But the point I want to make is that although there is no enduring kinship group here, there is 'alliance' in my sense: a relatively permanent assignment of mates operates to produce distinct breeding units.

The Multi-Male Group

Multi-male systems have been noted for the following: *Cercocebus albigena*; *Cercopithecus aethiops*; *C. sabaenus*; *C. talopin*: *Macaca fuscata*; *M. mulatta*; *M. silenus*; *M. radiata*; *M. uris*; *Papio anubis*; *P. cynocephalus*; *P. papio*; *P. ursinus*. [. . .] [Among the better studied multi-male groups are the] chimpanzees and gorillas (Goodall, 1965, 1968, 1971; Reynolds 1965; Schaller 1963). [. . .]

The multi-male system contrasts with the one-male system in a rather startling way to produce a different form of social cohesion. The three 'interest groups' are the same, but the way they accommodate to each other is different. The adult males form a cohesive unit in direct contact with each other and arranged in a hierarchy. They are not divided from each other by their 'family responsibilities'. There are no distinct breeding units; the whole group is the breeding unit, with the rank-order to some extent determining mating preferences. In a sense, *all* the females in the group belong to *all* the males; consort relationships occur during the peak of oestrus, that is, during ovulation, but after that the female is returned to the pool. Recent work on chimpanzees – most of it still in progress – shows that they too have consort relationships; that high-ranking males may well get preference with females in oestrus; that older males restrict the mating behaviour of younger; and so on (personal communications from D. Hamburg, J. van Lawick-Goodall, D. Bygott, P. McGinnis, M. Thorndahl). It is possible that middle-ranking males may do better than those of highest rank. A really high-ranking male who is the centre of attention for his group may find it difficult to detach himself in order to go off with a female; his partners are not so handicapped. But older males as a body have first choice *vis-à-vis* younger.

Thus the mating relationship is quite the opposite of that in the one-male system. It is brief and non-exclusive. There is then, in my sense, no alliance: no relatively permanent assignment of mates. While this is not altogether primitive promiscuity, it could be construed as a kind of group marriage. However, the main point is that there is no alliance function at work.

There is, however, kinship. If the sexual relationship is brief and unenduring, the consanguineal relationship is long lasting and of central importance. Earlier reports of this type concentrated heavily on the male hierarchy as the central feature, and it is indeed very important. But the existence of enduring kinship groups has now come to assume as great a significance. These groups are basically units of uterine kin – or not to put too fine a point on it, matrilineages. They were missed in earlier work simply because the longitudinal data were lacking. Now we know that in macaques and chimpanzees, for example, they are the enduring core of the group. It is the interplay between the male hierarchy, on the one hand, and the matrilines, on the other, that provides the dynamics of the social system.

The classic group consists of an old mother, her sons and daughters, and the children of her daughters. How long the continuity of a group will last we are not yet sure (after the old mother dies that is), but four-generation groups have been observed, and five or six are certainly possible. Sometimes, of course, we may be missing a matriline, since we have to infer that, e.g., two older females who are very close are 'sisters' – we do not know. But taking the typical three-generation group which is known, we find it in all multi-male systems of macaques and chimpanzees.

Studies of Japanese macaques (*Macaca fuscata*) and rhesus macaques (*Macaca mulatta*) have shown that members of matrilines act differently towards each other and towards non-members for many social purposes.

Yamada (1963) noted that related animals would tolerate greater proximity when feeding than would non-related, females being more kinship biased than males. He studied the effects of matriline membership on three categories of behaviour: (1) co-feeding (by which he means animals tolerating each other while feeding close together), (2) play, and (3) grooming. Animals which co-feed have a special tolerance relationship which permits contiguous feeding without tension. This relationship is almost exclusively found between members of the same matriline. The general rule is that frequent co-feeders are uterine kin while animals that are not blood relatives feed together rarely. In some cases, animals of equal social rank co-feed irrespective of kinship ties. Play is very seldom influenced by kinship and young animals play with whomever they can. Like feeding, grooming follows kinship lines in general but not so strictly. Co-feeding, he concludes, has to do with a 'family-making tendency' while playing, and to a lesser extent grooming, have to do with a 'group-making tendency'. Yamada also noted an interesting effect of rank: '...a higher individual has in general less tolerance of an individual not in kinship, while he gives his relatives special treatment.' In summary, and focusing on sex differences: 'With females, the higher the social status of the individual, the more frequently she co-fed with individuals in kinship and the more exclusively she behaved toward other individuals. Accordingly it may be supposed that the more prominent the status of the kinship group, the tighter its unity. With males, however, this fact does not always apply.' Males, for example, showed a smaller tendency to co-feed with maternal relatives.

Loy (1972), studying 33 juveniles separated from the rest of their group, could predict 95.6 per cent of dominance relationships solely on the basis of the known rank of the mother. Also, grooming between related monkeys was over five times more frequent than would be expected from a random selection of grooming partners. This is a more exact finding than Yamada's and shows that, while grooming is certainly 'group-making', grooming acts can cluster significantly among kin. Related animals were more likely to sit together, and on sitting to touch, than were unrelated animals. He concludes: 'These findings serve primarily to demonstrate the far-reaching effects of matrilineal relationships on rhesus behaviour and to reinforce the view that the matrilineal genealogy is the basis of rhesus monkey social organization.'

Kaufmann (1966) studied the maturation of infant macaques on Cayo Santiago. He found increasing interaction with members of the 'matrifocal family' as the young progressed from infancy through the juvenile period.

Sade (1965) notes that 79 per cent of touching or lying together occurred, in one sample, between matriline members. In a later paper (1967) he comments on rank:

> Offspring begin to fight as old infants or young yearlings. They defeat their age peers whose mothers rank below their own and are defeated by their age peers whose mothers rank above their own. The hierarchy thus established persists for several years, either because the first few fights set precedents which cannot easily be broken, or because the offspring continue to associate with their mothers or other older monkeys who rank near their mothers, or because of both reasons. As females become adult they come to rank just below mothers in the hierarchy of adults. This means they defeat not only their age mates but also older females who were adults when they were growing up. As males become adult they tend to rank near their mothers in the adult hierarchy, but at puberty or later, if they remain with the group, they may lose or gain rank. I speculate that at about puberty physiological differences between males become more important in fighting and that the difference that derives from past experience and continued association with adults of differing rank become less overriding in determining the winners of fights.

[...] Miller *et al.* (1973), on Cayo Santiago, studied various categories of behaviour in 18 male macaques between 2 and 8, under the general headings of 'joining', 'grooming', and 'threatening'. They found that: 'Statistical analysis revealed that the male subjects engaged in more positive social interactions with the matrifocal family (mother and offspring) than with other members of the genealogy (matriline), and, in turn, more such behaviour was observed within the genealogy than with unrelated monkeys. Threatening behaviour within the genealogies was infrequent.' They conclude that the socialization of the males within their matrilines contrasts markedly in its non-agonistic nature with the socialization of the males into the non-kin group at large, where threat becomes most important. [...]

Kawamura (1958), in his classic paper, described the 'matriarchal' order of the Minoo-B troop. He distinguished basic rank – that determined by open competition between animals for food – from dependent rank – the rank derived from the mother. He observed that in the troop (in which the leader was, unusually, a female) the children rank, without exception, according to the rank of their mothers. Among brothers and sisters, the younger rank higher than the older presumably because of their closer association with the mother and the protected-threat status they derive from that association. He concludes:

> This troop has a rank system based on the matriarchal order.... The matriarchal order is very stable, and conclusive evidence has been collected to support the fact that this order not only appears when ranking is tested by giving food, but that the troop lives its daily life under this order.... Classes of this troop arose, based on lineages. These classes form a social organisation transcending generations and they decide the social future of new-born babies.

This conclusion has been supported by the studies already cited and by Imanishi (1960) and Itani *et al.* (1963).

'Classes based on lineages' – this, more than any other finding about individual status, is the crux of the material we are summarizing here. Marsden (1968) followed this up with his observations on rhesus monkeys:

> With only one exception, all offspring directly reflected each change in the rank of their mothers, falling or rising to the position in the hierarchy occupied by the mother in relation to other family groups. More importantly, perhaps, patterns of aggression toward other adults and their young support the hypothesis that offspring often assist the mother directly in aggression toward other monkeys, and in turn are assisted by the mother. Therefore, it is more meaningful to think of families (mothers and offspring) as constituting social units which show or receive aggression from other family units in establishing a new hierarchy, or in maintaining an existing one. Thus a new concept of dominance based on family units is probably more realistic than a straight linearity of individuals when describing social dominance in rhesus bands.

If we add to this what is now known about the cohesion of expanded units of related mothers and offspring, that is, matrilineages, then a forceful picture emerges of the dynamics of a social system based on the interplay between ranked lineages, on the one hand, and the linear hierarchy of males, on the other.

Jane van Lawick-Goodall, in the several papers and books already cited, has described for chimpanzees the strong and enduring bonds between mothers and offspring and among the offspring themselves. The qualitative aspect of these relationships comes out clearly and graphically in her work (see also Goodall 1967). [. . .]

Finally, we should look at the most extensive data so far on the Japanese macaque, that of Koyama (1967, 1970). I will deal with this in more detail later under the discussion of group fission; for now, it is enough to note that he found sixteen lineages ranked in order one through sixteen. He comments (1970) on dependent rank generally: ' . . . concerning 54 females 3–10 years of age, rank among the same-age monkeys always corresponds to the rank of their mother and is the same as that of 1964 referred to in the first report. Accordingly, no change in rank among females of the same age occurred during these two years.' Among males 3–10 years old in March (n = 39) only two males had a rank higher than that of their consanguineal group. Rank among age-mates was the same as the rank of their mothers. Older monkeys tended to rank higher, but in all exceptional cases the younger monkeys had mothers ranking higher than those of the older monkeys.

I have taken the trouble to lay out these data in some detail (although space limits the discussion of finer points) in order to establish the 'reality' of this kinship organization, an organization based on matrilineal ties between units of mothers and offspring. The cumulative evidence shows clearly that matrilineages exist; the lineages are ranked; behaviour between members of a lineage is significantly different from that with non-members; membership affects the rank of individuals; membership is very important in the socialization of males in particular. It is not simply that a high-ranking mother will ensure a high rank for her son; the matrilineages themselves being ranked, if lineage A ranks over lineage B, then all members of A rank over all members of B. This remains true over long periods for females and is initially true for males. Male rank may change later, but even then, membership in the lineage may be important, as when brothers help each other to rise in rank even when they change groups (Kaufmann 1967). If Chance's thesis concerning attention as the basis of rank-orders is correct, then, clearly, being of a high-ranking lineage is an important source of attention for males (Chance 1967; see the extension of this idea in Tiger and Fox 1971: ch. 2). The low level of aggression, on the one hand, and the performance of 'altruistic' acts for near kin, on the other, make sense in terms of the theory of kin selection and inclusive fitness put forward by Hamilton (1963; 1964; 1972) and developed by Trivers (1971; 1972).

Thus the female-with-young block here is linked to the males not only by a breeding relationship, but also by uterine kinship. But although we have kinship, we do not yet quite have exogamy. The relationship between mating and lineage is uncertain. [. . .]

[We do know that incestuous matings (mother–son, brother–sister) within lineages are rare.] What we have is a set of tendencies which make it probable that these animals will display (a) patterns of grouping and behaviour which significantly discriminate between uterine kin and other animals, and (b) a statistical trend away from the probability of mating regularly with uterine kin over the 'breeding lifetime'. In the multi-male system, then, to use the jargon, we have *descent* but no *alliance*; kinship, but no marriage. There is assignment of kin to kinship groups, but not even a relatively permanent assignment of mates. The kinship system seems to have a discouraging effect on mating within the group – the beginnings of a negative marriage rule – but nothing more. There is thus a crucial difference between the two systems and between either and the human system, which combines both lasting kinship groups and polygynous and nuclear families; that is, to use the jargon again, both descent and alliance, kinship and marriage – and which uses the descent to determine, negatively or positively, the alliance. [. . .]

Models of the Two Systems

In order to show graphically both the similarities and the differences between the two types,

I have diagrammed them according to the same plan – the concentric circle of the 'classical' description. *Figure* 23.1 shows the multi-male model as originally described for the common baboons. In the inner circle are the males of the hierarchy – one through six (the usual maximum number). In the intermediate circle are the females with and without offspring. In the outer circle are the peripheral males. Outside the circle – literally – are the consort pairs, and one must imagine various of the hierarchical males (here 1 and 3) temporarily out of the system for a few days at a time consorting with females in oestrus. The model is not totally accurate since in reality there would be more females per male. Before the information on lineages came in, this model would have served to illustrate discussion of the multi-male type.

Figure 23.2, which can be totally superimposed on *Figure* 23.1, shows the same system with the kinship ties added. I have envisaged four lineages ranked one through four, one in each quadrant. In the less senior lineages I have put fewer animals, but numbers and dominance are not necessarily connected. The rank of the males is seen to be determined by the rank of their respective lineages, although there will be exceptions to this with older males. Again, the consorting pairs are outside the system. The peripheral males in lineage 1 will be more likely than those in the other lineages to reach top status in the group, thus succeeding their maternal uncles and great-uncles.

Figure 23.3 is the one-male group model drawn to the same ground plan to show how the peripheries are linked to the centre. Again I have envisaged four groups. In the centre are the harem-owning males – unranked. Attached to them are their mates and their infants. At the peripheries are the young males, some of whom have kidnapped young females in order to start their own harems. In some of the one-male groups there are apprentices, waiting to take over the group on the death or retirement of the senior male.

What I hope this illustrates better than any verbal description, is the structural similarity that lies in the existence of the three 'blocks' as I have called them – senior males, females-with-young, and junior males, and the dissimilarity in the way in which the peripheries are linked to the centre; both in the way the females are attached to the males for breeding purposes and the way in which the junior males make it into the hierarchy. In the multi-male model the link is that of matrilineal kinship. Females are the link between the centre and the periphery in their role as the pivots of the kinship system. Males almost 'succeed' their maternal uncles and their brothers; and while they have to prove themselves, their birth status is an enormous help. Mating has no place in the cohesion of the system. Indeed it can be seen as virtually a divisive force and, almost symbolically, it has to take place physically outside the group. With the one-male system, on the other hand, the mating link is all that joins the centre to the periphery. Females are again the link but in their role as wives. There is no kinship link between the dominant males in the centre and the peripheral candidates, who must either kidnap their way back in or ingratiate themselves with an older harem chief. Kinship plays no part in the cohesion of this system, while mating is thoroughly institutionalized.

Group Fission

Leaving aside for the moment the question why the evolving hominids put these systems together (if it can ever be answered), let us look more deeply into another feature of these multi-male, matrilineal systems: group fission. Primate groups split up from time to time when they get too large (a relative matter). We have one excellent account of such fission by Koyama (1967, 1970) – more are coming in (see Furuya 1969). In Koyama's group of macaques the lineages were ranked from 1 to 16. While they stayed together, each lineage would periodically feed new males into the status system and support them in their rise. Koyama suggests that as long as the rank order is stable all is well, but that if, for example, a high-ranking male habitually consorts with a low-ranking female this may cause a rise in the status of her offspring and hence upset the balance of the group. In any case, the group split, and lineages 1–7 formed group A, while lineages 8–16 formed group B. As Koyama points out, when a male leaves a group – and they often do – he leaves alone; when a female leaves she takes all her consanguines, and starts

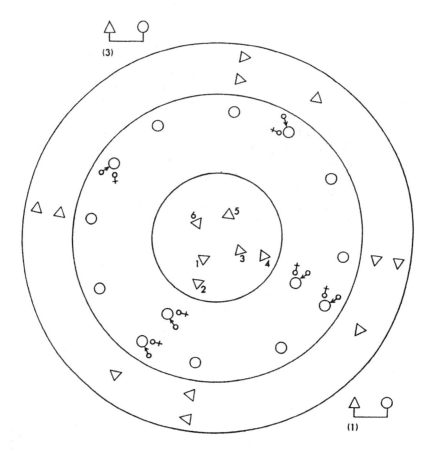

Inner circle: male hierarchy (1=α etc.)
Intermediate circle: females, infants, juveniles
Outer circle: peripheral males
Outside: consort pairs

♂♀ infants still with mother

Figure 23.1   *Multi-male group model*

an exodus of those lineages ranking below hers. The tendency of the males to move about, however, has an interesting consequence. Most of the males from group A eventually ended up in group B and vice versa. Thus, we have a picture, in effect, of two 're- lated' groups, each consisting of ranked matri- lineages, which exchanged males over a period. Had these males been involved in some system of alliance, in my terms, that is, had they ended up as relatively permanent mates in a matriline of the other group, then there would have been little difference, except at the symbolic level, between this and an 'Iroquoian' system of two moieties each composed of ranked matrili- neages, and a rule of moiety exogamy plus matrilocal residence – all very human, and yet little more than a naming system away from the Japanese monkeys. If groups A and B were called 'Eaglehawk' and 'Crow', and the various lineages 'Snake', 'Beaver', 'Bear', 'Antelope', etc., then a picture emerges of a proto-society on a clan–moiety basis which would have delighted Morgan and McLennan (and Bachofen), but depressed Westermarck and Maine for sure. For one thing, it would have

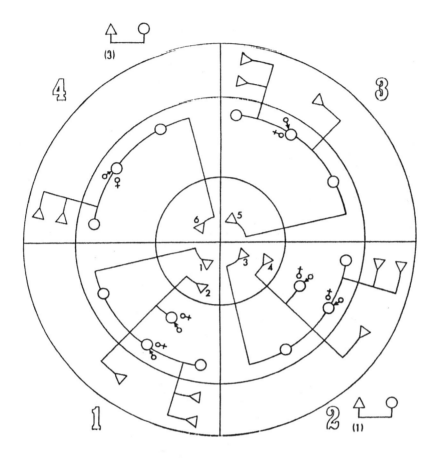

Inner circle: male hierarchy (1=α etc.)
Intermediate circle: females, infants, juveniles
Outer circle: peripheral males
Outside: consort pairs
Quadrants: matrilineages ranked 1 through 4

♂♀ infants still with mother

Figure 23.2 *Multi-male group model with kinship connections*

completely bypassed the nuclear family, and would not even require an incest taboo, much less a 'pair bond'.

We do not need to rehash the matriarchy–patriarchy debate here. But while there is some support given to Bachofen's contention that matriarchy is based on deep biological principles, we have to allow that, for our one-male-group species, so is patriarchy. But this is not a matter of paternity, as earlier thinkers maintained. Patriarchal baboons are not interested in offspring *per se* – in fact they can be quite hostile

to them. They are interested in obtaining and controlling mates. Maternity may well be the basis of descent, but paternity has little to do with alliance. If we marry the alliance principle as we find it in primates to the descent principle as we find it, we do not get patriarchy or patrilineal lineages; we get something more like sororal polygyny and a system of matrilineages with a possibility of lineage and even band exogamy. To put it brutally: females are interested in offspring, males are interested in females, at least at this stage of the game.

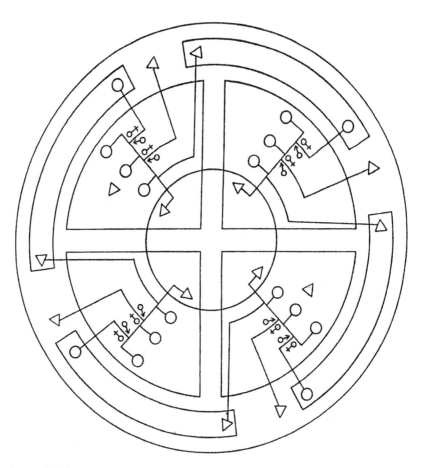

Inner circle: harem-owning males
Intermediate circle: females, infants, apprentices
Outer circle: peripheral males, kidnap pairs
Quadrants: One-male groups

♂♀ infants still with mother
 ♀

Figure 23.3 *One-male group model*

It would be of intense interest to find any species or population of non-human primates combining the two principles. This would mean that even more was attributable to 'nature' than has been envisaged here. The question would then be: on what basis was the combination made? And my own feeling is that it would not be on the basis of exogamy as we understand it in human kinship systems. That the descent system itself should determine the allocation of mates will probably remain the uniquely human distinction.

Conclusions

The position we are at is this. If we look at the range of non-human primate social systems we find several possibilities represented there: fairly stable, ranked matrilineages; a movement of males between groups – and in chimpanzees of females between groups; stable mating associations of a male and several females. As we have seen, the last is not found in conjunction with the others, but they all exist in the primate order, they all have good adaptive reasons for existing, and they represent the raw material out of which primate kinship systems, including our own, are woven. The question for us to explore in the future is why the hominids put together the alliance and descent functions when no other primates had found this necessary, and what form this putting-together took. For various reasons it is unlikely that it could have been a pattern of dispersed nuclear families. This leaves the possibility of some kind of system such as that envisaged above, with males being attached to multiple unrelated females for mating purposes, and yet remaining attached to related females for 'kinship' purposes. In the male–male relationships, again, there would be one relationship to consanguineous males – in the matrilines – and another to unrelated males in the hierarchy. Patterns of elementary exchange between lineages on the one hand, and moieties on the other (originating in simple band-splitting), are easy to envisage – the monkeys are already almost doing it anyway.

The 'why?' question I have tried to answer elsewhere (Fox 1972). It is clearly to do with the severe ecological changes consequent upon the adoption of hunting on the open savannas. I have here been more concerned with the 'how?' question; the question of the raw material that would have been available to our ancestors in making the change. If this gives credence to the matriarchal theory – that earliest kinship was matrilineal, that earliest sex was promiscuous, and that polygyny came next and eventually that patrilineality was 'invented' by the men – then so be it. I would rather see human kinship systems as symbolic methods of working out the tension inherent in trying to marry the polygynous (alliance) principle with its male emphasis, and the matrilineal (descent) principle with its focus on the female. Clearly, in the one the males are well in control; in the other the females are at least covertly exercising great influence. But in any case, to return to the original point, the dynamics of human kinship systems may well lie as much in deep and inherited biological tendencies as in the logic of human imagination – perhaps even more so.

The more general point being made here is that kinship groups and the alliances between them are not merely matters of rules, categories, laws, prescriptions, etc. They are more than results of the free play of human imagination. They are embedded in natural processes such as those described by Hamilton and Trivers. Relatedness – the sharing of common genes – is crucial to the process of natural selection, to the determination of what genes will dominate in any breeding population and ultimately what features will characterize the form and behaviour of an evolving species. Thus kinship groups are the outcome of natural processes; they are as natural as limbs and digestion; they are the outcome of adaptive responses and natural selection over millions of years; they are not peculiar to human society. They do not depend for their existence on the equally natural ability to classify and name which characterizes our species; in the absence of language and rules, they would still occur. It is only their elaboration that depends on the classificatory propensity and the evolution of true language. And even this elaboration itself, stemming from ecological circumstances, historical contingencies, and the vagaries of human inventiveness, is only a variation upon themes. Anthropology has been obsessed with the variations; I am suggesting a new look at the themes – not by a deduction of abstract 'functions' but by careful assessment of what 'nature' presents us with in conjunction with what we know about the selection pressures operating on our own species. Without a knowledge of the themes, we will never properly understand the variations – although we can get pretty close almost by accident.

Thus when Lévi-Strauss (1963) says that

$$\triangle = \overset{\frown}{\bigcirc} \quad \triangle$$
$$\searrow$$
$$\triangle$$

is the 'atom of kinship', he is more or less right, although it might have been better diagrammed:

$$\triangle = \overset{\frown}{\bigcirc} \quad \triangle$$
$$\triangle$$

He is also right when he sees this as a pattern to which, under stress, societies revert. But the question is, why is he right? His basic point is that this follows from the incest taboo – the culture–nature divide – which forbids ♂ △ as a mating relationship and so forces the △ = ♂ △ situation. This 'builds in' the mother's brother/sister's son relationship. But we have seen that the latter relationship already exists in the multi-male system; also, the one-male group system has the △=○ formula. Both elements of his equation, then, exist in nature, but not in the same system together. Putting them together may or may not have required an incest taboo *per se*. The taboo may be simply the result of the evolution of inhibition I have described (Fox 1972). That same evolution, however, as I have argued, both facilitated and required the exchange of spouses, hence exogamy – a factor independent of who has sex with whom (a point made in Fox 1967b, to which Leach called attention in his critique of Lévi- Strauss; see Leach 1970). The relatively permanent mating bond already existed in nature – our 'alliance'; the permanent kinship group already existed in nature – our 'descent'. It only remained for the two to be put together by the evolving hominids.

The possible ways of doing this nowhere *require* an incest taboo, a nuclear family, or the faculty of speech – those much-touted 'origins' of truly human kinship. Logically it would have been much simpler for the hominids to move from primate kinship to human kinship by going directly to the most elementary of elementary kinship systems described by Lévi-Strauss (1969) – and this without any invention, without any intrusion of culture into nature, but with all the possibilities that speech added to the raw material so richly presents.

NOTE

It will be clear from the many references to it that this article should be read as an extension of my 'Alliance and Constraint: Sexual Selection in the Evolution of Human Kinship Systems'. It is also a continuation of the themes discussed by Imanishi, Reynolds, Sahlins, Powell, *et al.* Space precludes any discussion of these here, but it will be obvious where I agree and where I differ. I would like to acknowledge the research assistance of Anthony Pfeiffer and Richard Diener. So much have they contributed both of information and ideas, that they should properly be co-authors, except that I am solely responsible for the final formulation of the argument from which they might well wish to dissent. I was enabled to write the article as a result of leave granted by Rutgers University, and the generous support of the Harry Frank Guggenheim Foundation, New York, NY.

BIBLIOGRAPHY

Chance, M. R. A. 1967. Attention structure as the basis of primate rank orders. *Man* n.s. 2: 503–518.

Crook, J. H., & Gartlan, J. S. 1966. Evolution of primate societies. *Nature Lond.* 210: 1200–3.

Fox, R. 1967a. In the beginning: Aspects of hominid behavioural evolution. *Man* n.s. 2: 415–433.

——1967b. *Kinship and Marriage: An Anthropological Perspective*. Harmondsworth and Baltimore: Penguin.

——1972. Alliance and constraint: sexual selection in the evolution of human kinship systems. In: B. Campbell (ed.), *Sexual Selection and the Descent of Man 1871–1971*. Chicago: Aldine.

Furuya, Y. 1969. On the fission of troops of Japanese monkeys. II. General view of troop fission of Japanese monkeys. *Primates* 10: 47–69.

Goodall, J. van Lawick. 1965. Chimpanzees of the Gombe Stream Reserve. In: I. DeVore (ed.), *Primate Behavior*. N.Y.: Holt, Rinehart and Winston.

——1967. Mother–offspring relationships in free-ranging chimpanzees. In: D. Morris (ed.), *Primate Ethology*. London: Weidenfeld and Nicolson.

——1968. The behaviour of free-living chimpanzees in the Gombe Stream Reserve. *Animal Behaviour Monogr.* 1, part 3.

——1971. *In the Shadow of Man*. Boston: Houghton Mifflin.

Hall, K. R. L. 1965. Behaviour and ecology of the wild patas monkey, *Erythrocebus patas*. *J. Zool.* 148: 15–87.

Hamilton, W. D. 1963. The evolution of altruistic behaviour. *Amer. Nat.* 97: 354–356.

——1964. The genetical evolution of social behaviour. *J. Theoretical Biol.* 7: 1–52.

——1970. Selfish and spiteful behaviour in an evolutionary model. *Nature Lond.* 228: 1218–1220.

——1971. Selection of selfish and altruistic behaviour in extreme models. In: J. P. Eisenberg and W. S. Dillon (eds.), *Man and Beast: Com-*

parative *Social Behavior*. Washington, D.C.: Smithsonian Press.

——1972. Altruism and related phenomena, mainly in social insects. *Annual Review of Ecology and Systematics* **3**: 193–232.

Imanishi, K. 1960. Social organization of sub-human primates in their natural habitat. *Current Anthrop.* **1**: 393–407.

Itani, J., Tokunda, K., Furuya, Y., Kano, K., & Shin, Y. 1963. The social construction of natural troops of Japanese monkeys in Takasakiyama. *Primates* **4** (3): 1–42.

Kaufmann, J. H. 1966. Behaviour of infant rhesus monkeys and their mothers in a free-ranging band. *Zoologica* **51**: 17–28.

Kawamura, S. 1958. Matriarchal social ranks in the Minoo-B troup: A study of the rank system of Japanese monkeys. *Primates* **1**: 149–156. Also S. A. Altmann (ed.), *Japanese Monkeys*. Atlanta: The Editor, 1965, pp. 105–112.

Koyama, N. 1967. On dominance rank and kinship of a wild Japanese monkey troop in Arashiyama. *Primates* **8** (3): 189–216.

——1970. Changes in dominance rank and division of a wild Japanese monkey troop in Arashiyama. *Primates* **11** (4): 335–390.

Leach, E. 1970. *Lévi-Strauss*. London: Fontana/Collins.

Lévi-Strauss, C. 1963. *Structural Anthropology*. Translated from the French by Clarke Jacobsen and Brooke Grundfest Schoepf. New York: Basic Books.

——1969. *The Elementary Structures of Kinship*. Edited by Rodney Needham. Translated from the French by J. H. Bell, J. R. von Sturmer, and Rodney Needham. Boston: Beacon Press; London: Eyre and Spottiswoode.

Loy, J. 1972. The effects of matrilineal relationships on the behaviour of juvenile rhesus monkeys. *Abstracts of the 71st Annual Meeting of the American Anthropological Association*.

Marsden, H. M. 1968. Agonistic behaviour of young rhesus monkeys after changes induced in the social rank of their mothers. *Animal Behaviour* **16**: 38–44.

Miller, M. H., Kling, A., & Dicks, D. 1973. Familial interactions of male rhesus monkeys in a semi-free-ranging troop. *Amer. J. Phys. Anthrop.* **38**: 605–611.

Omar, A., & Devos, A. 1971. Annual reproductive cycle of an African monkey (*Cercopithecus mitis kolbi*, Neumann). *Folia primat.* **16**: 206–215.

Poirier, F. E. 1970. Niligri langur (*Presbytis johni*) of South India. In: L. A. Rosenblum (ed.), *Primate Behaviour*. Vol. I. N.Y.: Academic Press.

Reynolds, V. 1965. *Budongo: A Forest and its Chimpanzees*. London: Methuen.

Sade, D. S. 1965. Some aspects of parent–offspring relations in a group of rhesus monkeys with a discussion of grooming. *Amer. J. Phys. Anthrop.* **23**: 1–17.

——1967. Determinants of dominance in a group of free-ranging rhesus monkeys. In: S. A. Altmann (ed.), *Social Communication among Primates*. Chicago: U. of Chicago Press.

Schaller, G. B. 1963. *The Mountain Gorilla*. Chicago: U. of Chicago Press.

Sugiyama, Y., & Parathasanathy, M. D. 1969. A brief account of the social life of hanuman langurs. *Proceedings of the National Institute of Sciences, India.* **35**, B: 306–319.

Tiger, L., & Fox, R. 1971. *The Imperial Animal*. New York: Holt, Rinehart and Winston.

Trivers, R. L. 1971. The evolution of reciprocal altruism. *Quarterly Review of Biology.* **46**: 35–57.

——1972. Parental investment and sexual selection. In: B. Campbell (ed.), *Sexual Selection and the Descent of Man 1871–1971*. Chicago: Aldine.

Washburn, S. L., & Devore, I. 1961. Social life of baboons. *Scient. Amer.* **204**: 62–71.

Yamada, M. 1963. A study of blood-relationship in the natural society of the Japanese macaque. *Primates* **4** (3).

24

Kinship and Evolved Psychological Dispositions: The Mother's Brother Controversy Reconsidered[1]

Maurice Bloch and Dan Sperber

One of the most discussed topics in the history of anthropology has been the significance of the relationship between mother's brother and sister's son in patrilineal societies. However, the subject seems to have entirely faded from the hot topics of the discipline since the sixties. We believe that, in reviewing this academic story of strange excitement and then total neglect, we can both understand some of the fundamental epistemological problems of anthropology and suggest some of the ways in which new approaches might throw light on questions which have tended to be abandoned rather than resolved.

The History of the Mother's Brother Controversy

The behavior which so intrigued anthropologists involved the rights, recognized in many unrelated patrilineal societies, of a male member of the junior generation over the property and even the persons and wives of senior male members of his mother's lineage, typically the mother's brother.[2] The example which came to be most discussed was that of the BaThonga of Southern Africa because of the particularly full and surprising description of the customs involved given by the early mis-sionary ethnographer Henri Junod in 1912. There the relation primarily concerned the right of mutual insult between the sister's son and the mother's brother and his wives and unclear claims to the property of the mother's brother by the sister's son. The tolerated violence of the behavior, as well as its sexual overtones, contributed to the fascination with the custom and probably titillated the various scholars who discussed the subject. But it was not so much this one example which interested scholars as the conviction that they were dealing with a peculiar relationship which occurred again and again in many totally unrelated societies, something which was all the more unexpected in that it contradicted patrilineal organizational principles – since mothers' brothers and sisters' sons must usually belong to different lineages – and the respect usually accorded to senior generations.

Examples of this peculiar relationship were thought to have been found among Australian Aborigines and in Amazonia, southern Europe, Oceania, and India, not to mention other parts of Africa. Even today recent ethnographers have been struck, again and again, by the prominence accorded to this relationship by the people they have studied in many different places, for example, northern India (Jamous

1991), Amazonia (Viveiros de Castro 1992), and Melanesia (Gillison 1993). But this apparent recurrence itself raises a problem. The various manifestations which so many anthropologists have recognized as instances of the peculiar mother's brother/sister's son relationship are clearly cognate. At the same time, these cases turn out, on closer examination, to be very varied – sometimes involving symmetrical joking, sometimes asymmetrical joking, sometimes avoidance, sometimes significant economic privileges, sometimes sexual rights, sometimes only ritual manifestations – and, furthermore, while in some cases it is actual mothers' brothers and sisters' sons who have the rights in question, the relation sometimes involves broad classificatory groups. The variation is in fact so great that it becomes very difficult to say exactly what it is that the various examples share, and this inevitably has made many wonder whether the scholars who have turned their attention to the question have not been dealing with a nonexistent category.

At first, anthropologists assuming a universal history for humankind along a single evolutionary path and, implicitly, a universal cognitive representation of filiation and marriage saw in such practices as the aggressive claim of the sister's son to his mother's brother's property a survival of mother right and proof of the existence of an earlier matrilineal stage (Rivers 1968 [1914]). This explanation was then famously dismissed by Radcliffe-Brown (1924), who, using his refutation to demonstrate the character of structural-functional accounts, supplied a synchronic explanation for the practice. Thus the controversy over the mother's brother could not have been more central to the short history of social anthropological theory, and the success of Radcliffe-Brown's argument was a key element in the gradual marginalization of notions of evolution from the mainstream of the discipline.

Radcliffe-Brown's explanation was, at first, mainly in terms of the extension of sentiment. He argued that the sentiments of a child toward its mother were extended to the mother's family, making the mother's brother a kind of male mother who acted accordingly in a maternal fashion and so gave gifts to his sister's son. More important, however, was the argument that such customs could only be understood in terms of their function as part of the total social structure. Radcliffe-Brown's argument therefore not only went against evolutionism but also was to be a dramatic demonstration of the value of what has come to be known as structural-functionalism. For Radcliffe-Brown, therefore, the idea of an identical and single history of humankind was to be abandoned, but a universalistic element remained in that he assumed a universal cognitive basis for the representation of kinship; mothers were always mothers, and patriliny's attempt to underplay this caused problems which had to be resolved by strange customs. Furthermore, because of the commonality of the fundamental building blocks of kinship systems, large-scale comparisons could be made between societies, which were to be the foundations of the new "natural science of society."

In turn, Radcliffe-Brown was criticized by Fortes (1953) and then by Goody (1959), who, while retaining the fundamental principle of a synchronic explanation in terms of a systematic social structure, criticized Radcliffe-Brown's explanation for being overgeneral, since it would predict a much greater degree of universality and uniformity than the evidence warranted. Goody's criticism took the form of noting that, although the sentiments of children toward their mothers were everywhere the same, the specific practice in question was found only in certain societies that had patrilineal descent groups without the counterbalance of matrilineal inheritance and that any explanation had to be tied to the occurrence of this type of group. Furthermore, and here following the later Radcliffe-Brown, he specified the character of the institution much more narrowly than the earlier evolutionist writers, insisting on the element of privileged aggression in the snatching of property by the sister's son in ritual contexts. This strange custom he explained, as did Fortes, in terms of the contradiction between what he argued was a universally bilateral kinship system and the occasionally occurring unilineal descent system. He argued that sisters' sons were grandchildren of their mothers' fathers in the kinship system and therefore their heirs, while in the descent system they were in no way their successors, since descent was traced only in the patrilineal line. The tolerated snatching of meat by the sister's son at his mother's brother's sacrifices resolved this contradiction because in this way he recovered some of his grandparental inheritance from the son of his maternal grandparents, who had (abusively in terms of the kinship system but legitimately in terms of the descent system) received all of that inheritance. Goody clinched this argument with a comparison of two closely related groups with different property systems in which the degree of inheritance "deprivation" of the sister's son was correlated with the importance of meat snatching.

This piece of work is a particularly fine example of the structural-functional analyses of its time. It assumes, with a characteristically confident tone, that comparison of the social structures of different societies will reveal recurring connections between different features which, it can then be assumed, are related in a synchronic causal way. This sort of comparison also implies a belief that the basic institutions of societies are everywhere of much the same kind, that they are represented in much the same way, and that we know that all human societies have men and women, marriage, and filiation. According to this way of thinking, patriliny is a particular perspective imposed on the universally recognized facts of procreation. The belief in the universality of the basic representations of kinship of Radcliffe-Brown is thus modified but not abandoned, since these representations, when they occur, are about natural, objective facts that exist independently. Furthermore, the emotional reaction to a certain state of affairs, in this case ambiguity over filiation, is assumed to be basically the same for all humans irrespective of culture and to produce, therefore, similar behaviors in similar circumstances. These different but related assumptions of a common ground are what made the use of comparison as a discovery procedure possible. Variations were significant because it could be assumed that they occurred within the same natural field consisting of identifiable elements; thus the general principles of Radcliffe-Brown's natural comparative science of society remained possible.

This identity of the basic building blocks of kinship systems is precisely what came under challenge in the subsequent development of the discipline. The first clearly expressed formulation of the coming epistemological shift is to be found in Leach's 1955 paper on marriage, and this shift was emphatically repeated and expanded in Needham's introduction to *Rethinking Kinship and Marriage* (1971). The basis of their arguments was that marriage and kinship, as understood by social and cultural anthropologists, were not externally existing phenomena but merely glosses for loosely similar notions found in different cultures. As Needham put it, there was no such thing as kinship. Subsequently, in a more empirical mood, Schneider (1984) attempted to demonstrate that Austronesian kinship was a fundamentally different phenomenon from European kinship and therefore aiming at understanding the former with the words appropriate for the latter was a source of confusion. Thus, generalizing comparisons of kinship systems were impossible because they did not, as was previously assumed, involve comparisons of like with like.

Similar in inspiration but even more startling – though to many less convincing in its extreme forms – was the point made by a number of feminists that there were no such things as women and men beyond a specific cultural context. Explicitly drawing on Schneider's critique of kinship, Collier and Yanagisako (1987) argued that the differentiation between female and male that anthropologists had incorporated into their analyses was a "cultural construction" and of a quite different order from any sexual difference between organisms that might exist in nature. These anti-naïve-empiricist points had two consequences for the kind of argument that Radcliffe-Brown, Fortes, and Goody had presented. First of all, as was noted above, it could be argued that the grand comparisons of structural-functionalism involved operations like adding apples and pears, and, secondly, the social units, for example, lineages, were not similar "natural things" occurring in different societies but different and unique historical/cultural representations constructed in different settings and therefore incommensurable (see Kuper 1982). The only reason, according to these writers, that kinship had seemed so similar among different human groups across the globe was an ethnocentric tendency to see similarities and overlook differences. Finally, the last universalistic element in the Goody argument, the similarity of behavioral response in all humans to similar situations, also came under attack by anthropologists who claimed that emotions too were culturally constructed (Rosaldo 1980) and could therefore not be intuited from introspective sympathy.

The implication of all this for the type of comparative enterprise that Goody and others had been engaged in seemed clear: it made it impossible. It led, if not necessarily at least quite directly, to the deep relativism of much modern anthropology. The systematic comparison which for the structural-functionalists was to be a first step toward scientific generalizations became clearly illegitimate if there could be no assurance that the units of analyses were commensurate. Those who studied kinship had deluded themselves that they had been dealing with biological facts, which it would be reasonable to assume would be severely constrained by nature and therefore comparable, while in reality they had been dealing with representations which, it was implicitly assumed, were the product of unique histories and therefore could take any form at all. In the case of the particular example of the mother's brother controversy, the recurrence of the institution which had intrigued the earlier writers was a mirage. Every case was different, and the very terms of the relationship – mother, brother, sister, and son – did not indicate the same kind of thing in different cultural contexts. Thus, just as structural-functionalism had dealt the first blow to anthropology as a natural science, the culturalist attack on structural-functionalism seemed to have destroyed any hope of generalization. We had been left with nothing but anecdotes about the infinity of specific situations in which human beings find themselves.

The theoretical history we have just traced can be seen as unidirectional: it is the history of the gradual abandonment of belief in the possibility of anthropology as a generalizing science. It assumes that because human beings can transmit information between individuals through symbolic communication they are entirely free of any natural constraints and essentially different from other animals, who transmit most, if not all, information genetic-

ally. Animals must wait for changes in their genomes to become different; humans, in contrast, change with their representations. The existence of these representations is made possible by the learning and computational potential of the human brain, but their contents, it is implicitly assumed, are not at all constrained or even influenced by genetically inherited brain "hardware." These contents are determined, rather, by historico-cultural processes. Human history is therefore liberated from biology, and people may represent the world and each other as they please. The belief in the need for cross-cultural regularities resisting historical specificity becomes simply wrong, the product of a category mistake. The extension of the aims of natural science to the study of culture and society would be like studying smells with rulers.

The aim of this paper is not to deny the validity of at least some of the criticisms of earlier anthropological approaches which have just been touched on. Indeed, we recognize the relevance of those arguments, and there is no doubt that the whole enterprise of Radcliffe-Brownian structural-functional analysis rested in part on the dubious foundations of misplaced naïve realism. We agree with Leach, Needham, and Schneider that the phenomena described by anthropologists under the label of "kinship" are cultural and therefore historical constructions and that people's thoughts and actions are about these constructions rather than about unmediated facts of biological kinship. The implicit argument which would see representations of kinship, marriage, and gender as merely the inevitable recognition of "the way things are" will not do. We will argue, however, that this does not mean that the attempt to invoke natural factors or even biological factors as explanations of such cultural representations must be abandoned as though these representations and the people who hold them had somehow floated free from the earth into the immaterial clouds of history. Antirealism too can be utterly naïve.

We choose the example of the mother's brother/sister's son relationship in patrilineal societies to demonstrate our argument simply because it has been so critical in the history of the discipline, and we try to show that it is possible to envisage, in a case such as this, an approach which combines the particular with the general, although we must recognize that the actual carrying out of such a study lies beyond what we can do here.

The abandonment of overpowerful theories in anthropology came, in the first place, from the realization that the implicit and explicit cultural "universals" of traditional anthropology were not as uniform as they had been assumed to be. But anthropologists who argue for a radically relativistic constructivism often seem to lack confidence in their own arguments. Their reasoning has taken them to a point that negates what all those with a reasonable acquaintance with the ethnographic record know – which is that the regularities which have fascinated the discipline since its inception are surprisingly evident. Thus, it is common for younger anthropologists, reared on the diet of relativism which the studies mentioned above exemplify, to be shocked by discovering the old chestnuts of traditional anthropology in their fieldwork just when they had been convinced that these were merely antique illusions.[3]

The dilemma that this particular history reveals is, in fact, typical of the subject matter of anthropology as a whole. What happens is that, first of all, some cross-cultural regularities are recognized: the incest taboo, for example. These lead to quick explanations in terms of the evolution of culture and their "function" for society as a whole, for individual well-being, or for reproductive success. These explanations are then shown to be based on a gross exaggeration of the unity of the phenomena to be explained. Then explanation is abandoned altogether and declared impossible, leaving anthropologists and, even more, the wider public, with the feeling that the original question has been more evaded than faced. In this way the very idea of the possibility of anthropology is destroyed.

The Epidemiological Approach to Representations

The aim of this paper is to shun such evasion and to sketch a theoretical model applied to a particular case – in other words, to see how a possible explanation might be framed in the case of a particular example of one of these

"obvious" regularities, the varied but similar peculiar relationships of the mother's brother and the sister's son in different societies. We want to do this without either exaggerating the unity of the phenomenon or avoiding the problems discussed above concerning misplaced realism, which recent theoretical criticism has well illuminated.

What is involved in explaining a cultural phenomenon? Here is a way of framing the question. All members of a human community are linked to one another across time and space by a flow of information. The information is about themselves, their environment, their past, their beliefs, their desires and fears, their skills and practices. The flow has rapid and slow currents, narrow rivulets and large streams, confluence and divisions. All the information in this flow is subject to distortion and decay. Most of it is about some here-and-now situation and does not flow much beyond it. Still, some of it is more stable in content and more widely distributed, being shared by many or even most members of the community. When anthropologists talk of culture, they refer to this widely shared information.

What explains the existence and contents of culture in the social flow of information? An answer of a sort is provided by modern interpretive anthropology, which aims to show that the elements of a culture (or of a cultural subsystem) cohere and constitute an integrated worldview (see in particular Geertz 1973). This is not the approach we favor. Without denying the insightfulness of such interpretive scholarship and the relative systematicity of culture, we are among those who have argued that this systematicity is often much greater in the anthropologists' interpretation than in the culture itself (e.g., Leach 1954, Bloch 1977, Sperber 1985a) and therefore is exaggerated (as is acknowledged by James Boon [1982: 326], who speaks approvingly of the "exaggeration of cultures"). More important, even if cultures were as systematic as claimed, this would fall far short of explaining the spread and stability of these coherent wholes, unless one were to take as given that there are factors and mechanisms in the flow of information that somehow promote systematicity. Rather than assuming their existence, we favor studying the factors and mechanisms actually at work in the spread and stabilization of cultural phenomena and leaving as an open question the degree and manner in which they may indeed promote systematicity.

Our explanatory approach to this flow of information in society is that of the "epidemiology of representations" (Sperber 1985b, 1996). It is naturalistic – that is, it aims at describing and explaining cultural phenomena in terms of processes and mechanisms the causal powers of which are wholly grounded in their natural (or "material") properties. More specifically, the kind of naturalistic explanation of cultural phenomena we favor invokes two kinds of small-scale processes: psychological processes within individuals and physical, biological, and psycho-physical interactions between individuals and their immediate environment (including interactions with other individuals) that we call "ecological" processes. Typically, the scale of the processes invoked is much smaller than that of the cultural phenomena described and explained in terms of them. It is the articulation of large numbers of these microprocesses that allows one to redescribe and explain cultural macrophenomena. This contrasts with more standard social science accounts that explain cultural macrophenomena in terms of other social and cultural macrophenomena.[4]

We view, then, the flow of information as a natural process occurring in the form of causal chains of microevents that take place both in individual mind/brains and in the shared environment of the individuals involved. Inside minds, we are dealing with processes of perception, inference, remembering, decision, and action planning and with the mental representations (memories, beliefs, desires, plans) that these processes deploy. In the environment, we are dealing with a variety of behaviors often involving artifacts and in particular with the production and reception of public representations that can take the form of behaviors such as gestures or utterances or of artifacts such as writings. We call these representations "public" because, unlike mental representations, they occur not within brains but in the shared environment of several persons. Thus not just discourse addressed to a crowd but also words whispered in someone's ear are "public" in the intended sense. Mental events

cause public events, which in turn cause mental events, and these chains of alternating mind-internal and mind-external events carry information from individual to individual. A simple example is provided by a folktale, in which the main mental events are those of comprehension, remembering, recall, and speech planning and the main public events are tellings of the tale. What makes a particular story a folktale is the fact that repeated sequences of these mental and public events succeed in distributing a stable story across a population over time.

All these events taking place inside and outside individual minds are material events: changes in brain states, on the one hand, and changes in the immediate environment of individuals, on the other. As material events, they possess causal powers and can be invoked as causes and effects in naturalistic causal explanations. They differ in this respect from the abstract meanings invoked in interpretive explanation (see Sperber 1985a: ch. 1). That meanings can be causes is contentious, and what kind of causal power they might have, if any, is obscure (see Jacob 1997). For instance, attributing to a folktale a meaning that coheres with, say, basic values of the culture in which it is told may, in a way, "make sense" of the tale, but it does not come near explaining its distribution and hence its existence as a folktale in that particular culture.

It could be objected that the microevents invoked in an epidemiological approach are at the level of individual minds and behaviors. How, then, can their study help explain cultural macrophenomena that exist not on an individual but on a societal scale? We have already suggested that these macrocultural phenomena are made up, at a microscopic level, of these causally linked microevents. To this it is sometimes objected that the vast majority of these microevents cannot be observed: anthropologists will never witness more than a very small sample of the public microevents involved, and mental events cannot be observed at all. Here, however, the comparison with medical epidemiology should help dispose of this objection.

Epidemiological phenomena such as epidemics are macrophenomena occurring at the level of populations, but they are made up of microphenomena of individual pathology and interindividual transmission. In most cases individual pathological processes are not directly observable and are known only through symptoms and tests, while the vast majority of microevents of disease transmission go unobserved. This, however, has been a challenge rather than an impediment to the development of medical epidemiology. In the epidemiology of representations the situation is, if anything, better than in the epidemiology of diseases. Our communicative and interpretive abilities give us a great amount of fine-grained information about the representations we entertain and about the process they undergo, whereas pain and other perceptible symptoms generally provide much coarser and harder-to-interpret information about our pathologies. Also, most events of cultural transmission require the attention of the participants, whereas pathological contagion is typically stealthy. Hence cultural transmission is much easier to spot and observe than disease transmission.

In spite of the limited evidence at its disposal, medical epidemiology has provided outstanding causal explanations of epidemiological phenomena. It has done so only occasionally by following actual causal chains of transmission and much more often by helping to identify the causal factors and mechanisms at work both within and across individual organisms. Mutatis mutandis, the task of the epidemiology of representations is not to describe in any detail the actual causal chains that stabilize (or destabilize) a particular cultural representation (although in some cases it is of great historical interest to be able to do so) but to identify factors and processes that help explain the existence and effect of these causal chains. For instance, showing that a particular folktale has an optimal structure for human memory and that there are recurring social situations in a given society in which people are motivated to tell it or to have it told helps explain why the tale is told again and again with little or no distortion of content in that society.

The central question on which an epidemiological approach focuses is what causes some representations and practices to become and remain widespread and relatively stable in content in a given society at a given time.[5] In so framing the question, we depart from the goal of generally explaining all or even most socio-cultural phenomena in one and the same way, either as fulfilling a function (a coarse functionalist approach) or as contributing to reproductive success (a coarse sociobiological approach). True, from an epidemiological point of view, all explanations of sociocultural phenomena will have to invoke both mind-external ecological factors linked to the transmission of cultural contents and mind-internal psychological factors linked to the mental representation and processing of these contents. However, the particular factors at play and the way they combine vary with each case (just as, in medical epidemiology, a different combination of organism-internal physiological factors and of organism-external environmental factors characterizes each disease). Because of this multiplicity of co-occurring causes, we aim only at identifying some of the factors that contribute to explaining particular instances. These factors play a causal role only in specific historical and environmental circumstances and therefore can never be sufficient to explain the local cultural forms. Caused in part by the same factors, these forms have recognizable similarities – which we aim to help explain. However, we merely identify a couple of important and recurring factors among many other diverging factors: each cultural form in its full local specifics is therefore unique to its particular historical context.

This, of course, is, first of all, simply to return, though more explicitly and critically, to the general multifactorial explanations that were typical of anthropology before its recent relativist turn. Two things may be new, though. Rather than accepting implicitly some nondescript naturalism or objectivism about kinship, we appeal quite explicitly to naturalistic considerations about evolved, genetically transmitted psychological predispositions. The result of this explicitly naturalistic account is, however, weaker in its predictive pretensions than the type of account found, for example, in Goody's functionalist thesis. There the sister's son's privilege seemed an almost necessary solution to a structural problem found in certain patrilineal societies. Similarly, this solution was to account for the particular form of the institution, for example, the snatching of significant property. According to our more explicitly naturalistic but at the same time more modest account, there are some factors that increase the chances that the sister's son privilege will stabilize as a cultural form in these societies, and we can expect and not be disturbed by a wide range of unexplained variation in practices because these will always be combined with many other factors and many different histories. We avoid, or so we hope, the too-strong explanations of functionalism, old-style cultural evolutionism, and sociobiology without giving up on causal explanation.

A few simple examples will give an idea of the range of factors that an epidemiological approach would consider relevant and the complex interrelation between mind-internal and mind-external factors. Density of population is a mind-external factor in the stabilization of drumming as a means of communication. The fact that percussion sounds tend to preempt human attention is a mind-internal factor in the culturally stabilized uses of percussion instruments. The relative ease with which human memory retains texts with specific prosodies is a mind-internal factor in the stabilization of various forms of poetry; familiarity with specific, historically evolved poetic forms is a mind-internal factor in the acceptability, learnability, and therefore chances of cultural stabilization of new poetic works. The effectiveness of internal combustion engines for moving vehicles is a mind-external factor contributing to the stabilization of the techniques involved in constructing and maintaining these engines. Untutored human minds do not, however, spontaneously or even easily acquire these techniques; hence the recognition of the effectiveness of internal combustion is a mind-internal motivating factor in the setting up of appropriate institutional teaching without which the relevant technologies would not stabilize. Institutional teaching itself involves a complex articulation of mind-internal and mind-external factors.

As these examples illustrate, both mind-external and mind-internal factors explaining cultural phenomena can pertain just to the natural history of the human species and its environment or involve also the sociocultural history of the populations involved. On the mind-external side, density of population is a natural factor that is found in all living species but can be modified by cultural factors. Demographic density has a wide variety of cultural effects, the stabilization of drummed communication in some low-density populations being a marginal but obvious illustration. On the mind-external side again, the presence in the environment of vehicles powered by internal combustion engines is a wholly cultural factor – which does not mean that it is nonnatural (it is, after all, the product of evolved mental mechanisms exploiting natural laws) – that contributes, among many other sociocultural effects, to the stabilization of the techniques necessary for their construction and maintenance. On the mind-internal side, the tendency of human attention to be preempted by percussion sounds, although it can be culturally modified, is basically a natural trait that humans share with other animals. The ability to organize knowledge in a hierarchy of concepts is typically human, and although it is likely to have a strong natural basis it is certainly enhanced by language, writing, and formal teaching. Familiarity with specific poetic forms is a wholly cultural trait. This illustrates an important difference, among several, between the epidemiology of diseases and the epidemiology of representations: culture occurs both inside and outside of minds, whereas diseases qua diseases occur only inside organisms.

The epidemiological model therefore does not deny the complexity of the process of human history. It fully recognizes that culture is both in us and outside – that it is not (even remotely) just a matter of human beings with genetically determined mind/brains reacting to diverse environments according to the dictates of their nature. But the recognition of this complexity and of the unique fact that humans are beings that, in a strong and important sense, make themselves still leaves room for considering, inter alia, the role of factors such as human psychological dispositions resulting from natural evolution. However, just as cultural patterns are never simple phenotypic expressions of genes, they are never simple social-scale projections of the individual mind. Culture is not human mentation writ large. It is, rather, the interaction of psychological dispositions with mind-external factors in a population that can best explain the sporadic recurrence of certain types of behaviors and norms in a whole variety of guises. The inability of other models to do this – an inability common in the social sciences – has left anthropology ill-equipped to explain many of the cross-cultural regularities which have, in the past, rightly fascinated it.

A rich example of the relationship between evolved psychological dispositions, mind-external factors, and cultural phenomena is afforded by the case of language. A common assumption in cognitive psychology is that humans come equipped with a language faculty. This language faculty is neither a language nor a disposition that generates a language in the individual ex nihilo but a disposition to acquire a specific language on the basis of external linguistic inputs. The disposition is assumed to work like this: Infants react differently to sound patterns typical of human speech: they pay particular attention to these sounds, analyze them differently from other sounds, look for special evidence such as speaker's gaze in order to associate meaning with sound, structure meaning in partly preformed ways, test their knowledge by themselves producing speech, and generally develop a competence in the language of their community. That the language acquired by the members of a community depends on the public linguistic productions encountered in this community is a truism. However, the languages found in all human communities depend on the psychological disposition that individuals bring to the task of language acquisition. Generally, human languages have to be learnable on the basis of this disposition. More specifically, phonetic, syntactic, and semantic forms are more likely to stabilize when they are more easily learnable. All so-called natural human languages – that is, languages the evolution of which is essentially the output of spontaneous collective linguistic activity – will therefore exhibit structural features that make them highly learnable as a first language by humans.

Languages – Chinese, English, Maori, and so forth – differ because they have different histories, with a variety of factors such as population movements, social stratification, and the presence or absence of writing affecting these histories in subtle ways. However, these mind-external, place-and-time-specific factors interact in every generation with the language fac-ulty found in every human. It is this interaction that determines the relative stability and the slow transformation of languages and puts limits on their variability. For a variety of sociohistorical reasons, topics of conversation, preferred words, socially valued patterns of speech, and so on, vary continuously over time in such a way that every generation is presented with a somewhat different sampling of linguistic inputs, to which it reacts, in the acquisition process, by unconsciously bringing about minor changes in the underlying grammar. Generally, whereas day-to-day cultural changes in language use may introduce new idiosyncrasies and difficulties such as hard-to-pronounce borrowed words, the language-learning disposition operating at the generational time scale pulls the mental representations of these inputs toward more regular and more easily remembered forms. For instance, the more difficult phonology of borrowed words or the more difficult semantics of meanings stipulated as part of sophisticated theories are likely to be normalized by language learners in the direction of easier forms. This determines a slow evolution of languages that is constrained both by the necessity of intergenerational communication and by the universal constraints of language acquisition.

The case of language learning, therefore, illustrates how the existence of a genetically inherited disposition is a factor in the stabilization of cultural forms not by directly generating these forms but by causing learners to pay special attention to certain types of stimuli and to use – and sometimes distort – the evidence provided by these stimuli in specific ways. This, of course, leaves room for much cultural variability. Moreover, dispositions capable of affecting cultural contents may be more or less rigidly constraining, the language-acquisition device envisaged by Chomskyans being on the more constraining side. In general, cultural representations departing from those favored by underlying dispositions, though possible, do not stabilize as easily. In the absence of other stabilizing factors counterbalancing the dispositions (e.g., institutional support), hard-to-learn representations tend to get transformed in the process of transmission in the direction favored by the dispositions.

The epidemiological approach to culture provides a way of understanding the relationship between psychology and culture that neither denies the role of psychology nor reduces culture to mind. In a nutshell, the idea is that psychological dispositions in general (whether evolved basic dispositions or culturally developed dispositions) modify the probability – and only the probability – that representations or practices of some specific tenor will spread, stabilize, and maintain a cultural level of distribution.

How might all this help explain the regularities in the relationship between mother's brother and sister's son in patrilineal societies that are the topic of this article? To this we now turn.

Applying the Theory to the Mother's Brother/Sister's Son Relation

Underlying the theories of the structural-functionalists concerning the mother's brother/sister's son relation in patrilineal societies was the assumption that all human beings really reckon kinship bilaterally. This made the occurrence of unilineal rules to form descent groups something which somehow "went against nature." Thus Fortes (1969) contrasted the domestic domain, in which relations were governed by biology and natural emotions, with the lineage domain, which was constrained by politico-jural considerations in conflict with this biology. For him, therefore, the claims of the sister's son were a kind of reassertion of underlying bilaterality. Goody, although distancing himself somewhat from the Fortesian formulation, seemed to imply something similar in that the reason the sister's son was being "cheated" of his inheritance by the patrilineal rule was that in reality he, like the maternal uncle's children, was a true descendant of his mother's parents. The objection to Fortes's and Goody's position, however, has been, as we have seen, that they seemed to assume that people acted in terms of genetic relations rather than in terms of a very different thing, their representation of socially specified relations. But what if there were some indirect causal link between social representations and genetic relations? Then the accusation of naïve empiricism might fall away and the Fortes/Goody argument might be partly reinstated. How this might be possible is what much of the rest of this paper is about.

We begin by noting that support for the structural-functionalists' assumption of the universal bilaterality of kinship seems to come from an unexpected source. This is Hamilton's (1964) neo-Darwinian explanation of kin altruism and its development in sociobiological theory. However, this kind of theory has been rejected out of hand by most social and cultural anthropologists (e.g., Sahlins 1976). It is necessary to outline the theory of kin altruism and why it has been rejected to see if, after all, it might not be used legitimately in favor of the kind of argument implicit in the writings of Goody and Fortes.

The by-now familiar kin-altruism argument can be summarized as follows: Genealogical relationships in the strict biological sense exist among all organisms, including humans. The transmission of heritable biological traits through genealogical relationships is what makes natural selection possible. Natural selection favors genes which have the effect, given the environment, of rendering more probable more replications of themselves in future generations. This includes genes that promote the reproduction of the organism in which they are located, genes that promote behaviors favorable to the survival and reproduction of descendants of the organism in which they are located, and also – and this is fundamental to Hamilton's thesis – genes that promote survival and reproduction in yet other organisms which, being genealogically related, are likely to carry copies of the same genes. A gene causing an organism to pay a cost or even to sacrifice itself for the benefit of its lateral kin may thereby increase the number of copies of itself in the next generation not through the descendants of the cost-paying or self-sacrificing organism (which may thereby lose its chance of reproducing at all) but through the descendants of the "altruistic" organism's kin, who are likely to carry the very same gene.

The potential contribution of kin altruism to what is known as "inclusive fitness" favors the emergence of a disposition to helpful behavior adjusted to the genealogical distance between the altruist and the beneficiary. For such a disposition to exert itself, the organism must have the possibility of discriminating kin from non-kin and, among kin, degrees of relatedness. This does not mean, of course, that the organism must have the conceptual resources to represent genealogical relatedness and its degrees precisely and as such. What it means is that, if the ecology is such that degree of relatedness can, at least roughly, be discriminated thanks to some simple criterion such as smell, appearance, or habitat, then a disposition exploiting this possibility may be selected for.

The importance of the theory of kin altruism for evolutionary biology and for the sociobiological study of animal behavior is not in dispute, but what are its consequences, if any, for the study of human behavior? At first sight this theory, transposed directly to humans, would predict that the requirements of this altruism should, in humans, favor an instinctually based universal bilateral recognition of kinship. This would be a priori support for the structural-functionalists' assumption. Here, however, is where the objections of most anthropologists come in.

These objections are fundamentally two. First, the great variability in kinship systems throughout the globe seems unaccountable in terms of panhuman characteristics. Second, humans live in the world via their representations, and how one gets from genes to representations or norms has simply not been thought through in the sociobiological literature (which has been criticized precisely on this ground by evolutionary psychologists [see Tooby and Cosmides 1992]).

The first objection means that the explanation in terms of genes is far too direct. One should note, however, that the sociobiological position not only is compatible with the recognition of some degree of variability but also purports to explain it. The expression of genes is always contingent on environmental factors, and it may be part of the contribution of a gene to the fitness of the organism that it has different phenotypic expressions in different environments. For instance, the sex of many reptiles is determined not directly by their genes but by the temperature at which eggs are incubated, females developing better, it seems, and being more often born in a warmer environment and males in a colder one (Shine, Elphick, and Harlow 1995).

Closer to our present concern, Alexander (1979) offers an explanation of both matrilineal inheritance and sister's-son rights in patrilineal societies in terms of uncertainty of paternity. An evolved disposition to favor kin should be sensitive to degrees of doubt or certainty of relatedness. In particular, a man's investment in his putative children should be sensitive to his degree of confidence that he is actually their biological father. If there are reasons that this degree of confidence should be low, then a man's closest relatives in the next generation may well be his sister's children. On this basis, Alexander predicts "that a general society-wide lowering of confidence of paternity will lead to a society-wide prominence, or institutionalization, of mother's brother as an appropriate male dispenser of parental benefits" (1979: 172). One may accept the premise that there is an evolved disposition to favor kin that is sensitive to confidence in relatedness and yet doubt Alexander's conclusion, in particular regarding the institutionalization of matrilineal inheritance. True, there is ethnographic evidence that confidence in paternity tends, with exceptions, to be lower in matrilineal than in patrilineal society, as the case of the 19th-century Nayars illustrates (Gough 1959), but it is most probably even lower in societies which have neither matrilineal nor patrilineal descent groups (Gibson 1986; Stack 1983). Furthermore, a correlation is not sufficient to determine that there is a direct causal relationship, let alone what the direction of such a causal relationship might be.

The ethnographic and historical record shows that matrilineality and patrilineality and related patterns of inheritance are fairly stable systems, with very rare documented examples (such as Barnes 1951) of a society's shifting from one to the other. In contrast, changes in sexual mores toward or away from greater permissiveness and associated lower confidence in paternity are very common and may be caused by rapidly shifting economic, demographic, or ideological factors. It cannot be the case, then, that a lowering of confidence in paternity systematically or even frequently leads to the institutionalization of matrilineality. Alexander's claim, therefore, is at best unconvincing. One could, for that matter, argue that the lower confidence in paternity in matrilineal society is an effect rather than (or as much as) a cause of the descent system. When the inheritance system is matrilineal, then a man knows that his heirs will be his sister's children rather than those of his wife. His chances of investing in his wife's children's welfare may be further reduced by rules of separate residence of the spouses such as are often found in matrilineal societies. To the extent that the opportunities for a man to invest resources in his wife's children are limited, it may matter relatively less whether these children are biologically his own, especially if the counterpart of greater paternity doubts is a greater chance of having children with other men's wives. This fits well with the common ethnographic observation that in most matrilineal societies there is less control over the sexual fidelity of women.

Extending Alexander's line of reasoning to the case with which we are concerned here, one would predict that the chances of having institutionalized privileges for the sister's son in an otherwise truly patrilineal system will be greater when paternity doubts are greater (but not great enough to tip the system over toward matrilineality). In this case, however, we know of no evidence of a correlation between institutionalized privileges of sister's son and paternity doubts, let alone a causal link in the hypothesized direction.

The second standard anthropological objection to a biological account implies that, even if we accept that a disposition to Hamiltonian kin altruism is biologically advantageous and therefore likely to have somehow evolved (something which is clearly plausible), it is not clear at all what would follow regarding cultural norms of human behavior. The answer is probably nothing directly and unconditionally, since dispositions to behavior need not actually lead to behavior, let alone to culturally codified behavior; they may be offset or inhibited in many ways. Moreover, assuming that a disposition is not inhibited, it still need not be reflected in a cultural norm. In most human society, for instance, the disposition to use, under certain conditions, an eyebrow flash as a sign of recognition is both uninhibited and culturally uncodified (see Eibl-Eibesfeldt 1975). Should we, then, as do most cultural and social anthropologists, simply forget

about all this biological stuff and, along with the theologians and philosophers of old, recognize that the categorical uniqueness of human beings frees them completely from animality?

The epidemiological approach offers a way of avoiding this type of dismissal while taking into account what is valuable in the objections. Let us accept, as a hypothesis, that there is an evolved disposition to try to differentiate people in a way sensitive to their degree of genealogical relatedness to self. It is most unlikely that such a disposition would be such as to cause the individual to seek actual genealogical information. It would be rather a disposition merely to seek whatever available information might indicate relatedness to self.[6] Now, such a disposition would favor the cultural stabilization of systems of representation providing for such ego-centered differentiation without determining their exact nature. The disposition would not be the source of these representations; these would arise as part of the process of distribution of ideas and practices – the historical dialectic of thought and communications, so to speak – and its interaction with the individual cognitive development of the members of every new generation. The epidemiological approach seeks factors explaining the transformation and stabilization of representations in the process of their transmission, including biological factors. It does not pretend, as might a classical sociobiological approach, that these biological factors somehow generate the representations or that culturally sanctioned behaviors are phenotypic expressions of genes.

One prediction that would follow from the hypothesis we are considering is that individuals would tend to show interest in evidence of relatedness, whether or not culturally codified. For instance, if a single kinship category included full sibling, half-sibling, and more distant relatives, with the same cultural norms of behavior vis-à-vis all, individuals would nevertheless tend to differentiate both cognitively and behaviorally between the different types of individual falling into this category (see, e.g., Bloch 1998). This further interest could be carried out individually without being particularly culturally condoned, as we have just envisaged, or it could contribute to the stabilization of further cultural representations (e.g., folk theories, tales, alternative or complementary terminologies for kin) drawing finer-grained distinctions than the basic kinship-terms system. In other words, whenever representations involving classifications and norms which distinguish kin in terms of closeness appeared amidst the babble and multiplicity of other representations caused either by individual imaginations and circumstances or by more general sociohistorical circumstances, these particular representations would seem strangely "right," "attractive," "natural," or "obvious" to people. This would be the case without individuals' being at all sure why these representations had these qualities, and even if they gave reasons these reasons would often be merely post hoc rationalizations.

Assuming this general framework, we would make the following predictions: In unilineal systems where transmission of rights and good and generally helpful behavior creates an inequality of treatment among individuals that are equally closely related to ego and therefore goes against the predisposition in question, there should be a general, nondeterministic tendency to compensate for this imbalance. Norms or institutions capable of playing, in such a system, a compensatory role would simply stand a greater chance of stabilizing than in systems where the imbalance did not exist in the first place. The special rights of the sister's son found in some patrilineal cultures could well be a case in point.

The relationship between biological disposition and cultural norm that we are envisaging in this case is one between a biological causal factor that is obviously not sufficient and maybe not necessary but such as to render more probable the emergence and stabilization of norms of the type in question. We emphasize that this more sophisticated naturalism makes, in this case, weaker claims than the common-sense naturalism of anthropologists such as the 19th-century cultural evolutionists and Malinowski, Radcliffe-Brown, Fortes, and Goody. According to their common-sense naturalism, there are natural kinship facts that people are somehow aware of and that guide their sentiments and behaviors. This makes a strong universalistic claim about human cognition, emotion, and behavior, which are taken to be neatly attuned to natural facts. If these

classical claims appear misleadingly weaker and more acceptable than those we are tentatively considering here, it is only because they are made, for the most part, implicitly, whereas we have tried to spell out a possible naturalistic approach.

According to the approach we are considering, there are indeed biological facts and, in particular, genealogical relationships. These, however, need not be cognized as such by people. A predisposition to attend to reliable correlates of these relationships cognitively, emotionally, or behaviorally in one or several of a multiplicity of possible ways is likely to have evolved in many species, including the human species. In humans, this attention to relatedness encounters a wealth of relevant cultural inputs. More specifically, developing children, searching their environment for evidence of relatedness to others, find kinship terms ("kinship" now in the cultural rather than the biological sense), people identified as related to them by means of these terms, do's and don'ts relating to kinship categories, folk theories, etc. Because of their evolved disposition, they attend to this information or even seek it, retain it, use it to guide their behavior, and become, in turn, transmitters of such information.

At this stage we seem to be just defending a weakened, updated, and explicit version of the implicit or less explicit naturalistic claims of Fortes and Goody regarding the mother's brother/sister's son relation in certain patrilineal societies. In fact, given the sweeping and careless way in which these claims have been dismissed, this is worth doing in any case. We are defending them, however, in a way that is not contradicted by the very real uniqueness of each case. Furthermore, in contrast to sociobiologists assuming a fairly direct connection between genes and culture, we claim only an indirect relationship of genetically favored receptivity to specific information, favoring in turn the stabilization of cultural representations of a more or less specific tenor.

Why Ritualized Transgression?

From Junod to Goody, ethnographers have stressed the transgressive style in which the sister's son's rights are exerted. This may take many forms, from ritualized insults among the

BaThonga to ritualized snatching of meat among the Lo Dagaba. Why should it be so? The general approach we are proposing might help us understand not just the recurrence of the recognition of the subsidiary rights of the sister's son in his mother's brother's property but also the ritualized transgressions so often involved in exerting those rights.

From a cultural-epidemiological point of view, cultural norms (such as the norm that authorizes a Lo Dagaba man to snatch meat from his mother's brother) are just a kind of representation that is widely distributed in a population through various processes of transmission. What makes them norms is the fact that they represent the way things are required or allowed to be. In the social science literature, norms are mostly envisaged as causes of behaviors conforming to them. However, norms play other causal roles which may be no less important. In particular, they serve to confer approval or blame on behaviors attributed to oneself or to others or just on behaviors that occur very rarely, if at all, but the very possibility of which captures the imagination and defines the limits of what is acceptable. In most societies, for instance, norms against cannibalism are much more important as a topic of narrative and conversation than as a guide for behavior. It would be interesting to know how much the norm permitting a sister's son to take his mother's brother's goods in one or another ritualized way results in actual taking of goods with significant economic effects as opposed to being a topic of conversation with occasional symbolic enactments, serving to define social roles more than to reallocate economic resources. Alas, the literature does not seem to offer the kind of data that would answer this question. Moreover, things are likely to differ in this respect across different societies and times.

Norms are not just causes of behaviors but also effects of behaviors. Their spreading is caused by the different types of behaviors that they promote. In other words, norms are cultural to the extent that they are distributed by causal chains in which mental representations of the norms and public behaviors (including public statements of the norm) alternate. Again, it would be interesting to know how much a norm such as that permitting goods

snatching is maintained by actual acts of snatching and how much by statements of and about the norm.

Both universal and culture-specific factors may contribute to the acceptability and attractiveness of a norm and therefore to its chance of reaching, in a given socio-historical situation, a cultural level of distribution. Whatever the extent to which a norm permitting ritualized transgression causes behaviors that conform to it, the cultural stability of the norm is a sign of its psychological acceptability and attractiveness – which have to be explained. Here we propose some considerations relevant to such an explanation.

Suppose that there is a type of behavior that, for different reasons, is simultaneously attractive and unattractive in the same society. As a result, there are, in that society, factors that would favor the stabilization of a norm approving this behavior and other factors that would favor the stabilization of a norm prohibiting it. Under such conditions, the stabilization of one of the two types of norm is an obvious obstacle to the stabilization of the other, opposite type.

In such a case, things can go in one of three ways. The first possibility is that indeed the stabilization of one norm effectively counteracts factors that would have favored the stabilization of the other. For instance, religious iconoclastic movements have, in different societies, effectively suppressed any type of image even though receptivity to iconic representations, we assume, was still psychologically present and would otherwise have favored the cultural approval of image production. Here a psychological disposition, although present, fails to favor any direct cultural expression. The second possibility is that the factors favoring opposite norms end up stabilizing some compromise norm, as when images are accepted and even encouraged but only with religious themes. Then there is a third possibility, in which the stabilization of one norm contributes to the stabilization of a well-contained, ritualized form of the opposite norm. One norm dominates, but the other norm applies in clearly insulated circumstances. This state of affairs may actually contribute to the stability of the dominant norm by highlighting the exceptional character of its occasional violation. Thus Bloch (1987) has argued that the sexual chaos expected at certain stages of Malagasy royal rituals must be seen as "scene setting" for the extreme domestic order dramatized in the next stage.

The behavior studied by Goody might well be such a case of a potential conflict of norms that results in the stabilization of two sharply contrasting cultural norms caused by very different factors. One, patrilineal descent and inheritance, is wholly dominant, while the other, the rights of the sister's son, takes the form of an authorized transgression with ritual aspects the very transgressive character of which contributes to the stabilization of the dominant patrilineal norm. This suggestion is, of course, reminiscent of a line of argument famously initiated by Gluckman (1954) and developed by the Manchester school, in particular in the work of Victor Turner (1969). What the epidemiological approach does and the Gluckman-type explanation does not, however, is seek to explain the macrocultural fact of the asymmetrical equilibrium between a dominant norm and its authorized or even prescribed transgression in terms of factors affecting the microprocesses of cultural transmission.

Given the stabilization of a patrilineal norm (the explanation of which is not the topic of this article) and the persistence of evolved psychological factors favoring investment of resources in all close kin, whether patrilineally or matrilineally related, we may expect individuals to welcome expressions of these psychological factors provided that they are not incompatible with the patrilineal norm they have internalized. These psychological factors may find an expression through the informal helping by the mother's brother of his sister's children. Here, however, we are talking of individual attitudes rather than of a culturally sanctioned practice. A cultural practice that acknowledges the rights of one's sister's children would normally go against the patrilineal norm and would be unlikely to stabilize (unless the patrilineal norm itself was in the process of destabilization). Expressing interest in the sister's son/mother's brother relationship while highlighting the fact that this relationship does not ground normal, regular rights of sharing or inheritance is a way of reasserting by

contrast that very patrilineal norm. More specifically, ritualized transgression practices of the type we are discussing here underscore the out-of-the-ordinary character of a sister's son's rights over his mother's brother's goods and thereby contribute to highlighting the normal character of patrilineal transmission of goods. Thus the combination of the dominant patrilineal norm internalized by all members of the society and the psychological factors favoring all close kin renders people receptive and welcoming to a norm of ritualized expression of sister's-son rights.

The norms and practices of ritualized transgression that are likely thus to stabilize are "catchy" because of their psychological rather than because of their economic effects. These are first and foremost "symbolic" practices that need not have any significant – let alone any major – effect regarding the actual allocation of resources between direct and lateral descendants. This is a further contrast between the epidemiological account we are sketching here and any sociobiological account that would explain such practices in terms of their putative effects, through reallocation of economic resources, on social stability or biological fitness.

All that we have said, of course, does not amount to a comprehensive explanation of the particular forms of the sister's son's privileges in any one of the societies discussed by so many ethnographers, and it is important to understand why. There are two reasons for this – besides the very sketchy character of our attempt. First, we have relied on the hypothesis that there is an evolved human disposition that is aimed at modulating behavior in a way sensitive to degrees of biological relatedness, but this hypothesis is based on speculation, however well-motivated, more than on conclusive hard evidence. Secondly, we are not offering an explanation for why, for example, Lo Dagaba sister's sons behave in precisely the way they do. Indeed, we think a unifactorial or bifactorial explanation of such an ethnographic datum would inevitably be insufficient. Actual cultural practices, as performed by specific individuals at a given time, are embedded in the sociohistorical processes that have distributed, stabilized, and transformed cultural representations and practices in the population to which these individuals belong. Each of these historical flows is unique. These processes are influenced by many types of factors, evolved psychological predispositions being only one of them. Mostly, cultural processes are influenced by other cultural processes. People's behavior, in particular their conformity or nonconformity to norms, is guided by the representations they have of the world rather than by the way the world is. People's representations are influenced in several ways by the phenomena they are about, but they are influenced also – and to a greater extent in most cases of interest to anthropologists – by other representations, in particular culturally transmitted ones.

All these difficulties and caveats do not mean that we need to abandon generalizing explanations of the kind we have attempted here. In other words, the recognition of the value of the objections to kinship studies of such as Needham and Schneider need not lead to a denial of the relevance of general unifying causes, amongst which are some universal human dispositions likely to have been naturally selected in the course of evolution. Such a method, precisely because it sets nonabsolute conditions for the expression of general factors, can overcome the difficulty which we highlighted at the beginning of this paper and which seems to have overwhelmed anthropology. Reasoning in terms of such things as evolved human dispositions has all too often produced too powerful explanations, while the refusal to try to explain obvious though partial recurrences across cultures in the end seems perverse and inevitably leaves anthropological questions to be naïvely answered by others.

and it is your duty to give me a drink." He then felt haunted by Radcliffe-Brown.

4 Of course, explaining cultural phenomena in terms of microinteractions is not new in anthropology. The work of Fredrik Barth (e.g., 1975, 1987), for example, has been a source of inspiration to the epidemiological approach.

5 How stable do representations have to be to count as "stable"? From the epidemiological viewpoint, there is no expectation that there will be a neat bipartition, among all representations that inhabit a human population, between individual representations that never stabilize in the community, on the one hand, and cultural representations that are transmitted over time and social space with relatively little modification, on the other. We expect, on the contrary, to have a continuum of cases between the idiosyncratic and the widely cultural. This viewpoint differs quite radically from the memetic approach to culture of Richard Dawkins and others (e.g., Dawkins 1976; Blackmore 1999), for which memes are true replicators and other mental contents are not. One might wonder, then, when a representation is stable enough to be seen as a cultural representation. We argue, against that very question, that, from an anthropological point of view, representations are best viewed as more or less cultural depending on the breadth, duration, and stability of their distribution.

6 Hirschfeld (1984) can be read as suggesting a similar approach and insisting, quite rightly, that an essential relatedness and not just any kind of relatedness is aimed at, but his description of this kind of relatedness in terms of a "natural resemblance" seems to us inadequate.

NOTES

1 For Jack Goody.
2 In a way that is typical of the time, the focus was almost exclusively on male roles.
3 Maurice Bloch remembers how, as a student, he was bored with the mother's brother controversy and convinced that it was an insignificant aberration in the history of the subject but subsequently, during fieldwork in Madagascar, had to listen all night to a drunk endlessly repeating, "I am your sister's son,

REFERENCES

ALEXANDER, R. D. 1979. *Darwinism and Human Affairs*. Seattle: University of Washington Press.

BARNES, J. 1951. *Marriage in a Changing Society*. Cape Town: Oxford University Press. Rhodes-Livingstone Paper 20.

BARTH, F. 1975. *Ritual and Knowledge among the Baktaman of New Guinea*. New Haven: Yale University Press.

BARTH, F. 1987. *Cosmologies in the Making: A Generative Approach to Cultural Variation in New Guinea.* Cambridge: Cambridge University Press.

BLACKMORE, S. 1999. *The Meme Machine.* Oxford: Oxford University Press.

BLOCH, M. 1977. The past and the present in the present. *Man* 12 (n.s.): 279–292.

BLOCH, M. 1987. "The Ritual of the Royal Bath in Madagascar: the Dissolution of Death, Birth and Fertility into Authority," in D. Cannadine and S. Price (eds.), *Rituals of Royalty: Power and Ceremonial in Traditional Societies.* Cambridge: Cambridge University Press.

BLOCH, M. 1998. Commensality and poisoning. *Social Research* 66(1): 133–151. Special Number. *Food: Nature and Culture.*

BOON, J. A. 1982. *Other Tribes, Other Scribes: Symbolic Anthropology in the Comparative Study of Cultures, Histories, Religion and Texts.* Cambridge: Cambridge University Press.

COLLIER, J. & YANAGISAKO, S. 1987. "Towards a Unified Analysis of Gender and Kinship," in *Gender and Kinship.* Standford: Stanford University Press.

DAWKINS, R. 1976. *The Selfish Gene.* Oxford: Oxford University Press.

EIBL-EIBELSFELDT, I. 1975. *Ethology, the Biology of Behavior.* New York: Holt, Rinehart and Winston.

FORTES, M. 1953. The structure of unilineal descent groups. *American Anthropologist* 55: 17–41.

FORTES, M. 1969. *Kinship and the Social Order.* Routledge: London.

GEERTZ, C. 1973. *The Interpretation of Cultures.* New York: Basic Books.

GIBSON, T. 1986. *Sacrifice and Sharing in the Philippine Highlands.* London: Athlone.

GILLISON, G. 1993. *Between Culture and Fantasy: A New Guinea Highlands Mythology.* Chicago: University of Chicago Press.

GOODY, J. 1959. The mother's brother and the sister's son in West Africa. *Journal of the Royal Anthropological Institute* 89: 61–88.

GLUCKMAN, M. 1954. *Rituals of Rebellion in South-East Africa.* Manchester: Manchester University Press.

GOUGH, K. 1959. The Nayars and the definition of marriage. *Journal of the Royal Anthropological Institute* 89: 23–34.

HAMILTON, W. D. 1964. The genetical theory of social behavior. *Journal of Theoretical Biology* 7: 1–52.

HIRSCHFELD, L. 1984. Kinship and cognition. *Current Anthropology* 27(3): 217–242.

JACOB, P. 1997. *What Minds Can Do.* Cambridge: Cambridge University Press.

JAMOUS, R. 1991. *La Relation Frère–Sœur.* Paris: Ecole des Hautes Etudes en Sciences Sociales.

JUNOD, H. 1912. *Life of a South African Tribe.* Neuchâtel, Switzerland: Attinger Bros.

KUPER, A. 1982. Lineage theory: A critical retrospect. *Annual Review of Anthropology for 1982* 11: 71–95.

LEACH, E. 1954. *Political Systems of Highland Burma.* London: Bell.

LEACH, E. 1955. Polyandry, inheritance and the definition of marriage. *Man* 55: 182–186.

NEEDHAM, R. 1971. "Remarks on the Analysis of Kinship and Marriage," in R. Needham (ed.), *Rethinking Kinship and Marriage.* London: Tavistock.

RADCLIFFE-BROWN, A. 1924. The mother's brother in South Africa. *South African Journal of Science* 21: 542–555.

RIVERS, W. H. R. 1968 [1914]. *Kinship and Social Organization.* London: Athlone Press.

ROSALDO, M. 1980. *Knowledge and Passion.* Cambridge: Cambridge University Press.

SAHLINS, M. 1976. *The Use and Abuse of Biology.* London: Tavistock.

SCHNEIDER, D. 1984. *A Critique of the Study of Kinship.* Ann Arbor: University of Michigan Press.

SHINE, R., ELPHICK, M. J. & HARLOW, P. S. 1995. Sisters like it hot. *Nature* 378: 451–452.

SPERBER, D. 1985a. *On Anthropological Knowledge.* Cambridge: Cambridge University Press.

SPERBER, D. 1985b. Anthropology and psychology: Towards an epidemiology of representations. The Malinowski Memorial Lecture (1984). *Man* (n.s.) 20: 73–89.

SPERBER, D. 1996. *Explaining Culture: A Naturalistic Approach.* Oxford: Blackwell.

STACK, C. 1983. *All Our Kin: Strategies for Survival in a Black American Community.* New York: HarperCollins.

TOOBY, J., & COSMIDES, L. 1992. "The Psychological Foundations of Culture," in J. Barkow, L. Cosmides & J. Tooby (eds.), *The Adapted Mind: Evolutionary Psychology and the Generation of Culture.* New York: Oxford University Press.

TURNER, V. 1969. *The Ritual Process*. London: Routledge.

VIVEIROS DE CASTRO, E. 1992. *From the Enemy's Point of View: Humanity and Diver-sity in an Amazonian Society*. Trans. Catherine V. Howard. Chicago: University of Chicago Press.

Glossary

affinal   related through marriage.

affinal alliance   *see* **marriage alliance**.

affines   relatives through marriage.

agnates, or patrikin   kin traced through male links (cf. **cognates, uterine kin**).

agnatic descent   descent traced through males; patrilineal.

alliance theory   theory of social organization stressing the properties of marriage systems (cf. **descent theory**).

ambilineal descent   descent traced through both males and females but not equally in both directions; descent traced back and forth between males and females.

apical ancestor   the most remote common ancestor linking two or more kin or groups of kin.

artificial insemination   a process of placing donor sperm into the vaginal cavity of a female in an attempt to achieve pregnancy.

avunculate   a special relationship between a male and his mother's brother which allows the nephew to take certain liberties with the maternal uncle and/or grants him privileged access to the uncle's property or resources.

bilateral descent   descent traced equally through both males and females.

bride capture   a marriage practice whereby the groom's kin or friends abduct (usually only symbolically or ritually) a woman from another group to become his spouse.

bride service   a marriage practice whereby a groom lives with the bride's kin and performs labor for them for a period of time, either before or during the early stage of the marriage.

bridewealth   wealth transferred from the groom and/or kin of a groom to the kin of the bride as part of a marriage transaction.

clan   a group or category of people who claim to share descent from a common ancestor, but whose more remote genealogical links are obscure or no longer traceable.

classificatory kinship terminology   Any kinship terminology system in which some lineal kin are linguistically classified together with some collateral kin.

cognates   kin traced through both male and female links (cf. **agnates, uterine kin**).

cognatic descent   descent traced through any combination of male or female links.

collateral kin   kin outside of a person's own line of descent, e.g., siblings, cousins.

conjugal   pertaining to marriage or the husband–wife relationship.

consanguineal   related through descent ("blood" ties in English usage).

consanguines   kin (as opposed to **affines**).

corporate group   a group of people who collectively share property, rights, privileges, and/or liabilities.

cross cousins   the children of two opposite-sex siblings; one's cross cousins are one's mother's brother's children and one's father's sister's children (cf. **parallel cousins**).

cultural constructivism a theoretical approach in anthropology which emphasizes that cultures construct their own realities; hence, innumerable concepts (e.g., "male," "female," "gender," "kinship") are best seen as cultural constructions rather than as realities external to all cultures.

cultural relativism the contention that (1) each culture can only be understood on its own (emic) terms, or from within; (2) no culture is superior to another, or that all values are relative to cultural contexts; or (3) no one mode of knowledge (for example, science) is intrinsically superior to another mode of knowledge or understanding.

descent the notion of relationship downward from a common ancestor, often forming a clan or lineage.

descent group social group formed by the principle of descent; *see* **clan, lineage**.

descent theory theory of social organization stressing the properties of descent systems (cf. **alliance theory**).

diffusionism the position that major elements of particular cultures have been learned or borrowed from neighboring peoples, or through travel or communication, rather than independently invented; a reaction against nineteenth-century evolutionism.

double descent the existence in one society of both patrilineal and matrilineal descent groups; each person in the society simultaneously belongs to descent groups of both kinds.

dowry wealth from the kin of a bride that accompanies the bride to her marriage. In some cases this wealth is jointly managed by the husband and wife; in other cases part or all of this wealth becomes the property of the husband's kin.

dual organization a system of exogamous marriage between two moieties.

ego an individual person who serves as a reference point for a kinship or marriage tie.

elementary structures Lévi-Strauss's term for systems of cross-cousin marriage.

emic pertaining to categories, concepts, or terms indigenous to a particular culture; the local meanings of such categories, concepts or terms; native perspectives (cf. **etic**).

endogamy marriage within a certain social group or category; the requirement that spouses come from the same social group or category (cf. **exogamy**).

ethnocentrism the view that one's own cultural or ethnic group is superior to or more natural than another or to others generally; the tendency to interpret ideas or practices of other cultures in terms of one's own cultural categories or values.

etic pertaining to the analytical categories, concepts, or terms used by anthropologists to describe and compare cultures, or cultural phenomena (cf. **emic**).

Eurocentric characterized by the interpretation or evaluation of other cultures in terms of the central cultural concepts or values of European ones.

exogamy marriage outside of a certain social group or category; the requirement that spouses come from different social groups or categories (cf. **endogamy**).

fictive kinship a relationship that a cultural group recognizes as modeled on kinship, e.g., God-parenthood or ritually sealed blood-brotherhood.

filiation ties between parents and children.

functionalism a theoretical approach especially popular in anthropology in the early to mid-twentieth century which emphasized that certain parts of a culture (social institutions, religious beliefs, rituals, kinship, forms of government, etc.) either (1) serve to fulfill basic human needs (following Bronislaw Malinowski), or (2) serve to maintain each other and so maintain and perpetuate the whole social system (following A. R. Radcliffe-Brown).

genealogy the network of kinship links (biological or social) between persons; a diagrammatic representation of kinship links between persons.

genitor, genetrix biological father, mother (cf. **mater, pater**).

ghost marriage the practice whereby a patrilineal kinsman takes a wife in the name of a deceased man in order to produce children by the woman in that man's name.

house society a society consisting of corporate domestic estates that transmit their titles, property, and prerogatives to their members over the generations.

hypergamy   marriage where the kin group of the bride is of lower status than that of the groom.

hypogamy   marriage where the kin group of the bride is of higher status than that of the groom.

incest taboo   prohibition on sexual relations (and often, by implication therefore, on marriage) between kin deemed too closely related.

inclusive fitness   the process whereby an individual enhances his or her reproductive success through acts that favor the fitness of others who share some genes with that individual, as in the case of close relatives.

in vitro fertilization (IVF)   the process of incubating oocytes with sperm in a receptacle such as a petri dish to produce fertilization.

isogamy   marriage between kin groups of equal status.

kindred   a set of relatives traced to a particular person (ego).

kin selection   the process whereby natural selection acts on inclusive fitness such that the fitness of one's close kin is enhanced (*see* **inclusive fitness**).

kinship terminology   an inventory of terms for relatives in a particular language.

kin terms   words for relatives.

levirate   the marriage of a man to the widow of his deceased brother.

lineage   a line of descent or (in anthropology) a group of people who trace descent to a common ancestor through known links.

lineal kin   a person's direct ancestors or descendants

marriage alliance, affinal alliance   the notion of links between groups (descent groups, village communities, etc.) being formed through marriage.

mater   social mother (as opposed to biological mother; cf. **genetrix**).

matriarchy   a society in which women hold dominant authority; female dominance.

matrikin   *see* **uterine kin**.

matrilineal descent   descent traced through females only.

matrilocal   a postmarital residence pattern in which a married couple lives with or near the bride's kin (*also* **uxorilocal**).

moiety   one of two exogamous subdivisions (often clans or groups of clans) that together comprise a whole society.

monogamy   marriage between two persons, generally a man and a woman.

neolocal   a postmarital residence pattern in which a married couple moves to a new location, living with the kin of neither the bride nor the groom.

nuclear family   a familial unit consisting of a married couple and their unmarried children.

parallel cousins   the children of two same-sex siblings; one's parallel cousins are one's mother's sister's children and one's father's brother's children (cf. **cross cousins**).

parental investment   the contributions of parents to the survival and reproductive success of their offspring.

pater   social father (as opposed to biological father; cf. **genitor**).

paternity certainty   the extent to which an individual male is led to believe that he is the biological father of a particular child.

patriarchy   a society in which men hold dominant authority; male dominance.

patrikin *see* **agnates**.

patrilineal descent   descent traced through males only; agnatic descent.

patrilocal   a postmarital residence pattern in which a married couple lives with or near the groom's kin (*also* **virilocal**).

phoneme   a minimal speech sound in a given language.

phratry   an exogamous subdivision of a society consisting of two or more clans (*see* **moiety**).

polyandry   the marriage of a woman to two or more men at the same time.

polygamy   the marriage to more than one partner at the same time, male or female.

polygyny   the marriage of a man to two or more women at the same time.

primogeniture   a pattern of inheritance in which only the eldest child, usually the eldest male child, receives an inheritance (cf. **ultimogeniture**).

reciprocal altruism   the behavior of an organism that favors the biological fitness of another, unrelated organism, carried out in the expectation that this favoring behavior will be reciprocated on some other occasion such that the fitness of the first organism is potentially benefited.

sociobiology the application of evolutionary theory to animal behavior, including that of humans.

sororate the marriage of a man to the sister of his deceased wife.

structuralism a theoretical approach that posits a universal structure in human unconscious thought processes (especially a tendency to think in terms of binary oppositions) which underlies what appear as variable cultural expressions; in anthropology this approach was elaborated by Claude Lévi-Strauss.

superorganic a characteristic of culture that, according to some anthropologists (notably Alfred L. Kroeber), allows it to develop a momentum of its own, such that "culture" cannot be reduced to or accounted entirely by other biological, social, economic, or material factors.

surrogate motherhood the role of a woman who bears another couple's genetic child.

totemism the symbolic identification of a group of people with a particular type of animal, plant, mythical being, or object.

ultimogeniture a pattern of inheritance in which only the youngest child, usually the youngest son, receives an inheritance (cf. **primogeniture**).

unilineal descent descent traced through only one sex, as in the cases of matrilineal or patrilineal descent.

uterine kin, matrikin kin traced exclusively through female links (cf. **agnates, cognates**).

uxorilocal *see* **matrilocal.**

virilocal *see* **patrilocal.**

woman–woman marriage the marriage of a barren woman (who counts as a "husband") to another woman; a genitor is arranged for the "wife," and the barren woman becomes the legal father of the children.

Standard Abbreviations for Relations

F	father	M	mother	P	parent
B	brother	Z	sister	G	sibling
H	husband	W	wife	E	spouse
S	son	D	daughter	C	child
e	elder	y	younger	os	opposite-sex
ss	same-sex	ms	male speaker	ws or fs	female speaker

These abbreviations may be used in combination, e.g., MeBD, "mother's elder brother's daughter."

Index

CPSIA information can be obtained
at www.ICGtesting.com
Printed in the USA
FSHW020127141218
54410FS